Complete Set
11 vol.

THE COLLECTED WORKS

OF

DUGALD STEWART.

THE COLLECTED WORKS

OF

DUGALD STEWART, ESQ., F.R.SS.,

HONORARY MEMBER OF THE IMPERIAL ACADEMY OF SCIENCES AT ST PETERSBURG,
MEMBER OF THE ROYAL ACADEMIES OF BERLIN AND OF NAPLES, OF THE
AMERICAN SOCIETIES OF PHILADELPHIA AND OF BOSTON;
HONORARY MEMBER OF THE PHILOSOPHICAL SOCIETY OF
CAMBRIDGE, PROFESSOR OF MORAL PHILOSOPHY
IN THE UNIVERSITY OF EDINBURGH

EDITED BY

SIR WILLIAM HAMILTON, BART.,

ADVOCATE, A M (OXON), ETC , CORRESPONDING MEMBER OF THE INSTITUTE OF FRANCE,
HONORARY MEMBER OF THE LATIN SOCIETY OF JENA, ETC , PROFESSOR OF
LOGIC AND METAPHYSICS IN THE UNIVERSITY OF EDINBURGH

VOL. I.

EDINBURGH THOMAS CONSTABLE AND CO.
HAMILTON, ADAMS, & CO, LONDON.

MDCCCLIV

EDINBURGH T CONSTABLE, PRINTER TO HER MAJESTY

DISSERTATION:

EXHIBITING THE PROGRESS OF

METAPHYSICAL, ETHICAL, AND POLITICAL PHILOSOPHY,

SINCE THE REVIVAL OF LETTERS IN EUROPE.

WITH NUMEROUS AND IMPORTANT ADDITIONS NOW FIRST PUBLISHED

BY

DUGALD STEWART, ESQ.

EDITED BY

SIR WILLIAM HAMILTON, BART.

EDINBURGH: THOMAS CONSTABLE AND CO.
HAMILTON, ADAMS, & CO., LONDON.
MDCCCLIV.

ADVERTISEMENT BY THE EDITOR

Of Mr. Stewart's historical Dissertation on the progress of Philosophy, there are two editions; which being both prepared with the participation of the Author, must, consequently, both be consulted by an Editor in the constitution of a comprehensive and authoritative text. In both also the Dissertation is prefixed to re-impressions of the Encyclopædia Britannica; for the right has not hitherto been exercised of publishing it separately, or in a collection of Mr. Stewart's writings.

The First Part of the Dissertation originally appeared in 1815; the Second Part, in 1821. The two were reprinted continuously in a second edition several years subsequently, and stereotyped. The editions are substantially identical; but in the second there are found a few additions, and at least two omissions, (pp. 201, 613.) The present volume is printed from the second edition, collated, however, with the first. The omitted passages have been reinstated, but explicitly distinguished; it has not, however, been thought necessary to discriminate the *printed* additions.—So much as to the published sources; it is now requisite to add somewhat in regard to the unpublished.

In the present edition of the Dissertation, beside the concluding Chapter of Part Third and its relative Note, which now appear for the first time, there are given numerous and extensive additions, both in the body of the work, and in the notes. These, as inserted, are all marked by their enclosure within square brackets. They are, however, to be divided into two classes, as derived from different sources. In the first place, Mr. Stewart's own interleaved copy of the *original* edition of *both* Parts of the Dissertation, contributes various corrections and amplifications. These have all been made use of, and their insertion is simply indicated by the brackets. In the second place, the other authorities from which new matter has been obtained, (but for Part *Second* only,) stand on a less favourable footing; in so far as whatever they afford was, after being written, omitted by Mr. Stewart himself from the Dissertation as published These omissions, however, seem to have been made under an anxiety to bring the work, as connected with the Encyclopædia, within a narrower compass, (see p. 201,) and not in consequence of any rejection of the passages as in themselves either erroneous or redundant. Their insertion is, therefore, now marked not only by the brackets, but expressly as *restorations;* and though printed without other distinction, it should be mentioned that they also are founded on *two* several documents. They are partly taken from the original *proof* of the Dissertation; it being explained that Mr. Stewart was in use to have the whole, or a large portion of an intended publication, set up at once in type, and on this, at his leisure, he made any alterations which he thought expedient. Such a proof of Part Second is preserved, and it supplies much that is new and valuable. Again, there remains of the same Part a copy of the author's *original manuscript*, which exhibits, in like manner, many passages which, though unpublished, merit preservation. Of this, it indeed appears that Mr. Stewart was fully sensible. For he, has not only printed in the second edition some insertions drawn from all the three sources, (insertions which, as stated, do not in the present publication show any sign of discrimination;) but on the third document—the original manuscript, it is prominently noted in his daughter's handwriting, that " this particularly is to be preserved with care," as containing "some valuable passages not printed." Accordingly, these omissions have, in a great measure, been recovered, and as already noticed, those from the two last sources are indifferently marked out by the word *restored*.

In the historical development of a series of opinions so complex, conflictive, and recondite, it could not but happen, be their general agreement what it might, that the conclusions of the author should to the editor appear occasionally to require, beside defence,* perhaps supplement, qualification, or even correction. But as I am persuaded of its propriety, so I have

* I may take this opportunity of supplying an example —Mr Fearn, in his ingenious work, *First Lines of the Human Mind*, (1820,) has, throughout a long preface, made a vehement attack on Mr Stewart, for statements contained in the First Part of his Dissertation, in regard to colours, (*infra*, pp 131-134,) asserting, that the fact which is supposed to be there *first* alleged, had been taken, without acknowledgment, from his (Mr. Fearn's) writings Mr Fearn says, (p. xix.)—"To justify most conclusively my assertions, made at different times, that the original notice of even the *generic fact* resides with myself, I now proceed to observe, that, although I have had occasion to peruse, and make very frequent references to, the works of BERKELEY, of HUME, of DR. REID, and of PROFESSOR STEWART, between whom it is a l i ll the t ntr versy concerning Perception has been carried on during near a century, I will venture to believe, there is not the most distant hint, in any one of their volumes, that *a* VARIETY *of colours* is necessary for the act of perceiving *visible figure or outline* nor do they at all hint at any such assertion as being made by any writer, ancient or modern" The italics and capitals are Mr. Fearn's —The letter to Dr. Reid, "of forty years before, and now first printed, (p. 133, *seq*,) completely vindicates,—what he himself could not condescend to do,—Mr Stewart's statements He therein, *inter alia*, expressly maintains —"To this opinion [Reid's] I cannot subscribe, because it appears to me to be evident, that our perceptions of colour and figure are not only received by the same organ of sense, but that the *varieties in our per- c ti s f l t i s of ou*

undertaken the office of his editor under the condition—that Mr. Stewart's writings should, in this collective edition, be published without note or comment. The only annotations, therefore, which I have deemed it necessary or even proper to append, are such as were required in the execution of my editorial functions. By exception, however, one or two bibliographical facts of some importance, but generally unknown, have been simply supplied. Where also Mr. Stewart had neglected a useful reference, such has been silently filled up; while verbal inaccuracies and imperfections have, in like manner, been emended. Beside, therefore, the principal value bestowed on this edition of the Dissertation by the extent and importance of its new matter; it is hoped, that the book has thus been rendered more convenient for study, to say nothing of the useful subsidiaries of a well digested Index, and of an appropriate disposition of minuter running titles.

W. H.

EDINBURGH, *April* 1854.

---

perception of visible figure." Compare also his doctrine on p 552.

It may here be added, that the whole speculation concerning the realizing, not only to imagination but to sight, of *breadthless lines*, (a speculation, in fact, hardly contemplated by Mr Stewart,) can be traced to *Aristotle*, but more explicitly to *Proclus* and his scholar, *Ammonius Hermiæ*, while in modern times, I find the phænomenon signalized, among others, by *Clavius*, by *D'Alembert*, and by *Dr Thomas Young*. Nor should it now remain a paradox, nor even an unemployed truth

CONTENTS.

DISSERTATION.

PROGRESS OF METAPHYSICAL, ETHICAL, AND POLITICAL PHILOSOPHY.

	PAGE
PREFACE, containing some Critical Remarks on the Discourse prefixed to the French Encyclopédie, ...	1
PART FIRST.—INTRODUCTION, ...	23
CHAPTER I. Progress of Philosophy from the Revival of Letters to the publication of Bacon's Philosophical Works, .	25
CHAPTER II Progress of Philosophy from the publication of Bacon's Philosophical Works till that of the Essay on Human Understanding.	
SECT 1. Progress of Philosophy in England during this period—	
Bacon, ...	63
Hobbes, ...	79
Antagonists of Hobbes, . .	85
SECT 2 Progress of Philosophy in France during the Seventeenth Century.—	
Montaigne.—Charron—La Rochefoucauld, . .	98
Descartes.—Gassendi.—Malebranche, . .	112
SECT 3 Progress of Philosophy during the Seventeenth Century in some parts of Europe not included in the preceding Review, ...	170
PART SECOND.—INTRODUCTION, . .	203
Progress of Metaphysics during the Eighteenth Century—	
SECT. 1. Historical and Critical Review of the Philosophical Works of Locke and Leibnitz —Locke, . .	206
SECT 2 Continuation of the Review of Locke and Leibnitz.—Leibnitz,	252

		PAGE
SECT 3	Of the Metaphysical Speculations of Newton and Clarke — Digression with respect to the System of Spinoza, Collins, and Jonathan Edwards —Anxiety of both to reconcile the scheme of Necessity with Man's Moral Agency —Departure of some later Necessitarians from their views,	287
SECT 4	Of some Authors who have contributed, by their Critical or Historical Writings, to diffuse a taste for Metaphysical Studies — Bayle.— Fontenelle —Addison —Metaphysical Works of Berkeley,	313
SECT. 5.	Hartleian School,	352
SECT 6.	Condillac, and other French Metaphysicians of a later date,	358
SECT 7	Kant, and other Metaphysicians of the New German School,	389
SECT. 8.	Metaphysical Philosophy of Scotland,	427

PART THIRD —

Progress of Ethical and Political Philosophy during the Eighteenth Century —

CHAPTER.—(Fragment in conclusion)—Progress, Tendencies, Results, . . . 487

NOTES AND ILLUSTRATIONS,
    To Part I, . . . 529
    To Part II, ... 550
    To Part III, ... 614

SUPPLEMENT, ... 615

INDEX, ... 619

PREFACE.

CONTAINING SOME CRITICAL REMARKS ON THE DISCOURSE
PREFIXED TO THE FRENCH ENCYCLOPÉDIE.

When I ventured to undertake the task of contributing a Preliminary Dissertation to these Supplemental Volumes of the *Encyclopædia Britannica*, my original intention was, after the example of D'Alembert, to have begun with a general survey of the various departments of human knowledge. The outline of such a survey, sketched by the comprehensive genius of Bacon, together with the corrections and improvements suggested by his illustrious disciple, would, I thought, have rendered it comparatively easy to adapt their intellectual map to the present advanced state of the sciences; while the unrivalled authority which their united work has long maintained in the republic of letters, would, I flattered myself, have softened those criticisms which might be expected to be incurred by any similar attempt of a more modern hand. On a closer examination, however, of their labours, I found myself under the necessity of abandoning this design. Doubts immediately occurred to me with respect to the justness of their logical views, and soon terminated in a conviction, that these views are radically and essentially erroneous. Instead, therefore, of endeavouring to give additional currency to speculations which I conceived to be fundamentally unsound, I resolved to avail myself of the present opportunity to point out their most important defects,—defects which, I am nevertheless very ready to acknowledge, it is much more easy to remark than to supply. The critical strictures which, in the course of this discussion, I shall have occasion to offer on my predecessors, will, at the same time, account for my forbearing to substitute a new map of my own, instead of that to which the names of Bacon and D'Alembert have lent so great and so well-merited a celebrity; and may perhaps suggest a doubt, whether the period be yet arrived for hazarding again, with any reasonable prospect of success, a repetition of their bold experiment. For the length to which these strictures are likely to extend, the only apology I have to offer is the peculiar importance of the questions to which they relate, and the high authority of the writers whose opinions I presume to controvert.

Before entering on his main subject, D'Alembert is at pains to explain a distinction, which he represents as of considerable importance, between the Genealogy of the sciences, and the Encyclopedical arrangement of the objects of human knowledge.[1] "In examining the former," he observes, "our aim is, by remounting to the origin and genesis of our ideas, to trace the causes to which the sciences owe their birth; and to mark the characteristics by which they are distinguished from each other. In order to ascertain the latter, it is necessary to comprehend, in one general *scheme*, all the various departments of study; to arrange them into proper classes; and to point out their mutual relations and dependencies." Such a *scheme* is sometimes likened by D'Alembert to a map or chart of the intellectual world; sometimes to a genealogical[2] or encyclopedical tree, indicating the manifold and complicated affinities of those studies, which, however apparently remote and unconnected, are all the common offspring of the human understanding. For

---

[1] "Il ne faut pas confondre l'ordre Encyclopédique des connoissances humaines avec la Généalogie des Sciences."— *Avertissement*, p. 7.

[2] It is to be regretted that the epithet *genealogical* should have been employed on this occasion, where the author's wish was to contradistinguish the idea denoted by it, from that historical view of the sciences to which the word *genealogy* had been previously applied.

executing successfully this chart or tree, a philosophical delineation of the natural progress of the mind may (according to him) furnish very useful lights; although he acknowledges that the results of the two undertakings cannot fail to differ widely in many instances—the laws which regulate the generation of our ideas often interfering with that systematical order in the relative arrangement of scientific pursuits, which it is the purpose of the Encyclopedical Tree to exhibit.[1]

In treating of the first of these subjects, it cannot be denied that D'Alembert has displayed much ingenuity and invention; but the depth and solidity of his general train of thought may be questioned. On various occasions, he has evidently suffered himself to be misled by a spirit of false refinement; and on others, where probably he was fully aware of his inability to render the theoretical chain complete, he seems to have aimed at concealing from his readers the faulty links, by availing himself of those epigrammatic points, and other artifices of style, with which the genius of the French language enables a skilful writer to smooth and varnish over his most illogical transitions.

The most essential imperfections, however, of this historical sketch, may be fairly ascribed to a certain vagueness and indecision in the author's idea, with regard to the scope of his inquiries. What he has in general pointed at is to trace, from the theory of the Mind, and from the order followed by nature in the development of its powers, the successive steps by which

---

[1] The true reason of this might perhaps have been assigned in simpler terms, by remarking that the order of invention is, in most cases, the reverse of that fitted for didactic communication. This observation applies not only to the analytical and synthetical processes of the *individual*, but to the progressive improvements of the *species*, when compared with the arrangements prescribed by logical method for conveying a knowledge of them to students. In an enlightened age, the sciences are justly considered as the basis of the arts, and, in a course of liberal education, the former are always taught prior to the latter. But, in the order of invention and discovery, the arts preceded the sciences. Men measured land before they studied speculative geometry, and governments were established before politics were studied as a science. A remark somewhat similar is made by Celsus concerning the history of medicine: "Non medicinam rationi esse posteriorem, sed post medicinam inventam, rationem esse quæsitam"

the curiosity may be conceived to have been gradually conducted from one intellectual pursuit to another; but, in the execution of this design, (which in itself is highly philosophical and interesting,) he does not appear to have paid due attention to the essential difference between the history of the human species, and that of the civilized and inquisitive individual. The former was undoubtedly that which principally figured in his conceptions; and to which, I apprehend, he ought to have confined himself exclusively; whereas, in fact, he has so completely blended the two subjects together, that it is often impossible to say which of them was uppermost in his thoughts. The consequence is, that instead of throwing upon either those strong and steady lights which might have been expected from his powers, he has involved both in additional obscurity. This indistinctness is more peculiarly remarkable in the beginning of his Discourse, where he represents men in the earliest infancy of science, before they had time to take any precautions for securing the means of their subsistence, or of their safety,—as philosophizing on their sensations,—on the existence of their own bodies,—and on that of the material world. His Discourse, accordingly, sets out with a series of Meditations, precisely analogous to those which form the introduction to the philosophy of Descartes; meditations which, in the order of time, have been uniformly posterior to the study of external nature; and which, even in such an age as the present, are confined to a comparatively small number of recluse metaphysicians.

Of this sort of *conjectural* or *theoretical* history, the most unexceptionable specimens which have yet appeared, are indisputably the fragments in Mr. Smith's posthumous work on the History of Astronomy, and on that of the Ancient Systems of Physics and Metaphysics. That, in the latter of these, he may have occasionally accommodated his details to his own peculiar opinions concerning the object of Philosophy, may perhaps, with some truth, be alleged; but he must at least be allowed the merit of completely avoiding the error by which D'Alembert was misled; and even in those instances where he himself seems to wander a little from the right path, of furnishing his successors with a thread, leading by easy and almost insensible steps, from the first gross perceptions of sense, to the most abstract refinements of the Grecian schools. Nor is this the only praise to which these fragments are entitled. By seizing on the different points of view from whence the same object was contemplated by different sects, they often bestow a certain degree of unity and of interest on what before seemed calculated merely to bewilder and to confound; and render the apparent aberrations and caprices of the understanding subservient to the study of its operations and laws.

To the foregoing strictures on D'Alembert's view of the origin of the sciences, it may be added, that this introductory part of his Discourse does not seem to have any immediate connexion with the sequel. We are led, indeed, to expect, that it is to prepare the way for the study of the Encylopedical Tree afterwards to be exhibited; but in this expectation we are completely disappointed;—no reference to it whatever being made by the author in the farther prosecution of his subject. It forms, accordingly, a portion of his Discourse altogether foreign to the general design; while, from the metaphysical obscurity which pervades it, the generality of readers are likely to receive an impression, either unfavourable to the perspicuity of the writer, or to their own powers of comprehension and of reasoning. It were to be wished, therefore, that instead of occupying the first pages of the *Encyclopédie*, it had been reserved for a separate article in the body of that work. There it might have been read by the logical student, with no small interest and advantage; for, with all its imperfections, it bears numerous and precious marks of its author's hand.

In delineating his Encyclopedical Tree, D'Alembert has, in my opinion, been still more unsuccessful than in the speculations which have been hitherto under our review. His veneration for Bacon seems, on this occasion, to have prevented him from giving due scope to his own powerful and fertile genius, and has engaged him in the fruitless task of attempting, by means of arbitrary definitions, to draw a veil over incurable defects and blemishes. In this part of Bacon's logic, it must, at the same time, be owned, that there is something peculiarly captivating to the fancy; and, accordingly, it has united in its favour the suffrages of almost all the succeeding authors who have treated of the same subject. It will be necessary for me, therefore, to explain fully the grounds of that censure, which, in opposition to so many illustrious names, I have presumed to bestow on it.

Of the leading ideas to which I more particularly object, the following statement is given by D'Alembert. I quote it in preference to the corresponding passage in Bacon, as it contains various explanatory clauses and glosses, for which we are indebted to the ingenuity of the commentator.

" The objects about which our minds are occupied, are either spiritual or material, and the media employed for this purpose are our ideas, either directly received, or derived from reflection. The system of our direct knowledge consists entirely in the passive and mechanical accumulation of the particulars it comprehends; an accumulation which belongs exclusively to the province of Memory. Reflection is of two kinds, according as it is employed in reasoning on the objects of our direct ideas, or in studying them as models for imitation.

" Thus, Memory, Reason, strictly so called, and Imagination, are the three modes in which the mind operates on the subjects of its thoughts. By Imagination, however, is here to be understood, not the faculty of conceiving or representing to ourselves what we have formerly perceived, a faculty which differs in nothing from the memory of these perceptions, and which, if it were not relieved by the invention of signs, would be in a state of continual exercise. The power which we denote by this name has a nobler province allotted to it, that of rendering imitation subservient to the creations of genius.

" These three faculties suggest a corresponding division of human knowledge into three branches:—1. History, which derives its materials from Memory; 2. Philosophy, which is the product of Reason; and 3 Poetry, (comprehending under this title all the Fine Arts,) which is the offspring of Imagination.[1] If we place Reason before Imagination, it is because this order appears to us conformable to the natural progress of our intellectual operations.[2] The Imagination is a creative faculty, and the mind, before it attempts to create, begins by reasoning upon what it sees and knows. Nor is this all. In the faculty of Imagination, both Reason and Memory are, to a certain extent, combined—the mind never imagining or creating objects but such as are analogous to those whereof it has had previous experience. Where this analogy is wanting, the combinations are extravagant and displeasing; and, consequently, in that agreeable imitation of nature, at which the fine arts aim in common, invention is necessarily subjected to the control of rules which it is the business of the philosopher to investigate.

"In farther justification of this arrangement, it may be remarked, that Reason, in the course of its successive operations on the subjects of thought, by creating abstract and general ideas, remote from the perceptions of sense, leads to the exercise of Imagination as the last step of the process. Thus metaphysics and geometry are, of all the sciences belonging to Reason, those in which Imagination has the greatest share. I ask pardon for this observation from those men of taste, who, little aware of the near affinity of geometry to their own pursuits, and still less suspecting that the only intermediate step

---

[1] The latitude given by D'Alembert to the meaning of the word *Poetry* is a real and very important improvement on Bacon, who restricts it to fictitious History or Fables.—(*De Aug. Scient.* lib. II cap 1) D'Alembert, on the other hand, employs it in its natural signification, as synonymous with *invention* or *creation*. "La Peinture, la Sculpture, l'Architecture, la Poésie, la Musique, et leurs différentes divisions, composent la troisième distribution générale qui naît de l'Imagination, et dont les parties sont comprises sous le nom de Beaux-Arts On peut les rapporter tous à la Poésie, en prenant ce mot dans sa signification naturelle, qui n'est autre chose qu'invention ou création."

[2] In placing Reason before Imagination, D'Alembert departs from the order in which these faculties are arranged by Bacon "Si nous n'avons pas placé, comme lui, la Raison après l'Imagination, c'est que nous avons suivi, dans le système Encyclopédique, l'ordre métaphysique des opérations de l'esprit, plutôt que l'ordre historique de ses progrès depuis la renaissance des lettres." —(*Disc. Prélim.*) How far the motive here assigned for the change is valid, the reader will be enabled to judge from the sequel of the above quotation.

between them is formed by metaphysics, are disposed to employ their wit in depreciating its value. The truth is, that, to the geometer who invents, Imagination is not less essential than to the poet who creates. They operate, indeed, differently on their object, the former abstracting and analyzing, where the latter combines and adorns;—two processes of the mind, it must, at the same time, be confessed, which seem from experience to be so little congenial, that it may be doubted if the talents of a great geometer and of a great poet will ever be united in the same person. But whether these talents be, or be not mutually exclusive, certain it is, that they who possess the one, have no right to despise those who cultivate the other. Of all the great men of antiquity, Archimedes is perhaps he who is the best entitled to be placed by the side of Homer."

D'Alembert afterwards proceeds to observe, that of these three general branches of the Encyclopedical Tree, a natural and convenient subdivision is afforded by the metaphysical distribution of things into Material and Spiritual. "With these two classes of existences," he observes farther, "history and philosophy are equally conversant; but *as for the Imagination, her imitations are entirely confined to the material world;* —a circumstance," he adds, "which conspires with the other arguments above stated, in justifying Bacon for assigning to her the *last* place in his enumeration of our intellectual faculties."[1] Upon this subdivision he enlarges at some length, and with considerable ingenuity, but on the present occasion it would be quite superfluous to follow him any farther, as more than enough has been already quoted to enable my readers to

---

[1] In this exclusive limitation of the province of Imagination to things material and sensible, D'Alembert has followed the definition given by Descartes in his second Meditation:—"*Imaginari nihil aliud est quam rei corporeæ figuram seu imaginem contemplari;*"—a power of the mind, which (as I have elsewhere observed) appears to me to be most precisely expressed in our language by the word *Conception.* The province assigned to Imagination by D'Alembert is more extensive than this, for he ascribes to her also a creative and combining power, but still his definition agrees with that of Descartes, inasmuch as it excludes entirely from her dominion both the intellectual and the moral worlds

judge, whether the objections which I am now to state to the foregoing extracts be as sound and decisive as I apprehend them to be.

Of these objections a very obvious one is suggested by a consideration, of which D'Alembert himself has taken notice,—that the three faculties to which he refers the whole operations of the understanding are perpetually blended together in their actual exercise, insomuch that there is scarcely a branch of human knowledge which does not, in a greater or less degree, furnish employment to them all. It may be said, indeed, that some pursuits exercise and invigorate particular faculties *more* than others; that the study of History, for example, although it may occasionally require the aid both of Reason and of Imagination, yet chiefly furnishes occupation to the Memory; and that this is sufficient to justify the logical division of our mental powers as the ground-work of a corresponding Encyclopedical classification.[1] This, however, will be found more specious than solid. In what respects is the faculty of Memory more essentially necessary to the student of history than to the philosopher or to the poet; and, on the other hand, of what value, in the circle of the sciences, would be a collection of historical details, accumulated without discrimination, without a scrupulous examination of evidence, or without any attempt to compare and to generalize? For the cultivation of that species of history, in particular, which alone deserves a place in the Encyclopedical Tree, it may be justly affirmed, that the rarest and most comprehensive combination of all our mental gifts is indispensably requisite.

Another, and a still more formidable objection to Bacon's

---

[1] I allude here to the following apology for Bacon, suggested by a very learned and judicious writer:—

"On a fait cependant à Bacon quelques reproches assez fondés On a observé que sa classification des sciences repose sur une distinction qui n'est pas rigoureuse, puisque la mémoire, la raison, et l'Imagination concourent nécessairement dans chaque art, comme dans chaque science. Mais on peut répondre, que l'une ou l'autre de ces trois facultés, quoique secondée par les deux autres, peut cependant jouer le rôle principal. En prenant la distinction de Bacon dans ce sens, sa classification reste exacte, et devient très utile."—Degerando, *Hist. Comp* tome i p 298

classification, may be derived from the very imperfect and partial analysis of the mind which it assumes as its basis. Why were the powers of Abstraction and Generalization passed over in silence?—powers which, according as they are cultivated or neglected, constitute the most essential of all distinctions between the intellectual characters of individuals. A corresponding distinction, too, not less important, may be remarked among the objects of human study, according as our aim is to treasure up particular facts, or to establish general conclusions. Does not this distinction mark out, with greater precision, the limits which separate philosophy from mere historical narrative, than that which turns upon the different provinces of Reason and of Memory?

I shall only add one other criticism on this celebrated enumeration, and that is, its want of distinctness, in confounding together the Sciences and the Arts under the same general titles. Hence a variety of those capricious arrangements, which must immediately strike every reader who follows Bacon through his details; the reference, for instance, of the mechanical arts to the department of History; and, consequently, according to his own analysis of the mind, the ultimate reference of these arts to the faculty of Memory: while, at the same time, in his tripartite division of the whole field of human knowledge, the art of Poetry has one entire province allotted to itself.

These objections apply in common to Bacon and to D'Alembert. That which follows has a particular reference to a passage already cited from the latter, where, by some false refinements concerning the nature and functions of Imagination, he has rendered the classification of his predecessor incomparably more indistinct and illogical than it seemed to be before.

That all the creations, or new combinations of Imagination, imply the previous process of decomposition or analysis, is abundantly manifest; and, therefore, without departing from the common and popular use of language, it may undoubtedly be said, that the faculty of abstraction is not less essential to the Poet, than to the Geometer and the Metaphysician.[1] But this is not the doctrine of D'Alembert. On the contrary, he affirms, that Metaphysics and Geometry are, of all the sciences connected with Reason, those in which Imagination has the greatest share; an assertion which, it will not be disputed, has at first sight somewhat of the air of a paradox; and which, on closer examination, will, I apprehend, be found altogether inconsistent with fact. If indeed D'Alembert had, in this instance, used (as some writers have done) the word Imagination as synonymous with Invention, I should not have thought it worth while (at least so far as the geometer is concerned) to dispute his proposition. But that this was not the meaning annexed to it by the author, appears from a subsequent clause, where he tells us, that the most refined operations of reason, consisting in the creation of *generals* which do not fall under the cognizance of our senses, naturally lead to the exercise of Imagination. His doctrine, therefore, goes to the identification of Imagination with Abstraction; two faculties so very different in the direction which they give to our thoughts, that (according to his own acknowledgment) the man who is habitually occupied in exerting the one, seldom fails to impair both his capacity and his relish for the exercise of the other.

This identification of two faculties, so strongly contrasted in their characteristical features, was least of all to be expected from a logician, who had previously limited the province of Imagination to the imitation of material objects; a limitation, it may be remarked in passing, which is neither sanctioned by common use, nor by just views of the philosophy of the Mind. Upon what ground can it be alleged that Milton's portrait of

---

[1] This assertion must, however, be understood with some qualifications; for, although the poet, as well as the geometer and the metaphysician, be perpetually called upon to decompose, by means of abstraction, the complicated objects of perception, it must not be concluded that the abstractions of all the three are exactly of the same kind. Those of the poet amount to nothing more than to a separation into parts of the realities presented to his senses; which separation is only a preliminary step to a subsequent recomposition into new and ideal forms of the things abstracted; whereas the abstractions of the metaphysician and of the geometer form the very objects of their respective sciences.

Satan's intellectual and moral character was not the offspring of the same creative faculty which gave birth to his Garden of Eden? After such a definition, however, it is difficult to conceive how so very acute a writer should have referred to Imagination the abstractions of the geometer and of the metaphysician; and still more, that he should have attempted to justify this reference, by observing, that these abstractions do not fall under the cognizance of the senses. My own opinion is, that in the composition of the whole passage he had a view to the unexpected parallel between Homer and Archimedes, with which he meant, at the close, to surprise his readers.

If the foregoing strictures be well founded, it seems to follow, not only that the attempt of Bacon and of D'Alembert to classify the sciences and arts according to a logical division of our faculties, is altogether unsatisfactory, but that every future attempt of the same kind may be expected to be liable to similar objections. In studying, indeed, the Theory of the Mind, it is necessary to push our analysis as far as the nature of the subject admits of; and, wherever the thing is possible, to examine its constituent principles separately and apart from each other: but this consideration itself, when combined with what was before stated on the endless variety of forms in which they may be blended together in our various intellectual pursuits, is sufficient to shew how ill adapted such an analysis must for ever remain to serve as the basis of an Encyclopedical distribution.[1]

The circumstance to which this part of Bacon's philosophy is

[1] In justice to the authors of the Encyclopedical Tree prefixed to the French Dictionary, it ought to be observed, that it is spoken of by D'Alembert, in his Preliminary Discourse, with the utmost modesty and diffidence, and that he has expressed not only his own conviction, but that of his colleague, of the impossibility of executing such a task in a manner likely to satisfy the public. "Nous sommes trop convaincus de l'arbitraire qui régnera toujours dans une pareille division, pour croire que notre système soit l'unique ou le meilleur; il nous suffira que notre travail ne soit pas entièrement désapprouvé par les bons esprits" And, some pages afterwards—" Si le public éclairé donne son approbation à ces changemens, elle sera la récompense de notre docilité, et s'il ne les approuve pas, nous n'en serons que plus convaincus de l'impossibilité de former un arbre encyclopédique qui soit au gré de tout le monde."

chiefly indebted for its popularity, is the specious simplicity and comprehensiveness of the distribution itself—not the soundness of the logical views by which it was suggested. That all our intellectual pursuits may be referred to one or other of these three heads—History, Philosophy, and Poetry, may undoubtedly be said with considerable plausibility; the word history being understood to comprehend all our knowledge of particular facts and particular events; the word philosophy, all the general conclusions or laws inferred from these particulars by induction; and the word poetry, all the arts addressed to the imagination. Not that the enumeration, even with the help of this comment, can be considered as complete, for (to pass over entirely the other objections already stated) under which of these three heads shall we arrange the various branches of pure mathematics?

Are we therefore to conclude, that the magnificent design conceived by Bacon, of enumerating, defining, and classifying the multifarious objects of human knowledge—(a design, on the successful accomplishment of which he himself believed that the advancement of the sciences essentially depended)—are we to conclude that this design was nothing more than the abortive offspring of a warm imagination, unsusceptible of any useful application to enlighten the mind, or to accelerate its progress? My own idea is widely different. The design was, in every respect, worthy of the sublime genius by which it was formed. Nor does it follow, because the execution was imperfect, that the attempt has been attended with no advantage. At the period when Bacon wrote, it was of much more consequence to exhibit to the learned a comprehensive sketch, than an accurate survey of the intellectual world; such a sketch as, by pointing out to those whose views had been hitherto confined within the limits of particular regions, the relative positions and bearings of their respective districts, as parts of one great whole, might invite them all, for the common benefit, to a reciprocal exchange of their local riches. The societies or academies which, soon after, sprung up in different countries of Europe, for the avowed purpose of contributing to the general mass of information, by the collection of insulated facts, conjectures, and queries, afford sufficient proof that the anticipations of Bacon were not, in this instance, altogether chimerical.

In examining the details of Bacon's survey, it is impossible not to be struck (more especially when we reflect on the state of learning two hundred years ago) with the minuteness of his information, as well as with the extent of his views; or to forbear admiring his sagacity in pointing out, to future adventurers, the unknown tracts still left to be explored by human curiosity. If his classifications be sometimes artificial and arbitrary, they have at least the merit of including, under one head or another, every particular of importance; and of exhibiting these particulars with a degree of method and of apparent connexion, which, if it does not always satisfy the judgment, never fails to interest the fancy, and to lay hold of the memory. Nor must it be forgotten, to the glory of his genius, that what he failed to accomplish remains to this day a desideratum in science,—that the intellectual chart delineated by him is, with all its imperfections, the only one of which modern philosophy has yet to boast;—and that the united talents of D'Alembert and of Diderot, aided by all the lights of the eighteenth century, have been able to add but little to what Bacon performed.

After the foregoing observations, it will not be expected that an attempt is to be made, in the following essay, to solve a problem which has so recently baffled the powers of these eminent writers; and which will probably long continue to exercise the ingenuity of our successors. How much remains to be previously done for the improvement of that part of logic, whose province it is to fix the limits by which contiguous departments of study are defined and separated! And how many unsuspected affinities may be reasonably presumed to exist among sciences, which, to our circumscribed views, appear at present the most alien from each other! The abstract geometry of Apollonius and Archimedes was found, after an interval of two thousand years, to furnish a torch to the physical inquiries of Newton; while, in the farther progress of knowledge, the Etymology of Languages has been happily employed to fill up the chasms of Ancient History; and the conclusions of Comparative Anatomy, to illustrate the Theory of the Earth. For my own part, even if the task were executed with the most complete success, I should be strongly inclined to think, that its appropriate place in an Encyclopædia would be as a branch of the article on Logic ;—certainly *not* as an *exordium* to the Preliminary Discourse ; the enlarged and refined views which it necessarily presupposes being peculiarly unsuitable to that part of the work which may be expected, in the first instance, to attract the curiosity of every reader. As, upon this point, however, there may be some diversity of opinion, I have prevailed on the Editor to add to these introductory Essays a translation of D'Alembert's Discourse, and of Diderot's Prospectus. No English version of either has, as far as I know, been hitherto published ; and the result of their joint ingenuity, exerted on Bacon's ground-work, must for ever fix no inconsiderable era in the history of learning.

Before concluding this preface, I shall subjoin a few slight strictures on a very concise and comprehensive division of the objects of Human Knowledge, proposed by Mr. Locke, as the basis of a new classification of the sciences. Although I do not know that any attempt has ever been made to follow out in detail the general idea, yet the repeated approbation which has been lately bestowed on a division essentially the same, by several writers of the highest rank, renders it in some measure necessary, on the present occasion, to consider how far it is founded on just principles; more especially as it is completely at variance, not only with the language and arrangement adopted in these preliminary essays, but with the whole of that plan on which the original projectors, as well as the continuators, of the *Encyclopædia Britannica* appear to have proceeded. These strictures will, at the same time, afford an additional proof of the difficulty, or rather of the impossibility, in the actual state of logical science, of solving this great problem, in a manner calculated to unite the general suffrages of philosophers.

" All that can fall," says Mr. Locke, " within the compass of Human Understanding being either, first, The nature of things as they are in themselves, their relations, and their manner of operation; or, secondly, That which man himself ought to do, as a rational and voluntary agent, for the attainment of any end, especially happiness; or, thirdly, The ways and means whereby the knowledge of both the one and the other of these is attained and communicated: I think science may be divided properly into these three sorts:—

"1. Φυσική, or Natural Philosophy. The end of this is bare speculative truth; and whatsoever can afford the mind of man any such falls under this branch, whether it be God himself, angels, spirits, bodies, or any of their affections, as number and figure, &c.

"2. Πρακτική, The skill of right applying our own powers and actions for the attainment of things good and useful. The most considerable under this head is *Ethics*, which is the seeking out those rules and measures of human actions which lead to happiness, and the means to practise them. The end of this is not bare speculation, but right, and a conduct suitable to it.[1]

"3. Σημειωτική, or *the doctrine of signs*, the most usual whereof being words, it is aptly enough termed also Λογική, *Logic*. The business of this is to consider the nature of signs the mind makes use of for the understanding of things, or conveying its knowledge to others.

"This seems to me," continues Mr. Locke, "*the first and most general, as well as natural*, division of the objects of our understanding; for a man can employ his thoughts about nothing but either the contemplation of *things* themselves, for the discovery of truth, or about the things in his own power, which are his own *actions*, for the attainment of his own ends, or the *signs* the mind makes use of, both in one and the other, and the right ordering of them for its clearer information. All which three, viz., things as they are in themselves knowable; actions as they depend on us, in order to happiness; and the

---

[1] From this definition it appears, that as Locke included under the title of *Physics*, not only *Natural Philosophy*, properly so called, but *Natural Theology*, and the *Philosophy of the Human Mind*, so he meant to refer to the head of *Practics*, not only *Ethics*, but all the various *Arts* of life, both mechanical and liberal

right use of *signs*, in order to knowledge; being *toto cœlo* different, they seemed to me to be the three great provinces of the intellectual world, wholly separate and distinct one from another."[1]

From the manner in which Mr. Locke expresses himself in the above quotation, he appears evidently to have considered the division proposed in it as an original idea of his own; and yet the truth is, that it coincides exactly with what was generally adopted by the philosophers of ancient Greece. "The ancient Greek Philosophy," says Mr. Smith, "was divided into three great branches, Physics, or Natural Philosophy; Ethics, or Moral Philosophy; and Logic. *This general division,*" he adds, "*seems perfectly agreeable to the nature of things.*" Mr. Smith afterwards observes, in strict conformity to Locke's definitions, (of which, however, he seems to have had no recollection when he wrote this passage,) "That, as the human mind and the Deity, in whatever their essence may be supposed to consist, are parts of the great system of the universe, and parts, too, productive of the most important effects, whatever was taught in the ancient schools of Greece concerning their nature, made a part of the system of physics."[2]

Dr. Campbell, in his *Philosophy of Rhetoric*, has borrowed from the Grecian schools the same very extensive use of the words *physics* and *physiology*, which he employs as synonymous terms; comprehending under this title "not merely Natural History, Astronomy, Geography, Mechanics, Optics, Hydrostatics, Meteorology, Medicine, Chemistry, but also Natural Theology and Psychology, which," he observes, "have been, in his opinion, most unnaturally disjoined from Physiology by philosophers." "Spirit," he adds, "which here comprises only the Supreme Being and the human soul, is surely as much included under the notion of natural object as body is; and is knowable to the philosopher purely in the same way, by observation and experience."[3]

---

[1] See the concluding chapter of the *Essay on the Human Understanding*, entitled, "Of the Division of the Sciences"

[2] *Wealth of Nations*, Book V chap i

[3] *Philosophy of Rhetoric*, Book I. chap. v Part iii § 1.

A similar train of thinking led the late celebrated M. Turgot to comprehend under the name of Physics, not only Natural Philosophy, (as that phrase is understood by the Newtonians,) but Metaphysics, Logic, and even History.[1]

Notwithstanding all this weight of authority, it is difficult to reconcile one's self to an arrangement which, while it classes with Astronomy, with Mechanics, with Optics, and with Hydrostatics, the strikingly contrasted studies of Natural Theology and of the Philosophy of the Human Mind, disunites from the two last the far more congenial sciences of Ethics and of Logic. The human mind, it is true, as well as the material world which surrounds it, forms a part of the great system of the Universe; but is it possible to conceive two parts of the same whole more completely dissimilar, or rather more diametrically opposite, in all their characteristical attributes? Is not the one the appropriate field and province of *observation*,—a power habitually awake to all the perceptions and impressions of the bodily organs? and does not the other fall exclusively under the cognizance of *reflection*,—an operation which inverts all the ordinary habits of the understanding,—abstracting the thoughts from every sensible object, and even striving to abstract them from every sensible image? What abuse of language can be greater than to apply a common name to departments of knowledge which invite the curiosity in directions precisely contrary, and which tend to form intellectual talents, which, if not altogether incompatible, are certainly not often found united in the same individual? The word *Physics*, in particular, which, in our language, long and constant use has restricted to the phe-

---

[1] "Sous le nom de sciences physiques je comprends la logique, qui est la connoissance des opérations de notre esprit et de la génération de nos idées, la métaphysique, qui s'occupe de la nature et de l'origine des êtres, et enfin la physique, proprement dite, qui observe l'action mutuel des corps les uns sur les autres, et les causes et l'enchainement des phénomènes sensibles. *On pourroit y ajouter l'histoire.*"—

Œuvres de Turgot, tome ii. pp 284, 285

In the year 1795, a quarto volume was published at Bath, entitled *Intellectual Physics* It consists entirely of speculations concerning the human mind, and is by no means destitute of merit. The publication was anonymous, but I have reason to believe that the author was the late well-known Governor Pownall

nomena of Matter, cannot fail to strike every ear as *anomalously*, and therefore *illogically*, applied, when extended to those of Thought and of Consciousness.

Nor let it be imagined that these observations assume any particular theory about the nature or essence of Mind. Whether we adopt, on this point, the language of the Materialists, or that of their opponents, it is a proposition equally certain and equally indisputable, that the phenomena of Mind and those of Matter, as far as they come under the cognizance of our faculties, appear to be more completely heterogeneous than any other classes of facts within the circle of our knowledge; and that the sources of our information concerning them are in every respect so radically different, that nothing is more carefully to be avoided, in the study of either, than an attempt to assimilate them, by means of analogical or metaphorical terms, applied to both in common In those inquiries, above all, where we have occasion to consider Matter and Mind as conspiring to produce the same joint effects, (in the constitution, for example, of our own compounded frame,) it becomes more peculiarly necessary to keep constantly in view the distinct province of each, and to remember, that the business of philosophy is not to resolve the phenomena of the one into those of the other, but merely to ascertain the general laws which regulate their mutual connexion. *Matter* and *Mind*, therefore, it should seem, are the two most general heads which ought to form the ground-work of an Encyclopedical classification of the sciences and arts No branch of human knowledge, no work of human skill, can be mentioned, which does not obviously fall under the former head or the latter.

Agreeably to this twofold classification of the sciences and arts, it is proposed, in the following introductory Essays, to exhibit a rapid sketch of the progress made since the revival of letters—*First*, in those branches of knowledge which relate to mind; and, *secondly*, in those which relate to matter. D'Alembert, in his Preliminary Discourse, has boldly attempted to embrace both subjects in one magnificent design; and never, certainly, was there a single mind more equal to such an undertaking. The historical outline which he has there traced forms by far the most valuable portion of that performance, and will for ever remain a proud monument to the depth, to the comprehensiveness, and to the singular versatility of his genius. In the present state of science, however, it has been apprehended that, by dividing so great a work among different hands, something might perhaps be gained, if not in point of reputation to the authors, at least in point of instruction to their readers. This division of labour was, indeed, in some measure rendered necessary (independently of all other considerations) by the important accessions which mathematics and physics have received since D'Alembert's time; by the innumerable improvements which the spirit of mercantile speculation, and the rivalship of commercial nations, have introduced into the mechanical arts; and, above all, by the rapid succession of chemical discoveries which commences with the researches of Black and of Lavoisier. The part of this task which has fallen to my share is certainly, upon the whole, the least splendid in the results which it has to record; but I am not without hopes that this disadvantage may be partly compensated by its closer connexion with (what ought to be the ultimate end of all our pursuits) the intellectual and moral improvement of the species.

I am, at the same time, well aware that, in proportion as this last consideration increases the importance, it adds to the difficulty of my undertaking. It is chiefly in judging of questions "coming home to their business and bosoms," that casual associations lead mankind astray, and of such associations how incalculable is the number arising from false systems of religion, oppressive forms of government, and absurd plans of education! The consequence is, that while the physical and mathematical discoveries of former ages present themselves to the hand of the historian like masses of pure and native gold, the truths which we are here in quest of may be compared to *iron*, which, although at once the most necessary and the most widely diffused of all the metals, commonly requires a discriminating eye to detect its existence, and a tedious, as well as nice process, to extract it from the ore.

To the same circumstance it is owing, that improvements in moral and in political science do not strike the imagination with nearly so great force as the discoveries of the mathematician or of the chemist. When an inveterate prejudice is destroyed by extirpating the casual associations on which it was grafted, how powerful is the new impulse given to the intellectual faculties of man! Yet how slow and silent the process by which the effect is accomplished! Were it not, indeed, for a certain class of learned authors, who from time to time heave the log into the deep, we should hardly believe that the reason of the species is progressive. In this respect, the religious and academical establishments in some parts of Europe are not without their use to the historian of the human mind. Immovably moored to the same station by the strength of their cables and the weight of their anchors, they enable him to measure the rapidity of the current by which the rest of the world are borne along.

This, too, is remarkable in the history of our prejudices, that as soon as the film falls from the intellectual eye, we are apt to lose all recollection of our former blindness. Like the fantastic and giant shapes which, in a thick fog, the imagination lends to a block of stone or to the stump of a tree, they produce, while the illusion lasts, the same effect with truths and realities; but the moment the eye has caught the exact form and dimensions of its object, the spell is broken for ever, nor can any effort of thought again conjure up the spectres which have vanished.

As to the subdivisions of which the sciences of matter and of mind are susceptible, I have already said that this is not the proper place for entering into any discussion concerning them. The passages above quoted from D'Alembert, from Locke, and from Smith, are sufficient to shew how little probability there is, in the actual state of logical science, of uniting the opinions of the learned in favour of any one scheme of partition. To prefix, therefore, such a scheme to a work which is professedly to be carried on by a set of unconnected writers, would be equally presumptuous and useless; and, on the most favourable supposition, could tend only to fetter, by means of dubious definitions, the subsequent freedom of thought and of expression. The example of the French *Encyclopédie* cannot be here justly alleged as a precedent. The preliminary pages by which it is introduced were written by the two persons who projected the whole plan, and who considered themselves as responsible, not only for their own admirable articles, but for the general conduct of the execution; whereas, on the present occasion, a porch was to be adapted to an irregular edifice, reared at different periods by different architects. It seemed, accordingly, most advisable to avoid as much as possible, in these introductory Essays, all innovations in language, and, in describing the different arts and sciences, to follow scrupulously the prevailing and most intelligible phraseology. The task of defining them with a greater degree of precision properly devolves upon those to whose province it belongs, in the progress of the work, to unfold in detail their elementary principles.

The Sciences to which I mean to confine my observations are Metaphysics, Ethics, and Political Philosophy; understanding, by Metaphysics, not the Ontology and Pneumatology of the schools, but the inductive Philosophy of the Human Mind; and limiting the phrase Political Philosophy almost exclusively to the modern science of Political Economy; or (to express myself in terms at once more comprehensive and more precise) to that branch of the theory of legislation which, according to Bacon's definition, aims to ascertain those " Leges legum, ex quibus informatio peti potest quid in singulis legibus bene aut perperam positum aut constitutum sit." The close affinity between these three departments of knowledge, and the easy transitions by which the curiosity is invited from the study of any one of them to that of the other two, will sufficiently appear from the following Historical Review.

DISSERTATION.

PART I.

In the following Historical and Critical Sketches, it has been judged proper by the different writers, to confine their views entirely to the period which has elapsed since the *revival of letters*. To have extended their retrospects to the ancient world, would have crowded too great a multiplicity of objects into the limited canvass on which they had to work. For my own part, I might perhaps, with still greater propriety, have confined myself exclusively to the two last centuries, as the Sciences of which I am to treat present but little matter for useful remark, prior to the time of Lord Bacon. I shall make no apology, however, for devoting, in the first place, a few pages to some observations of a more general nature; and to some scanty gleanings of literary detail, bearing more or less directly on my principal design.

On this occasion, as well as in the sequel of my Discourse, I shall avoid, as far as is consistent with distinctness and perspicuity, the minuteness of the mere bibliographer; and, instead of attempting to amuse my readers with a series of critical epigrams, or to dazzle them with a rapid succession of evanescent portraits, shall study to fix their attention on those great *lights of the world* by whom the torch of science has been successively seized and transmitted.[1] It is, in fact, such leading characters alone which furnish matter for philosophical history. To enumerate the names and the labours of obscure or even secondary authors, (whatever amusement it might afford to men of curious erudition,) would contribute but little to illustrate the origin and filiation of consecutive systems, or the gradual development and progress of the human mind.

---

[1] I have ventured here to combine a scriptural expression with an allusion of Plato's to a Grecian game, an allusion which, in his writings, is finely and pathetically applied to the rapid succession of generations, through which the continuity of human life is maintained from age to age, and which are perpetually transferring from hand to hand the concerns and duties of this fleeting scene Γεννῶντις καὶ ἐκτρίφοντις παῖδας, καθάπερ λαμπάδα τὸν βίον παραδιδόντις ἄλλοις ἐξ ἄλλων. — (Plato, *Leg.* lib vi)

"Et quasi cursores vitaï lampada tradunt."
Lucret

CHAPTER I.

FROM THE REVIVAL OF LETTERS TO THE PUBLICATION OF BACON'S
PHILOSOPHICAL WORKS.

THE long interval, commonly known by the name of the *middle ages*, which immediately preceded the revival of letters in the western part of Europe, forms the most melancholy blank, which occurs, from the first dawn of recorded civilisation, in the intellectual and moral history of the human race. In one point of view alone, the recollection of it is not altogether unpleasing, inasmuch as, by the proof it exhibits of the inseparable connexion between ignorance and prejudice on the one hand, and vice, misery, and slavery on the other, it affords, in conjunction with other causes, which will afterwards fall under our review, some security against any future recurrence of a similar calamity.

It would furnish a very interesting and instructive subject of speculation, to record and to illustrate (with the spirit, however, rather of a philosopher than of an antiquary) the various abortive efforts, which, during this protracted and seemingly hopeless period of a thousand years, were made by enlightened individuals, to impart to their contemporaries the fruits of their own acquirements. For in no one age from its commencement to its close, does *the continuity of knowledge* (if I may borrow an expression of Mr. Harris) seem to have been entirely interrupted: "There was always a faint twilight, like that auspicious gleam which, in a summer's night, fills up the interval between the setting and the rising sun."[1] On the present occa-

---
[1] *Philological Inquiries*, Part III chap. i.

sion, I shall content myself with remarking the important effects produced by the numerous monastic establishments all over the Christian world, in preserving, amidst the general wreck, the inestimable remains of Greek and Roman refinement, and in keeping alive, during so many centuries, those scattered sparks of truth and of science, which were afterwards to kindle into so bright a flame. I mention this particularly, because, in our zeal against the vices and corruptions of the Romish Church, we are too apt to forget, how deeply we are indebted to its superstitious and apparently useless foundations, for the most precious advantages that we now enjoy.

The study of the Roman Law, which, from a variety of causes, natural as well as accidental, became, in the course of the twelfth century, an object of general pursuit, shot a strong and auspicious ray of intellectual light across the surrounding darkness. No study could then have been presented to the curiosity of men, more happily adapted to improve their taste, to enlarge their views, or to invigorate their reasoning powers; and although, in the first instance, prosecuted merely as the object of a weak and undistinguishing idolatry, it nevertheless conducted the student to the very confines of ethical as well as of political speculation; and served, in the meantime, as a substitute of no inconsiderable value for both these sciences. Accordingly we find that, while in its *immediate* effects it powerfully contributed, wherever it struck its roots, by ameliorating and systematizing the administration of justice, to accelerate the progress of order and of civilisation, it afterwards furnished, in the farther career of human advancement, the parent stock on which were grafted the first rudiments of pure ethics and of liberal politics taught in modern times. I need scarcely add, that I allude to the systems of *natural jurisprudence* compiled by Grotius and his successors; systems which, for a hundred and fifty years, engrossed all the learned industry of the most enlightened part of Europe; and which, however unpromising in their first aspect, were destined, in the last result, to prepare the way for that never to be forgotten change in the literary taste of the eighteenth century, " which has everywhere turned the spirit of philosophical inquiry from frivolous or abstruse speculations, to the business and affairs of men."[1]

The revival of letters may be considered as coeval with the fall of the Eastern empire, towards the close of the fifteenth century. In consequence of this event, a number of learned Greeks took refuge in Italy, where the taste for literature already introduced by Dante, Petrarch, and Boccaccio, together with the liberal patronage of the illustrious House of Medicis, secured them a welcome reception. A knowledge of the Greek tongue soon became fashionable; and the learned, encouraged by the rapid diffusion which the art of printing now gave to their labours, vied with each other in rendering the Greek authors accessible, by means of Latin translations, to a still wider circle of readers.

For a long time, indeed, after the era just mentioned, the progress of useful knowledge was extremely slow. The passion for logical disputation was succeeded by an unbounded admiration for the wisdom of antiquity; and in proportion as the pedantry of the schools disappeared in the universities, that of erudition and philology occupied its place.

Meanwhile an important advantage was gained in the immense stock of materials which the ancient authors supplied to the reflections of speculative men; and which, although frequently accumulated with little discrimination or profit, were much more favourable to the development of taste and of genius than the unsubstantial subtleties of ontology or of dialectics. By such studies were formed Erasmus,[2] Ludovicus

[1] Dr Robertson, from whom I quote these words, has mentioned this change as the glory of the *present age*, meaning, I presume, the period which has elapsed since the time of Montesquieu. By what steps the philosophy to which he alludes took its rise from the systems of jurisprudence previously in fashion, will appear in the sequel of this Discourse.

[2] The writings of Erasmus probably contributed still more than those of Luther himself to the progress of the Reformation among men of education and taste; but, without the co-operation of bolder and more decided characters than his, little would to this day have been effected in Europe among the lower orders. "Erasmus imagined," as is observed by his biographer, "that at length, by training up youth in learning and useful knowledge, those religious improvements would gradually be

Vives,[1] Sir Thomas More,[2] and many other accomplished scholars of a similar character, who, if they do not rank in the same line with the daring reformers by whom the errors of the Catholic Church were openly assailed, certainly exhibit a very striking contrast to the barbarous and unenlightened writers of the preceding age

The Protestant Reformation, which followed immediately after, was itself one of the natural consequences of the revival of letters, and of the invention of printing. But although, in one point of view, only an *effect*, it is not, on the present occasion, less entitled to notice than the *causes* by which it was produced.

The renunciation, in a great part of Europe, of theological

---

brought about, which the princes, the prelates, and the divines of his days could not be persuaded to admit or to tolerate."—(Jortin, p 279) In yielding, however, to this pleasing expectation, Erasmus must have flattered himself with the hope, not only of a perfect freedom of literary discussion, but of such reforms in the prevailing modes of instruction, as would give complete scope to the energies of the human mind:—for, where books and teachers are subjected to the censorship of those who are hostile to the dissemination of truth, they become the most powerful of all auxiliaries to the authority of established errors

It was long a proverbial saying among the ecclesiastics of the Romish Church, that "Erasmus laid the egg, and Luther hatched it;" and there is more truth in the remark, than in most of their sarcasms on the same subject.

[1] Ludovicus Vives was a learned Spaniard, intimately connected both with Erasmus and More; with the former of whom he lived for some time at Louvain, "where they both promoted literature as much as they could, though not without great opposition from some of the divines"—Jortin, p. 255.

"He was invited into England by Wolsey in 1523: and coming to Oxford, he read the Cardinal's lecture of *Humanity*, and also lectures of Civil Law, which Henry VIII. and his Queen, Catharine, did him the honour of attending."—(*Ibid* p 207.) He died at Bruges in 1554

In point of good sense and acuteness, wherever he treats of philosophical questions, he yields to none of his contemporaries; and in some of his anticipations of the future progress of science, he discovers a mind more comprehensive and sagacious than any of them Erasmus appears, from a letter of his to Budæus, (dated in 1521,) to have foreseen the brilliant career which Vives, then a very young man, was about to run. "Vives in stadio literario, non minus feliciter quam gnaviter decertat, et si satis ingenium hominis novi, non conquiescet, donec omnes a tergo reliquerit"—For this letter, (the whole of which is peculiarly interesting, as it contains a character of Sir Thomas More, and an account of the extraordinary accomplishments of his daughters,) see Jortin's *Life of Erasmus*, vol. ii. p. 366, *et seq.*

[2] See Note A.

opinions so long consecrated by time, and the adoption of a creed more pure in its principles, and more liberal in its spirit, could not fail to encourage, on all other subjects, a congenial freedom of inquiry. These circumstances operated still more directly and powerfully, by their influence in undermining the authority of Aristotle; an authority which for many years was scarcely inferior in the schools to that of the Scriptures, and which, in some Universities, was supported by statutes, requiring the teachers to promise upon oath, that, in their public lectures, they would follow no other guide.

Luther,[1] who was perfectly aware of the corruptions which the Romish Church had contrived to connect with their veneration for the Stagirite,[2] not only threw off the yoke himself, but, in various parts of his writings, speaks of Aristotle with most unbecoming asperity and contempt.[3] In one very remarkable passage, he asserts, that the study of Aristotle was wholly useless, not only in Theology, but in Natural Philosophy. "What does it contribute," he asks, "to the knowledge of things, to trifle and cavil in language conceived and prescribed by Aristotle, concerning matter, form, motion, and time?"[4] The same

---

[1] Born 1483, died 1546.

[2] In one of his letters he writes thus: "Ego simpliciter credo, quod impossibile sit ecclesiam reformari, nisi funditus canones, decretales, scholastica theologia, philosophia, logica, ut nunc habentur, eradicentur, et alia instituantur"—Bruckeri *Hist Crit Phil.* tom iv p 95

[3] For a specimen of Luther's scurrility against Aristotle, see Bayle, Art *Luther*, Note HH

In Luther's *Colloquia Mensalia* we are told, that "he abhorred the schoolmen, and called them sophistical locusts, caterpillars, frogs, and lice" From the same work we learn, that "he hated Aristotle, but highly esteemed Cicero, as a wise and good man"—See Jortin's *Life of Erasmus*, p 121

[4] "Nihil adjumenti ex ipso haberi posse non solum ad theologiam seu sacras literas, verum etiam ad ipsam naturalem philosophiam. Quid enim juvet ad rerum cognitionem, si de materia, forma, motu, tempore, nugari et cavillari queas verbis ab Aristotele conceptis et præscriptis?"—Bruck *Hist. Phil* tom iv p 101

The following passage to the same purpose is quoted by Bayle. "Non mihi persuadebitis, philosophiam esse garrulitatem illam de materia, motu, infinito, loco, vacuo, tempore, quæ ferè in Aristotele sola discimus, talia quæ nec intellectum, nec affectum, nec communes hominum mores quidquam juvent; tantum contentionibus serendis, seminandisque idonea"—Bayle, Art *Luther*, Note HH

I borrow from Bayle another short extract from Luther: "Nihil ita ardet animus, quàm histrionem illum, (Aristotelem,) qui tam verè Græca larva ecclesiam lusit, multis revelare, igno-

freedom of thought on topics not strictly theological, formed a prominent feature in the character of Calvin. A curious instance of it occurs in one of his letters, where he discusses an ethical question of no small moment in the science of political economy:—" How far it is consistent with morality to accept of interest for a pecuniary loan ?" On this question, which, even in Protestant countries, continued, till a very recent period, to divide the opinions both of divines and lawyers, Calvin treats the authority of Aristotle, and that of the Church, with equal disregard. To the former, he opposes a close and logical argument, not unworthy of Mr Bentham. To the latter he replies, by shewing, that the Mosaic law on this point was not a moral but a municipal prohibition; a prohibition not to be judged of from any particular text of Scripture, but upon the principles of natural equity.[1] The example of these two Fathers of the Reformation, would probably have been followed by consequences still greater and more immediate, if Melanchthon had not unfortunately given the sanction of his name to the doctrines of the Peripatetic school;[2] but still, among the Reformers in general, the credit of these doctrines gradually declined, and a spirit of research and of improvement prevailed

The invention of printing, which took place very nearly at the same time with the fall of the Eastern Empire, besides adding greatly to the efficacy of the causes above-mentioned, must have been attended with very important effects of its own, on the progress of the human mind. For us who have been accus-

---

miniamque ejus cunctis ostendere, si otium esset Habeo in manus commentariolos in 1 Physicorum, quibus fabulam Aristæi denuò agere statui in meum istum Protea (Aristotelem) Pars crucis meæ vel maxima est, quod videre cogor fratrum optima ingenia, bonis studiis nata, in istis cœnis vitam agere, et operam perdere "—*Ibid.*

That Luther was deeply skilled in the scholastic philosophy we learn from very high authority, that of Melanchthon, who tells us farther, that he was a strenuous partisan of the sect of *Nominalists*, or, as they were then generally called, *Terminists*—Bruck tom iv pp 93, 94, *et seq*.

[1] See Note B.

[2] " Et Melanchthoni quidem præcipue debetur conservatio philosophiæ Aristotelicæ in academiis protestantium Scripsit is compendia plerarumque disciplinarum philosophiæ Aristotelicæ, quæ in Academiis diu regnarunt "—Heineccii, *Elem Hist Phil* §ciii See also *Bayle's Dict*, Art *Melanchthon*

tomed, from our infancy, to the use of books, it is not easy to form an adequate idea of the disadvantages which those laboured under, who had to acquire the whole of their knowledge through the medium of universities and schools;—blindly devoted as the generality of students must then have been to the peculiar opinions of the teacher, who first unfolded to their curiosity the treasures of literature and the wonders of science. Thus error was perpetuated; and, instead of yielding to time, acquired additional influence in each successive generation.[1] In modern times, this influence of names is, comparatively speaking, at an end. The object of a public teacher is no longer to inculcate a particular system of dogmas, but to prepare his pupils for exercising their own judgments; to exhibit to them an outline of the different sciences, and to suggest subjects for their future examination. The few attempts to establish schools, and to found sects, have all (after perhaps a temporary success) proved abortive. Their effect, too, during their short continuance, has been perfectly the reverse of that of the schools of antiquity; for whereas these were instrumental, on many occasions, in establishing and diffusing error in the world, the founders of our modern sects, by mixing up important truths with their own peculiar tenets, and by disguising them under the garb of a technical phraseology, have fostered such prejudices against themselves, as have blinded the public mind to all the lights

---

[1] It was in consequence of this mode of conducting education, by means of oral instruction alone, that the different sects of philosophy arose in ancient Greece; and it seems to have been with a view of counteracting the obvious inconveniences resulting from them, that Socrates introduced his peculiar method of questioning, with an air of sceptical diffidence, those whom he was anxious to instruct; so as to allow them, in forming their conclusions, the complete and unbiassed exercise of their own reason. Such, at least, is the apology offered for the apparent indecision of the Academic school, by one of its wisest, as well as most eloquent adherents. "As for other sects," says Cicero, "who are bound in fetters, before they are able to form any judgment of what is right or true, and who have been led to yield themselves up, in their tender years, to the guidance of some friend, or to the captivating eloquence of the teacher whom they have first heard, they assume to themselves the right of pronouncing upon questions of which they are completely ignorant; adhering to whatever creed the wind of doctrine may have driven them, as if it were the only rock on which their safety depended."—Cic. *Lucullus*, 3

they were able to communicate. Of this remark a melancholy illustration occurs (as M Turgot long ago predicted) in the case of the French economists ; and many examples of a similar import might be produced from the history of science in our country ; more particularly from the history of the various medical and metaphysical schools which successively rose and fell during the last century

With the circumstances already suggested, as conspiring to accelerate the progress of knowledge, another has co-operated very extensively and powerfully ; the rise of the lower orders in the different countries of Europe,—in consequence partly of the enlargement of commerce, and partly of the efforts of the Sovereigns to reduce the overgrown power of the feudal aristocracy.

Without this emancipation of the lower orders, and the gradual diffusion of wealth by which it was accompanied, the advantages derived from the invention of printing would have been extremely limited. A certain degree of ease and independence is essentially requisite to inspire men with the desire of knowledge, and to afford the leisure necessary for acquiring it ; and it is only by the encouragement which such a state of society presents to industry and ambition, that the selfish passions of the multitude can be interested in the intellectual improvement of their children. It is only, too, in such a state of society, that education and books are likely to increase the sum of human happiness ; for while these advantages are confined to one privileged description of individuals, they but furnish them with an additional engine for debasing and misleading the minds of their inferiors. To all which it may be added, that it is chiefly by the shock and collision of different and opposite prejudices, that truths are gradually cleared from that admixture of error which they have so strong a tendency to acquire, wherever the course of public opinion is forcibly constrained and guided within certain artificial channels, marked out by the narrow views of human policy. The diffusion of knowledge, therefore, occasioned by the rise of the lower orders, would necessarily contribute to the improvement of useful

CHAP. I.—PHILOSOPHY FROM THE REVIVAL TO BACON.   33

science, not merely in proportion to the arithmetical number of cultivated minds now combined in the pursuit of truth, but in a proportion tending to accelerate that important effect with a far greater rapidity.

Nor ought we here to overlook the influence of the foregoing causes, in encouraging among authors the practice of addressing the multitude in their own vernacular tongues. The zeal of the Reformers first gave birth to this invaluable innovation; and imposed on their adversaries the necessity of employing, in their own defence, the same weapons [1] From that moment the prejudice began to vanish which had so long confounded knowledge with erudition; and a revolution commenced in the republic of letters, analogous to what the invention of gunpowder produced in the art of war. "All the splendid distinctions of mankind," as the Champion and Flower of Chivalry indignantly exclaimed, "were thereby thrown down; and the naked shepherd levelled with the knight clad in steel."

To all these considerations may be added the gradual effects of time and experience in correcting the errors and prejudices which had misled philosophers during so long a succession of ages. To this cause, chiefly, must be ascribed the ardour with which we find various ingenious men, soon after the period in question, employed in prosecuting *experimental* inquiries; a species of study to which nothing analogous occurs in the history of ancient science.[2] The boldest and most successful of this new school was the celebrated Paracelsus; born in 1493, and consequently only ten years younger than Luther. " It is impossible to doubt," says Le Clerc, in his *History of Physic,* "that he possessed an extensive knowledge of what

[1] "The sacred books were, in almost all the kingdoms and states of Europe, translated into the language of each respective people, particularly in Germany, Italy, France, and Britain "— (Mosheim's *Eccles. Hist* vol. iii. p. 265) The effect of this single circumstance in multiplying the number of readers and of thinkers, and in giving a certain stability to the mutable forms of oral speech, may be easily imagined The vulgar translation of the Bible into English, is pronounced by Dr Lowth to be still the best standard of our language

[2] "Hæc nostra (ut sæpe diximus) felicitatis cujusdam sunt potius quam facultatis, *et potius temporis partus quam ingenii*"—*Nov Org* lib. 1 c. xxiii

is called the *Materia Medica,* and that he had employed much time in working on the animal, the vegetable, and the mineral substances of which it is composed. He seems, besides, to have tried an immense number of experiments in chemistry; but he has this great defect, that he studiously conceals or disguises the results of his long experience." The same author quotes from Paracelsus a remarkable expression, in which he calls the philosophy of Aristotle *a wooden foundation.* " He ought to have attempted," continues Le Clerc, "to have laid a better; but if he has not done it, he has at least, by discovering its weakness, invited his successors to look out for a firmer basis."[1]

Lord Bacon himself, while he censures the moral frailties of Paracelsus, and the blind empiricism of his followers, indirectly acknowledges the extent of his experimental information: "The ancient sophists may be said to have hid, but Paracelsus extinguished the light of nature. The sophists were only deserters of experience, but Paracelsus has betrayed it. At the same time, he is so far from understanding the right method of conducting experiments, or of recording their results, that he has added to the trouble and tediousness of experimenting. By wandering through the wilds of experience, his disciples sometimes stumble upon useful discoveries, not by reason, but by accident, whence rashly proceeding to form theories, they carry the smoke and tarnish of their art along with them, and, like childish operators at the furnace, attempt to raise a structure of philosophy with a few experiments of distillation."

Two other circumstances, of a nature widely different from those hitherto enumerated, although, probably, in no small degree to be accounted for on the same principles, seconded, with an incalculable accession of power, the sudden inpulse which the human mind had just received. The same century which the invention of printing and the revival of letters have made for ever memorable, was also illustrated by the discovery of the New World and of the passage to India by the Cape of Good Hope;—events which may be justly regarded as fixing a new

[1] *Histoire de la Médecine,* (à la Haye, 1729) p 819

era in the political and moral history of mankind, and which still continue to exert a growing influence over the general condition of our species. "It is an era," as Raynal observes, "which gave rise to a revolution, not only in the commerce of nations, but in the manners, industry, and government of the world. At this period new connexions were formed by the inhabitants of the most distant regions, for the supply of wants which they had never before experienced. The productions of climates situated under the equator were consumed in countries bordering on the pole; the industry of the north was transplanted to the south, and the inhabitants of the west were clothed with the manufactures of the east; a general intercourse of opinions, laws, and customs, diseases and remedies, virtues and vices, was established among men.

"Everything," continues the same writer, "has changed, and must yet change more. But it is a question whether the revolutions that are past, or those which must hereafter take place, have been, or can be, of any utility to the human race. Will they add to the tranquillity, to the enjoyments, and to the happiness of mankind? Can they improve our present state, or do they only change it?"

I have introduced this quotation, not with the design of attempting at present any reply to the very interesting question with which it concludes, but merely to convey some slight notion of the political and moral importance of the events in question. I cannot, however, forbear to remark, in addition to Raynal's eloquent and impressive summary, the inestimable treasure of new facts which these events have furnished for illustrating the versatile nature of man and the history of civil society. In this respect (as Bacon has well observed) they have fully verified the Scripture prophecy, *Multi pertransibunt, et augebitur scientia;* or, in the still more emphatic words of our English version, "Many shall go to and fro, and knowledge shall be increased."[1] The same prediction may be applied to the gra-

---

[1] "Neque omittenda est prophetia Danielis de ultimis mundi temporibus; *multi pertransibunt, et augebitur scientia* Manifeste innuens et significans, esse in fatis, id est, in providentia, ut pertransitus mundi (qui per tot longin-

dual renewal (in proportion as modern governments became effectual in securing order and tranquillity) of that intercourse between the different states of Europe which had, in a great measure, ceased during the anarchy and turbulence of the middle ages.

In consequence of these combined causes, aided by some others of secondary importance,[1] the Genius of the human race

---

quas navigationes impletur plane, aut jam in opere esse videtur) et augmenta scientiarum in eandem ætatem incidant"—*Nov. Org* lib 1 § xcii.

[1] Such as the *accidental* inventions of the telescope and of the microscope The powerful influence of these inventions may be easily conceived, not only in advancing the sciences of astronomy and of natural history, but in banishing many of the scholastic prejudices then universally prevalent The effects of the telescope, in this respect, have been often remarked, but less attention has been given to those of the microscope—which, however, it is probable, contributed not a little to prepare the way for the modern revival of the Atomic or Corpuscular Philosophy, by Bacon, Gassendi, and Newton That, on the mind of Bacon, the wonders disclosed by the microscope produced a strong impression in favour of the Epicurean physics, may be inferred from his own words "Perspicillum (microscopicum) si vidisset Democritus, exsiluisset forte, et modum videndi Atomum (quem ille invisibilem omnino affirmavit) inventum fuisse putasset "—*Nov Org*. lib ii § 39

We are told in the Life of Galileo, that when the telescope was invented, some individuals carried to so great a length their devotion to Aristotle, that they positively refused to look through that instrument so averse were they to open their eyes to any truths inconsistent with their favourite creed.—(*Vita del Galileo*, Venezia, 1744) It is amusing to find some other followers of the Stagirite, a very few years afterwards, when they found it impossible any longer to call in question the evidence of sense, asserting that it was from a passage in Aristotle (where he attempts to explain why stars become visible in the daytime when viewed from the bottom of a deep well) that the invention of the telescope was borrowed. The two facts, when combined together, exhibit a truly characteristical portrait of one of the most fatal weaknesses incident to humanity, and form a moral apologue, daily exemplified on subjects of still nearer and higher interest than the phenomena of the heavens

In ascribing to *accident* the inventions of the telescope and of the microscope, I have expressed myself in conformity to common language, but it ought not to be overlooked, that an invention may be accidental with respect to the particular author, and yet may be the natural result of the circumstances of society at the period when it took place As to the instruments in question, the combination of lenses employed in their structure is so simple, that it could scarcely escape the notice of *all* the experimenters and mechanicians of that busy and inquisitive age. A similar remark has been made by Condorcet concerning the invention of printing "L'invention de l'imprimerie a sans doute avancé le progrès de l'espèce humaine; mais cette invention étoit elle-même une suite de l'usage de la lecture répandu dans un grand nombre de pays " — *Vie de Turgot*

seems, all at once, to have awakened with renovated and giant strength from his long sleep. In less than a century from the invention of printing and the fall of the Eastern empire, Copernicus discovered the true theory of the planetary motions, and a very few years afterwards, was succeeded by the three great precursors of Newton—Tycho Brahe, Kepler, and Galileo.

The step made by Copernicus may be justly regarded as one of the proudest triumphs of human reason;—whether we consider the sagacity which enabled the author to obviate, to his own satisfaction, the many plausible objections which must have presented themselves against his conclusions, at a period when the theory of motion was so imperfectly understood; or the bold spirit of inquiry which encouraged him to exercise his private judgment, in opposition to the authority of Aristotle,—to the decrees of the Church of Rome,—and to the universal belief of the learned, during a long succession of ages. He appears, indeed, to have well merited the encomium bestowed on him by Kepler, when he calls him "a man of vast genius, and, what is of still greater moment in these researches, a man of a free mind."

The establishment of the Copernican system, beside the new field of study which it opened to Astronomers, must have had great effects on philosophy in all its branches, by inspiring those sanguine prospects of future improvement, which stimulate curiosity and invigorate the inventive powers. It afforded to the common sense, even of the illiterate, a palpable and incontrovertible proof, that the ancients had not exhausted the stock of possible discoveries; and that, in matters of science, the creed of the Romish Church was not infallible. In the conclusion of one of Kepler's works, we perceive the influence of these prospects on his mind. "Hæc et cetera hujusmodi latent in pandectis ævi sequentis, non antea discenda, quam librum hunc Deus arbiter seculorum recluserit mortalibus."[1]

I have hitherto taken no notice of the effects of the revival

[1] *Epit. Astron Copernic.*

of letters on Metaphysical, Moral, or Political science. The truth is, that little deserving of our attention occurs in any of these departments prior to the seventeenth century; and nothing which bears the most remote analogy to the rapid strides made, during the sixteenth, in mathematics, astronomy, and physics. The influence, indeed, of the Reformation on the *practical* doctrines of ethics appears to have been great and immediate. We may judge of this from a passage in Melanchthon, where he combats the pernicious and impious tenets of those theologians who maintained, that moral distinctions are created entirely by the arbitrary and revealed will of God. In opposition to this heresy he expresses himself in these memorable words:—" Wherefore our decision is this; that those precepts which learned men have committed to writing, transcribing them from the common reason and common feelings of human nature, are to be accounted as not less divine, than those contained in the tables given to Moses; and that it could not be the intention of our Maker to supersede, by a law graven upon stone, that which is written with his own finger on the table of the heart."[1]—This language was, undoubtedly, a most important step towards a just system of Moral Philosophy; but still, like the other steps of the Reformers, it was only a return to common sense, and to the genuine spirit of Christianity, from the dogmas imposed on the credulity of mankind by an ambitious priesthood.[2] Many

---

[1] " Proinde sic statuimus, nihilo minus divina præcepta esse ea, quæ a sensu communi et naturæ judicio mutuati docti homines gentiles literis mandarunt, quam quæ extant in ipsis saxeis Mosis tabulis Neque ille ipse cælestis Pater pluris a nobis fieri eas leges voluit, quas in saxo scripsit, quam quas in ipsos animorum nostrorum sensus impresserat."

Not having it in my power at present to consult Melanchthon's works, I have transcribed the foregoing paragraph on the authority of a learned German Professor, Christ Meiners

See his *Historia Doctrinæ de Vero Deo* Lemgoviæ, 1780, p. 12.

[2] It is observed by Dr. Cudworth, that the doctrine which refers the origin of moral distinctions to the arbitrary appointment of the Deity, was strongly reprobated by the ancient fathers of the Christian church, and that it crept up afterward in the scholastic ages, Occam being among the first that maintained, that there is no act evil, but as it is prohibited by God, and which cannot be made good, if it be commanded by him. In this doctrine he was quickly

years were yet to elapse before any attempts were to be made to trace, with analytical accuracy, the moral phenomena of human life to their first principles in the constitution and condition of man; or even to disentangle the plain and practical lessons of ethics from the speculative and controverted articles of theological systems.[1]

followed by Petrus Alliacus, Andreas de Novo Castro, and others. See *Treatise of Immutable Morality*

It is pleasing to remark, how very generally the heresy here ascribed to Occam is now reprobated by good men of all persuasions. The Catholics have even begun to recriminate on the Reformers as the first broachers of it; and it is to be regretted, that in *some* of the writings of the latter, too near approaches to it are to be found. The truth is, (as Burnet long ago observed,) that the effects of the Reformation have not been confined to the reformed churches,—to which it may be added, that both Catholics and Protestants have, since that era, profited very largely by the general progress of the sciences and of human reason

I quote the following sentence from a highly respectable Catholic writer on the law of nature and nations:—" Qui rationem exsulare jubent a moralibus præceptis quæ in sacris literis traduntur, et in absurdam enormemque LUTHERI sententiam imprudentes incidunt (quam egregie et elegantissime refutavit Melchior Canus *Loc Theolog* lib ix. and x) et ea docent, quæ si sectatores inveniant moralia omnia susque deque miscere, et revelationem ipsam inutilem omnino et inefficacem reddere possent "—(Lampredi Florentini *Juris Naturæ et Gentium Theoremata*, tom ii. p. 195 Pisis, 1782) For the continuation of the passage, which would do credit to the most liberal Protestant, I must refer to the original work The zeal of Luther for the doctrine of the Nominalists had probably prepossessed him, in his early years, in favour of some of the theological tenets of Occam, and afterwards prevented him from testifying his disapprobation of them so explicitly and decidedly as Melanchthon and other reformers have done

[1] " The theological system (says the learned and judicious Mosheim) that *now* prevails in the Lutheran academies, is not of the same tenor or spirit with that which was adopted in the infancy of the Reformation. The glorious defenders of religious liberty, to whom we owe the various blessings of the Reformation, could not, at once, behold the truth in all its lustre, and in all its extent, but, as usually happens to persons that have been long accustomed to the darkness of ignorance, their approaches towards knowledge were but slow, and their views of things but imperfect."—(Maclaine's *Transl. of Mosheim* London, 2d ed. vol iv p 19) He afterwards mentions one of Luther's early disciples, (Amsdorff,) "who was so far transported and infatuated by his excessive zeal for the supposed doctrine of his master, as to maintain that *good works are an impediment to salvation*" —*Ibid.* p 39.

Mosheim, after remarking that "there are more excellent rules of conduct in the few practical productions of Luther and Melanchthon, than are to be found in the innumerable volumes of all the ancient *casuists* and *moralizers*," candidly acknowledges, "that the notions of these great men concerning the im-

A similar observation may be applied to the powerful appeals, in the early Protestant writers, to the moral judgment and moral feelings of the human race, from those casuistical subtleties, with which the schoolmen and monks of the middle ages had studied to obscure the light of nature, and to stifle the voice of conscience. These subtleties were precisely analogous in their spirit to the *pia et religiosa calliditas*, afterwards adopted in the casuistry of the Jesuits, and so inimitably exposed by Pascal in the *Provincial Letters*. The arguments against them employed by the Reformers, cannot, in strict propriety, be considered as positive accessions to the stock of human knowledge; but what scientific discoveries can be compared to them in value![1]

From this period may be dated the decline[2] of that worst of

portant science of morality were far from being sufficiently accurate or extensive. Melanchthon himself, whose exquisite judgment rendered him peculiarly capable of reducing into a compendious system the elements of every science, never seems to have thought of treating morals in this manner, but has inserted, on the contrary, all his practical rules and instructions, under the theological articles that relate to the *law, sin, free-will, faith, hope, and charity*"—Mosheim's *Eccles Hist* vol. iv pp. 23, 24

The same author elsewhere observes, that "the progress of morality among the reformed was obstructed by the very same means that retarded its improvement among the Lutherans, and that it was left in a rude and imperfect state by Calvin and his associates It was neglected amidst the tumult of controversy, and, while every pen was drawn to maintain certain systems of doctrine, few were employed in cultivating that master science which has *virtue, life,* and *manners* for its objects."—*Ibid.* pp. 120, 121

[1] "Et tamen ni doctores, *angelici, cherubici, seraphici* non modo uni-versam philosophiam ac theologiam erroribus quam plurimis inquinarunt; verum etiam in philosophiam moralem invexere sacerrima ista principia *probabilismi, methodi dirigendi intentionem, reservationis mentalis, peccati philosophici*, quibus *Jesuitæ* etiamnum mirifice delectantur "—Heinecc *Elem. Histor. Phil* § cii. See also the references

With respect to the ethics of the Jesuits, which exhibit a very fair picture of the general state of that science, prior to the Reformation, see the *Provincial Letters*, Mosheim's *Ecclesiastical History*, vol. iv p. 354, Dornford's *Translation of Putter's Historical Development of the Present Political Constitution of the Germanic Empire*, vol. ii p 6, and the Appendix to Penrose's *Bampton Lectures*.

[2] I have said, *the decline of this heresy*, for it was by no means *immediately* extirpated even in the reformed churches "As late as the year 1598, Daniel Hoffman, Professor of Divinity in the University of Helmstadt, laying hold of some particular opinions of Luther, extravagantly maintained, that philosophy was the mortal enemy of

all heresies of the Romish Church, which, by opposing revelation to reason, endeavoured to extinguish the light of both; and the absurdity (so happily described by Locke) became every day more manifest, of attempting "to persuade men to put out their eyes, that they might the better receive the remote light of an invisible star by a telescope."

In the meantime, a powerful obstacle to the progress of practical morality and of sound policy, was superadded to those previously existing in Catholic countries, by the rapid growth and extensive influence of the Machiavellian school. The founder of this new sect (or to speak more correctly, the systematizer and apostle of its doctrines) was born as early as 1469, that is, about ten years before Luther; and, like that reformer, acquired by the commanding superiority of his genius, an astonishing ascendant (though of a very different nature) over the minds of his followers. No writer, certainly, either in ancient or in modern times, has ever united, in a more remarkable degree, a greater variety of the most dissimilar and seemingly the most discordant gifts and attainments;—a profound acquaintance with all those arts of dissimulation and intrigue, which, in the petty cabinets of Italy, were then universally confounded with political wisdom; an imagination familiarized to the cool contemplation of whatever is perfidious or atrocious in the history of conspirators and of tyrants;—combined with a graphical skill in holding up to laughter the comparatively harmless follies of ordinary life. His dramatic humour has been often compared to that of Molière; but it resembles it rather in comic force, than in benevolent gaiety, or in chastened morality. Such as it is, however, it forms an extraordinary contrast to that strength of intellectual character, which, in one page, reminds us of the deep sense of Tacitus, and in the next, of the dark and infernal policy of Cæsar Borgia. To all this must be superadded a purity of taste, which has enabled him, as an his-

religion; that truth was divisible into two branches, the one *philosophical*, and the other *theological*; and that what was *true* in philosophy, was *false* in theology "—Mosheim, vol. iv. p 18

torian, to rival the severe simplicity of the Grecian masters, and a sagacity in combining historical facts, which was afterwards to afford lights to the school of Montesquieu.—[The opinion of the Cardinal de Retz on the character and talents of Machiavel is entitled to much attention. It is expressed fully by himself in the following sentences. " Un des plus grands malheurs que l'autorité Despotique des Ministres du dernier siècle ait causé dans l'Etat, c'est la pratique que leurs intérêts particuliers mal entendus y ont introduite, de soutenir toujours le supérieur contre l'inférieur. Cette maxime est de Machiavel, que la plupart des gens qui le lisent n'entendent pas, et que les autres croient avoir été habile, parce qu'il a toujours été méchant. Il s'en faut de beaucoup qu'il ne fut habile, et il s'est très souvent trompé, mais en nul endroit à mon opinion plus qu'en celui-ci." [1]]

Eminent, however, as the talents of Machiavel unquestionably were, he cannot be numbered among the benefactors of mankind. In none of his writings does he exhibit any marks of that lively sympathy with the fortunes of the human race, or of that warm zeal for the interests of truth and justice, without the guidance of which, the highest mental endowments, when applied to moral or to political researches, are in perpetual danger of mistaking their way. What is still more remarkable, he seems to have been altogether blind to the mighty changes in human affairs, which, in consequence of the recent invention of printing, were about to result from the progress of Reason and the diffusion of Knowledge. Through the whole of his *Prince* (the most noted as well as one of the latest of his publications) he proceeds on the supposition, that the sovereign has no other object in governing but his own advantage; the very circumstance which, in the judgment of Aristotle, constitutes the essence of the worst species of tyranny.[2] He assumes also

---

[1] [*Mémoires du Cardinal de Retz.* Liv iii (1650)]

[2] "There is a third kind of tyranny, which most properly deserves that odious name, and which stands in direct opposition to royalty: it takes place when one man, the worst and perhaps the basest in the country, governs a kingdom, with no other view than the advantage of himself and his family."—Aristotle's *Politics*, Book vi. chap. x See Dr. Gillies's Translation.

the possibility of retaining mankind in perpetual bondage by the old policy of the *double doctrine;* or, in other words, by enlightening the few, and hoodwinking the many;—a policy less or more practised by statesmen in all ages and countries; but which (wherever the freedom of the Press is respected) cannot fail, by the insult it offers to the discernment of the multitude, to increase the insecurity of those who have the weakness to employ it. It has been contended, indeed, by some of Machiavel's apologists, that his real object in unfolding and systematizing the mysteries of *King-craft*, was to point out indirectly to the governed the means by which the encroachments of their rulers might be most effectually resisted; and, at the same time, to satirize, under the ironical mask of loyal and courtly admonition, the characteristical vices of princes.[1] But, although this hypothesis has been sanctioned by several distinguished names, and derives some verisimilitude from various incidents in the author's life, it will be found, on examination, quite untenable; and accordingly it is now, I believe, very generally rejected. One thing is certain, that if such were actually Machiavel's views, they were much too refined for the capacity of his royal pupils. By many of these his book has been adopted as a manual for daily use; but I have never heard of a single instance, in which it has been regarded by this class of students as a disguised panegyric upon liberty and virtue. The question concerning the *motives* of the author is surely of little moment, when experience has enabled us to pronounce so decidedly on the practical *effects* of his precepts

"About the period of the Reformation," says Condorcet, "the principles of religious Machiavelism had become the *only* creed of princes, of ministers, and of pontiffs; and the same opinions had contributed to corrupt philosophy. What code, indeed, of morals," he adds, "was to be expected from a system, of which one of the principles is,—that it is necessary to support the morality of the people by false pretences,—and that men of enlightened minds have a right to retain others in the chains from which they have themselves contrived to escape!" The fact is

[1] See Note C

perhaps stated in terms somewhat too unqualified; but there are the best reasons for believing, that the exceptions were few, when compared with the general proposition.—[The Christian charity of John Calvin, in judging of the Roman Pontiffs, does not seem to have exceeded that of Condorcet. "Ad homines autem si veniamus, satis scitur quales reperturi simus Christi vicarios; Julius, scilicet, et Leo, et Clemens, et Paulus Christianæ fidei Columnæ erunt, primique religionis interpretes, qui nihil aliud de Christo tenuerunt nisi quod didicerant in schola Luciani. Sed quid tres aut quatuor Pontifices enumero, quasi vero dubium sit qualem religionis speciem professi sint jampridem Pontifices cum toto Cardinalium collegio? Primum enim arcanæ illius Theologiæ quæ inter eos regnat, caput est; nullum esse Deum; cæterum, quæcunque de Christo scripta sunt docentur mendacia esse et imposturas"[1]]

The consequences of the prevalence of such a creed among the rulers of mankind were such as might be expected. "Infamous crimes, assassinations, and poisonings, (says a French historian,) prevailed more than ever. They were thought to be the growth of Italy, where the rage and weakness of the opposite factions conspired to multiply them. Morality gradually disappeared, and with it all security in the intercourse of life. The first principles of duty were obliterated by the joint influence of atheism and of superstition."[2]

And here, may I be permitted to caution my readers against the common error of confounding the double doctrine of Machiavellian politicians, with the benevolent reverence for established opinions, manifested in the noted maxim of Fontenelle,—"that a wise man, even when his hand was full of truths, would often content himself with opening his little finger?" Of the advocates for the former, it may be justly said, that "they love darkness rather than light, *because their deeds are evil;*" well knowing (if I may borrow the words of Bacon) "that the open day-light doth not shew the masks and mummeries, and triumphs of the world, half so stately as candle-light." The philosopher, on the other hand, who is duly impressed with the

---

[1] [Calvini *Instit* lib iv cap 7, § 17.]   [2] Millot.

latter, may be compared to the oculist, who, after removing the cataract of his patient, prepares the still irritable eye, by the glimmering dawn of a darkened apartment, for enjoying in safety the light of day.[1]

Machiavel is well known to have been, at bottom, no friend to the priesthood; and his character has been stigmatized by many of the order, with the most opprobrious epithets. It is nevertheless certain, that to *his* maxims the royal defenders of the Catholic faith have been indebted for the spirit of that policy which they have uniformly opposed to the innovations of the Reformers. The *Prince* was a favourite book of the Emperor Charles V., and was called the *Bible* of Catharine of Medicis. At the court of the latter, while Regent of France, those who approached her are said to have professed openly its most atrocious maxims, particularly *that* which recommends to sovereigns not to commit crimes by halves. The Italian cardinals, who are supposed to have been the secret instigators of the massacre of St. Bartholomew, were bred in the same school.[2]

[1] How strange is the following misrepresentation of Fontenelle's fine and deep saying, by the comparatively coarse hand of the Baron de Grimm! "Il disoit, que s'il eût tenu la vérité dans ses mains comme un oiseau, il l'auroit etouffée, tant il regardoit le plus beau présent du ciel inutile et dangereux pour le genre humain."—(*Mémoires Historiques*, &c par le Baron de Grimm Londres, 1814. Tome 1 p. 340) Of the complete inconsistency of this statement, not only with the testimony of his most authentic biographers, but with the general tenor both of his life and writings, a judgment may be formed from an expression of D'Alembert, in his very ingenious and philosophical parallel between Fontenelle and La Motte. "Tous deux ont porté trop loin leur révolte décidée, quoique douce en apparence, contre les dieux et les lois du Parnasse; mais la liberté des opinions de la Motte semble tenir plus intimement à l intérêt personnel qu'il avoit de les soutenir, et la liberté des opinions de Fontenelle à *l'intérêt général, peut être quelquefois mal entendu, qu'il prenoit au progrès de la raison dans tous les genres*" What follows may be regarded in the light of a comment on the maxim above quoted: "La finesse de la Motte est plus développée, celle de Fontenelle laisse plus à deviner à son lecteur La Motte, sans jamais en trop dire, n'oublie rien de ce que son sujet lui présente, met habilement tout en œuvre, et semble craindre perdre par des réticences trop subtiles quelqu'un de ses avantages; Fontenelle, sans jamais être obscur, excepté pour ceux qui ne méritent pas même qu'on soit clair, se menage à la fois et le plaisir de sous-entendre, et celui d'espérer qu'il sera pleinement entendu par ceux qui en sont dignes'—*Eloge de la Motte.*

[2] Voltaire, *Essay on Universal History.*

It is observed by Mr. Hume, that "there is scarcely any maxim in the *Prince* which subsequent experience has not entirely refuted" "Machiavel," says the same writer, "was certainly a great genius; but having confined his study to the furious and tyrannical governments of ancient times, or to the little disorderly principalities of Italy, his reasonings, especially upon monarchical governments, have been found extremely defective. The errors of this politician proceeded, in a great measure, from his having lived in too early an age of the world, to be a good judge of political truth."[1]

To these very judicious remarks, it may be added, that the bent of Machiavel's mind seems to have disposed him much more strongly to combine and to generalize his historical reading, than to remount to the first principles of political science, in the constitution of human nature, and in the immutable truths of morality. His conclusions, accordingly, ingenious and refined as they commonly are, amount to little more (with a few very splendid exceptions) than empirical results from the events of past ages. To the student of ancient history they may be often both interesting and instructive; but, to the modern politician, the most important lesson they afford is, the danger, in the present circumstances of the world, of trusting to such results, as maxims of universal application, or of permanent utility.

The progress of political philosophy, and along with it of morality and good order, in every part of Europe, since the period of which I am now speaking, forms so pleasing a comment on the profligate and short-sighted policy of Machiavel, that I cannot help pausing for a moment to remark the fact. In stating it, I shall avail myself of the words of the same profound writer, whose strictures on Machiavel's *Prince* I had already occasion to quote. "Though all kinds of government," says Mr. Hume, "be improved in modern times, yet monarchical government seems to have made the greatest advances towards perfection. It may now be affirmed of civilized monarchies, what was formerly said of republics alone, that

[1] *Essay on Civil Liberty.*

they are a government of laws, not of men. They are found susceptible of order, method, and constancy, to a surprising degree. Property is there secure, industry encouraged, the arts flourish, and the Prince lives secure among his subjects, like a father among his children. There are, perhaps, and have been for two centuries, near two hundred absolute princes, great and small, in Europe; and allowing twenty years to each reign, we may suppose that there have been in the whole two thousand monarchs or *tyrants*, as the Greeks would have called them. Yet of these there has not been one, not even Philip II. of Spain, so bad as Tiberius, Caligula, Nero, or Domitian, who were four in twelve among the Roman Emperors."[1]

For this very remarkable fact, it seems difficult to assign any cause equal to the effect, but the increased diffusion of knowledge (imperfect, alas! as this diffusion still is) by means of the Press; which, while it has raised, in free states, a growing bulwark against the oppression of rulers, in the light and spirit of the people, has, even under the most absolute governments, had a powerful influence—by teaching princes to regard the wealth, and prosperity, and instruction of their subjects, as the firmest basis of their grandeur—in directing their attention to objects of national and permanent utility How encouraging the prospect thus opened of the future history of the world! And what a motive to animate the ambition of those, who, in the solitude of the closet, aspire to bequeath their contributions, how slender soever, to the progressive mass of human improvement and happiness!—[The true interest of an absolute monarch, (says Gibbon,) generally coincides with that of his people. Their numbers, their wealth, their order, and their security, are the best and only foundations of real greatness; and were he totally devoid of virtue, prudence might supply its place, and would dictate the same rule of conduct.—*Decline of the Roman Empire*, c. v.]

In the bright constellation of scholars, historians, artists, and wits, who shed so strong a lustre on Italy during that splendid period of its history which commences with the revival of

[1] *Essay on Civil Liberty.*

letters, it is surprising how few names occur, which it is possible to connect, by any palpable link, with the philosophical or political speculations of the present times. As an original and profound thinker, the genius of Machiavel completely eclipses that of all his contemporaries. Not that Italy was then destitute of writers who pretended to the character of philosophers; but as their attempts were, in general, limited to the exclusive illustration and defence of some one or other of the ancient systems for which they had conceived a predilection, they added but little of their own to the stock of useful knowledge; and are now remembered chiefly from the occasional recurrence of their names in the catalogues of the curious, or in works of philological erudition. The zeal of Cardinal Bessarion, and of Marsilius Ficinus, for the revival of the Platonic philosophy, was more peculiarly remarkable; and, at one time, produced so general an impression, as to alarm the followers of Aristotle for the tottering authority of their master. If we may credit Launoius, this great revolution was on the point of being actually accomplished, when Cardinal Bellarmine warned Pope Clement VIII. of the peculiar danger of shewing any favour to a philosopher whose opinions approached so nearly as those of Plato to the truths revealed in the Gospel. In what manner Bellarmine connected his conclusions with his premises, we are not informed. To those who are uninitiated in the mysteries of the conclave, his inference would certainly appear much less logical than that of the old Roman Pagans, who petitioned the Senate to condemn the works of Cicero to the flames, as they predisposed the minds of those who read them for embracing the Christian faith.—[That the apprehensions of these Pagans were not altogether groundless, appears from the account given by St. Augustine of the progress of his own religious opinions (Not having the works of this father within my reach at present, I am obliged to quote him at second hand.) " Augustinus profecto lecto Ciceronis Hortensio, qui liber de laudibus erat Philosophiæ a deo admirari se solitum scribit nihil ut requireret hic amplius, præter Jesu Christi nomen. Hujus etiam libri lectione ad Christianæ, hoc est veræ Philosophiæ contemplationem incensum se fuisse ingenue confitetur. (Lib. iii. *Confess.* cap. 4, et lib. viii. cap 7, et principio Libri de *Vita Beata*).[1]

By a small band of bolder innovators, belonging to this golden age of Italian literature, the Aristotelian doctrines were more directly and powerfully assailed. Laurentius Valla, Marius Nizolius, and Franciscus Patricius,[2] have all of them transmitted their names to posterity as philosophical reformers, and, in particular, as revolters against the authority of the Stagirite. Of the individuals just mentioned, Nizolius is the only one who seems entitled to maintain a permanent place in the annals of modern science. His principal work, entitled *Antibarbarus*,[3] is not only a bold invective against the prevailing ignorance and barbarism of the schools, but contains so able an argument against the then fashionable doctrine of the Realists concerning *general ideas*, that Leibnitz thought it worth while, a century afterwards, to republish it, with the addition of a long and valuable preface written by himself.

At the same period with Franciscus Patricius, flourished

---

[1] [Cicero a Calumniis Vindicatus, auctore Andrea Schotto —Vide *Ciceronis Opera*. Edit. Verburgii, tom. i. p. 59]

[2] His *Discussiones Peripateticæ* were printed at Venice in 1571. Another work, entitled *Nova de Universis Philosophia*, also printed at Venice, appeared in 1593 I have never happened to meet with either: but from the account given of the author by Thuanus, he does not seem to have attracted that notice from his contemporaries to which his learning and talents entitled him (Thuan *Hist.* lib. cxix. xvii.) His *Discussiones Peripateticæ*, are mentioned by Brucker in the following terms: " *Opus egregium, doctum, varium, luculentum, sed invidia odioque in Aristotelem plenum satis superque* "—(*Hist. Phil* tom. iv p. 425.) The same very laborious and candid writer acknowledges the assistance he had derived from *Patricius* in his account of the Peripatetic philosophy —" In qua tractatione fatemur egregiam enitere Patricii doctrinam, ingenii elegantiam prorsus admirabilem, et quod primo loco ponendum est, insolitam veteris philosophiæ cognitionem, cujus ope nos Peripateticæ disciplinæ historiæ multoties lucem attulisse, grati suis locis professi sumus."—*Ibid* p. 426

[3] *Antibarbarus, sive de Veris Principiis et Vera Ratione Philosophandi contra Pseudo-philosophos*. Parmæ, 1553. " Les faux philosophos," dit Fontenelle, " étoient tous les scholastiques passés et présens , et Nizolius s'élève avec la dernière hardiesse contre leurs idées monstrueuses et leur langage barbare. La longue et constante admiration qu'on avoit eu pour Aristote, ne prouvoit, disoit-il, que la multitude des sots et la durée de la sottise " The merits of this writer are much too lightly estimated by Brucker.—See *Hist. Phil*. tom. iv. Pars I. pp. 91, 92.

another learned Italian, Albericus Gentilis, whose writings seem to have attracted more notice in England and Germany than in his own country. His attachment to the reformed faith having driven him from Italy, he sought an asylum at Oxford, where, in 1587, he was appointed professor of the Civil Law, an office which he held till the period of his death in 1611 [1] He was the author of a treatise *De Jure Belli*, in three books, which appeared successively in 1588 and 1589, and were first published together at Hanau in 1598. His name has already sunk into almost total oblivion; and I should certainly not have mentioned it on the present occasion, were it not for his indisputable merits as the precursor of Grotius, in a department of study which, forty years afterwards, the celebrated treatise *de Jure Belli et Pacis* was to raise to so conspicuous a rank among the branches of academical education. The avowed aim of this new science, when combined with the anxiety of Gentilis to counteract the effect of Machiavel's *Prince*, by representing it as a warning to subjects rather than as a manual of instruction for their rulers, may be regarded as satisfactory evidence of the growing influence, even at that era, of better ethical principles than those commonly imputed to the Florentine Secretary.[2]

The only other Italian of whom I shall take notice is Campanella,[3] a philosopher now remembered chiefly in consequence of his eccentric character and eventful life, but of whom Leibnitz has spoken in terms of such high admiration, as to place him in the same line with Bacon. After looking into several of his works with some attention, I must confess I am at a loss to conceive upon what grounds the eulogy of Leibnitz proceeds; but as it is difficult to suppose that the praise of this great man

[1] Wood's *Athenæ Oxonienses*, vol ii col 90 Dr Bliss's edition.

[2] The claims of Albericus Gentilis to be regarded as the father of *Natural Jurisprudence*, are strongly asserted by his countryman Lampredi, in his very judicious and elegant work, entitled, *Juris Publici Theoremata*, published at Pisa in 1782. " Hic primus jus aliquod Belli et esse et tradi posse excogitavit, et Belli et Pacis regulas explicavit primus, et fortasse in causa fuit cur Grotius opus suum conscribere aggrederetur, dignus sane qui præ ceteris memoretur, Italiæ enim, in qua ortus erat, et unde Juris Romani disciplinam hauserat, gloriam auxit, effecitque ut quæ fuerat bonarum artium omnium restitutrix et altrix, eadem esset et prima Jurisprudentiæ Naturalis magistra"

[3] Born 1568, died 1639

was, in any instance, the result of mere caprice, I shall put it in the power of my readers to judge for themselves, by subjoining a faithful translation of his words. I do this the more willingly, as the passage itself (whatever may be thought of the critical judgments pronounced in it) contains some general remarks on *intellectual character*, which are in every respect worthy of the author.

" Some men, in conducting operations where an attention to minutiæ is requisite, discover a mind vigorous, subtile, and versatile, and seem to be equal to any undertaking, how arduous soever. But when they are called upon to act on a greater scale, they hesitate, and are lost in their own meditations; distrustful of their judgment, and conscious of their incompetency to the scene in which they are placed; men, in a word, possessed of a genius rather acute than comprehensive. A similar difference may be traced among authors. What can be more acute than Descartes in Physics, or than Hobbes in Morals! And yet, if the one be compared with Bacon and the other with Campanella, the former writers seem to grovel upon the earth—the latter to soar to the heavens, by the vastness of their conceptions, their plans, and their enterprises, and to aim at objects beyond the reach of the human powers. The former, accordingly, are best fitted for delivering the first elements of knowledge, the latter for establishing conclusions of important and general application." [1]

---

[1] Leibnit *Opera*, vol. vi p. 303, Ed. Dutens.—It is probable that, in the above passage, Leibnitz alluded more to the elevated tone of Campanella's reasoning on moral and political subjects, when contrasted with that of Hobbes, than to the intellectual superiority of the former writer above the latter. No philosopher, certainly, has spoken with more reverence than Campanella has done, on various occasions, of the dignity of human nature. A remarkable instance of this occurs in his eloquent comparison of the *human hand* with the organs of touch in other animals (*Vide* Campan *Physiolog.* cap. xx art 2) Of his *Political Aphorisms,* (which form the third part of his treatise on *Morals,*) a sufficient idea for our purpose is conveyed by the concluding *corollary*,—" Probitas custodit regem populosque, non autem indocta Machiavellistarum astutia" On the other hand, Campanella's works abound with immoralities and extravagancies far exceeding those of Hobbes. In his idea of a perfect commonwealth, (to which he gives the name of *Civitas Solis,*) the impurity of his imagination and the unsoundness of his judgment are equally conspicuous.

The annals of France, during this period, present very scanty materials for the history of Philosophy. The name of the Chancellor De l'Hopital, however, must not be passed over in silence. As an author, he does not rank high, nor does he seem to have at all valued himself on the careless effusions of his literary hours; but as an upright and virtuous magistrate, he has left behind him a reputation unrivalled to this day.[1] His wise and indulgent principles on the subject of religious liberty, and the steadiness with which he adhered to them under circumstances of extraordinary difficulty and danger, exhibit a splendid contrast to the cruel intolerance which, a few years before, had disgraced the character of an illustrious Chancellor of England. The same philosophical and truly catholic spirit distinguished his friend, the President de Thou,[2] and gives the principal charm to the justly admired preface prefixed to his history. In tracing the progress of the human mind during the sixteenth century, such insulated and anomalous examples of the triumph of reason over superstition and bigotry deserve attention, not less than what is due, in a history of the experimental arts, to Friar Bacon's early anticipation of gunpowder and of the telescope.

Contemporary with these great men was Bodin, (or Bodinus,)[3] an eminent French lawyer, who appears to have been one of the first that united a philosophical turn of thinking with an extensive knowledge of jurisprudence and of history. His learning is often ill digested, and his conclusions still oftener rash and unsound; yet it is but justice to him to acknowledge that, in his views of the philosophy of law, he has approached very

He recommends, under certain regulations, a community of women, and in everything connected with procreation, lays great stress on the opinions of astrologers.

[1] "Magistrat au-dessus de tout éloge, et d'après lequel on a jugé tous ceux qui ont osé s'asseoir sur ce même tribunal sans avoir son courage ni ses lumières."—Henault, *Abrégé Chronologique.*

[2] "One cannot help admiring," says Dr. Jortin, "the *decent* manner in which the illustrious Thuanus hath spoken of Calvin: Acri vir ac vehementi ingenio, et admirabili facundia præditus; tum inter protestantes magni nominis Theologus"—(*Life of Erasmus,* p. 555.) The same writer has remarked the *great decency and moderation* with which Thuanus speaks of Luther.—*Ibid* p. 113

[3] Born 1530, died 1596.

nearly to some leading ideas of Lord Bacon,[1] while, in his refined combinations of historical facts, he has more than once struck into a train of speculation bearing a strong resemblance to that afterwards pursued by Montesquieu.[2] Of this resemblance, so remarkable an instance occurs in his chapter on the moral effects of Climate, and on the attention due to this circumstance by the legislator, that it has repeatedly subjected the author of *The Spirit of Laws* (but in my opinion without any good reason) to the imputation of plagiarism.[3] A resemblance to Montesquieu, still more honourable to Bodinus, may be traced in their common attachment to religious as well as to civil liberty. To have caught, in the sixteenth century, somewhat of the philosophical spirit of the eighteenth, reflects less credit on the force of his mind, than to have imbibed, in the midst of the theological controversies of his age, those lessons of mutual forbearance and charity, which a long and sad experience of the fatal effects of persecution has to this day so imperfectly taught to the most enlightened nations of Europe.

As a specimen of the liberal and moderate views of this philosophical politician, I shall quote two short passages from his treatise *De la République*, which seem to me objects of considerable curiosity, when contrasted with the general spirit of the age in which they were written. The first relates to liberty of

---

[1] See, in particular, the preface to his book entitled *Methodus ad facilem Historiarum cognitionem*

[2] See the work *De la République*, *passim*. In this treatise there are two chapters singularly curious, considering the time when they were written—the second and third chapters of the sixth book. The first is entitled *Des Finances;* the second, *Le Moyen d'empêcher que les Monnoyes soyent altérées de Prix ou falsifiées*. The reasonings of the author, on various points there treated of, will be apt to excite a smile among those who have studied the *Inquiry into the Wealth of Nations;* but it reflects no small credit on a lawyer of the sixteenth century to have subjected such questions to philosophical examination, and to have formed so just a conception, as Bodin appears evidently to have done, not only of the object, but of the importance of the modern science of political economy

Thuanus speaks highly of Bodin's dissertations *De re Monetaria*, which I have never seen. The same historian thus expresses himself with respect to the work *De Republica:* "Opus in quo ut omni scientiarum genere non tincti sed imbuti ingenii fidem fecit, sic nonnullis, qui recte judicant, non omnino ab *ostentationis innato genti vitio* vacuum se probavit."—*Hist* lib cxvii ix.

[3] See Note D.

conscience, for which he was a strenuous and intrepid advocate, not only in his publications, but as a member of the *Etats Généraux*, assembled at Blois in 1576. "The mightier that a man is," says Bodin, "the more justly and temperately he ought to behave himself towards all men, but especially towards his subjects. Wherefore the senate and people of Basil did wisely, who, having renounced the Bishop of Rome's religion, would not, upon the sudden, thrust the monks and nuns, with the other religious persons, out of their abbeys and monasteries, but only took order that, as they died, they should die both for themselves and their successors, expressly forbidding any new to be chosen in their places; so that, by that means, their colleges might by little and little, by the death of the fellows, be extinguished. Whereby it came to pass, that all the rest of the Carthusians, of their own accord, forsaking their cloisters, yet one of them all alone for a long time remained therein, quietly and without any disturbance, holding the right of his convent, being never enforced to change either his place, or habit, or old ceremonies, or religion before by him received. The like order was taken at Coire in the diet of the Grisons; wherein it was decreed, that the ministers of the reformed religion should be maintained of the profits and revenues of the church, the religious men, nevertheless, still remaining in their cloisters and convents, to be by their death suppressed, they being now prohibited to choose any new instead of them which died. By which means, they which professed the new religion, and they who professed the old, were both provided for."[1]

The aim of the chapter from which I have extracted the foregoing passage is to shew, that "it is a most dangerous thing, at

[1] Book iv. chap. iii.—The book from which this quotation is taken was published only twenty-three years after the murder of Servetus at Geneva, [on which consult Gibbon's *Misc. Works*, vol. ii p 214,] an event which leaves so deep a stain on the memory not only of Calvin, but on that of the milder and more charitable Melanchthon. The epistle of the latter to Bullinger, where he applauds the conduct of the judges who condemned to the flames this incorrigible heretic, affords the most decisive of all proofs, how remote the sentiments of the most enlightened Fathers of the Reformation were from those Christian and philosophical principles of toleration to which their noble exertions have gradually, and now almost universally, led the way.

one and the same time, to change the form, laws, and customs of a commonwealth." The scope of the author's reasonings may be judged of from the concluding paragraph.

"We ought then, in the government of a well ordered estate and commonwealth, to imitate and follow the great God of Nature, who in all things proceedeth easily, and by little and little; who of a little seed causeth to grow a tree, for height and greatness right admirable, and yet for all that insensibly; and still by means conjoining the extremities of nature, as by putting the spring between winter and summer, and autumn betwixt summer and winter, moderating the extremities of the terms and seasons, with the self-same wisdom which it useth in all other things also, and that in such sort as that no violent force or course therein appeareth."[1]

---

[1] Book iv. chap iii —The substance of the above reflection has been compressed by Bacon into the following well-known aphorisms :—

"Time is the greatest innovator; shall we then not imitate time?

"What innovator imitates time, which innovates so silently as to mock the sense?"

The resemblance between the two passages is still more striking in the Latin versions of their respective authors.

"Deum igitur præpotentem naturæ parentem imitemur, qui omnia paulatim : namque semina perquam exigua in arbores excelsas excrescere jubet, idque tam occultè ut nemo sentiat."—*Bodinus.*

"Novator maximus tempus; quidni igitur tempus imitemur?

"Quis novator tempus imitatur, quod novationes ita insinuat, ut sensus fallant?"—*Bacon.*

The treatise of Bodin, *De la République*, (by far the most important of his works,) was first printed at Paris in 1576, and was reprinted seven times in the space of three years It was translated into Latin by the author himself, with a view chiefly (as is said) to the accommodation of the scholars of England, among whom it was so highly esteemed, that lectures upon it were given in the University of Cambridge as early as 1580. In 1579, Bodin visited London in the suite of the Duc D'Alençon; a circumstance which probably contributed not a little to recommend his writings, so very soon after their publication, to the attention of our countrymen. In 1606, the treatise of *The Republic* was *done into English* by Richard Knolles, who appears to have collated the French and Latin copies so carefully and judiciously, that his version is, in some respects, superior to either of the originals. It is from this version, accordingly, that I have transcribed the passages above quoted, trusting that it will not be unacceptable to my readers, while looking back to the intellectual attainments of our forefathers, to have an opportunity, at the same time, of marking the progress which had been made in England, more than two centuries ago, in the arts of writing and of translation

For Dr Johnson's opinion of Knolles's merits as an historian and as an English writer, see the *Rambler*, No 123

Notwithstanding these wise and enlightened maxims, it must be owned, on the other hand, that Bodin has indulged himself in various speculations, which would expose a writer of the present times to the imputation of insanity. One of the most extraordinary of these, is his elaborate argument to prove, that, in a well constituted state, the father should possess the right of life and death over his children;—a paradox which forms an unaccountable contrast to the general tone of humanity which characterizes his opinions. Of the extent of his credulity on the subject of witchcraft, and of the deep horror with which he regarded those who affected to be sceptical about the reality of that crime, he has left a lasting memorial in a learned and curious volume entitled *Démonomanie;*[1] while the eccentricity of his religious tenets was such as to incline the candid mind of Grotius to suspect him of a secret leaning to the Jewish faith.[2]

In contemplating the characters of the eminent persons who appeared about this era, nothing is more interesting and instructive than to remark the astonishing combination, in the same minds, of the highest intellectual endowments, with the most deplorable aberrations of the understanding; and even, in numberless instances, with the most childish superstitions of the multitude. Of this apparent inconsistency, Bodinus does not furnish a solitary example. The same remark may be extended, in a greater or less degree, to most of the other celebrated names hitherto mentioned. Melanchthon, as appears

---

[1] *De la Démonomanie des Sorciers* Par J. Bodin Angevin, à Paris, 1580. This book, which exhibits so melancholy a contrast to the mental powers displayed in the treatise *De la République*, was dedicated by the author to his friend, the President de Thou; and it is somewhat amusing to find, that it exposed Bodin himself to the imputation of being a magician. For this we have the testimony of the illustrious historian just mentioned (Thuanus, lib. cxvii. ix.) Nor did it recommend the author to the good opinion of the Catholic Church, having been formally condemned and prohibited by the Roman Inquisition. The reflection of the Jesuit Martin del Rio on this occasion is worth transcribing "*Adeo lubricum et periculosum de his disserere, nisi Deum semper, et catholicam fidem, ecclesiæque Romanæ censuram tanquam cynosuram sequaris.*"—*Disquisitionum Magicarum*, libri sex. Auctore Martino del Rio, Societatis Jesu Presbytero Venet 1640, p. 8.

[2] *Epist ad Cordesium*, (quoted by Bayle.)

from his letters, was an interpreter of dreams, and a caster of nativities;[1] [Erasmus, as Mr. Gibbon has remarked, " who could see through much more plausible fables, believed firmly in witchcraft ,"[2]] and Luther not only sanctioned, by his authority, the popular fables about the sexual and prolific intercourse of Satan with the human race, but seems to have seriously believed that he had himself frequently seen the *arch-enemy* face to face, and held arguments with him on points of theology.[3] Nor was the study of the severer sciences, on all occasions, an effectual remedy against such illusions of the imagination The *sagacious* Kepler was an astrologer and a visionary; and his friend Tycho Brahe, *the Prince of Astronomers*, kept an idiot in his service, to whose prophecies he listened as revelations from above.[4] During the long night of Gothic barbarism, the intellectual world had again become, like the primitive earth, " without form and void;" the light had already appeared; " and God had seen the light that it was good," but the time was not yet come to " divide it from the darkness."[5]

---

[1] Jortin's *Life of Erasmus*, p 156

[2] [Gibbon's *Miscell Works*, vol. II. p. 76.—The character of Erasmus, both intellectual and moral, is drawn in the passage here referred to, with an impartial and masterly hand. The critical reflections on his Ciceronianus are entitled to particular attention.]

[3] See Note E.

[4] See *the Life of Tycho Brahe*, by Gassendi.

[5] I have allotted to Bodin a larger space than may seem due to his literary importance; but the truth is, I know of no political writer, of the same date, whose extensive and various and discriminating reading appears to me to have contributed more to facilitate and to guide the researches of his successors; or whose references to ancient learning have been more frequently transcribed without acknowledgment. Of late, his works have fallen into very general neglect, otherwise it is impossible that so many gross mistakes should be current about the scope and spirit of his principles. By many he has been mentioned as a zealot for republican forms of government, (probably for no better reason than that he chose to call his book a Treatise *De Republica:*) whereas, in point of fact, he is uniformly a warm and able advocate for monarchy, and, although no friend to tyranny, has, on more than one occasion, carried his monarchical principles to a very blameable excess (See, in particular, chapter fourth and fifth of the Sixth Book) On the other hand, Grouvelle, a writer of some note, has classed Bodin with Aristotle, as an advocate for domestic slavery. " The reasonings of both," he says, " are refuted by Montesquieu "— (*De l'autorité de Montesquieu dans la Révolution présente.* Paris, 1789) Whoever has the curiosity to compare Bodin

In the midst of the disorders, both political and moral, of that unfortunate age, it is pleasing to observe the anticipations of brighter prospects, in the speculations of a few individuals. Bodinus himself is one of the number;[1] and to his name may be added that of his countryman and predecessor Budæus.[2] But, of all the writers of the sixteenth century, Ludovicus Vives seems to have had the liveliest and the most assured foresight of the new career on which the human mind was about to enter. The following passage from one of his works would have done no discredit to the *Novum Organon:* " The similitude which many have fancied between the superiority of the moderns to the ancients, and the elevation of a dwarf on the back of a giant, is altogether false and puerile. Neither were *they* giants, nor are we dwarfs, but all of us men of the same standard,—and *we* the taller of the two, by adding their height to our own: Provided always, that we do not yield to them in study, attention, vigilance, and love of truth; for, if

and Montesquieu together, will be satisfied, that, on this point, their sentiments were exactly the same, and that, so far from refuting Bodin, Montesquieu has borrowed from him more than one argument in support of his general conclusion.

The merits of Bodin have been, on the whole, very fairly estimated by Bayle, who pronounces him " one of the ablest men that appeared in France during the sixteenth century." " Si nous voulons disputer à Jean Bodin la qualité d'écrivain exact et judicieux, laissons lui sans controverse, un grand génie, un vaste savoir, une mémoire et une lecture prodigieuses "

[1] See, in particular, his *Method of Studying History*, chap. vii. entitled, *Confutatio eorum qui quatuor Monarchias Aureaque Secula statuerunt* In this chapter, after enumerating some of the most important discoveries and inventions of the moderns, he concludes with mentioning the art of printing, of the value of which he seems to have formed a very just estimate. " Una Typographia cum omnibus veterum inventis certare facile potest. Itaque non minus peccant, qui à veteribus aiunt omnia comprehensa, quam qui illos de veteri multarum artium possessione deturbant Habet Natura scientiarum thesauros innumerabiles, qui nullis ætatibus exhauriri possunt " In the same chapter Bodinus expresses himself thus: " Ætas illa quam *auream* vocant, si ad nostram conferatur, *ferrea* videri possit."

[2] The works of Budæus were printed at Basle, in four volumes folio, 1557. My acquaintance with them is much too slight to enable me to speak of them from my own judgment. No scholar certainly stood higher in the estimation of his age " Quo viro," says Ludovicus Vives, " Gallia acutiore ingenio, acriore judicio, exactiore diligentia, majore eruditione nullum unquam produxit, hac vero ætate nec Italia quidem " The praise bestowed on him by other contemporary writers of the highest eminence is equally lavish.

these qualities be wanting, so far from mounting on the giant's shoulders, we throw away the advantages of our own just stature, by remaining prostrate on the ground."[1]

I pass over, without any particular notice, the names of some French logicians who flourished about this period, because, however celebrated among their contemporaries, they do not seem to form essential links in the History of Science. The bold and persevering spirit with which Ramus disputed, in the University of Paris, the authority of Aristotle, and the persecutions he incurred by this philosophical heresy, entitle him to an honourable distinction from the rest of his brethren. He was certainly a man of uncommon acuteness as well as eloquence, and placed in a very strong light some of the most vulnerable parts of the Aristotelian logic; without, however, exhibiting any marks of that deep sagacity which afterwards enabled Bacon, Descartes, and Locke, to strike at the very roots of the system. His copious and not inelegant style as a writer, recommended his innovations to those who were disgusted with the barbarism of the schools;[2] while his avowed partiality for the reformed faith (to which he fell a martyr in

---

[1] Vives *de Caus. Corrupt Artium*, lib 1. Similar ideas occur in the works of Roger Bacon: " Quanto juniores tanto perspicaciores, quia juniores posteriores successione temporum ingrediuntur labores priorum "—(*Opus Majus*, Edit Jebb. p 9) Nor were they altogether overlooked by ancient writers. " Veniet tempus, quo ista quæ latent nunc in lucem dies extrahet, et longioris ævi diligentia. Veniet tempus, quo posteri nostri tam aperta nos ignorasse mirabuntur."—(Seneca, *Quæst. Nat.* lib. vii. c 25) This language coincides exactly with that of the Chancellor Bacon; but it was reserved for the latter to illustrate the connexion between the progress of human *knowledge*, and of human *happiness;* or (to borrow his own phraseology) the connexion between the progress of knowledge, and the enlargement of man's power over the destiny of his own species Among other passages to this purpose, see *Nov Org.* lib. i cxxix.

[2] To the accomplishments of Ramus as a writer, a very flattering testimony is given by an eminent English scholar, by no means disposed to overrate his merits as a logician. " Pulsa tandem barbarie, Petrus Ramus politioris literaturæ vir, ausus est Aristotelem acrius ubique et liberius incessere, universamque Peripateticam philosophiam exagitare Ejus *dialectica* exiguo tempore fuit apud plurimos summo in pretio, maxime eloquentiæ studiosos, idque odio scholasticorum, quorum dictio et *stylus* ingrata fuerant auribus Ciceronianis "—*Logicæ Artis Compendium*, auctore R. Sanderson, Episc Lincoln, pp 250, 251 Edit. Decima. Oxon. The first edition was printed in 1618

the massacre of Paris) procured many proselytes to his opinions in all the Protestant countries of Europe. In England his logic had the honour, in an age of comparative light and refinement, to find an expounder and methodizer in the author of Paradise Lost; and in some of our northern universities, where it was very early introduced, it maintained its ground till it was supplanted by the logic of Locke.

It has been justly said of Ramus, that, "although he had genius sufficient to shake the Aristotelian fabric, he was unable to substitute anything more solid in its place:" but it ought not to be forgotten, that even *this* praise, scanty as it may *now* appear, involves a large tribute to his merits as a philosophical reformer. Before human reason was able to advance, it was necessary that it should first be released from the weight of its fetters.[1]

It is observed, with great truth, by Condorcet, that, in the

---

[1] Dr. Barrow, in one of his mathematical lectures, speaks of Ramus in terms far too contemptuous. "Homo, ne quid gravius dicam, *argutulus et dicaculus.*"—" Sane vix indignationi meæ tempero, quin illum accipiam pro suo merito, regeramque validius in ejus caput, quæ contra veteres jactat convicia." Had Barrow confined this censure to the weak and arrogant attacks made by Ramus upon Euclid, (particularly upon Euclid's definition of Proportion,) it would not have been more than Ramus deserved, but it is evident he meant to extend it also to the more powerful attacks of the same reformer upon the logic of Aristotle. Of these there are many which may be read with profit even in the present times. I select one passage as a specimen, recommending it strongly to the consideration of those logicians who have lately stood forward as advocates for Aristotle's *abecedarian* demonstrations of the syllogistic rules. " In Aristotelis arte, unius præcepti unicum exemplum est, ac sæpissime nullum: Sed unico et singulari exemplo non potest artifex effici, pluribus opus est et dissimilibus. Et quidem, ut Aristotelis exempla tantummodo non falsa sint, qualia tamen sunt? Omne b est a. omne c est b: ergo omne c est a. Exemplum Aristotelis est puero à grammaticis et oratoribus venienti, et istam mutorum Mathematicorum linguam ignoranti, novum et durum. et in totis Analyticis istâ non Atticâ, non Ionicâ, non Doricâ, non Æolicâ, non communi, sed geometricâ linguâ usus est Aristoteles, odiosâ pueris, ignotâ populo, à communi sensu remotâ, à rhetoricæ usu et ab humanitatis usu alienissimâ."—(P. Rami *pro Philosophica Parisiensis Academiæ Disciplina Oratio,* 1550) If these strictures should be thought too loose and declamatory, the reader may consult the fourth chapter (*De Conversionibus*) of the seventh book of Ramus's *Dialectics,* where the same charge is urged, in my opinion, with irresistible force of argument.

times of which we are now speaking, "the science of political economy did not exist. Princes estimated not the number of men, but of soldiers in the state;—finance was merely the art of plundering the people, without driving them to the desperation that might end in revolt;—and governments paid no other attention to commerce but that of loading it with taxes, of restricting it by privileges, or of disputing for its monopoly"

The internal disorders then agitating the whole of Christendom were still less favourable to the growth of this science, considered as a branch of speculative study. Religious controversies everywhere divided the opinions of the multitude;—involving those collateral discussions concerning the liberty of conscience, and the relative claims of sovereigns and subjects, which, by threatening to resolve society into its first elements, present to restless and aspiring spirits the most inviting of all fields for enterprise and ambition. Amidst the shock of such discussions, the calm inquiries which meditate in silence the slow and gradual amelioration of the social order, were not likely to possess strong attractions, even to men of the most sanguine benevolence; and, accordingly, the political speculations of this period turn almost entirely on the comparative advantages and disadvantages of different forms of government; or on the still more alarming questions concerning the limits of allegiance and the right of resistance.

The dialogue of our illustrious countryman Buchanan, *De Jure Regni apud Scotos,* though occasionally disfigured by the keen and indignant temper of the writer, and by a predilection (pardonable in a scholar warm from the schools of ancient Greece and Rome) for forms of policy unsuitable to the circumstances of modern Europe, bears, nevertheless, in its general spirit, a closer resemblance to the political philosophy of the eighteenth century, than any composition which had previously appeared. The ethical paradoxes afterwards inculcated by Hobbes as the ground-work of his slavish theory of government, are anticipated and refuted, and a powerful argument is urged against that doctrine of utility which has attracted so much notice in our times. The political reflections, too, incidentally introduced by the same author in his History of Scotland, bear marks of a mind worthy of a better age than fell to his lot. Of this kind are the remarks with which he closes his narrative of the wanton cruelties exercised in punishing the murderers of James the First. In reading them, one would almost imagine, that one is listening to the voice of Beccaria or of Montesquieu. "After this manner," says the historian, "was the cruel death of James still more cruelly avenged. For punishments so far exceeding the measure of humanity, have less effect in deterring the multitude from crimes, than in rousing them to greater efforts, both as actors and as sufferers. Nor do they tend so much to intimidate by their severity, as by their frequency to diminish the terrors of the spectators. The evil is more peculiarly great, when the mind of the criminal is hardened against the sense of pain; for in the judgment of the unthinking vulgar, a stubborn confidence generally obtains the praise of heroic constancy."

After the publication of this great work, the name of Scotland, so early distinguished over Europe by the learning and by the *fervid genius*[1] of her sons, disappears for more than a century and a half from the History of Letters. But from this subject, so pregnant with melancholy and humiliating recollections, our attention is forcibly drawn to a mighty and auspicious light which, in a more fortunate part of the island, was already beginning to rise on the philosophical world.[2]

---

[1] Præfervidum Scotorum ingenium

[2] That, at the end of the sixteenth century, the Scottish nation were advancing not less rapidly than their neighbours, in every species of mental cultivation, is sufficiently attested by their literary remains, both in the Latin language and in their own vernacular tongue. A remarkable testimony to the same purpose occurs in the dialogue above quoted, the author of which had spent the best years of his life in the most polished society of the Continent. "As often," says Buchanan, "as I turn my eyes to the niceness and elegance of our own times, the ancient manners of our forefathers appear sober and venerable, but withal rough and horrid"—" Quoties oculos ad nostri temporis munditias et elegantiam refero, antiquitas illa sancta et sobria, sed *horrida* tamen, et nondum *satis expolita*, fuisse videtur."—*De Jure Regni apud Scotos* One would think, that he conceived the taste of his countrymen to have then arrived at the *ne plus ultra* of national refinement,

Aurea nunc, olim sylvestribus *horrida* dumis

CHAPTER II

FROM THE PUBLICATION OF BACON'S PHILOSOPHICAL WORKS, TILL THAT OF THE ESSAY ON THE HUMAN UNDERSTANDING.

SECT. I.—PROGRESS OF PHILOSOPHY IN ENGLAND DURING THIS PERIOD.

BACON.[1]

THE state of science towards the close of the sixteenth century, presented a field of observation singularly calculated to attract the curiosity, and to awaken the genius of Bacon; nor was it the least of his personal advantages, that, as the son of one of Queen Elizabeth's ministers, he had a ready access, wherever he went, to the most enlightened society in Europe. While yet only in the seventeenth year of his age, he was removed by his father from Cambridge to Paris, where it is not to be doubted, that the novelty of the literary scene must have largely contributed to cherish the natural liberality and independence of his mind. Sir Joshua Reynolds has remarked, in one of his Academical Discourses, that "every seminary of learning is surrounded with an atmosphere of floating knowledge, where every mind may imbibe somewhat congenial to its own original conceptions."[2] He might have added, with still greater truth, that it is an atmosphere, of which it is more peculiarly salutary for those who have been elsewhere reared to breathe the air. The remark is applicable to higher pursuits than were in the contemplation of this philosophical artist; and

---

[1] Born 1561, died 1626.
[2] Discourse delivered at the opening of the Royal Academy, January 2, 1769.

it suggests a hint of no inconsiderable value for the education of youth.

The merits of Bacon, as the father of Experimental Philosophy, are so universally acknowledged, that it would be superfluous to touch upon them here. The lights which he has struck out in various branches of the Philosophy of Mind, have been much less attended to; although the whole scope and tenor of his speculations shew, that to *this* study his genius was far more strongly and happily turned, than to that of the Material World. It was not, as some seem to have imagined, by sagacious anticipations of particular discoveries afterwards to be made in physics, that his writings have had so powerful an influence in accelerating the advancement of that science. In the extent and accuracy of his *physical* knowledge, he was far inferior to many of his predecessors; but he surpassed them all in his knowledge of the laws, the resources, and the limits of the human understanding. The sanguine expectations with which he looked forward to the future, were founded solely on his confidence in the untried *capacities of the mind;* and on a conviction of the possibility of invigorating and guiding, by means of logical rules, those faculties which, in all our researches after truth, are the organs or instruments to be employed. "Such rules," as he himself has observed, "do in some sort equal men's wits, and leave no great advantage or pre-eminence to the perfect and excellent motions of the spirit. To draw a straight line, or to describe a circle, by aim of hand only, there must be a great difference between an unsteady and unpractised hand, and a steady and practised; but to do it by rule or compass it is much alike."

Nor is it merely as a logician that Bacon is entitled to notice on the present occasion. It would be difficult to name another writer prior to Locke, whose works are enriched with so many just observations on the intellectual phenomena. Among these, the most valuable relate to the laws of Memory and of Imagination; the latter of which subjects he seems to have studied with peculiar care. In one short but beautiful paragraph concerning *Poetry,* (under which title may be comprehended all the various creations of this faculty,) he has exhausted everything that philosophy and good sense have yet had to offer, on what has been since called the *Beau Ideal;* a topic, which has furnished occasion to so many over-refinements among the French critics, and to so much extravagance and mysticism in the *cloud-capt* metaphysics of the new German school.[1] In considering imagination as connected with the nervous system, more particularly as connected with that species of sympathy to which medical writers have given the name of *imitation,* he has suggested some very important hints, which none of his successors have hitherto prosecuted; and has, at the same time, left an example of cautious inquiry, worthy to be studied by all who may attempt to investigate the laws regulating the union between Mind and Body.[2] His illustration of the different

[1] "Cum mundus sensibilis sit anima rationali dignitate inferior, videtur Poesis hæc humanæ naturæ largiri quæ historia denegat, atque animo umbris rerum utcunque satisfacere, cum solida haberi non possint. Si quis enim rem acutius introspiciat, firmum ex *Poesi* sumitur argumentum, magnitudinem rerum magis illustrem, ordinem magis perfectum, et varietatem magis pulchram, animæ humanæ complacere, quam in natura ipsa, post lapsum, reperiri ullo modo possit Quapropter, cum res gestæ et eventus, qui veræ historiæ subjiciuntur, non sint ejus amplitudinis, in qua anima humana sibi satisfaciat, præsto est *Poesis,* quæ facta magis heroica confingat. Cum historia vera successus rerum, minime pro meritis virtutum et scelerum narret, corrigit eam *Poesis,* et exitus, et fortunas, secundum merita, et ex lege Nemeseos, exhibet. Cum historia vera obvia rerum satietate et similitudine, animæ humanæ fastidio sit, reficit eam Poesis, inexpectata, et varia, et vicissitudinum plena canens. Adeo ut *Poesis* ista non solum ad delectationem, sed ad animi magnitudinem, et ad mores conferat."—*De Aug. Scient.* lib ii cap xiii

[2] To this branch of the philosophy of mind, Bacon gives the title of *Doctrina de fœdere, sive de communi vinculo animæ et corporis.*—(*De Aug Scient* lib iv cap 1) Under this article, he mentions, among other *desiderata,* an inquiry (which he recommends to physicians) concerning the influence of imagination over the body. His own words are very remarkable, more particularly the clause in which he remarks the effect of fixing and concentrating the attention, in giving to ideal objects the power of realities over the belief. "Ad aliud quippiam, quod huc pertinet, parce admodum, nec pro rei subtilitate, vel utilitate, inquisitum est; quatenus scilicet *ipsa imaginatio animæ vel cogitatio perquam fixa, et veluti in fidem quandam exaltata,* valeat ad immutandum corpus imaginantis "—(*Ibid*) He suggests also, as a curious problem, to ascertain how far it is possible to fortify and exalt the imagination; and by what means this may most effectually be done. The class of facts here alluded to, are manifestly of the same description with those to which the attention of philosophers has been lately called by the pretensions of Mesmer and of Perkins "Atque

classes of prejudices incident to human nature, is, in point of practical utility, at least equal to anything on that head to be found in Locke, of whom it is impossible to forbear remarking, as a circumstance not easily explicable, that he should have resumed this important discussion, without once mentioning the name of his great predecessor. The chief improvement made by Locke, in the farther prosecution of the argument, is the application of Hobbes's theory of association, to explain in what manner these prejudices are originally generated.

In Bacon's scattered hints on topics connected with the Philosophy of the Mind, strictly so called, nothing is more remarkable than the precise and just ideas they display of the proper aim of this science. He had manifestly reflected much and successfully on the operations of his own understanding, and had studied with uncommon sagacity the intellectual characters of others. Of his reflections and observations on both subjects, he has recorded many important results; and has in general stated them without the slightest reference to any physiological theory concerning their causes, or to any analogical explanations founded on the caprices of metaphorical language. If, on some occasions, he assumes the existence of *animal spirits*, as the medium of communication between Soul and Body, it must be remembered, that this was *then* the universal belief of the learned; and that it was at a much later period not less confidently avowed by Locke. Nor ought it to be overlooked, (I mention it to the credit of *both* authors,) that in such instances the *fact* is commonly so stated, as to render it easy for the reader to detach it from the *theory*. As to the scholastic questions concerning the nature and essence of mind, —whether it be extended or unextended? whether it have any relation to space or to time? or whether (as was contended by others) it exist in *every ubi*, but in *no place?*—Bacon has

huic conjuncta est disquisitio, quomodo imaginatio intendi et fortificari possit? Quippe, si imaginatio fortis tantarum sit virium, operæ pretium fuerit nosse, quibus modis eam exaltari, et se ipsa majorem fieri detur? Atque hic oblique, nec minus periculose se insinuat palliatio quædam et defensio maximæ partis *Magiæ Ceremonialis*," &c. &c — *De Aug. Scient.* lib iv cap iii

uniformly passed them over with silent contempt; and has probably contributed not less effectually to bring them into general discredit, by this indirect intimation of his own opinion, than if he had descended to the ungrateful task of exposing their absurdity.[1]

While Bacon, however, so cautiously avoids these unprofitable discussions about the nature of Mind, he decidedly states his conviction, that the *faculties* of Man differ not merely in degree, but in kind, from the instincts of the brutes. "I do not, therefore," he observes on one occasion, " approve of that confused and promiscuous method in which philosophers are accustomed to treat of pneumatology; as if the human Soul ranked above those of brutes, merely like the sun above the stars, or like gold above other metals."

Among the various topics started by Bacon for the consideration of future logicians, he did not overlook (what may be justly regarded, in a practical view, as the most interesting of all logical problems) the question concerning the mutual influence of Thought and of Language on each other. "Men believe," says he, "that their reason governs their words; but, it often happens, that words have power enough to *re-act* upon reason." This aphorism may be considered as the text of by far the most valuable part of Locke's Essay,—*that* which relates to the imperfections and abuse of words; but it was not till within the last twenty years, that its depth and im-

---

[1] Notwithstanding the extravagance of Spinoza's own philosophical creed, he is one of the very few among Bacon's successors, who seem to have been fully aware of the justness, importance, and originality of the method pointed out in the *Novum Organon* for the study of the Mind. " Ad hæc intelligenda, non est opus *naturam mentis* cognoscere, sed sufficit, mentis sive *perceptionum* historiolam concinnare modo illo quo Verulamius docet "—*Spin Epist* 42

In order to comprehend the whole merit of this remark, it is necessary to know that, according to the Cartesian phraseology, which is here adopted by Spinoza, the word *perception* is a general term, equally applicable to all the intellectual operations The words of Descartes himself are these · " Omnes modi cogitandi, quos in nobis experimur, ad duos generales referri possunt quorum unus est, *perceptio*, sive operatio intellectus; alius verò, *volitio*, sive operatio voluntatis. *Nam sentire, imaginari, et pure intelligere, sunt tantum diversi modi percipiendi;* ut et cupere, aversari, affirmare, negare, dubitare, sunt diversi modi volendi "—*Princ Phil* Pars I § 32

portance were perceived in all their extent. I need scarcely say, that I allude to the excellent Memoirs of M. Prevost and of M Degerando, on "Signs considered in their connexion with the Intellectual Operations" The anticipations formed by Bacon of that branch of modern logic which relates to *Universal Grammar,* do no less honour to his sagacity. "Grammar," he observes, "is of two kinds, the one literary; the other philosophical The former has for its object to trace the analogies running through the structure of a particular tongue, so as to facilitate its acquisition to a foreigner, or to enable him to speak it with correctness and purity. The latter directs the attention, *not* to the analogies which words bear to words, but to the analogies which words bear to things;"[1] or, as he afterwards explains himself more clearly, "to language considered as the sensible portraiture or image of the mental processes." In farther illustration of these hints, he takes notice of the lights which the different genius of different languages reflect on the characters and habits of those by whom they were respectively spoken. "Thus," says he, "it is easy to perceive, that the Greeks were addicted to the culture of the arts, the Romans engrossed with the conduct of affairs; inasmuch as the technical distinctions introduced in the progress of refinement require the aid of compounded words; while the real business of life stands in no need of so artificial a phraseology."[2] Ideas of this sort have, in the course of a very few years, already become common, and almost tritical; but how different was the case two centuries ago!

With these sound and enlarged views concerning the Philosophy of the Mind, it will not appear surprising to those who have attended to the slow and irregular advances of human reason, that Bacon should occasionally blend incidental remarks, savouring of the habits of thinking prevalent in his time. A curious example of this occurs in the same chapter which contains his excellent definition or description of universal grammar. "This too," he observes, "is worthy of notice, that the ancient languages were full of declensions, of cases, of conjugations, of

[1] *De Aug Scient* lib vi. cap i   [2] *Ibid.*

tenses, and of other similar inflections; while the modern, almost entirely destitute of these, indolently accomplish the same purpose by the help of prepositions, and of auxiliary verbs   Whence," he continues, "may be inferred, (however we may flatter ourselves with the idea of our own superiority,) that the human intellect was much more acute and subtile in ancient, than it now is in modern times."[1]   How very unlike is this last reflection to the usual strain of Bacon's writings! It seems, indeed, much more congenial to the philosophy of Mr. Harris and of Lord Monboddo; and it has accordingly been sanctioned with the approbation of both these learned authors. If my memory does not deceive me, it is the only passage in Bacon's works which Lord Monboddo has anywhere condescended to quote.

These observations afford me a convenient opportunity for remarking the progress and diffusion of *the philosophical spirit* since the beginning of the seventeenth century. In the short passage just cited from Bacon, there are involved no less than two capital errors, which are now almost universally ranked, by men of education, among the grossest prejudices of the multitude. The one, that the declensions and conjugations of the ancient languages, and the modern substitution in their place of prepositions and auxiliary verbs, are both of them the deliberate and systematical contrivances of speculative grammarians; the other, (still less analogous to Bacon's general style of reasoning,) that the faculties of man have declined as the world has grown older. Both of these errors may be now said to have disappeared entirely. The latter, more particularly, must to the rising generation seem so absurd, that it almost requires an apology to have mentioned it. That the capacities of the human mind have been in all ages the same, and that the diversity of phenomena exhibited by our species is the result merely of the different circumstances in which men are placed, has been long received as an incontrovertible logical maxim; or rather, such is the influence of early instruction, that we are apt to regard it as one of the most obvious suggestions of com-

[1] *De Aug. Scient* lib vi cap 1

mon sense. And yet, till about the time of Montesquieu, it was by no means so generally recognised by the learned as to have a sensible influence on the fashionable tone of thinking over Europe. The application of this fundamental and leading idea to the natural or *theoretical history* of society in all its various aspects;—to the history of languages, of the arts, of the sciences, of laws, of government, of manners, and of religion,—is the peculiar glory of the latter half of the eighteenth century, and forms a characteristical feature in its philosophy, which even the imagination of Bacon was unable to foresee.

It would be endless to particularize the original suggestions thrown out by Bacon on topics connected with the science of Mind. The few passages of this sort already quoted are produced merely as a specimen of the rest. They are by no means selected as the most important in his writings; but, as they happened to be those which had left the strongest impression on my memory, I thought them as likely as any other to invite the curiosity of my readers to a careful examination of the rich mine from which they are extracted.

The Ethical disquisitions of Bacon are almost entirely of a practical nature. Of the two theoretical questions so much agitated, in both parts of this island, during the eighteenth century, concerning the *principle* and the *object* of moral approbation, he has said nothing; but he has opened some new and interesting views with respect to the influence of *custom* and the formation of *habits*—a most important article of moral philosophy, on which he has enlarged more ably and more usefully than any writer since Aristotle.[1] Under the same head of *Ethics* may be mentioned the small volume to which he has given the title of *Essays*, the best known and the most popular of all his works. It is also one of those where the superiority of his genius appears to the greatest advantage, the novelty and depth of his reflections often receiving a strong relief from the triteness of his subject. It may be read from beginning to end in a few hours; and yet, after the twentieth perusal, one seldom fails to remark in it something overlooked before. This, indeed,

[1] *De Aug. Scient.* lib vii. cap. iii

is a characteristic of all Bacon's writings, and is only to be accounted for by the inexhaustible aliment they furnish to our own thoughts, and the sympathetic activity they impart to our torpid faculties.

The suggestions of Bacon for the improvement of Political Philosophy, exhibit as strong a contrast to the narrow systems of contemporary statesmen as the Inductive Logic to that of the Schools. How profound and comprehensive are the views opened in the following passages, when compared with the scope of the celebrated treatise *De Jure Belli et Pacis;* a work which was first published about a year before Bacon's death, and which continued, for a hundred and fifty years afterwards, to be regarded, in all the Protestant universities of Europe, as an inexhaustible treasure of moral and jurisprudential wisdom!

" The ultimate object which legislators ought to have in view, and to which all their enactments and sanctions ought to be subservient, is, *that the citizens may live happily.* For this purpose, it is necessary that they should receive a religious and pious education; that they should be trained to good morals; that they should be secured from foreign enemies by proper military arrangements; that they should be guarded by an effectual police against seditions and private injuries, that they should be loyal to government, and obedient to magistrates; and finally, that they should abound in wealth, and in other national resources."[1]—" The science of such matters certainly belongs more particularly to the province of men who, by habits of public business, have been led to take a comprehensive survey of the social order, of the interests of the community at large; of the rules of natural equity; of the manners of nations; of the different forms of government; and who are

---

[1] *Exemplum Tractatus de Fontibus Juris,* Aphor. 5 This enumeration of the different objects of law approaches very nearly to Mr. Smith's ideas on the same subject, as expressed by himself in the concluding sentence of his *Theory of Moral Sentiments* " In another Discourse, I shall endeavour to give an account of the general principles of law and government, and of the different revolutions they have undergone in the different ages and periods of society, not only in what concerns justice, but in what concerns police, revenue, and arms, and whatever else is the object of law."

thus prepared to reason concerning the wisdom of laws, both from considerations of justice and of policy. The great desideratum, accordingly, is, by investigating the principles of *natural justice,* and those of *political expediency,* to exhibit a theoretical model of legislation, which, while it serves as a standard for estimating the comparative excellence of municipal codes, may suggest hints for their correction and improvement, to such as have at heart the welfare of mankind."[1]

How precise the notion was that Bacon had formed of a philosophical system of jurisprudence, (with which as a standard the municipal laws of different nations might be compared,) appears from a remarkable expression, in which he mentions it as the proper business of those who might attempt to carry his plan into execution, to investigate those " LEGES LEGUM, ex quibus informatio peti possit, quid in singulis legibus bene aut perperam positum aut constitutum sit."[2] I do not know if, in Bacon's prophetic anticipations of the future progress of physics, there be anything more characteristical, both

---

[1] *De Aug Scient.* lib viii. cap iii.

[2] *De Fontibus Juris,* Aphor. 6
From the preface to a small tract of Bacon's, entitled *The Elements of the Common Laws of England,* (written while he was Solicitor-General to Queen Elizabeth,) we learn, that the phrase *legum leges* had been previously used by some "great Civilian." To what *civilian* Bacon here alludes, I know not; but, whoever he was, I doubt much if he annexed to it the comprehensive and philosophical meaning, so precisely explained in the above definition. Bacon himself, when he wrote his Tract on the Common Laws, does not seem to have yet risen to this vantage-ground of Universal Jurisprudence. His great object (he tells us) was " to collect the rules and grounds dispersed throughout the body of the same laws, in order to see more profoundly into the reason of such judgments and ruled cases, and thereby to make more use of them for the decision of other cases more doubtful ; so that the uncertainty of law, which is the principal and most just challenge that is made to the laws of our nation at this time, will, by this new strength laid to the foundation, be somewhat the more settled and corrected." In this passage, no reference whatever is made to the *Universal Justice* spoken of in the aphorisms *de Fontibus Juris,* but merely to the leading and governing rules which give to a municipal system whatever it possesses of analogy and consistency To these rules Bacon gives the title of *leges legum;* but the meaning of the phrase, on this occasion, differs from that in which he afterwards employed it, not less widely than the rules of Latin or of Greek syntax differ from the principles of universal grammar —[The phrase " *Legum leges,*" occurs also in Cicero ; *vide* lib. ii *De Legibus,* cap vii]

of the grandeur and of the justness of his conceptions, than this short definition; more particularly, when we consider how widely Grotius, in a work professedly devoted to this very inquiry, was soon after to wander from the right path, in consequence of his vague and wavering idea of the aim of his researches.

The sagacity, however, displayed in these, and various other passages of a similar import, can by no means be duly appreciated, without attending, at the same time, to the cautious and temperate maxims so frequently inculcated by the author, on the subject of political innovation. " A stubborn retention of customs is a turbulent thing, not less than the introduction of new."—" Time is the greatest innovator; shall we then not imitate time, which innovates so silently as to mock the sense ?" Nearly connected with these aphorisms, are the profound reflections in the first book *De Augmentis Scientiarum*, on the necessity of accommodating every new institution to the character and circumstances of the people for whom it is intended; and on the peculiar danger which literary men run of overlooking this consideration, from the familiar acquaintance they acquire, in the course of their early studies, with the ideas and sentiments of the ancient classics.

The remark of Bacon on the systematical policy of Henry VII., was manifestly suggested by the same train of thinking. " His laws (whoso marks them well) were deep and not vulgar; not made on the spur of a particular occasion for the present, but out of providence for the future; to make the estate of his people still more and more happy, after the manner of the legislators in ancient and heroic times." How far this noble eulogy was merited, either by the legislators of antiquity, or by the modern prince on whom Bacon has bestowed it, is a question of little moment. I quote it merely on account of the important philosophical distinction which it indirectly marks, between " deep and vulgar laws ," the former invariably aiming to accomplish their end, not by giving any sudden shock to the feelings and interests of the existing generation, but by allowing to natural causes time and opportunity to operate; and by removing those artificial obstacles which check the progressive tendencies of society. It is probable, that, on this occasion, Bacon had an eye more particularly to the memorable *statute of alienation;* to the effects of which, (whatever were the motives of its author,) the above description certainly applies in an eminent degree.

After all, however, it must be acknowledged that it is rather in his general views and maxims, than in the details of his political theories, that Bacon's sagacity appears to advantage. His notions with respect to commercial policy seem to have been more peculiarly erroneous, originating in an overweening opinion of the efficacy of law, in matters where natural causes ought to be allowed a free operation. It is observed by Mr. Hume, that the statutes of Henry VII. relating to the police of his kingdom, are generally contrived with more judgment than his commercial regulations. The same writer adds, that "the more simple ideas of order and equity are sufficient to guide a legislator in everything that regards the internal administration of justice; but that the principles of commerce are much more complicated, and require long experience and deep reflection to be well understood in any state. The real consequence is *there* often contrary to first appearances. No wonder that, during the reign of Henry VII, these matters were frequently mistaken; and it may safely be affirmed that, even in the age of Lord Bacon, very imperfect and erroneous ideas were formed on that subject."

The instances mentioned by Hume in confirmation of these general remarks, are peculiarly gratifying to those who have a pleasure in tracing the slow but certain progress of reason and liberality. "During the reign," says he, "of Henry VII. it was prohibited to export horses, as if that exportation did not encourage the breed, and make them more plentiful in the kingdom. Prices were also affixed to woollen cloths, to caps and hats, and the wages of labourers were regulated by law. IT IS EVIDENT *that these matters ought always to be left free, and be entrusted to the common course of business and commerce."—*
" For a like reason," the historian continues, " the law enacted

against enclosures and for the keeping up of farm-houses, scarcely deserves the praises bestowed on it by Lord Bacon. If husbandmen understand agriculture, and have a ready vent for their commodities, we need not dread a diminution of the people employed in the country. During a century and a half after this period, there was a frequent renewal of laws and edicts against depopulation; whence we may infer that none of them were ever executed. *The natural course of improvement at last provided a remedy."*

These acute and decisive strictures on the impolicy of some laws highly applauded by Bacon, while they strongly illustrate the narrow and mistaken views in political economy entertained by the wisest statesmen and philosophers two centuries ago, afford, at the same time, a proof of the general diffusion which has since taken place, among the people of Great Britain, of juster and more enlightened opinions on this important branch of legislation. Wherever such doctrines find their way into the page of history, it may be safely inferred that the public mind is not indisposed to give them a welcome reception.

The ideas of Bacon concerning the education of youth were such as might be expected from a philosophical statesman. On the conduct of education in general, with a view to the development and improvement of the intellectual character, he has suggested various useful hints in different parts of his works; but what I wish chiefly to remark at present is, the paramount importance which he has attached to the education of the people, comparing (as he has repeatedly done) the effects of early culture on the understanding and the heart to the abundant harvest which rewards the diligent husbandman for the toils of the spring. To this analogy he seems to have been particularly anxious to attract the attention of his readers, by bestowing on education the title of *the Georgics of the Mind;* identifying, by a happy and impressive metaphor, the two proudest functions entrusted to the legislator—the encouragement of agricultural industry and the care of national instruction. In both instances, the legislator exerts a power which is literally *productive* or *creative;* compelling, in the one case, the unprofitable desert to pour forth its latent riches; and in the other, vivifying the dormant seeds of genius and virtue, and redeeming, from the neglected wastes of human intellect, a new and unexpected accession to the common inheritance of mankind.

When from such speculations as these we descend to the treatise *De Jure Belli et Pacis*, the contrast is mortifying indeed. And yet, so much better suited were the talents and accomplishments of Grotius to the taste, not only of his contemporaries, but of their remote descendants, that while the merits of Bacon failed, for a century and a half, to command the general admiration of Europe,[1] Grotius continued, even in our British universities, the acknowledged Oracle of Jurisprudence and of Ethics, till long after the death of Montesquieu. Nor was Bacon himself unapprized of the slow growth of his posthumous fame. No writer seems ever to have felt more deeply that he properly belonged to a later and more enlightened age—a sentiment which he has pathetically expressed in that clause of his testament, where he "bequeaths his name to posterity, after some generations shall be past."[2]

Unbounded, however, as the reputation of Grotius was on the Continent, even before his own death, it was not till many years after the publication of the treatise *De Jure Belli et Pacis*, that the science of natural jurisprudence became, in this island, an object of much attention, even to the learned. In order, therefore, to give to the sequel of this section some degree of continuity, I shall reserve my observations on Grotius and his successors, till I shall have finished all that I think it necessary to mention further, with respect to the literature of our own country, prior to the appearance of Mr. Locke's Essay.

---

[1] "La célébrité en France des écrits du Chancelier Bacon n'a guère pour date que celle de l'Encyclopédie."—(*Histoire des Mathématiques par Montucla*, Preface, p ix.) It is an extraordinary circumstance that Bayle, who has so often wasted his erudition and acuteness on the most insignificant characters, and to whom Le Clerc has very justly ascribed the merit of *une exactitude étonnante dans des choses de néant*, should have devoted to Bacon only twelve lines of his Dictionary

[2] See Note F.

The rapid advancement of intellectual cultivation in England, between the years 1588 and 1640, (a period of almost uninterrupted peace,) has been remarked by Mr. Fox. "The general improvement," he observes, "in all arts of civil life, and above all, the astonishing progress of literature, are the most striking among the general features of that period; and are in themselves causes sufficient to produce effects of the utmost importance A country whose language was enriched by the works of Hooker, Raleigh, and Bacon, could not but experience a sensible change in its manners, and in its style of thinking; and even to speak the same language in which Spencer and Shakespeare had written, seemed a sufficient plea to rescue the Commons of England from the appellation of *Brutes*, with which Henry the Eighth had addressed them."— The remark is equally just and refined. It is by the mediation of an improving language, that the progress of the mind is chiefly continued from one generation to another; and that the acquirements of the enlightened few are insensibly imparted to the many. Whatever tends to diminish the ambiguities of speech, or to fix, with more logical precision, the import of general terms;—above all, whatever tends to embody, in popular forms of expression, the ideas and feelings of the wise and good, augments the natural powers of the human understanding, and enables the succeeding race to start from a higher ground than was occupied by their fathers. The remark applies with peculiar force to the study of the Mind itself; a study, where the chief source of error is the imperfection of words, and where every improvement on this great instrument of thought may be justly regarded in the light of a discovery.[1]

---

[1] It is not so foreign as may at first be supposed to the object of this Discourse, to take notice here of the extraordinary demand for books on *Agriculture* under the government of James I. The fact is thus very strongly stated by Dr Johnson, in his introduction to the Harleian Miscellany "It deserves to be remarked, because it is not generally known, that the treatises on husbandry and agriculture, which were published during the reign of King James, are so numerous, that it can scarcely be imagined by whom they were written, or to whom they were sold" Nothing can illustrate more strongly the effects of a pacific system of policy, in encouraging a general taste for reading, as well as

In the foregoing list of illustrious names, Mr. Fox has, with much propriety, connected those of Bacon and Raleigh; two men, who, notwithstanding the diversity of their professional pursuits, and the strong contrast of their characters, exhibit, nevertheless, in their capacity of authors, some striking features of resemblance. Both of them owed to the force of their own minds, their emancipation from the fetters of the schools; both were eminently distinguished above their contemporaries, by the originality and enlargement of their philosophical views; and both divide, with the venerable Hooker, the glory of exemplifying to their yet unpolished countrymen, the richness, variety, and grace, which might be lent to the English idiom by the hand of a master.[1]

It is not improbable that Mr. Fox might have included the name of Hobbes in the same enumeration, had he not been prevented by an aversion to his slavish principles of government, and by his own disrelish for metaphysical theories. As a writer, Hobbes unquestionably ranks high among the older English classics; and is so peculiarly distinguished by the simplicity and ease of his manner, that one would naturally have expected from Mr. Fox's characteristical taste, that he would have relished *his* style still more than that of Bacon[2] or

---

an active spirit of national improvement. At all times, and in every country, the extensive sale of *books on agriculture* may be regarded as one of the most pleasing symptoms of mental cultivation in the great body of a people

[1] To prevent being misunderstood, it is necessary for me to add, that I do not speak of the *general style* of these old authors, but only of detached passages, which may be selected from all of them, as earnests or first-fruits of a new and brighter era in English literature. It may be safely affirmed, that in *their* works, and in the prose compositions of Milton, are to be found some of the finest sentences of which our language has yet to boast. To propose them *now* as models for imitation, would be quite absurd. Dr Lowth certainly went much too far when he said, "That in *correctness, propriety*, and *purity* of English style, Hooker hath hardly been surpassed, or even equalled, by any of his successors."—*Preface to Lowth's English Grammar*.

[2] According to Dr Burnet, (no contemptible judge of style,) Bacon was "the first that *writ* our language correctly." The same learned prelate pronounces Bacon to be "*still* our best author," and *this* at a time when the works of Sprat, and many of the prose compositions of Cowley and of Dryden, were already in the hands of the public. It is difficult to conceive on what grounds Burnet proceeded, in hazarding so extraordinary an opinion. See

of Raleigh.—It is with the *philosophical* merits, however, of Hobbes, that we are alone concerned at present; and, in this point of view, what a space is filled in the subsequent history of our domestic literature, by his own works, and by those of his innumerable opponents! Little else, indeed, but the systems which he published, and the controversies which they provoked, occurs, during the interval between Bacon and Locke, to mark the progress of English Philosophy, either in the study of the mind, or in the kindred researches of Ethical and Political Science.

Of the few and comparatively trifling exceptions to this remark, furnished by the metaphysical tracts of Glanvill, of Henry More, and of John Smith, I must delay taking notice, till some account shall be given of the Cartesian philosophy; to which their most interesting discussions have a constant reference, either in the way of comment or refutation.

Hobbes.[1]

"The philosopher of Malmesbury," says Dr. Warburton, "was the terror of the last age, as Tindall and Collins are of this. The press sweat with controversy; and every young churchman militant, would try his arms in thundering on Hobbes's steel cap."[2] Nor was the opposition to Hobbes confined to the clerical order, or to the controversialists of his own

---

the Preface to Burnet's translation of More's *Utopia*

It is still more difficult, on the other hand, to account for the following very bold decision of Mr Hume I transcribe it from an essay first published in 1742, but the same passage is to be found in the last edition of his works, corrected by himself "The first polite prose we have was *writ* by a man (Dr Swift) who is still alive As to Sprat, Locke, and even Temple, they knew too little of the rules of art to be esteemed elegant writers The prose of Bacon, Harrington, and Milton, is altogether stiff and pedantic, though their sense be excellent "

How insignificant are the petty grammatical improvements proposed by Swift, when compared with the inexhaustible riches imparted to the English tongue by the writers of the seventeenth century; and how inferior, in all the higher qualities and graces of style, are his prose compositions, to those of his immediate predecessors, Dryden, Pope, and Addison!

[1] Born 1588, died 1679
[2] *Divine Legation*, Preface to vol ii p 9

times. The most eminent moralists and politicians of the eighteenth century may be ranked in the number of his antagonists, and even at the present moment, scarcely does there appear a new publication on Ethics or Jurisprudence, where a refutation of Hobbism is not to be found.

The period when Hobbes began his literary career, as well as the principal incidents of his life, were, in a singular degree, favourable to a mind like his; impatient of the yoke of authority, and ambitious to attract attention, if not by solid and useful discoveries, at least by an ingenious defence of paradoxical tenets. After a residence of five years at Oxford, and a very extensive tour through France and Italy, he had the good fortune, upon his return to England, to be admitted into the intimacy and confidence of Lord Bacon; a circumstance which, we may presume, contributed not a little to encourage that bold spirit of inquiry, and that aversion to scholastic learning, which characterize his writings. Happy, if he had, at the same time, imbibed some portion of that love of truth and zeal for the advancement of knowledge, which seem to have been Bacon's ruling passions! But such was the obstinacy of his temper, and his overweening self-conceit, that, instead of co-operating with Bacon in the execution of his magnificent design, he resolved to rear, on a foundation exclusively his own, a complete structure both of Moral and Physical Science; disdaining to avail himself even of the materials collected by his predecessors, and treating the *experimentarian* philosophers as objects only of contempt and ridicule![1]

In the *political* writings of Hobbes, we may perceive the influence also of other motives. From his earliest years he seems to have been decidedly hostile to all the forms of popular government; and it is said to have been with the design of impressing his countrymen with a just sense of the disorders incident to democratical establishments, that he published, in 1618, an English translation of Thucydides. In these opinions he was more and more confirmed by the events he afterwards witnessed in England; the fatal consequences of which he early

[1] See Note G.

foresaw with so much alarm, that, in 1640, he withdrew from the approaching storm, to enjoy the society of his philosophical friends at Paris. It was here he wrote his book *De Cive*, a few copies of which were printed, and privately circulated in 1642. The same work was afterwards given to the public, with material corrections and improvements, in 1647, when the author's attachment to the royal cause being strengthened by his personal connexion with the exiled King, he thought it incumbent on him to stand forth avowedly as an advocate for those principles which he had long professed. The great object of this performance was to strengthen the hands of sovereigns against the rising spirit of democracy, by arming them with the weapons of a new philosophy.

The fundamental doctrines inculcated in the political works of Hobbes, are contained in the following propositions. I recapitulate them here, not on their own account, but to prepare the way for some remarks which I mean afterwards to offer on the coincidence between the principles of Hobbes and those of Locke In their practical conclusions, indeed, with respect to the rights and duties of citizens, the two writers differ widely; but it is curious to observe how very nearly they set out from the same hypothetical assumptions.

All men are by nature equal; and, prior to government, they had all an equal right to enjoy the good things of this world. Man, too, is (according to Hobbes) by nature a solitary and purely selfish animal; the social union being entirely an interested league, suggested by prudential views of personal advantage. The necessary consequence is, that a state of nature must be a state of perpetual warfare, in which no individual has any other means of safety than his own strength or ingenuity; and in which there is no room for regular industry, because no secure enjoyment of its fruits. In confirmation of this view of the origin of society, Hobbes appeals to facts falling daily within the circle of our own experience. " Does not a man (he asks) when taking a journey, arm himself, and seek to go well accompanied ? When going to sleep, does he not lock his doors ? Nay, even in his own house, does he not lock his chests? Does he not *there* as much accuse mankind by his actions, as I do by my words?"[1] An additional argument to the same purpose may, according to some later Hobbists, be derived from the instinctive aversion of infants for strangers; and from the apprehension which (it is alleged) every person feels, when he hears the tread of an unknown foot in the dark.

For the sake of peace and security, it is necessary that each individual should surrender a part of his natural right, and be contented with such a share of liberty as he is willing to allow to others; or, to use Hobbes's own language, "every man must divest himself of the right he has to all things by nature; the right of all men to all things being in effect no better than if no man had a right to any thing"[2] In consequence of this transference of natural rights to an individual, or to a body of individuals, the multitude become one person, under the name of a State or Republic, by which person the common will and power are exercised for the common defence. The ruling power cannot be withdrawn from those to whom it has been committed; nor can they be punished for misgovernment. The interpretation of the laws is to be sought, not from the comments of philosophers, but from the authority of the ruler; otherwise society would every moment be in danger of resolving itself into the discordant elements of which it was at first composed. The will of the magistrate, therefore, is to be regarded as the ultimate standard of right and wrong, and his voice to be listened to by every citizen as the voice of conscience.

Not many years afterwards,[3] Hobbes pushed the argument for the absolute power of princes still further, in a work to which he gave the name of *Leviathan*. Under this appellation he means the *body politic;* insinuating, that man is an untameable beast of prey, and that government is the strong chain by which he is kept from mischief. The fundamental principles here maintained are the same as in the book *De Cive;* but as it inveighs more particularly against *ecclesiastical* tyranny, with the view of subjecting the consciences of men to

---

[1] *Of Man*, Part I chap xiii
[2] *De Corpore Politico*, Part I chap i
[3] In 1651 §10

the civil authority, it lost the author the favour of some powerful protectors he had hitherto enjoyed among the English divines who attended Charles II. in France; and he even found it convenient to quit that kingdom, and to return to England, where Cromwell (to whose government his political tenets were *now* as favourable as they were meant to be to the royal claims) suffered him to remain unmolested The same circumstances operated to his disadvantage after the Restoration, and obliged the King, who always retained for him a very strong attachment, to confer his marks of favour on him with the utmost reserve and circumspection [1]

The details which I have entered into, with respect to the history of Hobbes's political writings, will be found, by those who may peruse them, to throw much light on the author's reasonings. Indeed, it is only by thus considering them in their connexion with the circumstances of the times, and the fortunes of the writer, that a just notion can be formed of their spirit and tendency.

The ethical principles of Hobbes are so completely interwoven with his political system, that all which has been said of the one may be applied to the other. It is very remarkable, that Descartes should have thought so highly of the former, as to pronounce Hobbes to be " a much greater master of morality than of metaphysics ;" a judgment which is of itself sufficient to mark the very low state of ethical science in France about the middle of the seventeenth century.—[It must be observed, however, to the honour of Descartes, that he qualifies this eulogy by adding in the next sentence: " I can by no means approve of his principles or maxims, which are very bad and very dangerous, because they suppose all men to be wicked, or give them occasion to be so. His whole design is to write in favour of monarchy, which might be done to more advantage than he has done, upon maxims more virtuous and solid [2]] Mr. Addison, on the other hand, gives a decided preference (among all the books written by Hobbes) to his *Treatise on*

[1] See Note H.
[2] [*Life of Hobbes;* prefixed to his Moral and Political Works Lond. 1750. Fol]

Human Nature; and to *his* opinion on this point I most implicitly subscribe; including, however, in the same commendation, some of his other philosophical essays on similar topics. They are the only part of his works which it is possible now to read with any interest; and they everywhere evince in their author, even when he thinks most unsoundly himself, that power of setting his reader a-thinking, which is one of the most unequivocal marks of original genius. They have plainly been studied with the utmost care both by Locke and Hume. To the former they have suggested some of his most important observations on the Association of Ideas, as well as much of the sophistry displayed in the first book of his Essay, on the Origin of our Knowledge, and on the factitious nature of our moral principles; to the latter, (among a variety of hints of less consequence,) his theory concerning the nature of those established connexions among physical events, which it is the business of the natural philosopher to ascertain,[1] and the substance of his argument against the scholastic doctrine of general conceptions. It is from the works of Hobbes, too, that our later Necessitarians have borrowed the most formidable of those weapons with which they have combated the doctrine of moral liberty; and from the same source has been derived the leading idea which runs through the philological materialism of Mr. Horne Tooke. It is probable, indeed, that this last author borrowed it, at second hand, from a hint in Locke's

---

[1] The same doctrine, concerning the proper object of natural philosophy, (commonly ascribed to Mr Hume, both by his followers and by his opponents,) is to be found in various writers contemporary with Hobbes. It is stated, with uncommon precision and clearness, in a book entitled *Scepsis Scientifica,* or Confessed Ignorance the way to Science; by Joseph Glanvill, (printed in 1665.) The whole work is strongly marked with the features of an acute, an original, and (in matters of science) a somewhat sceptical genius; and, when compared with the treatise on witchcraft, by the same author, adds another proof to those already mentioned, of the possible union of the highest intellectual gifts with the most degrading intellectual weaknesses.

With respect to the *Scepsis Scientifica,* it deserves to be noticed, that the doctrine maintained in it concerning *physical* causes and effects does not occur in the form of a detached observation, of the value of which the author might not have been fully aware, but is the very basis of the general argument running through all his discussions.

Essay; but it is repeatedly stated by Hobbes, in the most explicit and confident terms. Of this idea, (than which, in point of fact, nothing can be imagined more puerile and unsound,) Mr Tooke's etymologies, when he applies them to the solution of metaphysical questions, are little more than an ingenious expansion, adapted and levelled to the comprehension of the multitude

The speculations of Hobbes, however, concerning the theory of the understanding, do not seem to have been nearly so much attended to during his own life, as some of his other doctrines, which, having a more immediate reference to human affairs, were better adapted to the unsettled and revolutionary spirit of the times. It is by these doctrines, chiefly, that his name has since become so memorable in the annals of modern literature; and although they now derive their whole interest from the extraordinary combination they exhibit of acuteness and subtlety with a dead-palsy in the powers of taste and of moral sensibility, yet they will be found, on an attentive examination, to have had a far more extensive influence on the subsequent history both of political and of ethical science, than any other publication of the same period.

ANTAGONISTS OF HOBBES.

Cudworth[1] was one of the first who successfully combated this new philosophy. As Hobbes, in the frenzy of his political zeal, had been led to sacrifice wantonly all the principles of religion and morality to the establishment of his conclusions, his works not only gave offence to the friends of liberty, but excited a general alarm among all sound moralists. His doctrine, in particular, that there is no *natural* distinction between Right and Wrong, and that these are dependent on the arbitrary will of the civil magistrate, was so obviously subversive of all the commonly received ideas concerning the moral constitution of human nature, that it became indispensably necessary, either to expose the sophistry of the attempt,

[1] Born 1617, died 1688

or to admit, with Hobbes, that man is a beast of prey, incapable of being governed by any motives but fear, and the desire of self-preservation.

Between some of these tenets of the courtly Hobbists, and those inculcated by the Cromwellian Antinomians, there was a very extraordinary and unfortunate coincidence; the latter insisting, that, in expectation of Christ's second coming, "the obligations of morality and natural law were suspended; and that the elect, guided by an internal principle, more perfect and divine, were superior to the *beggarly elements* of justice and humanity."[1] It was the object of Cudworth to vindicate, against the assaults of both parties, the immutability of moral distinctions.

In the prosecution of his very able argument on this subject, Cudworth displays a rich store of enlightened and choice erudition, penetrated throughout with a peculiar vein of sobered and subdued Platonism, from whence some German systems, which have attracted no small notice in our own times, will be found, when stripped of their deep neological disguise, to have borrowed their most valuable materials.[2]

---

[1] Hume.——For a more particular account of the English Antinomians, see Mosheim, vol. iv. p 534, *et seq.*

[2] The mind (according to Cudworth) perceives, by occasion of outward objects, as much more than is represented to it by sense, as a learned man does in the best written book, than an illiterate person or brute. "To the eyes of both the same characters will appear, but the learned man, in those characters, will see heaven, earth, sun, and stars; read profound theorems of philosophy or geometry, learn a great deal of new knowledge from them, and admire the wisdom of the composer, while, to the other, nothing appears but black strokes drawn on white paper The reason of which is, that the mind of the one is furnished with certain previous inward anticipations, ideas, and instruction, that the other wants."—"In the room of this book of *human* composition, let us now substitute the book of Nature, written all over with the characters and impressions of *divine* wisdom and goodness, but legible only to an intellectual eye. To the sense both of man and brute, there appears nothing else in it, but, as in the other, so many inky scrawls, that is, nothing but figures and colours But the mind, which hath a participation of the divine wisdom that made it, upon occasion of those sensible delineations, exerting its own inward activity, will have not only a wonderful scene, and large prospects of other thoughts laid open before it, and variety of knowledge, logical, mathematical, and moral displayed, but also clearly read the divine wisdom and goodness in every page of this great

CHAP. II.—PHILOSOPHY FROM BACON TO LOCKE.

Another coincidence between the Hobbists and the Antinomians, may be remarked in their common zeal for the scheme of *necessity ;* which both of them stated in such a way as to be equally inconsistent with the moral agency of man, and with the moral attributes of God.[1] The strongest of all presumptions against this scheme is afforded by the other tenets with which it is almost universally combined ; and accordingly, it was very shrewdly observed by Cudworth, that *the licentious system* which flourished in his time, (under which title, I presume, he comprehended the immoral tenets of the fanatics, as well as of the Hobbists,) " grew up from the doctrine of the fatal neces-

volume, as it were written in large and legible characters "

I do not pretend to be an adept in the philosophy of Kant ; but I certainly think I pay it a very high compliment, when I suppose that, in the *Critic of pure Reason,* the leading idea is somewhat analogous to what is so much better expressed in the foregoing passage. To Kant it was probably suggested by the following very acute and decisive remark of Leibnitz on Locke's Essay. " Nempe, nihil est in intellectu, quod non fuerit in sensu, *nisi ipse intellectus.*"

In justice to Aristotle, it may be here observed, that, although the general strain of his language is strictly conformable to the scholastic maxim just quoted, he does not seem to have altogether overlooked the important exception to it pointed out by Leibnitz Indeed, this exception or limitation is very nearly a translation of Aristotle's words Καὶ αὐτὸς δὲ νοῦς νοητός ἐστιν, ὥσπερ τὰ νοητά ἐπὶ μὲν γὰρ τῶν ἄνευ ὕλης, τὸ αὐτό ἐστι τὸ νοοῦν καὶ τὸ νοούμενον. " And the mind itself is an object of knowledge, as well as other things which are intelligible. For, in immaterial beings, that which understands is the same with that which is understood."—(*De Anima,* lib iii cap v) I quote this very curious, and, I suspect, very little known sentence, in order to vindicate Aristotle against the misrepresentations of some of his present idolaters, who, in their anxiety to secure to him all the credit of Locke's doctrine concerning the Origin of our Ideas, have overlooked the occasional traces which occur in his works, of that higher and sounder philosophy in which he had been educated

[1] " The doctrines of fate or destiny were deemed by the Independents essential to all religion. In these rigid opinions, *the whole sectaries,* amidst all their other differences, unanimously concurred."—Hume's *History,* chap lvii — [A Sermon of Dr Cudworth's, " preached before the Honourable the House of Commons, on March 31, 1647, being a day of public humiliation," has been lately reprinted (1812) by the Philanthropic Society It is levelled from beginning to end against the Predestinarians and Antinomians of those days, and, considering the audience to which it was addressed, (including among others Oliver Cromwell himself,) discovers no common intrepidity in the preacher. In the advertisement prefixed to this publication, we are told, " that the sermon is called in the votes of the House, *a painstaking and heart-searching sermon,* and that the preacher had the sum of £20 voted to him."]

sity of all actions and events, as from its proper root." The unsettled, and, at the same time, disputatious period during which Cudworth lived, afforded him peculiarly favourable opportunities of judging from experience, of the practical tendency of this metaphysical dogma; and the result of his observations deserves the serious attention of those who may be disposed to regard it in the light of a fair and harmless theme for the display of controversial subtilty. To argue, in this manner, against a speculative principle from its palpable effects, is not always so illogical as some authors have supposed. "You repeat to me incessantly," says Rousseau to one of his correspondents, "that truth can never be injurious to the world I myself believe so as firmly as you do; and it is for this very reason I am satisfied that your proposition is false."[1]

But the principal importance of Cudworth, as an ethical writer, arises from the influence of his argument concerning the immutability of right and wrong on the various theories of morals which appeared in the course of the eighteenth century To this argument may, more particularly, be traced the origin of the celebrated question, Whether the principle of moral approbation is to be ultimately resolved into Reason, or into Sentiment?—a question which has furnished the chief ground of difference between the systems of Cudworth and of Clarke, on the one hand, and those of Shaftesbury, Hutcheson, Hume, and Smith, on the other. The remarks which I have to offer on this controversy must evidently be delayed, till the writings of these more modern authors shall fall under review.

The *Intellectual System* of Cudworth embraces a field much wider than his treatise of *Immutable Morality*. The latter is particularly directed against the ethical doctrines of Hobbes, and of the Antinomians; but the former aspires to tear up by the roots all the principles, both physical and metaphysical, of the Epicurean philosophy. It is a work, certainly, which re-

[1] "Vous répétez sans cesse que la vérité ne peut jamais faire de mal aux hommes, je le crois, et c'est pour moi la preuve que ce que vous dites n'est pas la vérité"

flects much honour on the talents of the author, and still more on the boundless extent of his learning; but it is so ill suited to the taste of the present age, that, since the time of Mr. Harris and Dr. Price, I scarcely recollect the slightest reference to it in the writings of our British metaphysicians. Of its faults, (beside the general disposition of the author to discuss questions placed altogether beyond the reach of our faculties,) the most prominent is the wild hypothesis of a *plastic nature;* or, in other words, "of a vital and spiritual, but unintelligent and necessary agent, created by the Deity for the execution of his purposes." Notwithstanding, however, these, and many other abâtements of its merits, *the Intellectual System* will for ever remain a precious mine of information to those whose curiosity may lead them to study the spirit of the ancient theories; and to *it* we may justly apply what Leibnitz has somewhere said, with far less reason, of the works of the schoolmen, "Scholasticos agnosco abundare ineptiis, *sed aurum est in illo cœno.*"[1]

Before dismissing the doctrine of Hobbes, it may be worth while to remark, that all his leading principles are traced by Cudworth to the remains of the ancient sceptics, by some of whom, as well as by Hobbes, they seem to have been adopted from a wish to flatter the uncontrolled passions of sovereigns Not that I am disposed to call in question the originality of Hobbes; for it appears, from the testimony of all his friends, that he had much less pleasure in reading than in thinking. "If I had read," he was accustomed to say, "as much as some others, I should have been as ignorant as they are."—[If, however, the reading of Hobbes was not extensive, it is probable that his favourite authors were perused with a proportionably greater degree of care. He was certainly well-informed on some subjects very foreign to his philosophical pursuits The following testimony to his knowledge of the Common Law of England, is borne by a very competent judge.—"It appears by

[1] The *Intellectual System* was published in 1678 The *Treatise concerning Eternal and Immutable Morality* did not appear till a considerable number of years after the author's death

Hobbes's Dialogue between a Lawyer and a Philosopher, that this very acute writer had considered most of the fundamental principles of English Law, and had read Sir Edward Coke's Institutes with great care and attention."[1]] But similar political circumstances invariably reproduce similar philosophical theories; and it is one of the numerous disadvantages attending an inventive mind, not properly furnished with acquired information, to be continually liable to a waste of its powers on subjects previously exhausted.

The sudden tide of licentiousness, both in principles and in practice, which burst into this island at the moment of the Restoration, conspired with the paradoxes of Hobbes, and with the no less dangerous errors recently propagated among the people by their religious instructors, to turn the thoughts of sober and speculative men towards ethical disquisitions. The established clergy assumed a higher tone than before in their sermons; sometimes employing them in combating that Epicurean and Machiavellian philosophy which was then fashionable at court, and which may be always suspected to form the secret creed of the enemies of civil and religious liberty; on other occasions, to overwhelm, with the united force of argument and learning, the extravagancies by which the ignorant enthusiasts of the preceding period had exposed Christianity itself to the scoffs of their libertine opponents. Among the divines who appeared at this era, it is impossible to pass over in silence the name of Barrow, whose theological works (adorned throughout by classical erudition, and by a vigorous, though unpolished eloquence) exhibit, in every page, marks of the same inventive genius which, in mathematics, has secured to him a rank second alone to that of Newton. As a writer, he is equally distinguished by the redundancy of his matter, and by the pregnant brevity of his expression; but what more peculiarly characterizes his manner, is a certain air of powerful and of conscious facility in the execution of whatever he undertakes. Whether the subject be mathematical, metaphysical, or theolo-

[1] [*Barrington on Ancient Statutes*, p 275]

gical, he seems always to bring to it a mind which feels itself superior to the occasion; and which, in contending with the greatest difficulties, "puts forth but half its strength." He has somewhere spoken of his *Lectiones Mathematicæ* (which it may, in passing, be remarked, display *metaphysical* talents of the highest order) as extemporaneous effusions of his pen; and I have no doubt that the same epithet is still more literally applicable to his pulpit discourses. It is, indeed, only thus we can account for the variety and extent of his voluminous remains, when we recollect that the author died at the age of forty-six.[1]

To the extreme rapidity with which Barrow committed his thoughts to writing, I am inclined to ascribe the hasty and not altogether consistent opinions which he has hazarded on some important topics. I shall confine myself to a single example, which I select in preference to others, as it bears directly on the most interesting of all questions connected with the theory of morals. "If we scan," says he, "the particular nature, and search into the original causes of the several kinds of naughty dispositions in our souls, and of miscarriages in our lives, we shall find inordinate self-love to be a main ingredient and a common source of them all; so that a divine of great name had some reason to affirm, that *original sin* (or that innate distemper from which men generally become so very prone to evil and averse to good) doth consist in self-love, disposing us to all kinds of irregularity and excess." In another passage, the same author expresses himself thus. "Reason dictateth and prescribeth to us, that we should have a sober regard to our true good and welfare; to our best interests and solid content; to

---

[1] In a note annexed to an English translation of the Cardinal Maury's *Principles of Eloquence*, it is stated, upon the authority of a manuscript of Dr Doddridge, that *most* of Barrow's sermons were transcribed three times, and some much oftener. They seem to me to contain very strong intrinsic evidence of the incorrectness of this anecdote. Mr. Abraham Hill (in his *Account of the Life of Barrow*, addressed to Dr Tillotson) contents himself with saying, that "*Some* of his sermons were written four or five times over," mentioning, at the same time, a circumstance which may account for this fact, in perfect consistency with what I have stated above, that "Barrow was very ready to *lend* his sermons as often as desired."

that which (all things being rightly stated, considered, and computed) will, in the final event, prove most beneficial and satisfactory to us. a self-love working in prosecution of such things, common sense cannot but allow and approve."

Of these two opposite and irreconcilable opinions, the latter is incomparably the least wide of the truth; and accordingly Mr. Locke and his innumerable followers, both in England and on the Continent, have maintained that virtue and an enlightened self-love are one and the same. I shall afterwards find a more convenient opportunity for stating some objections to the latter doctrine, as well as to the former. I have quoted the two passages here merely to shew the very little attention that had been paid, at the era in question, to ethical science, by one of the most learned and profound divines of his age. This is the more remarkable, as his works everywhere inculcate the purest lessons of practical morality, and evince a singular acuteness and justness of eye in the observation of human character. Whoever compares the views of Barrow, when he touches on the theory of morals, with those opened about fifty years afterwards by Dr. Butler, in his *Discourses on Human Nature*, will be abundantly satisfied that in this science, as well as in others, the progress of the philosophical spirit during the intervening period was not inconsiderable.—[I am at a loss to comprehend the import of the following judgment on *the works of Dr. Barrow*, pronounced by Mr. Gibbon: "Barrow was as much of a philosopher as a divine could well be."—Note, p. 76.[1]]

The name of Wilkins (although he too wrote with some reputation against the Epicureans of his day) is now remembered chiefly in consequence of his treatises concerning *a universal language and a real character*. Of these treatises I shall hereafter have occasion to take some notice, under a different article. With all the ingenuity displayed in them, they cannot be considered as accessions of much value to science; and the long period since elapsed, during which no attempt has been made to turn them to any practical use, affords of itself no slight presumption against the solidity of the project.

[1] [*Miscell Works*, vol ii p 61]

A few years before the death of Hobbes, Dr. Cumberland (afterwards Bishop of Peterborough) published a book, entitled, *De Legibus Naturæ, Disquisitio Philosophica;* the principal aim of which was to confirm and illustrate, in opposition to Hobbes, the conclusions of Grotius, concerning *Natural Law* The work is executed with ability, and discovers juster views of the object of moral science, than any modern system that had yet appeared; the author resting the strength of his argument, not, as Grotius had done, on an accumulation of authorities, but on the principles of the human frame, and the mutual relations of the human race. The circumstance, however, which chiefly entitles this publication to *our* notice is, that it seems to have been the earliest on the subject which attracted, in any considerable degree, the attention of English scholars. From this time, the writings of Grotius and of Puffendorff began to be generally studied, and soon after made their way into the Universities. In Scotland, the impression produced by them was more peculiarly remarkable. They were everywhere adopted as the best manuals of ethical and of political instruction that could be put into the hands of students; and gradually contributed to form that memorable school, from whence so many Philosophers and Philosophical Historians were afterwards to proceed.

From the writings of Hobbes to those of Locke, the transition is easy and obvious; but, before prosecuting farther the history of philosophy in England, it will be proper to turn our attention to its progress abroad, since the period at which this section commences.[1] In the first place, however, I shall add a

[1] Through the whole of this Discourse, I have avoided touching on the discussions which, on various occasions, have arisen with regard to the theory of government, and the comparative advantages or disadvantages of different political forms Of the scope and spirit of these discussions it would be seldom possible to convey a just idea, without entering into details of a local or temporary nature, inconsistent with my general design In the present circumstances of the world, besides, the theory of government (although, in one point of view, the most important of all studies) seems to possess a very subordinate interest to inquiries connected with political economy, and with the fundamental principles of legislation What is it, indeed, that renders one

few miscellaneous remarks on some important events which occurred in this country during the lifetime of Hobbes, and of which his extraordinary longevity prevented me sooner from taking notice.

Among these events, that which is most immediately connected with our present subject, is the establishment of the Royal Society of London in 1662, which was followed a few years afterwards by that of the Royal Academy of Sciences at Paris The professed object of both institutions was the improvement of Experimental Knowledge, and of the auxiliary science of Mathematics; but their influence on the general progress of human reason has been far greater than could possibly have been foreseen at the moment of their foundation. On the happy effects resulting from them in this respect, La Place has introduced some just reflections in his *System of the World*, which, as they discover more originality of thought than he commonly displays, when he ventures to step beyond the circumference of his own magic circle, I shall quote, in a literal translation of his words.

" The chief advantage of learned societies, is the *philosophical*

form of government more favourable than another to human happiness, but the superior security it provides for the enactment of wise laws, and for their impartial and vigorous execution? These considerations will sufficiently account for my passing over in silence, not only the names of Needham, of Sidney, and of Milton, but that of Harrington, whose *Oceana* is justly regarded as one of the boasts of English literature, and is pronounced by Hume to be "the only valuable model of a commonwealth that has yet been offered to the public."— *Essays and Treatises*, vol i Essay xvi.

· A remark which Hume has elsewhere made on the *Oceana*, appears to me so striking and so instructive, that I shall give it a place in this note " Harrington," he observes, " thought himself so sure of his general principle,—*that the balance of power depends on that of property*, that he ventured to pronounce it impossible ever to re-establish monarchy in England· But this book was scarcely published when the King was restored, and we see that monarchy has ever since subsisted on the same footing as before. So dangerous is it for a politician to venture to foretell the situation of public affairs a few years hence."—*Ibid* Essay vii.

How much nearer the truth (even in the science of *politics*) is Bacon's cardinal principle, that *knowledge is power*' —a principle, which applies to Man not less in his corporate than in his individual capacity, and which may be safely trusted to as the most solid of all foundations for our reasonings concerning the future history of the world.

spirit to which they may be expected to give birth, and which they cannot fail to diffuse over all the various pursuits of the nations among whom they are established. The insulated scholar may without dread abandon himself to the spirit of system; he hears the voice of contradiction only from afar. But in a learned society, the collision of systematic opinions soon terminates in their common destruction; while the desire of mutual conviction creates among the members a tacit compact, to admit nothing but the results of observation, or the conclusions of mathematical reasoning. Accordingly, experience has shown, how much these establishments have contributed, since their origin, to the spread of true philosophy. By setting the example of submitting everything to the examination of a severe logic, they have dissipated the prejudices which had too long reigned in the sciences, and which the strongest minds of the preceding centuries had not been able to resist. They have constantly opposed to empiricism a mass of knowledge, against which the errors adopted by the vulgar, with an enthusiasm which, in former times, would have perpetuated their empire, have spent their force in vain. In a word, it has been in their bosoms that those grand theories have been conceived, which, although far exalted by their generality above the reach of the multitude, are for this very reason entitled to special encouragement, from their innumerable applications to the phenomena of nature, and to the practice of the arts."[1]

In confirmation of these judicious remarks, it may be farther observed, that nothing could have been more happily imagined than the establishment of learned corporations for correcting those prejudices which (under the significant title of *Idola Specus*) Bacon has described as incident to the retired student.

[1] The Royal Society of London, though not incorporated by charter till 1662, may be considered as virtually existing, at least as far back as 1638, when some of the most eminent of the original members began first to hold regular meetings at Gresham College, for the purpose of philosophical discussion. Even these meetings were but a continuation of those previously held by the same individuals, at the apartments of Dr Wilkins in Oxford. See Sprat's *History of the Royal Society*.

While these *idols of the den* maintain their authority, the cultivation of the philosophical spirit is impossible; or rather, it is in a renunciation of this idolatry that the philosophical spirit essentially consists. It was accordingly in this great school of the learned world, that the characters of Bacon, Descartes, Leibnitz, and Locke were formed; the four individuals who have contributed the most to diffuse the philosophical spirit over Europe. The remark applies more peculiarly to Bacon, who first pointed out the inconveniences to be apprehended from a minute and mechanical subdivision of literary labour; and anticipated the advantages to be expected from the institution of learned academies, in enlarging the field of scientific curiosity, and the correspondent grasp of the emancipated mind For accomplishing this object, what means so effectual as habits of daily intercourse with men whose pursuits are different from our own; and that expanded knowledge, both of man and of nature, of which such an intercourse must necessarily be productive!

Another event which operated still more forcibly and universally on the intellectual character of our countrymen, was the civil war which began in 1640, and which ultimately terminated in the usurpation of Cromwell. It is observed by Mr. Hume, that " the prevalence of democratical principles, under the Commonwealth, engaged the country gentlemen to bind their sons apprentices to merchants; and that commerce has ever since been more honourable in England, than in any other European Kingdom."[1] "The higher and the lower ranks (as a later writer has remarked) were thus brought closer together, and all of them inspired with an activity and vigour that, in former ages, had no example."[2]

To this combination of the pursuits of trade, with the advantages of a liberal education, may be ascribed the great multitude of ingenious and enlightened speculations on commerce, and on the other branches of national industry, which issued from the press, in the short interval between the Restoration

---

[1] *History of England*, chap. lxii.
[2] Chalmers's *Political Estimate*, &c (London, 1804,) p 44.

and the Revolution; an interval during which the sudden and immense extension of the trade of England, and the corresponding rise of the commercial interest, must have presented a spectacle peculiarly calculated to awaken the curiosity of inquisitive observers. It is a very remarkable circumstance with respect to these economical researches, which now engage so much of the attention both of statesmen and of philosophers, that they are altogether of modern origin. "There is scarcely," says Mr. Hume, "any ancient writer on politics who has made mention of trade; nor was it ever considered as an affair of state till the seventeenth century."[1]—The work of the celebrated John de Witt, entitled, "The true interest and political maxims of the Republic of Holland and West Friesland," is the earliest publication of any note in which commerce is treated of as an object of *national* and *political* concern, in opposition to the partial interests of corporations and of monopolists

Of the English publications to which I have just alluded, the greater part consists of anonymous pamphlets, now only to be met with in the collections of the curious. A few bear the names of eminent English merchants. I shall have occasion to refer to them more particularly afterwards, when I come to speak of the writings of Smith, Quesnay, and Turgot. At present, I shall only observe, that, in these fugitive and now neglected tracts, are to be found the first rudiments of that science of *Political Economy* which is justly considered as the boast of the present age; and which, although the aid of learning and philosophy was necessary to rear it to maturity, may be justly said to have had its cradle in the Royal Exchange of London.

Mr. Locke was one of the first retired theorists (and this singular feature in his history has not been sufficiently attended to by his biographers) who condescended to treat of *trade* as an object of liberal study. Notwithstanding the manifold errors into which he fell in the course of his reasonings concerning it, it may be fairly questioned, if he has anywhere else given greater proofs, either of the vigour or of the originality of his

[1] *Essay of Civil Liberty.*

genius. But the name of Locke reminds me, that it is now time to interrupt these national details; and to turn our attention to the progress of science on the Continent, since the times of Bodinus and of Campanella.

SECT. II.—PROGRESS OF PHILOSOPHY IN FRANCE DURING THE SEVENTEENTH CENTURY.

MONTAIGNE—CHARRON—LA ROCHEFOUCAULD.

AT the head of the French writers who contributed, in the beginning of the seventeenth century, to turn the thoughts of their countrymen to subjects connected with the Philosophy of Mind, Montaigne may, I apprehend, be justly placed. Properly speaking, he belongs to a period somewhat earlier; but his tone of thinking and of writing classes him much more naturally with his successors, than with any French author who had appeared before him.[1]

In assigning to Montaigne so distinguished a rank in the history of modern philosophy, I need scarcely say, that I leave entirely out of the account what constitutes (and justly constitutes) to the generality of readers the principal charm of his Essays; the good nature, humanity, and unaffected sensibility, which so irresistibly attach us to his character,—lending, it must be owned, but too often, a fascination to his *talk*, when he cannot be recommended as the safest of companions. Nor do I lay much stress on the inviting frankness and vivacity with which he unbosoms himself about all his domestic habits and concerns; and which render his book so expressive a portrait, not only of the author, but of the Gascon country-gentleman, two hundred years ago. I have in view chiefly the minuteness and good faith of his details concerning his own personal qualities, both intellectual and moral. The only study which seems ever to have engaged his attention was that of *man;* and for this he was singularly fitted, by a rare combination of that talent for observation which belongs to men of the world,

[1] Montaigne was born in 1533, and died in 1592.

with those habits of abstracted reflection, which men of the world have commonly so little disposition to cultivate. "I study myself," says he, "more than any other subject. This is my metaphysic; this my natural philosophy."[1] He has accordingly produced a work, *unique* in its kind; valuable, in an eminent degree, as an authentic record of many interesting facts relative to human nature; but more valuable by far, as holding up a mirror in which every individual, if he does not see his own image, will at least occasionally perceive so many traits of resemblance to it, as can scarcely fail to invite his curiosity to a more careful review of himself. In this respect, Montaigne's writings may be regarded in the light of what painters call *studies;* in other words, of those slight sketches which were originally designed for the improvement or amusement of the artist; but which, on that account, are the more likely to be useful in developing the germs of similar endowments in others.

Without a union of these two powers, (reflection and observation,) the study of Man can never be successfully prosecuted. It is only by retiring within ourselves that we can obtain a key to the characters of others; and it is only by observing and comparing the characters of others that we can thoroughly understand and appreciate our own.

After all, however, it may be fairly questioned, notwithstanding the scrupulous fidelity with which Montaigne has endeavoured to delineate his own portrait, if he has been always sufficiently aware of the secret folds and reduplications of the human heart. That he was by no means exempted from the common delusions of self-love and self-deceit, has been fully evinced in a very acute, though somewhat uncharitable, section of the *Port-Royal* logic; but this consideration, so far from diminishing the value of his Essays, is one of the most instructive lessons they afford to those who, after the example of the author, may undertake the salutary but humiliating task of self-examination.

As Montaigne's scientific knowledge was, according to his

[1] *Essays,* Book III chap xiii.

own account, "very vague and imperfect,"[1] and his booklearning rather sententious and gossiping than comprehensive and systematical, it would be unreasonable to expect, in his philosophical arguments, much either of depth or of solidity.[2] The sentiments he hazards are to be regarded but as the impressions of the moment; consisting chiefly of the more obvious doubts and difficulties which, on all metaphysical and moral questions, are apt to present themselves to a speculative mind, when it first attempts to dig below the surface of common opinions In reading Montaigne, accordingly, what chiefly strikes us, is not the novelty or the refinement of his ideas, but the liveliness and felicity with which we see embodied in words the previous wanderings of our own imaginations. It is probably owing to this circumstance, rather than to any direct plagiarism, that his Essays appear to contain the germs of so many of the paradoxical theories which, in later times, Helvetius and others have laboured to systematize and to support with the

---

[1] Book i chap xxv

[2] Montaigne's education, however, had not been neglected by his father. On the contrary, he tells us himself, that "George Buchanan, the great poet of Scotland, and Marcus Antonius Muretus, the best orator of his time, were among the number of his domestic preceptors"—"Buchanan," he adds, "when I saw him afterwards in the retinue of the late Mareschal de Brissac, told me, that he was about to write a treatise on the education of children, and that he would take the model of it from mine."—Book i chap xxv—[Traces of Buchanan's tuition may be perceived in various opinions adopted by Montaigne, strongly at variance with the political ideas then commonly received. "All (says Montaigne) that exceeds a simple death appears to me mere cruelty; neither can our justice expect, that he whom the fear of death, by being beheaded or hanged, will not restrain, should be any more awed by the imagination of a slow fire, burning pincers, or the wheel And, I know not, in the meantime, whether we do not drive them to despair, &c."—Book ii chap xxvii Compare this with the passage quoted from Buchanan, p 62

The remark of Montaigne on *Substitutions* or Entails, savours also of Buchanan's principles. "In general, the most judicious distribution of our estates, when we come to die, is, in my opinion, to leave them to be disposed of according to the custom of the country. We are too fond of *masculine substitutions*, and ridiculously think to make our names thereby last to eternity."—Book ii chap viii. The following is Buchanan's reflection on the vanity and shortsightedness of those princes who have laboured to establish *a perpetuity of their race and name*. "Adversus naturam rerum certamen sibi et rem maxime fluxam et fragilem, omniumque casuum momentis obnoxiam, æternitate, quam ipsi nec habent nec habere possunt, donare contendunt"]

parade of metaphysical discussion. In the mind of Montaigne, the same paradoxes may be easily traced to those deceitful *appearances* which, in order to stimulate our faculties to their best exertions, nature seems purposely to have thrown in our way, as stumbling-blocks in the pursuit of truth; and it is only to be regretted on such occasions, for the sake of his own happiness, that his genius and temper qualified and disposed him more to start the problem than to investigate the solution

When Montaigne touches on religion, he is, in general, less pleasing than on other subjects. His constitutional temper, it is probable, predisposed him to scepticism; but this original bias could not fail to be mightily strengthened by the disputes, both religious and political, which during his lifetime convulsed Europe, and more particularly his own country. On a mind like his, it may be safely presumed that the writings of the Reformers and the instructions of Buchanan were not altogether without effect; and hence, in all probability, the perpetual struggle, which he is at no pains to conceal, between the creed of his infancy and the lights of his mature understanding. He speaks, indeed, of "reposing tranquilly on the *pillow of doubt;*" but this language is neither reconcilable with the general complexion of his works, nor with the most authentic accounts we have received of his dying moments. It is a maxim of his own, that "in forming a judgment of a man's life, particular regard should be paid to his behaviour at the end of it;" to which he pathetically adds, "that the chief study of his own life was, that his latter end might be decent, calm, and silent." The fact is, (if we may credit the testimony of his biographers,) that, in his declining years, he exchanged his boasted *pillow of doubt* for the more powerful opiates prescribed by the infallible church, and that he expired in performing what his old preceptor Buchanan would not have scrupled to describe as an act of idolatry.[1]

---

[1] "Sentant sa fin approcher, il fit dire la messe dans sa chambre. A l'élévation de l'hostie, il se leva sur son lit pour l'adorer, mais une foiblesse l'enleva dans ce moment même, le 13 Sep tembre 1592, à 60 ans"—*Nouveau Dict Histor*, à Lyon, 1804.—Art Montaigne

The scepticism of Montaigne seems to have been of a very peculiar cast, and to have had little in common with that either of Bayle or of Hume. The great aim of the two latter writers evidently was, by exposing the uncertainty of our reasonings whenever we pass the limit of sensible objects, to inspire their readers with a complete distrust of the human faculties on all moral and metaphysical topics. Montaigne, on the other hand, never thinks of forming a sect, but, yielding passively to the current of his reflections and feelings, argues at different times, according to the varying state of his impressions and temper, on opposite sides of the same question. On all occasions he preserves an air of the most perfect sincerity; and it was to *this*, I presume, much more than to the superiority of his reasoning powers, that Montesquieu alluded, when he said, "In the greater part of authors I see the *writer;* in Montaigne I see nothing but the *thinker.*" The radical fault of his understanding consisted in an incapacity of forming, on disputable points, those decided and fixed opinions which can alone impart either force or consistency to intellectual character. For remedying this weakness, the religious controversies, and the civil wars recently engendered by the Reformation, were but ill calculated The minds of the most serious men, all over Christendom, must have been then unsettled in an extraordinary degree; and where any predisposition to scepticism existed, every external circumstance must have conspired to cherish and confirm it. Of the extent to which it was carried, about the same period, in England, some judgment may be formed from the following description of a *Sceptic* by a writer not many years posterior to Montaigne:—

"A sceptic in religion is one that hangs in the balance with all sorts of opinions; whereof not one but stirs him, and none sways him. A man guiltier of credulity than he is taken to be; for it is out of his belief of everything that he believes nothing. Each religion scares him from its contrary, none persuades him to itself. He would be wholly a Christian, but that he is something of an Atheist; and wholly an Atheist, but that he is partly a Christian; and a perfect Heretic, but that there are so many to distract him. He finds *reason* in all opinions, *truth* in none; indeed, the least reason perplexes him, and the best will not satisfy him. He finds doubts and scruples better than resolves them, and *is always too hard for himself.*"[1] If this portrait had been presented to Montaigne, I have little doubt that he would have had the candour to acknowledge that he recognised in it some of the most prominent and characteristical features of his own mind.[2]

The most elaborate, and seemingly the most serious, of all Montaigne's essays, is his long and somewhat tedious *Apology for Raimond de Sebonde*, contained in the twelfth chapter of his second book. This author appears, from Montaigne's account, to have been a Spaniard, who professed physic at Toulouse, towards the end of the fourteenth century; and who published a treatise, entitled *Theologia Naturalis*, which was put into the hands of Montaigne's father by a friend, as a useful antidote against the innovations with which Luther was then beginning to disturb the ancient faith. That, in this particular instance, the book answered the intended purpose, may be presumed from the request of old Montaigne to his son, a few days before his death, to translate it into French from the Spanish original. His request was accordingly complied with, and the translation is referred to by Montaigne in the first edition of his *Essays*, printed at Bourdeaux in 1580; but the execution of this filial duty seems to have produced on Montaigne's own mind very different effects from what his father had anticipated.[3]

[1] *Micro-cosmography*, or a Piece of the World Discovered, in Essays and Characters For a short notice of the author of this very curious book, (Bishop Earle,) see the edition published at London in 1811. The chapter containing the above passage is entitled *A Sceptic in Religion;* and it has plainly suggested to Lord Clarendon some of the ideas, and even expressions, which occur in his account of Chillingworth

[2] "The writings of the best authors among the ancients," Montaigne tells us on one occasion, " being full and solid, tempt and carry me which way almost they will He that I am reading seems always to have the most force; and I find that every one in turn has reason, though they contradict one another "—Book ii chap xii

[3] The very few particulars known with respect to Sebonde have been collected by Bayle See his *Dictionary,*—Art Sebonde

The principal aim of Sebonde's book, according to Montaigne, is to shew that "Christians are in the wrong to make human reasoning the basis of their belief, since the object of it is only conceived by faith, and by a special inspiration of the divine grace." To this doctrine Montaigne professes to yield an implicit assent; and, under the shelter of it, contrives to give free vent to all the extravagances of scepticism The essential distinction between the reason of man and the instincts of the lower animals, is at great length, and with no inconsiderable ingenuity, disputed; the powers of the human understanding, in all inquiries, whether physical or moral, are held up to ridicule; a universal Pyrrhonism is recommended; and we are again and again reminded, that "*the senses are the beginning and the end of all our knowledge.*" Whoever has the patience to peruse this chapter with attention, will be surprised to find in it the rudiments of a great part of the licentious philosophy of the eighteenth century; nor can he fail to remark the address with which the author avails himself of the language afterwards adopted by Bayle, Helvetius, and Hume: —" That, to be a philosophical sceptic, is the first step towards becoming a sound believing Christian "[1] It is a melancholy fact in ecclesiastical history, that this insidious maxim should have been sanctioned, in our times, by some theologians of no common pretensions to orthodoxy; who, in direct contradiction to the words of Scripture, have ventured to assert, that "he who comes to God must first believe that He is NOT." Is it necessary to remind these grave retailers of Bayle's sly and ironical sophistry, that every argument for Christianity, drawn from its *internal* evidence, tacitly recognises the authority of human reason; and assumes, as the ultimate *criteria* of truth and of falsehood, of right and of wrong, certain fundamental articles of belief, discoverable by the light of Nature?[2]

---

[1] This expression is Mr Hume's, but the same proposition, in substance, is frequently repeated by the two other writers, and is very fully enlarged upon by Bayle in the *Illustration upon the Sceptics,* annexed to his Dictionary

[2] "I once asked *Adrian Turnebus,*"

Charron is well known as the chosen friend of Montaigne's latter years, and as the confidential depositary of his philosophical sentiments. Endowed with talents far inferior in force and originality to those of his master, he possessed, nevertheless, a much sounder and more regulated judgment; and as his reputation, notwithstanding the liberality of some of his peculiar tenets, was high among the most respectable and conscientious divines of his own church, it is far from improbable, that Montaigne committed to him the guardianship of his posthumous fame, from motives similar to those which influenced Pope, in selecting Warburton as his literary executor. The discharge of this trust, however, seems to have done less good to Montaigne than harm to Charron; for, while the unlimited scepticism, and the indecent levities of the former, were viewed by the zealots of those days with a smile of tenderness and indulgence, the slighter heresies of the latter were marked with a severity the more rigorous and unrelenting, that, in points of essential importance, they deviated so very little from the standard of the Catholic faith. It is not easy to guess the motives of this inconsistency; but such we find from the fact to have been the

says Montaigne, 'what he thought of Sebonde's treatise? The answer he made to me was, That he believed it to be some extract from *Thomas Aquinas*, for that none but a genius like his was capable of such ideas."

I must not, however, omit to mention, that a very learned Protestant, *Hugo Grotius*, has expressed himself to his friend *Bignon* not unfavourably of Sebonde's intentions, although the terms in which he speaks of him are somewhat equivocal, and imply but little satisfaction with the execution of his design. "Non ignoras quantum excoluerint istam materiam (*argumentum scil. pro Religione Christiana*) philosophica substitute Raimundus Sebundus, dialogorum varietate Ludovicus Vives, maxima autem tum eruditione tum facundia vestras Philippus Mornæus." The authors of the *Nouveau Dictionnaire Historique* (Lyons, 1804) have entered much more completely into the spirit and drift of Sebonde's reasoning, when they observe, "Ce livre offre des singularités hardies, qui plurent dans le temps aux philosophes de ce siècle, et *qui ne déplairoient pas à ceux du notre.*"

It is proper to add, that I am acquainted with Sebonde only through the *medium* of Montaigne's version, which does not lay claim to the merit of strict fidelity, the translator himself having acknowledged, that he had given to the Spanish philosopher "un accoutrement à la Françoise, et qu'il l'a dévêtu de son port farouche et maintien barbaresque, de manière qu'il a mes hui assez de façon pour se présenter en toute bonne compagnie."

temper of religious bigotry, or, to speak more correctly, of political religionism, in all ages of the world.[1]

As an example of Charron's solicitude to provide an antidote against the more pernicious errors of his friend, I shall only mention his ingenious and philosophical attempt to reconcile, with the moral constitution of human nature, the apparent discordancy in the judgments of different nations concerning right and wrong. His argument on this point is in substance the very same with that so well urged by Beattie, in opposition to Locke's reasonings against the existence of innate practical principles. It is difficult to say, whether, in this instance, the coincidence between Montaigne and Locke, or that between Charron and Beattie, be the more remarkable [2]

Although Charron has affected to give to his work a systematical form, by dividing and subdividing it into books and chapters, it is in reality little more than an unconnected series of essays on various topics, more or less distantly related to the science of Ethics. On the powers of the understanding he has touched but slightly; nor has he imitated Montaigne, in anatomizing, for the edification of the world, the peculiarities of his own moral character. It has probably been owing to the desultory and popular style of composition common to both, that so little attention has been paid to either by those who have treated of the history of French philosophy. To Montaigne's merits, indeed, as a lively and amusing essayist, ample justice has been done; but his influence on the subsequent habits of thinking among his countrymen remains still to be illustrated. He has done more, perhaps, than any other author,

---

[1] Montaigne, cet auteur charmant,
Tour à-tour profond et frivole,
Dans son chateau paisiblement,
Loin de tout frondeur malévole
Doutoit de tout impunément,
Et se moquoit très librement
Des bavards fourrés de l'école
Mais quand son élève Charron,
Plus retenu, plus méthodique,
De sagesse donna leçon,
Il fut près de périr, dit on,
Par la haine théologique
—Voltaire, *Epître au Président Hénault.*

[2] See Beattie's *Essay on Fable and Romance;* and Charron *de la Sagesse,* liv ii c 8 It may amuse the curious reader also to compare the theoretical reasonings of Charron with a Memoir in the *Phil. Trans.* for 1773, (by Sir Roger Curtis,) containing *some particulars with respect to the country of Labrador*

(I am inclined to think with the most honest intentions,) to introduce *into men's houses* (if I may borrow an expression of Cicero) what is now called the *new philosophy*,—a philosophy certainly very different from that of Socrates. In the fashionable world, he has, for more than two centuries, maintained his place as the first of moralists; a circumstance easily accounted for, when we attend to the singular combination, exhibited in his writings, of a semblance of erudition, with what Malebranche happily calls his *air du monde*, and *air cavalier*.[1] As for the graver and less attractive Charron, his name would probably before now have sunk into oblivion, had it not been so closely associated, by the accidental events of his life, with the more celebrated name of Montaigne.[2]

The preceding remarks lead me, by a natural connexion of ideas, (to which I am here much more inclined to attend than to the order of dates,) to another writer of the seventeenth century, whose influence over the literary and philosophical taste of France has been far greater than seems to be commonly imagined. I allude to the Duke of La Rochefoucauld, author of the *Maxims* and *Moral Reflections*.

Voltaire was, I believe, the first who ventured to assign to La Rochefoucauld the pre-eminent rank which belongs to him among the French classics. "One of the works," says he, "which contributed most to form the taste of the nation to a

---

[1] "Ah l'aimable homme, *qu'il est de bonne compagnie!* C'est mon ancien ami, mais, à force d'être ancien, il m'est nouveau."—Madame de Sevigné

[2] Montaigne himself seems, from the general strain of his writings, to have had but little expectation of the posthumous fame which he has so long continued to enjoy One of his reflections on this head is so characteristical of the author as a man, and, at the same time, affords so fine a specimen of the graphical powers of his now antiquated style, that I am tempted to transcribe it in his own words —"J'écris mon livre à peu d'hommes et à peu d'années, s'il c'eût été une matière de durée, il l'eût fallu commettre à un langage plus ferme Selon la variation continuelle qui a suivi le nôtre jusqu'à cette heure, qui peut espérer que sa forme présente soit en usage d'ici à cinquante ans? il écoule tous les jours de nos mains, et depuis que je vis, s'est altéré de moitié. Nous disons qu'il est à cette heure parfait Autant en dit du sien chaque siècle. *C'est aux bons et utiles écrits de le clouer à eux, et ira sa fortune selon le crédit de notre état*"

How completely have both the predictions in the last sentence been verified by the subsequent history of the French language!

justness and precision of thought and expression, was the small collection of maxims by Francis Duke of La Rochefoucauld. Although there be little more than one idea in the book, that *self-love is the spring of all our actions,* yet this idea is presented in so great a variety of forms, as to be always amusing. When it first appeared, it was read with avidity; and it contributed, more than any other performance since the revival of letters, to improve the vivacity, correctness, and delicacy of French composition."

Another very eminent judge of literary merit (the late Dr. Johnson) was accustomed to say of La Rochefoucauld's *Maxims,* that it was almost the only book written by a man of fashion, of which professed authors had reason to be jealous. Nor is this wonderful, when we consider the unwearied industry of the very accomplished writer, in giving to every part of it the highest and most finished polish which his exquisite taste could bestow. When he had committed a maxim to paper, he was accustomed to circulate it among his friends, that he might avail himself of their critical animadversions, and, if we may credit Segrais, altered some of them no less than thirty times, before venturing to submit them to the public eye.

That the tendency of these maxims is, upon the whole, unfavourable to morality, and that they always leave a disagreeable impression on the mind, must, I think, be granted. At the same time, it may be fairly questioned, if the motives of the author have in general been well understood, either by his admirers or his opponents. In affirming that self-love is the spring of all our actions, there is no good reason for supposing that he meant to deny the reality of moral distinctions as a philosophical truth;—a supposition quite inconsistent with his own fine and deep remark, that *hypocrisy is itself a homage which vice renders to virtue.* He states it merely as *a position,* which, in the course of his experience as a man of the world, he had found very *generally verified* in the higher classes of society; and which he was induced to announce without any qualification or restriction, in order to give more force and poignancy to his satire. In adopting this mode of writing, he has unconsciously conformed himself, like many other French authors, who have since followed his example, to a suggestion which Aristotle has stated with admirable depth and acuteness in his Rhetoric. "Sentences or apophthegms lend much aid to eloquence. One reason of this is, that they flatter the *pride* of the hearers, who are delighted when the speaker, making use of general language, touches upon opinions which they had before known to be true in part. Thus, a person who had the misfortune to live in a bad neighbourhood, or to have worthless children, would easily assent to the speaker who should affirm, that *nothing* is more vexatious than to have any neighbours ; *nothing* more irrational than to bring children into the world."[1] This observation of Aristotle, while it goes far to account for the imposing and dazzling effect of these rhetorical exaggerations, ought to guard us against the common and popular error of mistaking them for the serious and profound generalizations of science. As for La Rochefoucauld, we know, from the best authorities, that, in private life, he was a conspicuous example of all those moral qualities of which he seemed to deny the existence ; and that he exhibited, in this respect, a striking contrast to the Cardinal de Retz, who has presumed to censure him for his want of faith in the reality of virtue.

In reading La Rochefoucauld, it should never be forgotten, that it was within the vortex of a court he enjoyed his chief opportunities of studying the world ; and that the narrow and exclusive circle in which he moved was not likely to afford him the most favourable specimens of human nature in general. Of the Court of Lewis XIV. in particular, we are told by a very nice and reflecting observer, (Madame de la Fayette,) that "ambition and gallantry were *the soul*, actuating alike both

---

[1] Ἔχουσι δὲ (γνῶμαι) εἰς τοὺς λόγους βοήθειαν μεγάλην, μίαν μὲν δὴ διὰ φορτικότητα τῶν ἀκροατῶν· χαίρουσι γὰρ, ἐάν τις καθόλου λέγων, ἐπιτύχῃ τῶν δοξῶν, ἃς ἐκεῖνοι κατὰ μέρος ἔχουσιν.—Ἡ μὲν γὰρ γνώμη, ὥσπερ εἴρηται, καθόλου ἀπόφανσίς ἐστι· χαίρουσι δὲ καθόλου λεγομένου, ὃ κατὰ μέρος προυπολαμβάνοντες τυγχάνουσιν. Οἷον εἴ τις γείτοσι τύχοι κεχρημένος ἢ τέκνοις φαύλοις, ἀποδέξαιτ' ἂν τοῦ εἰπόντος, ὅτι οὐδὲν γειτονίας χαλεπώτερον· ἢ, ὅτι οὐδὲν ἠλιθιώτερον τεκνοποιίας.—Arist. *Rhet* lib. ii. c. xxi

The whole chapter is interesting and instructive, and shews how profoundly Aristotle had meditated the principles of the rhetorical art.

men and women. So many contending interests, so many different cabals were constantly at work, and in all of these women bore so important a part, that love was always mingled with business, and business with love Nobody was tranquil or indifferent. Every one studied to advance himself by pleasing, serving, or ruining others. Idleness and languor were unknown, and nothing was thought of but intrigues or pleasures."

In the passage already quoted from Voltaire, he takes notice of the effect of La Rochefoucauld's maxims, in improving the style of French composition. We may add to this remark, that their effect has not been less sensible in vitiating the tone and character of French philosophy, by bringing into vogue those false and degrading representations of human nature and of human life, which have prevailed in that country, more or less, for a century past. Mr. Addison, in one of the papers of the *Tatler*, expresses his indignation at this general bias among the French writers of his age "It is impossible," he observes, "to read a passage in Plato or Tully, and a thousand other ancient moralists, without being a greater and better man for it. On the contrary, I could never read any of our modish French authors, or those of our own country, who are the imitators and admirers of that nation, without being, for some time, out of humour with myself, and at everything about me. Their business is to depreciate human nature, and to consider it under the worst appearances; they give mean interpretations, and base motives to the worthiest actions. In short, they endeavour to make no distinction between man and man, or between the species of man and that of the brutes."[1]

It is very remarkable, that the censure here bestowed by Addison on the fashionable French wits of his time, should be so strictly applicable to Helvetius, and to many other of the most admired authors whom France has produced in our own day. It is still more remarkable to find the same depressing

---

[1] *Tatler*, No. 103. The last paper of the *Tatler* was published in 1711, and, consequently, the above passage must be understood as referring to the *modish* tone of French philosophy, prior to the death of Louis XIV.

spirit shedding its malignant influence on French literature, as early as the time of La Rochefoucauld, and even of Montaigne; and to observe how very little has been done by the successors of these old writers, but to expand into grave philosophical systems their loose and lively paradoxes;—disguising and fortifying them by the aid of those logical principles, to which the name and authority of Locke have given so wide a circulation in Europe.

In tracing the origin of that false philosophy on which the excesses of the French Revolutionists have entailed such merited disgrace, it is usual to remount no higher than to the profligate period of the Regency; but the seeds of its most exceptionable doctrines had been sown in that country at an earlier era, and were indebted for the luxuriancy of their harvest, much more to the political and religious soil where they struck their roots, than to the skill or foresight of the individuals by whose hands they were scattered.

I have united the names of Montaigne and of La Rochefoucauld, because I consider their writings as rather addressed to the world at large, than to the small and select class of speculative students. Neither of them can be said to have enriched the stock of human knowledge by the addition of any one important general conclusion; but the maxims of both have operated very extensively and powerfully on the taste and principles of the higher orders all over Europe, and predisposed them to give a welcome reception to the same ideas, when afterwards reproduced with the imposing appendages of logical method, and of a technical phraseology. The foregoing reflections, therefore, are not so foreign as might at first be apprehended, to the subsequent history of ethical and of metaphysical speculation. It is time, however, now to turn our attention to a subject far more intimately connected with the general progress of human reason—the philosophy of Descartes

DESCARTES—GASSENDI—MALEBRANCHE.

According to a late writer,[1] whose literary decisions (excepting where he touches on religion or politics) are justly entitled to the highest deference, Descartes has a better claim than any other individual to be regarded as the father of that spirit of free inquiry which, in modern Europe, has so remarkably displayed itself in all the various departments of knowledge. Of Bacon he observes, "that though he possessed, in a most eminent degree, the genius of philosophy, he did not unite with it the genius of the sciences; and that the methods proposed by him for the investigation of truth, consisting entirely of precepts which he was unable to exemplify, had little or no effect in accelerating the rate of discovery." As for Galileo, he remarks, on the other hand, "that his exclusive taste for mathematical and physical researches disqualified him for communicating to the general mind that impulse of which it stood in need."

"This honour," he adds, "was reserved for Descartes, who combined in himself the characteristical endowments of both his predecessors. If, in the physical sciences, his march be less sure than that of Galileo—if his logic be less cautious than that of Bacon,—yet the very temerity of his errors was instrumental to the progress of the human race. He gave activity to minds which the circumspection of his rivals could not awake from their lethargy. He called upon men to throw off the yoke of authority, acknowledging no influence but what reason should avow: And his call was obeyed by a multitude of followers, encouraged by the boldness and fascinated by the enthusiasm of their leader."

In these observations, the ingenious author has rashly generalized a conclusion deduced from the literary history of his own country. That the works of Bacon were but little read there till after the publication of D'Alembert's *Preliminary Discourse* is, I believe, an unquestionable fact;[2] *not* that it necessarily

---

[1] Condorcet

[2] One reason for this is well pointed out by D'Alembert :—"Il n'y a que les chefs de secte en tout genre, dont les

follows from this, that, even in France, no previous effect had been produced by the labours of Boyle, of Newton, and of the other English experimentalists trained in Bacon's school With respect to England, it is a fact not less certain, that at no period did the philosophy of Descartes produce such an impression on public opinion, either in Physics or in Ethics, as to give the slightest colour to the supposition that it contributed, in the most distant degree, to the subsequent advances made by our countrymen in these sciences. In Logic and Metaphysics, indeed, the case was different. Here the writings of Descartes did much; and if they had been studied with proper attention, they might have done much more But of *this* part of their merits Condorcet seems to have had no idea. His eulogy, therefore, is rather misplaced than excessive. He has extolled Descartes as the father of Experimental Physics: he would have been nearer the truth, if he had pointed him out as the father of the Experimental Philosophy of the Human Mind

In bestowing this title on Descartes, I am far from being inclined to compare him, in the number or importance of *the facts* which he has remarked concerning our intellectual powers, to various other writers of an earlier date I allude merely to his clear and precise conception of that operation of the understanding (distinguished afterwards in Locke's *Essay* by the name of *Reflection*) through the medium of which all our knowledge of Mind is exclusively to be obtained. Of the essential subserviency of this power to every satisfactory conclusion that can be formed with respect to the mental phenomena, and of the futility of every theory which would attempt to explain them by metaphors borrowed from the material world, no other philosopher prior to Locke seems to have been fully aware; and from the moment that these truths were recognised as logical principles in the study of *mind*, a new era commences in the history of that branch of science. It will be necessary, therefore, to allot to the illustration of this part of the Cartesian philosophy a larger space than the limits of my undertaking will permit

ouvrages puissent avoir un certain éclat, Bacon n'a pas été du nombre, et la forme de sa philosophie s'y opposoit elle étoit trop sage pour étonner personne "—*Disc Prél*.

me to afford to the researches of some succeeding inquirers, who may, at first sight, appear more worthy of attention in the present times.

It has been repeatedly asserted by the Materialists of the last century, that Descartes was the first Metaphysician by whom the pure immateriality of the human soul was taught; and that the ancient philosophers, as well as the schoolmen, went no farther than to consider *mind* as the result of a material organization, in which the constituent elements approached to evanescence, in point of subtlety. Both of these propositions I conceive to be totally unfounded. That many of the schoolmen, and that the wisest of the ancient philosophers, when they described the mind as a *spirit* or as a *spark of celestial fire*, employed these expressions, *not* with any intention to materialize its essence, but merely from want of more unexceptionable language, might be shewn with demonstrative evidence, if this were the proper place for entering into the discussion. But what is of more importance to be attended to, on the present occasion, is the effect of Descartes' writings in disentangling the *logical principle* above mentioned, from the *scholastic* question about the nature of *mind,* as contradistinguished from *matter.* It were indeed to be wished, that he had perceived still more clearly and steadily the essential importance of keeping this distinction constantly in view; but he had at least the merit of illustrating, by his own example, in a far greater degree than any of his predecessors, the possibility of studying the mental phenomena, without reference to any facts but those which rest on the evidence of consciousness. The metaphysical question about the *nature* of mind he seems to have considered as a problem, the solution of which was an easy corollary from these *facts*, if distinctly apprehended; but still as a problem, whereof it was possible that different views might be taken by those who agreed in opinion, as far as *facts* alone were concerned. Of this a very remarkable example has since occurred in the case of Mr. Locke, who, although he has been at great pains to shew, that the power of *reflection* bears the same relation to the study of the mental phenomena, which the power of *observation* bears to the study of the material world, appears, nevertheless, to have been far less decided than Descartes with respect to the essential distinction between Mind and Matter, and has even gone so far as to hazard the unguarded proposition, that there is no absurdity in supposing the Deity to have superadded to the other qualities of matter *the power of thinking*. His scepticism, however, on this point, did not prevent his good sense from perceiving, with the most complete conviction, the indispensable necessity of abstracting from the analogy of matter, in studying the laws of our intellectual frame.

The question about the nature or essence of the soul, has been, in all ages, a favourite subject of discussion among Metaphysicians, from its supposed connexion with the argument in proof of its immortality. In this light it has plainly been considered by both parties in the dispute; the one conceiving, that if Mind could be shewn to have no quality in common with Matter, its *dissolution* was physically impossible; the other, that if this assumption could be disproved, it would necessarily follow, that the *whole man* must perish at death. For the last of these opinions Dr. Priestley and many other speculative theologians have of late very zealously contended; flattering themselves, no doubt, with the idea, that they were thus preparing a triumph for their own peculiar schemes of Christianity. Neglecting, accordingly, all the presumptions for a future state, afforded by a comparison of the course of human affairs with the moral judgments and moral feelings of the human heart; and overlooking, with the same disdain, the presumptions arising from the narrow sphere of human knowledge, when compared with the indefinite improvement of which our intellectual powers seem to be susceptible; this acute but superficial writer attached himself exclusively to the old and hackneyed pneumatological argument; tacitly assuming as a principle, that the future prospects of man depend entirely on the determination of a *physical* problem, analogous to that which was then dividing chemists about the existence or non-existence of Phlogiston. In the actual state of science, these speculations might well have been spared. Where is the sober metaphysician to be found, who now speaks of the immortality of the soul as a logical consequence of its immateriality, instead of considering it as depending on the will of that Being by whom it was at first called into existence? And, on the other hand, is it not universally admitted by the best philosophers, that whatever hopes the light of nature encourages beyond the present scene, rest solely (like all our other anticipations of future events) on the general tenor and analogy of the laws by which we perceive the universe to be governed? The proper use of the argument concerning *the immateriality of mind*, is not to establish any positive conclusion as to its destiny hereafter; but to repel the reasonings alleged by materialists, as proofs that its annihilation must be the obvious and necessary effect of the dissolution of the body.[1]

I thought it proper to state this consideration pretty fully, lest it should be supposed that the logical method recommended by Descartes for studying the phenomena of mind, has any necessary dependence on his metaphysical opinion concerning its being and properties, as a separate substance.[2] Between

---

[1] "We shall here be content," says the learned John Smith of Cambridge, "with that sober thesis of Plato, in his *Timæus*, who attributes the perpetuation of all substances to the benignity and liberality of the Creator, whom he therefore brings in thus speaking, ὑμεῖς οὐκ ἐστι ἀθάνατοι οὐδὶ ἄλυτοι, &c *You are not of yourselves immortal nor indissoluble, but would relapse and slide back from that being which I have given you, should I withdraw the influence of my own power from you, but yet you shall hold your immortality by a patent from myself*"—(*Select Discourses*, Cambridge, 1660.) I quote this passage from one of the oldest partisans of Descartes among the English philosophers.

Descartes himself is said to have been of a different opinion 'On a été étonné,' says Thomas, "que dans ses *Méditations Métaphysiques*, Descartes n'ait point parlé de l'immortalité de l'âme Mais il nous apprend lui-même par une de ses lettres, qu'ayant établi clairement, dans cet ouvrage, la distinction de l'âme et de la matière, il suivoit nécessairement de cette distinction, que l'âme par sa nature ne pouvoit périr avec le corps."—*Eloge de Descartes*. Note 21—[On this point Leibnitz agreed with Descartes. "Je ne demeure point d'accord, que l'Immortalité est seulement probable par la lumière naturelle, car je crois qu'il est certain que l'âme ne peut être éteinte que par miracle."—Leibnitii *Opera*, tom vi p. 274.]

[2] I employ the scholastic word *substance*, in conformity to the phraseology of Descartes, but I am fully aware of the strong objections to which it is liable, not only as a wide deviation from popular use, which has appropriated it

these two parts of his system, however, there is, if not a demonstrative connexion, at least a natural and manifest affinity; inasmuch as a steady adherence to his logical method, (or, in other words, the habitual exercise of patient *reflection*,) by accustoming us to break asunder the obstinate associations to which materialism is indebted for the early hold it is apt to take of the fancy, gradually and insensibly predisposes us in favour of his metaphysical conclusion. It is to be regretted, that, in stating this conclusion, his commentators should so frequently make use of the word *spirituality;* for which I do not recollect that his own works afford any authority. The proper expression is *immateriality*, conveying merely a negative idea; and, of consequence, implying nothing more than a rejection of that hypothesis concerning the nature of Mind, which the scheme of materialism so gratuitously, yet so dogmatically assumes.[1]

The power of Reflection, it is well known, is the last of our intellectual faculties that unfolds itself; and, in by far the greater number of individuals, it never unfolds itself in any considerable degree. It is a fact equally certain, that, long before the period of life when this power begins to exercise its appropriate functions, the understanding is already preoccupied with a chaos of opinions, notions, impressions, and associations, bearing on the most important objects of human inquiry; not to mention the innumerable sources of illusion and error connected with the use of a vernacular language, learned in infancy by rote, and identified with the first processes of thought and perception. The consequence is, that when Man begins to reflect, he finds himself (if I may borrow an allusion of M. Turgot's) lost in a labyrinth, into which he had been led blindfolded.[2] To the same purpose, it was long ago complained of by Bacon, "that no one has yet been found of so constant and severe a

to things material and tangible, but as implying a greater degree of positive knowledge concerning the nature of *mind*, than our faculties are fitted to attain —For some farther remarks on this point, see Note I

[1] See Note K

[2] "Quand l'homme a voulu se replier sur lui-même il s'est trouvé dans un labyrinthe où il étoit entré les yeux bandés."—*Œuvres* de Turgot, tom II p 261.

mind, as to have determined and tasked himself utterly to abolish theories and common notions, and to apply his intellect, altogether smoothed and even, to particulars anew. Accordingly, that human reason which we have, is a kind of medley and unsorted collection, from much trust and much accident, and the childish notions which we first drank in Whereas, if one of ripe age and sound senses, and a mind thoroughly cleared, should apply himself freshly to experiment and particulars, of him were better things to be hoped."

What Bacon has here recommended, Descartes attempted to execute; and so exact is the coincidence of his views on this fundamental point with those of his predecessor, that it is with difficulty I can persuade myself that he had never read Bacon's works.[1] In the prosecution of this undertaking, the first steps of Descartes are peculiarly interesting and instructive; and it is *these* alone which merit our attention at present. As for the details of his system, they are now curious only as exhibiting an amusing contrast to the extreme rigour of the principle from whence the author sets out; a contrast so very striking, as fully to justify the epigrammatic saying of D'Alembert, that "Descartes began with doubting of everything, and ended in believing that he had left nothing unexplained."

Among the various articles of common belief which Descartes proposed to subject to a severe scrutiny, he enumerates particularly, the conclusiveness of mathematical demonstration; the existence of God; the existence of the material world; and even the existence of his own body. The only thing that appeared to him certain and incontrovertible, was his own existence; by which he repeatedly reminds us, we are to understand merely the existence of *his mind*, abstracted from all consideration of the material organs connected with it. About every other proposition, he conceived, that doubts might reasonably be entertained; but to suppose the non-existence of *that* which thinks, at the very moment it is conscious of thinking, appeared to him a contradiction in terms. From this single postulatum, accordingly, he took his departure; resolved to admit nothing as a

[1] See Note L.

philosophical truth, which could not be deduced from it by a chain of logical reasoning.[1]

Having first satisfied himself of his own existence, his next step was to inquire, how far his perceptive and intellectual faculties were entitled to credit. For this purpose, he begins with offering a proof of the existence and attributes of God;— truths which he conceived to be necessarily involved in the idea he was able to form of a perfect, self-existent, and eternal Being. His reasonings on this point it would be useless to state. It is sufficient to observe, that they led him to conclude, that God cannot possibly be supposed to deceive His creatures; and therefore, that the intimations of our senses, and the decisions of our reason, are to be trusted to with entire confidence, wherever they afford us *clear and distinct ideas* of their respective objects.[2]

---

[1] "Sic autem rejicientes illa omnia, de quibus aliquo modo possumus dubitare, ac etiam falsa esse fingentes, facile quidem supponimus nullum esse Deum, nullum cœlum, nulla corpora, nosque etiam ipsos, non habere manus, nec pedes, nec denique ullum corpus; non autem ideo nos qui talia cogitamus nihil esse: repugnat enim, ut putemus id quod cogitat, eo ipso tempore quo cogitat, non existere. Ac proinde hæc cognitio, *ego cogito, ergo sum*, est omnium prima et certissima, quæ cuilibet ordine philosophanti occurrat."—*Princip Philos* Pars i § 7.

[2] The substance of Descartes' argument on these fundamental points, is thus briefly recapitulated by himself in the conclusion of his third Meditation:—"Dum in meipsum mentis aciem converto, non modo intelligo me esse rem incompletam, et ab alio dependentem, remque ad majora et meliora indefinite aspirantem, sed simul etiam intelligo illum, à quo pendeo, majora ista omnia non indefinite et potentia tantum, sed reipsa infinite in se habere, atque ita Deum esse, totaque vis argumenti in eo est, quod agnoscam fieri non posse ut existam talis naturæ qualis sum, nempe ideam Dei in me habens, nisi revera Deus etiam existeret, Deus, inquam, ille idem cujus idea in me est, hoc est habens omnes illas perfectiones quas ego non comprehendere sed quocunque modo attingere cogitatione possum, et nullis plane defectibus obnoxius. Ex his satis patet, illum fallacem esse non posse: omnem enim fraudem et deceptionem à defectu aliquo pendere lumine naturali manifestum est."

The above argument for the existence of God, (very improperly called by some foreigners an argument *a priori*,) was long considered by the most eminent men in Europe as quite demonstrative. For my own part, although I do not think that it is by any means so level to the apprehension of common inquirers, as the argument from the marks of *design* everywhere manifested in the universe, I am still less inclined to reject it as altogether unworthy of attention. It is far from being so metaphysically abstruse as the reasonings of Newton and Clarke, founded on our conceptions of *space* and of *time*, nor would it appear, perhaps, less logical and conclu-

As Descartes conceived the existence of God (next to the existence of his own mind) to be the most indisputable of all truths, and rested his confidence in the conclusions of human reason entirely on his faith in the divine veracity, it is not surprising that he should have rejected the argument from *final causes* as superfluous and unsatisfactory. To have availed himself of its assistance, would not only have betrayed a want of confidence in what he professed to regard as much more certain than any mathematical theorem; but would obviously have exposed him to the charge of first appealing to the divine attributes in proof of the authority of his faculties, and afterwards, of appealing to these faculties in proof of the existence of God.

It is wonderful that it should have escaped the penetration of this most acute thinker, that a *vicious circle* of the same description is involved in every appeal to the intellectual powers, in proof of their own credibility; and that unless this credibility be assumed as unquestionable, the farther exercise of human reason is altogether nugatory. The evidence for the existence of God seems to have appeared to Descartes too irresistible and overwhelming to be subjected to those logical canons which apply to all the other conclusions of the understanding.[1]

Extravagant and hopeless as these preliminary steps must now appear, they had nevertheless an obvious tendency to direct the attention of the author, in a singular degree, to the pheno-

---

sive than that celebrated demonstration, if it were properly unfolded, and stated in more simple and popular terms. The two arguments, however, are, in no respect, exclusive of each other; and I have always thought, that, by combining them together, a proof of the point in question might be formed, more impressive and luminous than is to be obtained from either, when stated apart

[1] How painful is it to recollect, that the philosopher who had represented his faith in the veracity of God as the sole foundation of his confidence in the demonstrations of mathematics, was accused and persecuted by his contemporaries as an atheist, and *that*, too, in the same country (Holland) where, for more than half a century after his death, his doctrines were to be taught in all the universities with a blind idolatry! A zeal without knowledge, and the influence of those earthly passions from which even Protestant divines are not always exempted, may, it is to be hoped, go far to account for this inconsistency and injustice, without adopting the uncharitable insinuation of D'Alembert " Malgré toute la sagacité qu'il avoit employée pour prouver l'existence de Dieu, il fut accusé de la nier par *des ministres, qui peut-être ne la croyoient pas* "

mena of thought; and to train him to those habits of abstraction from external objects which, to the bulk of mankind, are next to impossible. In this way he was led to perceive, with the evidence of consciousness, that the attributes of Mind were still more clearly and distinctly knowable than those of Matter; and that, in studying the former, so far from attempting to explain them by analogies borrowed from the latter, our chief aim ought to be, to banish as much as possible from the fancy every analogy, and even every analogical expression, which, by inviting the attention abroad, might divert it from its proper business at home. In one word, that the only right method of philosophizing on this subject was comprised in the old stoical precept, (understood in a sense somewhat different from that originally annexed to it,) *nec te quæsiveris extra.* A just conception of this rule, and a steady adherence to its spirit, constitutes the groundwork of what is properly called the Experimental Philosophy of the Human Mind. It is thus that all our facts relating to Mind must be ascertained; and it is only upon facts thus attested by our own consciousness, that any just theory of Mind can be reared.

Agreeably to these views, Descartes was, I think, the first who clearly saw that our idea of Mind is not direct but relative;—relative to the various operations of which we are conscious. What am I? he asks, in his second Meditation: A thinking being; that is, a being doubting, knowing, affirming, denying, consenting, refusing, susceptible of pleasure and of pain.[1] Of all these things I might have had complete experience, without any previous acquaintance with the qualities and laws of matter, and therefore it is impossible that the study of matter can avail me aught in the study of myself. This, accordingly, Descartes laid down as a first principle,—that *nothing comprehensible by the imagination can be at all subservient to the knowledge of Mind;* and that the sensible

---

[1] "Non sum compages illa membrorum, quæ corpus humanum appellatur, non sum etiam tenuis aliquis aer istis membris infusus, non ventus, non ignis, non vapor, non halitus... Quid igitur sum ? *res cogitans ;* quid est hoc ? nempe dubitans, intelligens, affirmans, negans, volens, nolens," &c —*Med. Sec*

images involved in all our common forms of speaking concerning its operations, are to be guarded against with the most anxious care, as tending to confound, in our apprehensions, two classes of phenomena which it is of the last importance to distinguish accurately from each other.[1]

To those who are familiarly acquainted with the writings of Locke, and of the very few among his successors who have thoroughly entered into the spirit of his philosophy, the foregoing observations may not appear to possess much either of originality or of importance; but when first given to the world, they formed the greatest step ever made in the science of Mind by a single individual. What a contrast do they exhibit, not only to the discussions of the schoolmen, but to the analogical

---

[1] "Itaque cognosco, nihil eorum quæ possum *Imaginatione* comprehendere, ad hanc quam de me habeo notitiam pertinere; mentemque ab illis diligentissime esse avocandam, ut suam ipsa naturam quàm distinctissime percipiat"—*Ibid* A few sentences before, Descartes explains with precision in what sense *Imagination* is here to be understood "Nihil aliud est *imaginari* quam rei corporeæ figuram seu imaginem contemplari"

The following extracts from a book published at Cambridge in 1660, (precisely ten years after the death of Descartes,) while they furnish a useful comment on some of the above remarks, may serve to shew how completely the spirit of the Cartesian philosophy of Mind had been seized, even *then*, by some of the members of that university.

"The souls of men exercising themselves first of all κινήσει προβατικῇ, as the Greek philosopher expresseth himself, merely by a *progressive kind of motion*, spending themselves about bodily and material acts, and conversing only with sensible things, they are apt to acquire such deep stamps of material phantasms to themselves, that they cannot imagine their own *Being* to be any other than *material* and *divisible*, though of a fine ethereal nature It is not possible for us well to know what our souls are, but only by their κινήσεις κυκλικαί, their *circular or reflex motions*, and converse with themselves, which can only steal from them their own secrets."—Smith's *Select Discourses*, pp 65, 66.

"If we reflect but upon our own souls, how manifestly do the notions of *reason, freedom, perception,* and the like, offer themselves to us, whereby we may *know* a thousand times *more distinctly* what our souls are than what our bodies are For the former, we know by an immediate converse with ourselves, and a distinct sense of their operations; whereas all our knowledge of the body is little better than merely historical, which we gather up by scraps and piecemeal, from more doubtful and uncertain experiments which we make of them; but the notions which we have of a *mind, i e,* something within us that thinks, apprehends, reasons, and discourses, are so clear and distinct from all those notions which we can fasten upon a body, that we can easily conceive that if all *body-being* in the world were destroyed, yet we might then as well subsist as now we do"—*Ibid* p 98

theories of Hobbes at the very same period! and how often have they been since lost sight of, notwithstanding the clearest speculative conviction of their truth and importance, by Locke himself, and by the greatest part of his professed followers! Had they been duly studied and understood by Mr. Horne Tooke, they would have furnished him with a key for solving those etymological riddles, which, although mistaken by many of his contemporaries for profound philosophical discoveries, derive, in fact, the whole of their mystery, from the strong bias of shallow reasoners to *relapse* into the same scholastic errors, from which Descartes, Locke, Berkeley, Hume, and Reid, have so successfully laboured to emancipate the mind.

If anything can add to our admiration of a train of thought manifesting in its author so unexampled a triumph over the strongest prejudices of sense, it is the extraordinary circumstance of its having first occurred to a young man, who had spent the years commonly devoted to academical study, amid the dissipation and tumult of camps.[1] Nothing could make this conceivable, but the very liberal education which he had previously received under the Jesuits, at the college of *La Flèche*;[2] where, we are told, that while yet a boy, he was so distinguished by habits of deep meditation, that he went among his companions by the name of *the Philosopher*. Indeed, it is only at that early age that such habits are to be cultivated with complete success.

---

[1] "Descartes porta les armes, d'abord en Hollande, sous le célèbre Maurice de Nassau, de-là en Allemagne, sous Maximilien de Bavière, au commencement de la guerre de trente ans Il passa ensuite au service de l'Empereur Ferdinand II pour voir de plus près les troubles de la Hongrie. On croit aussi, qu'au siège de la Rochelle, il combattit, comme volontaire, dans une bataille contre la flotte Angloise"— Thomas, *Eloge de Descartes*, Note 8

When Descartes quitted the profession of arms, he had arrived at the age of twenty-five

[2] It is a curious coincidence, that it was in the same village of *La Flèche* that Mr. Hume fixed his residence, while composing his Treatise of Human Nature Is it not probable, that he was partly attracted to it by associations similar to those which presented themselves to the fancy of Cicero, when he visited the walks of the Academy?

In the beginning of Descartes' dissertation upon *Method*, he has given a very interesting account of the pursuits which occupied his youth, and of the considerations which suggested to him the bold undertaking of reforming philosophy.

The glory, however, of having pointed out to his successors the true method of studying the theory of *Mind*, is almost all that can be claimed by Descartes in logical and metaphysical science. Many important hints, indeed, may be gleaned from his works; but, on the whole, he has added very little to our knowledge of human nature. Nor will this appear surprising, when it is recollected, that he aspired to accomplish a similar revolution in all the various departments of physical knowledge;—not to mention the time and thought he must have employed in those mathematical researches, which, however lightly esteemed by himself, have been long regarded as the most solid basis of his fame.[1]

Among the principal articles of the Cartesian philosophy, which are now incorporated with our prevailing and most accredited doctrines, the following seem to me to be chiefly entitled to notice:—

1. His luminous exposition of the common logical error of attempting to define words which express notions too simple to admit of analysis. Mr. Locke claims this improvement as entirely his own; but the merit of it unquestionably belongs to Descartes, although it must be owned that he has not always sufficiently attended to it in his own researches.[2]

2. His observations on the different classes of our prejudices—

---

[1] Such too is the judgment pronounced by D'Alembert. "Les mathématiques dont Descartes semble avoir fait assez peu de cas, font néanmoins aujourd'hui la partie la plus solide et la moins contestée de sa gloire." To this he adds a very ingenious reflection on the comparative merits of Descartes, considered as a geometer and as a philosopher "Comme philosophe, il a peut-être été aussi grand, mais il n'a pas été si heureux La Géométrie, qui par la nature de son objet doit toujours gagner sans perdre, ne pouvoit manquer, étant maniée par un aussi grand génie, de faire des progrès très-sensibles et apparens pour tout le monde. La philosophie se trouvoit dans un état bien différent, tout y étoit à commencer; et que ne coûtent point les premiers pas en tout genre! le mérite de les faire dispense de celui d'en faire de grands"
—*Disc Prél*

[2] "The names of simple ideas are not capable of any definitions; the names of all complex ideas' are It has not, that I know, been yet observed by anybody, what words are, and what are not capable of being defined"—(Locke's *Essay*, Book iii chap iv § 4) Compare this with the *Principia* of Descartes, I. 10, and with Lord Stair's *Physiologia Nova Experimentalis*, pp 9 and 79, printed at Leyden in 1686

particularly on the errors to which we are liable in consequence of a careless use of language as the instrument of thought. The greater part of these observations, if not the whole, had been previously hinted at by Bacon; but they are expressed by Descartes with greater precision and simplicity, and in a style better adapted to the taste of the present age.

3 The paramount and indisputable authority which, in all our reasonings concerning the human mind, he ascribes to the evidence of consciousness. Of this logical principle he has availed himself, with irresistible force, in refuting the scholastic sophisms against the liberty of human actions, drawn from the prescience of the Deity, and other considerations of a theological nature.

4. The most important, however, of all his improvements in metaphysics, is the distinction which he has so clearly and so strongly drawn between the *primary* and the *secondary* qualities of matter. This distinction was not unknown to some of the ancient schools of philosophy in Greece; but it was afterwards rejected by Aristotle, and by the schoolmen; and it was reserved for Descartes to place it in such a light, as (with the exception of a very few sceptical, or rather paradoxical theorists) to unite the opinions of all succeeding inquirers. For this step, so apparently easy, but so momentous in its consequences, Descartes was not indebted to any long or difficult processes of reasoning, but to those habits of accurate and patient attention to the operations of his own mind, which, from his early years, it was the great business of his life to cultivate. It may be proper to add, that the epithets *primary* and *secondary*, now universally employed to mark the distinction in question, were first introduced by Locke,—a circumstance which may have contributed to throw into the shade the merits of those inquirers who had previously struck into the same path.

As this last article of the Cartesian system has a close connexion with several of the most refined conclusions yet formed concerning the intellectual phenomena, I feel it due to the memory of the author to pause for a few moments, in order to

vindicate his claim to some leading ideas commonly supposed by the present race of metaphysicians to be of much later origin. In doing so, I shall have an opportunity, at the same time, of introducing one or two remarks which, I trust, will be useful in clearing up the obscurity which is allowed, by some of the ablest followers of Descartes and Locke, still to hang over this curious discussion.

I have elsewhere observed, that Descartes has been very generally charged, by the writers of the last century, with a sophistical play upon words in his doctrine concerning the non-existence of secondary qualities; while, in fact, he was the first person by whom the fallacy of this scholastic paralogism was exposed to the world.[1] In proof of this, it might be sufficient to refer to his own statement in the first part of the *Principia*;[2] but, for a reason which will immediately appear, I think it more advisable, on this occasion, to borrow the words of one of his earliest and ablest commentators. "It is only (says Father Malebranche) since the time of Descartes, that to those con-

---

[1] "Descartes, Malebranche, and Locke revived the distinction between primary and secondary qualities. But they made the secondary qualities mere sensations, and the primary ones resemblances of our sensations They maintained that colour, sound, and heat, are not anything in bodies, but sensations of the mind . . The paradoxes of these philosophers were only an abuse of words For when they maintain, *as an important modern discovery*, that there is no heat in the fire, they mean no more than that the fire does not feel heat, which every one knew before"— Reid's *Inquiry*, chap v sect viii

[2] See sections lxix lxx lxxi The whole of these three paragraphs is highly interesting, but I shall only quote two sentences, which are fully sufficient to shew that, in the above observations, I have done Descartes no more than strict justice.

"Patet itaque in re idem esse, cum dicimus nos percipere colores in objectis, ac si diceremus nos percipere aliquid in objectis, quod quidem quid sit ignoramus, sed a quo efficitur in nobis ipsis sensus quidam valde manifestus et perspicuus, qui vocatur sensus colorum . . Cum vero putamus nos percipere colores in objectis, etsi revera nesciamus quidnam sit quod tunc nomine coloris appellamus, nec ullam similitudinem intelligere possimus, inter colorem quem supponimus esse in objectis, et illum quem experimur esse in sensu, quia tamen hoc ipsum non advertimus, et multa alia sunt, ut magnitudo, figura, numerus, &c quæ clare percipimus non aliter a nobis sentiri vel intelligi, quam ut sunt, aut saltem esse possunt in objectis, facile, in eum errorem delabimur, ut judicemus id, quod in objectis vocamus *colorem*, esse quid omnino simile colori quem sentimus, atque ita ut id quod nullo modo percipimus, a nobis clare percipi arbitraremur"

fused and indeterminate questions, whether fire is hot, grass green, and sugar sweet, philosophers are in use to reply, by distinguishing the equivocal meaning of the words expressing sensible qualities. If by heat, cold, and savour, you understand such and such a disposition of parts, or some unknown motion of sensible qualities, then fire is hot, grass green, and sugar sweet. But if by heat and other qualities you understand what I feel by fire, what I see in grass, &c., fire is not hot, nor grass green; for the heat I feel, and the colours I see, are only in the soul."[1] It is surprising how this, and other passages to the same purpose in Malebranche, should have escaped the notice of Dr. Reid, for nothing more precise on the ambiguity in the names of secondary qualities is to be found in his own works. It is still more surprising that Buffier, who might be expected to have studied with care the speculations of his illustrious countrymen, should have directly charged, not only Descartes, but Malebranche, with maintaining a paradox, which they were at so much pains to banish from the schools of philosophy [2]

The important observations of Descartes upon this subject, made their way into England very soon after his death. They are illustrated at considerable length, and with great ingenuity, by Glanvill, in his *Scepsis Scientifica*, published about thirteen years before Malebranche's *Search after Truth*. So slow, however, is the progress of good sense, when it has to struggle against the prejudices of the learned, that, as lately as 1713, the paradox so clearly explained and refuted by Descartes,

---

[1] *Recherche de la Vérité*, livre vi chap ii

[2] "J'ai admiré souvent que d'aussi grands hommes que Descartes et Malebranche, avec leurs sectateurs, fissent valoir, comme une rare découverte de leur philosophie, que *la chaleur étoit dans nous-mêmes et nullement dans le feu*, au lieu que le commun des hommes trouvoient que *la chaleur étoit dans le feu aussi bien que dans nous* . Mais en ce fameux débat, de quoi s'agit il? Uniquement de l'imperfection du langage, qui causoit une idée confuse par le mot de *chaleur*, ce mot exprimant également deux choses, qui à la vérité ont quelque rapport ou analogie, et pourtant qui sont très différentes savoir, 1 le sentiment de chaleur que nous éprouvons en nous, 2 la disposition qui est dans le feu à produire en nous ce sentiment de chaleur"—*Cours de Sciences*, par le Père Buffier, p 819 A Paris, 1732.

appears to have kept some footing in the English Universities.* In a paper of *the Guardian,* giving an account of a visit paid by Jack Lizard to his mother and sisters, after a year and a half's residence at Oxford, the following *précis* is given of his logical attainments. " For the first week (it is said) Jack dealt wholly in paradoxes. It was a common jest with him to pinch one of his sister's lap-dogs, and afterwards prove he could not feel it When the girls were sorting a set of knots, he would demonstrate to them that all the ribbons were of the same colour; or rather, says Jack, of no colour at all. My Lady Lizard herself, though she was not a little pleased with her son's improvements, was one day almost angry with him; for, having accidentally burnt her fingers as she was lighting the lamp for her tea-pot, in the midst of her anguish, Jack laid hold of the opportunity to instruct her, that there was no such thing as heat in the fire "

This miserable quibble about the non-existence of secondary qualities, never could have attracted the notice of so many profound thinkers, had it not been for a peculiar difficulty connected with our notions of *colour,* of which I do not know any one English philosopher who seems to have been sufficiently aware. That this quality belongs to the same class with sounds, smells, tastes, heat and cold, is equally admitted by the partisans of Descartes and of Locke; and must, indeed, appear an indisputable fact to all who are capable of reflecting accurately on the subject. But still, between *colour* and the other qualities now mentioned, a very important distinction must be allowed to exist. In the case of smells, tastes, sounds, heat and cold, every person must immediately perceive, that his senses give him only *a relative idea* of the external quality; in other words, that they only convey to him the knowledge of the existence of certain properties or powers in external objects, which fit them to produce certain sensations in his mind; and accordingly, nobody ever hesitated a moment about the truth

---

* Mr Stewart substitutes "the English Universities" for what stood in the first edition — " that University from which, about thirty years before, Mr Locke had been expelled," as, in point of fact, Locke was not expelled from Oxford but from Christ Church — *Editor.*

of this part of the Cartesian philosophy, in so far as *these* qualities alone are concerned. But, in the application of the same doctrine to *colour*, I have conversed with many, with whom I found it quite in vain to argue; and *this*, not from any defect in their reasoning powers, but from their incapacity to reflect steadily on the subjects of their consciousness; or rather, perhaps, from their incapacity to separate, as objects of the understanding, two things indissolubly combined by early and constant habit, as objects of the imagination. The silence of modern metaphysicians on this head is the more surprising, that D'Alembert long ago invited their attention to it as one of the most wonderful phenomena in the history of the human mind. " The bias we acquire," I quote his own words, " in consequence of habits contracted in infancy, to refer to a substance material and divisible, what really belongs to a substance spiritual and simple, is a thing well worthy of the attention of metaphysicians. Nothing," he adds, " is perhaps more extraordinary, in the operations of the mind, than to see it transport its sensations out of itself, and to spread them, as it were, over a substance to which they cannot possibly belong." It would be difficult to state the fact in question in terms more brief, precise, and perspicuous.

That the illusion, so well described in the above quotation, was not overlooked by Descartes and Malebranche, appears unquestionable, from their extreme solicitude to reconcile it with that implicit faith, which, from religious considerations, they conceived to be due to the testimony of those faculties with which our Maker has endowed us. Malebranche, in particular, is at pains to distinguish between the sensation, and the judgment combined with it " The sensation never deceives us; it differs in no respect from what we conceive it to be. The *judgment*, too, is natural, or rather (says Malebranche) *it is only a sort of compounded sensation ;*[1] but this judgment leads us into no error with respect to philosophical truth. The

---

[1] He would have expressed himself more accurately, if he had said, that the judgment is indissolubly combined with the sensation, but his meaning is sufficiently obvious

moment we exercise our reason, we see the fact in its true light, and can account completely for that illusive appearance which it presents to the imagination."

Not satisfied, however, with this solution of the difficulty, or rather perhaps apprehensive that it might not appear quite satisfactory to some others, he has called in to his assistance the doctrine of *original sin;* asserting, that all the mistaken judgments which our constitution leads us to form concerning external objects and their qualities, are the consequences of the fall of our first parents; since which *adventure* (as it is somewhat irreverently called by Dr Beattie) it requires the constant vigilance of reason to guard against the numberless tricks and impostures practised upon us by our external senses.[1] In another passage, Malebranche observes very beautifully, (though not very consistently with his theological argument on the same point,) that our senses being given us for the preservation of our bodies, it was requisite for our wellbeing, that we should judge as we do of sensible qualities "In the case of the sensations of *pain* and of *heat*, it was much more advantageous that we should *seem* to feel them in those parts of the body which are immediately affected by them, than that we should associate them with the external objects by which they are occasioned; because pain and heat, having the power to injure our members, it was necessary that we should be warned in what place to apply the remedy; whereas *colours* not being likely, in ordinary cases, to hurt the eye, it would have been superfluous for us to know that they are painted on the *retina*. On the contrary, as they are only useful to us, from the information they convey with respect to things external, it was essential that we should be so formed as to attach them to the corresponding objects on which they depend."[2]

---

[1] "We are informed by Father Malebranche, that the senses were at first as honest faculties as one could desire to be endued with, till after they were debauched by original sin; *an adventure* from which they contracted such an invincible propensity to cheating, that they are now continually lying in wait to deceive us."—*Essay on Truth*, p 241, second edition.

[2] *Recherche de la Vérité*, liv i chap. xiii § 5 In Dr Reid's strictures on Descartes and Locke there are two remarks which I am at a loss how to re-

The two following remarks, which I shall state with all possible brevity, appear to me to go far towards a solution of the problem proposed by D'Alembert

1. According to the *new* theory of vision, *commonly* (but, as I shall afterwards shew, not altogether *justly*) ascribed to Dr. Berkeley, lineal distance from the eye is not an original perception of sight. In the meantime, from the first moment that the eye opens, the most intimate connexion must necessarily be established between the notion of colour and those of visible extension and figure. At first, it is not improbable that all of them may be conceived to be merely *modifications* of the mind; but, however this may be, the manifest consequence is, that when a comparison between the senses of Sight and of Touch has taught us to refer to a distance the objects of the one, the indissolubly associated sensations of the other must of course accompany them, how far soever that distance may extend [1]

2. It is well known to be a general law of our constitution, when one thing is destined, either by nature or by convention, to be *the sign* of another, that the mind has a disposition to pass on, as rapidly as possible, to the thing signified, without dwelling on *the sign* as an object worthy of its attention. The most

---

concile "Colour," says he, "differs from other secondary qualities in this, that whereas the name of the quality is sometimes given to the sensation which indicates it, and is occasioned by it, we never, as far as I can judge, give the name of *colour* to the sensation, but to the quality only" A few sentences before, he had observed, "That when we think or speak of any particular colour, however simple the notion may seem to be which is presented to the imagination, it is really in some sort compounded It involves an unknown cause, and a known effect. The name of *colour* belongs indeed to the cause only, and not to the effect But as the cause is unknown, we can form no distinct conception of it, but by its relation to the known effect And, therefore,

both go together in the imagination, and are so closely united, that they are mistaken for one simple object of thought."—*Inquiry*, chap vi § 4

These two passages seem quite inconsistent with each other If in the perception of colour, the sensation and the quality "be so closely united as to be mistaken for one single object of thought," does it not obviously follow, that it is to this compounded notion the name of *colour* must, in general, be given? On the other hand, when it is said *that the name of colour is never given to the sensation, but to the quality only*, does not this imply, that every time the word is pronounced the quality is separated from the sensation, even in the imaginations of the vulgar?

[1] See Note M.

remarkable of all examples of this occurs in the acquired perceptions of sight, where our estimates of distance are frequently the result of an intellectual process, comparing a variety of different *signs* together, without a possibility on our part, the moment afterwards, of recalling one single step of the process to our recollection. Our inattention to the sensations of colour, considered as affections of the Mind, or as modifications of our own being, appears to me to be a fact of precisely the same description; for all these sensations were plainly intended by nature to perform the office of *signs*, indicating to us the figures and distances of things external. Of their essential importance in this point of view, an idea may be formed, by supposing for a moment the whole face of nature to exhibit only one uniform colour, without the slightest variety even of light and shade. Is it not self-evident that, on this supposition, the organ of sight would be entirely useless, inasmuch as it is by the *varieties* of colour alone that the outlines or visible figures of bodies are so defined, as to be distinguishable one from another? Nor could the eye, in this case, give us any information concerning diversities of *distance;* for all the various signs of it, enumerated by optical writers, presuppose the antecedent recognition of the bodies around us, as separate objects of perception. It is not therefore surprising, that *signs* so indispensably subservient to the exercise of our noblest sense, should cease, in early infancy, to attract notice as the subjects of our consciousness; and that afterwards they should present themselves to the imagination rather as qualities of Matter, than as attributes of Mind.[1]

---

[1] In Dr Reid's Inquiry, he has introduced a discussion concerning the perception of *visible figure*, which has puzzled me since the first time (more than forty years ago) that I read his work. The discussion relates to this question, Whether "there be any sensation proper to visible figure, by which it is suggested in vision?" The result of the argument is, that "our eye *might* have been so framed as to suggest the figure of the object, without suggesting colour, or any other quality; and, of consequence, that there seems to be *no sensation* appropriated to visible figure, this quality being suggested *immediately* by the material impression upon the organ, of which impression we are not conscious."—(*Inquiry*, &c chap vi § 8.) To my apprehension, nothing can appear more manifest than this, that, if there had been no *variety* in our sensa-

To this reference of the sensation of colour to the external object, I can think of nothing so analogous as the feelings we experience in surveying a library of books. We speak of the volumes piled up on its shelves, as *treasures* or *magazines* of

tions of colour, and still more, if we had had no sensation of colour whatsoever, the organ of sight could have given us no information, either with respect to *figures* or to *distances;* and, of consequence, would have been as useless to us, as if we had been afflicted, from the moment of our birth, with a *gutta serena.*

[The following, which was found amongst Mr. Stewart's manuscripts, seems the scroll of a letter to Reid himself, in which Stewart states "what puzzled him in the discussion, more than forty years ago."—*Editor.*

"SIR,—I had the honour of your letter some time ago, and would sooner have returned you my thanks for it, if I had not accidentally lent your *Inquiry* to a gentleman who lives at a considerable distance from me, and did not choose to trouble you again, till I should have an opportunity of reviewing the observations which you have there made on the subject of our correspondence.

"The illustration which you sent me of the notion which you annex to the word *suggest*, has not only satisfied me with respect to the propriety of the use which you have made of it in the passage to which I referred, but has given me a clearer notion of your sentiments concerning the manner in which perception is carried on than I ever had before. I was led to object to your use of the word in this instance, from observing the sense in which you generally use it through the whole of your book. As far as I am able to recollect, the passage which I quoted is the only one in the *Inquiry* in which you have used the word *suggest* to express the communication of knowledge to the

mind by means of something of which we are not conscious. In general you employ it to express the conveyance of knowledge to the mind by means of natural or of artificial signs. This led me to suspect, that the use which you have made of it in this particular case had proceeded from inadvertence. The observations with which you have favoured me have convinced me of my mistake, and at the same time have pointed out to me the reason of your confining the use of it in general in the manner which you have done.

"As to the other point, I am not so fully satisfied. I am happy to find, indeed, that our sentiments upon the subject are not so different as I at first apprehended, but I do not imagine that they yet entirely coincide. You seem to acknowledge that the mode in which we obtain the perception of visible figure is precisely similar to the mode in which we obtain the perception of tangible figure. So far I perfectly agree with you. And I apprehend you will likewise acknowledge the reasonings which you have advanced upon the perception of visible figure are applicable to our perception of extension both by sight and touch. This observation had occurred to me before the first time I wrote to you. But as you have taken no notice of it in your *Inquiry*, and as, in another part of your book, (p. 306 of the 3d Edition,) you have spoken of our perception of visible figure, as an exception from all our perceptions, I was led to conclude that you had conceived some peculiarity about it which I did not fully comprehend. It was this which first turned my attention particularly to the subject, and gave rise to the obser-

the knowledge of past ages; and contemplate them with gratitude and reverence, as inexhaustible *sources* of instruction and delight to the mind. Even in looking at a page of print or of manuscript, we are apt to say, that the ideas we acquire are received by the sense of sight; and we are scarcely conscious of a metaphor, when we employ this language. On such occasions we seldom recollect, that nothing is perceived by the eye but a multitude of *black strokes drawn upon white paper*, and that it is our own acquired habits which communicate to these *strokes* the whole of that significancy whereby they are distinguished from the unmeaning scrawling of an infant or a changeling. The knowledge which we conceive to be preserved in books, like the fragrance of a rose, or the gilding of the clouds, depends, for its existence, on the *relation* between the object and the percipient mind; and the only difference between the two cases is, that in the one, this relation is the local and temporary effect of conventional habits; in the other,

vations which I sent you in my last letter

"Although, however, I flatter myself we agreed in this general point, that our perception of visible figure is obtained in a way similar to that in which we obtain the perception of tangible figure, I cannot help being of opinion that the perception in neither case is obtained without the intervention of a sensation You have said, indeed, that you allow it to be impossible for us in our present state, to perceive figure without colour, and consequently, without the sensation of colour; but I am inclined to suspect that you imagine the impossibility in the case to arise, not from any connexion or dependence between these perceptions established by nature, but merely from their happening to be received by the same organ of sense, so that they always enter the mind in company To this opinion I cannot subscribe, because it appears to me to be evident, that our perceptions of colour and figure are not only received by the same organ of sense, but that the varieties in our perceptions of colour are the *means* of our perception of visible figure.

"I formerly observed, that our perception of visible figure appears to me to be a necessary consequence of that law of our nature, that every visible point is seen in the direction of a straight line passing from the picture of that point on the retina through the centre of the eye If a blind man was made acquainted with this law of our nature, he could of himself infer the necessity of our perceiving visible figure. If it is allowed, then, that our perception of the visible figure of an object is the result of our perceiving the position of all the different points of its boundary, it is evident, that if visible figure can be perceived without any other quality, then position may likewise be perceived without any other quality]

it is the universal and the unchangeable work of nature. The art of printing, it is to be hoped, will in future render the former relation, as well as the latter, coëval with our species; but, in the past history of mankind, it is impossible to say how often it may have been dissolved. What vestiges can now be traced of those scientific attainments which, in early times, drew to *Egypt*, from every part of the civilized world, all those who were anxious to be initiated in the mysteries of philosophy? The symbols which still remain in that celebrated country, inscribed on eternal monuments, have long lost the correspondent *minds* which reflected upon them their own intellectual attributes. To us they are useless and silent, and serve only to attest the existence of arts, of which it is impossible to unriddle the nature and the objects.

―――――――― Variis nunc sculpta figuris
Marmora, trunca tamen visuntur mutaque nobis,
Signa repertorum tumuli, cecidere reperta.

What has now been remarked with respect to *written characters*, may be extended very nearly to *oral language*. When we listen to the discourse of a public speaker, eloquence and persuasion seem to issue from his lips; and we are little aware, that we ourselves infuse the soul into every word that he utters. The case is exactly the same when we enjoy the conversation of a friend. We ascribe the charm entirely to his voice and accents; but without our co-operation, its potency would vanish. How very small the comparative proportion is, which, in such cases, the words spoken contribute to the intellectual and moral effect, I have elsewhere endeavoured to show.

I have enlarged on this part of the Cartesian system, *not* certainly on account of its intrinsic value, as connected with the theory of our external perceptions, (although even in *this* respect of the deepest interest to every philosophical inquirer,) but because it affords the most palpable and striking example I know of, to illustrate the indissoluble associations established during the period of infancy, between the intellectual and the material worlds. It was plainly the intention of nature, that our thoughts should be habitually directed to things external, and accordingly, the bulk of mankind are not only indisposed to study the intellectual phenomena, but are incapable of that degree of reflection which is necessary for their examination. Hence it is, that when we begin to analyze our own internal constitution, we find the facts it presents to us so very intimately combined in our conceptions with the qualities of matter, that it is impossible for us to draw distinctly and steadily the line between them; and that, when Mind and Matter are concerned in the same result, the former is either entirely overlooked, or is regarded only as an accessory principle, dependent for its existence on the latter. To the same cause it is owing, that we find it so difficult (if it be at all practicable) to form an idea of any of our intellectual operations, abstracted from *the images* suggested by their metaphorical names. It was objected to Descartes by some of his contemporaries, that the impossibility of accomplishing the *abstractions* which he recommended, furnished of itself a strong argument against the soundness of his doctrines.[1] The proper answer to this objection does not seem to have occurred to him; nor, so far as I know, to any of his successors;—that the abstractions of the *understanding* are totally different from the abstractions of the *imagination;* and that we may *reason* with most logical correctness about things considered apart, which it is impossible, even in thought, to *conceive* as separated from each other. His own speculations concerning the indissolubility of the union established in the mind between the sensations of colour and the primary qualities of extension and figure, might have furnished him, on this occasion, with a triumphant reply to his adversaries; not to mention that the variety of metaphors, equally fitted to denote the same intellectual powers and operations, might have been urged as a demonstrative proof, that none of these metaphors have any connexion with the general laws to which it is the business of the philosopher to trace the mental phenomena.

When Descartes established it as a general principle, that *nothing conceivable by the power of imagination could throw*

[1] See, in particular, *Gassendi Opera*, tom iii pp 300, 301. Lugduni, 1658.

any light on the operations of thought, (a principle which I consider as exclusively his own,) he laid the foundation-stone of the Experimental Philosophy of the Human Mind. That the same truth had been previously perceived more or less distinctly, by Bacon and others, appears probable from the general complexion of their speculations; but which of them has expressed it with equal precision, or laid it down as a fundamental maxim in their logic? It is for this reason, that I am disposed to date the origin of the true Philosophy of Mind from the *Principia* of Descartes rather than from the *Organon* of Bacon, or the *Essay* of Locke; without, however, meaning to compare the French author with our two countrymen, either as a contributor to our stock of *facts* relating to the intellectual phenomena, or as the author of any important conclusion concerning the general laws to which they may be referred. It is mortifying to reflect on the inconceivably small number of subsequent inquirers by whom the spirit of this cardinal maxim has been fully seized; and that, even in our own times, the old and inveterate prejudice to which it is opposed, should not only have been revived with success, but should have been very generally regarded as an original and profound discovery in metaphysical science. These circumstances must plead my apology for the space I have assigned to the Cartesian Metaphysics in the crowded historical picture which I am at present attempting to sketch. The fulness of illustration which I have bestowed on the works of the master, will enable me to pass over those of his disciples, and even of his antagonists, with a correspondent brevity.[1]

---

[1] The Cartesian doctrine concerning the secondary qualities of matter, is susceptible of various other important applications Might it not be employed, at least as an *argumentum ad hominem* against Mr Hume and others, who, admitting *this* part of the Cartesian system, seem nevertheless to have a secret leaning to the scheme of materialism? Mr Hume has somewhere spoken of *that little agitation of the brain we call thought.* If it be unphilosophical to confound our *sensations* of colour, of heat, and of cold, with such qualities as extension, figure, and solidity, is it not, if possible, still more so, to confound with these qualities the phenomena of thought, of volition, and of moral emotion?

After having said so much of the singular merits of Descartes as the father of genuine metaphysics, it is incumbent on me to add, that his errors in this science were on a scale of proportionate magnitude. Of these the most prominent (for I must content myself with barely mentioning a few of essential importance) were his obstinate rejection of all speculations about final causes;[1] his hypothesis concerning the lower animals, which he considered as mere machines;[2] his doctrine of *innate* ideas, *as understood and expounded by himself;*[3] his noted paradox of placing the *essence* of mind in thinking, and of matter in extension;[4] and his new modification of the ideal theory of perception, adopted afterwards, with some very slight changes, by Malebranche, Locke, Berkeley, and Hume.[5] To

---

[1] It is not unworthy of notice, that, in spite of his own logical rules, Descartes sometimes seems insensibly to adopt, on this subject, the common ideas and feelings of mankind. Several instances of this occur in his Treatise on the Passions, where he offers various conjectures concerning the *uses* to which they are subservient. The following sentence is more peculiarly remarkable: "Mihi persuadere nequeo, naturam indedisse hominibus ullum affectum qui semper vitiosus sit, nullumque usum bonum et laudabile habeat."—Art. clxxv

[2] This hypothesis never gained much ground in England, and yet a late writer of distinguished eminence in *some* branches of science, has plainly intimated that, in his opinion, the balance of probabilities inclined in its favour. "I omit mentioning other animals here," says Mr. Kirwan in his *Metaphysical Essays,* "*as it is at least doubtful whether they are not mere automatons*"—*Met Essays,* p 41 Lond. 1809

[3] I have added the clause in *Italics,* because in Descartes' reasonings on this question, there is no inconsiderable portion of most important truth debased by a large and manifest alloy of error

[4] To this paradox may be traced many of the conclusions of the author, both on physical and on metaphysical subjects. One of the most characteristical features, indeed, of his genius, is the mathematical concatenation of his opinions, even on questions which, at first sight, seem the most remote from each other; a circumstance which, when combined with the extraordinary perspicuity of his style, completely accounts for the strong hold his philosophy took of every mind, thoroughly initiated, at an early period of life, in its principles and doctrines. In consequence of conceiving the essence of matter to consist in extension, he was necessarily obliged to maintain the doctrine of a universal *plenum,* upon which doctrine the theory of the vortices came to be grafted by a very short and easy process The same idea forced him, at the very outset of his *Metaphysical Meditations,* to assert, much more dogmatically than his premises seem to warrant, the *non-extension* of Mind; and led him on many occasions to blend, very illogically, this *comparatively* disputable dogma, with the facts he has to state concerning the mental phenomena

[5] See Note N.

some of these errors I shall have occasion to refer in the sequel of this Discourse The foregoing slight enumeration is sufficient for my present purpose.

In what I have hitherto said of Descartes, I have taken no notice of his metaphysico-physiological theories relative to the connexion between soul and body. Of these theories, however, groundless and puerile as they are, it is necessary for me, before I proceed farther, to say a few words, on account of their extensive and lasting influence on the subsequent history of the science of Mind, not only upon the Continent, but in our own Island.

The hypothesis of Descartes, which assigns to the soul for its principal seat the *pineal gland* or *conarion*, is known to every one who has perused the *Alma* of Prior. It is not, perhaps, equally known, that the circumstance which determined him to fix on this particular spot, was the very plausible consideration, that, among the different parts of the brain, *this* was the only one he could find, which, being single and central, was fitted for the habitation of a being, of which he conceived unity and indivisibility to be essential and obvious attributes.[1] In what manner the *animal spirits*, by their motions forwards and backwards in the nervous tubes, keep up the communication between this gland and the different parts of the body, so as to produce the phenomena of perception, memory, imagination, and muscular motion, he has attempted particularly to explain; describing the processes by which these various effects are accomplished, with as decisive a tone of authority, as if he had been demonstrating experimentally the circulation of the blood. How curious to meet with such speculations in the works of the same philosopher, who had so clearly perceived the necessity, in studying the laws of Mind, of abstracting entirely from the analogies of Matter; and who, at the outset of his inquiries, had carried his scepticism so far, as to require a proof even of the existence of his own body! To those, however, who reflect with attention on the *method* adopted by Descartes, this inconsistency will not appear so inexplicable as

[1] See in particular, the *Treatise de Passionibus*, Art. 31, 32 —See also Note O.

at first sight may be imagined; inasmuch as the same scepticism which led him to suspend his faith in his intellectual faculties till he had once proved to his satisfaction, from the necessary veracity of God, that these faculties were to be regarded as the divine oracles, prepared him, in all the subsequent steps of his progress, to listen to the suggestions of his own fallible judgment, with more than common credulity and confidence.

The ideas of Descartes, respecting the communication between soul and body, are now so universally rejected, that I should not have alluded to them here, had it not been for their manifest influence in producing, at the distance of a century, the rival hypothesis of Dr. Hartley. The first traces of this hypothesis occur in some *queries* of Sir Isaac Newton, which he was probably induced to propose, less from the conviction of his own mind, than from a wish to turn the attention of philosophers to an examination of the correspondent part of the Cartesian system. Not that I would be understood to deny that this great man seems, on more than one occasion, to have been so far misled by the example of his predecessor, as to indulge himself in speculating on questions altogether unsusceptible of solution. In the present instance, however, there cannot, I apprehend, be a doubt, that it was the application made by Descartes of the old theory of *animal spirits*, to explain the mental phenomena, which led Newton into that train of thinking which served as the groundwork of Hartley's Theory of *Vibrations*.[1]

---

[1] The physiological theory of Descartes, concerning the connexion between soul and body, was adopted, together with some of his sounder opinions, by a contemporary English philosopher, Mr. Smith of Cambridge, whom I had occasion to mention in a former note; and that, for some time after the beginning of the eighteenth century, it continued to afford one of the chief subjects of controversy between the two English universities, the *Alma* of Prior affords incontestable evidence. From the same poem it appears, how much the reveries of Descartes about the *seat of the soul*, contributed to wean *the wits of Cambridge* from their former attachment to the still more incomprehensible pneumatology of the schoolmen.

—————— Here Matthew said,
Alma in verse, in prose the mind
By Aristotle's pen defin'd,
Throughout the body, squat or tall,
Is, *bona fide*, all in all.
And yet, slap-dash, is all again
In every sinew, nerve, and vein,
Runs here and there like Hamlet's Ghost
While everywhere she rules the roast

It would be useless to dwell longer on the reveries of a philosopher, much better known to the learned of the present age by the boldness of his exploded errors, than by the profound and important truths contained in his works. At the period when he appeared, it may perhaps be questioned, Whether the truths which he taught, or the errors into which he fell, were most instructive to the world? The controversies provoked by the latter had certainly a more immediate and palpable effect in awakening a general spirit of free inquiry. To this consideration may be added an ingenious and not altogether unsound remark of D'Alembert, that "when absurd opinions are become inveterate, it is sometimes necessary to replace them by other errors, if nothing better can be done. Such (he continues) are the uncertainty and the vanity of the human mind, that it has always need of *an opinion* on which it may lean; it is a child to whom a play-thing must occasionally be presented in order to get out of its hands a mischievous weapon: the play-thing will soon be abandoned, when the light of reason begins to dawn."[1]

Among the opponents of Descartes, Gassendi was one of the earliest, and by far the most formidable. No two philosophers were ever more strongly contrasted, both in point of talents and of temper; the former as far superior to the latter in originality of genius—in powers of concentrated attention to the phenomena of the internal world—in classical taste—in moral sensi-

---

This system, Richard, we are told,
The men of Oxford firmly hold,
The Cambridge wits, you know, deny
With *ipse dixit* to comply
They say (for in good truth they speak
With small respect of that old Greek)
That, putting all his words together,
'Tis three blue beans in one blue bladder
Alma, they strenuously maintain,
Sits cock-horse on her throne the brain,
And from that seat of thought dispenses
Her sovereign pleasure to the senses, &c. &c.

The whole poem, from beginning to end, is one continued piece of ridicule upon the various hypotheses of physiologists concerning the nature of the communication between soul and body The amusing contrast between the solemn absurdity of these disputes, and the light pleasantry of the excursions to which they lead the fancy of the poet, constitutes the principal charm of this performance, by far the most original and characteristical of all Prior's Works.

[1] See Note P.—[For Dr Barrow's opinion of the philosophical merits of Descartes, see his *Opuscula*, p 156]

bility, and in all the rarer gifts of the mind, as he fell short of him in erudition—in industry as a book-maker—in the justness of his logical views, so far as the phenomena of the *material* universe are concerned—and, in general, in those literary qualities and attainments, of which the bulk of mankind either are, or think themselves best qualified to form an estimate. The reputation of Gassendi, accordingly, seems to have been at its height in his own lifetime; that of Descartes made but little progress, till a considerable time after his death.

The comparative justness of Gassendi's views in natural philosophy, may be partly, perhaps chiefly, ascribed to his diligent study of Bacon's works, which Descartes (if he ever read them) has nowhere alluded to in his writings. This extraordinary circumstance in the character of Descartes, is the more unaccountable, that not only Gassendi, but some of his other correspondents, repeatedly speak of Bacon in terms which one should think could scarcely have failed to induce him to satisfy his own mind whether their encomiums were well or ill founded. One of these, while he contents himself, from very obvious feelings of delicacy, with mentioning the Chancellor of England, as the person who, *before the time of Descartes*, had entertained the justest notions about the method of prosecuting physical inquiries, takes occasion, in the same letter, to present him, in the form of a friendly admonition from himself, with the following admirable summary of the *instauratio magna* " To all this it must be added, that no architect, however skilful, can raise an edifice, unless he be provided with proper materials. In like manner, your *method*, supposing it to be perfect, can never advance you a single step in the explanation of natural causes, unless you are in possession of the facts necessary for determining their effects. They who, without stirring from their libraries, attempt to discourse concerning the works of nature, may indeed tell us what sort of world they would have made, if God had committed that task to their ingenuity; but, without a wisdom truly divine, it is impossible for them to form an idea of the universe, at all approaching to that in the mind of its Creator. And, although your *method* promises everything that can be expected from human genius, it does not, therefore, lay any claim to the art of divination; but only boasts of deducing from the assumed *data*, all the truths which follow from them as legitimate consequences; which *data* can, in physics, be nothing else but principles previously established by experiment."[1] In Gassendi's controversies with Descartes, the name of Bacon seems to be studiously introduced on various occasions, in a manner still better calculated to excite the curiosity of his antagonist; and in his historical review of logical systems, the *heroical attempt which gave birth to the Novum Organon* is made the subject of a separate chapter, immediately preceding that which relates to the *Metaphysical Meditations* of Descartes.

The partiality of Gassendi for the Epicurean physics, if not originally imbibed from Bacon, must have been powerfully encouraged by the favourable terms in which he always mentions the Atomic or Corpuscular theory. In its conformity to that luminous simplicity which everywhere characterizes the operations of nature, this theory certainly possesses a decided superiority over all the other conjectures of the ancient philosophers concerning the material universe; and it reflects no small honour on the sagacity both of Bacon and of Gassendi, to have perceived so clearly the strong analogical presumption which this conformity afforded in its favour, prior to the unexpected lustre thrown upon it by the researches of the Newtonian school. With all his admiration, however, of the Epicurean physics, Bacon nowhere shews the slightest leaning towards the metaphysical or ethical doctrines of the same sect; but, on the contrary, considered (and, I apprehend, rightly considered) the atomic theory as incomparably more hostile to atheism, than the hypothesis of four mutable elements, and of one immutable fifth essence. In this last opinion, there is every reason to believe that Gassendi fully concurred; more especially, as he was a zealous advocate for the investigation of *final causes*, even in inquiries strictly physical. At the same time, it cannot be

[1] See the first Epistle to Descartes, prefixed to his *Treatise on the Passions* Amstel 1664.

denied, that, on many questions, both of Metaphysics and of Ethics, this very learned theologian (one of the most orthodox, *professedly*, of whom the Catholic Church has to boast) carried his veneration for the authority of Epicurus to a degree bordering on weakness and servility; and although, on such occasions, he is at the utmost pains to guard his readers against the dangerous conclusions commonly ascribed to his master, he has nevertheless retained more than enough of his system to give a plausible colour to a very general suspicion, that he secretly adopted more of it than he chose to avow.

As Gassendi's attachment to the physical doctrines of Epicurus predisposed him to give an easier reception than he might otherwise have done to his opinions in Metaphysics and in Ethics, so his unqualified contempt for the hypothesis of the Vortices seems to have created in his mind an undue prejudice against the speculations of Descartes on all other subjects. His objections to the argument by which Descartes has so triumphantly established the distinction between Mind and Matter, as separate and heterogeneous objects of human knowledge, must now appear, to every person capable of forming a judgment upon the question, altogether frivolous and puerile, amounting to nothing more than this, that all our knowledge is received by the channel of the external senses—insomuch, that there is not a single object of the understanding which may not be ultimately analyzed into *sensible images;*[1] and of consequence, that when Descartes proposed to abstract from these images in studying the mind, he rejected the only materials out of which it is possible for our faculties to rear any superstructure. The sum of the whole matter is, (to use his own language,) that "there is no real distinction between *imagination* and *intellection;*" meaning, by the former of these words, the power which the mind possesses of *representing* to itself the material objects

---

[1] ["Deinde omnis nostra notitia videtur plane ducere originem à sensibus; et quamvis tu neges quicquid est in intellectu præesse debere in sensu, videtur et esse nihilominus verum, cum nisi sola incursione, κατὰ περίπτωσιν, ut loquuntur, fiat, perficiatur tamen analogia, compositione, divisione, ampliatione, extenuatione, aliisque similibus modis, quos commemorare nihil est necesse"—*Objectiones in Meditationem Secundam.*]

CHAP. II—PHILOSOPHY FROM BACON TO LOCKE. 145

and qualities it has previously perceived. It is evident that this conclusion coincides exactly with the tenets inculcated in England at the same period by his friend Hobbes,[1] as well as with those revived at a later period by Diderot, Horne Tooke, and many other writers, both French and English, who, while they were only repeating the exploded dogmas of Epicurus, fancied they were pursuing, with miraculous success, the new path struck out by the genius of Locke.

It is worthy of remark, that the argument employed by Gassendi against Descartes is copied almost *verbatim* from his own version of the account given by *Diogenes Laertius* of the sources of our knowledge, according to the principles of the Epicurean philosophy;[2]—so very little is there of novelty in the consequences deduced by modern materialists from the scholastic proposition, *Nihil est in intellectu quod non fuit prius in sensu.* The same doctrine is very concisely and explicitly stated in a maxim formerly quoted from Montaigne, that " the senses are the *beginning* and *end* of all our knowledge;—a maxim which Montaigne learned from his oracle Raymond de Sebonde ;—which, by the present race of French philosophers, is almost universally supposed to be sanctioned by the authority of Locke ;—and which, if true, would at once cut up by the roots, not only all metaphysics, but all ethics, and all religion, both natural and revealed. It is, accordingly, with this very maxim that Madame du Deffand (in a letter which rivals anything that the fancy of Molière has conceived in his *Femmes Savantes*) assails Voltaire for his imbecility in attempting a reply to an atheistical book then recently published. In justice to this celebrated lady, I shall transcribe part of it in her own words, as a precious and authentic document of the philosophical tone

---

[1] The affection of Gassendi for Hobbes, and his esteem for his writings, are mentioned in very strong terms by Sorbière "Thomas Hobbius Gassendo charissimus, cujus libellum *De Corpore* paucis ante obitum mensibus accipiens, osculatus est subjungens, *mole quidem parvus est iste liber, verùm totus, ut opinor, medullâ scatet!*"—(Sorberi *Pref.*) Gassendi's admiration of Hobbes's treatise *De Cive*, was equally warm, as we learn from a letter of his to Sorbière, prefixed to that work.

[2] Compare *Gassendi Opera*, tom. iii. pp. 300, 301, and tom v p 12.

affected by the higher orders in France during the reign of Louis XV.

"J'entends parler d'une réfutation d'un certain livre, (*Système de la Nature*.) Je voudrois l'avoir. Je m'en tiens à connoître ce livre par vous. Toutes réfutations de système doivent être bonnes, surtout quand c'est vous qui les faites. Mais, mon cher Voltaire, ne vous ennuyez-vous pas de tous les raisonnemens métaphysiques sur les matières inintelligibles. *Peut-on donner des idées, ou peut-on en admettre d'autres que celles que nous recevons par nos sens ?*"—If the Senses be *the beginning* and *end* of all our knowledge, the inference here pointed at is quite irresistible.[1]

A learned and profound writer has lately complained of the injustice done by the present age to Gassendi; in whose works, he asserts, may be found the whole of the doctrine commonly ascribed to Locke concerning the origin of our knowledge[2] The remark is certainly just, if restricted to Locke's doctrine as interpreted by the greater part of philosophers on the Continent; but it is very wide of the truth, if applied to it as now explained and modified by the most intelligent of his disciples in this

---

[1] Notwithstanding the evidence (according to *my* judgment) of this conclusion, I trust it will not be supposed that I impute the slightest bias in its favour to the generality of those who have adopted the premises. If an author is to be held chargeable with all the consequences logically deducible from his opinions, who can hope to escape censure ? And, in the present instance, how few are there among Montaigne's disciples, who have ever reflected for a moment on the real meaning and import of the proverbial maxim in question !

[2] " Gassendi fut le premier auteur de la nouvelle philosophie de l'esprit humain, car il est tems de lui rendre, à cet égard, une justice qu'il n'a presque jamais obtenue de ses propres compatriotes Il est très singulier en effet, qu'en parlant de la nouvelle philosophie de l'esprit humain, nous disions toujours, *la philosophie de Locke*. D'Alembert et Condillac ont autorisé cette expression, en rapportant l'un et l'autre à Locke exclusivement, la gloire de cette invention," &c &c —De Gerando, *Hist Comp des Systêmes*, tome i p. 301 — [The blind and idolatrous admiration of the French philosophers for Locke can be accounted for only by their very imperfect acquaintance with his writings If Voltaire had ever read the *Essay on Human Understanding*, his estimate of the merits of that excellent work would probably have been somewhat more discriminating "Locke seul a développé *l'entendement humain* dans un livre où il n'y a que des vérités, et ce qui rend l'ouvrage parfait, toutes ces vérités sont claires "—(*Siècle de Louis XIV*)]

country. The main scope, indeed, of Gassendi's argument against Descartes, is to materialize that class of our ideas which the Lockists as well as the Cartesians consider as the exclusive objects of the power of *reflection;* and to shew that these ideas are all ultimately resolvable into images or conceptions borrowed from things external. It is not, therefore, what is sound and valuable in this part of Locke's system, but the errors grafted on it in the comments of some of his followers, that can justly be said to have been borrowed from Gassendi. Nor has Gassendi the merit of originality, even in these errors; for scarcely a remark on the subject occurs in his works, but what is copied from the accounts transmitted to us of the Epicurean metaphysics.

Unfortunately for Descartes, while he so clearly perceived that the origin of those ideas which are the most interesting to human happiness, could not be traced to our external senses, he had the weakness, instead of stating this fundamental proposition in plain and precise terms, to attempt an explanation of it by the extravagant hypothesis of *innate ideas.* This hypothesis gave Gassendi great advantages over him, in the management of their controversy; while the subsequent adoption of Gassendi's reasonings against it by Locke, has led to a very general but ill-founded belief, that the latter, as well as the former, rejected, along with the doctrine of *innate ideas,* the various important and well-ascertained truths combined with it in the Cartesian system.[1]

The hypothetical language afterwards introduced by Leibnitz concerning the human soul, (which he sometimes calls a *living mirror of the universe,* and sometimes supposes to contain within itself *the seeds* of that knowledge which is gradually unfolded in the progressive exercise of its faculties,) is another impotent attempt to explain a mystery unfathomable by human reason. The same remark may be extended to some of Plato's reveries on this question, more particularly to his supposition, that those ideas which cannot be traced to any of our external senses, were acquired by the soul in its state of pre-existence.

[1] [See Note Q.]

In all of these theories, as well as in that of Descartes, the cardinal truth is assumed as indisputable, that the Senses *are not* the only sources of human knowledge; nor is anything wanting to render them correctly logical, but the statement of this truth as an ultimate fact (or at least as a fact hitherto unexplained) in our intellectual frame.

It is very justly observed by Mr. Hume, with respect to Sir Isaac Newton, that "while he seemed to draw off the veil from some of the mysteries of nature, he showed, at the same time, the imperfections of the mechanical philosophy, and thereby restored her ultimate secrets to that obscurity in which they ever did, and ever will remain."[1] When the justness of this remark shall be as universally acknowledged in the science of Mind as it now is in Natural Philosophy, we may reasonably expect that an end will be put to those idle controversies which have so long diverted the attention of metaphysicians from the proper objects of their studies.

The text of Scripture, prefixed by Dr. Reid as a motto to his *Inquiry*, conveys, in a few words, the result of his own modest and truly philosophical speculations on the origin of our knowledge, and expresses this result in terms strictly analogous to those in which Newton speaks of the law of gravitation:— "*The Inspiration of the Almighty hath given them understanding.*" Let our researches concerning the development of the Mind, and the *occasions* on which its various notions are first formed, be carried back ever so far towards the commencement of its history, in *this* humble confession of human ignorance they must terminate at last.

I have dwelt thus long on the writings of Gassendi, much less from my own idea of their merits, than out of respect to an author, in whose footsteps Locke has frequently condescended to tread. The epigrammatic encomium bestowed on him by Gibbon, who calls him "le meilleur philosophe des littérateurs, et le meilleur littérateur des philosophes," appears to me quite extravagant.[2] His learning, indeed, was at once vast and accu-

[1] *History of Great Britain*, chap. lxxi

[2] *Essai sur l'Etude de la Littérature*

rate; and, as a philosopher, he is justly entitled to the praise of being one of the first who entered thoroughly into the spirit of the Baconian logic. But his inventive powers, which were probably not of the highest order, seem to have been either dissipated amidst the multiplicity of his literary pursuits, or laid asleep by his indefatigable labours, as a Commentator and a Compiler. From a writer of this class, new lights were not to be expected in the study of the human Mind; and accordingly, *here* he has done little or nothing, but to revive and to repeat over the doctrines of the old Epicureans. His works amount to six large volumes in folio, but the substance of them might be compressed into a much smaller compass, without any diminution of their value.

In *one* respect Gassendi had certainly a great advantage over his antagonist—the good humour which never forsook him in the heat of a philosophical argument. The comparative indifference with which he regarded most of the points at issue between them, was perhaps the chief cause of that command of temper so uniformly displayed in all his controversies, and so remarkably contrasted with the constitutional irritability of Descartes. Even the faith of Gassendi in his own favourite master, Epicurus, does not seem to have been very strong or dogmatical, if it be true that he was accustomed to allege, as the chief ground of his preferring the Epicurean physics to the theory of the Vortices, "that chimera for chimera, he could not help feeling some partiality for that which was two thousand years older than the other."

About twenty years after the death of Gassendi, (who did not long survive Descartes,) Malebranche entered upon his philosophical career. The earlier part of his life had, by the advice of some of his preceptors, been devoted to the study of ecclesiastical history, and of the learned languages; for neither of which pursuits does he seem to have felt that marked predilection which afforded any promise of future eminence. At length, in the twenty-fifth year of his age, he accidentally met

[1] See Note R

with Descartes' *Treatise on Man,* which opened to him at once a new world, and awakened him to a consciousness of powers, till then unsuspected either by himself or by others. Fontenelle has given a lively picture of the enthusiastic ardour with which Malebranche first read this performance; and describes its effects on his nervous system as sometimes so great, that he was forced to lay aside the book till the palpitation of his heart had subsided.

It was only ten years after this occurrence when he published *The Search after Truth;* a work which, whatever judgment may now be passed on its philosophical merits, will always form an interesting study to readers of taste, and a useful one to students of human nature. Few books can be mentioned, combining, in so great a degree, the utmost depth and abstraction of thought, with the most pleasing sallies of imagination and eloquence; and none, where they who delight in the observation of intellectual character may find more ample illustrations, both of the strength and weakness of the human understanding. It is a singular feature in the history of Malebranche, that, notwithstanding the poetical colouring which adds so much animation and grace to his style, he never could read, without disgust, a page of the finest verses;[1] and that, although Imagination was manifestly the predominant ingredient in the composition of his own genius, the most elaborate passages in his works are those where he inveighs against this treacherous faculty, as the prolific parent of our most fatal delusions.[2]

In addition to the errors more or less incident to all men, from the unresisted sway of imagination during the infancy of reason, Malebranche had, in his own case, to struggle with

---

[1] Bayle.—Fontenelle.—D'Alembert

[2] In one of his arguments on this head, Malebranche refers to the remarks previously made on the same subject by an English philosopher, who, like himself, has more than once taken occasion, while warning his readers against the undue influence of imagination over the judgment, to exemplify the boundless fertility and originality of his own. The following allusion of Bacon's, quoted by Malebranche, is eminently apposite and happy. "Omnes perceptiones tam sensus quam mentis sunt ex analogia hominis, non ex analogia universi Estque intellectus humanus instar speculi inæqualis ad radios rerum, qui suam naturam naturæ rerum immiscet, eamque distorquet et inficit."

all the prejudices connected with the peculiar dogmas of the Roman Catholic faith. Unfortunately, too, he everywhere discovers a strong disposition to blend his theology and his metaphysics together; availing himself of the one as an auxiliary to the other, wherever, in either science, his ingenuity fails him in establishing a favourite conclusion. To this cause is chiefly to be ascribed the little attention now paid to a writer formerly so universally admired, and, in point of fact, the indisputable author of some of the most refined speculations claimed by the theorists of the eighteenth century. As for those mystical controversies about *Grace* with Anthony Arnauld, on which he wasted so much of his genius, they have long sunk into utter oblivion; nor should I have here revived the recollection of them, were it not for the authentic record they furnish of the passive bondage in which, little more than a hundred years ago, two of the most powerful minds of that memorable period were held by a creed, renounced at the Reformation, by all the Protestant countries of Europe; and the fruitful source, wherever it has been retained, of other prejudices, not less to be lamented, of an opposite description.[1]

When Malebranche touches on questions not positively decided by the church, he exhibits a remarkable boldness and freedom of inquiry, setting at nought those human authorities

---

[1] Of this disposition to blend theological dogmas with philosophical discussions, Malebranche was so little conscious in himself, that he has seriously warned his readers against it, by quoting an aphorism of Bacon's, peculiarly applicable to his own writings:—"Ex divinorum et humanorum malesana admixtione non solum educitur philosophia phantastica, sed etiam religio hæretica Itaque salutare admodum est si mente sobria fidei tantum dentur quæ fidei sunt" In transcribing these words, it is amusing to observe, that Malebranche has slily suppressed the name of the author from whom they are borrowed, manifestly from an unwillingness to weaken their effect, by the suspicious authority of a philosopher not in communion with the Church of Rome.—*Recherche de la Vérité*, liv ii chap ix

Dr. Reid, proceeding on the supposition that Malebranche was a Jesuit, has ascribed to the antipathy between this order and the Jansenists, the warmth displayed on both sides, in his disputes with Arnauld, (*Essays on the Int. Powers*, p. 124), but the fact is, that Malebranche belonged to the Congregation of the *Oratory;* a society much more nearly allied to the Jansenists than to the Jesuits; and honourably distinguished, since its first origin, by the moderation as well as learning of its members

which have so much weight with men of unenlightened erudition; and sturdily opposing his own reason to the most inveterate prejudices of his age. His disbelief in the reality of sorcery, which, although cautiously expressed, seems to have been complete, affords a decisive proof of the soundness of his judgment, where he conceived himself to have any latitude in exercising it. The following sentences contain more good sense on the subject, than I recollect in any contemporary author. I shall quote them, as well as the other passages I may afterwards extract from his writings, in his own words, to which it is seldom possible to do justice in an English version.

"Les hommes même les plus sages se conduisent plutôt par l'imagination des autres, je veux dire par l'opinion et par la coûtume, que par les règles de la raison. Ainsi dans les lieux où l'on brule les sorciers, on ne voit autre chose, parce que dans les lieux où l'on les condamne au feu, on croit véritablement qu'ils le sont, et cette croyance se fortifie par les discours qu'on en tient. Que l'on cesse de les punir et qu'on les traite comme des fous, et l'on verra qu'avec le tems ils ne seront plus sorciers; parce que ceux qui ne le sont que par imagination, qui font certainement le plus grand nombre, deviendront comme les autres hommes.

"C'est donc avec raison que plusieurs Parlemens ne punissent point les sorciers : ils s'en trouve beaucoup moins dans les terres de leur ressort· Et l'envie, la haine, et la malice des méchans ne peuvent se servir de ce prétexte pour accabler les innocens."

How strikingly has the sagacity of these anticipations and reflections been verified by the subsequent history of this popular superstition in our own country, and indeed in every other instance where the experiment recommended by Malebranche has been tried! Of this sagacity much must, no doubt, be ascribed to the native vigour of a mind struggling against and controlling early prejudices; but it must not be forgotten, that, notwithstanding his retired and monastic life, Malebranche had breathed the same air with the associates and friends of Descartes and of Gassendi, and that no philosopher

seems ever to have been more deeply impressed with the truth of that golden maxim of Montaigne—" Il est bon de frotter et limer notre cervelle contre celle d'autrui."

Another feature in the intellectual character of Malebranche, presenting an unexpected contrast to his powers of abstract meditation, is the attentive and discriminating eye with which he appears to have surveyed the habits and manners of the comparatively little circle around him; and the delicate yet expressive touches with which he has marked and defined some of the nicest shades and varieties of genius.[1] To this branch of the Philosophy of Mind, not certainly the least important and interesting, he has contributed a greater number of original remarks than Locke himself;[2]—since whose time, with the

---

[1] See among other passages, *Rech. de la Vérité*, liv. ii. chap. ix.

[2] In one of Locke's most noted remarks of this sort, he has been anticipated by Malebranche, on whose clear yet concise statement, he does not seem to have thrown much new light by his very diffuse and wordy commentary. "If in having our ideas in the memory ready at hand, consists quickness of parts, in this of having them unconfused, and being able nicely to distinguish one thing from another, where there is but the least difference, consists, in a great measure, the exactness of judgment and clearness of reason, which is to be observed in one man above another And hence, perhaps, may be given some reason of that common observation, that men who have a great deal of wit, and prompt memories, have not always the clearest judgment, or deepest reason. For Wit, lying most in the assemblage of ideas, and putting those together with quickness and variety, *wherein* can be found any resemblance or congruity, *thereby* to make up pleasant pictures, and agreeable visions in the fancy; Judgment, on the contrary, lies quite on the other side, in separating carefully, one from another, ideas *wherein* can be found the least difference, *thereby* to avoid being misled by similitude, and by affinity to take one thing for another "—*Essay*, &c., b. ii c xi § 2

"Il y a donc des esprits de deux sortes Les uns remarquent aisément les différences des choses, et ce sont les bons esprits Les autres imaginent et supposent de la ressemblance entr'elles, et ce sont les esprits superficiels."—*Rech. de la Vérité*, liv. ii. *Seconde Partie*, chap. ix.

At a still earlier period, Bacon had pointed out the same cardinal distinction in the intellectual characters of individuals

"Maximum et velut radicale discrimen ingeniorum, quoad philosophiam et scientias, illud est, quod alia ingenia sint fortiora et aptiora ad notandas rerum differentias; alia, ad notandas rerum similitudines. Ingenia enim constantia et acuta, figere contemplationes, et morari, et hærere in omni subtilitate differentiarum possunt Ingenia autem sublimia, et discursiva, etiam tenuissimas et catholicas rerum similitudines et cognoscunt, et componunt. Utrumque autem ingenium facile labitur in exces-

single exception of Helvetius, hardly any attention has been paid to it, either by French or English metaphysicians. The same practical knowledge of the human understanding, modified and diversified, as we everywhere see it, by education and external circumstances, is occasionally discovered by his very able antagonist Arnauld; affording, in both cases, a satisfactory proof, that the narrowest field of experience may disclose to a superior mind those refined and comprehensive results, which common observers are forced to collect from an extensive and varied commerce with the world.

In some of Malebranche's incidental strictures on men and manners, there is a lightness of style and fineness of *tact*, which one would scarcely have expected from the mystical divine, who believed that *he saw all things in God*. Who would suppose that the following paragraph forms part of a profound argument on the influence of the external senses over the human intellect?

"Si par exemple, celui qui parle s'énonce avec facilité, s'il garde une mesure agréable dans ses périodes, s'il a l'air d'un honnête homme et d'un homme d'esprit, si c'est une personne de qualité, s'il est suivi d'un grand train, s'il parle avec autorité et avec gravité, si les autres l'écoutent avec respect et en silence, s'il a quelque réputation, et quelque commerce avec les esprits du premier ordre, enfin, s'il est assez heureux pour plaire, ou pour être estimé, il aura raison dans tout ce qu'il avancera; et il n'y aura pas jusqu'à son collet et à ses manchettes, qui ne prouvent quelque chose."[1]

In his philosophical capacity, Malebranche is to be considered

---

sum, prensando aut gradus rerum, aut umbras."

That strain I heard was of a higher mood! It is evident, that Bacon has here seized, in its most general form, the very important truth perceived by his two ingenious successors in particular cases. *Wit*, which Locke contrasts with *judgment*, is only one of the various talents connected with what Bacon calls the *discursive genius*, and indeed, a talent very subordinate in dignity to most of the others.

[1] I shall indulge myself only in one other citation from Malebranche, which I select partly on account of the curious extract it contains from an English publication long since forgotten in this country, and partly as a proof that this learned and pious father was not altogether insensible to the ludicrous.

"Un illustre entre les Sçavans, qui a

in two points of view, 1. As a commentator on Descartes; and, 2. As the author of some conclusions from the Cartesian principles, not perceived or not avowed by his predecessors of the same school.

1. I have already taken notice of Malebranche's comments on fondé des chaires de Géometrie et d'Astronomie dans l'Université d'Oxford,* commence un livre, qu'il s'est avisé de faire sur les huit premières propositions d'Euclide, par ces paroles *Consilium meum est, auditores, si vires et valetudo suffecerint, explicare definitiones, petitiones, communes sententias, et octo priores propositiones primi libri elementorum, cætera post me venientibus relinquere:* et il le finit par celles-ci: *Exsolvi per Dei gratiam, Domini auditores, promissum, liberavi fidem meam, explicavi pro modulo meo definitiones, petitiones, communes sententias, et octo priores propositiones elementorum Euclidis Hic annis fessus cyclos artemque repono Succedent in hoc munus alii fortasse magis vegeto corpore et vivido ingenio.* Il ne faut pas une heure à un esprit médiocre, pour apprendre par lui même, ou par le secours du plus petit géometre qu'il y ait, les définitions, demandes, axiomes, et les huit premières propositions d'Euclide: et voici un auteur qui parle de cette entreprise, comme de quelque chose de fort grand, et de fort difficile Il a peur que ses forces lui manquent, *Si vires et valetudo suffecerint* Il laisse à ses successeurs à pousser ces choses: *cætera post me venientibus relinquere* Il remercie Dieu de ce que, par une grace particulière, il a exécuté ce qu il avoit promis: *exsolvi per Dei gratiam promissum, liberavi fidem meam, explicavi pro modulo meo* Quoi ? la quadrature du cercle? la duplication du cube? Ce grand homme a expliqué *pro modulo suo*, les définitions, les demandes, les axiomes, et les huit premières propositions du premier livre des *Élémens* d'Euclide. Peut-être qu'entre ceux qui lui succéderont, il s'en trouvera qui auront plus de santé, et plus de force que lui pour continuer ce bel ouvrage: *Succedent in hoc munus alii* FORTASSE *magis vegeto corpore, et vivido ingenio* Mais pour lui il est tems qu'il se repose, *hic annis fessus cyclos artemque repono*"

After reading the above passage, it is impossible to avoid reflecting, with satisfaction, on the effect which the progress of philosophy has since had in removing those obstacles to the acquisition of useful knowledge which were created by the pedantic taste prevalent two centuries ago. What a contrast to a quarto commentary on the definitions, postulates, axioms, and first eight propositions of Euclid's First Book, is presented by Condorcet's estimate of the time now sufficient to conduct a student to the highest branches of mathematics! "Dans le siècle dernier, il suffisoit de quelques années d'étude pour savoir tout ce qu'Archimède et Hipparque avoient pu connoître, et aujourd'hui deux années de l'enseignement d'un professeur vont au delà de ce que savoient Leibnitz ou Newton."—(*Sur l'Instruction Publique*) In this particular science, I am aware that much is to be ascribed to the subsequent invention of new and more general *methods*, but, I apprehend, not a little also to the improvements gradually suggested by experience, in what Bacon calls the *traditive* part of logic

---

* Sir Henry Savile The work here referred to is a 4to volume, entitled, *Prælectiones xiii in Principium Elementorum Euclidis*, Oxoniæ habitæ, Anno 1620

the Cartesian doctrine concerning the *sensible*, or, as they are now more commonly called, *the secondary qualities* of matter. The same fulness and happiness of illustration are everywhere else to be found in his elucidations of his master's system; to the popularity of which he certainly contributed greatly by the liveliness of his fancy, and the charms of his composition. Even in *this* part of his writings, he always preserves the air of an original thinker; and, while pursuing the same path with Descartes, seems rather to have accidentally struck into it from his own casual choice, than to have selected it out of any deference for the judgment of another. Perhaps it may be doubted, if it is not on such occasions, that the inventive powers of his genius, by being somewhat restrained and guided in their aim, are most vigorously and most usefully displayed.

In confirmation of this last remark, I shall only mention, by way of examples, his comments on the Cartesian theory of Vision,—more especially on that part of it which relates to our experimental estimates of the distances and magnitudes of objects; and his admirable illustration of the errors to which we are liable from the illusions of sense, of imagination, and of the passions. In his physiological reveries on the union of soul and body, he wanders, like his master, in the dark, from the total want of facts as a foundation for his reasonings; but even here his genius has had no inconsiderable influence on the inquiries of later writers. The fundamental principle of Hartley is most explicitly stated in *The Search after Truth*;[1] as well

---

[1] "Toutes nos différentes perceptions sont attachées aux différens changemens qui arrivent dans les fibres de la partie principale du cerveau dans laquelle l'âme réside plus particulièrement."—(*Rech. de la Vérité*, lib. ii chap v)' These *changes* in the fibres of the brain are commonly called by Malebranche *ébranlemens ;*—a word which is frequently rendered by his old English translator (Taylor) *vibrations* "La seconde chose," says Malebranche, "qui se trouve dans chacune des sensations, est *l'ébranlement* des fibres de nos nerfs, qui se communique jusqu'au cerveau." thus translated by Taylor· "The second thing that occurs in every sensation is the *vibration* of the fibres of our nerves, which is communicated to the brain"—(Liv. 1 chap xii) Nor was the theory of *association* overlooked by Malebranche. See, in particular, the third chapter of his second book, entitled, *De la liaison mutuelle des idées de l'esprit, et des traces du cerveau; et de la liaison mutuelle des traces avec les traces, et des idées avec les idées*

as a hypothesis concerning the nature of *habits*, which, rash and unwarranted as it must now appear to every novice in science, was not thought unworthy of adoption in *The Essay on Human Understanding*.[1]

2. Among the opinions which chiefly characterize the system of Malebranche, the leading one is, that the *causes* which it is the aim of philosophy to investigate are only *occasional causes*, and that the Deity is himself the *efficient* and the *immediate cause* of every effect in the universe.[2] From this single principle, the greater part of his distinguishing doctrines may be easily deduced, as obvious corollaries.

That we are completely ignorant of the manner in which *physical causes* and *effects* are connected, and that all our knowledge concerning them amounts merely to a perception of *constant conjunction*, had been before remarked by Hobbes, and more fully shown by Glanvill in his *Scepsis Scientifica*. Malebranche, however, has treated the same argument much more profoundly and ably than any of his predecessors, and has, indeed, anticipated Hume in some of the most ingenious reasonings contained in his Essay on *Necessary Connexion*. From these *data*, it was not unnatural for his pious mind to conclude, that what are commonly called *second causes* have no

---

[1] " Mais afin de suivre notre explication, il faut remarquer que les esprits ne trouvent pas toujours les chemins, par où ils doivent passer, assez ouverts et assez libres, et que cela fait que nous avons de la difficulté à remuer, par exemple, les doigts avec la vitesse qui est nécessaire pour jouer des instrumens de musique, ou les muscles qui servent à la prononciation, pour prononcer les mots d'une langue étrangère Mais que peu-à-peu *les esprits animaux par leur cours continuel ouvrent et applanissent ces chemins,* en sorte qu'avec le tems ils n'y trouvent plus de résistance Car c'est dans cette facilité que les esprits animaux ont de passer dans les membres de notre corps, que consistent les habitudes "—*Rech de la Vérité,* liv ii chap v.

" Habits seem to be but trains of motion in the animal spirits, which, once set a-going, continue in the same steps they have been used to, *which, by often treading, are worn into a smooth path* "—Locke, book ii chap. xxxiii. § 6.

[2] " Afin qu'on ne puisse plus douter de la fausseté de cette misérable philosophie, il est nécessaire de prouver qu'il n'y a qu'un vrai Dieu, parce qu'il n'y a qu'une vraie cause, que la nature ou la force de chaque chose n'est que la volonté de Dieu: que toutes les causes naturelles ne sont point de véritable causes, mais seulement des causes occasionelles "—*De la Vérité,* livre vi 2de Partie, chap iii.

existence; and that the Divine power, incessantly and universally exerted, is, in truth, the connecting link of all the phenomena of nature. It is obvious, that, in this conclusion, he went farther than his premises warranted; for, although no necessary connexions among physical events can be traced by our faculties, it does not therefore follow that such connexions are impossible. The only sound inference was, that the laws of nature are to be discovered, *not*, as the ancients supposed, by *a priori* reasonings from causes to effects, but by experience and observation. It is but justice to Malebranche to own, that he was one of the first who placed in a just and strong light this fundamental principle of the inductive logic.

On the other hand, the objections to the theory of *occasional causes*, chiefly insisted on by Malebranche's opponents, were far from satisfactory. By some it was alleged, that it ascribed every event to a miraculous interposition of the Deity; as if this objection were not directly met by the general and constant *laws* everywhere manifested to our senses,—in a departure from which laws, the very essence of a *miracle* consists. Nor was it more to the purpose to contend, that the beauty and perfection of the universe were degraded by excluding the idea of *mechanism;* the whole of this argument turning, as is manifest, upon an application to Omnipotence of ideas borrowed from the limited sphere of human power.[1] As to the study of natural philosophy, it is plainly not at all affected by the hypothesis in question; as the investigation and generalization of the laws of nature, which are its only proper objects, present exactly the same field to our curiosity, whether we suppose these *laws* to be the immediate effects of the Divine agency, or

---

[1] This objection, frivolous as it is, was strongly urged by Mr Boyle, (*Inquiry into the Vulgar Idea concerning Nature,*) and has been copied from him by Mr. Hume, Lord Kames, and many other writers. Mr. Hume's words are these "It argues more wisdom to contrive at first the fabric of the world with such perfect foresight, that, of itself, and by its proper operation, it may serve all the purposes of providence, than if the great Creator were obliged every moment to adjust its parts, and animate by his breath all the wheels of that stupendous machine."—(*Essay on the Idea of Necessary Connexion*) An observation somewhat similar occurs in the Treatise *De Mundo,* commonly ascribed to Aristotle

the effects of *second causes*, placed beyond the reach of our faculties.[1]

Such, however, were the chief reasonings opposed to Malebranche by Leibnitz, in order to prepare the way for the system of *Pre-established Harmony;* a system more nearly allied to that of *occasional causes* than its author seems to have suspected, and encumbered with every solid difficulty connected with the other.

From the theory of *occasional causes*, it is easy to trace the process which led Malebranche to conclude, *that we see all things in God.* The same arguments which convinced him, that the Deity carries into execution every *volition* of the mind, in the movements of the body, could not fail to suggest, as a farther consequence, that every *perception* of the mind is the immediate effect of the divine illumination As to the *manner* in which this illumination is accomplished, the extraordinary hypothesis adopted by Malebranche was forced upon him, by the opinion then universally held, that the immediate objects of our perceptions are not things external, but their *ideas* or images. The only possible expedient for reconciling these two articles of his creed, was to transfer the seat of our *ideas* from our own minds to that of the Creator.[2]

[1] In speaking of the theory of *occasional causes*, Mr Hume has committed a historical mistake, which it may be proper to rectify. "Malebranche," he observes, "and other Cartesians, made the doctrine of the universal and sole efficacy of the Deity, the foundation of all their philosophy. *It had, however, no authority in England* Locke, Clarke, and Cudworth, never so much as take notice of it, but suppose all along that matter has a real, though subordinate and derived power"—*Hume's Essays*, vol ii. p 475, edition of 1784.

Mr. Hume was probably led to connect, in this last sentence, the name of Clarke with those of Locke and Cudworth, by taking for granted that his metaphysical opinions agreed exactly with those commonly ascribed to Sir Isaac Newton. In fact, on the point now in question, his creed was the same with that of Malebranche The following sentence is very nearly a translation of a passage already quoted from the latter. "The course of nature, truly and properly speaking, is nothing but the will of God producing certain effects in a continued, regular, constant, and uniform manner"—*Clarke's Works*, vol ii p 698, fol ed

[2] We are indebted to La Harpe for the preservation of an epigrammatic line (*un vers fort plaisant*, as he justly calls it) on this celebrated hypothesis · "*Lui, qui voit tout en Dieu, n'y voit-il pas qu'il est fou ?*—C'étoit au moins," La Harpe adds, "un fou qui avoit beaucoup d'esprit."

In this theory of Malebranche, there is undoubtedly, as Bayle has remarked,[1] an approach to some speculations of the latter Platonists; but there is a much closer coincidence between it and the system of those Hindoo philosophers, who (according to Sir William Jones) "believed that the whole creation was rather an *energy* than a *work;* by which the infinite Mind, who is present at all times, and in all places, exhibits to his creatures a set of perceptions, like a wonderful picture, or piece of music, always varied, yet always uniform."[2]

In some of Malebranche's reasonings upon this subject, he has struck into the same train of thought which was afterwards pursued by Berkeley, (an author to whom he bore a very strong resemblance in some of the most characteristical features of his genius;) and, had he not been restrained by religious scruples, he would, in all probability, have asserted, not less confidently than his successor, that the existence of matter was demonstrably inconsistent with the principles then universally admitted by philosophers. But this conclusion Malebranche rejects, as not reconcilable with the words of Scripture, that "in the beginning God created the heavens and the earth" "La foi m'apprend que Dieu a créé le ciel et la terre. Elle m'apprend que l'Ecriture est un livre divin. Et ce livre ou son apparence me dit nettement et positivement, qu'il y a mille et mille créatures. Donc voilà toutes mes apparences changées en réalités. Il y a des corps; cela est démontré en toute rigueur la foy supposée."[3]

In reflecting on the repeated reproduction of these, and other

---

[1] See his Dictionary, article *Amelius*

[2] Introduction to a Translation of some Hindoo verses

[3] *Entretiens sur la Métaphysique,* p 207.

The celebrated *doubt* of Descartes concerning all truths but the existence of his own *mind*, (it cannot be too often repeated,) was the real source, not only of the inconsistency of Malebranche on this head, but of the chief metaphysical *puzzles* afterwards started by Berkeley and Hume. The illogical transition by which he attempted to pass from this first principle to other truths, was early remarked by some of his own followers, who were accordingly led to conclude, that no man can have full assurance of anything but of his own individual existence. If the fundamental doubt of Descartes be admitted as reasonable, the conclusion of these philosophers (who were distinguished by the name of *Egoists*) is unavoidable.

CHAP II.—PHILOSOPHY FROM BACON TO LOCKE.

ancient paradoxes, by modern authors, whom it would be highly unjust to accuse of plagiarism;—still more, in reflecting on the affinity of some of our most refined theories to the popular belief in a remote quarter of the globe, one is almost tempted to suppose, that human invention is limited, like a barrel-organ, to a specific number of tunes. But is it not a fairer inference, that the province of pure Imagination, unbounded as it may at first appear, is narrow, when compared with the regions opened by truth and nature to our powers of observation and reasoning?[1] Prior to the time of Bacon, the physical systems of the learned performed their periodical revolutions in orbits as small as the metaphysical hypotheses of their successors; and yet, who would now set any bounds to our curiosity in the study of the material universe? Is it reasonable to think, that the phenomena of the intellectual world are less various, or less marked with the signatures of Divine wisdom?

It forms an interesting circumstance in the history of the two memorable persons who have suggested these remarks, that they had *once*, and only *once*, the pleasure of a short interview. "The conversation," we are told, "turned on the non-existence of matter. Malebranche, who had an inflammation in his lungs, and whom Berkeley found preparing a medicine in his cell, and cooking it in a small pipkin, exerted his voice so violently in the heat of their dispute, that he increased his disorder, which carried him off a few days after."[2] It is impossible not to regret; that of this interview there is no other record;— or rather, that Berkeley had not made it the groundwork of one of his own dialogues. Fine as his imagination was, it could scarcely have added to the picturesque effect of the real scene.[3]

---

[1] The limited number of fables, of humorous tales, and even of jests, which, it should seem, are in circulation over the face of the globe, might perhaps be alleged as an additional confirmation of this idea

[2] *Biog Brit* vol ii. p 251

[3] This interview happened in 1715, when Berkeley was in the thirty-first, and Malebranche in the seventy-seventh year of his age What a change in the state of the philosophical world (whether for the better or worse is a different question) has taken place in the course of the intervening century!

Dr Warburton, who, even when he thinks the most unsoundly, always possesses the rare merit of thinking for

Anthony Arnauld, whom I have already mentioned as one of the theological antagonists of Malebranche, is also entitled to a distinguished rank among the French philosophers of this period. In his book *On true and false ideas*, written in opposition to Malebranche's scheme of our seeing all things in God, he is acknowledged by Dr. Reid to have struck the first mortal blow at the *ideal theory*, and to have approximated very nearly to his own refutation of this ancient and inveterate prejudice.[1]

himself, is one of the very few English authors who have spoken of Malebranche with the respect due to his extraordinary talents. "All you say of Malebranche," he observes in a letter to Dr Hurd, "is strictly true, he is an admirable writer. There is something very different in the fortune of Malebranche and Locke. When Malebranche first appeared, it was with a general applause and admiration; when Locke first published his *Essay*, he had hardly a single approver. Now Locke is universal, and Malebranche sunk into obscurity. All this may be easily accounted for. The intrinsic merit of either was out of the question. But Malebranche supported his first appearance on a philosophy in the highest vogue; that philosophy has been overturned by the Newtonian, and Malebranche has fallen with his master. It was to no purpose to tell the world, that Malebranche could stand without him. The public never examines so narrowly. Not but that there was another cause sufficient to do the business; and that is, his debasing his noble work with his system of seeing all things in God. When this happens to a great author, one half of his readers out of folly, the other out of malice, dwell only on the unsound part, and forget the other, or use all their arts to have it forgotten.

"But the sage Locke supported himself by no system on the one hand, nor, on the other, did he dishonour himself by any whimsies. The consequence of which was, that, neither following the fashion, nor striking the imagination, he, at first, had neither followers nor admirers, but being everywhere clear, and everywhere solid, he at length worked his way, and afterwards was subject to no reverses. He was not affected by the new fashions in philosophy, who leaned upon none of the old, nor did he afford ground for the after attacks of envy and folly by any fanciful hypotheses, which, when grown stale, are the most nauseous of all things."

The foregoing reflections on the opposite fates of these two philosophers, do honour on the whole to Warburton's penetration; but the unqualified panegyric on Locke will be now very generally allowed to furnish an additional example of "that national spirit, which," according to Hume "forms the great happiness of the English, and leads them to bestow on all their eminent writers such praises and acclamations, as may often appear partial and excessive."

[1] The following very concise and accurate summary of Arnauld's doctrine concerning *ideas*, is given by Brucker. "Antonius Arnaldus, ut argumenta Malebranchii eo fortius everteret, peculiarem sententiam defendit, asseruitque, ideas earumque perceptiones esse unum idemque, et non nisi relationibus differre. Ideam scilicet esse, quatenus ad objectum refertur quod mens considerat; perceptionem vero, quatenus ad ipsam mentem quæ percipit, duplicem tamen

A step so important would of itself be sufficient to establish his claim to a place in literary history; but what chiefly induces me again to bring forward his name, is the reputation he has so justly acquired by his treatise, entitled *The Art of Thinking;*[1] a treatise written by Arnauld in conjunction with his friend Nicole, and of which (considering the time when it appeared) it is hardly possible to estimate the merits too highly. No publication certainly, prior to Locke's *Essay*, can be named, containing so much good sense and so little nonsense on the science of Logic; and very few have *since* appeared on the same subject, which can be justly preferred to it in point of practical utility. If the author had lived in the present age, or had been less fettered by a prudent regard to existing prejudices, the technical part would probably have been reduced within a still narrower compass; but even there he has contrived to substitute, for the puerile and contemptible examples of common logicians, several interesting illustrations from the physical discoveries of his immediate predecessors; and has indulged himself in some short excursions which excite a lively regret that he had not more frequently and freely given scope to his original reflections. Among these excursions, the most valuable, in my opinion, is the twentieth chapter of the third part, which deserves the attention of every logical student, as an important and instructive supplement to the enumeration of sophisms given by Aristotle.[2]

illam relationem ad unam pertinere mentis modificationem."—(*Hist Phil de Ideis*, pp 247, 248) Anthony Arnauld farther held, that "material things are perceived *immediately* by the mind, without the intervention of *ideas*."—(*Hist de Ideis*, p 261) In this respect his doctrine coincided exactly with that of Reid.

[1] More commonly known by the name of the *Port-Royal Logic*.

[2] According to Crousaz, *The Art of Thinking* contributed more than either the *Organon* of Bacon, or the *Method* of Descartes, to improve the established modes of academical education on the Continent (See the Preface to his *Logic*, printed at Geneva, 1724.) Leibnitz himself has mentioned it in the most flattering terms, coupling the name of the author with that of Pascal, a still more illustrious ornament of the *Port-Royal* Society:—"Ingeniosissimus Pascalius in præclara dissertatione de ingenio Geometrico, cujus fragmentum extat in egregio libro celeberrimi viri Antonii Arnaldi de Arte bene Cogitandi," &c, but lest this encomium

The soundness of judgment so eminently displayed in *The Art of Thinking,* forms a curious contrast to that passion for theological controversy, and that zeal for what he conceived to be the purity of the Faith, which seem to have been the ruling passions of the author's mind. He lived to the age of eighty-three, continuing to write against Malebranche's opinions concerning *Nature and Grace* to his last hour. "He died," says his biographer, "in an obscure retreat at Brussels, in 1692, without fortune, and even without the comfort of a servant; *he*, whose nephew had been a Minister of State, and who might himself have been a Cardinal. The pleasure of being able to *publish* his sentiments was to him a sufficient recompense." Nicole, his friend and companion in arms, worn out at length with these incessant disputes, expressed a wish to retire from the field, and to enjoy repose. "*Repose!*" replied Arnauld; "won't you have the whole of eternity to repose in?"

An anecdote which is told of his infancy, when considered in connexion with his subsequent life, affords a good illustration of the force of impressions received in the first dawn of reason. He was amusing himself one day with some childish sport, in the library of the Cardinal du Perron, when he requested of the Cardinal to give him a pen.—And for what purpose? said the Cardinal.—To write books, like you, against the Huguenots

---

from so high an authority should excite a curiosity somewhat out of proportion to the real value of the two works here mentioned, I think it right to add, that the praises bestowed by Leibnitz, whether on living or dead authors, are not always to be strictly and literally interpreted. "No one," says Hume, "is so liable to an excess of admiration as a truly great genius." Wherever Leibnitz has occasion to refer to any work of solid merit, this remark applies to him with peculiar force, partly, it is probable, from his quick and sympathetic perception of congenial excellence, and partly from a generous anxiety to point it out to the notice of the world. It affords, on the other hand, a remarkable illustration of the force of prejudice, that Buffier, a learned and most able Jesuit, should have been so far influenced by the hatred of his order to the Jansenists, as to distinguish the *Port-Royal Logic* with the cold approbation of being "a judicious *compilation* from former works on the same subject,—particularly from a treatise by a Spanish Jesuit, *Fonseca*" —(*Cours de Sciences*, p 873 Paris, 1732) Gibbon also has remarked how much "the learned Society of Port-Royal contributed to establish in France a taste for just reasoning, simplicity of style, and philosophical method."—*Misc. Works*, vol ii p 70

The Cardinal, it is added, who was then old and infirm, could not conceal his joy at the prospect of so hopeful a successor; and, as he was putting the pen into his hand, said, " I give it to *you*, as the dying shepherd Damœtas bequeathed his pipe to the little Corydon."

The name of Pascal (*that prodigy of parts*, as Locke calls him) is more familiar to modern ears, than that of any of the other learned and polished anchorites, who have rendered the sanctuary of *Port-Royal* so illustrious ; but his writings furnish few materials for philosophical history. Abstracting from his great merits in mathematics and in physics, his reputation rests chiefly on the *Provincial Letters;* a work from which Voltaire, notwithstanding his strong prejudices against the author, dates the *fixation* of the French language ; and of which the same excellent judge has said, that " Molière's best comedies do not excel them in wit, nor the compositions of Bossuet in sublimity." The enthusiastic admiration of Gibbon for this book, which he was accustomed from his youth to read once a year, is well known ; and is sufficient to account for the rapture with which it never fails to be spoken of by *the erudite vulgar*[1] in this country. I cannot help, however, suspecting, that it is now more praised than read in Great Britain ; so completely have those disputes, to which it owed its first celebrity, lost their interest. Many passages in it, indeed, will always be perused with delight ; but it may be questioned, if Gibbon himself would have read it so often from beginning to end, had it not been for the strong hold which ecclesiastical controversies, and the Roman Catholic faith, had early taken of his mind.

In one respect, the *Provincial Letters* are well entitled to the attention of philosophers, inasmuch as they present so faithful and lively a picture of the influence of false religious views in perverting the moral sentiments of mankind. The overwhelming ridicule lavished by Pascal on the whole system of jesuitical casuistry, and the happy effects of his pleasantry

[1] *Eruditum Vulgus*—Plin *Nat Hist* lib ii.

in preparing, from a distance, the fall of that formidable order, might be quoted as proofs, that there are at least *some* truths, in whose defence this weapon may be safely employed;—perhaps with *more* advantage than the commanding voice of Reason herself. The mischievous absurdities which it was his aim to correct, scarcely admitted of the gravity of logical discussion; requiring only the extirpation or the prevention of those early prejudices which choke the growth of common sense and of conscience: And for this purpose, what so likely to succeed with the open and generous minds of youth, as Ridicule, managed with decency and taste; more especially when seconded, as in the *Provincial Letters,* by acuteness of argument, and by the powerful eloquence of the heart? In this point of view, few practical moralists can boast of having rendered a more important service than Pascal to the general interests of humanity. Were it not, indeed, for his exquisite satire, we should already be tempted to doubt, if, at so recent a date, it were possible for such extravagancies to have maintained a dangerous ascendant over the human understanding.

The unconnected fragment of Pascal, entitled *Thoughts on Religion,* contains various reflections which are equally just and ingenious; some which are truly sublime; and not a few which are false and puerile: the whole, however, deeply tinctured with that ascetic and morbid melancholy, which seems to have at last produced a partial eclipse of his faculties. Voltaire has animadverted on this fragment with much levity and petulance; mingling, at the same time, with many very exceptionable strictures, several of which it is impossible to dispute the justness. The following reflection is worthy of Addison, and bears a strong resemblance in its spirit to the amiable lessons inculcated in his papers on Cheerfulness:[1]—" To consider the world as a dungeon, and the whole human race as so many criminals doomed to execution, is the idea of an enthusiast; to suppose the world to be a seat of delight, where we are to expect nothing but pleasure, is the dream of a Sybarite; but to conclude that the Earth, Man, and the lower

[1] *Spectator,* No. 381 and 387.

Animals, are, all of them, subservient to the purposes of an unerring Providence, is, in my opinion, the system of a wise and good man."

From the sad history of this great and excellent person, (on whose deep superstitious gloom it is the more painful to dwell, that, by an unaccountable, though not singular coincidence, it was occasionally brightened by the inoffensive play of a lively and sportive fancy,) the eye turns with pleasure to repose on the *mitis sapientia,* and the Elysian imagination of Fenelon. The interval between the deaths of these two writers is indeed considerable, but that between their births does not amount to thirty years; and, in point of education, both enjoyed nearly the same advantages.

The reputation of Fenelon as a philosopher would probably have been higher and more universal than it is, if he had not added to the depth, comprehension, and soundness of his judgment, so rich a variety of those more pleasing and attractive qualities, which are commonly regarded rather as the flowers than the fruits of study. The same remark may be extended to the Fenelon of England, whose ingenious and original essays on the *Pleasures of Imagination* would have been much more valued by modern metaphysicians, had they been less beautifully and happily written. The characteristical excellence, however, of the Archbishop of Cambray, is that *moral wisdom* which (as Shaftesbury has well observed) "comes more from the heart than from the head;" and which seems to depend less on the reach of our reasoning powers, than on the absence of those narrow and malignant passions, which, on all questions of ethics and politics, (perhaps I might add of religion also,) are the chief source of our speculative errors.

The *Adventures of Telemachus,* when considered as a production of the seventeenth century, and still more as the work of a Roman Catholic Bishop, is a sort of prodigy; and it may, to this day, be confidently recommended as the best manual extant for impressing on the minds of youth the leading truths both of practical morals and of political economy. Nor ought it to be concluded, because these truths appear to lie so near the surface, and command so immediately the cordial assent of the understanding, that they are therefore obvious or trite; for the case is the same with *all* the truths most essential to human happiness. The importance of agriculture and of religious toleration to the prosperity of states; the criminal impolicy of thwarting the kind arrangements of Providence, by restraints upon commerce; and the duty of legislators to study the laws of the moral world as the groundwork and standard of their own, appear, to minds unsophisticated by inveterate prejudices, as approaching nearly to the class of axioms,—yet how much ingenious and refined discussion has been employed, even in our own times, to combat the prejudices which everywhere continue to struggle against them; and how remote does the period yet seem, when there is any probability that these prejudices shall be completely abandoned!

"But how," said Telemachus to Narbal, "can such a commerce as this of Tyre be established at Ithaca?" "By the same means," said Narbal, "that have established it here. Receive all strangers with readiness and hospitality, let them find convenience and liberty in your ports; and be careful never to disgust them by avarice or pride. above all, never restrain the freedom of commerce, by rendering it subservient to your own immediate gain. The pecuniary advantages of commerce should be left wholly to those by whose labour it subsists; lest this labour, for want of a sufficient motive, should cease. There are more than equivalent advantages of another kind, which must necessarily result to the Prince from the wealth which a free commerce will bring into his state; and commerce is a kind of spring, which to divert from its natural channel is to lose."[1] Had the same question been put to Smith or to Franklin in the present age, what sounder advice could they have offered?

In one of Fenelon's *Dialogues of the Dead*, the following remarkable words are put into the mouth of Socrates: "It is necessary that a people should have written laws, always the

[1] Hawkesworth's Translation.

same, and consecrated by the whole nation; that these laws should be paramount to everything else; that those who govern should derive their authority from *them* alone; possessing an unbounded power to do all the good which the laws prescribe, and restrained from every act of injustice which the laws prohibit."

But it is chiefly in a work which did not appear till many years after his death, that we have an opportunity of tracing the enlargement of Fenelon's political views, and the extent of his Christian charity It is entitled *Direction pour la Conscience d'un Roi;* and abounds with as liberal and enlightened maxims of government as, under the freest constitutions, have ever been offered by a subject to a sovereign. Where the variety of excellence renders selection so difficult, I must not venture upon any extracts; nor, indeed, would I willingly injure the effect of the whole by quoting detached passages. A few sentences on *liberty of conscience* (which I will not presume to translate) may suffice to convey an idea of the general spirit with which it is animated. " Sur toute chose, ne forcez jamais vos sujets à changer de religion. Nulle puissance humaine ne peut forcer le retranchement impénétrable de la liberté du cœur. La force ne peut jamais persuader les hommes; elle ne fait que des hypocrites. Quand les lois se mêlent de religion, au lieu de la protéger, ils la mettent en servitude. Accordez à tous la tolérance civile, non en approuvant tout comme indifférent, mais en souffrant avec patience tout ce que Dieu souffre, et en tâchant de ramener les hommes par une douce persuasion."

AND SO MUCH for the French philosophy of the seventeenth century. The extracts last quoted forewarn us that we are fast approaching to a new era in the history of the Human Mind. *The glow-worm 'gins to pale his ineffectual fire;* and we *scent the morning air* of the coming day. This era I propose to date from the publications of Locke and of Leibnitz; but the remarks which I have to offer on their writings, and on those of their most distinguished successors, I reserve for the Second Part of this Discourse, confining myself, at present, to a very short retrospect of the state of philosophy, during the preceding period, in some other countries of Europe.[1]

SECT. III.—PROGRESS OF PHILOSOPHY DURING THE SEVENTEENTH CENTURY, IN SOME PARTS OF EUROPE, NOT INCLUDED IN THE PRECEDING REVIEW.

DURING the first half of the seventeenth century, the philosophical spirit which had arisen with such happy auspices in England and in France, has left behind it few or no traces of its existence in the rest of Europe. On all questions connected with *the science of mind*; (a phrase which I here use in its largest acceptation,) authority continued to be everywhere mistaken for argument; nor can a single work be named, bearing, in its character, the most distant resemblance to the *Organon* of Bacon; to the *Meditations* of Descartes; or to the bold theories of that sublime genius who, soon after, was to shed so dazzling a lustre on the north of Germany. Kepler and Galileo still lived; the former languishing in poverty at Prague; the latter oppressed with blindness, and with ecclesiastical persecution at Florence; but their pursuits were of a nature altogether foreign to our present subject.

One celebrated work alone, the Treatise of Grotius, *De Jure Belli et Pacis*, (first printed in 1625,) arrests our attention among the crowd of useless and forgotten volumes, which were then issuing from the presses of Holland, Germany, and Italy. The influence of this treatise, in giving a new direction to the studies of the learned, was so remarkable, and continued so long to operate with undiminished effect, that it is necessary to

---

[1] I have classed *Télémaque* and the *Direction pour la Conscience d'un Roi* with the philosophy of the seventeenth century, although the publication of the former was not permitted till after the death of Louis XIV., nor that of the latter till 1748 The tardy appearance of both only shews how far the author had shot ahead of the orthodox religion and politics of his times

allot to the author, and to his successors, a space considerably larger than may, at first sight, seem due to their merits. Notwithstanding the just neglect into which they have lately fallen in our Universities, it will be found, on a close examination, that they form an important link in the history of modern literature. It was from their school that most of our best writers on Ethics have proceeded, and many of our most original inquirers into the Human Mind; and it is to the same school (as I shall endeavour to shew in the Second Part of this Discourse) that we are chiefly indebted for the modern science of Political Economy.[1]

For the information of those who have not read the Treatise *De Jure Belli et Pacis*, it may be proper to observe, that, under this title, Grotius has aimed at a complete system of Natural Law. Condillac says, that he chose the title, in order to excite a more general curiosity; adding, (and, I believe, very justly,) that many of the most prominent defects of his work may be fairly ascribed to a compliance with the taste of his age. "The author," says Condillac, "was able to think for himself; but he constantly labours to support his conclusions by the authority of others; producing, on many occasions, in support of the most obvious and indisputable propositions, a long string of quotations from the Mosaic law; from the Gospels; from the Fathers of the Church; from the Casuists; and not unfrequently, in the very same paragraph, from Ovid and Aristophanes." In consequence of this cloud of witnesses, always at hand to attest the truth of his axioms, not only is the attention perpetually interrupted and distracted; but the author's reasonings, even when perfectly solid and satisfactory, fail in making a due impression on the reader's mind; while the very little that there probably was of systematical arrangement in the general plan of the book, is totally kept out of view.

---

[1] From a letter of Grotius, quoted by Gassendi, we learn, that the Treatise *De Jure Belli et Pacis* was undertaken at the request of his learned friend Peireskius. "Non otior, sed in illo de jure gentium opere pergo, quod si tale futurum est, ut lectores demereri possit, habebit quod tibi debeat posteritas, qui me ad hunc laborem et auxilio et hortatu tuo excitasti"—*Gassendi Opera*, tom. v p 294

In spite of these defects, or rather, perhaps, in consequence of some of them, the impression produced by the treatise in question, on its first publication, was singularly great. The stores of erudition displayed in it, recommended it to the classical scholar, while the happy application of the author's reading to the affairs of human life, drew the attention of such men as Gustavus Adolphus; of his Prime-Minister, the Chancellor Oxenstiern; and of the Elector Palatine, Charles Lewis. The last of these was so struck with it, that he founded at Heidelberg a Professorship for the express purpose of teaching the Law of Nature and Nations;—an office which he bestowed on Puffendorff; the most noted, and, on the whole, the most eminent of those who have aspired to tread in the footsteps of Grotius.

The fundamental principles of Puffendorff possess little merit in point of originality, being a sort of medley of the doctrines of Grotius, with some opinions of Hobbes; but his book is entitled to the praise of comparative conciseness, order, and perspicuity, and accordingly came very generally to supplant the Treatise of Grotius, as a manual or institute for students, notwithstanding its immense inferiority in genius, in learning, and in classical composition.

The authors who, in different parts of the Continent, have since employed themselves in commenting on Grotius and Puffendorff; or in abridging their systems; or in altering their arrangements, are innumerable; but notwithstanding all their industry and learning, it would be very difficult to name any class of writers, whose labours have been of less utility to the world. The same ideas are constantly recurring in an eternal circle; the opinions of Grotius and of Puffendorff, where they are at all equivocal, are anxiously investigated, and sometimes involved in additional obscurity; while, in the meantime, the science of Natural Jurisprudence never advances one single step; but, notwithstanding its recent birth, seems already sunk into a state of dotage.[1]

[1] I have borrowed, in this last paragraph, some expressions from Lamprech 'Grotii et Puffendorfii interpretes, viri quidem diligentissimi, sed qui vix fruc-

In perusing the systems now referred to, it is impossible not to feel a very painful dissatisfaction, from the difficulty of ascertaining the precise object aimed at by the authors. So vague and indeterminate is the general scope of their researches, that not only are different views of the subject taken by different writers, but even by the same writer in different parts of his work,—a circumstance which, of itself, sufficiently accounts for the slender additions they have made to the stock of useful knowledge; and which is the real source of that chaos of heterogeneous discussions, through which the reader is perpetually forced to fight his way. A distinct conception of these different views will be found to throw more light than might at first be expected on the subsequent history of Moral and of Political Science; and I shall therefore endeavour, as accurately as I can, to disentangle and separate them from each other, at the risk perhaps of incurring, from some readers, the charge of prolixity. The most important of them may, I apprehend, be referred to one or other of the following heads:—

1. Among the different ideas which have been formed of Natural Jurisprudence, one of the most common (particularly in the earlier systems) supposes its object to be—to lay down those rules of justice which *would* be binding on men living in a social state, without any positive institutions; or (as it is frequently called by writers on this subject) living together in a *state of nature*. This idea of the province of Jurisprudence seems to have been uppermost in the mind of Grotius, in various parts of his Treatise.

To this speculation about the state of nature, Grotius was manifestly led by his laudable anxiety to counteract the attempts then recently made to undermine the foundations of morality. That moral distinctions are created entirely by the

tum aliquem tot commentariis, adnotationibus, compendiis, tabulis, ceterisque ejusmodi aridissimis laboribus attulerunt perpetuo circulo eadem res circumagitur, quid uterque senserit quæritur, interdum etiam utrisque sententiæ obscurantur, disciplina nostra tamen ne latum quidem unguem progreditur, et dum aliorum sententiæ disquiruntur et explanantur, Rerum Natura quasi senio confecta squalescit, neglectaque jacet et inobservata omnino."—*Juris Publici Theoremata,* p 34

arbitrary and revealed will of God, had, before his time, been zealously maintained by some theologians even of the Reformed Church; while, among the political theorists of the same period, it was not unusual to refer these distinctions (as was afterwards done by Hobbes) to the positive institutions of the civil magistrate. In opposition to both, it was contended by Grotius, that there is a natural law coëval with the human constitution, from which positive institutions derive all their force; a truth which, how obvious and trite soever it may now appear, was so opposite in its spirit to the illiberal systems taught in the monkish establishments, that he thought it necessary to exhaust in its support all his stores of ancient learning. The older writers on Jurisprudence must, I think, be allowed to have had great merit in dwelling so much on this fundamental principle; a principle which renders "*Man a Law to Himself;*" and which, if it be once admitted, reduces the metaphysical question concerning the nature of the moral faculty to an object merely of speculative curiosity.[1] To this faculty the ancients frequently give the name of *reason;* as in that noted passage of Cicero, where he observes, that " right reason is itself *a law;* congenial to the feelings of nature; diffused among all men; uniform; eternal; calling us imperiously to our duty, and peremptorily prohibiting every violation of it Nor does it speak," continues the same author, " one language at Rome and another at Athens, varying from place to place, or time to time; but it addresses itself to all nations, and to all ages; deriving its authority from the common sovereign of the

---

[1] " Upon whatever we suppose that our moral faculties are founded, whether upon a certain modification of reason, upon an original instinct, called a moral sense, or upon some other principle of our nature, it cannot be doubted that they were given us for the direction of our conduct in this life. They carry along with them the most evident badges of this authority, which denote that they were set up within us to be the supreme arbiters of all our actions, to superintend all our senses, passions, and appetites, and to judge how far each of them was either to be indulged or restrained The rules, therefore, which they prescribe, are to be regarded as the commands and *laws of the Deity*, promulgated by those vicegerents which he has set up within us."—(Smith's *Theory of Moral Sentiments*, Part iii. chap. v) See also Dr Butler's very original and philosophical *Discourses on Human Nature*

universe, and carrying home its sanctions to every breast, by the inevitable punishment which it inflicts on transgressors."[1]

The habit of considering morality under the similitude of *a law*, (*a law* engraved on the human heart,) led not unnaturally to an application to ethical subjects of the technical language and arrangements of the Roman jurisprudence; and this innovation was at once facilitated and encouraged, by certain peculiarities in the nature of the most important of all the virtues, —that of justice; peculiarities which, although first explained fully by Hume and Smith, were too prominent to escape altogether the notice of preceding moralists.

The circumstances which distinguish justice from the other virtues, are chiefly two. In the first place, its rules may be laid down with a degree of accuracy whereof moral precepts do not, in any other instance, admit. Secondly, its rules may be enforced, inasmuch as every transgression of them implies a violation of the rights of others. For the illustration of both propositions, I must refer to the eminent authors just mentioned.

As, in the case of justice, there is always a right, on the one hand, corresponding to an obligation on the other, the various rules enjoined by it may be stated in two different forms; either as a system of duties, or as a system of rights. The former view of the subject belongs properly to the moralist—the latter to the lawyer. It is this last view that the writers on Natural Jurisprudence (most of whom were lawyers by profession) have in general chosen to adopt, although, in the same works, both views will be found to be not unfrequently blended together.

To some indistinct conception among the earlier writers on Natural Law, of these peculiarities in the nature of justice, we may probably ascribe the remarkable contrast pointed out by Mr. Smith between the ethical systems of ancient and of modern times "In none of the ancient moralists," he observes, "do we find any attempt towards a particular enumeration of the rules of justice. On the contrary, Cicero in his *Offices*, and

[1] *Frag* lib iii. *de Rep.*

Aristotle in his *Ethics*, treat of justice in the same general manner in which they treat of generosity or of charity."[1]

But although the rules of justice are in every case precise and indispensable, and although their authority is altogether independent of that of the civil magistrate, it would obviously be absurd to spend much time in speculating about the principles of this natural law, as applicable to men, before the establishment of government. The same state of society which diversifies the condition of individuals to so great a degree as to suggest problematical questions with respect to their rights and their duties, necessarily gives birth to certain conventional laws or customs, by which the conduct of the different members of the association is to be guided; and agreeably to which the disputes that may arise among them are to be adjusted. The imaginary state referred to under the title of the *State of Nature*, though it certainly does not exclude the idea of *a moral right of property arising from labour*, yet excludes all that variety of cases concerning its alienation and transmission, and the mutual covenants of parties, which the political union alone could create;—an order of things, indeed, which is virtually supposed in almost all the speculations about which the law of nature is commonly employed.

2. It was probably in consequence of the very narrow field of study which Jurisprudence, considered in this light, was found to open, that its province was gradually enlarged, so as to comprehend, not merely the rules of justice, but the rules enjoining all our other moral duties. Nor was it only the *province* of Jurisprudence which was thus enlarged. A corresponding extension was also given, by the help of arbitrary definitions, to its *technical phraseology*, till at length the whole doctrines of practical ethics came to be moulded into an artificial form, originally copied from the Roman code. Although justice is the only branch of virtue in which every moral Obligation implies a corresponding Right, the writers on Natural Law have contrived, by fictions of *imperfect rights* and of *external rights*, to treat indirectly of all our various duties, by pointing out the rights

[1] *Theory of Moral Sentiments*, Part vii sect. iv.

which are supposed to be their correlates —in other words, they have contrived to exhibit, in the form of a system of rights, a connected view of the whole duty of man. This idea of Jurisprudence, which identifies its object with that of Moral Philosophy, seems to coincide nearly with that of Puffendorff; and some vague notion of the same sort has manifestly given birth to many of the digressions of Grotius.

Whatever judgment may now be pronounced on the effects of this innovation, it is certain that they were considered, not only at the time, but for many years afterwards, as highly favourable. A very learned and respectable writer, Mr. Carmichael of Glasgow, compares them to the improvements made in Natural Philosophy by the followers of Lord Bacon. "No person," he observes, "liberally educated, can be ignorant that, within the recollection of ourselves and of our fathers, philosophy has advanced to a state of progressive improvement hitherto unexampled; in consequence partly of the rejection of scholastic absurdities, and partly of the accession of new discoveries. Nor does this remark apply solely to Natural Philosophy, in which the improvements accomplished by the united labours of the learned have forced themselves on the notice even of the vulgar, by their palpable influence on the mechanical arts The other branches of philosophy also have been prosecuted during the last century with no less success, and none of them in a more remarkable degree than the science of Morals.

"This science, so much esteemed, and so assiduously cultivated by the sages of antiquity, lay for a length of time, in common with all the other useful arts, buried in the rubbish of the dark ages, till (soon after the commencement of the seventeenth century) the incomparable Treatise of Grotius, *De Jure Belli et Pacis*, restored to more than its ancient splendour that part of it which defines the relative duties of individuals; and which, in consequence of the immense variety of cases comprehended under it, is by far the most extensive of any. Since that period, the most learned and polite scholars of Europe, as if suddenly roused by the alarm of a trumpet, have vied with each other in the prosecution of this study,—so strongly recommended to their attention, not merely by its novelty, but by the importance of its conclusions and the dignity of its object."[1]

I have selected this passage, in preference to many others that might be quoted to the same purpose from writers of higher name; because, in the sequel of this historical sketch,

---

[1] The last sentence is thus expressed in the original: "Ex illo tempore, quasi classico dato, ab eruditissimis passim et politissimis viris excoli certatim cœpit, utilissima hæc nobilissimaque doctrina"—(See the edition of Puffendorff, *De Officio Hominis et Civis*, by Professor Gerschom Carmichael of Glasgow, 1724,) an author whom Dr Hutcheson pronounces to be "by far the best commentator on Puffendorff," and "whose notes," he adds, "are of much more value than the *text*" See his short *Introduction to Moral Philosophy*

Puffendorff's principal work, entitled *De Jure Naturæ et Gentium*, was first printed in 1672, and was afterwards abridged by the author into the small volume referred to in the foregoing paragraph The idea of Puffendorff's aim, formed by Mr Carmichael, coincides exactly with the account of it given in the text: "Hoc demum tractatu edito, facile intellexerunt æquiores harum rerum arbitri, non aliam esse genuinam *Morum Philosophiam*, quam quæ ex evidentibus principiis, in ipsa rerum natura fundatis, hominis atque civis officia, in singulis vitæ humanæ circumstantiis debita, eruit ac demonstrat, atque adeo Juris Naturalis scientiam, quantumvis diversam ab Ethica quæ in scholis dudum obtinuerat, præ se ferret faciem, non esse, quod ad scopum et rem tractandam, verè aliam disciplinam, sed eandem rectius duntaxat et solidius traditam, ita ut, ad quam prius male collineaverit, tandem reipsâ feriret scopum"—See Carmichael's edition of the Treatise *De Officio Hominis et Civis*, p 7

To so late a period did this admiration of the Treatise, *De Officio Hominis et Civis*, continue in our Scotch Universities, that the very learned and respectable Sir John Pringle (afterwards President of the Royal Society of London) adopted it as the text-book for his lectures, while he held the Professorship of Moral Philosophy at Edinburgh Nor does the case seem to have been different in England "I am going," says Gray, in a letter written while a student at Cambridge, "to attend a lecture on *one* Puffendorff" And, much in the same spirit, Voltaire thus expresses himself with respect to the schools of the Continent "On est partagé, dans les écoles, entre Grotius et Puffendorff Croyez moi, lisez les Offices de Cicéron" From the contemptuous tone of these two writers, it should seem that the old systems of Natural Jurisprudence had entirely lost their credit among men of taste and of enlarged views, long before they ceased to form an essential part of academical instruction, thus affording an additional confirmation of Mr Smith's complaint, that "the greater part of universities have not been very forward to adopt improvements after they were made; and that several of those learned societies have chosen to remain, for a long time, the sanctuaries in which exploded systems found shelter and protection, after they had been hunted out of every other corner of the world" Considering his own successful exertions, in his academical capacity, to remedy this evil, it is more than probable that Mr. Smith had Grotius and Puffendorff in his view when he wrote the foregoing sentence

it appears to me peculiarly interesting to mark the progress of Ethical and Political speculation in that seat of learning, which, not many years afterwards, was to give birth to the *Theory of Moral Sentiments*, and to the *Inquiry into the Nature and Causes of the Wealth of Nations*. The powerful effect which the last of these works has produced on the political opinions of the whole civilized world, renders it unnecessary, in a Discourse destined to form part of a Scottish *Encyclopædia*, to offer any apology for attempting to trace, with some minuteness, the train of thought by which an undertaking, so highly honourable to the literary character of our country, seems to have been suggested to the author.

The extravagance of the praise lavished on Grotius and Puffendorff, in the above citation from Carmichael, can be accounted for only by the degraded state into which Ethics had fallen in the hands of those who were led to the study of it, either as a preparation for the casuistical discussions subservient to the practice of auricular confession, or to justify a scheme of morality which recommended the useless austerities of an ascetic retirement, in preference to the manly duties of social life. The practical doctrines inculcated by the writers on Natural Law, were all of them favourable to active virtue; and, how reprehensible soever in point of form, were not only harmless, but highly beneficial in their tendency. They were at the same time so diversified (particularly in the work of Grotius) with beautiful quotations from the Greek and Roman classics, that they could not fail to present a striking contrast to the absurd and illiberal systems which they supplanted; and perhaps to these passages, to which they thus gave a sort of systematical connexion, the progress which the science made in the course of the eighteenth century, may, in no inconsiderable degree, be ascribed. Even now, when so very different a taste prevails, the treatise *De Jure Belli et Pacis* possesses many charms to a classical reader; who, although he may not always set a very high value on the author's reasonings, must at least be dazzled and delighted with the splendid profusion of his learning.

The field of Natural Jurisprudence, however, was not long to remain circumscribed within the narrow limits commonly assigned to the province of Ethics. The contrast between natural law and positive institution, which it constantly presents to the mind, gradually and insensibly suggested the idea of comprehending under it every question concerning right and wrong, on which positive law is silent. Hence the origin of two different departments of Jurisprudence, little attended to by some of the first authors who treated of it, but afterwards, from their practical importance, gradually encroaching more and more on those ethical disquisitions by which they were suggested. Of these departments, the one refers to the conduct of individuals in those violent and critical moments when the bonds of political society are torn asunder; the other, to the mutual relations of independent communities. The questions connected with the former article, lie indeed within a comparatively narrow compass; but on the latter so much has been written, that what was formerly called Natural Jurisprudence, has been, in later times, not unfrequently distinguished by the title of the *Law of Nature and Nations*. The train of thought by which both subjects came to be connected with the systems now under consideration, consists of a few very simple and obvious steps.

As an individual who is a member of a political body necessarily gives up his will to that of the governors who are entrusted by the people with the supreme power, it is his duty to submit to those inconveniences which, in consequence of the imperfection of all human establishments, may incidentally fall to his own lot. This duty is founded on the Law of Nature, from which, indeed, (as must appear evident on the slightest reflection,) conventional law derives all its *moral* force and obligation. The great end, however, of the political union being a sense of general utility, if this end should be manifestly frustrated, either by the injustice of laws, or the tyranny of rulers, individuals must have recourse to the principles of natural law, in order to determine how far it is competent for them to withdraw themselves from their country, or to resist its governors by force. To Jurisprudence, therefore, considered in this light, came with great propriety to be referred all those practical discussions which relate to the limits of allegiance, and the right of resistance.

By a step equally simple, the province of the science was still farther extended. As independent states acknowledge no superior, the obvious inference was, that the disputes arising among them must be determined by an appeal to the Law of Nature; and accordingly, this law, when applied to states, forms a separate part of Jurisprudence, under the title of the Law of Nations. By some writers we are told, that the general principles of the Law of Nature and of the Law of Nations, are one and the same, and that the distinction between them is merely verbal. To this opinion, which is very confidently stated by Hobbes,[1] Puffendorff has given his sanc-

---

[1] "Lex Naturalis dividi potest in naturalem hominum quæ sola obtinuit dici Lex Naturæ, et naturalem civitatum, quæ dici potest Lex Gentium, vulgo autem Jus Gentium appellatur. Præcepta utriusque eadem sunt, sed quia civitates semel institutæ induunt proprietates hominum personales, lex quam loquentes de hominum singulorum officio naturalem dicimus, applicata totis civitatibus, nationibus, sive gentibus, vocatur Jus Gentium "—*De Cive*, cap. xiv. § 4.

In a late publication, from the title of which some attention to dates might have been expected, we are told, that "Hobbes's book, *De Cive*, appeared but a little time *before* the Treatise of Grotius;" whereas, in point of fact, Hobbes's book did not *appear* till twenty-two years *after* it. A few copies were indeed printed at Paris, and privately circulated by Hobbes, as early as 1642, but the book was not published till 1647.—(See "*An Inquiry into the Foundation and History of the Law of Nations in Europe,*" &c., by Robert Ward of the Inner Temple, Esq., London, 1795) This inaccuracy, however, is trifling, when compared with those committed in the same work, in stating the distinguishing doctrines of the two systems.

As a writer on the Law of Nations, Hobbes is now altogether unworthy of notice. I shall therefore only remark on this part of his philosophy, that its aim is precisely the *reverse* of that of Grotius, the latter labouring through the whole of his treatise, to extend, as far as possible, among independent states, the same laws of justice and of humanity, which are universally recognised among individuals; while Hobbes, by *inverting* the argument, exerts his ingenuity to shew, that the moral repulsion which commonly exists between independent and neighbouring communities, is an exact picture of that which existed among individuals prior to the origin of government. The inference, indeed, was most illogical, inasmuch as it is the social attraction among individuals which is the source of the mutual repulsion among nations and as this attraction invariably ope-

tion; and, in conformity to it, contents himself with laying down the general principles of natural law, leaving it to the reader to apply it as he may find necessary, to individuals or to societies.

The later writers on Jurisprudence have thought it expedient to separate the law of nations from that part of the science which treats of the duties of individuals;[1] but without being at sufficient pains to form to themselves a definite idea of the object of their studies. Whoever takes the trouble to look into their systems, will immediately perceive, that their leading aim is not (as might have been expected,) to ascertain the great principles of morality binding on all nations in their intercourse with each other; or to point out with what limitations the ethical rules recognised among individuals must be understood, when extended to political and unconnected bodies; but to exhibit a digest of those laws and usages, which, partly from considerations of utility, partly from accidental circumstances, and partly from positive conventions, have gradually arisen among those states of Christendom, which, from their mutual connexions, may be considered as forming one great republic. It is evident, that such a digest has no more connexion with the Law of Nature, properly so called, than it has

---

rates with the greatest force, where the individual is the most completely independent of his species, and where the advantages of the political union are the least sensibly felt. If, in any state of human nature, it be in danger of becoming quite evanescent, it is in large and civilized empires, where man becomes indispensably necessary to man, depending for the gratification of his artificial wants on the co-operation of thousands of his fellow-citizens.

Let me add, that the theory, so fashionable at present, which resolves the whole of morality into the principle of *utility*, is more nearly akin to Hobbism, than some of its partisans are aware of.

[1] The credit of this improvement is ascribed by Vattel (one of the most esteemed writers on the subject) to the celebrated German philosopher Wolfius, whose labours in this department of study he estimates very highly.—(*Questions de Droit Naturel* Berne, 1762.) Of this great work I know nothing but the title, which is not calculated to excite much curiosity in the present times.—"Christiani Wolfii *jus Naturæ methodo scientifica pertractatum*, in 9 tomos distributum '—(Francof 1740) "Non est," says Lampredi, *himself* a professor of public law, "qui non deterreatur tanta librorum farragine, quasi vero Herculeo labore opus esset, ut quis honestatem et justitiam addiscat."

with the rules of the Roman law, or of any other municipal code. The details contained in it are highly interesting and useful in themselves; but they belong to a science altogether different; a science, in which the ultimate appeal is made, not to abstract maxims of right and wrong, but to precedents, to established customs, and to the authority of the learned.

The intimate alliance, however, thus established between the Law of Nature and the conventional Law of Nations, has been on the whole attended with fortunate effects. In consequence of the discussions concerning questions of justice and of expediency which came to be blended with the details of public law, more enlarged and philosophical views have gradually presented themselves to the minds of speculative statesmen; and, in the last result, have led, by easy steps, to those liberal doctrines concerning commercial policy, and the other mutual relations of separate and independent states, which, if they should ever become the creed of the rulers of mankind, promise so large an accession to human happiness.

3. Another idea of Natural Jurisprudence, essentially distinct from those hitherto mentioned, remains to be considered. According to this, its object is to ascertain the general principles of justice which *ought to be* recognised in every municipal code; and to which it *ought to be* the aim of every legislator to accommodate his institutions. It is to this idea of Jurisprudence that Mr. Smith has given his sanction in the conclusion of his Theory of Moral Sentiments; and this he seems to have conceived to have been likewise the idea of Grotius, in the Treatise *De Jure Belli et Pacis.*

"It might have been expected," says Mr Smith, "that the reasonings of lawyers upon the different imperfections and improvements of the laws of different countries, should have given occasion to an inquiry into what were the natural rules of justice, independent of all positive institution. It might have been expected, that these reasonings should have led them to aim at establishing a system of what might properly be called Natural Jurisprudence, or *a theory of the principles which ought to run through, and to be the foundation of the laws of all nations.* But, though the reasonings of lawyers did produce something of this kind, and though no man has treated systematically of the laws of any particular country, without intermixing in his work many observations of this sort, it was very late in the world before any such general system was thought of, or before the philosophy of laws was treated of by itself, and without regard to the particular institutions of any nation. Grotius seems to have been the first who attempted to give the world anything like a system of those principles which ought to run through, and be the foundation of the laws of all nations; and his Treatise of the Laws of Peace and War, with all its imperfections, is perhaps, at this day, the most complete work that has yet been given on the subject."

Whether this was, or was not, the leading object of Grotius, it is not material to decide; but if this *was* his object, it will not be disputed that he has executed his design in a very desultory manner, and that he often seems to have lost sight of it altogether, in the midst of those miscellaneous speculations on political, ethical, and historical subjects, which form so large a portion of his Treatise, and which so frequently succeed each other without any apparent connexion or common aim.[1]

Nor do the views of Grotius appear always enlarged or just, even when he is pointing at the object described by Mr. Smith. The Roman system of Jurisprudence seems to have warped, in no inconsiderable degree, his notions on all questions connected with the theory of legislation, and to have diverted his attention from that philosophical idea of law, so well expressed by Cicero,—"Non à prætoris edicto, neque à duodecim tabulis, sed penitus ex intimâ philosophiâ, hauriendam juris disciplinam." In this idolatry, indeed, of the Roman law, he has

---

[1] "Of what stamp," says a most ingenious and original thinker, "are the works of Grotius, Puffendorff, and Burlamaqui? Are they political or ethical, historical or juridical, expository or censorial?—Sometimes one thing, sometimes another, they seem hardly to have settled the matter with themselves."—Bentham's *Introduction to the Principles of Morals and Legislation*, p 327.

not gone so far as some of his commentators, who have affirmed, that it is only a different name for the Law of Nature; but that his partiality for his professional pursuits has often led him to overlook the immense difference between the state of society in ancient and modern Europe, will not, I believe, be now disputed. It must, at the same time, be mentioned to his praise, that no writer appears to have been, *in theory*, more completely aware of the essential distinction between Natural and Municipal laws. In one of the paragraphs of his *Prolegomena*, he mentions it as a part of his general plan, to illustrate the Roman code, and to systematize those parts of it which have their origin in the Law of Nature. "The task," says he, "of moulding it into the form of a system, has been projected by many, but hitherto accomplished by none. Nor indeed was the thing possible, while so little attention was paid to the distinction between natural and positive institutions; for the former being everywhere the same, may be easily traced to a few general principles, while the latter, exhibiting different appearances at different times, and in different places, elude every attempt towards methodical arrangement, no less than the insulated facts which individual objects present to our external senses."

This passage of Grotius has given great offence to two of the most eminent of his commentators, Henry and Samuel de Cocceii, who have laboured much to vindicate the Roman legislators against that indirect censure which the words of Grotius appear to convey. "My chief object," says the latter of those writers, "was, by deducing the Roman law from its source in the nature of things, to reconcile Natural Jurisprudence with the civil code; and, at the same time, to correct the supposition implied in the foregoing passage of Grotius, which is indeed one of the most exceptionable to be found in his work. The remarks on this subject, scattered over the following commentary, the reader will find arranged in due order in my twelfth Preliminary Dissertation, the chief design of which is to systematize the whole Roman law, and to demonstrate its beautiful coincidence with the Law of Nature."

In the execution of this design, Cocceii must, I think, be allowed to have contributed a very useful supplement to the jurisprudential labours of Grotius, the Dissertation in question being eminently distinguished by that distinct and luminous method, the want of which renders the study of the Treatise *De Jure Belli et Pacis* so peculiarly irksome and unsatisfactory.

The superstitious veneration for the Roman code expressed by such writers as the Cocceii, will appear less wonderful, when we attend to the influence of the same prejudice on the liberal and philosophical mind of Leibnitz; an author, who has not only gone so far as to compare the civil law (considered as a monument of human genius) with the remains of the ancient Greek geometry; but has strongly intimated his dissent from the opinions of those who have represented its principles as being frequently at variance with the Law of Nature. In one very powerful paragraph, he expresses himself thus: " I have often said, that, after the writings of geometricians, there exists nothing which, in point of strength, subtilty, and depth, can be compared to the works of the Roman lawyers. And as it would be scarcely possible, from mere intrinsic evidence, to distinguish a demonstration of Euclid's from one of Archimedes or of Apollonius, (the style of all of them appearing no less uniform than if reason herself were speaking through their organs,) so also the Roman lawyers all resemble each other like twin-brothers; insomuch that, from the style alone of any particular opinion or argument, hardly any conjecture could be formed about its author. Nor are the traces of a refined and deeply meditated system of Natural Jurisprudence anywhere to be found more visible, or in greater abundance. And even in those cases where its principles are departed from, either in compliance with the language consecrated by technical forms, or in consequence of new statutes, or of ancient traditions, the conclusions which the assumed hypothesis renders it necessary to incorporate with the eternal dictates of right reason, are deduced with the soundest logic, and with an ingenuity that excites admiration *Nor are these deviations from the Law of Nature so frequent as is commonly apprehended.*"

In the last sentence of this passage, Leibnitz had probably an eye to the works of Grotius and his followers; which, however narrow and timid in their views they may now appear, were, for a long time, regarded among civilians as savouring somewhat of theoretical innovation, and of political heresy.

To all this may be added, as a defect still more important and radical in the systems of Natural Jurisprudence considered as models of universal legislation, that their authors reason concerning laws too abstractedly, without specifying the particular circumstances of the society to which they mean that their conclusions should be applied. It is very justly observed by Mr. Bentham, that " if there are any books of universal Jurisprudence, they must be looked for within very narrow limits." He certainly, however, carries this idea too far, when he asserts, that " to be susceptible of a universal application, *all* that a book of the expository kind can have to treat of, is *the import of words;* and that, to be strictly speaking universal, it must confine itself to terminology; that is, to an explanation of such words connected with law, as *power, right, obligation, liberty,* to which are words pretty exactly correspondent in all languages."[1] His expressions, too, are somewhat unguarded, when he calls the *Law of Nature* " an obscure phantom, which, in the imaginations of those who go in chase of it, points sometimes to *manners,* sometimes to *laws,* sometimes to what law *is,* sometimes to what it *ought to be* "[2] Nothing, indeed, can be more exact and judicious than this description, when restricted to the *Law of Nature,* as commonly treated of by writers on Jurisprudence; but if extended to the *Law of Nature,* as originally understood among ethical writers, it is impossible to assent to it, without abandoning all the principles on which the science of morals ultimately rests. With these obvious, but, in my opinion, very essential limitations, I perfectly agree with Mr Bentham, in considering an abstract code of laws as a thing equally unphilosophical in the design, and useless in the execution.

[1] *Introduction to the Principles of Morals and Legislation,* p 323
[2] *Ibid* p. 327.

In stating these observations, I would not be understood to dispute the utility of turning the attention of students to a comparative view of the municipal institutions of different nations; but only to express my doubts whether this can be done with advantage, by referring these institutions to that abstract theory called the *Law of Nature*, as to a common standard. The code of some particular country must be fixed on as a groundwork for our speculations; and its laws studied, not as consequences of any abstract principles of justice, but in their connexion with the circumstances of the people among whom they originated. A comparison of these laws with the corresponding laws of other nations, considered also in their connexion with the circumstances whence they arose, would form a branch of study equally interesting and useful; not merely to those who have in view the profession of law, but to all who receive the advantages of a liberal education. In fixing on such a standard, the preference must undoubtedly be given to the Roman law, if for no other reason than this, that its technical language is more or less incorporated with all our municipal regulations in this part of the world: and the study of this language, as well as of the other technical parts of Jurisprudence, (so revolting to the taste when considered as the arbitrary jargon of a philosophical theory,) would possess sufficient attractions to excite the curiosity, when considered as a necessary passport to a knowledge of that system, which so long determined the rights of the greatest and most celebrated of nations.

"Universal grammar," says Dr. Lowth, "cannot be taught abstractedly; it must be done with reference to some language already known, in which the terms are to be explained and the rules exemplified"[1] The same observation may be applied (and for reasons strikingly analogous) to the science of Natural or Universal Jurisprudence.

Of the truth of this last proposition Bacon seems to have been fully aware; and it was manifestly some ideas of the same kind which gave birth to Montesquieu's historical speculations

[1] Preface to his *English Grammar*.

with respect to the origin of laws, and the reference which they may be expected to bear, in different parts of the world, to the physical and moral circumstances of the nations among whom they have sprung up. During this long interval, it would be difficult to name any intermediate writer, by whom the important considerations just stated were duly attended to.

In touching formerly on some of Bacon's ideas concerning the philosophy of law, I quoted a few of the most prominent of those fortunate anticipations, so profusely scattered over his works, which, outstripping the ordinary march of human reason, associate his mind with the luminaries of the eighteenth century, rather than with his own contemporaries. These anticipations, as well as many others of a similar description, hazarded by his bold yet prophetic imagination, have often struck me as resembling the *pierres d'attente* jutting out from the corners of an ancient building, and inviting the fancy to complete what was left unfinished of the architect's design ;—or the slight and broken sketches traced on the skirts of an American map, to connect its chains of hills and branches of rivers with some future survey of the contiguous wilderness Yielding to such impressions, and eager to pursue the rapid flight of his genius, let me abandon for a moment the order of time, while I pass from the *Fontes Juris* to the *Spirit of Laws*. To have a just conception of the comparatively limited views of Grotius, it is necessary to attend to what was planned by his immediate predecessor, and first executed (or rather first *begun* to be executed) by one of his remote successors.

The main object of the *Spirit of Laws* (it is necessary here to premise) is to show, not, as has been frequently supposed, what laws *ought* to be,—but how the diversities in the physical and moral circumstances of the human race have contributed to produce diversities in their political establishments, and in their municipal regulations.[1] On this point, indeed, an appeal

---

[1] This, though somewhat ambiguously expressed, *must*, I think, have been the idea of D'Alembert in the following sentence "Dans cet ouvrage, M. de Montesquieu s'occupe moins des loix qu'on a faites, que de celles qu'on a du

may be made to the author himself. "I write not," says he, "to censure anything established in any country whatsoever; every nation will here find the *reasons* on which its maxims are founded." This plan, however, which, when understood with proper limitations, is highly philosophical, and which raises Jurisprudence, from the uninteresting and useless state in which we find it in Grotius and Puffendorff, to be one of the most agreeable and important branches of useful knowledge, (although the execution of it occupies by far the greater part of his work,) is prosecuted by Montesquieu in so very desultory a manner, that I am inclined to think he rather fell into it insensibly, in consequence of the occasional impulse of accidental curiosity, than from any regular design he had formed to himself when he began to collect materials for that celebrated performance. He seems, indeed, to confess this in the following passage of his preface: "Often have I begun, and as often laid aside, this undertaking I have followed my observations without any fixed plan, and without thinking either of rules or exceptions. I have found the truth only to lose it again."

But whatever opinion we may form on this point, Montesquieu enjoys an unquestionable claim to the grand idea of connecting Jurisprudence with History and Philosophy, in such a manner as to render them all subservient to their mutual illustration. Some occasional disquisitions of the same kind may, it is true, be traced in earlier writers, particularly in the works of Bodinus; but they are of a nature too trifling to detract from the glory of Montesquieu. When we compare the jurisprudential researches of the latter with the systems previously in possession of the schools, the step which he made appears to have been so vast as almost to justify the somewhat too ostentatious motto prefixed to them by the author; *Prolem sine Matre creatam*. Instead of confining himself, after the example of his predecessors, to an interpretation of one part of the Roman code by another, he studied the SPIRIT of these laws

---

faire."—(*Eloge de M de Montesquieu*) According to the most obvious interpretation of his words, they convey a meaning which I conceive to be the very reverse of the truth

in the political views of their authors, and in the peculiar circumstances of that extraordinary race. He combined the science of law with the history of political society, employing the latter to account for the varying aims of the legislator; and the former, in its turn, to explain the nature of the government, and the manners of the people. Nor did he limit his inquiries to the Roman law and to Roman history; but, convinced that the general principles of human nature are everywhere the same, he searched for new lights among the subjects of every government, and the inhabitants of every climate; and, while he thus opened inexhaustible and unthought-of resources to the student of Jurisprudence, he indirectly marked out to the legislator the extent and the limits of his power, and recalled the attention of the philosopher from abstract and useless theories, to the only authentic monuments of the history of mankind.[1]

This view of law, which unites History and Philosophy with Jurisprudence, has been followed out with remarkable success by various authors since Montesquieu's time; and for a considerable number of years after the publication of the *Spirit of Laws*, became so very fashionable (particularly in this country) that many seem to have considered it, *not* as a step towards a farther end, but as exhausting the whole science of Jurisprudence. For such a conclusion there is undoubtedly some foundation, so long as we confine our attention to the ruder periods of society, in which governments and laws may be universally regarded as the gradual result of time and experience, of circumstances and emergencies. In enlightened ages, however, there cannot be a doubt, that political wisdom comes in for its share in the administration of human affairs; and there is reasonable ground for hoping, that its influence will

---

[1] As examples of Montesquieu's peculiar and characteristical style of thinking in *The Spirit of Laws*, may be mentioned his *Observations on the Origin and Revolutions of the Roman Laws on Successions;* and what he has written on the *History of the Civil Laws in his own Country;* above all, his *Theory of the Feudal Laws among the Franks*, considered in relation to the revolutions of their monarchy. On many points connected with these researches, his conclusions have been since controverted, but all his successors have agreed in acknowledging him as their common master and guide.

continue to increase, in proportion as the principles of legislation are more generally studied and understood. To suppose the contrary, would reduce us to be mere *spectators* of the progress and decline of society, and put an end to every species of patriotic exertion.

Montesquieu's own aim in his historical disquisitions, was obviously much more deep and refined. In various instances, one would almost think he had in his mind the very shrewd aphorism of Lord Coke, that, "to trace an error to its fountainhead, is to refute it;"—a species of refutation, which, as Mr Bentham has well remarked, is, with many understandings, the only one that has any weight.[1] To men prepossessed with a blind veneration for the wisdom of antiquity, and strongly impressed with a conviction that everything they see around them is the result of the legislative wisdom of their ancestors, the very existence of a legal principle, or of an established custom, becomes an argument in its favour; and an argument to which no reply can be made, but by tracing it to some acknowledged prejudice, or to a form of society so different from that existing at present, that the same considerations which serve to account for its first origin, demonstrate indirectly the expediency of now accommodating it to the actual circumstances of mankind.

According to this view of the subject, the speculations of Montesquieu were ultimately directed to the same practical conclusion with that pointed out in the prophetic suggestions of Bacon; aiming, however, at this object, by a process more circuitous; and, perhaps, on that account, the more likely to be

---

[1] "*If our ancestors have been all along under a mistake, how came they to have fallen into it?* is a question that naturally occurs upon all such occasions The case is, that, in matters of law more especially, such is the dominion of authority over our minds, and such the prejudice it creates in favour of whatever institution it has taken under its wing, that, after all manner of reasons that can be thought of in favour of the institution have been shewn to be insufficient, we still cannot forbear looking to some unassignable and latent reason for its efficient cause. But if, instead of any such reason, we can find a cause for it in some notion, of the erroneousness of which we are already satisfied, then at last we are content to give it up without further struggle, and then, and not till then, our satisfaction is complete."—*Defence of Usury,* pp. 94, 95

CHAP. II.—PHILOSOPHY FROM BACON TO LOCKE.

effectual. The plans of both have been since combined with extraordinary sagacity, by some of the later writers on Political Economy;[1] but with *their* systems we have no concern in the present section. I shall therefore only remark, in addition to the foregoing observations, the peculiar utility of these researches concerning the *history* of laws, in repressing the folly of sudden and violent innovation, by illustrating the reference which laws must necessarily have to the actual circumstances of a people,—and the tendency which natural causes have to improve gradually and progressively the condition of mankind, under every government which allows them to enjoy the blessings of peace and of liberty.

The well-merited popularity of the *Spirit of Laws*, gave the first fatal blow to the study of *Natural Jurisprudence;* partly by the proofs which, in every page, the work afforded, of the absurdity of all schemes of Universal Legislation; and partly by the attractions which it possessed, in point of eloquence and taste, when contrasted with the insupportable dulness of the systems then in possession of the schools. It is remarkable, that Montesquieu has never once mentioned the name of Grotius;—in *this*, probably, as in numberless other instances, conceiving it to be less expedient to attack established prejudices openly and in front, than gradually to undermine the unsuspected errors upon which they rest.

If the foregoing details should appear tedious to some of my readers, I must request them to recollect, that they relate to a science which, for much more than a hundred years, constituted the whole philosophy, both ethical and political, of the largest portion of civilized Europe. With respect to Germany, in par-

[1] Above all, by Mr Smith; who, in his *Wealth of Nations*, has judiciously and skilfully combined with the investigation of general principles, the most luminous sketches of *Theoretical History* relative to that form of political society, which has given birth to so many of the institutions and customs peculiar to modern Europe. — " The strong ray of philosophic light on this interesting subject," which, according to Gibbon, " broke from Scotland in our times," was but a *reflection*, though with a far steadier and more concentrated force, from the scattered but brilliant sparks kindled by the genius of Montesquieu I shall afterwards have occasion to take notice of the mighty influence which his writings have had on the subsequent history of Scottish literature

ticular, it appears from the Count de Hertzberg, that this science continued to maintain its undisputed ground, till it was supplanted by that growing passion for Statistical details, which, of late, has given a direction so different, and in some respects so opposite, to the studies of his countrymen [1]

When from Germany we turn our eyes to the south of Europe, the prospect seems not merely sterile, but afflicting and almost hopeless. Of Spanish literature I know nothing but through the medium of translations; a very imperfect one, undoubtedly, when a judgment is to be passed on compositions addressed to the powers of imagination and taste, yet fully sufficient to enable us to form an estimate of works which treat of science and philosophy. On such subjects it may be safely concluded, that whatever is unfit to stand the test of a literal version, is not worth the trouble of being studied in the original. The progress of the Mind in Spain, during the seventeenth century, we may therefore confidently pronounce, if not entirely suspended, to have been too inconsiderable to merit attention.

" The only good book," says Montesquieu, " which the Spaniards have to boast of, is that which exposes the absurdity of all the rest." In this remark, I have little doubt that there is a considerable sacrifice of truth to the pointed effect of an antithesis. The unqualified censure, at the same time, of this great man is not unworthy of notice, as a strong expression of his feelings with respect to the general insignificance of the Spanish writers.[2]

---

[1] " La connoissance des États qu'on se plait aujourd'hui d'appeller *Statistique*, est une de ces sciences qui sont devenues à la mode, et qui ont pris une vogue générale depuis quelques années, elle a presque dépossédé celle du Droit Public, qui régnoit au commencement et jusques vers le milieu du siècle présent "—*Reflexions sur la Force des États* Par M le Comte de Hertzberg Berlin, 1782

[2] " Lord Bolingbroke told Mr. Spence, as he informs us in his Anecdotes, that Dryden assured him he was more indebted to the Spanish critics than to the writers of any other nation "—Malone, in a note on Dryden's *Essay on Dramatic Poesy*.

The same anecdote is told, though with a considerable difference in the circumstances, by Warton, in his *Essay on the Writings of Pope* " Lord Bolingbroke assured Pope, that Dryden often declared to him, that he got more

CHAP. II.—PHILOSOPHY FROM BACON TO LOCKE.

The inimitable work here referred to by Montesquieu, is itself entitled to a place in this Discourse, not only as one of the happiest and most wonderful creations of human fancy, but as the record of a force of character and an enlargement of mind which, when contrasted with the prejudices of the author's age and nation, seem almost miraculous. It is not merely against Books of Chivalry that the satire of Cervantes is directed. Many other follies and absurdities of a less local and temporary nature have their share in his ridicule, while not a single expression escapes his pen that can give offence to the most fastidious moralist. Hence those amusing and interesting contrasts by which Cervantes so powerfully attaches us to the hero of his story; chastising the wildest freaks of a disordered imagination by a stateliness yet courtesy of virtue, and (on all subjects but one) by a superiority of good sense and of philosophical refinement, which, even under the most ludicrous circumstances, never cease to command our respect and to keep alive our sympathy.

In Italy, notwithstanding the persecution undergone by Galileo, physics and astronomy continued to be cultivated with success by Torricelli, Borelli, Cassini, and others; and in pure geometry, Viviani rose to the very first eminence, as the restorer, or rather as the diviner, of ancient discoveries; but in all those studies which require the animating spirit of civil and religious liberty, this once renowned country exhibited the most melancholy symptoms of mental decrepitude. "Rome," says a French historian, "was too much interested in maintaining her principles, not to raise every imaginable barrier against what might destroy them. Hence that *index* of prohibited books, into which were put the history of the President de Thou; the works on the liberties of the Gallican church; and (who could have believed it?) the translations of the Holy Scriptures. Meanwhile,

from the Spanish critics than from the Italian, French, and all other critics put together."

I suspect that there is some mistake in this story. A Spanish gentleman, equally well acquainted with the literature of his own country and with that of England, assures me, that he cannot recollect a single Spanish critic from whom Dryden can reasonably be supposed to have derived any important lights.

this tribunal, though always ready to condemn judicious authors upon frivolous suspicions of heresy, approved those seditious and fanatical theologists whose writings tended to the encouragement of regicide and the destruction of government. The approbation and censure of books," it is justly added, " deserve a place in the history of the human mind."

The great glory of the Continent towards the end of the seventeenth century (I except only the philosophers of France) was Leibnitz. He was born as early as 1646; and distinguished himself, while still a very young man, by a display of those talents which were afterwards to contend with the united powers of Clarke and of Newton. I have already introduced his name among the writers on Natural Law; but in every other respect he ranks more fitly with the contemporaries of his old age than with those of his youth. My reasons for thinking so will appear in the sequel. In the meantime, it may suffice to remark, that Leibnitz the jurist belongs to one century, and Leibnitz the philosopher to another.

In this and other analogous distributions of my materials, as well as in the order I have followed in the arrangement of particular facts, it may be proper, once for all, to observe, that much must necessarily be left to the *discretionary*, though not to the *arbitrary* decision of the author's judgment; that the dates which separate from each other the different stages in the progress of Human Reason do not, like those which occur in the history of the exact sciences, admit of being fixed with chronological and indisputable precision; while, in adjusting the perplexed rights of the innumerable claimants in this intellectual and shadowy region, a task is imposed on the writer, resembling not unfrequently the labour of *him*, who should have attempted to circumscribe, by mathematical lines, the melting and intermingling colours of Arachne's web;

> In quo diversi niteant cum mille colores,
> Transitus ipse tamen spectantia lumina fallit,
> Usque adeo quod tangit idem est, tamen ultima distant.

But I will not add to the number (already too great) of the foregoing pages, by anticipating, and attempting to obviate, the criticisms to which they may be liable Nor will I dissemble the confidence with which, amid a variety of doubts and misgivings, I look forward to the candid indulgence of those who are best fitted to appreciate the difficulties of my undertaking. I am certainly not prepared to say with Johnson, that "I dismiss my work with frigid indifference, and that to me success and miscarriage are empty sounds." My feelings are more in unison with those expressed by the same writer in the conclusion of the admirable preface to his edition of Shakespeare. One of his reflections, more particularly, falls in so completely with the train of my own thoughts, that I cannot forbear, before laying down the pen, to offer it to the consideration of my readers.

"Perhaps I may not be more censured for doing wrong, than for doing little, for raising in the public, expectations which at last I have not answered. The expectation of ignorance is indefinite, and that of knowledge is often tyrannical. It is hard to satisfy those who know not what to demand, or those who demand by design what they think impossible to be done."

DISSERTATION.

PART SECOND.

ADVERTISEMENT.

[Only in First Edition.—Editor]

Some apology, I am afraid, is necessary for the length to which this Dissertation has already extended My original design (as is well known to my friends) was to comprise in ten or twelve sheets all the preliminary matter which I was to contribute to this Supplement. But my work grew insensibly under my hands, till it assumed a form which obliged me either to destroy all that I had written, or to continue my Historical Sketches on the same enlarged scale. In selecting the subjects on which I have chiefly dwelt, I have been guided by my own idea of their pre-eminent importance, when considered in connexion with the present state of Philosophy in Europe. On some, which I have passed over unnoticed, it was impossible for me to touch, without a readier access to public libraries than I can command in this retirement. The same circumstance will, I trust, account, in the opinion of candid readers, for various other omissions in my performance

The time unavoidably spent in consulting, with critical care, the numerous Authors referred to in this and in the former part of my Discourse, has encroached so deeply, and to myself so painfully, on the leisure which I had destined for a different purpose, that, at my advanced years, I can entertain but a very faint expectation (though I do not altogether abandon the hope) of finishing my intended Sketch of the Progress of Ethical and Political Philosophy during the Eighteenth Century. An undertaking of a much earlier date has a prior and stronger claim on my attention. At all events, whatever may be wanting to complete my plan, it cannot be difficult for another hand to supply. An Outline is all that should be attempted on such a subject; and the field which it has to embrace will be found incomparably more interesting to most readers than that which has fallen under my review.

KINNIEL HOUSE, *August* 7, 1821

DISSERTATION.

PART II.

INTRODUCTION

In the farther prosecution of the plan of which I traced the outline in the Preface to the First Part of this Dissertation, I find it necessary to depart considerably from the arrangement which I adopted in treating of the Philosophy of the seventeenth century. During that period, the literary intercourse between the different nations of Europe was comparatively so slight, that it seemed advisable to consider, separately and successively, the progress of the mind in England, in France, and in Germany But from the era at which we are now arrived, *the Republic of Letters* may be justly understood to comprehend, not only these and other countries in their neighbourhood, but every region of the civilized earth. Disregarding, accordingly, all diversities of language and of geographical situation, I shall direct my attention to the intellectual progress of the species in general; enlarging, however, chiefly on the Philosophy of those parts of Europe, from whence the rays of science have, in modern times, diverged to the other quarters of the globe. I propose also, in consequence of the thickening crowd of useful authors, keeping pace in their numbers with the diffusion of knowledge and of liberality, to allot separate discourses to the history of Metaphysics, of Ethics, and of Politics; a distribution which, while it promises a more distinct and connected view of these different subjects, will furnish convenient resting-places, both to the writer and to the reader, and can scarcely fail to place, in a stronger and more concentrated light, whatever general conclusions may occur in the course of this survey.

The foregoing considerations, combined with the narrow limits assigned to the sequel of my work, will sufficiently account for the contracted scale of some of the following sketches, when compared with the magnitude of the questions to which they relate, and the peculiar interest which they derive from their immediate influence on the opinions of our own times.

In the case of Locke and Leibnitz, with whom the metaphysical history of the eighteenth century opens, I mean to allow myself a greater degree of latitude. The rank which I have assigned to both in my general plan seems to require, of course, a more ample space for their leading doctrines, as well as for those of some of their contemporaries and immediate successors, than I can spare for metaphysical systems of a more modern date; and as the rudiments of the most important of these are to be found in the speculations either of one or of the other, I shall endeavour, by connecting with my review of their works, those longer and more abstract discussions which are necessary for the illustration of fundamental principles, to avoid, as far as possible, in the remaining part of my discourse, any tedious digressions into the thorny paths of scholastic controversy. The critical remarks, accordingly, which I am now to offer on their philosophical writings, will, I trust, enable me to execute the very slight sketches which are to follow, in a manner at once more easy to myself, and more satisfactory to the bulk of my readers.

But what I have chiefly in view in these preliminary observations, is to correct certain misapprehensions concerning the opinions of Locke and of Leibnitz, which have misled (with very few exceptions) all the later historians who have treated of the literature of the eighteenth century. I have felt a more particular solicitude to vindicate the fame of Locke, not only against the censures of his opponents, but against the mistaken comments and eulogies of his admirers, both in England and on the Continent. Appeals to his authority are so frequent in the reasonings of all who have since canvassed the same subjects, that, without a precise idea of his distinguishing tenets, it is impossible to form a just estimate, either of the merits or demerits of his successors. In order to assist my readers in this previous study, I shall endeavour, as far as I can, to make Locke his own commentator; earnestly entreating them, before they proceed to the sequel of this dissertation, to collate carefully those scattered extracts from his works, which, in the following section, they will find brought into contact with each other, with a view to their mutual illustration. My own conviction, I confess, is, that the *Essay on Human Understanding* has been much more generally applauded than read; and if I could only flatter myself with the hope of drawing the attention of the public from the glosses of commentators to the author's text, I should think that I had made a considerable step towards the correction of some radical and prevailing errors, which the supposed sanction of his name has hitherto sheltered from a free examination.

PROGRESS OF METAPHYSICS DURING THE EIGHTEENTH CENTURY.

SECT. I.—HISTORICAL AND CRITICAL REVIEW OF THE PHILOSOPHICAL WORKS OF LOCKE AND LEIBNITZ.

LOCKE.

BEFORE entering on the subject of this section, it is proper to premise, that, although my design is to treat separately of Metaphysics, Ethics, and Politics, it will be impossible to keep these sciences wholly unmixed in the course of my reflections. They all run into each other by insensible gradations; and they have all been happily united in the comprehensive speculations of some of the most distinguished writers of the eighteenth century. The connexion between Metaphysics and Ethics is more peculiarly close; the theory of Morals having furnished, ever since the time of Cudworth, several of the most abstruse questions which have been agitated concerning the general principles, both intellectual and active, of the human frame. The inseparable affinity, however, between the different branches of the Philosophy of the Mind, does not afford any argument against the arrangement which I have adopted. It only shows, that it cannot, in every instance, be rigorously adhered to. It shall be my aim to deviate from it as seldom, and as slightly, as the miscellaneous nature of my materials will permit.

JOHN LOCKE, from the publication of whose *Essay on Human Understanding* a new era is to be dated in the History of Philosophy, was born at Wrington in Somersetshire, in 1632. Of his father nothing remarkable is recorded, but that he was a captain in the Parliament's army during the civil wars; a circumstance which, it may be presumed from the son's political opinions, would not be regarded by him as a stain on the memory of his parent.

In the earlier part of Mr. Locke's life, he prosecuted for some years, with great ardour, the study of medicine; an art, however, which he never actually exercised as a profession. According to his friend Le Clerc, the delicacy of his constitution rendered this impossible. But that his proficiency in the study was not inconsiderable, we have good evidence in the dedication prefixed to Dr. Sydenham's *Observations on the History and Cure of Acute Diseases* ;[1] where he boasts of the approbation bestowed on his METHOD by Mr. John Locke, who (to borrow Sydenham's own words) "examined it to the bottom; and who, if we consider his genius and penetrating and exact judgment, has scarce any superior, and few equals, now living." The merit of this METHOD, therefore, which still continues to be regarded as a model by the most competent judges, may be presumed to have belonged *in part* to Mr. Locke,[2]—a circumstance which deserves to be noticed, as an additional confirmation of what Bacon has so sagaciously taught, concerning the dependence of all the sciences relating to the phenomena, either of Matter or of Mind, on principles and rules derived from the resources of a higher philosophy. On the other hand, no science could have been chosen, more happily calculated than Medicine, to prepare such a mind as that of Locke for the prosecution of those speculations which have immortalized his name; the complicated, and fugitive, and often equivocal phenomena of disease, requiring in the observer a far greater

---

[1] Published in the year 1676.

[2] It is remarked of Sydenham, by the late Dr John Gregory, "That though full of hypothetical reasoning, it had not the usual effect of making him less attentive to observation; and that his hypotheses seem to have sat so loosely about him, that either they did not influence his practice at all, or he could easily abandon them, whenever they would not bend to his experience."

This is precisely the idea of Locke concerning the true use of hypotheses "Hypotheses, if they are well made, are at least great helps to the memory, and often direct us to new discoveries." —(Locke's *Works*, vol iii p 81) See also some remarks on the same subject in one of his letters to Mr. Molyneux (The edition of Locke to which I uniformly refer, is that printed at London in 1812, in ten volumes 8vo)

portion of discriminating sagacity, than those of Physics, strictly so called; resembling, in this respect, much more nearly, the phenomena about which Metaphysics, Ethics, and Politics, are conversant.

I have said, that the study of Medicine forms one of the best preparations for the study of Mind, *to such an understanding as Locke's.* To an understanding less comprehensive, and less cultivated by a liberal education, the effect of this study is likely to be similar to what we may trace in the works of Hartley, Darwin, and Cabanis; to all of whom we may more or less apply the sarcasm of Cicero on Aristoxenus, the Musician, who attempted to explain the nature of the soul by comparing it to a *Harmony;* HIC AB ARTIFICIO SUO NON RECESSIT.[1] In Locke's *Essay,* not a single passage occurs savouring of the Anatomical Theatre or of the Chemical Laboratory.

In 1666, Mr. Locke, then in his thirty-fifth year, formed an intimate acquaintance with Lord Ashley, afterwards Earl of Shaftesbury; from which period a complete change took place, both in the direction of his studies and in his habits of life. His attention appears to have been then turned, for the first time, to political subjects; and his place of residence transferred from the university to the metropolis. From London (a scene which gave him access to a society very different from what he had previously lived in)[2] he occasionally passed over to the Continent, where he had an opportunity of profiting by the conversation of some of the most distinguished persons of his age. In the course of his foreign excursions, he visited France, Germany, and Holland; but the last of these countries seems to have been his favourite place of residence; the blessings which the people there enjoyed, under a government peculiarly favourable to civil and religious liberty, amply compensating, in his view, for what their uninviting territory wanted in point of scenery and of climate. In this respect, the

---

[1] Tusc Quæst. lib. i

[2] Villiers Duke of Buckingham, and the Lord Halifax, are particularly mentioned among those who were delighted with his conversation.

coincidence between the taste of Locke and that of Descartes, throws a pleasing light on the characters of both.

The plan of the *Essay on Human Understanding* is said to have been formed as early as 1670; but the various employments and avocations of the Author prevented him from finishing it till 1687, when he fortunately availed himself of the leisure which his exile in Holland afforded him, to complete his long meditated design. He returned to England soon after the Revolution, and published the first edition of his work in 1690; the busy and diversified scenes through which he had passed during its progress, having probably contributed, not less than the academical retirement in which he had spent his youth, to enhance its peculiar and characteristical merits.

Of the circumstances which gave occasion to this great and memorable undertaking, the following interesting account is given in the *Prefatory Epistle to the Reader* —" Five or six friends, meeting at my chamber, and discoursing on a subject very remote from this, found themselves quickly at a stand, by the difficulties that rose on every side. After we had a while puzzled ourselves, without coming any nearer a resolution of those doubts which perplexed us, it came into my thoughts that we took a wrong course, and that, before we set ourselves upon inquiries of that nature, it was necessary to examine our own abilities, and see what objects our understandings were, or were not, fitted to deal with. This I proposed to the company, who all readily assented, and thereupon it was agreed, that this should be our first inquiry. Some hasty and undigested thoughts on a subject I had never before considered, which I set down against our next meeting, gave the first entrance into this discourse, which having been thus begun by chance, was continued by entreaty; written by incoherent parcels, and, after long intervals of neglect, resumed again as my humour or occasions permitted; and at last in retirement, where an attendance on my health gave me leisure, it was brought into that order thou now seest it"

Mr. Locke afterwards informs us, that "when he first put pen to paper, he thought all he should have to say on this matter would have been contained in one sheet, but that the farther he went the larger prospect he had;—new discoveries still leading him on, till his book grew insensibly to the bulk it now appears in "

On comparing the *Essay on Human Understanding* with the foregoing account of its origin and progress, it is curious to observe, that it is the fourth and last book alone which bears directly on the author's principal object. In this book, it is further remarkable, that there are few, if any, references to the preceding parts of the Essay; insomuch that it might have been published separately, without being less intelligible than it is. Hence, it seems not unreasonable to conjecture, that it was the *first* part of the work in the order of composition, and that it contains those leading and fundamental thoughts which offered themselves to the author's mind, when he first began to reflect on the friendly conversation which gave rise to his philosophical researches The inquiries in the first and second books, which are of a much more abstract, as well as scholastic nature, than the sequel of the work, probably opened gradually on the author's mind in proportion as he studied his subject with a closer and more continued attention. They relate chiefly to the origin and to the technical classification of our ideas, frequently branching out into *collateral*, and sometimes into *digressive* discussions, without much regard to method or connexion. The third book, (by far the most important of the whole,) where the nature, the use, and the abuse of language are so clearly and happily illustrated, seems, from Locke's own account, to have been a sort of *after-thought;* and the two excellent chapters on the *Association of Ideas* and on *Enthusiasm* (the former of which has contributed as much as anything else in Locke's writings, to the subsequent progress of Metaphysical Philosophy) were printed, for the first time, in the fourth edition of the Essay.

I would not be understood, by these remarks, to undervalue the two first books. All that I have said amounts to this, that the subjects which they treat of are seldom susceptible of any practical application to the conduct of the understanding; and that the author has adopted a new phraseology of his own, where, in some instances, he might have much more clearly conveyed his meaning without any departure from the ordinary forms of speech.[1] But although these considerations render the two first books inferior in point of general utility to the two last, they do not materially detract from their merit, as a precious accession to the theory of the Human Mind. On the contrary, I do not hesitate to consider them as the richest contribution of well-observed and well-described facts, which was ever bequeathed to this branch of science by a single individual, and as the indisputable, though not always acknowledged, source of some of the most refined conclusions, with respect to the intellectual phenomena, which have been since brought to light by succeeding inquirers.

After the details given by Locke himself, of the circumstances in which his Essay was begun and completed; more especially, after what he has stated of the "discontinued way of writing" imposed on him by the avocations of a busy and unsettled life, it cannot be thought surprising that so very little of method should appear in the disposition of his materials; or that the opinions which, on different occasions, he has pronounced on the same subject, should not always seem perfectly steady and consistent. In these last cases, however, I am inclined to think that the inconsistencies, if duly reflected on, would be found rather apparent than real. It is but seldom that a writer possessed of the powerful and upright mind of Locke, can reasonably be suspected of stating propositions in direct contradiction to each other. The presumption is, that in each of these propositions there is a mixture of truth, and that the error lies chiefly in the unqualified manner in which the truth is stated; proper allowances not being made, during the fervour of composition, for the partial survey taken of the objects from a particular point of view. Perhaps it would not be going too far to assert, that most of the seeming contradictions which occur

---

[1] [*I allude here to such phrases as *simple and mixed modes, adequate and inadequate ideas*, &c. &c]

* Restored —*Ed*

in authors animated with a sincere love of truth, might be fairly accounted for by the different aspects which the same object presented to them upon different occasions. In reading such authors, accordingly, when we meet with discordant expressions, instead of indulging ourselves in the captiousness of verbal criticism, it would better become us carefully and candidly to collate the questionable passages; and to study so to reconcile them by judicious modifications and corrections, as to render the oversights and mistakes of our illustrious guides subservient to the precision and soundness of our own conclusions. In the case of Locke, it must be owned, that this is not always an easy task, as the limitations of some of his most exceptionable propositions are to be collected, not from the context, but from different and widely separated parts of his Essay.[1]

In a work thus composed *by snatches*, (to borrow a phrase of the author's,) it was not to be expected that he should be able accurately to draw the line between his own ideas and the hints for which he was indebted to others. To those who are well acquainted with his speculations, it must appear evident that he had studied diligently the metaphysical writings both of Hobbes and of Gassendi; and that he was no stranger to the *Essays* of Montaigne, to the philosophical works of Bacon, or to Malebranche's *Inquiry after Truth*.[2] That he was familiarly conversant with the Cartesian system may be presumed from what we are told by his biographer, that it was *this* which first inspired him with a disgust at the jargon of the schools, and led

---

[1] That Locke himself was sensible that some of his expressions required explanation, and was anxious that his opinions should be judged of rather from the general tone and spirit of his work, than from detached and isolated propositions, may be inferred from a passage in one of his notes, where he replies to the animadversions of one of his antagonists, (the Reverend Mr. Lowde,) who had accused him of calling in question the immutability of moral distinctions. " But (says Locke) the good man does well, and as becomes his calling, to be watchful in such points, and to take the alarm even at expressions which, standing alone by themselves, might sound ill, and be suspected "—Locke's *Works*, vol ii. p 93, note.

[2] Mr. Addison has remarked, that Malebranche had the start of Locke, by several years, in his notions on the subject of *Duration*.—(*Spectator*, No 94.) Some other coincidences, not less remarkable, might be easily pointed out in the opinions of the English and of the French philosopher.

him into that train of thinking which he afterwards prosecuted so successfully. I do not, however, recollect that he has anywhere in his Essay mentioned the name of any one of these authors.[1] It is probable that, when he sat down to write, he found the result of his youthful reading so completely identified with the fruits of his subsequent reflections, that it was impossible for him to attempt a separation of the one from the other; and that he was thus occasionally led to mistake the treasures of memory for those of invention. That this was really the case may be farther presumed from the peculiar and original cast of his phraseology, which, though in general careless and unpolished, has always the merit of that characteristical unity and *raciness* of style, which demonstrate that, while he was writing, he conceived himself to be drawing only from his own resources.

With respect to his style, it may be further observed, that it resembles that of a well-educated and well-informed man of the world, rather than of a recluse student who had made an object of the art of composition. It everywhere abounds with colloquial expressions, which he had probably caught by the ear from those whom he considered as models of good conversation, and hence, though it now seems somewhat antiquated, and not altogether suited to the dignity of the subject, it may be presumed to have contributed its share towards his great object of turning the thoughts of his contemporaries to logical and metaphysical inquiries. The author of the *Characteristics*, who will not be accused of an undue partiality for Locke, acknowledges in strong terms the favourable reception which his book had met with among the higher classes. " I am not sorry, however," says Shaftesbury to one of his correspondents, "that I lent you Locke's Essay, a book that may as well qualify men for business and the world, as for the sciences and a university. No one has

---

[1] The name of Hobbes occurs in Mr Locke's *Reply to the Bishop of Worcester* See the Notes on his Essay, b iv c 3. It is curious that he classes Hobbes and Spinoza together, as writers of the same stamp, and that he disclaims any intimate acquaintance with the works of either. " I am not so well read in *Hobbes* and *Spinoza* as to be able to say what were their opinions in this matter, but possibly there be those who will think your Lordship's authority of more use than those justly decried names," &c. &c.

done more towards the recalling of philosophy from barbarity, into use and practice of the world, and into the company of the better and politer sort, who might well be ashamed of it in its other dress. No one has opened a better and clearer way to reasoning."[1]

In a passage of one of Warburton's letters to Hurd, which I had occasion to quote in the first part of this Dissertation, it is stated as a fact, that "when Locke first published his Essay, he had neither followers nor admirers, and hardly a single approver." I cannot help suspecting very strongly the correctness of this assertion, not only from the flattering terms in which the Essay is mentioned by Shaftesbury in the foregoing quotation, and from the frequent allusions to its doctrines by Addison and other popular writers of the same period, but from the unexampled sale of the book during the fourteen years which elapsed between its publication and Locke's death. Four editions were printed in the space of ten years, and three others must have appeared in the space of the next four; a reference being made to the *sixth* edition by the author himself, in the epistle to the reader prefixed to all the subsequent impressions. A copy of the thirteenth edition, printed as early as 1748, is now lying before me. So rapid and so extensive a circulation of a work, on a subject so little within the reach of common readers, is the best proof of the established popularity of the author's name, and of the respect generally entertained for his talents and his opinions.

That the *Essay on Human Understanding* should have excited some alarm in the University of Oxford, was no more than the author had reason to expect from his boldness as a philosophical reformer; from his avowed zeal in the cause of liberty, both civil and religious; from the suspected orthodoxy of his theological creed; and (it is but candid to add) from the apparent coincidence of his ethical doctrines with those of Hobbes.[2] It is more difficult to account for the long continuance, in that illustrious seat of learning, of the prejudice against

[1] See Shaftesbury's First Letter to a Student at the University.

[2] "It was proposed, at a meeting of the heads of houses of the University of

the *logic* of Locke, (by far the most valuable part of his work,) and of that partiality for the logic of Aristotle, of which Locke has so fully exposed the futility.[1] In the University of Cambridge, on the other hand, the *Essay on Human Understanding* was for many years regarded with a reverence approaching to idolatry; and to the authority of some distinguished persons connected with that learned body may be traced (as will afterwards appear) the origin of the greater part of the extravagancies which, towards the close of the last century, were grafted on Locke's errors, by the disciples of Hartley, of Law, of Priestley, of Tooke, and of Darwin.[2]

Oxford, to censure and discourage the reading of Locke's Essay, and, after various debates among themselves, it was concluded, that each head of a house should endeavour to prevent its being read in his college, without coming to any public censure."— See Des Maizeaux's note on a letter from Locke to Collins.—Locke's *Works*, vol x. p 284.

[1] [* "The Logic of Aristotle," says a late writer, whose taste, learning, and liberality entitle him to a distinguished rank among the eminent men of whom Oxford has to boast during the last fifty years,— "the Logic of Aristotle, however at present neglected for those redundant and verbose systems which took their rise from Locke's *Essay on the Human Understanding*, is a mighty effort of the mind, in which are discovered the principal sources of the art of reasoning, and the dependencies of one thought on another, and where, by the different combinations *he* hath made of all the forms the understanding can assume in reasoning, which *he* hath traced *for it*, *he* hath so closely confined *it*, that *it* cannot depart from *them* without arguing inconsequentially.' — Warton's *Essay on the Writings of Pope*, vol i p 168.

This luminous account of the scope of Aristotle's Logic may serve to illustrate the superiority of *this* logic to that of Locke, in training the mind to habits of correct thinking and of precise expression]

[2] I have taken notice, with due praise, in the former part of this Discourse, of the metaphysical speculations of John Smith, Henry More, and Ralph Cudworth, all of them members and ornaments of the University of Cambridge about the middle of the seventeenth century They were deeply conversant in the Platonic Philosophy, and applied it with great success in combating the Materialists and Necessitarians of their times They carried, indeed, some of their Platonic notions to an excess bordering on mysticism, and may, perhaps, have contributed to give a bias to some of their academical successors towards the opposite extreme A very pleasing and interesting account of the characters of these amiable and ingenious men, and of the spirit of their philosophy, is given by Burnet in the *History of his Own Times.*

To the credit of Smith and of More, it may be added, that they were among the first in England to perceive and to acknowledge the merits of the Cartesian Metaphysics

* Restored.—*Ed.*

To a person who now reads with attention and candour the work in question, it is much more easy to enter into the prejudices which at first opposed themselves to its complete success, than to conceive how it should so soon have acquired its just celebrity. Something, I suspect, must be ascribed to the political importance which Mr. Locke had previously acquired as the champion of religious toleration; as the great apostle of the Revolution; and as the intrepid opposer of a tyranny which had been recently overthrown.

In Scotland, where the liberal constitution of the universities has been always peculiarly favourable to the diffusion of a free and eclectic spirit of inquiry, the philosophy of Locke seems very early to have struck its roots, deeply and permanently, into a kindly and congenial soil. Nor were the errors of this great man implicitly adopted from a blind reverence for his name. The works of Descartes still continued to be studied and admired; and the combined systems of the English and the French metaphysicians served, in many respects, to correct what was faulty, and to supply what was deficient, in each. As to the *ethical* principles of Locke, where they appear to lean towards Hobbism, a powerful antidote against them was already prepared in the Treatise *De Jure Belli et Pacis*, which was then universally and deservedly regarded in this country as the best introduction that had yet appeared to the study of moral science If Scotland, at this period, produced no eminent authors in these branches of learning, it was not from want of erudition or of talents; nor yet from the narrowness of mind incident to the inhabitants of remote and insulated regions; but from the almost insuperable difficulty of writing in a dialect, which imposed upon an author the double task of at once acquiring a new language, and of unlearning his own [1]

The success of Locke's Essay, in some parts of the Continent, was equally remarkable; owing, no doubt, in the first instance, to the very accurate translation of it into the French language by Coste, and to the eagerness with which everything proceed-

[1] See Note S

ing from the author of the *Letters on Toleration*[1] may be presumed to have been read by the multitude of learned and enlightened refugees, whom the revocation of the edict of Nantz forced to seek an asylum in Protestant countries In Holland, where Locke was personally known to the most distinguished characters, both literary and political, his work was read and praised by a discerning few, with all the partiality of friendship;[2] but it does not seem to have made its way into the schools till a period considerably later. The doctrines of Descartes, at first so vehemently opposed in that country, were now

---

[1] The principle of religious toleration was at that time very imperfectly admitted, even by those philosophers who were the most zealously attached to the cause of civil liberty. The great Scottish lawyer and statesman, Lord Stair, himself no mean philosopher, and, like Locke, a warm partisan of the Revolution, seems evidently to have regretted the impunity which Spinoza had experienced in Holland, and Hobbes in England. "Execrabilis ille Atheus Spinosa adeo impudens est, ut affirmet omnia esse absolute necessaria, et nihil quod est, fuit, aut erit, aliter fieri potuisse, in quo omnes superiores Atheos excessit, aperte negans omnem Deitatem, nihilque præter potentias naturæ agnoscens.

"Vaninus Deitatem non aperte negavit, sed causam illius prodidit, in tractatu quem edidit, argumenta pro Dei existentia tanquam futilia et vana rejiciens, adferendo contrarias omnes rationes per modum objectionum, easque prosequendo ut indissolubiles videantur, postea tamen larvam exuit, et atheismum clare professus est, ET JUSTISSIME IN INCLYTA URBE THOLOSA DAMNATUS EST ET CREMATUS.

"Horrendus Hobbesius tertius erat atheismi promotor, qui omnia principia moralia et politica subvertit, eorumque loco naturalem vim et humana pacta, ut prima principia moralitatis, societatis, et politici regiminis substituit· NEC TAMEN SPINOSA AUT HOBBIUS, QUAMVIS IN REGIONIBUS REFORMATIS VIXERINT ET MORTUI SINT, NEDUM EXEMPLA FACTI SUNT IN ATHEORUM TERROREM, UT NE VEL ULLAM PŒNAM SENSERINT."—*Physiol. Nova Experimentalis* Lugd. Batav. 1666, pp 16, 17.

[2] Among those whose society Locke chiefly cultivated while in Holland, was the celebrated Le Clerc, the author of the *Bibliothèque Universelle*, and the *Bibliothèque Choisie*, besides many other learned and ingenious publications. He appears to have been warmly attached to Locke, and embraced the fundamental doctrines of his Essay without any slavish deference for his authority Though he fixed his residence at Amsterdam, where he taught Philosophy and the Belles Lettres, he was a native of Geneva, where he also received his academical education. He is, therefore, to be numbered with Locke's *Swiss* disciples I shall have occasion to speak of him more at length afterwards, when I come to mention his controversy with Bayle. At present, I shall only observe, that his Eloge on Locke was published in the *Bibliothèque Choisie*, (Année 1705,) tom vi ; and that some important remarks on the *Essay on Human Understanding*, particularly on the chapter on Power, are to be found in the 12th vol of the same work, (Année 1707)

so completely triumphant, both among philosophers and divines,[1] that it was difficult for a new reformer to obtain a hearing. The case was very nearly similar in Germany, where Leibnitz (who always speaks coldly of Locke's Essay)[2] was then looked up to as the great oracle in every branch of learning and of science. If I am not mistaken, it was in Switzerland where (as Gibbon observes) "the intermixture of sects had rendered the clergy acute and learned on controversial topics," that Locke's real merits were first appreciated on the Continent with a discriminating impartiality. In Crousaz's Treatise of Logic, (a book which, if not distinguished by originality of genius, is at least strongly marked with the sound and unprejudiced judgment of the author,) we everywhere trace the influence of Locke's doctrines; and, at the same time, the effects of the Cartesian Metaphysics, in limiting those hasty expressions of Locke, which have been so often misinterpreted by his followers.[3] Nor do

---

[1] "Quamvis huic sectæ (Cartesianæ) initio acriter se opponerent Theologi et Philosophi Belgæ, in Academiis tamen eorum *hodie* (1727,) vix alia, quam Cartesiana principia inculcantur"—(Heineccii *Elem. Hist Philosoph*) In Gravesande's *Introductio ad Philosophiam*, published in 1736, the name of Locke is not once mentioned It is probable that this last author was partly influenced by his admiration for Leibnitz, whom he servilely followed even in his *physical* errors

[2] "In Lockio sunt quædam particularia non male exposita, sed in summa longe aberravit a janua, nec naturam mentis veritatisque intellexit"—Leibnitz *Op* tom v p 355, ed Dutens.

"M. Locke avoit de la subtilité et de l'addresse, et quelque espèce de métaphysique superficielle qu'il savoit relever"—*Ibid* pp 11, 12

Heineccius, a native of Saxony, in a Sketch of the History of Philosophy, printed in 1728, omits altogether the name of Locke in his enumeration of the logical and metaphysical writers of modern Europe In a passage of his logic, where the same author treats of *clear* and *obscure*, *adequate* and *inadequate ideas*, (a subject on which little or nothing of any value had been advanced before Locke,) he observes, in a note, "Debemus hanc doctrinam Leibnitio, eamque deinde sequutus est illust Wolfius"*

[3] Of the *Essay on Human Understanding* Crousaz speaks in the following terms "Clarissimi, et merito celebratissimi Lockii de Intellectu Humano eximium opus, et auctore suo dignissimum, *logicis* utilissimis semper annumerabitur"—(*Præfat*) If Pope had ever looked into this Treatise, he could not have committed so gross a mistake, as to introduce the author into the Dunciad, among Locke's Aristotelian opponents; a distinction for which Crousaz was probably indebted to his acute strictures on those passages in *The Essay on Man*, which seem favourable to fatalism —

* Rightly.—Leibnitz's relative *Meditationes de Cogn Verit et Ideis* were published six years before the first edition of the Essay —*Ed*

Crousaz's academical labours appear to have been less useful than his writings; if a judgment on this point may be formed from the sound philosophical principles which he diffused among a numerous race of pupils. One of these, (M. Allamand,)

Prompt at the call, around the goddess roll
Broad hats, and hoods, and caps, a sable shoal,
Thick and more thick the black blockade extends,
A hundred head of Aristotle's friends.
Nor wert thou, Isis¹ wanting to the day,
(Though Christ-church long kept prudishly away)
Each staunch Polemic, stubborn as a rock,
Each fierce Logician, still expelling Locke,
Came whip and spur, and dash'd through thin and thick
On German Crousaz, and Dutch Burgersdyck.

[* To the honour of Crousaz it may be farther mentioned, that he was among the first (if not the first) who introduced into a Treatise of Logic, an account of Bacon's classification of our prejudices The first sentences of this account shew at once how fully the author was aware of Bacon's merits, and how sensible at the same time of the sacrifices which, in point of diction, he occasionally made to the pedantic taste of his age

"*Idola* vocavit Præjudicia VERULAMIUS, nunquam satis laudandus, veræ scientiæ restaurator, quia videlicet qui honor solis debetur Principiis ad Præjudicia, acquiescentiâ nostrâ maxime indigna, defertur

"Pro more sui temporis, singularibus et technicis titulis, ingeniosis tamen, Prejudiciorum singula genera designavit,—*Idola Tribus*," &c. &c.]

Warburton, with his usual scurrility towards all Pope's adversaries as well as his own, has called Crousaz *a blundering Swiss* † A very different estimate of Crousaz's merits has been formed by Gibbon, who seems to have studied his works much more carefully than the Right Reverend Commentator on the Dunciad.

"M. de Crousaz, the adversary of Bayle and Pope, is not distinguished by lively fancy or profound reflection; and even in his own country, at the end of a few years, his name and writings are almost obliterated But his Philosophy had been formed in the school of Locke, his Divinity in that of Limborch and Le Clerc, in a long and laborious life, several generations of pupils were taught to think, and even to write, his lessons rescued the Academy of Lausanne from Calvinistic prejudices, and he had the rare merit of diffusing a more liberal spirit among the people of the *Pays de Vaud*"—Gibbon's *Memoirs*

In a subsequent passage Gibbon says, "The logic of Crousaz had prepared me to engage with his master Locke, and his antagonist Bayle, of whom the former may be used as a bridle, and the latter applied as a spur to the curiosity of a young philosopher."—*Ibid*

The following details, independently of their reference to Crousaz, are so interesting in themselves, and afford so strong a testimony to the utility of logical studies, when rationally conducted, that I am tempted to transcribe them.

"December, 1755 In finishing this year, I must remark how favourable it was to my studies In the space of eight months, I learned the principles of drawing; made myself completely master of the French and Latin languages, with which I was very superficially acquainted before, and wrote and translated a great deal in both, read Cicero's Epistles ad Familiares, his Brutus, all his Orations, his Dialogues de Amicitia

* Restored —*Ed*
† [The epithet blundering may with far greater justice be retorted on Warburton himself, as it describes exactly that unsoundness of understanding, which rendered his talents, powerful as they certainly were, far more dangerous to his friends than to his opponents]

the friend and correspondent of Gibbon, deserves particularly to be noticed here, on account of two letters published in the posthumous works of that historian, containing a criticism on Locke's argument against innate ideas, so very able and judicious, that it may still be read with advantage by many logicians of no small note in the learned world. Had these letters happened to have sooner attracted my attention, I should not have delayed so long to do this tardy justice to their merits.[1]

I am not able to speak with confidence of the period at which Locke's Essay began to attract public notice in France. Voltaire, in a letter to Horace Walpole, asserts, that he was the first person who made the name of Locke known to his countrymen;[2] but I suspect that this assertion must be re-

---

et de Senectute; Terence twice, and Pliny's Epistles In French, Giannoni's History of Naples, l'Abbé Banier's Mythology, and M Rochat's Mémoires sur la Suisse, and wrote a very ample relation of my tour I likewise began to study Greek, and went through the grammar I began to make very large collections of what I read But what I esteem most of all,—from the perusal and meditation of De Crousaz's logic, I not only understood the principles of that science, but formed my mind to a habit of thinking and reasoning, I had no idea of before"

' After all, I very readily grant, that Crousaz's logic is chiefly to be regarded as the work of a sagacious and enlightened compiler, but even this (due allowance being made for the state of philosophy when it appeared) is no mean praise. "Good sense (as Gibbon has very truly observed) is a quality of mind hardly less rare than genius "

[1] For some remarks of M Allamand, which approach very near to Reid's Objections to the Ideal Theory, see Note T

Of this extraordinary man Gibbon gives the following account in his *Journal*, " C'est un ministre dans le Pays de Vaud, et un des plus beaux génies que je connoisse Il a voulu embrasser tous les genres; mais c'est la Philosophie qu'il a le plus approfondi Sur toutes les questions il s'est fait des systêmes, ou du moins des argumens toujours originaux et toujours ingénieux. Ses idées sont fines et lumineuses, son expression heureuse et facile On lui reproche avec raison trop de rafinement et de subtilité dans l'esprit, trop de fierté, trop d'ambition, et trop de violence dans le caractère. Cet homme, qui auroit pu éclairer ou troubler une nation, vit et mourra dans l'obscurité."

It is of the same person that Gibbon sneeringly says, in the words of Vossius, " *Est sacrificulus in pago, et rusticos decipit.*"

[2] " Je peux vous assurer qu'avant moi personne en France ne connoissoit la poésie Angloise; à peine avoit on entendu parler de Locke. J'ai été persécuté pendant trente ans par une nuée de fanatiques pour avoir dit que Locke est l'Hercule de la Métaphysique, qui a posé les bornes de l'Esprit Humain."— Ferney, 1768.

In the following passage of *the Age of Louis XIV.*, the same celebrated writer is so lavish and undistinguishing

ceived with considerable qualifications. The striking coincidence between some of Locke's most celebrated doctrines and those of Gassendi, can scarcely be supposed to have been altogether overlooked by the followers and admirers of the latter; considering the immediate and very general circulation given on the Continent to the *Essay on Human Understanding*, by Coste's French version. The *Gassendists*, too, it must be remembered, formed, even before the death of their master, a party formidable in talents as well as in numbers; including, among other distinguished names, those of Molière,[1] Chapelle,[2]

---

[1] Molière was in his youth so strongly attached to the Epicurean theories, that he had projected a translation of Lucretius into French. He is even said to have made some progress in executing his design, when a trifling accident determined him, in a moment of ill humour, to throw his manuscript into the fire. The plan on which he was to proceed in this bold undertaking does honour to his good sense and good taste, and seems to me the only one on which a successful version of Lucretius can ever be executed. The didactic passages of the poem were to be translated into prose, and the descriptive passages into verse. Both parts would have gained greatly by this compromise; for, where Lucretius wishes to unfold the philosophy of his master, he is not less admirable for the perspicuity and precision of his expressions, than he is on other occasions, where his object is to detain and delight the imaginations of his readers, for the charms of his figurative diction, and for the bold relief of his images. In instances of the former kind, no modern language can

in his praise of Locke, as almost to justify a doubt whether he had ever read the book which he extols so highly. "Locke seul a développé *l'entendement human*, dans un livre où il n'y a que des vérités, et ce qui rend l'ouvrage parfait, toutes ces vérités sont claires."

give even the *semblance* of poetry to the theories of Epicurus, while, at the same time, in the vain attempt to conquer this difficulty, the rigorous precision and simplicity of the original are inevitably lost.

The influence of Gassendi's instructions may be traced in several of Molière's comedies; particularly in the *Femmes Savantes*, and in a little piece *Le Mariage Forcé*, where an Aristotelian and a Cartesian doctor are both held up to the same sort of ridicule, which, in some other of his performances, he has so lavishly bestowed on the medical professors of his time.

[2] The joint author, with Bachaumont, of the *Voyage en Provence*, which is still regarded as the most perfect model of that light, easy, and graceful *badinage* which seems to belong exclusively to French poetry. Gassendi, who was an intimate friend of his father, was so charmed with his vivacity while a boy, that he condescended to be his instructor in philosophy; admitting, at the same time, to his lessons, two other illustrious pupils, Molière and Bernier. The life of Chapelle, according to all his biographers, exhibited a complete contrast to the simple and ascetic manners of his master; but, if the following account is to be credited, he missed no opportunity of propagating, as widely as he could, the speculative principles

and Bernier,[1] all of them eminently calculated to give the tone, on disputed questions of Metaphysics, to that numerous class of Parisians of both sexes, with whom the practical lessons, vulgarly imputed to Epicurus, were not likely to operate to the prejudice of his speculative principles. Of the three persons just mentioned, the two last died only a few years before Locke's *Essay* was published; and may be presumed to have left behind them many younger pupils of the same school. One thing is certain, that, long before the middle of the last century, the *Essay on Human Understanding* was not only read by the learned, but had made its way into the circles of fashion at Paris.[2] In what manner this is to be accounted for, it is not easy to say; but the fact will not be disputed by those who are at all acquainted with the history of French literature.

In consequence of this rapid and extensive circulation of the work in question, and the strong impression that it everywhere produced, by the new and striking contrast which it exhibited to the doctrines of the schools, a very remarkable change soon manifested itself in the prevailing habits of thinking on philo-

---

in which he had been educated. "Il étoit fort éloquent dans l'ivresse. Il restoit ordinairement le dernier à table, et se mettoit à expliquer aux valets la philosophie d'Epicure."— *Biographie Universelle*, article *Chapelle*. Paris, 1813. He died in 1686.

[1] The well-known author of one of our most interesting and instructive books of travels. After his return from the East, where he resided twelve years at the Court of the Great Mogul, he published at Lyons, an excellent *Abridgment of the Philosophy of Gassendi*, in 8 vols. 12mo, a second edition of which, corrected by himself, afterwards appeared, in seven volumes. To this second edition (which I have never met with) is annexed a Supplement, entitled *Doutes de M. Bernier sur quelques uns des principaux Chapitres de son Abrégé de la Philosophie de Gassendi*. It is to this work, I presume, that Leibnitz alludes in the following passage of a letter to John Bernouilli, and, from the manner in which he speaks of its contents, it would seem to be an object of some curiosity. "Frustra quæsivi apud typographos librum cui titulus; *Doutes de M Bernier sur la Philosophie*, in Gallia ante annos aliquot editum et mihi visum, sed nunc non repertum. Vellem autem ideo iterum legere, quia ille *Gassendistorum* fuit Princeps, sed paullo ante mortem, libello hoc edito ingenue professus est, in quibus nec Gassendus nec Cartesius satisfaciant."— Leibnitii et Jo Bernouilli *Commerc Epist.* 2 vols 4to Laussanæ et Genevæ, 1745 Bernier died in 1688.

[2] A decisive proof of this is afforded by the allusions to Locke's doctrines in the dramatic pieces then in possession of the French stage See Note U

sophical subjects. Not that it is to be supposed that the opinions of men, on particular articles of their former creed, underwent a sudden alteration. I speak only of the *general effect* of Locke's discussions, in preparing the thinking part of his readers, to a degree till then unknown, for the unshackled use of their own reason. This has always appeared to me the most characteristical feature of Locke's Essay; and *that* to which it is chiefly indebted for its immense influence on the philosophy of the eighteenth century. Few books can be named, from which it is possible to extract more exceptionable passages; but, such is the liberal tone of the author; such the manliness with which he constantly appeals to *reason*, as the paramount authority which, even in religious controversy, every candid disputant is bound to acknowledge; and such the sincerity and simplicity with which, on all occasions, he appears to inquire after truth, that the *general effect* of the whole work may be regarded as the best of all antidotes against the errors involved in some of its particular conclusions.[1]

To attempt any general review of the doctrines sanctioned, or supposed to be sanctioned, by the name of Locke, would be obviously incompatible with the design of this Discourse; but, among these doctrines, there are *two*, of fundamental importance, which have misled so many of his successors, that a few remarks on each form a necessary preparation for some historical details which will afterwards occur. The first of these doctrines relates to the ORIGIN OF OUR IDEAS; the second to THE POWER OF MORAL PERCEPTION, AND THE IMMUTABILITY OF MORAL DISTINCTIONS. On *both* questions, the real opinion of

[1] The maxim which he constantly inculcates is, that "Reason must be our last judge and guide in everything."—(Locke's *Works*, vol iii p 145.) To the same purpose, he elsewhere observes, that "he who makes use of the light and faculties God has given him, and seeks sincerely to discover truth by those helps and abilities he has, may have this satisfaction in doing his duty as a rational creature; that, though he should miss truth, he will not miss the reward of it. For *he* governs his assent right, and places it as he should, who in any case or matter whatsoever, believes or disbelieves, according as reason directs him. He that does otherwise, transgresses against his own light, and misuses those faculties which were given him to no other end, but to search and follow the clearer evidence and greater probability."—*Ibid* p 125.

Locke has, if I am not widely mistaken, been very grossly misapprehended or misrepresented, by a large portion of his professed followers, as well as of his avowed antagonists.

1. The objections to which Locke's doctrine concerning the origin of our ideas, or, in other words, concerning the sources of our knowledge, are, in my judgment, liable, I have stated so fully in a former work,[1] that I shall not touch on them here. It is quite sufficient, on the present occasion, to remark, how very unjustly *this* doctrine (imperfect, on the most favourable construction, as it undoubtedly is) has been confounded with those of Gassendi, of Condillac, of Diderot, and of Horne Tooke. The substance of all that is common in the conclusions of these last writers, cannot be better expressed than in the words of their master, Gassendi. "All our knowledge (he observes in a letter to Descartes) appears plainly to derive its origin from the senses; and although you deny the maxim, 'Quicquid est in intellectu præesse debere in sensu,' yet this maxim appears, nevertheless, to be true; since our knowledge is all ultimately obtained by an *influx* or *incursion* from things external; which knowledge afterwards undergoes various modifications by means of analogy, composition, division, amplification, extenuation, and other similar processes, which it is unnecessary to enumerate."[2]

---

[1] *Philosophical Essays.*

[2] "Deinde omnis nostra notitia videtur plane ducere originem a sensibus; et quamvis tu neges quicquid est in intellectu præesse debere in sensu, videtur id esse nihilominus verum, cum nisi sola incursione κατὰ περίπτωσιν, ut loquuntur, fiat, perficiatur tamen analogia, compositione, divisione, ampliatione, extenuatione, aliisque similibus modis, quos commemorare nihil est necesse"— *Objectiones in Meditationem Secundam.*

This doctrine of Gassendi's is thus very clearly stated and illustrated, by the judicious authors of the *Port-Royal Logic:* "Un philosophe qui est estimé dans le monde commence sa logique par cette proposition *Omnis idea orsum ducit a sensibus. Toute idée tire son origine des sens.* Il avoue néanmoins que toutes nos idées n ont pas été dans nos sens telles qu'elles sont dans notre esprit mais il prétend qu'elles ont au moins été formées de celles qui ont passé par nos sens, ou par *composition*, comme lorsque des images separées de l'or et d'une montagne, on s'en fait une montagne d'or; ou par *ampliation* et *diminution*, comme lorsque de l'image d'un homme d'une grandeur ordinaire on s'en forme un géant ou un pigmée; ou par *accommodation* et *proportion*,

This doctrine of Gassendi's coincides exactly with that ascribed to Locke by Diderot and by Horne Tooke; and it differs only verbally from the more concise statement of Condillac, that " our ideas are nothing more than *transformed*

comme lorsque de l'idée d'une maison qu'on a vue, on s'en forme l'image d'une maison qu'on n'a pas vue. ET AINSI, dit il, NOUS CONCEVONS DIEU QUI NE PEUT TOMBER SOUS LES SENS, SOUS L'IMAGE D'UN VENERABLE VIEILLARD." " Selon cette pensée, quoique toutes nos idées ne fussent semblables à quelque corps particulier que nous ayons vu, ou qui ait frappé nos sens, elles seroient néanmoins toutes corporelles, et ne vous représenteroient rien qui ne fût entré dans nos sens, au moins par parties Et ainsi nous ne concevons rien que par des images, semblables à celles qui se forment dans le cerveau quand nous voyons, ou nous nous imaginons des corps "—*L'Art de Penser*, 1 Partie, c. 1.

The reference made, in the foregoing quotation, to Gassendi's illustration drawn from *the idea of God*, affords me an opportunity, of which I gladly avail myself, to contrast it with Locke's opinion on the same subject " How many amongst us will be found, upon inquiry, to fancy God, in the shape of a man, sitting in heaven, and to have many other absurd and unfit conceptions of him? Christians, as well as Turks, have had whole sects owning, or contending earnestly for it, that the Deity was corporeal and of human shape And although we find few amongst us, who profess themselves *Anthropomorphites* (though some I have met with that own it,) yet, I believe, he that will make it his business, may find amongst the ignorant and uninstructed Christians, many of that opinion."*—Vol 1 p 67

" Let the ideas of being and matter be strongly joined either by education or much thought, whilst these are still combined in the mind, what notions, what reasonings will there be about separate spirits? Let custom, from the very childhood, have joined figure and

---

* In the judgment of a very learned and pious divine, the bias towards *Anthropomorphism*, which Mr. Locke has here so severely reprehended, is not confined to " ignorant and uninstructed Christians." " If *Anthropomorphism* (says Dr Maclaine) was banished from theology, orthodoxy would be deprived of some of its most precious phrases, and our confessions of faith and systems of doctrine would be reduced within much narrower bounds."—*Note on* Mosheim's *Church History*, vol iv p 550

On this point I do not presume to offer any opinion, but one thing I consider as indisputable, that it is by means of *Anthropomorphism*, and other idolatrous pictures of the invisible world, that superstition lays hold of the infant mind Such pictures operate not upon Reason, but upon the Imagination, producing that temporary belief with which I conceive all the illusions of imagination to be accompanied.

In point of fact, the bias of which Locke speaks extends in a greater or less degree to all men of strong imaginations, whose education has not been very carefully superintended in early infancy

I have applied to *Anthropomorphism* the epithet idolatrous, as it seems to be essentially the same thing to bow down and worship a graven image of the Supreme Being, and to worship a supposed likeness of Him conceived by the Imagination.

In Bernier's *Abridgment of Gassendi's Philosophy*, (tom III p 13 *et seq*) an attempt is made to reconcile with the Epicurean account of the origin of our knowledge, that more pure and exalted idea of God to which the mind is gradually led by the exercise of its reasoning powers But I am very doubtful if Gassendi would have subscribed, in this instance, to the comments of his ingenious disciple

sensations" "Every idea," says the first of these writers, "must necessarily, when brought to its state of ultimate decomposition, resolve itself into a *sensible* representation or picture; and since every thing *in* our understanding has been introduced

shape to the idea of God, and what absurdities will that mind be liable to about the Deity?"—Vol. ii. p. 144.

The authors of the *Port-Royal Logic* have expressed themselves on this point to the very same purpose with Locke; and have enlarged upon it still more fully and forcibly (See the sequel of the passage above quoted.) Some of their remarks on the subject, which are more particularly directed against Gassendi, have led Brucker to rank them among the advocates for *innate ideas*, (Brucker, *Historia de Ideis*, p. 271,) although these remarks coincide exactly in substance with the foregoing quotation from Locke Like many other modern metaphysicians, this learned and laborious, but not very acute historian, could imagine no intermediate opinion between the theory of *innate ideas*, as taught by the Cartesians, and the Epicurean account of our knowledge, as revived by Gassendi and Hobbes, and accordingly thought himself entitled to conclude, that whoever rejected the one must necessarily have adopted the other. The doctrines of Locke and of his predecessor Arnauld will be found, on examination, essentially different from both.

Persons little acquainted with the metaphysical speculations of the two last centuries are apt to imagine, that when "all knowledge is said to have its origin in the senses," nothing more is to be understood than this, that it is by the impressions of external objects on our organs of perception, that the *dormant powers* of the understanding are at first awakened. The foregoing quotation from Gassendi, together with those which I am about to produce from Diderot and Condorcet, may, I trust, be useful in correcting this very common mistake; all of these quotations explicitly asserting, that the external senses furnish not only the *occasions* by which our intellectual powers are excited and developed, but all the *materials* about which our thoughts are conversant; or, in other words, that it is impossible for us to think of anything, which is not either a sensible image, or the result of sensible images combined together, and transmuted into new forms by a sort of logical chemistry That the powers of the understanding would for ever continue dormant, were it not for the action of things external on the bodily frame, is a proposition now universally admitted by philosophers. Even Mr Harris and Lord Monboddo, the two most zealous as well as most learned of Mr. Locke's adversaries in England, have, in the most explicit manner, expressed their assent to the common doctrine. "The first class of ideas (says Monboddo) is produced from ideas furnished by the senses; the second arises from the operations of the mind upon these materials. for I do not deny, that in this our present state of existence, all our ideas, and all our knowledge, are ultimately to be derived from sense and matter."—Vol i. p. 44, 2d Ed. Mr. Harris, while he holds the same language, points out, with greater precision, the essential difference between his philosophy and that of the Hobbists "Though sensible objects may be the destined medium to awaken the dormant energies of man's understanding, yet are those energies themselves no more contained in sense, than the explosion of a cannon in the spark

there by the channel of sensation, whatever proceeds *out* of the understanding is either chimerical, or must be able, in returning by the same road, to re-attach itself to its sensible archetype. Hence an important rule in philosophy,—that every expression which cannot find an external and a sensible object, to which it can thus establish its affinity, is destitute of signification."—*Œuvres de* Diderot, tom. vi.

Such is the exposition given by Diderot, of what is regarded in France as Locke's great and capital *discovery;* and precisely to the same purpose we are told by Condorcet, that " Locke was the first who proved that *all our ideas are compounded of sensations*"—*Esquisse Historique,* &c

If this were to be admitted as a fair account of Locke's opinion, it would follow, that he has not advanced a single step beyond Gassendi and Hobbes, both of whom have repeatedly expressed themselves in nearly the same words with Diderot and Condorcet. But although it must be granted, in favour of their interpretation of his language, that various detached passages may be quoted from his work, which seem, on a superficial view, to justify their comments, yet of what weight, it may be asked, are these passages, when compared with the stress laid by the author on *Reflection,* as an original source of our ideas, altogether different from *Sensation?* " The *other fountain,*" says Locke, " from which experience furnisheth the understanding with ideas, is the perception of the operations of our own mind within us, as it is employed about the ideas it has got; which operations, when the soul comes to *reflect on* and consider, do furnish the understanding with another set of ideas, which could not be had from things without; and such are *Perception, Thinking, Doubting, Believing, Reasoning, Knowing, Willing,* and all the different actings of our own minds, which, we being conscious of, and observing in our-

---

which gave it fire."—(Hermes) On this subject see *Elements of the Philosophy of the Human Mind,* vol. i. chap. i. sect. 4.

To this doctrine I have little doubt that Descartes himself would have assented, although the contrary opinion has been generally supposed by his adversaries to be virtually involved in his *Theory of Innate Ideas.* My reasons for thinking so, the reader will find stated in Note X.

selves, do from these receive into our understandings ideas as distinct as we do from bodies affecting our senses. This source of ideas every man has wholly in himself: And though it be not sense, *as having nothing to do with external objects,* yet it is very like it, and might properly enough be called *internal sense.* But as I call the other SENSATION, so I call this REFLECTION; the ideas it affords being such only as the mind gets by *reflecting* on its own operations within itself."[1]—Locke's *Works,* vol. i. p. 78.

" The understanding seems to me not to have the least glimmering of any ideas which it doth not receive from one of these two *External objects furnish the mind with the ideas of sensible qualities; and the mind furnishes the understanding with ideas of its own operations."—Ibid.* p. 79.

In another part of the same chapter, Locke expresses himself thus. "Men come to be furnished with fewer or more simple ideas from without, according as the objects they converse with afford greater or less variety, and from the operations of their minds within, according as they more or less REFLECT on them. For though he that contemplates the operations of his mind, cannot but have plain and clear ideas of them; yet, unless he turn his thoughts that way, and consider them *attentively,* he will no more have clear and distinct ideas of all the operations of his mind, and all that may be observed therein, than he will have all the particular ideas of any landscape, or of the parts and motions of a clock, who will not turn his eyes to it, and with attention heed all the parts of it. The picture or clock may be so placed that they may come in his way every day; but yet he will have but a confused idea of all the parts they are made up of, till he applies himself with attention to consider them in each particular

" And hence we see the reason why it is pretty late before most children get ideas of the operations of their own minds; and some have not any very clear or perfect ideas of the greatest part of them all their lives . . Children, when they first come into it, are surrounded with a world of new things, which,

---

[1] See Note Y.

by a constant solicitation of their senses, draw the mind constantly to them,—forward to take notice of new, and apt to be delighted with the variety of changing objects. Thus, the first years are usually employed and directed in looking abroad. Men's business in them is to acquaint themselves with what is to be found without; and so growing up in a constant attention to outward sensations, seldom make any considerable reflection on what passes within them, till they come to be of riper years; and some scarce ever at all."—*Ibid.* pp. 80, 81.

I beg leave to request more particularly the attention of my readers to the following paragraphs :—

"If it be demanded, *when a man begins to have any ideas?* I think the true answer is, when he first has any *sensation*. . . I conceive that ideas in the understanding are coeval with *sensation;* which is such an impression or motion, made in some part of the body, as produces some perception in the understanding. It is about these impressions made on our senses by outward objects, that the mind seems *first* to employ itself in such operations as we call *Perception, Remembering, Consideration, Reasoning,* &c.

"In time, the mind comes to reflect on its own operations, and about the ideas got by sensation, and thereby stores itself with a new set of ideas, which I call *ideas of reflection.* These impressions that are made on our senses by objects extrinsical to the mind; and *its own operations, proceeding from powers intrinsical and proper to itself,* (which, when reflected on by itself, become also objects of its contemplation,) are, as I have said, *the original of all knowledge.*"[1]—*Ibid* pp. 91, 92.

---

[1] The idea attached by Locke in the above passages to the word *Reflection,* is clear and precise But in the course of his subsequent speculations, he does not always rigidly adhere to it, frequently employing it in that more extensive and popular sense in which it denotes the attentive and deliberate consideration of any object of thought, whether relating to the external or to the internal world It is in this sense he uses it when he refers to Reflection our ideas of Cause and Effect, of Identity and Diversity, and of *all other relations* " All of these (he observes) *terminate in,* and are *concerned about,* those simple ideas, either of Sensation or Reflection, which I think to be the whole materials of all our knowledge "—(Book ii c xxv sect. 9) From this explanation it would appear that Locke conceived it sufficient to justify his account of the origin of our

A few other scattered sentences, collected from different parts of Locke's *Essay*, may throw additional light on the point in question.

"I know that people whose thoughts are immersed in matter, and have so subjected their minds to their senses, that they seldom reflect on anything beyond them, are apt to say they cannot comprehend a *thinking* thing, which perhaps is true: But I affirm, when they consider it well, they can no more comprehend an *extended* thing.

"If any one say, he knows not what 'tis thinks in him; he means he knows not what the substance is of that thinking thing: No more, say I, knows he what the substance is of that solid thing. Farther, if he says he knows not *how* he thinks; I answer, Neither knows he *how* he is extended; *how* the solid parts of body are united, or cohere together to make extension." —Vol. ii. p. 22.

"I think we have as many and as clear ideas belonging to mind as we have belonging to body, the substance of each being

---

knowledge, if it could be shewn that all our ideas *terminate in, and are concerned about,* ideas derived either from Sensation or Reflection, according to which comment, it will not be a difficult task to obviate every objection to which his fundamental principle concerning the two sources of our ideas may appear to be liable

In this lax interpretation of a principle so completely interwoven with the whole of his philosophy, there is undoubtedly a departure from logical accuracy; and the same remark may be extended to the vague and indefinite use which he occasionally makes of the word *Reflection*—a word which expresses the peculiar and characteristical doctrine by which his system is distinguished from that of the Gassendists and Hobbists. All this, however, serves only to prove still more clearly, how widely remote his real opinion on this subject was from that commonly ascribed to him by the French and German commentators. For my own part, I do not think, notwithstanding some casual expressions which may seem to favour the contrary supposition, that Locke would have hesitated for a moment to admit, with Cudworth and Price, that the *Understanding* is itself a source of new ideas That it is by *Reflection* (which, according to his own definition, means merely the exercise of the *Understanding* on the internal phenomena) that we get our ideas of memory, imagination, reasoning, and of all other intellectual powers, Mr Locke has again and again told us, and from this principle it is so obvious an inference, that all the simple ideas which are necessarily implied in our intellectual operations, are ultimately to be referred to the same source, that we cannot reasonably suppose a philosopher of Locke's sagacity to admit the former proposition, and to withhold his assent to the latter.

equally unknown to us; and the idea of thinking in mind is clear as of extension in body; and the communication of motion by thought, which we attribute to mind, is as evident as that by impulse, which we ascribe to body. Constant experience makes us sensible of both of these, though our narrow understanding can comprehend neither.[1]

" To conclude : Sensation convinces us, that there are solid extended substances; and Reflection, that there are thinking ones: Experience assures us of the existence of such beings; and that the one hath a power to move body by impulse, the other by thought; *this* we cannot doubt of. But beyond these ideas, as received from their proper sources, our faculties will not reach. If we would inquire farther into their nature, causes, and manner, we perceive not the nature of Extension clearer than we do of Thinking. If we would explain them any farther, one is as easy as the other; and there is no more difficulty to conceive *how* a substance we know not should, by *thought*, set body into motion, than how a substance we know not should, by *impulse*, set body into motion."—*Ibid.* pp. 26, 27.

The passage in Locke which, on a superficial view, appears the most favourable to the misinterpretation put on his account of the Sources of our Knowledge, by so many of his professed followers, is, in my opinion, the following :—

" It may also lead us a little towards the original of all our notions and knowledge, if we remark how great a dependence our words have on common sensible ideas, and how those which are made use of to stand for actions and notions quite removed from sense, have their rise from thence, and from obvious sensible ideas are transferred to more abstruse significations, and made to stand for ideas that come not under the cognizance of our senses ; *e. g.* to *imagine, apprehend, comprehend, adhere, conceive, instil, disgust, disturbance, tranquillity*, &c., are all

---

[1] In transcribing this paragraph, I have taken the liberty to substitute the word *Mind* instead of *Spirit* The two words were plainly considered by Locke, on the present occasion, as quite synonymous, and the latter (which *seems* to involve a theory concerning the nature of the thinking principle) is now almost universally rejected by English metaphysicians from their Philosophical Vocabulary

words taken from the operations of sensible things, and applied to certain modes of thinking *Spirit*, in its primary signification, is breath ; *angel*, a messenger : *and I doubt not, but if we could trace them to their sources, we should find, in all languages, the names which stand for things that fall not under our senses, to have had their first rise from sensible ideas.* By which we may give some kind of guess what kind of notions they were, and whence derived, which filled their minds, who were the first beginners of languages ; and how nature, even in the naming of things, unawares suggested to men the originals and principles of all their knowledge."

So far the words of Locke coincide very nearly, if not exactly, with the doctrines of Hobbes and of Gassendi ; and I have not a doubt, that a mistaken interpretation of the clause which I have distinguished by *italics*, furnished the germ of all the mighty *discoveries* contained in the Ἔπεα Πτερόεντα. If Mr. Tooke, however, had studied with due attention the import of what immediately follows, he must have instantly perceived how essentially different Locke's real opinion on the subject was from what he conceived it to be.—" Whilst to give names, that might make known to others any operations they felt in themselves, or any other ideas that came not under their senses, they were fain to borrow words from ordinary known ideas of sensation, by that means to make others the more easily to conceive those operations they experienced in themselves, which made no outward sensible appearances ; and then, when they had got known and agreed names, to signify those internal operations of their own minds, they were sufficiently furnished to make known by words all their other ideas ; since they could consist of nothing but either of outward sensible perceptions, or of the inward operations of their minds about them."— Vol. ii. pp 147, 148.

From the sentences last quoted it is manifest, that when Locke remarked the *material* etymology of all our language about mind, he had not the most distant intention to draw from it any inference which might tend to identify the sensible images which this language presents to the fancy, with the metaphysical notions which it figuratively expresses. Through the whole of his *Essay*, he uniformly represents *sensation* and *reflection* as radically distinct sources of knowledge; and, of consequence, he must have conceived it to be not less unphilosophical to attempt an explanation of the phenomena of mind by the analogy of matter, than to think of explaining the phenomena of matter by the analogy of mind. To this fundamental principle concerning the origin of our ideas, he has added, in the passage now before us,—That, as our knowledge of mind is posterior in the order of time to that of matter, (the first years of our existence being necessarily occupied about objects of sense,) it is not surprising, that "when men wished *to give names that might make known to others* any operations they felt in themselves, or any other ideas that came not under their senses, they should have been fain to borrow words from ordinary known ideas of sensation, by that means to make others the more easily to conceive those operations which make no outward sensible appearances." According to this statement, the purpose of these "borrowed" or metaphorical words is not (as Mr. Tooke concluded) to *explain* the nature of the operations, but to direct the attention of the hearer to that internal world, the phenomena of which he can only learn to comprehend by the exercise of his own power of reflection. If Locke has nowhere affirmed so explicitly as his predecessor Descartes, that "nothing conceivable by the power of imagination can throw any light on the operations of thought," it may be presumed that he considered this as unnecessary, after having dwelt so much on *reflection* as the exclusive source of all our ideas relating to mind; and on the peculiar difficulties attending the exercise of this power, in consequence of the effect of early associations in confounding together our notions of mind and of matter.

The misapprehensions so prevalent on the Continent, with respect to Locke's doctrine on this most important of all metaphysical questions, began during his own lifetime, and were countenanced by the authority of no less a writer than Leibnitz, who always represents Locke as a partisan of the scholastic maxim, *Nihil est in intellectu quod non fuerit in sensu.*— "Nempe (says Leibnitz, in reply to this maxim) nihil est in intellectu quod non fuerit in sensu, *nisi ipse intellectus.*"[1]

---

[1] *Opera*, tom v. pp 358, 359

That the same mistake still keeps its ground among many foreign writers of the highest class, the following passage affords a sufficient proof.—" Leibnitz a combattu avec une force de dialectique admirable le Système de Locke, qui attribue toutes nos idées à nos sensations. On avoit mis en avant cet axiome si connu, qu'il n'y avoit rien dans l'intelligence qui n'eut été d'abord dans les sensations, et Leibnitz y ajouta cette sublime restriction, *si ce n'est l'intelligence elle-même.* De ce principe derive toute la philosophie nouvelle qui exerce tant d'influence sur les esprits en Allemagne."—Madame de Staël *de l'Allemagne*, tom. iii. p 65.

I observed in the First Part of this Dissertation, (page 87,) that this *sublime restriction* on which so much stress has been laid by the partisans of the German school, is little more than a translation of the following words of Aristotle. Καὶ αὐτὸς δὲ νοῦς νοητός ἐστιν, ὥσπερ τὰ νοητά· ἐπὶ μὲν γὰρ τῶν ἄνευ ὕλης, τὸ αὐτό ἐστι τὸ νοοῦν καὶ τὸ νοούμενον.—*De Anima*, lib. iii. cap v.

As to Locke, the same injustice which he received from Leibnitz was very early done to him in his own country In a tract printed in 1697, by a mathematician of some note, the author of the *Essay on Human Understanding* is represented as holding the same opinion with Gassendi concerning the origin of our ideas. "*Ideæ* nomine sensu utor ; earum originem an a sensibus solum, ut Gassendo et Lockio nostrati, cæterisque plurimis visum est, an aliunde, hujus loci non est inquirere "—(*De Spatio Reali, seu Ente Infinito Conamen Mathematico-Metaphysicum* Auctore Josepho Raphson, Reg Soc.

Socio. This tract is annexed to the second edition of a work entitled *Analysis Æquationum Universalis.* Lond. 1702)

In order to enable my readers more easily to form a judgment on the argument in the text, I must beg leave once more to remind them of the distinction already pointed out between the Gassendists and the Cartesians; the former asserting, that, as all our ideas are derived from the external senses, the intellectual phenomena can admit of no other explanation than what is furnished by analogies drawn from the material world; the latter rejecting these analogies altogether, as delusive and treacherous lights in the study of mind, and contending, that the exercise of the power of reflection is the only medium through which any knowledge of its operations is to be obtained To the one or the other of these two classes, all the metaphysicians of the last century may be referred ; and even at the present day, the fundamental question which formed the chief ground of controversy between Gassendi and Descartes (I mean the question concerning the proper logical method of studying the mind) still continues the hinge on which the most important disputes relating to the internal world will be found ultimately to turn.

According to this distinction, Locke, notwithstanding some occasional slips of his pen, belongs indisputably to the class of Cartesians , as well as the very small number of his followers who have entered thoroughly into the spirit of his philosophy. To the class of Gassendists, on the other hand, belong all those French metaphysicians who, professing

The remark is excellent, and does honour to the acuteness of the critic; but it is not easy to conceive on what grounds it should have been urged as an objection to a writer, who has insisted so explicitly and so frequently on *reflection* as the

to tread in Locke's footsteps, have derived all their knowledge of the *Essay on Human Understanding* from the works of Condillac, together with most of the commentators on Locke who have proceeded from the school of Bishop Law. To these may be added (among the writers of later times) Priestley, Darwin, Beddoes, and, above all, Horne Tooke with his numerous disciples.

The doctrine of Hobbes on this cardinal question coincided entirely with that of Gassendi, and accordingly it is not unusual in the present times, among Hobbes's disciples, to ascribe to him the whole merit of that account of the origin of our knowledge which, from a strange misconception, has been supposed to have been claimed by Locke as his own discovery. But where, it may be asked, has Hobbes said anything about the origin of those ideas which Locke refers to the power of *reflection?* and may not the numerous observations which Locke has made on *this* power as a source of ideas peculiar to itself, be regarded as an indirect refutation of that theory which would resolve all the objects of our knowledge into *sensations,* as their ultimate elements? This was not merely a step *beyond* Hobbes, but the correction of an error which lies at the very root of Hobbes's system,—an error under which (it may be added) the greater part of Hobbes's eulogists have the misfortune still to labour.

It is with much regret I add, that a very large proportion of the English writers who call themselves *Lockists,* and who, I have no doubt, believe themselves to be so in reality, are at bottom (at least in their metaphysical opinions) *Gassendists* or *Hobbists.* In what re-

spect do the following observations differ from the Epicurean theory concerning the origin of our knowledge, as expounded by Gassendi? "The ideas conveyed by sight, and by our other senses, having entered the mind, intermingle, unite, separate, throw themselves into various combinations and postures, and thereby generate new ideas of reflection, strictly so called; such as those of comparing, dividing, distinguishing,—of abstraction, relation, with many others, all which remain with us as stock for our further use on future occasions." I do not recollect any passage, either in Helvetius or Diderot, which contains a more explicit and decided avowal of that Epicurean system of Metaphysics which it was the great aim both of Descartes and of Locke to overthrow.

In the following conjectures concerning the *nature* of our ideas, the same author has far exceeded in extravagance any of the metaphysicians of the French school. "What those *substances* are, whereof our ideas are the modifications, *whether parts of the mind, as the members are of our body, or contained in it like wafers in a box, or enveloped by it like fish in water;* whether *of a spiritual, corporeal, or middle nature between both,* I need not now ascertain. All I mean to lay down at present is this, that in every exercise of the understanding, that which discerns is *numerically and substantially distinct* from that which is discerned, and that an act of the understanding is not so much our own proper act, as the act of something else operating upon us"

I should scarcely have thought it worth while to take notice of these pas-

source of a class of ideas essentially different from those which are derived from *sensation.* To myself it appears, that the words of Leibnitz only convey in a more concise and epigrammatic form, the substance of Locke's doctrine. Is anything implied in them which Locke has not more fully and clearly stated in the following sentence? "External objects furnish the mind with the ideas of sensible qualities; and the mind furnishes the understanding with ideas of its own operations."—Locke's *Works,* vol. i. p. 79.

The extraordinary zeal displayed by Locke, at the very outset of his work, against the hypothesis of *innate ideas,* goes far to account for the mistakes committed by his commentators, in interpreting his account of the origin of our knowledge. It ought, however, to be always kept in view, in reading his argument on the subject, that it is the *Cartesian* theory of innate ideas which he is here combating; according to which theory, (as understood by Locke,) an *innate idea* signifies *something* coeval in its existence with the mind to which it belongs, and

---

sages, had not the doctrines contained in the work from which they are taken been sanctioned in the most unqualified terms by the high authority of Dr Paley "There is one work (he observes) to which I owe so much, that it would be ungrateful not to confess the obligation; I mean the writings of the late Abraham Tucker, Esq, part of which were published by himself, and the remainder since his death, under the title of the *Light of Nature Pursued,* by Edward Search, Esq" "*I have found, in this writer, more original thinking and observation, upon the several subjects that he has taken in hand, than in any other, not to say than in all others put together* His talent also for illustration is unrivalled. But his thoughts are diffused through a long, various, and irregular work I shall account it no mean praise, if I have been sometimes able to dispose into method, to collect into heads and articles, or to exhibit in more compact and tangible masses, what, in that excellent performance, is spread over too much surface "—*Principles of Moral and Political Philosophy,* Preface, pp 25, 26.

Of an author whom Dr Paley has honoured with so very warm an eulogy, it would be equally absurd and presumptuous to dispute the merits. Nor have I any wish to detract from the praise here bestowed on him as an original thinker and observer. I readily admit, also, his talent for illustration, although it sometimes leads him to soar into bombast, and more frequently to sink into buffoonery. As an honest inquirer after moral and religious truth, he is entitled to the most unqualified approbation But I must be permitted to add, that, as a metaphysician, he seems to me much more fanciful than solid, and, at the same time, to be so rambling, verbose, and excursive, as to be more likely to unsettle than to fix the principles of his readers.

illuminating the understanding before the external senses begin to operate. The very close affinity between this theory, and some of the doctrines of the Platonic school, prevented Leibnitz, it is probable, from judging of Locke's argument against it, with his usual candour; and disposed him hastily to conclude, that the opposition of Locke to Descartes proceeded from views essentially the same with those of Gassendi, and of his other Epicurean antagonists. How very widely he was mistaken in this conclusion, the numerous passages which I have quoted in Locke's own words sufficiently demonstrate.

In what respects Locke's account of the origin of our ideas *falls short* of the truth, will appear, when the metaphysical discussions of later times come under our review. Enough has been already said to show, how completely this account has been misapprehended, not only by his opponents, but by the most devoted of his admirers;—a misapprehension so very general, and at the same time so obviously at variance with the whole spirit of his Essay, as to prove to a demonstration that, in point of numbers, the *intelligent readers* of this celebrated work have hitherto borne but a small proportion to its purchasers and panegyrists. What an illustration of the folly of trusting, in matters of literary history, to the traditionary judgments copied by one commentator or critic from another, when recourse may so easily be had to the original sources of information![1]

[1] In justice to Dr Hartley I must here observe, that, although his account of the origin of our ideas is precisely the same with that of Gassendi, Hobbes, and Condillac—one of his fundamental principles being, that the *ideas* of sensation are the *elements* of which all the rest are compounded—(Hartley *on Man*, 4th Edit. p 2 of the Introduction)—he has not availed himself, like the other Gassendists of later times, of the name of Locke to recommend this theory to the favour of his readers On the contrary, he has very clearly and candidly pointed out the wide and essential distinction between the two opinions "It may not be amiss here to take notice how far the theory of these papers has led me to differ, in respect of logic, from Mr Locke's excellent *Essay on the Human Understanding*, to which the world is so much indebted for removing prejudices and encumbrances, and advancing real and useful knowledge

"First, then, it appears to me, that all the most complex ideas arise from sensation, and that *reflection is not a distinct source*, as Mr Locke makes it" —Hartley *on Man*, 4th Edit p 360 of the Introduction.

This last proposition Hartley seems to have considered as an important and

II. Another misapprehension, not less prevalent than the former, with respect to Locke's philosophical creed, relates to the power of moral perception, and the immutability of moral distinctions. The consideration of such questions, it may at

original improvement of his own on Locke's logic, whereas, in fact, it is only a relapse into the old Epicurean hypothesis, which it was one of the main objects of Locke's Essay to explode.

I would not have enlarged so fully on Locke's account of the origin of our ideas, had not a mistaken view of his argument on this head, served as a groundwork for the whole Metaphysical Philosophy of the French *Encyclopédie.* That all our knowledge is derived from our external senses, is everywhere assumed by the conductors of that work as a demonstrated principle, and the credit of this demonstration is uniformly ascribed to Locke, who, we are told, was the first that fully unfolded and established a truth, of which his predecessors had only an imperfect glimpse. La Harpe, in his *Lycée,* has, on this account, justly censured the metaphysical phraseology of the *Encyclopédie,* as tending to degrade the intellectual nature of man, while, with a strange inconsistency, he bestows the most unqualified praise on the writings of Condillac. Little did he suspect, when he wrote the following sentences, how much the reasonings of his favourite logician had contributed to pave the way to those conclusions which he reprobates with so much asperity in Diderot and D'Alembert.

"La gloire de Condillac est d'avoir été le premier disciple de Locke; mais si Condillac eut un maître, il mérita d'en servir à tous les autres, il répandit même une plus grande lumière sur les découvertes du philosophe Anglois; il les rendit pour ainsi dire sensibles, et c'est grace à lui qu'elles sont devenues communes et familières En un mot, la saine Métaphysique ne date en France, que des ouvrages de Condillac, et à ce titre il doit être compté dans le petit nombre d'hommes qui ont avancé la science qu'ils ont cultivée."—*Lycée,* tom. xv. pp. 136, 137.

La Harpe proceeds in the same panegyrical strain through more than seventy pages, and concludes his eulogy of Condillac with these words. "Le style de Condillac est clair et pur comme ses conceptions, c'est en général l'esprit le plus juste et le plus lumineux qui ait contribué, dans ce siècle, aux progrès de la bonne philosophie."—*Ibid.* p 214

La Harpe's account of the power of *Reflection* will form an appropriate supplement to his comments on Condillac. "L'impression sentie des objets se nomme *perception;* l'action de l'âme qui les considère, se nomme *reflexion.* Ce mot, il est vrai, exprime un mouvement physique, celui de se replier sur soi-même ou sur quelque chose, mais *toutes nos idées venant des sens,* nous sommes souvent obligés de nous servir de termes physiques pour exprimer les opérations de l'âme."—(*Ibid* p. 158) In another passage, he defines Reflection as follows "La faculté de réflexion, c'est-à-dire, le pouvoir qu'a notre âme, de comparer, d'assembler, de combiner les perceptions."—(*Ibid* p 183) How widely do these definitions of *reflection* differ from that given by Locke, and how exactly do they accord with the Philosophy of Gassendi, of Hobbes, and of Diderot!

In a lately published sketch *Of the State of French Literature during the Eighteenth Century,* (a work, to which the Author's taste and powers as a writer have attracted a degree of public atten-

first sight be thought, belongs rather to the history of Ethics than of Metaphysics; but it must be recollected, that, in introducing them here, I follow the example of Locke himself, who has enlarged upon them at considerable length, in his Argument against the Theory of *Innate Ideas*. An *Ethical* disquisition of this sort formed, it must be owned, an awkward introduction to a work on the Human Understanding; but the conclusion on which it is meant to bear is purely of a *Metaphysical* nature; and when combined with the premises from which it is deduced, affords a good illustration of the impossibility, in tracing the progress of these two sciences, of separating completely the history of the one from that of the other.

tion something beyond what was due to his philosophical depth and discernment,) there are some shrewd, and, in my opinion, sound remarks, on the *moral* tendency of that metaphysical system to which Condillac gave so much circulation and celebrity I shall quote some of his strictures which bear more particularly on the foregoing argument.

" Autrefois, négligeant d'examiner tout ce mécanisme des sens, tous ces rapports directs du corps avec les objets, les philosophes ne s'occupoient que de ce qui se passe au-dedans de l'homme. La science de l'âme, telle a été la noble étude de Descartes, de Pascal, de Malebranche, de Leibnitz (Why omit in this list the name of Locke?) . . . Peut-être se perdoient-ils quelquefois dans les nuages des hautes régions où ils avoient pris leur vol; peut-être leurs travaux étoient-ils sans application directe; mais du moins ils suivoient une direction élevée, leur doctrine étoit en rapport avec les pensées qui nous agitent quand nous réfléchissons profondément sur nous-mêmes. Cette route conduisoit nécessairement au plus nobles des sciences, à la religion, et à la morale. Elle supposoit dans ceux qui la cultivoient un génie élevé et de vastes méditations.

" On se lassa de les suivre, on traita de vaines subtilités, on flétrit du titre de rêveries scholastiques les travaux de ces grands esprits. On se jeta dans la science des sensations, espérant qu'elle seroit plus à la portée de l'intelligence humaine On s'occupa de plus en plus des rapports mécaniques de l'homme avec les objets, et de l'influence de son organisation physique De cette sorte, la métaphysique alla toujours se rabaissant, au point que maintenant, pour quelques personnes, elle se confond presque avec la physiologie. . . . Le dix-huitième siècle a voulu faire de cette manière d'envisager l'homme un de ses principaux titres de gloire. . . .

" Condillac est le chef de cette école C'est dans ses ouvrages que cette métaphysique exerce toutes les séductions de la méthode, et de la lucidité, d'autant plus claire, qu'elle est moins profonde. Peu d'écrivains ont obtenu plus de succès. Il réduisit à la portée du vulgaire la science de la pensée, en retranchant tout ce qu'elle avoit d'élevé. Chacun fut surpris et glorieux de pouvoir philosopher si facilement, et l'on eut une grande reconnoissance pour celui à qui l'on devoit ce bienfait. On ne s'apperçut pas qu'il avoit rabaissé la science, au lieu de rendre ses disciples capable d'y atteindre."—*Tableau de la Littérature Françoise pendant le dix huitième Siècle*, pp. 87, 88, 89, 92.

In what sense Locke's reasonings against *Innate Ideas* have been commonly understood, may be collected from the following passage of an author, who had certainly no wish to do injustice to Locke's opinions

" The First Book (says Dr. Beattie) of the *Essay on Human Understanding*, which, with submission, I think the worst, tends to establish this dangerous doctrine, that the human mind, previous to education and habit, is as susceptible of any one impression as of any other:—a doctrine which, if true, would go near to prove, that truth and virtue are no better than human contrivances, or at least, that they have nothing permanent in their nature, but may be as changeable as the inclinations and capacities of men." Dr. Beattie, however, candidly and judiciously adds, " Surely this is not the doctrine that Locke *meant* to establish; but his zeal against innate ideas, and innate principles, put him off his guard, and made him allow too little to instinct, for fear of allowing too much "

In this last remark, I perfectly agree with Dr. Beattie; although I am well aware, that a considerable number of Locke's English disciples have not only chosen to interpret the first book of his *Essay* in that very sense in which it appeared to Dr. Beattie to be of so mischievous a tendency, but have avowed Locke's doctrine, when thus interpreted, as their own ethical creed In this number, I am sorry to say, the respectable name of Paley must be included.[1]

It is fortunate for Locke's reputation, that, in other parts of his *Essay*, he has disavowed, in the most unequivocal terms, those dangerous conclusions which, it must be owned, the general strain of his first book has too much the appearance of favouring " He that hath the idea (he observes on one occasion) of an intelligent, but frail and weak being, made by and depending on another, who is omnipotent, perfectly wise, and good, will as certainly know, that man is to honour, fear, and obey God, as that the sun shines when he sees it; nor can he be surer, in a clear morning, that the sun is risen, if he will but

---

[1] See *Principles of Moral and Political Philosophy*, book i chap 5, where the author discusses the question concerning a *moral sense*

open his eyes, and turn them that way. But yet these truths being never so certain, never so clear, he may be ignorant of either, or all of them, who will never take the pains to employ his faculties as he should to inform himself about them." To the same purpose, he has elsewhere said, that " there is a *Law of Nature*, as intelligible to a *rational creature and studier of that law*, as the positive laws of commonwealths " Nay, he has himself, in the most explicit terms, anticipated and disclaimed those dangerous consequences which, it has been so often supposed, it was the chief scope of this introductory chapter to establish. " I would not be mistaken,—as if, because I deny an innate law, I thought there were none but positive laws. There is a great deal of difference between an innate law and a law of nature; between something imprinted on our minds in their very original, and something that we, being ignorant of, may attain to the knowledge of, by the use and due application of our natural faculties. And I think they equally forsake the truth, who, running into the contrary extremes, either affirm an innate law, or deny that there is a law knowable by the light of nature, without the help of a positive revelation "— (Vol i. p. 44.) Nor was Locke unaware of the influence on men's lives of their speculative tenets concerning these metaphysical and ethical questions. On this point, which can alone render such discussions interesting to human happiness, he has expressed himself thus: " Let that principle of some of the philosophers, that *all is matter, and that there is nothing else*, be received for certain and indubitable, and it will be easy to be seen, by the writings of some that have revived it again in our days, what consequences it will lead into. . . Nothing can be so dangerous as principles thus taken up without due questioning or examination; especially if they be such as influence men's lives, and give a bias to all their actions. He that with *Archelaus* shall lay it down as a principle, that right and wrong, honest and dishonest, are defined only by laws, and not by nature, will have other measures of moral rectitude and pravity, than those who take it for granted, that we are under obligations antecedent to all human constitutions."—(Vol. iii.

p. 75.) Is not the whole of this passage evidently pointed at the Epicurean maxims of Hobbes and of Gassendi?[1]

Lord Shaftesbury was one of the first who sounded the alarm against what he conceived to be the drift of that philosophy which denies the existence of *innate principles*. Various strictures on this subject occur in the *Characteristics;* particularly in the treatise entitled *Advice to an Author;* but the most direct of all his attacks upon Locke is to be found in his eighth Letter, addressed to a Student at the University. In this letter he observes, that "all those called *free writers* now-a-days have espoused those principles which Mr. Hobbes set afoot in this last age."—" Mr. Locke (he continues) as much as I honour him on account of other writings, (on Government, Policy, Trade, Coin, Education, Toleration, &c,) and as well as I knew him, and can answer for his sincerity as a most zealous Christian and believer, did however go in the self-same track; and is followed by the Tindals, and all the other free authors of our times!

" 'Twas Mr. Locke that struck the home blow: for Mr Hobbes's character, and base slavish principles of government took off the poison of his philosophy. 'Twas Mr. Locke that struck at all fundamentals, threw all *order and virtue* out of the world, and made the very ideas of these (which are the same with those of GOD) *unnatural*, and without foundation in our minds. *Innate* is a word he poorly plays upon: the right word, though less used, is *connatural*. For what has *birth* or progress of the fœtus out of the womb to do in this case?—the question is not about the *time* the ideas entered, or the moment that one body came out of the other; but whether the constitu-

---

[1] To the above quotations from Locke, the following deserves to be added: "Whilst the parties of men cram their tenets down all men's throats, whom they can get into their power, without permitting them to examine their truth or falsehood, and will not let truth have fair play in the world, nor men the liberty to search after it, what improvements can be expected of this kind? What greater light can be hoped for in the moral sciences? The subject part of mankind in most places might, instead thereof, with Egyptian bondage expect Egyptian darkness, *were not the candle of the Lord set up by himself in men's minds, which it is impossible for the breath or power of man wholly to extinguish.*"—Vol. II. pp 343, 344

tion of man be such, that, being adult and grown up,[1] at such a time, sooner or later (no matter when) the idea and sense of *order, administration,* and a GOD, will not infallibly, inevitably, necessarily spring up in him."

In this last remark Shaftesbury appears to me to place the question about *innate ideas* upon the right and only philosophical footing; and to afford a key to all the confusion running through Locke's argument against their existence. The sequel of the above quotation is not less just and valuable—but I must not indulge myself in any farther extracts. It is sufficient to mention the perfect coincidence between the opinion of Shaftesbury, as here stated by himself, and that formerly quoted in the words of Locke; and, of consequence, the injustice of concluding, from some unguarded expressions of the latter, that there was, at bottom, any essential difference between their real sentiments.[2]

---

[1] Lord Shaftesbury should have said, "grown up to the possession and exercise of his reasoning powers."

[2] I must, at the same time, again repeat, that the facts and reasonings contained in the introduction to Locke's *Essay,* go very far to account for the severity of Shaftesbury's censures on this part of his work. Sir Isaac Newton himself, an intimate friend of Locke's, appears, from a letter of his which I have read in his own handwriting, to have felt precisely in the same manner with the author of the *Characteristics.* Such, at least, were his *first* impressions; although he afterwards requested, with a humility and candour worthy of himself, the forgiveness of Locke, for this injustice done to his character. "I beg your pardon (says he) for representing that you struck at the root of morality in a principle you laid down in your book of ideas, and designed to pursue in another book, and that I took you for a Hobbist." In the same letter Newton alludes to certain unfounded suspicions which he had been led to entertain of the propriety of Locke's conduct in some of their private concerns adding, with an ingenuous and almost infantine simplicity, ' I was so much affected with this, that when one told me you was sickly and would not live, I answered, 'twere better if you were dead. I desire you to forgive me this uncharitableness." The letter is subscribed, *your most humble and most unfortunate servant, Is Newton.*

The rough draft of Mr. Locke's reply to these afflicting acknowledgments was kindly communicated to me by a friend some years ago. It is written with the magnanimity of a philosopher, and with the good-humoured forbearance of a man of the world; and it breathes throughout so tender and so unaffected a veneration for the good as well as great qualities of the excellent person to whom it is addressed, as de-

* It is dated *at the Bull in Shoreditch, London, September* 1693, and is addressed, *For John Locke, Esq., at Sir Fra Masham's, Bart, at Oates, in Essex.*

Under the title of Locke's *Metaphysical* (or, to speak with more strict precision, his *Logical*) writings, may also be classed his tracts on Education, and on the Conduct of the Understanding. These tracts are entirely of a practical nature, and were plainly intended for a wider circle of readers than his monstrates at once the conscious integrity of the writer, and the superiority of his mind to the irritation of little passions. I know of nothing from Locke's pen which does more honour to his temper and character, and I introduce it with peculiar satisfaction, in connexion with those strictures which truth has extorted from me on that part of his system which to the moralist stands most in need of explanation and apology.

MR. LOCKE TO MR NEWTON
"*Oaks, 5th October* 1693

"Sir,—I have been ever since I first knew you so kindly and sincerely your friend, and thought you so much mine, that I could not have believed what you tell me of yourself, had I had it from anybody else And though I cannot but be mightily troubled that you should have had so many wrong and unjust thoughts of me, yet, next to the return of good offices, such as from a sincere good will I have ever done you, I receive your acknowledgment of the contrary as the kindest thing you could have done me, since it gives me hopes I have not lost a friend I so much valued. After what your letter expresses, I shall not need to say anything to justify myself to you I shall always think your own reflection on my carriage both to you and all mankind will sufficiently do that Instead of that, give me leave to assure you, that I am more ready to forgive you than you can be to desire it; and I do it so freely and fully that I wish for nothing more than the opportunity to convince you that I truly love and esteem you; and that I have still the same good will for you as if nothing of this had happened. To confirm this to you more fully, I should be glad to meet you anywhere, and the rather, because the conclusion of your letter makes me apprehend it would not be wholly useless to you. I shall always be ready to serve you to my utmost, in any way you shall like, and shall only need your commands or permission to do it.

"My book is going to press for a second edition, and, though I can answer for the design with which I writ it, yet, since you have so opportunely given me notice of what you have said of it, I should take it as a favour if you would point out to me the places that gave occasion to that censure, that, by explaining myself better, I may avoid being mistaken by others, or unwillingly doing the least prejudice to truth or virtue I am sure you are so much a friend to both, that, were you none to me, I could expect this from you. But I cannot doubt but you would do a great deal more than this for my sake, who, after all, have all the concern of a friend for you, wish you extremely well, and am, without compliment," &c &c

(For the preservation of this precious memorial of Mr Locke, the public is indebted to the descendants of his friend and relation the Lord Chancellor King, to whom his papers and library were bequeathed The original is still in the possession of the present representative of that noble family, for whose flattering permission to enrich my Dissertation with the above extracts, I feel the more grateful, as I have not the honour of being personally known to his Lordship)

Essay; but they everywhere bear the strongest marks of the same zeal for extending the empire of Truth and of Reason, and may be justly regarded as parts of the same great design.[1] It has been often remarked, that they display less originality than might have been expected from so bold and powerful a thinker; and, accordingly, both of them have long fallen into very general neglect. It ought, however, to be remembered, that, on the most important points discussed in them, new suggestions are not now to be looked for; and that the great object of the reader should be, not to learn something which he never heard of before, but to learn, among the multiplicity of discordant precepts current in the world, *which* of them were sanctioned, and *which* reprobated by the judgment of Locke. The candid and unreserved thoughts of such a writer upon such subjects as Education, and the culture of the intellectual powers, possess an intrinsic value, which is not diminished by the consideration of their triteness They not only serve to illustrate the peculiarities of the author's own character and views, but, considered in a practical light, come recommended to us by all the additional weight of his discriminating experience In this point of view, the two tracts in question, but more especially that on the *Conduct of the Understanding*, will always continue to be interesting manuals to such as are qualified to appreciate the mind from which they proceeded.[2]

[1] Mr Locke, it would appear, had once intended to publish his thoughts on the Conduct of the Understanding, as an additional chapter to his Essay. " I have lately," says he, in a letter to Mr. Molyneux, " got a little leisure to think of some additions to my book against the next edition, and within these few days have fallen upon a subject that I know not how far it will lead me I have written several pages on it, but the matter, the farther I go, opens the more upon me, and I cannot get sight of any end of it. The title of the chapter will be, *Of the Conduct of the Understanding*, which, if I shall pursue as far as I imagine it will reach, and as it deserves, will, I conclude, make the largest chapter of my Essay." —Locke's *Works*, vol IX p. 407

[2] A similar remark may be extended to a letter from Locke to his friend Mr. Samuel Bold, who had complained to him of the disadvantages he laboured under from a weakness of memory. It contains nothing but what might have come from the pen of one of Newberry's authors, but with what additional interest do we read it, when considered as a comment by Locke on a suggestion of Bacon's '—Locke's *Works*, vol x p 317.

It is a judicious reflection of Shenstone's, that " every single observation

It must not, however, be concluded from the *apparent* triteness of some of Locke's remarks, to the present generation of readers, that they were viewed in the same light by his own contemporaries. On the contrary, Leibnitz speaks of the *Treatise on Education* as a work of still greater merit than the *Essay on Human Understanding*.[1] Nor will this judgment be wondered at by those who, abstracting from the habits of thinking in which they have been reared, transport themselves in imagination to the state of Europe a hundred years ago. How flat and nugatory seem now the cautions to parents about watching over those associations on which the dread of spirits in the dark is founded! But how different was the case (even in Protestant countries) till a very recent period of the last century!

I have, on a former occasion, taken notice of the slow but (since the invention of printing) certain steps by which Truth makes its way in the world: "The discoveries which, in one age, are confined to the studious and enlightened few, becoming, in the next, the established creed of the learned, and, in the third, forming part of the elementary principles of education." The harmony, in the meantime, which exists among truths of all descriptions, tends perpetually, by blending them into one common mass, to increase the joint influence of the whole; the contributions of individuals to this mass (to borrow the fine allusion of Middleton) "resembling the drops of rain, which, falling separately into the water, mingle at once with the stream, and strengthen the general current." Hence the ambition, so natural to weak minds, to distinguish themselves by paradoxical and extravagant opinions; for *these*, having no chance to incorporate themselves with the progressive reason of the species, are

published by a man of genius, be it ever so trivial, should be esteemed of importance, because he speaks from his own impressions; whereas common men publish common things, which they have perhaps *gleaned* from frivolous writers. I know of few authors to whom this observation applies more forcibly and happily than to Locke, when he touches on the culture of the intellectual powers. His precepts, indeed, are not all equally sound; but they, in general, contain a large proportion of truth, and may always furnish to a speculative mind matter of useful meditation.

[1] Leib. *Op.* tom vi. p 226

the more likely to immortalize the eccentricity of their authors, and to furnish subjects of wonder to the common compilers of literary history. This ambition is the more general, as so little expense of genius is necessary for its gratification. "Truth (as Mr. Hume has well observed) is *one thing*, but errors are numberless;" and hence (he might have added) the difficulty of seizing the former, and the facility of swelling the number of the latter.[1]

Having said so much in illustration of Locke's philosophical merits, and in reply to the common charge against his metaphysical and ethical principles, it now only remains for me to take notice of one or two defects in his intellectual character, which exhibit a strong contrast to the general vigour of his mental powers

Among these defects, the most prominent is, the facility with which he listens to historical evidence, when it happens to favour his own conclusions. Many remarkable instances of this occur in his long and rambling argument (somewhat in the style of Montaigne) against the existence of *innate practical principles;* to which may be added, the degree of credit he appears to have given to the popular tales about mermaids, and to Sir William Temple's idle story of Prince Maurice's "rational and intelligent parrot." Strange! that the same person who, in matters of reasoning, had divested himself, almost to a fault, of all reverence for the opinions of others, should have failed to perceive, that, of all the various sources of error, one of the most copious and fatal is an unreflecting faith in human testimony!

---

[1] Descartes has struck into nearly the same train of thinking with the above, but his remarks apply much better to the writings of Locke than to his own

"L'expérience m'apprit, que quoique mes opinions surprennent d'abord, parce qu'elles sont fort différentes des vulgaires, cependant, après qu'on les a comprises on les trouve si simples et si conformes au sens commun, qu'on cesse entièrement de les admirer, et par la même d'en faire cas: parceque tel est le naturel des hommes qu'ils n'estiment que les choses qui leur laissent d'admiration et qu'ils ne possèdent pas tout-à-fait. C'est ainsi que quoique la santé soit le plus grand de tous les biens qui concernent le corps, c'est pourtant celui auquel nous faisons le moins de réflexion, et que nous goutons le moins Or, la connoissance de la vérité est comme la santé de l'âme, lorsque on la possède on n'y pense plus"—*Lettres*, tome i Lettre xliii.

The disrespect of Locke for the wisdom of antiquity, is another prejudice which has frequently given a wrong bias to his judgment. The idolatry in which the Greek and Roman writers were held by his immediate predecessors, although it may help to account for this weakness, cannot altogether excuse it in a man of so strong and enlarged an understanding. Locke, as we are told by Dr Warton, "*affected* to depreciate the ancients; which circumstance, (he adds,) as I am informed from undoubted authority, was the source of perpetual discontent and dispute betwixt him and his pupil, Lord Shaftesbury; who, in many parts of the *Characteristics*, has ridiculed Locke's philosophy, and endeavoured to represent him as a disciple of Hobbes." To those who are aware of the direct opposition between the principles of Hobbes, of Montaigne, of Gassendi, and of the other *minute philosophers* with whom Locke sometimes seems unconsciously to unite his strength,—and the principles of Socrates, of Plato, of Cicero, and of all the soundest moralists, both of ancient and of modern times, the foregoing anecdote will serve at once to explain and to palliate the acrimony of some of Shaftesbury's strictures on Locke's Ethical paradoxes.[1]

With this disposition of Locke to depreciate the ancients, was intimately connected that contempt which he everywhere expresses for the study of Eloquence, and that perversion of taste which led him to consider Blackmore as one of the first of our English poets.[2] That his own imagination was neither sterile nor torpid, appears sufficiently from the agreeable colouring and animation which it has not unfrequently imparted to his style: but *this* power of the mind he seems to have regarded with a peculiarly jealous and unfriendly eye; confining his view exclusively to its occasional effects in misleading the judgment, and overlooking altogether the important purposes

[1] Plebeii Philosophi (says Cicero) qui a Platone et Socrate, et ab ea familia dissident.

[2] "All our English poets, except Milton," says Molyneux in a letter to Locke, 'have been mere ballad makers in comparison to Sir Richard Blackmore." In reply to which Locke says, "There is, I with pleasure find, a strange harmony throughout between your thoughts and mine."—*Locke's Works*, vol. ix. pp. 423, 426.

to which it is subservient, both in our intellectual and moral frame Hence, in all his writings, an inattention to those more attractive aspects of the mind, the study of which, as Burke has well observed, "while it communicates to the taste a sort of philosophical solidity, may be expected to reflect back on the severer sciences some of those graces and elegancies, without which the greatest proficiency in these sciences will always have the appearance of something illiberal."

To a certain hardness of character, not unfrequently united with an insensibility to the charms of poetry and of eloquence, may partly be ascribed the severe and forbidding spirit which has suggested some of the maxims in his *Tract on Education*[1] He had been treated himself, it would appear, with very little indulgence by his parents; and probably was led by that filial veneration which he always expressed for their memory, to ascribe to the early habits of self-denial imposed on him by their ascetic system of ethics, the existence of those moral qualities which he owed to the regulating influence of his own reason in fostering his natural dispositions; and which, under a gentler and more skilful culture, might have assumed a still more engaging and amiable form. His father, who had served in the Parliament's army, seems to have retained through life that austerity of manners which characterized his puritanical associates; and, notwithstanding the comparative enlargement and cultivation of Mr. Locke's mind, something of this hereditary leaven, if I am not mistaken, continued to operate upon many of his opinions and habits of thinking. If, in the *Conduct of the Understanding*, he trusted (as many have thought) too much to nature, and laid too little stress on logical rules, he certainly fell into the opposite extreme in everything connected with the culture of the heart; distrusting nature altogether, and placing his sole confidence in the effects of a systematical and vigilant discipline. That the great object of education is

---

[1] Such, for example, as this, that "a child should never be suffered to have what he craves, or *so much as speaks for*, much less if he cries for it!" A maxim (as his correspondent Molyneux observes) "which seems to bear hard on the tender spirits of children, and the natural affections of parents "—Locke's *Works*, vol ix p 319

not to thwart and disturb, but to study the aim, and to facilitate the accomplishment of her beneficial arrangements, is a maxim, one should think, obvious to common sense; and yet it is only of late years that it has begun to gain ground even among philosophers. It is but justice to Rousseau to acknowledge, that the zeal and eloquence with which he has enforced it, go far to compensate the mischievous tendency of some of his other doctrines.[1]

To the same causes it was probably owing, that Locke has availed himself so little in his *Conduct of the Understanding*, of his own favourite doctrine of the Association of Ideas. He has been, indeed, at sufficient pains to warn parents and guardians of the mischievous consequences to be apprehended from this part of our constitution, if not diligently watched over in our infant years But he seems to have altogether overlooked the positive and immense resources which might be derived from it, in the culture and amelioration, both of our intellectual and moral powers;—in strengthening, (for instance,) by early *habits* of right thinking, the authority of reason and of conscience;—in blending with our best feelings the congenial and ennobling sympathies of taste and of fancy;—and in identifying, with the first workings of the imagination, those pleasing views of the order of the universe, which are so essentially necessary to human happiness. A law of our nature, so mighty and so extensive in its influence, was surely not given to man in vain; and the fatal *purchase* which it has, in all ages, afforded to Machiavellian statesmen, and to political religionists, in carrying into effect their joint conspiracy against the improvement and welfare of our species, is the most decisive

---

[1] [* The most exceptionable part of the Treatise in question is, in my opinion, that which relates to the management of the temper and dispositions of children On this subject Locke seems to have written more from theory than from actual observation; nor, indeed, did the circumstances of his life enable him to do otherwise His remarks on the treatment of youth in their approach to manhood are of far greater value. They discover much knowledge of the world, as well as of human nature, and are totally uninfected with that spirit of false refinement by which so many of our later writers on education have been misled]

* Restored.—*Ed*

proof of the manifold uses to which it might be turned in the hands of instructors, well disposed and well qualified humbly to co-operate with the obvious and unerring purposes of Divine Wisdom.

A more convenient opportunity will afterwards occur for taking some notice of Locke's writings on Money and Trade, and on the Principles of Government. They appear to me to connect less naturally and closely with the literary history of the times when they appeared, than with the systematical views which were opened on the same subjects about fifty years afterwards, by some speculative politicians in France and in England. I shall, therefore, delay any remarks on them which I have to offer, till we arrive at the period when the questions to which they relate began everywhere to attract the attention of the learned world, and to be discussed on those general principles of expediency and equity, which form the basis of the modern science of Political Economy. With respect to his merits as a logical and metaphysical reformer, enough has been already said for this introductory section: but I shall have occasion, more than once, to recur to them in the following pages, when I come to review those later theories, of which the germs or rudiments may be distinctly traced in his works; and of which he is, therefore, entitled to divide the praise with such of his successors as have reared to maturity the prolific seeds scattered by his hand.[1]

---

[1] And yet with what modesty does Locke speak of his own pretensions as a Philosopher! "In an age that produces such masters as the great Huygenius and the incomparable Mr Newton, it is ambition enough to be employed as an under-labourer in clearing the ground a little, and removing some of the rubbish that lies in the way to knowledge."—*Essay on Human Understanding*. *Epistle to the Reader* See Note Z

SECT. II.—CONTINUATION OF THE REVIEW OF LOCKE
AND LEIBNITZ.

LEIBNITZ.

INDEPENDENTLY of the pre-eminent rank which the versatile talents and the universal learning of Leibnitz entitle him to hold among the illustrious men who adorned the Continent of Europe during the eighteenth century, there are other considerations which have determined me to unite his name with that of Locke, in fixing the commencement of the period, on the history of which I am now to enter. The school of which he was the founder was strongly discriminated from that of Locke by the general spirit of its doctrines; and to this school a large proportion of the metaphysicians, and also of the mathematicians of Germany, Holland, France, and Italy, have ever since his time had a decided leaning. On the fundamental question, indeed, concerning the *Origin of our Knowledge*, the philosophers of the Continent (with the exception of the Germans, and a few eminent individuals in other countries) have in general sided with Locke, or rather with Gassendi; but in most other instances, a partiality for the opinions, and a deference for the authority of Leibnitz, may be traced in their speculations, both on metaphysical and physical subjects. Hence a striking contrast between the characteristical features of the continental philosophy and those of the contemporary systems which have succeeded each other in our own island; the great proportion of our most noted writers, notwithstanding the opposition of their sentiments on particular points, having either attached themselves, or professed to attach themselves, to the method of inquiry recommended and exemplified by Locke.

But the circumstance which chiefly induced me to assign to Leibnitz so prominent a place in this historical sketch, is the extraordinary influence of his industry and zeal in uniting, by a mutual communication of intellectual lights and of moral sympathies, the most powerful and leading minds scattered over Christendom. Some preliminary steps towards such an union had been already taken by Wallis in England, and by Mersenne in France; but the *literary commerce*, of which they were the centres, was confined almost exclusively to Mathematics and to Physics; while the comprehensive correspondence of Leibnitz extended alike to every pursuit interesting to man, either as a speculative or as an active being. From this time forward, accordingly, the history of philosophy involves, in a far greater degree than at any former period, the general history of the human mind; and we shall find, in our attempts to trace its farther progress, our attention more and more irresistibly withdrawn from local details to more enlarged views of the globe which we inhabit. A striking change in this literary commerce among nations took place, at least in the western parts of Europe, before the death of Leibnitz; but during the remainder of the last century, it continued to proceed with an accelerated rapidity over the whole face of the civilized world. A multitude of causes, undoubtedly, conspired to produce it; but I know of no individual whose name is better entitled than that of Leibnitz to mark the era of its commencement.[1]

I have already, in treating of the philosophy of Locke, said enough, and perhaps more than enough, of the opinion of Leibnitz concerning the origin of our knowledge. Although expressed in a different phraseology, it agrees in the most essential points with the *innate ideas* of the Cartesians; but it approaches still more nearly to some of the mystical speculations of Plato. The very exact coincidence between the language of Leibnitz on this question, and that of his contemporary Cudworth, whose mind, like his own, was deeply tinctured with the Platonic

---

[1] The following maxims of Leibnitz deserve the serious attention of all who have at heart the improvement of mankind.—

' "On trouve dans le monde plusieurs personnes bien intentionnées; mais le mal est, qu'elles ne s'entendent point, et ne travaillent point de concert. S'il y avoit moyen de trouver une espèce de glu pour les réunir, on feroit quelque chose Le mal est souvent que les gens de bien ont quelques caprices ou opinions particulières, qui font qu'ils sont contraires entr' eux. . . . L'esprit sectaire consiste proprement dans cette prétention de vouloir que les autres se règlent sur nos maximes, au lieu qu'on se devroit contenter de voir qu'on aille au but principal."—Leib *Op.* tom i. p 740

Metaphysics, is not unworthy of notice here, as an historical fact; and it is the only remark on this part of his system which I mean to add at present to those in the preceding history.

"The *seeds* of our acquired knowledge," says Leibnitz, "or, in other words, our *ideas*, and the eternal truths which are derived from them, are contained in the mind itself; nor is this wonderful, since we know by our own consciousness that we possess within ourselves the ideas of *existence*, of *unity*, of *substance*, of *action*, and other ideas of a similar nature." To the same purpose, we are told by Cudworth, that "the mind contains in itself virtually (as the future plant or tree is contained in the *seed*) general notions of all things, which unfold and discover themselves as occasions invite, and proper circumstances occur."

The metaphysical theories, to the establishment of which Leibnitz chiefly directed the force of his genius, are the doctrine of *Pre-established Harmony*, and the scheme of *Optimism*, as new modelled by himself. On neither of these heads will it be necessary for me long to detain my readers.

1. According to the system of *Pre-established Harmony*, the human mind and human body are two independent but constantly correspondent machines;—adjusted to each other like two unconnected clocks, so constructed that, at the same instant, the one should *point* the hour, and the other *strike* it. Of this system the following summary and illustration are given by Leibnitz himself, in his Essay entitled *Theodicæa* :—

"I cannot help coming into this notion, that God created the *soul* in such manner at first, that it should *represent* within itself all the simultaneous changes in the body; and that he has made the body also in such manner, as that it must of itself do what the soul wills:—So that the laws which make the thoughts of the soul follow each other in regular succession, *must* produce *images* which shall be coincident with the impressions made by external objects upon our organs of sense; while the laws by which the motions of the body follow each other are likewise so coincident with the thoughts of the soul, as to give to our *volitions* and *actions* the very same appearance, as if the latter were really the natural and the necessary consequences of the former."—(Leib. *Op.* i. p. 163.) Upon another occasion he observes, that "everything goes on in the soul as if it had no body, and that everything goes on in the body as if it had no soul."—*Ibid.* ii. p. 44.

To convey his meaning still more fully, Leibnitz borrows from Mr Jaquelot[1] a comparison, which, whatever may be thought of its justness, must be at least allowed some merit in point of ingenuity. "Suppose that an intelligent and powerful being, who knew beforehand every particular thing that I should order my footman to do to-morrow, should make a machine to resemble my footman exactly, and punctually to perform, all day, whatever I directed. On this supposition, would not *my will* in issuing all the details of my orders remain, in every respect, in the same circumstances as before? And would not my machine-footman, in performing his different movements, have the appearance of acting only in obedience to my commands?" The inference to be drawn from this comparison is, that the movements of my body have no direct dependence whatever on the volitions of my mind, any more than the actions of my machine-footman would have on the words issuing from my lips. The same inference is to be extended to the relation which the *impressions* made on my different senses bear to the co-existent perceptions arising in my mind. The impressions and perceptions have no mutual *connexion*, resembling that of physical causes with their effects; but the one series of events is made to correspond invariably with the other, in consequence of an eternal *harmony* between them *pre-established* by their common Creator.

From this outline of the scheme of *Pre-established Harmony*, it is manifest that it took its rise from the very same train of thinking which produced Malebranche's doctrine of *Occasional Causes.* The authors of both theories saw clearly the impossibility of tracing the mode in which mind acts on body, or body on mind; and hence were led rashly to conclude, that the

[1] Author of a book entitled *Conformité de la Foi avec la Raison*

connexion or *union* which seems to exist between them is not real, but apparent. The inferences, however, which they drew from this common principle were directly opposite; Malebranche maintaining that the communication between mind and body was carried on by the immediate and incessant agency of the Deity; while Leibnitz conceived that the agency of God was employed only in the original contrivance and mutual adjustment of the two machines,—all the subsequent phenomena of each being the necessary results of its own independent mechanism, and, at the same time, the progressive evolutions of a comprehensive design, harmonizing the laws of the one with those of the other.

Of these two opposite hypotheses, that of Leibnitz is by far the more unphilosophical and untenable. The chief objection to the doctrine of *occasional causes* is, that it presumes to decide upon a question of which human reason is altogether incompetent to judge;—our ignorance of the mode in which matter acts upon mind, or mind upon matter, furnishing not the shadow of a proof that the one may not act directly and immediately on the other, in some way incomprehensible by our faculties.[1] But

---

[1] The mutual action, or (as it was called in the schools) the mutual *influence* (*influxus*) of soul and body, was, till the time of Descartes, the prevailing hypothesis, both among the learned and the vulgar. The reality of this *influx*, if not positively denied by Descartes, was at least mentioned by him as a subject of doubt, but by Malebranche and Leibnitz it was confidently rejected as absurd and impossible (See their works *passim*) Gravesande, who had a very strong leaning towards the doctrines of Leibnitz, had yet the good sense to perceive the inconclusiveness of his reasoning in this particular instance, and states in opposition to it the following sound and decisive remarks —"Non concipio, quomodo mens in corpus agere possit, non etiam video quomodo ex motu nervi perceptio sequatur; non tamen inde sequi mihi apparet, omnem *influxum* esse rejiciendum

"Substantiæ incognitæ sunt Jam videmus naturam mentis nos latere, scimus hanc esse aliquid, quod ideas habet, has confert, &c. sed ignoramus quid sit subjectum, cui hæ proprietates conveniant

"Hoc idem de corpore dicimus, est extensum, impenetrabile, &c sed quid est quod habet hasce proprietates? Nulla nobis via aperta est, qua ad hanc cognitionem pervenire possimus

"Inde concludimus, multa nos latere, quæ proprietates mentis et corporis spectant

"Invicta demonstratione constat, non mentem in corpus, neque hoc in illam agere, ut corpus in corpus agit, sed mihi non videtur inde concludi posse, omnem *influxum* esse impossibilem

the doctrine of *Pre-established Harmony*, besides being equally liable to this objection, labours under the additional disadvantage of involving a perplexed and totally inconsistent conception of the nature of *Mechanism;* an inconsistency, by the way, with which all those philosophers are justly chargeable who imagine that, by likening the universe to a machine, they get rid of the necessity of admitting the constant agency of powers essentially different from the known qualities of matter. The word *Mechanism* properly expresses a combination of natural powers to produce a certain effect. When such a combination is successful, a machine, once set a-going, will sometimes continue to perform its office for a considerable time, without requiring the interposition of the artist: and hence we are led to conclude, that the case may perhaps be similar with respect to the universe, when once put into motion by the Deity. This idea Leibnitz carried so far as to exclude the supposition of any

"Motu suo corpus non agit in aliud corpus, sine resistente, sed an non actio, omnino diversa, et cujus ideam non habemus, in aliam substantiam dari possit, et ita tamen, ut causa effectui respondeat, in re adeo obscura, determinare non ausim Difficile certe est influxum negare, quando exacte perpendimus, quomodo in minimis quæ mens percipit, relatio detur cum agitationibus in corpore, et quomodo hujus motus cum mentis determinationibus conveniant Attendo ad illa quæ medici, et anatomici, nos de his docent.

"Nihil, ergo, de systemate *influxus* determino, præter hoc, mihi nondum hujus impossibilitatem satis clare demonstratam esse videri."—*Introductio ad Philosophiam* See Note A A·

With respect to the *manner* in which the intercourse between Mind and Matter is carried on, a very rash assertion escaped Mr Locke in the first edition of his *Essay* "The next thing to be considered is, how bodies produce ideas in us, *and that is manifestly by impulse, the only way which we can conceive*

bodies *operate in*."—*Essay*, B ii ch viii. § 11.

In the course of Locke's controversial discussions with the Bishop of Worcester, he afterwards became fully sensible of this important oversight, and he had the candour to acknowledge his error in the following terms :—"'Tis true, I have said that bodies operate by impulse, and nothing else And so I thought when I writ it, and can yet conceive no other way of their operations But I am since convinced, by the judicious Mr. Newton's incomparable book, that it is too bold a presumption to limit God's power in this point by my narrow conceptions . . And, therefore, in the next edition of my book, I will take care to have that passage rectified"

It is a circumstance that can only be accounted for by the variety of Mr Locke's other pursuits, that in all the later editions of the *Essay* which have fallen in my way, the proposition in question has been allowed to remain as it originally stood

subsequent agency in the first contriver and mover, excepting in the case of a miracle. But the falseness of the analogy appears from this, that the moving force in every machine is some *natural power*, such as gravity or elasticity; and, consequently, the very idea of mechanism assumes the existence of those active powers, of which it is the professed object of a mechanical theory of the universe to give an explanation. Whether, therefore, with Malebranche, we resolve every effect into the immediate agency of God, or suppose, with the great majority of Newtonians, that he employs the instrumentality of second causes to accomplish his purposes, we are equally forced to admit with Bacon, the necessity not only of a first contriver and mover, but of his constant and efficient concurrence (either immediately or mediately) in carrying his design into execution:—"*Opus* (says Bacon) *quod operatur Deus a primordio usque ad finem.*"

In what I have now said I have confined myself to the idea of *Mechanism* as it applies to the material universe; for, as to this word, when applied by Leibnitz to the mind, which he calls a *Spiritual Automaton*, I confess myself quite unable to annex a meaning to it; I shall not, therefore, offer any remarks on this part of his system.[1]

To these visionary speculations of Leibnitz, a strong and instructive contrast is exhibited in the philosophy of Locke; a philosophy, the main object of which is less to enlarge our knowledge, than to make us sensible of our ignorance, or (as the author himself expresses it) "to prevail with the busy mind of man to be cautious in meddling with things exceeding its comprehension; to stop when it is at the utmost extent of

---

[1] Absurd as the hypothesis of a *Pre-established Harmony* may now appear, not many years have elapsed since it was the prevailing, or rather universal creed, among the philosophers of Germany. "Il fut un temps" (says the celebrated Euler) "où le système de l'harmonie préétablie étoit tellement en vogue dans toute l'Allemagne, que ceux qui en doutoient, passoient pour des ignorans, ou des esprits bornés"—(*Lettres de M. Euler à une Princesse d'Allemagne*, 83me Lettre.) It would be amusing to reckon up the succession of metaphysical creeds which have been since swallowed with the same implicit faith by this learned and speculative, and (in all those branches of knowledge where imagination has no influence over the judgment) profound and inventive nation

its tether; and to sit down in a quiet ignorance of those things which, upon examination, are found to be beyond the reach of our capacities" .... " My right hand writes," says Locke, in another part of his *Essay*, " whilst my left hand is still. What causes rest in one, and motion in the other ? Nothing but my will, a thought of my mind; my thought only changing, my right hand rests, and the left hand moves. *This is matter of fact which cannot be denied.* Explain this and make it intelligible, and then the next step will be to understand Creation.

. In the meantime, it is an overvaluing ourselves, to reduce all to the narrow measure of our capacities, and to conclude all things impossible to be done, whose manner of doing exceeds our comprehension . . . If you do not understand the operations of your own finite Mind, that thinking thing within you, do not deem it strange that you cannot comprehend the operations of that eternal infinite Mind, who made and governs all things, and whom the heaven of heavens cannot contain."[1]—Vol. ii. pp. 249, 250.

This contrast between the philosophical characters of Locke and of Leibnitz is the more deserving of notice, as something of the same sort has ever since continued to mark and to discriminate the metaphysical researches of the English and of the German schools Various exceptions to this remark may, no doubt, be mentioned; but these exceptions will be found of trifling moment, when compared with the indisputable extent of its general application.

The theory of pre-established harmony led, by a natural and

---

[1] That this is a fair representation of the scope of Locke's philosophy, according to the author's own view of it, is demonstrated by the two mottos prefixed to the *Essay on Human Understanding*. The one is a passage of the book of *Ecclesiastes*, which, from the place it occupies in the front of his work, may be presumed to express what he himself regarded as the most important moral to be drawn from his speculations "As thou knowest not what is the way of the spirit, nor how the bones do grow in the womb of her that is with child, even so, thou knowest not the works of God, who maketh all things." The other motto (from Cicero) strongly expresses a sentiment which every competent judge must feel on comparing the above quotations from Locke, with the *monads* and the *pre-established harmony* of Leibnitz " Quam bellum est velle confiteri potius nescire quod nescias, quam ista effutientem nauseare, atque ipsum sibi displicere!" See Note B B

obvious transition, to the scheme of Optimism. As it represented all events, both in the physical and moral worlds, as the necessary effects of a mechanism originally contrived and set a-going by the Deity, it reduced its author to the alternative of either calling in question the Divine power, wisdom, and goodness, or of asserting that the universe which he had called into being was the best of all possible systems. This last opinion, accordingly, was eagerly embraced by Leibnitz; and forms the subject of a work entitled *Theodicæa*, in which are combined together, in an extraordinary degree, the acuteness of the logician, the imagination of the poet, and the impenetrable, yet sublime darkness, of the metaphysical theologian.[1]

The modification of Optimism, however, adopted by Leibnitz, was, in some essential respects, peculiar to himself. It differed from that of Plato, and of some other sages of antiquity, in considering the human mind in the light of *a spiritual machine*, and, of consequence, in positively denying the freedom of human actions. According to Plato, every thing is right, so far as it is the work of God,—the creation of beings endowed with free will, and consequently liable to moral delinquency—and the government of the world by general laws, from which occasional evils *must* result,—furnishing no objection to the perfection of the universe, to which a satisfactory reply may not be found in the partial and narrow views of it, to which our faculties are at present confined. But he held, at the same time, that, although the permission of moral evil does not detract from the goodness of God, it is nevertheless imputable to man as a fault, and renders him justly obnoxious to punishment. This system (under a variety of forms) has been in all ages maintained by the wisest and best philosophers, who, while they were anxious to vindicate the perfections of God,

---

[1] " La Théodicée seule (says Fontenelle) suffiroit pour représenter M Leibnitz Une lecture immense, des anecdotes curieuses sur les livres ou les personnes, beaucoup d'équité et même de faveur pour tous les auteurs cités, fût-ce en les combattant, des vues sublimes et lumineuses, des raisonnemens au fond desquels on sent toujours l'esprit géométrique, un style où la force domine, et où cependant sont admis les agrémens d'une imagination heureuse "
—*Eloge de Leibnitz.*

saw the importance of stating their doctrine in a manner not inconsistent with man's free will and moral agency.

The scheme of Optimism, on the contrary, as proposed by Leibnitz, is completely subversive of these cardinal truths. It was, indeed, viewed by the great and excellent author in a very different light; but in the judgment of the most impartial and profound inquirers, it leads, by a short and demonstrative process, to the annihilation of all moral distinctions.[1]

---

[1] It is observed by Dr. Akenside, that "the Theory of Optimism has been delivered of late, especially abroad, in a manner which subverts the freedom of human actions; whereas Plato appears very careful to preserve it, and has been in that respect imitated by the best of his followers."—Notes on the 2d Book of the *Pleasures of the Imagination.*

I am perfectly aware, at the same time, that different opinions have been entertained of Plato's real sentiments on this subject, and I readily grant that passages with respect to Fate and Necessity may be collected from his works, which it would be very difficult to reconcile with any one consistent scheme —See the notes of Mosheim on his Latin Version of Cudworth's *Intellectual System,* tom i pp 10, 310, et seq. Lugd Batav. 1773.

Without entering at all into this question, I may be permitted here to avail myself, for the sake of conciseness, of Plato's name, to distinguish that modification of optimism which I have opposed in the text to the optimism of Leibnitz The following sentence, in the 10th Book *De Republica,* seems sufficient of itself to authorize this liberty : —'Ἀρετὴ δὲ ἀδέσποτον, ἣν τιμῶν καὶ ἀτιμάζων, πλέον καὶ ἔλαττον αὐτῆς ἕκαστος ἕξει. αἰτία ἑλομένου Θεὸς ἀναίτιος Virtus inviolabilis ac libera quam prout honorabit quis aut negliget, ita plus aut minus ex ea possidebit Eligentis qui-

dem culpa est omnis Deus vero extra culpam

A short abstract of the allegory with which Leibnitz concludes his *Theodicæa,* will convey a clearer idea of the scope of that work, than I could hope to do by any metaphysical comment The groundwork of this allegory is taken from a dialogue on Free-Will, written by Laurentius Valla, in opposition to Boethius ;—in which dialogue, Sextus, the son of Tarquin the Proud, is introduced as consulting Apollo about his destiny. Apollo predicts to him that he is to violate Lucretia, and afterwards, with his family, to be expelled from Rome (*Exul inopsque cades irata pulsus ub urbe*) Sextus complains of the prediction Apollo replies, that the fault is not his, that he has only the gift of seeing into futurity,* that all things are regulated by Jupiter; and that it is to him his complaint should be addressed (*Here finishes the allegory of Valla, which Leibnitz thus continues, agreeably to his own principles*) In consequence of the advice of the Oracle, Sextus goes to Dodona to complain to Jupiter of the crime which he is destined to perpetrate "Why, (says he,) O Jupiter! have you made me wicked and miserable? Either change my lot and my will, or admit that the fault is yours, not mine." Jupiter replies to him "Renounce all thoughts of Rome and of the crown, be wise, and

---

* "Futura novi, non facio"

It is of great importance to attend to the distinction between these two systems; because it has, of late, become customary among sceptical writers, to confound them studiously together, in order to extend to both that ridicule to which the latter is justly entitled. This, in particular, was the case with Voltaire, who, in many parts of his later works, and more especially in his *Candide*, has, under the pretence of exposing the extravagances of Leibnitz, indulged his satirical raillery against the order of the universe. The success of his attempt was much aided by the confused and inaccurate manner in which the scheme of optimism had been recently stated by various writers, who, in their zeal to "vindicate the ways of God," had been led to hazard principles more dangerous in their consequences, than the prejudices and errors which it was their aim to correct.[1]

you shall be happy. If you return to Rome you are undone." Sextus, unwilling to submit to such a sacrifice, quits the Temple, and abandons himself to his fate.

After his departure, the high priest, Theodorus, asks Jupiter why he had not given another *Will* to Sextus. Jupiter sends Theodorus to Athens to consult Minerva. The goddess shows him the Palace of the Destinies, where are representations of all possible worlds,[*] each of them containing a Sextus Tarquinius with a different *Will*, leading to a catastrophe more or less happy. In the last and best of these worlds, forming the summit of the pyramid composed by the others, the high priest sees Sextus go to Rome, throw every thing into confusion, and violate the wife of his friend. "You see" (says the Goddess of Wisdom) "it was not my father that made Sextus wicked. He was wicked from all eternity, and he was always so in consequence of his own will.[†] Jupiter has only bestowed on him that existence which he could not refuse him in the best of all possible worlds. He only transferred him from the region of *possible* to that of *actual* beings. What great events does the crime of Sextus draw after it? The liberty of Rome—the rise of a government fertile in civil and military virtues, and of an empire destined to conquer and to civilize the earth." Theodorus returns thanks to the goddess, and acknowledges the justice of Jupiter.

[1] Among this number must be included the author of the *Essay on Man*, who, from a want of precision in his metaphysical ideas, has unconsciously fallen into various expressions, equally inconsistent with each other and with his own avowed opinions.

If plagues and earthquakes break not Heaven's design,
Why then a Borgia or a Catiline?—
Who knows but He whose hand the lightning forms,

[*] *World* (it must be remembered) is here synonymous with *Universe*.

[†] "Vides Sextum a Patre meo non fuisse factum improbum, talis quippe ab omni æternitate fuit, et quidem semper libere, existere tantum ei concessit Jupiter, quod ipsum profecto ejus sapientia mundo, in quo ille continebatur, denegare non poterat ergo Sextum e regione possibilium ad rerum existentium classem transtulit."

The zeal of Leibnitz in propagating the dogma of Necessity, is not easily reconcilable with the hostility which, as I have already remarked, he uniformly displays against the congenial doctrine of Materialism. Such, however, is the fact, and I believe it to be quite unprecedented in the previous history of philosophy Spinoza himself has not pushed the argument for necessity further than Leibnitz,—the reasonings of both concluding not less forcibly against the free-will of God than against the free-will of man, and, of consequence, terminating ultimately in *this* proposition, that no event in the universe could possibly have been different from what has actually taken

Who heaves old Ocean, and who wings the storms,
Pours fierce ambition on a Cæsar's mind,
Or turns young Ammon loose to scourge mankind ?—
* * * *
—The general order since the whole began,
Is kept in Nature, and is kept in Man

[* "How this is to be reconciled," says Dr. Warton, "with the orthodox doctrine of the fall of man, we are not informed" It certainly required some explanation from the Right Reverend annotator, not less than many others which he has employed no small ingenuity to illustrate]
This approaches very nearly to the optimism of Leibnitz, and has certainly nothing in common with the optimism of Plato Nor is it possible to reconcile it with the sentiments inculcated by Pope in other parts of the same poem

What makes all physical and moral ill ?
There deviates Nature, and here wanders Will

In this last couplet he seems to admit, not only that *Will* may *wander*, but that *Nature* herself may *deviate* from the *general order*, whereas the doctrine of his universal prayer is, that, while the material world is subjected to established laws, man is left to be the arbiter of his own destiny

Yet gav'st me in this dark estate
To know the good from ill,
And, binding Nature fast in fate,
Left free the human will.

[* With respect to Pope's unguarded expressions in this poem, a curious anecdote is mentioned by Dr Warton in his Essay on the Genius and Writings of Pope The late Lord Bathurst (we are told) had read the whole scheme of the *Essay on Man*, in the handwriting of Bolingbroke, drawn up in a series of propositions which Pope was to verify and illustrate The same author mentions, upon what he thinks good authority, that Bolingbroke was accustomed to ridicule Pope as not understanding the drift of his own principles, in their full extent, a circumstance which will not seem improbable to those who shall compare together the import of the different passages quoted above.]
In the Dunciad, too, the scheme of *Necessity* is coupled with that of *Materialism*, as one of the favourite doctrines of the sect of free-thinkers.

Of nought so certain as our *Reason* still,
Of nought so doubtful as of *Soul* and *Will*

"Two things," says Warburton, who professes to speak Pope's sentiments, "the most self-evident, the existence of our souls and the freedom of our will!"

* Restored.—*Ed*

place.[1] The *distinguishing* feature of this article of the Leibnitzian creed is, that, while the Hobbists and Spinozists were employing their ingenuity in connecting together Materialism and Necessity, as branches springing from one common root, Leibnitz always speaks of the soul as a machine purely *spiritual*,[2]—a machine, however, as necessarily regulated by pre-ordained and immutable laws, as the movements of a clock or the revolutions of the planets. In consequence of holding this language, he seemed to represent Man in a less degrading light than other necessitarians; but, in as far as such speculative tenets may be supposed to have any practical effect on human conduct, the tendency of his doctrines is not less dangerous than that of the most obnoxious systems avowed by his predecessors.[3]

[1] So completely, indeed, and so mathematically linked, did Leibnitz conceive all truths, both physical and moral, to be with each other, that he represents the eternal geometrician as incessantly occupied in the solution of this problem, — *The State of one Monad (or elementary atom) being given, to determine the state, past, present, and future, of the whole universe.*

[2] "Cuncta itaque in homine certa sunt, et in antecessum determinata, uti in cæteris rebus omnibus, et anima humana est *spirituale quoddam automatum.*"— Leib. *Op.* tom. i p. 156.

In a note on this sentence, the editor quotes a passage from Bilfinger, a learned German, in which an attempt is made to vindicate the propriety of the phrase, by a reference to the etymology of the word *automaton*. This word, it is observed, when traced to its source, literally expresses something which contains within itself its principle of motion, and, consequently, it applies still more literally to *Mind* than to a machine. The remark, considered in a philological point of view, is indisputably just; but is it not evident that it leads to a conclusion precisely contrary to what this author would deduce from it? Whatever may have been the primitive meaning of the word, its common, or rather its universal meaning, even among scientific writers, is, a *material* machine, moving without any foreign impulse; and, that this was the idea annexed to it by Leibnitz, appears from his distinguishing it by the epithet *spirituale*,—an epithet which would have been altogether superfluous had he intended to convey the opinion ascribed to him by Bilfinger. In applying, therefore, this language to the mind, we may conclude, with confidence, that Leibnitz had no intention to contrast together mind and body, in respect of their moving or actuating principles, but only to contrast them in respect of the *substances* of which they are composed. In a word, he conceived both of them to be equally *machines*, made and wound up by the Supreme Being, but the machinery in the one case to be material, and in the other spiritual.

[3] The following remark in Madame de Staël's interesting and eloquent review of German philosophy, bears marks of a haste and precipitation with which her criticisms are seldom chargeable. "Les opinions de Leibnitz tendent sur-

The scheme of necessity was still farther adorned and sublimed in the *Theodicæa* of Leibnitz, by an imagination nurtured and trained in the school of Plato "May there not exist," he asks on one occasion, "an immense space beyond the region of the stars? and may not this *empyreal* heaven be filled with happiness and glory? It may be conceived to resemble an ocean, where the rivers of all those created beings that are destined for bliss shall finish their course, when arrived in the starry system, at the perfection of their respective natures."—Leib. *Op.* tom. i. p. 135.[1]

tout au perfectionnement moral, s'il est vrai, comme les philosophes Allemands ont taché de le prouver, que le libre arbitre repose sur la doctrine qui affranchit l'âme des objets extérieurs, et que la vertu ne puisse exister sans la parfaite indépendance du vouloir."

[*I cannot omit this opportunity of remarking an Historical inaccuracy which has escaped the pen of Madame de Stael, who, in one of her latest and most brilliant works, has pointed out Leibnitz as the first Philosopher who raised his voice against the prevailing Materialism and Necessitarianism of his contemporaries. To the *first* part of this praise he was certainly well entitled; but as to the *second* it is so completely at variance with the uniform tenor of his doctrines, that if I were called on to name the individual who had contributed the most during the last century to the propagation of the dogma in question, I would without hesitation fix upon Leibnitz. It not only forms the basis of the two theories which have been already mentioned, but is stated by the author with all the confidence of demonstration as an obvious and indisputable corollary from his favourite principle of the *Sufficient Reason*;—a principle on which I intend to offer hereafter some remarks. . . . The mistake of Madame de Stael with respect to the

spirit of the Leibnitzian system, is common to her with many French and even with some English writers The author of the *Tableau de la Littérature Françoise*, thus expresses himself "La science de l'âme, telle a été la noble étude de Descartes, de Pascal, de Malebranche, de Leibnitz Cette métaphysique les conduisait directement à toutes les questions qui importent le plus à notre cœur, . et aux plus nobles des sciences, à la religion et à la morale." —*Tableau*, &c pp 87, 88]

[1] The celebrated *Charles Bonnet*, in his work entitled, *Contemplation de la Nature*, has indulged his imagination so far, in following out the above conjecture of Leibnitz, as to rival some of the wildest flights of Jacob Behmen. "Mais l'échelle de la création ne se termine point au plus élevés des mondes planétaires. Là commence un autre univers, dont l'étendue est peut-être à celle de l'univers des *Fixes*, ce qu'est l'espace du système solaire à la capacité d'une noix

"Là, comme des Astres resplendissans, brillent les Hierarchies Celestes

"Là rayonnent de toutes parts les Anges, les Archanges, les Seraphins, les Cherubins, les Trones, les Vertus, les Principautes. les Dominations, les Puissances

* Restored —*Ed*

In various other instances, he rises from the deep and seemingly hopeless abyss of *Fatalism*, to the same lofty conceptions of the universe; and has thus invested the most humiliating article of the atheistic creed, with an air of Platonic mysticism. The influence of his example appears to me to have contributed much to corrupt the taste and to bewilder the speculations of his countrymen; giving birth in the last result, to that heterogeneous combination of all that is pernicious in Spinozism, with the transcendental eccentricities of a heated and exalted fancy, which, for many years past, has so deeply tinctured both their philosophy and their works of fiction.[1]

"Au centre de ces AUGUSTES SPHERES, éclate le SOLFIL DE JUSTICE, L'ORIENT D'ENHAUT, dont tous les ASTRES empruntent leur lumière et leur splendeur"

"La *Theodicée* de Leibnitz," the same author tells us in another passage, "est un de mes livres de dévotion : J'ai intitulé mon Exemplaire, *Manuel de Philosophie Chrétienne.*"

[1] "The gross appetite of Love (says Gibbon) becomes most dangerous when it is elevated, or rather disguised, by sentimental passion." The remark is strikingly applicable to some of the most popular novels and dramas of Germany, and something very similar to it will be found to hold with respect to those speculative extravagances which, in the German systems of philosophy, are *elevated or disguised* by the imposing cant of moral enthusiasm.

In one of Leibnitz's controversial discussions with Dr Clarke, there is a passage which throws some light on his taste, not only in matters of science, but in judging of works of imagination. "Du temps de M Boyle, et d'autres excellens hommes qui fleurissoient en Angleterre sous Charles II on n'auroit pas osé nous débiter *des notions si creuses. (The notions here alluded to are those of Newton concerning the law of gravitation)* J'espère que le beautemps reviendra sous un aussi bon gouvernement que celui d'à present. Le capital de M. Boyle étoit d'inculquer que tout se faisoit *mécaniquement* dans la physique Mais c'est un malheur des hommes, de se dégoûter enfin de la raison même, et de s'ennuyer do la lumière Les chimères commencent à revenir, et plaisent parce qu'elles ont quelque chose de merveilleux. Il arrive dans le pays philosophique ce qui est arrivé dans le pays poétique. On s'est lassé des romans raisonnables, tel que *la Clélie Françoise* ou *l'Aramène Allemande;* et on est revenu depuis quelque temps aux *Contes des Fées*"— *Cinquième Ecrit de* M. Leibnitz, p 266.

From this passage it would seem, that Leibnitz looked forward to the period when the dreams of the Newtonian philosophy would give way to some of the exploded mechanical theories of the universe, and when the *Fairy-tales* then in fashion (among which number must have been included those of Count Anthony Hamilton) would be supplanted by the revival of such *reasonable Romances* as the *Grand Clelia* In neither of these instances does there seem to be much probability, at present, that his prediction will be ever verified

The German writers, who, of late years, have made the greatest noise among the sciolists of this country, will

In other parts of Europe, the effects of the *Theodicæa* have not been equally unfavourable. In France, more particularly, it has furnished to the few who have cultivated with success the Philosophy of Mind, new weapons for combating the materialism of the Gassendists and Hobbists; and, in England, we are indebted to it for the irresistible reasonings by which Clarke subverted the foundations on which the whole superstructure of Fatalism rests.

be found less indebted for their fame to the new lights which they have struck out, than to the unexpected and grotesque forms in which they have combined together the materials supplied by the invention of former ages, and of other nations It is this combination of truth and error in their philosophical systems, and of right and wrong in their works of fiction, which has enabled them to perplex the understandings, and to unsettle the principles of so many, both in Metaphysics and Ethics. In point of profound and extensive erudition, the scholars of Germany still continue to maintain their long established superiority over the rest of Europe.

[1] A very interesting account is given by Leibnitz, of the circumstances which gave occasion to his *Theodicæa*, in a letter to a Scotch gentleman, Mr. Burnet of Kemney, to whom he seems to have unbosomed himself on all subjects without any reserve " Mon hvre intitulé *Essais de Théodicée*, sur la bonté de Dieu, la liberté de l'homme, et l'origine de mal, sera bientôt achevé La plus grande partie de cet ouvrage avoit été faite par lambeaux, quand je me trouvois chez la feue Reine de Prusse, où ces matières étoient souvent agitées à l'occasion du Dictionnaire et des autres ouvrages de M. Bayle, qu'on y lisoit beaucoup Après la mort de cette grande Princesse, j'ai rassemblé et augmenté ces pièces sur l'exhortation des amis qui en étoient informés, et j'en ai fait l'ouvrage dont je viens de parler. Comme j'ai médité sur cette matière depuis ma jeunesse, je prétends de l'avoir discutée à fond "— Leibnitii, *Opera*, tom. vi p 284

In another letter to the same correspondent, he expresses himself thus —

" La plupart de mes sentimens ont été enfin arrêtés après une délibération de 20 ans car j'ai commencé bien jeune à méditer, et je n'avois pas encore 15 ans, quand je me promenois des journées entières dans un bois, pour prendre parti entre Aristote et Démocrite. Cependant j'ai changé et rechangé sur des nouvelles lumières, et ce n'est que depuis environ 12 ans que je me trouve satisfait, et que je suis arrivé à des démonstrations sur ces matières qui n'en paroissent point capables Cependant de la manière que je m'y prends, ces démonstrations peuvent être sensibles comme celles des nombres, quoique le sujet passe l'imagination "— (*Ibid* p. 253)

The letter from which this last paragraph is taken is dated in the year 1697.

My chief reason for introducing these extracts, was to do away an absurd suspicion, which has been countenanced by some respectable writers, (among others by Le Clerc,) that the opinions maintained in the *Théodicée* of Leibnitz were not his real sentiments, and that his own creed, on the most important questions there discussed, was not very

It may be justly regarded as a proof of the progress of reason and good sense among the Metaphysicians of this country since the time of Leibnitz, that the two theories of which I have been speaking, and which, not more than a century ago, were honoured by the opposition of such an antagonist as Clarke, are now remembered only as subjects of literary history.—In the arguments, however, alleged in support of these theories, there are some *logical* principles involved, which still continue to have an extensive influence over the reasonings of the learned, on questions seemingly the most remote from all metaphysical conclusions. The two most prominent of these are, the principle of the *Sufficient Reason*, and the *Law of Continuity*; both of them so intimately connected with some of the most celebrated disputes of the last century, as to require a more particular notice than may, at first sight, seem due to their importance.

different from that of Bayle Gibbon has even gone so far as to say, that "in his defence of the attributes and providence of the Deity, he was suspected of a secret correspondence with his adversary"—(*Antiquities of the House of Brunswick*.) In support of this very improbable charge, I do not know that any evidence has ever been produced, except the following passage, in a letter of his addressed to a Professor of Theology in the University of Tubingen (Pfaffius).—" Ita prorsus est, vir summe reverende, uti scribis, de Theodicæa mea. Rem acu tetigisti; et miror, neminem hactenus fuisse, qui sensum hunc meum senserit Neque enim Philosophorum est rem serio semper agere; qui in fingendis hypothesibus, uti bene mones, ingenii sui vires experiuntur. Tu, qui Theologus, in refutandis erroribus Theologum agis" In reply to this it is observed, by the learned editor of Leibnitz's works, (Dutens,) that it is much more probable that Leibnitz should have expressed himself on this particular occasion in jocular and ironical terms, than that he should have wasted so much ingenuity and learning in support of an hypothesis to which he attached no faith whatever, an hypothesis, he might have added, with which the whole principles of his philosophy are systematically, and, as he conceived, mathematically connected It is difficult to believe, that among the innumerable correspondents of Leibnitz, he should have selected a Professor of Theology at Tubingen, as the sole depositary of a secret which he was anxious to conceal from all the rest of the world

Surely a solitary document such as this weighs less than nothing, when opposed to the details quoted in the beginning of this note; not to mention its complete inconsistency with the character of Leibnitz, and with the whole tenor of his writings

For my own part, I cannot help thinking, that the passage in question has far more the air of *persiflage*, provoked by the vanity of Pfaffius, than of a serious compliment to his sagacity and penetration No injunction to secrecy, it is to be observed, is here given by Leibnitz to his correspondent.

I. Of the principle of the *Sufficient Reason*, the following succinct account is given by Leibnitz himself, in his controversial correspondence with Dr. Clarke.—" The great foundation of Mathematics is the principle of *contradiction* or *identity;* that is, that a proposition cannot be true and false at the same time. But, in order to proceed from Mathematics to Natural Philosophy, another principle is requisite, (as I have observed in my *Theodicæa;*) I mean the principle of the *Sufficient Reason;* or, in other words, that nothing happens without a *reason* why it should be so, rather than otherwise: And, accordingly, Archimedes was obliged, in his book *De Æquilibrio*, to take for granted, that if there be a balance, in which everything is alike on both sides, and if equal weights are hung on the two ends of that balance, the whole will be at rest. It is because no *reason* can be given why one side should weigh down rather than the other Now, by this single principle of the *Sufficient Reason*, may be demonstrated the being of a God, and all the other parts of Metaphysics or Natural Theology; and even, in some measure, those physical truths that are independent of Mathematics, such as the Dynamical Principles, or the Principles of Forces."[1]

Some of the inferences deduced by Leibnitz from this almost gratuitous assumption are so paradoxical, that one cannot help wondering he was not a little staggered about its certainty. Not only was he led to conclude, that the mind is necessarily determined in all its elections by the influence of motives, insomuch that it would be impossible for it to make a choice between two things perfectly alike; but he had the boldness to extend this conclusion to the Deity, and to assert, that two

---

[1] [* The following sentence in a letter from Leibnitz to M. Des Maizeaux, affords a strong proof of the importance which he attached to the principle in question —(See Leib *Opera*, vol. v pp. 38, 39) " J'espère qu'il y a beaucoup de gens en Angleterre, qui ne seront pas de l'avis de Mr. Newton ou de Mr Clarke sur la Philosophie, et qui ne goûteront point les Attractions proprement dites, ni le Vuide, ni le *Sensorium* de Dieu, ni cette imperfection de l'Univers, qui oblige Dieu de le redresser de tems en tems ; ni la nécessité où les sectateurs de Newton se trouvent, de nier le grand Principe du besoin d'une *Raison Suffisante*, par lequel je les bats en ruine "]

* Restored —*Fd.*

things perfectly alike could not have been produced even by Divine Power. It was upon this ground that he rejected a *vacuum*, because all the parts of it would be perfectly like to each other; and that he also rejected the supposition of *atoms*, or similar particles of matter, and ascribed to each particle a *monad*, or active principle, by which it is discriminated from every other particle.[1] The application of his principle, however, on which he evidently valued himself the most, was that to which I have already alluded; the demonstrative evidence with which he conceived it to establish the impossibility of free-agency, not only in man, but in any other intelligent being:[2] a conclusion which, under whatever form of words it may be disguised, is liable to every objection which can be urged against the system of Spinoza.

---

[1] See Note C C

[2] The following comment on this part of the Leibnitzian system is from the pen of one of his greatest admirers, *Charles Bonnet*. " Cette Métaphysique transcendante deviendra un peu plus intelligible, si l'on fait attention, qu'en vertu du principe de la *raison suffisante*, tout est nécessairement lié dans l'univers Toutes les Actions des Etres Simples sont harmoniques, ou subordonnées les unes aux autres L'exercice actuel de l'activité d'une monade donnée, est déterminé par l'exercice actuel de l'activité des monades auxquelles elle correspond immédiatement. Cette correspondance continue d'un point quelconque de l'univers jusqu'à ses extrémités. Représentez-vous les ordres circulaires et concentriques qu'une pierre excite dans une eau dormante Elles vont toujours en s'élargissant et en s'affoiblissant

" Mais, l'état actuel d'une monade est nécessairement déterminé par son état antécédent Celui-ci par un état qui a précédé, et ainsi en remontant jusqu'à l'instant de la création. . . .

" Ainsi le passé, le présent. et le futur ne forment dans la même monade qu'une seule chaine Notre philosophe disoit ingénieusement, que *le présent est toujours gros de l'avenir*

" Il disoit encore que l'Eternel Géomètre résolvoit sans cesse ce Problème l'état d'une monade étant donné, en déterminer l'état passé, présent, et futur de tout l'univers."—BONNET, tom viii pp 303-305

[* For some account of the monads of Wolff, see *Euler*—Lettres, 76, 92

To this hypothesis Wolff was naturally led by the phrase *Spiritual machine*, which Leibnitz applied to the soul.

In a view of the Necessitarian or Best scheme, ascribed to Collins, and commonly annexed to his Inquiry concerning human liberty, I find the following sentence .—" That our bodies are machines is not denied, but I never heard that Leibnitz called spirits or intelligences *machines* " This single sentence affords a proof how imperfectly the writer was acquainted with Leibnitz's works.]

* Restored.—*Ed.*

With respect to the principle from which these important consequences were deduced, it is observable, that it is stated by Leibnitz in terms so general and vague, as to extend to all the different departments of our knowledge; for he tells us, that there must be a *sufficient reason* for every *existence*, for every *event*, and for every *truth*. This use of the word *reason* is so extremely equivocal, that it is quite impossible to annex any precise idea to the proposition. Of this it is unnecessary to produce any other proof than the application which is here made of it to things so very different as *existences, events*, and *truths;* in all of which cases, it must of necessity have different meanings ' It would be a vain attempt, therefore, to combat the maxim in the form in which it is commonly appealed to. nor, indeed, can we either adopt or reject it, without considering particularly how far it holds in the various instances to which it may be applied.

The multifarious discussions, however, of a physical, a metaphysical, and a theological nature,[1] necessarily involved in so detailed an examination, would, in the present times, (even if this were a proper place for introducing them,) be equally useless and uninteresting; the peculiar opinions of Leibnitz on most questions connected with these sciences having already fallen into complete neglect. But as the maxim still continues to be quoted by the latest advocates for the scheme of necessity, it may not be altogether superfluous to observe, that, when understood to refer to the changes that take place in the *material* universe, it coincides entirely with the common maxim, that " every change implies the operation of a *cause;*" and that it is in consequence of its intuitive evidence in this par-

---

[1] Since the time of Leibnitz, the principle of the *sufficient reason* has been adopted by some mathematicians as a legitimate mode of reasoning in plane geometry, in which case, the application made of it has been in general just and logical, notwithstanding the vague and loose manner in which it is expressed. In this science, however, the use of it can never be attended with much advantage; except perhaps in demonstrating a few elementary truths, (such as the 5th and 6th propositions of Euclid's first book,) which are commonly established by a more circuitous process and even in these instances, the spirit of the reasoning might easily be preserved under a different form, much less exceptionable in point of phraseology.

ticular case, that so many have been led to acquiesce in it, in the unlimited terms in which Leibnitz has announced it. One thing will be readily granted, that the maxim, when applied to the determinations of intelligent and moral *agents*, is not *quite* so obvious and indisputable, as when applied to the changes that take place in things altogether inanimate and passive.

What then, it may be asked, induced Leibnitz, in the enunciation of his maxim, to depart from the form in which it has generally been stated, and to substitute instead of the word *cause*, the word *reason*, which is certainly not only the more unusual, but the more ambiguous expression of the two ? Was it not evidently a perception of the impropriety of calling the motives from which we act the *causes* of our actions; or, at least of the inconsistency of this language with the common ideas and feelings of mankind? The word *reason* is *here* much less suspicious, and much more likely to pass current without examination. It was therefore with no small dexterity that Leibnitz contrived to express his general principle in such a manner, that the impropriety of his language should be most apparent in that case in which the proposition is instantaneously admitted by every reader as self-evident; and to adapt it, in its most precise and definite shape, to the case in which it was in the greatest danger of undergoing a severe scrutiny. In this respect he has managed his argument with more address than Collins, or Edwards, or Hume, all of whom have applied the maxim to *mind*, in the very same words in which it is usually applied to inanimate matter.

But on this article of Leibnitz's philosophy, which gave occasion to his celebrated controversy with Clarke, I shall have a more convenient opportunity to offer some strictures, when I come to take notice of another antagonist, more formidable still, whom Clarke had soon after to contend with on the same ground. The person I allude to is Anthony Collins, a writer certainly not once to be compared with Leibnitz in the grasp of his intellectual powers; but who seems to have studied this particular question with greater attention and accuracy, and who is universally allowed to have defended his opinions concerning it in a manner far more likely to mislead the opinions of the multitude.

II. The same remark which has been already made on the principle of the *Sufficient Reason,* may be extended to that of the *Law of Continuity.* In both instances the phraseology is so indeterminate, that it may be interpreted in various senses essentially different from each other; and, accordingly, it would be idle to argue against either principle as a general theorem, without attending separately to the specialties of the manifold cases which it may be understood to comprehend. Where such a latitude is taken in the enunciation of a proposition, which, so far as it is true, must have been inferred from an induction of particulars, it is at least possible that while it holds in *some* of its applications, it may yet be far from possessing any claim to that universality which seems necessarily to belong to it, when considered in the light of a metaphysical axiom, resting on its own intrinsic evidence

Whether this vagueness of language was the effect of artifice, or of a real vagueness in the author's notions, may perhaps be doubted; but that it has contributed greatly to extend his reputation among a very numerous class of readers, may be confidently asserted. The possession of a general maxim, sanctioned by the authority of an illustrious name, and in which, as in those of the schoolmen, *more* seems to *be meant than meets the ear,* affords of itself no slight gratification to the vanity of many; nor is it inconvenient for a disputant, that the maxims to which he is to appeal should be stated in so dubious a shape, as to enable him, when pressed in an argument, to shift his ground at pleasure, from one interpretation to another The extraordinary popularity which, in our own times, the philosophy of Kant enjoyed for a few years, among the countrymen of Leibnitz, may, in like manner, be in a great degree ascribed to the imposing aspect of his enigmatical oracles, and to the consequent facility of arguing without end, in defence of a system so transmutable and so elusive in its forms

The extension, however, given to the *Law of Continuity,* in the later publications of Leibnitz, and still more by some of his successors, has been far greater than there is any reason to think was originally in the author's contemplation. It first occurred to him in the course of one of his physical controversies, and was probably suggested by the beautiful exemplifications of it which occur in pure geometry. At that time it does not appear that he had the slightest idea of its being susceptible of any application to the objects of natural history, far less to the succession of events in the intellectual and moral worlds. The supposition of bodies *perfectly hard*, having been shown to be inconsistent with two of his leading doctrines, *that* of the constant maintenance of the same quantity of force in the Universe, and *that* of the proportionality of forces to the squares of the velocities,—he found himself reduced to the necessity of asserting, that all changes are produced by insensible gradations, so as to render it impossible for a body to have its state changed from motion to rest, or from rest to motion, without passing through all the intermediate states of velocity. From this assumption he argued, with much ingenuity, that the existence of atoms, or of perfectly hard bodies, is impossible; because, if two of them should meet with equal and opposite motions, they would necessarily stop at once, in violation of the *law of continuity*. It would, perhaps, have been still more logical, had he argued against the universality of a law so gratuitously assumed, from its incompatibility with an hypothesis, which, whether true or false, certainly involves nothing either contradictory or improbable: but as this inversion of the argument would have undermined some of the fundamental principles of his physical system, he chose rather to adopt the other alternative, and to announce the *law of continuity* as a metaphysical truth, which admitted of no exception whatever. The facility with which this *law* has been adopted by subsequent philosophers is not easily explicable; more especially, as it has been maintained by many who reject those physical errors, in defence of which Leibnitz was first led to advance it.

One of the earliest, and certainly the most illustrious, of all the partisans and defenders of this principle, was John Bernouilli, whose Discourse on Motion first appeared at Paris in 1727, having been previously communicated to the Royal Academy of Sciences in 1724 and 1726 [1] It was from this period it began to attract the general attention of the learned; although many years were yet to elapse before it was to acquire that authority which it now possesses among our most eminent mathematicians.

Mr. Maclaurin, whose Memoir on the *Percussion of Bodies* gained the prize from the Royal Academy of Sciences in 1724, continued from that time, till his death, the steady opposer of this new *law*. In his Treatise of *Fluxions*, published in 1742, he observes, that "the existence of hard bodies void of elasticity has been rejected for the sake of what is called the *Law of Continuity*; a law which has been *supposed* to be general, without sufficient ground." [2] And still more explicitly, in his *Posthumous Account of Newton's Philosophical Discoveries*, he complains of those who "have rejected hard bodies as impossible, from far-fetched and metaphysical considerations;" proposing to his adversaries this unanswerable question, "Upon what grounds is the *law of continuity* assumed as a universal law of nature?" [3]

[1] "En effet (says Bernouilli) un pareil principe de dureté (the supposition, to wit, of bodies perfectly hard) ne sçauroit exister; c'est une chimère qui répugne à cette loi générale que la nature observe constamment dans toutes ses opérations, je parle de cet ordre immuable et perpétuel établi depuis la création de l'univers, qu'on peut appeler LOI DE CONTINUITE, en vertu de laquelle tout ce qui s'exécute, s'exécute par des degrés infiniment petits Il semble que le bon sens dicte, qu'aucun changement ne peut se faire *par saut; natura non operatur per saltum;* rien ne peut passer d'une extrémité à l'autre, sans passer par tous les degrés du milieu," &c The continuation of this passage (which I have not room to quote) is curious, as it suggests an argument, in proof of the *law of continuity*, from the principle of the *sufficient reason*

It may be worth while to observe here, that though, in the above quotation, Bernouilli speaks of the *law of continuity* as an arbitrary arrangement of the Creator, he represents, in the preceding paragraph, the idea of perfectly hard bodies as involving a manifest contradiction

[2] Maclaurin's *Fluxions*, vol ii p 438

[3] Nearly to the same purpose Mr Robins, a mathematician and philosopher of the highest eminence, expresses himself thus "M. Bernouilli, (in his *Discours sur les Lois de la Communication du Mouvement,*) in order to prove that there are no bodies perfectly hard

In the speculations hitherto mentioned, the *law of continuity* is applied merely to such *successive* events in the material world as are connected together by the relation of *cause and effect;* and, indeed, *chiefly* to the changes which take place in the state of bodies with respect to *motion and rest.* But in the philosophy of Leibnitz, we find the same *law* appealed to as an indisputable principle in all his various researches, physical, metaphysical, and theological. He extends it with the same confidence to mind as to matter, urging it as a demonstrative proof, in opposition to Locke, that the soul never ceases to think even in sleep or in *deliquium ;*[1] nay, inferring from it the impossibility that, in the case of any animated being, there should be such a thing as *death,* in the literal sense of that word.[2] It is by no means probable that the author was at all aware, when he first introduced this principle into the theory of motion, how far it was to lead him in his researches concerning other ques-

---

and inflexible, lays it down as an immutable law of nature, that no body can pass from motion to rest instantaneously, or without having its velocity gradually diminished That this is a law of nature, M Bernouilli thinks is evident from that principle, *Natura non operatur per saltum,* and from good sense. BUT HOW GOOD SENSE CAN, OF ITSELF, WITHOUT EXPERIMENT, DETERMINE ANY OF THE LAWS OF NATURE, IS TO ME VERY ASTONISHING. Indeed, from anything M Bernouilli has said, it would have been altogether as conclusive to have begun at the other end, and have disputed, that no body can pass instantaneously from motion to rest, because it is an immutable law of nature that all bodies shall be flexible "
—Robins, vol ii pp. 174, 175.

In quoting these passages, I would not wish to be understood as calling in question the universality of the *Law of Continuity* in the phenomena of moving bodies, a point on which I am not led by the subject of this Discourse, to offer any opinion, but on which I intend to hazard some remarks in a Note at the end of it. (See Note D D) All that I would here assert is, that it is a *law,* the truth of which can be inferred only by an induction from the phenomena, and to which, accordingly, we are not entitled to say that there cannot possibly exist any exceptions.

[1] "Je tiens que l'âme, et même le corps, n'est jamais sans action, et que l'âme n'est jamais sans quelque perception, même en dormant on a quelque sentiment confus et sombre du lieu où l'on est, et d'autres choses *Mais quand l'expérience ne le confirmeroit pas, je crois qu'il y en a démonstration.* C'est à peu près comme on ne sçauroit prouver absolument par les expériences, s'il n'y a point de vuide dans l'espace, et s'il n'y a point de repos dans la matière. Et cependant ces questions me paroissent décidées démonstrativement, aussi bien qu'à M Locke "—Leib. *Op* tome ii. p. 220

[2] See Note E E.

tions of greater moment; nor does it appear that it attracted much notice from the learned, but as a new *mechanical* axiom, till a considerable time after his death.

Charles Bonnet of Geneva, a man of unquestionable talents and of most exemplary worth, was, as far as I know, the first who entered fully into the views of Leibnitz on this point; perceiving how inseparably the law of continuity (as well as the principle of the sufficient reason) was interwoven with his scheme of universal concatenation and mechanism; and inferring from thence not only all the paradoxical corollaries deduced from it by its author, but some equally bold conclusions of his own, which Leibnitz either did not foresee in their full extent, or to which the course of his inquiries did not particularly attract his attention. The most remarkable of these conclusions was, that all the various beings which compose the universe, form a scale descending downwards without any chasm or *saltus*, from the Deity to the simplest forms of unorganized matter;[1]

---

[1] " Leibnitz admettoit comme un principe fondamental de sa sublime philosophie, qu'il n'y a jamais de sauts dans la nature, et que tout est continu ou nuancé dans le physique et dans le moral C'étoit sa fameuse *Loi de Continuité*, qu'il croyoit retrouver encore dans les mathématiques, et ç'avoit été cette loi qui lui avoit inspiré la singulière prédiction dont je parlois "* "Tous les êtres, disoit il, ne forment qu'une seule chaine, dans laquelle les différentes classes, comme autant d'anneaux, tiennent si étroitement les unes aux autres, qu'il est impossible aux sens et à l'imagination de fixer précisément le point où quelqu'un commence ou finit toutes les espèces qui bordent ou qui occupent, pour ainsi dire, les régions d inflection, et de rebroussement, devoit être équivoques et douées de caractères qui peuvent se rapporter aux espèces voisines également Ainsi, l'existence des zoo-phytes ou *Plant-Animaux* n'a rien de monstrueux, mais il est même convenable à l'ordre de la nature qu'il y en ait. Et telle est la force du principe de continuité chez moi, que non seulement je ne serois point étonné d'apprendre, qu'on eut trouvé des êtres, qui par rapport à plusieurs propriétés, par exemple, celle de se nourrir ou de se multiplier, puissent passer pour des végétaux à aussi bon droit que pour des animaux, .

J'en serois si peu étonné, dis-je, que même je suis convaincu qu'il doit y en avoir de tels, que l'Histoire Naturelle parviendra peut-être à connoître un jour," &c &c —*Contemplation de la Nature*, pp 341, 342.

Bonnet, in the sequel of this passage, speaks of the words of Leibnitz as a prediction of the discovery of the *Polypus*, deduced from the *Metaphysical* principle of the Law of Continuity. But would it not be more philosophical to

* La prédiction de la découverte des Polypes.

a proposition not altogether new in the history of philosophy, but which I do not know that any writer before Bonnet had ventured to assert as a metaphysical and necessary truth. With what important limitations and exceptions it must be received, even when confined to the comparative anatomy of animals, has been fully demonstrated by Cuvier;[1] and it is of material consequence to remark, that these exceptions, how few soever, to a *metaphysical* principle, are not less fatal to its truth than if they exceeded in number the instances which are quoted in support of the general rule.[2]

regard it as a query founded on the *analogy* of nature, as made known to us by experience and observation?*

[† In another passage of the same work, Bonnet expresses himself thus: "La Nature paroit aller par degrés d'une production à une autre production, point de sauts dans sa marche, encore moins de cataractes. Il semble que la loi de *Continuité* soit la loi universelle, et le philosophe qui l'a introduite dans la physique, nous a ouvert un grand spectacle C'est en conséquence de cette loi que Leibnitz soutenait que la nature va toujours par nuances et par gradations, d'une production à une autre production, et que *tous les états par lesquels un être passe successivement, sont tous déterminés les uns par les autres, en sorte que l'état subséquent étoit renfermé dans l'état antécédent comme l'effet dans sa cause*"—Bonnet, tom. viii pp 350, 351]

[1] *Leçons d'Anatomie Comparée*

[2] While Bonnet was thus employing his ingenuity in generalizing, still farther than his predecessors had done, the law of continuity, one of the most distinguished of his fellow-citizens, with whom he appears to have been connected in the closest and most confidential friendship, (the very ingenious M Le Sage,) was led, in the course of his researches concerning the physical cause of gravitation, to deny the existence of the law, even in the descent of heavy bodies. "The action of gravity (according to him) is *not* continuous" In other words, "each of its impressions is finite, and the interval of time which separates it from the following impression is of a finite duration" Of this proposition he offers a proof, which he considers as demonstrative, and thence deduces the following very paradoxical corollary, That "Projectiles do not move in curvilinear paths, but in rectilinear polygons"‡—"C'est ainsi (he adds) qu'un pré, qui vu de près, se trouve couvert de parties vertes réellement séparées, offre cependant aux personnes qui le regardent de loin, la sensation d'une verdure continué Et qu'un corps poli, auquel le microscope découvre mille

* "Ad eum modum summus opifex rerum seriem concatenavit a planta ad hominem, ut quasi sine ullo cohæreant intervallo, sic Ζωόφυτα cum plantis bruta conjungunt; sic cum homine simia quadrupedes Itaque in hominis quaque specie invenimus divinos, humanos, feros"— Scaliger, (prefixed as a motto to Mr White's *Essay on the regular gradation in Man* London, 1799)

† Restored.—*Ed.*

‡ "Ullas vero curvas in rerum natura esse negavere multi Nominabo tantum, qui nunc occurrunt *Lubinum, Bassonem, Regium, Borartem,* et quem parum abest, quin addam *Hobbesium*"— Leibnitii *Op* tom ii p 47

At a period somewhat later, an attempt has been made to connect the *same law of continuity* with the history of human improvement, and more particularly with the progress of invention in the sciences and arts. Helvetius is the most noted writer in whom I have observed this last extension of the Leibnitzian principle; and I have little doubt, from his known opinions, that, when it occurred to him, he conceived it to afford a new illustration of the scheme of necessity, and of the mechanical concatenation of all the phenomena of human life. Arguing in support of his favourite paradox concerning the original equality of all men in point of mental capacity, he represents the successive advances made by different individuals in the career of discovery, as so many imperceptible or infinitesimal steps, each individual surpassing his predecessor by a trifle, till at length nothing is wanting but an additional mind, not superior to the others in natural powers, to combine together, and to turn to its own account, their accumulated labours. " It is upon *this* mind," he observes, " that the world is always ready to bestow the attribute of genius. From the tragedies of *The Passion,* to the poets Hardy and Rotrou, and to the *Marianne* of Tristan, the French theatre was always acquiring successively an infinite number of inconsiderable improvements. Corneille was born at a moment when the addition he made to the art could not fail to form an epoch; and accordingly Corneille is universally regarded as a Genius. I am far from wishing," Helvetius adds, " to detract from the glory of this great poet. I wish only to prove, that *Nature never proceeds* PER SALTUM, [*an old* and *common* axiom in philosophy —*Ed.*] *and that the Law of Continuity is always exactly observed.* The remarks, therefore, now made on the dramatic

solutions de continuité, paroit à l'oeil nu, posséder une continuité parfaite."

' Généralement, le simple bons sens, qui veut qu'on suspende son jugement sur ce qu'on ignore, et que l'on ne tranche pas hardiment sur la non-existence de ce qui échappe à nos sens, auroit dû empêcher des gens qui s'appeloient philosophes de décider si dogmatiquement, la continuité réelle, de ce qui avoit une continuité apparente, et la non-existence des intervalles qu'ils n'apercevoient pas "—*Essai de Chymie Mécanique.* Couronné en 1758, par l'Académie de Rouen Imprimé à Genève, 1761 Pp 94-96.

art, may also be applied to the sciences which rest on observation."[1]—*De l'Esprit,* dis. iv. chap. i.

With this last extension of the *Law of Continuity,* as well as with that of Bonnet, a careless reader is the more apt to be dazzled, as there is a large mixture in both of unquestionable truth. The mistake of the ingenious writers lay in pushing to *extreme cases* a doctrine, which, when kept within certain limits, is not only solid but important; a mode of reasoning which, although it may be always safely followed out in pure Mathematics (where the principles on which we proceed are mere definitions,) is a never-failing source of error in all the other sciences; and which, when practically applied to the concerns of life, may be regarded as an infallible symptom of an understanding better fitted for the subtle contentions of the schools, than for those average estimates of what is expedient and practicable in the conduct of affairs, which form the chief elements of political sagacity and of moral wisdom.[2]

---

[1] It may, perhaps, be alleged, that the above allusion to the *Law of Continuity* was introduced merely for the sake of illustration, and that the author did not mean his words to be strictly interpreted, but this remark will not be made by those who are acquainted with the philosophy of Helvetius

Let me add, that, in selecting Corneille as the only exemplification of this theory, Helvetius has been singularly unfortunate It would have been difficult to have named any other modern poet, in whose works, when compared with those of his immediate predecessors, the *Law of Continuity* has been more remarkably violated. " Corneille (says a most judicious French critic) est, pour ainsi dire, de notre tems, mais ses contemporains n'en sont pas. *Le Cid, les Horaces, Cinna, Polieucte,* forment le commencement de cette chaine brillante qui réunit notre littérature actuelle de celle du règne de Richelieu et de la minorité de Louis XIV ; mais autour de ces points lumineux règne encore une nuit profonde, leur éclat les rapproche en apparence de nos yeux, le reste, repoussé dans l'obscurité, semble bien loin de nous. Pour nous Corneille est moderne, et Rotrou ancien," &c. (For detailed illustrations and proofs of these positions, see a slight but masterly historical sketch of the French Theatre, by M Suard)

[2] Locke has fallen into a train of thought very similar to that of Bonnet, concerning the *Scale of Beings;* but has expressed himself with far greater caution,—stating it modestly as an inference deduced from an induction of particulars, not as the result of any abstract or metaphysical principle.— (See Locke's *Works,* vol III p 101) In one instance, indeed, he avails himself of an allusion, which, at first sight, may appear to favour the extension of the mathematical *Law of Continuity* to the works of creation, but it is evident, from the context, that he meant this allusion merely as a popular illustration of a fact in Natural History, not as the

' If on these two celebrated principles of Leibnitz, I have enlarged at greater length than may appear to some of my readers to be necessary, I must remind them, 1*st*, Of the illustration they afford of what Locke has so forcibly urged with respect to the danger of adopting, upon the faith of reasonings *a priori*, metaphysical conclusions concerning the laws by which the universe is governed: 2*dly*, Of the proof they exhibit of the strong bias of the human mind, even in the present advanced stage of experimental knowledge, to grasp at general maxims, without a careful examination of the grounds on which they rest; and of that less frequent, but not less unfortunate bias, which has led some of our most eminent mathematicians to transfer to sciences, resting ultimately on an appeal to *facts*, those habits of thinking which have been formed amidst the hypothetical abstractions of pure geometry: *Lastly*, Of the light they throw on the mighty influence which the name and authority of Leibnitz have, for more than a century past, exercised over the strongest and acutest understandings in the most enlightened countries of Europe.

It would be improper to close these reflections on the philosophical speculations of Leibnitz, without taking some notice of his very ingenious and original thoughts on the etymological study of languages, considered as a guide to our conclusions concerning the origin and migrations of different tribes of our species. These thoughts were published in 1710, in the *Memoirs* of the Berlin Academy, and form the first article of the first volume of that justly celebrated collection. I do not recollect any author of an earlier date, who seems to have been completely aware of the important consequences to which the

---

rigorous enunciation of a theorem applicable alike to all truths, mathematical, physical, and moral "It is a hard matter to say where sensible and rational begin, and where insensible and irrational end; and who is there quick-sighted enough to determine precisely, which is the lowest species of living things, and which is the first of those who have no life? Things, as far as we can observe, lessen and augment, as the quantity does in a *regular cone*, where, though there be a manifest odds betwixt the bigness of the diameter at a remote distance, yet the difference between the upper and under, where they touch one another, is hardly discernible."—*Ibid.*

See some Reflections on this speculation of Locke's in the *Spectator*, No 519.

prosecution of this inquiry is likely to lead; nor, indeed, was much progress made in it by any of Leibnitz's successors, till towards the end of the last century; when it became a favourite object of pursuit to some very learned and ingenious men, both in France, Germany, and England. *Now,* however, when our knowledge of the globe, and of its inhabitants, is so wonderfully enlarged by commerce, and by conquest; and when so great advances have been made in the acquisition of languages, the names of which, till very lately, were unheard of in this quarter of the world,—there is every reason to hope for a series of farther discoveries, strengthening progressively, by the multiplication of their mutual points of contact, the common evidence of their joint results; and tending more and more to dissipate the darkness in which the primeval history of our race is involved It is a field, of which only detached corners have hitherto been explored; and in which, it may be confidently presumed, that unthought of treasures still lie hid, to reward sooner or later the researches of our posterity [1]

My present subject does not lead me to speak of the mathematical and physical researches, which have associated so closely the name of Leibnitz with that of Newton, in the history of modern science; of the inexhaustible treasures of his erudition, both classical and scholastic; of his vast and manifold contributions towards the elucidation of German antiquities and of Roman jurisprudence; or of those theological controversies, in which, while he combated with one hand the enemies of revelation, he defended, with the other, the orthodoxy of his own dogmas against the profoundest and most learned divines of Europe Nor would I have digressed so far as to allude here to these particulars, were it not for the unparalleled example they display, of what a vigorous and versatile genius, seconded by habits of persevering industry, may accomplish, within the short span of human life Even the relaxations with which he was accustomed to fill up his moments of leisure, partook of the general character of his more serious engagements. By early and long habit, he had

[1] See Note F F.

acquired a singular facility in the composition of Latin verses; and he seems to have delighted in loading his muse with new fetters of his own contrivance, in addition to those imposed by the laws of classical prosody.[1] The number, besides, of his literary correspondents was immense, including all that was most illustrious in Europe: and the rich materials everywhere scattered over his letters are sufficient of themselves to show, that his amusements consisted rather in a change of objects, than in a suspension of his mental activity. Yet while we admire these stupendous monuments of his intellectual energy, we must not forget (if I may borrow the language of Gibbon) that " even the powers of Leibnitz were dissipated by the multiplicity of his pursuits. He attempted more than he could finish, he designed more than he could execute, his imagination was too easily satisfied with a bold and rapid glance on the subject which he was impatient to leave; and he may be compared to those heroes whose empire has been lost in the ambition of universal conquest."[2]

From some expressions which Leibnitz has occasionally dropped, I think it probable, that he himself became sensible, as he advanced in life, that his time might have been more profitably employed, had his studies been more confined in their aim. "If the whole earth (he has observed on one occasion) had continued to be of one language and of one speech, human life might be considered as extended beyond its present term, by the addition of all that part of it which is devoted to the acquisition of dead and foreign tongues. Many other branches of knowledge, too, may, in this respect, be classed with the languages; such as Positive Laws, Ceremonies, the Styles of

---

[1] A remarkable instance of this is mentioned by himself in one of his letters " Annos natus tredecim una die trecentos versus hexametros effudi, sine elisione omnes, quod hoc fieri facile posse forte affirmassem."—(Leib Op. tom v p 304.) He also amused himself occasionally with writing verses in German and in French

[2] May I presume to remark farther, that the native powers of Leibnitz's mind, astonishing and preternatural as they certainly were, seem sometimes oppressed and overlaid under the weight of his still more astonishing erudition? The influence of his scholastic reading is more peculiarly apparent in warping his judgment, and clouding his reason, on all questions connected with Metaphysical Theology

Courts, and a great proportion of what is called *critical erudition*. The utility of all these arises merely from opinion; nor is there to be found, in the innumerable volumes that have been written to illustrate them, a hundredth part, which contains anything subservient to the happiness or improvement of mankind."

The most instructive lesson, however, to be drawn from the history of Leibnitz, is the incompetency of the most splendid gifts of the understanding, to advance essentially the interests either of Metaphysical or of Ethical Science, unless accompanied with that rare devotion to truth, which may be regarded, if not as the basis, at least as one of the most indispensable elements, of moral genius. The chief attraction to the study of philosophy, in *his* mind, seems to have been (what many French critics have considered as a chief source of the charms of the imitative arts) the pride of *conquering difficulties*: a feature of his character which he had probably in his own eye, when he remarked, (not without some degree of conscious vanity,) as a peculiarity in the turn or cast of his intellect, that to *him* "all difficult things were easy, and all easy things difficult."[1] Hence the disregard manifested in his writings to the simple and obvious conclusions of experience and common sense; and the perpetual effort to unriddle mysteries over which an impenetrable veil is drawn. "Scilicet sublime et erectum ingenium, pulchritudinem ac speciem excelsæ magnæque gloriæ vehementius quam caute appetebat." It is to be regretted, that the sequel of this fine eulogy does not equally apply to him. "Mox mitigavit ratio et ætas; *retinuitque, quod est difficillimum, et in sapientia modum.*"[2] How happily does this last expression characterize the temperate wisdom of Locke, when contrasted with that towering, but impotent ambition, which, in the Theories of Optimism and of Pre-established Harmony, seemed to realize the fabled revolt of the giants against the sovereignty of the gods!

---

[1] "Sentio paucos esse mei characteris, et omnia facilia mihi difficilia, omnia contra difficilia mihi facilia esse." —Leib. *Op* tom vi. p 302.

[2] Tacitus, *Agric*

After all, a similarity may be traced between these two great men in *one* intellectual weakness common to both; a facility in the admission of facts, stamped sufficiently (as we should *now* think) by their own intrinsic evidence, with the marks of incredibility. The observation has been often made with respect to Locke;[1] but it would be difficult to find in Locke's writings, anything so absurd as an account gravely transmitted by Leibnitz to the Abbé de St Pierre, and by him communicated to the Royal Academy of Sciences at Paris, of a dog who spoke.[2] No person liberally educated could, I believe, be found at present in any *Protestant* country of Christendom, capable of such credulity. By what causes so extraordinary a revolution in the minds of men has been effected, within the short space of a hundred years, I must not here stop to inquire. Much, I apprehend, must be ascribed to our enlarged knowledge of nature, and more particularly to those scientific voyages and travels which have annihilated so many of the prodigies which exercised the wonder and subdued the reason of our ancestors. But, in whatever manner the revolution is to be explained, there can be no doubt that this growing disposition to weigh scrupulously the *probability* of alleged *facts* against the faith due to the testimonies brought to attest them, and, even in some cases, against the apparent evidence of our own senses, enters largely and essentially into the composition of that philosophical *spirit* or temper, which so strongly distinguishes the eighteenth century from all those which preceded it.[3] It is no small consolation to reflect, that some important maxims of good sense have been thus familiarized to the most ordinary understandings, which, at so very recent a period, failed in producing their due effect on two of the most powerful minds in Europe.

[1] [* The passages commonly cited in proof of Locke's credulity, are the references to the manners of savage nations introduced in the course of his argument against *innate Practical Principles* To these may be added, the degree of credit he appears to have given to the story of a rational parrot, and to the popular fables about mermaids — *Vide* p 247]

[2] See Note G G.

[3] See Note H H

* Restored.—*Ed*

On reviewing the foregoing paragraphs, I am almost tempted to retract part of what I have written, when I reflect on the benefits which the world has derived even from the *errors* of Leibnitz It has been well and justly said, that "every *desideratum* is an imperfect discovery," to which it may be added, that every new problem which is started, and still more every attempt, however abortive, towards its solution, strikes out a new path, which must sooner or later lead to the truth. If the problem be solvible, a solution will in due time be obtained: if insolvible, it will soon be abandoned as hopeless by general consent; and the legitimate field of scientific research will become more fertile, in proportion as a more accurate survey of its boundaries adapts it better to the limited resources of the cultivators.

In this point of view, what individual in modern times can be compared to Leibnitz! To how many of those researches, which still usefully employ the talents and industry of the learned, did he not point out and open the way! From how many more did he not warn the wise to withhold their curiosity, by his bold and fruitless attempts to burst the barriers of the invisible world!

The best *eloge* of Leibnitz is furnished by the literary history of the eighteenth century;—a history which, whoever takes the pains to compare with his works, and with his epistolary correspondence, will find reason to doubt whether, at the singular era when he appeared, he could have more accelerated the advancement of knowledge by the concentration of his studies, than he has actually done by the universality of his aims; and whether he does not afford one of the few instances to which the words of the poet may literally be applied:—

"Si non errasset, fecerat ille minus."[1]

[1] See Note I I

SECT. III.—OF THE METAPHYSICAL SPECULATIONS OF NEWTON AND CLARKE—DIGRESSION WITH RESPECT TO THE SYSTEM OF SPINOZA—COLLINS AND JONATHAN EDWARDS—ANXIETY OF BOTH TO RECONCILE THE SCHEME OF NECESSITY WITH MAN'S MORAL AGENCY—DEPARTURE OF SOME LATER NECESSITARIANS FROM THEIR VIEWS.[1]

The foregoing review of the philosophical writings of Locke and of Leibnitz naturally leads our attention, in the next place, to those of our illustrious countrymen Newton and Clarke; the former of whom has exhibited, in his *Principia* and *Optics*, the most perfect exemplifications which have yet appeared of

---

[1] In conformity to the plan announced in the preface to this *Dissertation*, I confine myself to those authors whose opinions have had a marked and general influence on the subsequent history of philosophy, passing over a multitude of other names well worthy to be recorded in the annals of metaphysical science. Among these I shall only mention the name of Boyle, to whom the world is indebted, beside some very acute remarks and many fine illustrations of his own upon metaphysical questions of the highest moment, for the philosophical arguments in defence of religion, which have added so much lustre to the names of Derham and Bentley, and, far above both, to that of Clarke.* The *remarks* and *illustrations*, which I here refer to, are to be found in his *Inquiry into the Vulgar Notion of Nature*, and in his *Essay, inquiring whether, and how, a Naturalist should consider Final Causes*. Both of these tracts display powers which might have placed their author on a level with Descartes and Locke, had not his taste and inclination determined him more strongly to other pursuits. I am inclined to think that neither of them is so well known as were to be wished. I do not even recollect to have seen it anywhere noticed, that some of the most striking and beautiful instances of design in the order of the material world, which occur in the Sermons preached at Boyle's *Lecture*, are borrowed from the works of the founder.†

Notwithstanding, however, these great merits, he has written too little on such abstract subjects to entitle him to a place among English metaphysicians, nor has he, like Newton, started any leading thoughts which have since given a new direction to the studies of metaphysical inquirers. From the slight specimens he has left, there is reason to conclude, that his mind was still more happily turned than that of Newton, for the prosecution of that branch of science to which their contemporary Locke was then beginning to invite the attention of the public.

* To the English reader it is unnecessary to observe, that I allude to the Sermons preached at the Lecture founded by the Honourable Robert Boyle.

† Those instances, more especially, which are drawn from the anatomical structure of animals, and the adaptation of their perceptive organs to the habits of life for which they are destined.

the cautious logic recommended by Bacon and Locke; while the other, in defending against the assaults of Leibnitz the metaphysical principles on which the Newtonian philosophy proceeds, has been led, at the same time, to vindicate the authority of various other truths, of still higher importance, and more general interest.

The chief subjects of dispute between Leibnitz and Clarke, so far as the principles of the Newtonian philosophy are concerned, have been long ago settled, to the entire satisfaction of the learned world. The *monads*, and the *plenum*, and the *pre-established harmony* of Leibnitz, already rank, in the public estimation, with the vortices of Descartes, and the plastic nature of Cudworth; while the theory of gravitation prevails everywhere over all opposition; and (as Mr. Smith remarks) "has advanced to the acquisition of the most universal empire that was ever established in philosophy." On these points, therefore, I have only to refer my readers to the collection published by Dr. Clarke, in 1717, of the controversial papers which passed between him and Leibnitz during the two preceding years;—a correspondence equally curious and instructive; and which it is to be lamented, that the death of Leibnitz in 1716 prevented from being longer continued [1]

Although Newton does not appear to have devoted much of his time to metaphysical researches, yet the general spirit of his physical investigations has had a great, though indirect,

---

[1] From a letter of Leibnitz to M. Remond de Montmort, it appears that he considered Newton, and not Clarke, as his real antagonist in this controversy. "M Clarke, ou plutôt M. Newton, dont M. Clarke soutient les dogmes, est en dispute avec moi sur la philosophie"—(Leib *Op* tom v. p. 33.) From another letter to the same correspondent we learn, that Leibnitz aimed at nothing less than the complete overthrow of the Newtonian philosophy; and that it was chiefly to his grand principle of the *sufficient reason* that he trusted for the accomplishment of this object "J'ai réduit l'état de notre dispute à ce grand axiome, que *rien n'existe ou n'arrive sans qu'il y ait une raison suffisante, pourquoi il en est plutôt ainsi qu'autrement.* S'il continue à me le nier, où en sera sa sincérité? S'il me l'accorde, adieu le vuide, les atomes, *et toute la philosophie de M Newton*"—(*Ibid*) See also a letter from Leibnitz to M des Maizeaux in the same volume of his works, p 39

influence on the metaphysical studies of his successors. It is justly and profoundly remarked by Mr. Hume, that "while Newton *seemed* to draw off the veil from some of the mysteries of nature, he showed, at the same time, the imperfections of the mechanical philosophy, and thereby restored her ultimate secrets to that obscurity in which they ever did, and ever will remain." In this way, his discoveries have co-operated powerfully with the reasonings of Locke, in producing a general conviction of the inadequacy of our faculties to unriddle those sublime enigmas on which Descartes, Malebranche, and Leibnitz had so recently wasted their strength, and which, in the ancient world, were regarded as the only fit objects of philosophical curiosity. It is chiefly too since the time of Newton, that the ontology and pneumatology of the dark ages have been abandoned for inquiries resting on the solid basis of experience and analogy; and that philosophers have felt themselves emboldened by his astonishing discoveries concerning the more distant parts of the material universe, to argue from the known to the unknown parts of the moral world. So completely has the prediction been verified which he himself hazarded, in the form of a query, at the end of his *Optics*, that "if natural philosophy should continue to be improved in its various branches, the bounds of moral philosophy would be enlarged also."

How far the peculiar cast of Newton's genius qualified him for prosecuting successfully the study of Mind, he has not afforded us sufficient *data* for judging; but such was the admiration with which his transcendent powers as a mathematician and natural philosopher were universally regarded, that the slightest of his hints on other subjects have been eagerly seized upon as indisputable axioms, though sometimes with little other evidence in their favour but the supposed sanction of his authority.[1] The part of his works, however, which chiefly led me to connect his name with that of Clarke,

---

[1] Witness Hartley's *Physiological Theory of the Mind*, founded on a query in Newton's *Optics;* and a long list of theories in medicine, grafted on a hint thrown out in the same query, in the form of a modest conjecture

is a passage in the *Scholium* annexed to his *Principia*,[1] which may be considered as the germ of the celebrated argument *a priori* for the existence of God, which is commonly, though, I apprehend, not justly, regarded as the most important of all Clarke's contributions to Metaphysical Philosophy. I shall quote the passage in Newton's own words, to the oracular conciseness of which no English version can do justice.

"Æternus est et infinitus, omnipotens et omnisciens . id est, durat ab æterno in æternum, et adest ab infinito in infinitum . . . Non est æternitas et infinitas, sed æternus et infinitus; non est duratio et spatium, sed durat et adest. Durat semper et adest ubique, et existendo semper et ubique durationem et

---

[1] This *Scholium*, it is to be observed, first appeared at the end of the second edition of the *Principia*, printed at Cambridge in 1713. The former edition, published at London in 1687, has no *Scholium* annexed to it. From a passage, however, in a letter of Newton's to Dr. Bentley, (dated 1692,) it seems probable, that as far back, at least, as that period, he had thoughts of attempting a proof *a priori* of the existence of God. After some new illustrations, drawn from his own discoveries, of the common argument from *final causes*, he thus concludes: "There is yet *another* argument for a Deity, which I take to be a very strong one; but, till the principles on which it is grounded are better received, I think it more advisable to let it sleep."—*Four Letters from Sir I Newton to Dr Bentley*, p. 11. London, Dodsley, 1756.

It appears from this passage, that Newton had no intention, like his predecessor Descartes, to supersede, by any new argument of his own for the existence of God, the common one drawn from the consideration of *final causes;* and, therefore, nothing could be more uncandid than the following sarcasm, pointed by Pope at the laudable attempts of his two countrymen to *add* to the evidence of this conclusion, by deducing it from *other* principles

"Let others creep by timid steps and slow.
On plain experience lay foundations low.
By common sense to common knowledge bred,
And last to Nature's cause through Nature led
We nobly take the high *priori* road,
And reason downwards till we doubt of God."

That Pope had Clarke in his eye when he wrote these lines, will not be doubted by those who recollect the various other occasions in which he has stepped out of his way, to vent an impotent spleen against this excellent person

"Let Clarke live half his life the poor's support,
But let him live the other half at court."

And again—

"Even in an ornament its place remark
Nor in a hermitage set Dr Clarke"

in which last couplet there is a manifest allusion to the bust of Clarke, placed in a hermitage by Queen Caroline, together with those of Newton, Boyle, Locke, and Wollaston. See some fine verses on these busts in a poem called the *Grotto*, by Matthew Green.

spatium constituit."[1] Proceeding on these principles, Dr. Clarke argued, that, as immensity and eternity (which force themselves irresistibly on our belief as *necessary* existences, or, in other words, as existences of which the annihilation is impossible) are not *substances*, but *attributes*, the immense and eternal Being, whose attributes they are, must exist of necessity also. The existence of God, therefore, according to Clarke, is a truth that follows with demonstrative evidence from those conceptions of space and time which are inseparable from the human mind. . . "These (says Dr. Reid) are the speculations of men of superior genius; but whether they be as solid as they are sublime, or whether they be the wanderings of imagination in a region beyond the limits of the human understanding, I am at a loss to determine." After this candid acknowledgment from Dr. Reid, I need not be ashamed to confess my own doubts and difficulties on the same question.[2]

But although the argument, as stated by Clarke, does not carry complete satisfaction to my mind, I think it must be granted that there is something peculiarly wonderful and overwhelming in those conceptions of immensity and eternity, which it is not less impossible to banish from our thoughts, than the consciousness of our own existence. Nay, further, I think that these conceptions are very intimately connected with the fundamental principles of Natural Religion For when once we have established, from the evidences of design everywhere manifested around us, the existence of an intelligent and powerful *cause*, we are unavoidably led to apply to this *cause* our conceptions of *immensity* and *eternity*, and to conceive Him as filling the infinite extent of both with his presence and with

---

[1] Thus translated by Dr. Clarke: "God is eternal and infinite, omnipotent and omniscient, that is, he endures from everlasting to everlasting, and is present from infinity to infinity. He is not eternity or infinity, but eternal and infinite. He is not duration or space, but he endures and is present He endures always, and is present everywhere, and by existing always and everywhere, constitutes duration and space."—See Clarke's *Fourth Reply to Leibnitz*

[2] An argument substantially the same with this for the existence of God, is hinted at very distinctly by Cudworth, *Intellect System*, chap v § 3, 4 Also by Dr Henry More, *Enchir Metaph* cap. 8, § 8. See Mosheim's *Transl. of Cudworth*, tom ii p 356

his power. Hence we associate with the idea of God those awful impressions which are naturally produced by the idea of infinite space, and perhaps still more by the idea of endless duration. Nor is this all. It is from the immensity of space that the notion of infinity is originally derived ; and it is hence that we transfer the expression, by a sort of metaphor, to other subjects. When we speak, therefore, of *infinite* power, wisdom, and goodness, our notions, if not wholly borrowed from space, are at least greatly aided by this analogy; so that the conceptions of Immensity and Eternity, if they do not of themselves *demonstrate* the existence of God, yet necessarily enter into the ideas we form of his nature and attributes.

To these various considerations it may be added, that the notion of *necessary existence* which we derive from the contemplation of Space and of Time, renders the same notion, when applied to the Supreme Being, much more easy to be apprehended than it would otherwise be.

It is not, therefore, surprising, that Newton and Clarke should have fallen into that train of thought which encouraged them to attempt a demonstration of the being of God from our conceptions of Immensity and Eternity ; and still less is it to be wondered at, that, in pursuing this lofty argument, they should have soared into regions where they were lost in the clouds.

I have said above, that Clarke's demonstration seems to have been suggested to him by a passage in Newton's *Scholium*. It is, however, more than probable that he had himself struck into a path very nearly approaching to it, at a much earlier period of his life. The following anecdote of his childhood, related, upon his own authority, by his learned and authentic, though, in many respects, weak and visionary biographer, (Whiston,) exhibits an interesting example of an anomalous development of the powers of reflection and abstraction, at an age when, in ordinary cases, the attention is wholly engrossed with sensible objects Such an inversion of the common process of nature in unfolding our different faculties, is perhaps one of the rarest phenomena in the intellectual world ; and, wherever it occurs, may be regarded as strongly symptomatic of something peculiar and decided in the philosophical character of the individual.

"One of his parents," says Whiston, "asked him when he was very young, Whether God could do every thing? He answered, Yes! He was asked again, Whether God could tell a lie? He answered, No! And he understood the question to suppose, that this was the only thing that God could not do; nor durst he say, so young was he then, that he thought there was any thing else which God could not do; while yet, well he remembered, that he had, *even then, a clear conviction in his own mind, that there was one thing which God could not do;—that he could not annihilate that space which was in the room where they were.*"[1]

[1] The question concerning the necessary existence of Space and of Time, formed one of the principal subjects of discussion between Clarke and Leibnitz According to the former, space and time are, both of them, infinite, immutable, and indestructible According to his antagonist, "space is nothing but the order of things co-existing," and "time nothing but the order of things successive" The notion of real absolute Space, in particular, he pronounces to be *a mere chimera and superficial imagination;* classing it with those prejudices which Bacon called *idola tribus.*—See his 4th *Paper,* § 14.

It has always appeared to me a thing quite inexplicable, that the great majority of philosophers, both in Germany and in France, have, on the above question, decided in favour of Leibnitz Even D'Alembert himself, who, on most metaphysical points, reasons so justly and so profoundly, has, in this instance, been carried along by the prevailing opinion (or, perhaps, it would be more correct to say, by the fashionable phraseology) among his countrymen. "Y auroit-il un espace, s'il n'y avoit point de corps, et une durée s'il n'y avoit rien? Ces questions viennent, ce me semble, de ce qu'on suppose au temps et à l'espace plus de réalité qu'ils n'en ont . . Les enfants, qui disent que le vuide n'est rien, ont raison parce qu'ils s'en tiennent au simples notions du sens commun * et les philosophes qui veulent réaliser le vuide se perdent dans leurs spéculations le vuide a été enfanté par les abstractions, et voilà l'abus d'une méthode si utile à bien des égards. *S'il n'y avoit point de corps et de succession, l'espace et le temps seroient possibles, mais ils n'existeroient pas*"— (*Mélanges,* &c. tom. v. § xvi) Bailly, a writer by no means partial to D'Alembert, quotes, with entire approbation, the foregoing observations, subjoining to them, in the following terms, his own judgment on the merits of this branch of the controversy between Clarke and Leibnitz "La notion du temps et de l'espace, est un des points sur lesquels Leibnitz a combattu contre Clarke,

* I quote the sequel of this passage on the authority of Bailly, (see his *Eloge on Leibnitz,*) for it is not to be found in the copy of the *Mélanges* before me printed at Amsterdam in 1767.

With this early and deep impression on his mind, it is easy to conceive how Newton's *Scholium* should have encouraged him to resume the musings of his *boyish days*, concerning the necessary existence of space, and to trace, as far as he could, its connexion with the principles of Natural Theology. But the above anecdote affords a proof how strongly his habits of thought had long before predisposed him for the prosecution of a metaphysical idea, precisely the same with that on which this Scholium proceeds.[1]

mais il nous semble que l'Anglois n'a rien opposé de satisfaisant aux raisons de Leibnitz."—*Eloge de Leibnitz*

As for the point here in dispute, I must own, that it does not seem to me a fit subject for argument; inasmuch as I cannot even form a conception of the proposition contended for by Leibnitz. The light in which the question struck Clarke in his childhood, is the same in which I am still disposed to view it, or rather, I should say, is the light in which I must ever view it, while the frame of my understanding continues unaltered. Of what *data* is human reason possessed, from which it is entitled to argue in opposition to truths, the contrary of which it is impossible not only to prove, but to express in terms comprehensible by our faculties?

For some remarks on the scholastic controversies concerning *space* and *time*, see the First Part of this *Dissertation*, Note I. See also Locke's *Essay*, book ii. chap. xiii. § 16, 17, 18

[1] [* An anecdote somewhat similar to this is told by Dr Henry More, of his own philosophical, or rather mystical habits of reflection, before he left Eton school. Though not immediately connected with my present subject, I cannot refrain from transcribing part of his very picturesque description of himself. "In a certain ground, belonging to Eton College, where the boys used to play and exercise themselves, walking as my manner was, slowly, and with my head on one side, and kicking now and then the stones with my feet, I used sometimes, with a sort of musical and melancholic murmur, to repeat to myself these verses of Claudian:—

' Sæpe mihi dubiam traxit sententia mentem,
Curarent superi terras; an nullus inesset
Rector, et incerto fluerent mortalia casu.'†

Yet that sound and entire sense of God, which nature herself had planted deeply in me, very easily silenced all such slight and poetical doubts as these Yea, even in my first childhood, an inward sense of the Divine presence was so strong upon my mind, that I then believed, that no action, word, or thought, could be concealed from him. Which thing since no distinct reason, philosophy, or instruction taught it me at that age, but only an internal sensation urged it upon me, I think is a very evident proof, that this was an innate sense or notion in me, contrary to some absurd and sordid pretenders to philosophy in our present age. And if these sophists shall reply, that I derived this sense *ex traduce*, or by way of propagation, as being born of parents of great piety, I demand, how it came to pass, I received not Calvinism also along with it? for my father, mother, and uncle, were all zeal-

* Restored.—*Ed*
† [So also the Psalmist, "My feet were ready to slip, when I saw the prosperity of the wicked"]

. It would be superfluous to dwell longer on the history of these speculations, which, whatever value they may possess in the opinion of persons accustomed to deep and abstract reasoning, are certainly not well adapted to ordinary or to uncultivated understandings. This consideration furnishes, of itself, no slight presumption, that they were not intended to be the *media* by which the bulk of mankind were to be led to the knowledge of truths so essential to human happiness;[1] and, accordingly, it was on this very ground that Bishop Butler and Dr. Francis Hutcheson were induced to strike into a different and more popular path for establishing the fundamental principles of religion and morality. Both of these writers appear to have communicated, in very early youth, their doubts and objections to Dr. Clarke; and to have had, even then, a glimpse of those inquiries by which they were afterwards to give so new and so fortunate a direction to the ethical studies of their countrymen. It is sufficient here to remark this circumstance as an important step in the progress of Moral Philosophy. The farther illustration of it properly belongs to another part of this discourse.

The chief glory of Clarke, as a metaphysical author, is due to the boldness and ability with which he placed himself in the breach against the Necessitarians and Fatalists of his times. With a mind far inferior to that of Locke, in comprehensiveness, in originality, and in fertility of invention, he was, nevertheless, the more wary and skilful disputant of the two, possessing, in a singular degree, that reach of thought in grasping remote consequences, which effectually saved him from those rash concessions into which Locke was frequently betrayed by the greater warmth of his temperament, and vivacity of his fancy. This logical foresight (the natural result of his habits of mathematical study) rendered him peculiarly fit to contend with adversaries, eager and qualified to take ad-

---

ous followers of Calvin, and withal very pious and good persons."—*Preface* to the first volume of his *Philosophical Works.*]

[1] [* Quicquid nos aut meliores aut beatiores facturum est vel in aperto, vel in proximo posuit natura —*Seneca*]

* Restored —*Ed*

vantage of every vulnerable point in his doctrines; but it gave, at the same time, to his style a tameness, and monotony, and want of colouring, which never appear in the easy and spirited, though often unfinished and unequal, sketches of Locke. Voltaire has somewhere said of him, that he was a mere reasoning machine, (*un moulin à raisonnement*,) and the expression, though doubtless much too unqualified, possesses a merit, in point of just discrimination, of which Voltaire was probably not fully aware.[1]

---

[1] In the extent of his learning, the correctness of his taste, and the depth of his scientific acquirements, Clarke possessed indisputable advantages over Locke, with which advantages he combined another not less important, the systematical steadiness with which his easy fortune and unbroken leisure enabled him to pursue his favourite speculations through the whole course of his life.

On the subject of Free Will, Locke is more indistinct, undecided, and inconsistent, than might have been expected from his powerful mind, when directed to so important a question. This was probably owing to his own strong feelings in favour of man's moral liberty, struggling with the deep impression left on his philosophical creed by the writings of Hobbes, and with his deference for the talents of his own intimate friend, Anthony Collins * That Locke conceived himself to be an advocate for *free-will*, appears indisputably from many expressions in his chapter on *Power;* and yet, in that very chapter, he has made various concessions to his adversaries, in which he seems to yield all that was contended for by Hobbes and Collins: And, accordingly, he is ranked, with some appearance of truth, by Priestley, with those who, while they opposed verbally the scheme of necessity, have adopted it substantially, without being aware of their mistake

In one of Locke's letters to Mr. Molyneux, he has stated, in the strongest possible terms, his conviction of man's free agency, resting this conviction entirely on our indisputable consciousness of *the fact*. This declaration of Locke I consider as well worthy of attention in the argument about Free Will; for, although in questions of pure speculation, the authority of great names is entitled to no weight, excepting in so far as it is supported by solid reasonings, the case is otherwise with *facts* relating to the phenomena of the human mind. The patient attention with which Mr Locke had studied these very nice phenomena during the course of a long life, gives to the results of his metaphysical experience a value of the same sort, but much greater in degree, with that which we attach to a delicate experiment in chemistry, when vouched by a Black or a Davy. The ultimate appeal, after all, must be made by every person to his own consciousness; but when we have the experience of Locke on the one hand, and that of Priestley and Belsham on the other, the contrast is surely sufficient to induce every cautious inquirer to re-examine his feelings before he allows himself to listen to the statements of the latter in preference to that of the former

* See Note K k

I have already taken notice of Clarke's defence of moral liberty in opposition to Leibnitz; but soon after this controversy was brought to a conclusion by the death of his antagonist, he had to resume the same argument, in reply to his countryman, Anthony Collins; who, following the footsteps of Hobbes, with logical talents not inferior to those of his master, and with a weight of personal character in his favour, to which his master had no pretensions,[1] gave to the cause which he so warmly espoused, a degree of credit among sober and serious inquirers, which it had never before possessed in England. I have reserved, therefore, for this place, the few general reflections which I have to offer on this endless subject of controversy. In stating these, I shall be the less anxious to condense my thoughts, as I do not mean to return to the discussion in the sequel of this historical sketch. Indeed, I do not know of anything that has been advanced by later writers, in support of

For the information of some of my readers, it may be proper to mention that it has of late become fashionable among a certain class of metaphysicians, boldly to assert, that the evidence of *their* consciousness is decidedly in favour of the scheme of necessity

But to return to Mr. Locke. The only consideration on this subject which seems to have staggered him, was the difficulty of reconciling this opinion with the prescience of God. As to this theological difficulty, I have nothing to say at present. The only question which I consider as of any consequence, is the matter of fact; and, on this point, nothing can be more explicit and satisfactory than the words of Locke In examining these, the attentive reader will be satisfied, that Locke's declaration is not (as Priestley asserts) in favour of the Liberty of Spontaneity, but in favour of the Liberty of Indifference; for as to the former, there seems to be no difficulty in reconciling it with the prescience of God "I own (says Mr Locke) freely to you the weakness of my understanding, that though it be unquestionable that there is omnipotence and omniscience in God our Maker, and though *I cannot have a clearer perception of anything than that I am free,* yet I cannot make freedom in man consistent with omnipotence and omniscience in God, though I am as fully persuaded of both as of any truth I most firmly assent to; and therefore I have long since given off the consideration of that question, resolving all into this short conclusion, that, *if it be possible for God to make a free agent, then man is free, though I see not the way of it."*

[1] In speaking disrespectfully of the personal character of Hobbes, I allude to the base servility of his political principles, and to the suppleness with which he adapted them to the opposite interests of the three successive governments under which his literary life was spent To his private virtues the most honourable testimony has been borne, both by his friends and by his enemies

the scheme of necessity, of which the germ is not to be found in the inquiry of Collins.

In order to enter completely into the motives which induced Clarke to take so zealous and so prominent a part in the dispute about Free Will, it is necessary to look back to the system of Spinoza; an author, with whose peculiar opinions I have hitherto avoided to distract my readers' attention. At the time when he wrote, he does not appear to have made many proselytes; the extravagant and alarming consequences in which his system terminated, serving with most persons as a sufficient antidote against it. Clarke was probably the first who perceived distinctly the logical accuracy of his reasoning; and that, if the principles were admitted, it was impossible to resist the conclusions deduced from them.[1] It seems to have been the object both of Leibnitz and of Collins, to obviate the force of this indirect argument against the scheme of necessity, by attempting to reconcile it with the moral agency of man; a task which, I think, it must be allowed, was much less ably and plausibly executed by the former than by the latter. Convinced, on the other hand, that Spinoza had reasoned from his premises much more rigorously than either Collins or Leibnitz, Clarke bent the whole force of his mind to demonstrate that these premises were false; and, at the same time, to put incautious reasoners on their guard against the seducing sophistry of his antagonists, by showing, that there was no medium between admitting the free agency of man, and of acquiescing in all the monstrous absurdities which the creed of Spinoza involves.

Spinoza,[2] it may be proper to mention, was an Amsterdam

---

[1] Dr Reid's opinion on this point coincides exactly with that of Clarke. See his Essays on the *Active Powers of Man*, (p. 289, 4to edition,) where he pronounces the system of Spinoza to be "the genuine, and the most tenable system of necessity."

[2] Born 1632, died 1677. It is observed by Bayle, that "although Spinoza was the first who reduced Atheism to a system, and formed it into a body of doctrine, connected according to the method of geometricians, yet, in other respects, his opinion is not new, the substance of it being the same with that of several other philosophers, both ancient and modern, European and Eastern"—See his *Dict*, Art. *Spinoza*, and the authorities in Note S.

It is asserted by a late German writer, that " Spinoza has been little heard of in England, and not at all in France,

Jew of Portuguese extraction, who (with a view probably to gain a more favourable reception to his philosophical dogmas) withdrew himself from the sect in which he had been educated, and afterwards appears to have lived chiefly in the society of Christians,[1] without, however, making any public profession of the Christian faith, or even submitting to the ceremony of baptism In his philosophical creed, he at first embraced the system of Descartes, and began his literary career with a work entitled, *Renati Descartes Principiorum Philosophiæ, Pars Prima et Secunda, More Geometrico Demonstratæ*, 1663. It was, however, in little else than his physical principles that he agreed with Descartes; for no two philosophers ever differed more widely in their metaphysical and theological tenets. Fontenelle characterizes his system as a "Cartesianism pushed to extravagance," (*une Cartésianisme outrée;*) an expression which, although far from conveying a just or adequate idea of the whole spirit of his doctrines, applies very happily to his boldness and pertinacity in following out his avowed principles to the most paradoxical consequences which he conceived them to involve. The reputation of his writings, accordingly, has fallen entirely (excepting perhaps in Germany and in Holland) with the philosophy on which they were grafted; although some of the most obnoxious opinions contained in them are still, from time to time, obtruded on the world, under the disguise of a new form, and of a phraseology less revolting to modern taste.[2]

and that he has been zealously defended and attacked by Germans alone." The same writer informs us, that "the philosophy of Leibnitz has been little studied in France, and not at all in England." — *Lectures on the History of Literature*, by FRED SCHLEGEL. English Transl. published at Edin 1818. Vol ii p 243.

Is it possible that an author who pronounces so dogmatically upon the philosophy of England, should never have heard the name of Dr. Clarke?

[1] The Synagogue were so indignant at his apostasy, that they pronounced against him their *highest* sentence of excommunication called *Schammata* The form of the sentence may be found in the Treatise of Selden, *De Jure Naturæ et Gentium*, lib iv c 7 It is a document of some curiosity, and will scarcely suffer by a comparison with the Popish form of excommunication recorded by Sterne. For some farther particulars with respect to Spinoza see Note L L.

[2] " On vient de proposer à l'Académie de Berlin, pour sujet de concours:

In no part of Spinoza's works has he avowed himself an atheist; but it will not be disputed, by those who comprehend the drift of his reasonings, that, in point of practical tendency, Atheism and Spinozism are one and the same. In this respect, we may apply to Spinoza (and I may add to Vanini also) what Cicero has said of Epicurus, *Verbis reliquit Deos, re sustulit;* a remark which coincides exactly with an expression of Newton's in the *Scholium* at the end of the *Principia:* "DEUS sine dominio, providentia, et causis finalibus, nihil aliud est quam FATUM et NATURA."[1]

Among other doctrines of natural and revealed religion which Spinoza affected to embrace, was that of the Divine Omnipresence; a doctrine which, combined with the Plenum of Descartes, led him, by a short and plausible process of reasoning, to the revival of the old theory which represented God as *the soul of the world;* or rather to that identification of God and of the material universe, which I take to be still more agreeable to the idea of Spinoza.[2] I am particularly anxious to direct

---

' Quels sont les points de contact du Cartésianisme et du système de Spinoza?' "—*Recherches Philosophiques,* par M de Bonald, 1818

[1] One of the most elaborate and acute refutations of Spinozism which has yet appeared, is to be found in Bayle's Dictionary, where it is described as "the most monstrous scheme imaginable, and the most diametrically opposite to the clearest notions of the mind." The same author affirms, that "it has been fully overthrown even by the weakest of its adversaries"—"It does not, indeed, appear possible," as Mr Maclaurin has observed, "to invent another system equally absurd; amounting (as it does in fact) to this proposition, that there is but one substance in the universe, endowed with infinite attributes, (particularly infinite extension and cogitation,) which produces all other things necessarily as its own modifications, and which alone is, in all events, both physical and moral, at once cause and effect, agent and patient."—*View of Newton's Discoveries,* book i. chap iv

[2] Spinoza supposes that there are in God two eternal properties, thought and extension; and as he held, with Descartes, that extension is the essence of matter, he must necessarily have conceived *materiality* to be an essential attribute of God. "Per Corpus intelligo modum, qui Dei essentiam quatenus ut res extensa consideratur, certo et determinato modo exprimit."—(*Ethica ordine Geometrico Demonstrata,* Pars ii Defin. 1 See also *Ethic.* Pars i Prop. 14) With respect to the other attributes of God, he held that God is the *cause* of all things; but that he acts not from choice, but from necessity, and of consequence, that he is the involuntary author of all the good and evil, virtue and vice, which are exhibited in human life "Res nullo alio modo, neque alio ordine a Deo produci potuerunt, quam

the attention of my readers to this part of his system, as I conceive it to be at present very generally misrepresented, or, at least, very generally misunderstood; a thing not to be wondered at, considering the total neglect into which his works have long

productæ sunt "—(*Ibid.* Pars i. Prop 33) In one of his letters to Mr Oldenburg, (Letter 21,) he acknowledges that his ideas of God and of nature were very different from those entertained by *modern* Christians, adding, by way of explanation, "Deum rerum omnium causam immanentem, non vero transeuntem statuo ;"—an expression to which I can annex no other meaning but this, that God is inseparably and essentially united with his works, and that they form together but one being [* The *transient* acts of God (according to Bishop Burnet) 'are those which are done in a succession of times, such as creation, providence, and miracles; whereas his *immanent* acts, his knowledge and decrees, are one with his essence."—*Exposit.* pp. 26, 27.]

The diversity of opinions entertained concerning the nature of Spinozism has been chiefly owing to this, that some have formed their notions of it from the books which Spinoza published during his life, and others from his posthumous remains. It is in the last alone (particularly in his *Ethics*) that his system is to be seen completely unveiled and undisguised In the former, and also in the letters addressed to his friends, he occasionally accommodates himself, with a very temporizing spirit, to what he considered as the prejudices of the world In proof of this, see his *Tractatus Theologico-Politicus*, and his epistolary correspondence, *passim;* above all, his letter to a young friend who had apostatized from Protestantism to the Catholic Church. The letter is addressed, "Nobilissimo Juveni, *Alberto Burgh.*"— Spin. *Op.* tom ii p. 695.

The edition of Spinoza's works to which my references are made, is the complete and very accurate one published at Jena, in 1802, by Henr. Eberh. Gottlob Paulus, who styles himself Doctor and Professor of Theology.

This learned divine is at no pains to conceal his admiration of the character as well as talents of his author, nor does he seem to have much to object to the system of Spinozism, as explained in his posthumous work upon Ethics, a work which, the editor admits, contains the only genuine exposition of Spinoza's creed "Sedes systematis quod sibi condidit in ethica est."— (*Præf. Iteratæ Editionis*, p. ix) In what manner all this was reconciled in his theological lectures with the doctrines either of natural or of revealed religion, it is not very easy to imagine. Perhaps he only affords a new example of what Dr. Clarke long ago remarked, that "Believing too much and too little have commonly the luck to meet together, like two things moving contrary ways in the same circle."—*Third Letter to Dodwell*

A late German writer, who, in his own opinions, has certainly no leaning towards Spinozism, has yet spoken of the moral tendency of Spinoza's writings in terms of the warmest praise. "The morality of Spinoza (says M. Fred. Schlegel) is not indeed that of the Bible, for he himself was no Christian, but it is still a pure and noble morality, resembling that of the ancient Stoics, perhaps possessing considerable advantages over that system. That which makes him strong when opposed to adversaries who do not understand or

* Restored.—*Ed*

fallen. It is only in this way I can account for the frequent use which has most unfairly been made of the term *Spinozism* to stigmatize and discredit some doctrines, or rather some modes of speaking, which have been sanctioned not only by the wisest

feel his depth, or who unconsciously have fallen into errors not much different from his, is not merely the scientific clearness and decision of his intellect, but in a much higher degree the openheartedness, strong feeling, and conviction, with which all that he says seems to gush from his heart and soul "— (*Lect. of Fred Schlegel*, Eng. Transl vol ii p. 244.) The rest of the passage, which contains a sort of apology for the system of Spinoza, is still more curious.

Although it is with the metaphysical tenets of Spinoza alone that we are immediately concerned at present, it is not altogether foreign to my purpose to observe, that he had also speculated much about the principles of government, and that the coincidence of his opinions with those of Hobbes, on this last subject, was not less remarkable than the similarity of their views on the most important questions of metaphysics and ethics Unconnected as these different branches of knowledge may at first appear, the theories of Spinoza and of Hobbes concerning *all* of them, formed parts of one and the same system, the whole terminating ultimately in the maxim with which, according to Plutarch, Anaxarchus consoled Alexander after the murder of Clytus: Πᾶν τὸ πραχθὲν ἀπὸ τοῦ κρατοῦντος δίκαιον εἶναι Even in discussing the question about Liberty and Necessity, Hobbes cannot help glancing at this political corollary "The *power of God alone* is a sufficient *justification* of any action he doth"   "That which he doth is made just by his doing it" . . . "Power irresistible justifies *all* actions really and properly, in whomsoever it be found "—(*Of Liberty and Necessity*, addressed to the Lord Marquis of Newcastle) Spinoza has expressed himself exactly to the same purpose —(See his *Tractatus Politicus*, cap 2, § 3, 4) So steadily, indeed, is this practical application of their abstract principles kept in view by both these writers, that not one generous feeling is ever suffered to escape the pen of either in favour of the rights, the liberties, or the improvement of their species.

The close affinity between those abstract theories which tend to degrade human nature, and that accommodating morality which prepares the minds of men for receiving passively the yoke of slavery, although too little attended to by the writers of literary history, has not been overlooked by those deeper politicians who are disposed (as has been alleged of the first of the Cæsars) to consider their fellow-creatures "but as rubbish in the way of their ambition, or tools to be employed in removing it" This practical tendency of the Epicurean philosophy is remarked by one of the wisest of the Roman statesmen, and we learn from the same high authority, how fashionable this philosophy was in the higher circles of his countrymen, at that disastrous period which immediately preceded the ruin of the Republic "Nunquam audivi in Epicuri schola, Lycurgum, Solonem, Miltiadem, Themistoclem, Epaminondam, nominari, qui in ore sunt cæterorum omnium philosophorum "—(*De Fin.* lib ii c. 21.) "Nec tamen Epicuri licet oblivisci, si cupiam, cujus imaginem non modo in tabulis nostri familiares, sed etiam in poculis, et annulis habent "—*Ibid* lib v c 1

The prevalence of Hobbism at the

of the ancients, but by the highest names in English philosophy and literature; and which, whether right or wrong, will be found, on a careful examination and comparison, not to have the most distant affinity to the absurd creed with which they have been confounded. I am afraid that Pope, in the following lines of the *Dunciad,* suffered himself so far to be misled by the malignity of Warburton, as to aim a secret stab at Newton and Clarke, by associating their figurative, and not altogether unexceptionable, language concerning *space* (when they called it the *sensorium* of the Deity) with the opinion of Spinoza, as I have just explained it.[1]

> "Thrust some Mechanic Cause into His place,
> Or bind in matter, or *diffuse in space.*"

How little was it suspected by the poet, when this sarcasm escaped him, that the charge of Spinozism and Pantheism was afterwards to be brought against himself, for the sublimest passage to be found in his writings!

court of Charles II, (a fact acknowledged by Clarendon himself,) is but one of the many instances which might be quoted from modern times in confirmation of these remarks.

The practical tendency of such doctrines as would pave the way to universal scepticism, by holding up to ridicule the extravagances and inconsistencies of the learned, is precisely similar. We are told by Tacitus, (*Annal* lib xiv.) that Nero was accustomed, at the close of a banquet, to summon a party of philosophers, that he might amuse himself with listening to the endless diversity and discordancy of their respective systems. nor were there wanting philosophers at Rome, the same historian adds, who were flattered to be thus exhibited as a spectacle at the table of the emperor What a deep and instructive moral is conveyed by this anecdote! and what a contrast does it afford to the sentiment of one of Nero's successors, who was himself a philosopher in the best sense of the word, and whose reign furnishes some of the fairest pages in the annals of the human race! "I search for truth, (says Marcus Antoninus,) by which no person has ever been injured.' Ζητῶ γὰρ τὴν ἀλήθειαν, ὑφ' ἧς ἐδεὶς πώποτε ἐϐλάβη.

[1] Warburton, indeed, always *professes* great respect for Newton, but of his hostility to Clarke it is unnecessary to produce any other proof than his note on the following line of the *Dunciad* —

"Where Tindal dictates, and Silenus snores"
—B iv l 492

May I venture to add, that the noted line of the *Essay on Man,*

" And shew d a Newton as we shew an ape,"

could not possibly have been written by any person impressed with a due veneration for this glory of his species?

> "All are but parts of one stupendous whole,
> Whose body Nature is, and God the soul
> * * * * *
> Lives through all Life, *extends through all extent,
> Spreads undivided,* operates unspent."[1]

Bayle was, I think, the writer who first led the way to this misapplication of the term *Spinozism;* and his object in doing so was plainly to destroy the effect of the most refined and philosophical conceptions of the Deity which were ever formed by the unassisted power of human reason.

> "Estne Dei sedes nisi terra, et pontus, et aër,
> Et cœlum, et virtus? Superos quid quærimus ultra?
> Jupiter est quodcumque vides, quocumque moveris"

> "Is there a place that God would choose to love
> Beyond this earth, the seas, yon Heaven above,
> And virtuous minds, the noblest throne for Jove,
> Why seek we farther then? Behold around,
> How all thou seest does with the God abound,
> Jove is alike to all, and always to be found"
>
> Rowe's *Lucan.*

Who but Bayle could have thought of extracting anything like Spinozism from such verses as these!

On a subject so infinitely disproportioned to our faculties, it is vain to expect language which will bear a logical and captious examination. Even the Sacred Writers themselves are forced to adapt their phraseology to the comprehension of those to whom it is addressed, and frequently borrow the figurative diction of poetry to convey ideas which must be interpreted, not according to the letter, but the spirit of the passage. It is thus that thunder is called the voice of God; the wind, His breath; and the tempest, the blast of His nostrils. Not attending to this circumstance, or rather not choosing to direct to it

---

[1] This passage, as Warton has remarked, bears a very striking analogy to a noble one in the old Orphic verses quoted in the treatise Περὶ κόσμου, ascribed to Aristotle, and it is not a little curious, that the same ideas occur in some specimens of *Hindoo* poetry, translated by Sir W. Jones, more particularly in the Hymn to *Narrayna*, or the Spirit of God, taken, as he informs us, from the writings of their ancient authors

Omniscient Spirit, whose all-ruling power
Bids from each sense bright emanations beam;
Glows in the rainbow, sparkles in the stream,
&c &c.

the attention of his readers, Spinoza has laid hold of the well-known expression of St. Paul, that " in God we live, and move, and have our being," as a proof that the ideas of the apostle, concerning the Divine Nature, were pretty much the same with his own; a consideration which, if duly weighed, might have protected some of the passages above quoted from the uncharitable criticisms to which they have frequently been exposed.[1]

To return, however, to Collins, from whose controversy with Clarke I was insensibly led aside into this short digression

---

[1] Mr. Gibbon, in commenting upon the celebrated lines of Virgil,

" Spiritus intus alit, totamque infusa per artus, Mens agitat molem, et magno se corpore miscet,"

observes, that " the mind which is INFUSED into the different parts of matter, and which MINGLES ITSELF with the mighty mass, scarcely retains any property of a spiritual substance, and bears too near an affinity to the principles which the impious Spinoza revived rather than invented" He adds, however, that " the poverty of human language, and the obscurity of human ideas, make it difficult to speak worthily of the GREAT FIRST CAUSE, and that our most religious poets, (particularly Pope and Thomson,) in striving to express the presence and energy of the Deity in every part of the universe, deviate unwarily into images which require a favourable construction But these writers (he candidly remarks) deserve that favour, by the sublime manner in which they celebrate the Great Father of the universe, and by those effusions of love and gratitude which are inconsistent with the materialist's system."
—*Misc. Works*, vol ii. pp 509, 510

May I be permitted here to remark, that it is not only *difficult* but *impossible* to speak of the omnipresence and omnipotence of God, without deviating into such images?

With the doctrine of the *Anima Mundi*, some philosophers, both ancient and modern, have connected another theory, according to which the souls of men are portions of the Supreme Being, with whom they are re-united at death, and in whom they are finally absorbed and lost. To assist the imagination in conceiving this theory, death has been compared to the breaking of a phial of water, immersed in the ocean It is needless to say, that this incomprehensible jargon has no *necessary* connexion with the doctrine which represents God as the soul of the world, and that it would have been loudly disclaimed, not only by Pope and Thomson, but by Epictetus, Antoninus, and all the wisest and soberest of the Stoical school Whatever objections, therefore, may be made to this doctrine, let not its supposed *consequences* be charged upon any but those who may expressly avow them On such a subject, as Gibbon has well remarked, " we should be slow to suspect, and still slower to condemn."
—*Ibid* p 510.

Sir William Jones mentions a very curious modification of this theory of *absorption*, as one of the doctrines of the *Vedanta* School " The Vedanta School represent *Elysian* happiness as a total absorption, *though not such as to destroy consciousness*, in the Divine Essence."—*Dissertation on the Gods of Greece, Italy, and India*.

about Spinoza: I have already said, that it seems to have been the aim of Collins to vindicate the doctrine of Necessity from the reproach brought on it by its supposed alliance with Spinozism; and to retort upon the partisans of free-will the charges of favouring atheism and immorality. In proof of this I have only to quote the account given by the author himself, of the plan of his work:—

"Too much care cannot be taken to prevent being misunderstood and prejudged, in handling questions of such nice speculation as those of Liberty and Necessity; and, therefore, though I might in justice expect to be read before any judgment be passed on me, I think it proper to premise the following observations.—

"1. *First*, Though I deny *liberty* in a certain meaning of that word, yet I contend for *liberty*, as it signifies *a power in man to do as he wills or pleases;* [*which is the notion of liberty maintained by Aristotle, Cicero,[1] Mr. Locke, and several other philosophers, ancient and modern.] . . .

"2 *Secondly*, When I affirm *necessity*, I contend only for *moral necessity;* meaning thereby, that man who is an intelligent and sensible being, is determined by his reason and his senses; and I deny man to be subject to such necessity as is in clocks, watches, and such other beings, which, for want of sensation and intelligence, are subject to an absolute, physical, or mechanical necessity.

"3. *Thirdly*, I have undertaken to show, that the notions I advance are so far from being inconsistent with, that they are the sole foundations of morality and laws, and of rewards and punishments in society; and that the notions I explode are subversive of them."[2]

---

[1] [* How far this is a just account of Cicero's notion of liberty, the reader may judge from his own words "Si omnia fato fiunt (says Cicero) omnia fiunt causa antecedente; et si causa appetitus non est sita in nobis," &c — *De Fato,* cap xvii.

Cicero, indeed, has elsewhere said, "*Quid est libertas? Potestas vivendi ut velis*" But Cicero is here speaking of that *liberty* which consists in exemption from *external* restraint, in which sense of the word, it has nothing in common with that *moral* liberty which has been so long the subject of dispute among metaphysicians]

[2] *A Philosophical Inquiry concerning Human Liberty,* 3d edit Lond 1735.

* Restored.—Ed.

In the prosecution of his argument on this question, Collins endeavours to show, that man is a necessary agent: 1. From our experience. (By *experience* he means our own consciousness that we *are* necessary agents.) 2. From the impossibility of liberty.[1] 3 From the consideration of the Divine prescience. 4. From the nature and use of rewards and punishments; and, 5. From the nature of morality.[2]

In this view of the subject, and, indeed, in the very selection of his premises, it is remarkable how completely Collins has anticipated Dr. Jonathan Edwards, the most celebrated and indisputably the ablest champion of the scheme of Necessity who has since appeared. The coincidence is so perfect, that the outline given by the former, of the plan of his work, might have served with equal propriety as a preface to that of the latter.

From the above summary, and still more from the whole tenor of the *Philosophical Inquiry*, it is evident that Collins (one of the most obnoxious writers of his day to divines of all denominations) was not less solicitous than his successor Edwards to reconcile his metaphysical notions with man's accountableness and moral agency. The remarks, accordingly, of Clarke upon Collins's work, are equally applicable to that of Edwards. It is to be regretted that they seem never to have fallen into the hands of this very acute and honest reasoner. As for Collins, it is a remarkable circumstance, that he attempted no reply to this tract of Clarke's, although he lived twelve years after its publication.* The reasonings contained in it, together with those on the same subject in his correspondence with Leibnitz, and in his *Demonstration of the Being*

---

[1] See Note M M
[2] See Note N N.

* [Not during Clarke's life. But in 1729, Collins published a treatise *On Liberty and Necessity*, being a vindication of his *Inquiry*. This defence, which seems now quite unknown, was, however, answered in the following year by two Anglican divines, (Jackson and Gretton) The author of *Reflections upon Liberty and Necessity*, &c , Lond. 1759, a book printed but never published, and containing " Cursory Remarks upon Dr Clarke's Answer to Mr. Collins's Inquiry concerning Human Liberty,"—this author says, (pp 6, 7, 61, 66,) that Collins was deterred from answering Clarke " *by a fear of the Civil Magistrate* " Bayle's *Dictionary* in English (Art. *Collins*) makes an unqualified assertion equivalent to Mr Stewart's —*Ed*]

and *Attributes of God,* form, in my humble opinion, the most important as well as powerful of all his metaphysical arguments.[1] The adversaries with whom he had to contend were, both of them, eminently distinguished by ingenuity and subtlety, and he seems to have put forth to the utmost his logical strength, in contending with such antagonists. " The liberty or moral agency of man (says his friend Bishop Hoadley) was a darling point to him. He excelled always, and showed a superiority to all, whenever it came into private discourse or public debate. But he never more excelled than when he was pressed with the strength Leibnitz was master of; which made him exert all his talents to set it once again in a clear light, to guard it against the evil of metaphysical obscurities, and to give the finishing stroke to a subject which must ever be the foundation of morality in man, and is the ground of the accountableness of intelligent creatures for all their actions."[2]

It is needless to say, that neither Leibnitz nor Collins admitted the fairness of the inferences which Clarke conceived to follow from the scheme of necessity: But almost every page in the subsequent history of this controversy may be regarded as an additional illustration of the soundness of Clarke's reasonings, and of the sagacity with which he anticipated the fatal errors likely to issue from the system which he opposed.

" Thus (says a very learned disciple of Leibnitz, who made his first appearance as an author about thirty years after the death of his master[3])—thus, the same chain embraces the

---

[1] Voltaire, who, in all probability, never read either Clarke or Collins, has said that the former replied to the latter only by *Theological* reasonings " *Clarke n'a répondu à Collins qu'en Théologien* "—(*Quest sur l'Encyclopédie,* Art *Liberté*) Nothing can be more remote from the truth The argument of Clarke is wholly *Metaphysical;* whereas, his antagonist, in various instances, has attempted to wrest to his own purposes the words of Scripture.

[2] Preface to the folio ed. of Clarke's *Works* —The vital importance which Clarke attached to this question, has given to the concluding paragraphs of his remarks on Collins, an earnestness and a solemnity of which there are not many instances in his writings These paragraphs cannot be too strongly recommended to the attention of those well-meaning persons, who, in our own times, have come forward as the apostles of Dr Priestley's "great and glorious Doctrine of Philosophical Necessity "

[3] Charles Bonnet, born 1720, died 1793

physical and moral worlds, binds the past to the present, the present to the future, the future to eternity."

"That wisdom which has ordained the existence of this chain, has doubtless willed that of every link of which it is composed. A CALIGULA is one of those links, and this link is of iron: a MARCUS AURELIUS is another link, and this link is of gold. *Both* are necessary parts of one whole, which could not but exist. Shall God then be angry at the sight of the iron link? What absurdity! God esteems this link at its proper value: He sees it in its cause, and he approves this cause, for it is good. God beholds moral monsters as he beholds physical monsters. Happy is the link of gold! Still more happy if he know that he is *only fortunate*.[1] He has attained the highest degree of moral perfection, and is nevertheless without pride, knowing that what he is, is the necessary result of the place which he must occupy in the chain."

"The gospel is the allegorical exposition of this system; the simile of the potter is its summary."[2]—BONNET, tom. viii. pp. 237, 238.

In what essential respect does this system differ from that of Spinoza? Is it not even more dangerous in its practical tendency, in consequence of the high strain of mystical devotion by which it is exalted?[3]

---

[1] The words in the original are, "Heureux le chainon d'or! plus *heureux* encore, s'il sait qu'il n'est qu' *heureux.*" The double meaning of *heureux*, if it render the expression less logically precise, gives it at least an epigrammatic turn, which cannot be preserved in our language.

[2] See Note O O

[3] Among the various forms which religious enthusiasm assumes, there is a certain prostration of the mind, which, under the specious disguise of a deep humility, aims at exalting the Divine perfections, by annihilating all the powers which belong to Human Nature. "Nothing is more usual for fervent devotion, (says Sir James Mackintosh, in speaking of some theories current among the Hindoos,) than to dwell so long and so warmly on the meanness and worthlessness of created things, and on the all-sufficiency of the Supreme Being, that it slides insensibly from comparative to absolute language, and in the eagerness of its zeal to magnify the Deity seems to annihilate everything else."—See *Philosophy of the Human Mind*, vol ii p 529, 2d. ed.

This excellent observation may serve to account for the zeal displayed by Bonnet, and many other devout men, in

This objection, however, does not apply to the quotations which follow. They exhibit, without any colourings of imagination or of enthusiasm, the scheme of necessity pushed to the remotest and most alarming conclusions which it appeared to Clarke to involve; and as they express the serious and avowed creed of two of our contemporaries, (both of them men of distinguished talents,) may be regarded as a proof, that the zeal displayed by Clarke against the metaphysical principles which led ultimately to such results, was not so unfounded as some worthy and able inquirers have supposed.

May I be permitted to observe farther on this head, that, as one of these writers spent his life in the pay of a German prince, and as the other was the favourite philosopher of another sovereign, still more illustrious, the sentiments which they were so anxious to proclaim to the world, may be presumed to have been not very offensive, in their judgments, to the ears of their protectors?

"All that is must be, (says the Baron de Grimm, addressing himself to the Duke of Saxe-Gotha)—all that is must be, even because it is; this is the only sound philosophy; as long as we do not know this universe *a priori*, (as they say in the schools,) ALL IS NECESSITY.[1] Liberty is a word without meaning, as you shall see in the letter of M. Diderot."

The following passage is extracted from Diderot's letter here referred to:—

favour of the Scheme of Necessity. "We have nothing (they frequently and justly remind us) but what we have received"—But the question here is simply a matter of fact, whether we have or have not *received* from *God* the gift of Free Will, and the only argument, it must be remembered, which they have yet been able to advance for the negative proposition, is, that this gift was *impossible*, even for the power of God; nay, the same argument which annihilates the power of Man, annihilates that of God also, and subjects him, as well as all his creatures, to the control of causes which he is unable to resist. So completely does this scheme defeat the pious views in which it has sometimes originated.—I say *sometimes;* for the very same argument against the liberty of the Will is employed by Spinoza, according to whom the free-agency of man involves the absurd supposition of an *imperium in imperio* in the universe —*Tractat Po't* cap. 11. sect. 6.

[1] The logical inference ought undoubtedly to have been, "as long as we know nothing of the universe *a priori*, we are not entitled to say of anything that it either is, or is not, necessary."

"I am now, my dear friend, going to quit the tone of a preacher, to take, if I can, that of a philosopher. Examine it narrowly, and you will see that the word *Liberty* is a word devoid of meaning,[1] that there are not, and that there cannot be free beings; that we are only what accords with the general order, with our organization, our education, and the chain of events. These dispose of us invincibly. We can no more conceive a being acting without a motive, than we can one of the arms of a balance acting without a weight. The motive is always exterior and foreign, fastened upon us by some cause distinct from ourselves. What deceives us, is the prodigious variety of our actions, joined to the habit which we catch at our birth, of confounding the voluntary and the free. We have been so often praised and blamed, and have so often praised and blamed others, that we contract an inveterate prejudice of believing that we and they will and act freely. But if there is no liberty, there is no action that merits either praise or blame; neither vice nor virtue, nothing that ought either to be rewarded or punished. What then is the distinction among men? The doing of good and the doing of ill! The doer of ill is one who must be destroyed, not punished. The doer of good is lucky, not virtuous. But though neither the doer of good or of ill be free, man is nevertheless a being to be modified; it is for this reason the doer of ill should be destroyed upon the scaffold. From thence the good effects of education, of pleasure, of grief, of grandeur, of poverty, &c.; from thence a philosophy full of pity, strongly attached to the good, nor more angry with the wicked, than with the whirlwind which fills one's eyes with dust. Strictly speaking, there is but one sort of causes, that is, physical causes. There is but one sort of necessity, which is the same for all beings. This is what reconciles me to humankind: it is for this reason I exhorted you to philanthropy. Adopt these principles if you think them good, or show me that they are bad. If you adopt them, they will reconcile *you* too with others and with yourself: you

---

[1] Does not this remark of Diderot apply with infinitely greater force to the word *necessity*, as employed in this controversy?

will neither be pleased nor angry with yourself for being what you are. Reproach others for nothing, and repent of nothing; this is the first step to wisdom. Besides this, all is prejudice and false philosophy."[1]

The prevalence of the principles here so earnestly inculcated among the higher orders in France, at a period somewhat later in the history of the monarchy, may be judged of from the occasional allusions to them in the dramatic pieces then chiefly in request at Paris In the *Mariage de Figaro*, (the popularity of which was quite unexampled,) the hero of the piece, an intriguing valet in the service of a Spanish courtier, is introduced as thus moralizing, in a soliloquy on his own free-agency and personal identity. Such an exhibition upon the English stage would have been universally censured as out of character and extravagant, or rather, would have been completely unintelligible to the crowds by which our theatres are filled.

"Oh bizarre suite d'évènemens! Comment cela m'a-t-il arrivé? Pourquoi ces choses et non pas d'autres? Qui les a fixées sur ma tête? Forcé de parcourir la route où je suis entré sans le savoir, comme j'en sortirai sans le vouloir, je l'ai jonchée d'autant de fleurs que ma gaieté me la permet : encore je dis *ma* gaieté, sans savoir si elle est à moi plus que le reste, ni même qui est ce *moi* dont je m'occupe."

That this soliloquy, though put into the mouth of Figaro, was meant as a picture of the philosophical jargon at that time affected by courtiers and men of the world, will not be doubted by those who have attended to the importance of the *rôles* commonly assigned to confidential valets in French comedies, and to the habits of familiarity in which they are always repre-

---

[1] Nearly to the same purpose, we are told by Mr. Belsham, that "the *fallacious* feeling of *remorse* is superseded by the doctrine of necessity."—(*Elem* p 284) And again, "*Remorse* supposes free will It is of little or no use in moral discipline In a degree, it is even pernicious"—*Ibid* p 406

Nor does the opinion of Hartley seem to have been different. "The doctrine of Necessity has a tendency to abate all resentment against men. Since all they do against us is by the appointment of God, it is rebellion against him to be offended with them "

For the originals of the quotations from Grimm and Diderot, see Note P P.

sented as living with their masters. The sentiments which they are made to utter may, accordingly, be safely considered as but an echo of the lessons which they have learned from their superiors.[1]

My anxiety to state, without any interruption, my remarks on some of the most important questions to which the attention of the public was called by the speculations of Locke, of Leibnitz, of Newton, and of Clarke, has led me, in various instances, to depart from the strict order of Chronology. It is time for me, however, now to pause, and, before I proceed farther, to supply a few chasms in the foregoing sketch.[2]

SECT. IV.—OF SOME AUTHORS WHO HAVE CONTRIBUTED, BY THEIR CRITICAL OR HISTORICAL WRITINGS, TO DIFFUSE A TASTE FOR METAPHYSICAL STUDIES — BAYLE — FONTENELLE — ADDISON. —METAPHYSICAL WORKS OF BERKELEY.

AMONG the many eminent persons who were either driven from France, or who went into voluntary exile, in consequence of the revocation of the edict of Nantz, the most illustrious by far was Bayle;[3] who, fixing his residence in Holland, and availing himself, to the utmost extent, of the religious toleration then enjoyed in that country, diffused from thence, over Europe, a greater mass of accurate and curious information, accompanied by a more splendid display of acute and lively

---

[1] A reflection of Voltaire's on the writings of Spinoza may, I think, be here quoted without impropriety. "Vous êtes très confus, Baruc Spinoza, mais êtes vous aussi dangereux qu'on le dit? Je soutiens que non, et ma raison c'est que vous êtes confus, que vous avez écrit en mauvais Latin, et qu'il n'y a pas dix personnes en Europe qui vous lisent d'un bout à l'autre Quel est l'auteur dangereux? C'est celui qui est lu par les Oisifs de la Cour, et par les Dames "— *Quest sur l'Encyclop* Art. *Dieu*.

Had Voltaire kept this last remark steadily in view in his own writings, how many of those pages would he have cancelled which he has given to the world!

[2] [If any of my readers wish for further information concerning the history of the controversy about Liberty and Necessity, I beg leave to refer them to a small work entitled *Theatrum Fati*. Notitia scriptorum de Providentia, Fortuna, et Fato, auctore Petr Frid Arpe. Roterodami, 1712.]

[3] Born in 1647, died 1705.

criticism, than had ever before come from the pen of a single individual.[1] Happy! if he had been able to restrain within due bounds his passion for sceptical and licentious discussion, and to respect the feelings of the wise and good, on topics connected with religion and morality. But, in the peculiar circumstances in which he was educated, combined with the seducing profession of a literary adventurer, to which his hard fortune condemned him, such a spirit of moderation was rather to be wished than expected.

When Bayle first appeared as an author, the opinions of the learned still continued to be divided between Aristotle and Descartes. A considerable number leaned, in secret, to the metaphysical creed of Spinoza and of Hobbes; while the clergy of the Roman Catholic and the Protestant churches, instead of uniting their efforts in defence of those truths which they professed in common, wasted their strength against each other in fruitless disputes and recriminations.

In the midst of these controversies, Bayle, keeping aloof as far as possible from all the parties, indulged his sceptical and ironical humour at the common expense of the various combatants. Unattached himself to any system, or, to speak more correctly, unfixed in his opinions on the most fundamental questions, he did not prosecute any particular study with suffi-

---

[1] The erudition of Bayle is greatly undervalued by his antagonist Le Clerc. "Toutes les lumières philosophiques de M. Bayle consistoient en quelque peu de Péripatétisme, qu'il avoit appris des Jésuites de Toulouse, et un peu de Cartésianisme, qu'il n'avoit jamais approfondi."—*Bibl. Choisie*, tom. xii p. 106.

[* Mr Gibbon, although he does not go so far on this point as his favourite author, Le Clerc, has yet carried his deference for Le Clerc's authority to an undue length in the following judgment upon Bayle's erudition.]

In the judgment of Gibbon, "Bayle's learning was chiefly confined to the Latin authors; and he had more of a certain multifarious reading than of real erudition. Le Clerc, his great antagonist, was as superior to him in that respect as inferior in every other."—*Extraits Raisonnés de mes Lectures*, p. 62.

[* The *Bibliothèques* of Le Clerc (his *Bibliothèque Universelle* and his *Bibliothèque Choisie*) are characterized by Gibbon as "an inexhaustible source of amusement and instruction"—(*Misc Works*, vol. ii. p. 55.) Of these two, the *Bibliothèque Choisie* is elsewhere pronounced by the same excellent judge to be "by far the better work."—Vol i. p. 100.]

* Restored —*Ed.*

cient perseverance to add materially to the stock of useful knowledge. The influence, however, of his writings on the taste and views of speculative men of all persuasions, has been so great, as to mark him out as one of the most conspicuous characters of his age; and I shall accordingly devote to him a larger space than may, at first sight, appear due to an author who has distinguished himself only by the extent of his historical researches, and by the sagacity and subtlety of his critical disquisitions.

We are informed by Bayle himself, that his favourite authors, during his youth, were Plutarch and Montaigne; and from *them*, it has been alleged by some of his biographers, he imbibed his first lessons of scepticism. In what manner the first of these writers should have contributed to inspire him with this temper of mind, is not very obvious. There is certainly no heathen philosopher or historian whose morality is more pure or elevated; and none who has drawn the line between superstition and religion with a nicer hand.[1] Pope has with perfect truth said of him, that " he abounds more in strokes of good nature than any other author;" to which it may be added, that he abounds also in touches of simple and exquisite *pathos*, seldom to be met with among the greatest painters of antiquity. In all these respects what a contrast does Bayle present to Plutarch!

Considering the share which Bayle ascribes to Montaigne's Essays in forming his literary taste, it is curious, that there is no separate article allotted to Montaigne in the *Historical and*

---

[1] See, in particular, his account of the effects produced on the character of Pericles by the sublime lessons of Anaxagoras.

Plutarch, it is true, had said before Bayle, that atheism is less pernicious than superstition, but how wide the difference between this paradox, as explained and qualified by the Greek philosopher, and as interpreted and applied in the *Reflections on the Comet!* Mr. Addison himself seems to give his sanction to Plutarch's maxim in one of his papers on Cheerfulness "An eminent Pagan writer has made a discourse to show, that the atheist, who denies a God, does him less dishonour than the man who owns his being, but, at the same time, believes him to be cruel, hard to please, and terrible to human nature. For my own part, says he, I would rather it should be said of me, that there was never any such man as Plutarch, than that Plutarch was ill-natured, capricious, and inhuman."— *Spectator*, No. 494

Critical Dictionary. What is still more curious, there is more than one reference to this article, as if it actually existed; without any explanation of the omission (as far as I recollect) from the author or the publisher of the work. Some very interesting particulars, however, concerning Montaigne's life and writings, are scattered over the *Dictionary*, in the notices of other persons, with whom his name appeared to Bayle to have a sufficient connexion to furnish an apology for a short episode.

It does not seem to me a very improbable conjecture, that Bayle had intended, and perhaps attempted, to write an account of Montaigne; and that he had experienced greater difficulties than he was aware of, in the execution of his design. Notwithstanding their common tendency to scepticism, no two characters were ever more strongly discriminated in their most prominent features; the doubts of the one resulting from the singular coldness of his moral temperament, combined with a subtlety and over-refinement in his habits of thinking, which rendered his ingenuity, acuteness, and erudition, more than a match for his good sense and sagacity;—the indecision of the other partaking more of the shrewd and soldier-like *étourderie* of Henry IV. when he exclaimed, after hearing two lawyers plead on opposite sides of the same question, "*Ventre St. Gris! il me semble que tous les deux ont raison.*"

Independently of Bayle's constitutional bias towards scepticism, some other motives, it is probable, conspired to induce him, in the composition of his *Dictionary*, to copy the spirit and tone of the old Academic school. On these collateral motives a strong and not very favourable light is thrown by his own candid avowal in one of his letters. "In truth, (says he to his correspondent Minutoli,) it ought not to be thought strange, that so many persons should have inclined to Pyrrhonism; for of all things in the world it is the most convenient. You may dispute with impunity against everybody you meet, without any dread of that vexatious argument which is addressed *ad hominem*. You are never afraid of a retort, for as you announce no opinion of your own, you are always ready to abandon those of others to the attacks of sophists of every description. In a word, you may dispute and jest on all subjects without incurring any danger from the *lex talionis*."[1] It is amusing to think, that the Pyrrhonism which Bayle himself has here so ingeniously accounted for, from motives of conveniency and of literary cowardice, should have been mistaken by so many of his disciples for the sportive triumph of a superior intellect over the weaknesses and errors of human reason.[2]

The profession of Bayle, which made it an object to him to turn to account even the sweepings of his study, affords an additional explanation of the indigested mass of heterogeneous

---

[1] "En verité, il ne faut pas trouver étrange que tant des gens aient donné dans le Pyrrhonisme Car c'est la chose du monde la plus commode. Vous pouvez impunément disputer contre tous venans, et sans craindre ces argumens *ad hominem*, qui font quelquefois tant de peine Vous ne craignez point la rétorsion, puisque ne soutenant rien, vous abandonnez de bon cœur à tous les sophismes et à tous les raisonnemens de la terre quelque opinion que ce soit Vous n'êtes jamais obligé d'en venir à la défensive En un mot, vous contestez et vous daubez sur toutes choses tout votre saoul, sans craindre la peine du talion "—*Œuv Div de Bayle*, iv p 537.

[2] The estimate formed by Warburton of Bayle's character, both intellectual and moral, is candid and temperate. "A writer whose strength and clearness of reasoning can only be equalled by the gaiety, easiness, and delicacy of his wit, who, pervading human nature with a glance, struck into the province of paradox, as an exercise for the restless vigour of his mind who, with a soul superior to the sharpest attacks of fortune, and a heart practised to the best philosophy, had not yet enough of real greatness to overcome that last foible of superior geniuses, the temptation of honour, which the academical exercise of wit is supposed to bring to its professors "—*Divine Legation*

If there be anything objectionable in this panegyric, it is the unqualified praise bestowed on Bayle's *wit*, which, though it seldom fails in copiousness, in poignancy, or in that grave argumentative irony, by which it is still more characteristically marked, is commonly as deficient in *gaiety* and *delicacy* as that of Warburton himself.

Leibnitz seems perfectly to have entered into the peculiar temper of his adversary Bayle, when he said of him, that " the only way to make Bayle write usefully, would be to attack him when he advances propositions that are sound and true, and to abstain from attacking him, when he says anything false or pernicious "

" Le vrai moyen de faire écrire utilement M Bayle, ce seroit de l'attaquer, lorsqu'il écrit des bonnes choses et vraies, car ce seroit le moyen de le piquer pour continuer. Au lieu qu'il ne faudroit point l'attaquer quand il en dit de mauvaises, car cela l'engagera à en dire d'autres aussi mauvaises pour soutenir les premières."—Tom vi p. 273.

Leibnitz elsewhere says of him:— *Ubi bene, nemo melius*—Tom i p. 257.

and inconsistent materials contained in his Dictionary. Had he adopted any one system exclusively, his work would have shrunk in its dimensions into a comparatively narrow compass.[1]

When these different considerations are maturely weighed, the omission by Bayle of the article *Montaigne* will not be much regretted by the admirers of the Essays. It is extremely doubtful if Bayle would have been able to seize the true spirit of Montaigne's character; and, at any rate, it is not in the delineation of character that Bayle excels. His critical acumen, indeed, in the examination of opinions and arguments, is unrivalled; but his portraits of persons commonly exhibit only the coarser lineaments which obtrude themselves on the senses of ordinary observers; and seldom, if ever, evince that discriminating and divining eye, or that sympathetic penetration into the retirements of the heart, which lend to every touch of a master artist, the never-to-be-mistaken expression of truth and nature.

It furnishes some apology for the unsettled state of Bayle's opinions, that his habits of thinking were formed prior to the discoveries of the Newtonian School. Neither the vortices of Descartes, nor the monads and pre-established harmony of Leibnitz, were well calculated to inspire him with confidence in the powers of the human understanding; nor does he seem to have been led, either by taste or by genius, to the study of those

---

[1] "The inequality of Bayle's voluminous works, (says Gibbon,) is explained by his alternately writing for himself, for the bookseller, and for posterity, and if a severe critic would reduce him to a single folio, that relic, like the books of the Sybils, would become still more valuable."—Gibbon's *Mem* p 50.

Mr Gibbon observes in another place, that, "if Bayle wrote his *Dictionary* to empty the various collections he had made, without any particular design, he could not have chosen a better plan It permitted him everything, and obliged him to nothing By the double freedom of a *Dictionary* and of Notes, he could pitch on what articles he pleased, and say what he pleased on those articles"—*Extraits Raisonnés de mes Lectures*, p 64

"How could such a genius as Bayle," says the same author, "employ three or four pages, and a great apparatus of learning, to examine whether Achilles was fed with marrow only, whether it was the marrow of lions and stags, or that of lions only?" &c —*Ibid* p. 66

For a long and interesting passage with respect to Bayle's history and character, see Gibbon's *Memoirs*, &c, vol. i pp. 49, 50, 51.

exacter sciences in which Kepler, Galileo, and others, had, in the preceding age, made such splendid advances. In Geometry he never proceeded beyond a few of the elementary propositions; and it is even said, (although I apprehend with little probability,) that his farther progress was stopped by some defect in his intellectual powers, which disqualified him for the successful prosecution of the study.

It is not unworthy of notice, that Bayle was the son of a Calvinist minister, and was destined by his father for his own profession; that during the course of his education in a college of Jesuits, he was converted to the Roman Catholic persuasion;[1] and that finally he went to Geneva, where, if he was not recalled to the Protestant faith, he was at least most thoroughly reclaimed from the errors of Popery.[2]

To these early fluctuations in his religious creed, may be ascribed his singularly accurate knowledge of controversial theology, and of the lives and tenets of the most distinguished divines of both churches;—a knowledge much more minute

---

[1] "For the benefit of education, the Protestants were tempted to risk their children in the Catholic Universities, and in the twenty-second year of his age young Bayle was seduced by the arts and arguments of the Jesuits of Thoulouse He remained about seventeen months in their hands a voluntary captive."—Gibbon's *Misc. Works*, vol. i p. 49.

[2] According to Gibbon, "the piety of Bayle was offended by the excessive worship of creatures, and *the study of physics* convinced him of the impossibility of transubstantiation, which is abundantly refuted by the testimony of our senses."—*Ibid* p 49

The same author, speaking of his own conversion from Popery, observes, (after allowing to his Preceptor Mr. Pavillard "a handsome share" of the honour,) "that it was principally effected by his private reflections;" adding the following very curious acknowledgment: "I still remember my solitary transport at the discovery of a *philosophical argument* against the doctrine of *Transubstantiation;* that the text of Scripture, which seems to inculcate the real presence, is attested only by a single sense —our sight, while the real presence itself is disproved by three of our senses —the sight, the touch, and the taste." —(*Ibid* p 58) That this "*philosophical* argument" should have had any influence on the mind of Gibbon, even at the early period of life when he made "the discovery," would appear highly improbable, if the fact were not attested by himself, but as for Bayle, whose logical acumen was of a far harder and keener edge, it seems quite impossible to conceive, "that the study of physics" was at all necessary to open his eyes to the absurdity of the *real presence;* or that he would not at once have perceived the futility of appealing to our senses or to our reason, against an article of faith which professedly disclaims the authority of both.

than a person of his talents could well be supposed to accumulate from the mere impulse of literary curiosity. In these respects he exhibits a striking resemblance to the historian of the *Decline and Fall of the Roman Empire:* Nor is the parallel between them less exact in the similar effects produced on their minds, by the polemical cast of their juvenile studies Their common propensity to indulge in indecency is not so easily explicable. In neither does it seem to have originated in the habits of a dissolute youth, but in the wantonness of a polluted and distempered imagination. Bayle, it is well known, led the life of an anchoret;[1] and the licentiousness of his pen is, on that very account, the more reprehensible. But everything considered, the grossness of Gibbon is certainly the more unaccountable, and perhaps the more unpardonable of the two.[2]

On the mischievous tendency of Bayle's work to unsettle the principles of superficial readers, and, what is worse, to damp the moral enthusiasm of youth, by shaking their faith in the reality of virtue, it would be superfluous to enlarge. The fact is indisputable, and is admitted even by his most partial admirers. It may not be equally useless to remark the benefits which (whether foreseen or not by the author, is of little consequence) have actually resulted to literature from his indefatigable labours. *One* thing will, I apprehend, be very generally granted in his favour, that, if he has taught men to suspend

---

[1] "Chaste dans ses discours, grave dans ses discours, sobre dans ses alimens, austère dans son genre de vie"—Portrait de Bayle, par M Saurin, dans son Sermon sur l'accord de la Religion avec la Politique

[2] In justice to Bayle, and also to Gibbon, it should be remembered, that over the most offensive passages in their works they have drawn the veil of the learned languages It was reserved for the translators of the *Historical and Critical Dictionary* to tear this veil asunder, and to expose the indelicacy of their author to every curious eye. It is impossible to observe the patient industry and fidelity with which they have executed this part of their task without feelings of indignation and disgust. For such an outrage on taste and decorum, their tedious and feeble attacks on the Manicheism of Bayle offer but a poor compensation. Of all Bayle's suspected heresies, it was perhaps that which stood the least in need of a serious refutation; and, if the case had been otherwise, their incompetency to contend with such an adversary would have only injured the cause which they professed to defend.

their judgment, he has taught them also to think and to reason for themselves; a lesson which appeared to a late philosophical divine of so great importance, as to suggest to him a doubt whether it would not be better for authors to state nothing but *premises*, and to leave to their readers the task of forming their own *conclusions*.[1] Nor can Bayle be candidly accused of often discovering a partiality for any particular sect of philosophers. He opposes Spinoza and Hobbes with the same spirit and ability, and apparently with the same good faith, with which he controverts the doctrines of Anaxagoras and of Plato. Even the ancient Sceptics, for whose mode of philosophizing he might be supposed to have felt some degree of tenderness, are treated with as little ceremony as the most extravagant of the dogmatists. He has been often accused of a leaning to the most absurd of all systems, that of the Manicheans; and it must be owned, that there is none in defence of which he has so often and so ably[2] exerted his talents; but it is easy to perceive that, when he does so, it is not from any serious faith which he attaches to it, (perhaps the contrary supposition would be nearer the truth,) but from the peculiarly ample field which it opened for the display of his controversial subtlety, and of his inexhaustible stores of miscellaneous information.[3] In one passage he has pronounced, with a tone of decision which he seldom assumes, that

---

[1] See the Preface to Bishop Butler's Sermons.

[2] Particularly in the article entitled *Paulicians*.

[3] One of the earliest as well as the ablest of those who undertook a reply to the passages in Bayle which *seem* to favour Manicheism, candidly acquits him of any serious design to recommend that system to his readers. "En répondant aux objections Manichéennes, je ne prétends faire aucun tort à M. Bayle: que je ne soupçonne nullement de les favoriser. Je suis persuadé qu'il n'a pris la liberté philosophique de dire, en bien des rencontres, le pour et le contre, sans rien dissimuler, que pour donner de l'exercice à ceux qui entendent les matières qu'il traite, et non pour favoriser ceux dont il explique les raisons"—(*Parrhasiana, ou Pensées Diverses*, p. 302 par M. Le Clerc. Amsterdam, 1699.) [* The testimony of Le Clerc on this point is of peculiar value, as he knew Bayle intimately. It may be thought trifling to add, but I cannot help mentioning it as a curious accident, that the copy of the *Parrhasiana* now lying before me is marked with the name of *John Locke* in his own handwriting, and appears to have been presented to him by the author.]

* Restore l.—*Ed*

"it is absurd, indefensible, and inconsistent with the regularity and order of the universe; that the arguments in favour of it are liable to be retorted; and that, granting it to be true, it would afford no solution of the difficulties in question."[1] The apparent zeal with which, on various occasions, he has taken up its defence, may, I think, be reasonably accounted for, by the favourable opportunity it afforded him of measuring his logical powers with those of Leibnitz.[2]

To these considerations it may be added, that, in consequence of the progress of the sciences since Bayle's time, the unlimited scepticism commonly, and perhaps justly, imputed to him, is much less likely to mislead than it was a century ago; while the value of his researches, and of his critical reflections, becomes every day more conspicuous, in proportion as more enlarged views of nature and of human affairs enable us to combine together that mass of rich but indigested materials, in the compilation of which his own opinions and principles seem to have been totally lost. Neither comprehension, indeed, nor generalization, nor metaphysical depth,[3] are to be numbered

---

[1] See the illustration upon the Sceptics at the end of the Dictionary.

[2] This supposition may be thought inconsistent with the well-known fact, that the *Theodicée* of Leibnitz was not published till after the death of Bayle But it must be recollected, that Bayle had previously entered the lists with Leibnitz in the article *Rorarius*, where he had urged some very acute and forcible objections against the scheme of *pre-established harmony*, a scheme which leads so naturally and obviously to that of Optimism, that it was not difficult to foresee what ground Leibnitz was likely to take in defending his principles The great aim of Bayle seems to have been to provoke Leibnitz to unfold *the whole* of his system and of its necessary consequences, well knowing what advantages, in the management of such a controversy, would be on the side of the assailant

The tribute paid by Leibnitz to the memory of his illustrious antagonist deserves to be quoted "Sperandum est, *Bælium* luminibus illis nunc circumdari, quod terris negatum est cum credibile sit, bonam voluntatem ei nequaquam defuisse."

" Candidus insuetum miratur limen Olympi,
Sub pedibusque videt nubes et sidera Daphnis "

[* " Charité rare (adds Fontenelle) parmi les Théologiens, à qui il est fort familier de damner leurs adversaires "]

[3] I speak of that metaphysical *depth* which is the exclusive result of what Newton called *patient thinking* In logical quickness and metaphysical subtlety, Bayle has never been surpassed

* Restored.—*Ed*

among the characteristical attributes of his genius. Far less does he ever anticipate, by the moral lights of the soul, the slow and hesitating decisions of the understanding, or touch with a privileged hand those mysterious chords to which all the social sympathies of our frame are responsive. Had his ambition, however, been more exalted, or his philanthropy more warm and diffusive, he would probably have attempted less than he actually accomplished; nor would he have stooped to enjoy that undisputed pre-eminence, which the public voice has now unanimously assigned him, among those inestimable though often ill-requited authors, whom Johnson has called " the pioneers of literature."

The suspense of judgment which Bayle's *Dictionary* inspires with respect to *facts* is, perhaps, still more useful than that which it encourages in matters of abstract reasoning. Fontenelle certainly went much too far, when he said of history that it was only a collection of *Fables Convenues;* a most significant and happy phrase, to which I am sorry that I cannot do justice in an English version But though Fontenelle pushed his maxim to an extreme, there is yet a great deal of important truth in the remark; and of this I believe every person's conviction will be stronger, in proportion as his knowledge of men and of books is profound and extensive.[1]

Of the various lessons of historical scepticism to be learned from Bayle, there is none more practically valuable (more especially in such revolutionary times as we have witnessed) than that which relates to the biographical portraits of distinguished persons, when drawn by their theological and political opponents. In illustration of this, I have only to refer to the copious and instructive extracts which he has produced from Roman Catholic writers, concerning the lives, and still more concerning the deaths, of Luther, Knox,[2] Buchanan, and various other leaders or partisans of the Reformation. It would be impossible for any well-informed Protestant to read these extracts

---

[1] Montesquieu has expressed himself on this subject in nearly as strong terms as Fontenelle " Les Histoires sont des faits faux composés sur des faits vrais, ou bien à l'occasion des vrais "—*Pensées Diverses* de Montesquieu, tom v de ses Œuvres Ed. de Paris, 1818.

[2] See Note Q Q.

without indulging a smile at their incredible absurdity, if every feeling of levity were not lost in a sentiment of deep indignation at the effrontery and falsehood of their authors. In stating this observation, I have taken my examples from Roman Catholic libellers, without any illiberal prejudices against the members of that church. The injustice done by Protestants to some of the conscientious defenders of the old faith has been, in all probability, equally great; but this we have no opportunity of ascertaining here, by the same direct evidence to which we can fortunately appeal in vindication of the three characters mentioned above. With the history of *two* of them every person in this country is fully acquainted; and I have purposely selected them in preference to others, as their *names* alone are sufficient to cover with disgrace the memory of their calumniators.[1]

A few years before the death of Bayle, Fontenelle began to attract the notice of Europe.[2] I class them together on account of the mighty influence of both on the literary taste of their contemporaries; an influence in neither case founded on any claims to original genius, or to important improvements, but on the attractions which they possessed in common, though in very different ways, as popular writers; and on the easy and agreeable access which their works opened to the opinions and speculations of the learned. Nor do I depart so far as might at first be supposed from the order of chronology, in passing from the one to the other. For though Fontenelle survived almost to our own times, (having very nearly completed a cen-

---

[1] Of all Bayle's works, "the most useful and the least sceptical," according to Gibbon, "is his *Commentaire Philosophique* on these words of the Gospel, *Compel them to come in*."

The great object of this Commentary is to establish the general principles of Toleration, and to remonstrate with the members of Protestant churches on the inconsistency of their refusing to those they esteem heretics, the same indulgence which they claim for themselves in Catholic countries. The work is diffuse and rambling, like all Bayle's compositions, but the matter is excellent, and well deserves the praise which Gibbon has bestowed on it.

[2] Bayle died in 1706. Fontenelle's first work in prose (the *Dialogues of the Dead*) was published as early as 1683, and was quickly followed by his *Conversations on the Plurality of Worlds*.

tury at the time of his death,) the interval between his birth and that of Bayle was only ten years, and he had actually published several volumes, both in prose and verse, before the *Dictionary* of Bayle appeared.

But my chief reason for connecting Fontenelle rather with the contemporaries of his youth than with those of his old age, is, that during the latter part of his life he was left far behind in his philosophical creed (for he never renounced his faith as a Cartesian[1]) by those very pupils to whose minds he had given so powerful an impulse, and whom he had so long taught by his example, the art (till then unknown in modern times) of blending the truths of the severer sciences with the lights and graces of eloquence. Even this *eloquence*, once so much admired, had ceased before his death to be regarded as a model, and was fast giving way to the purer and more manly taste in writing, recommended by the precepts, and exemplified in the historical compositions of Voltaire.

Fontenelle was a nephew of the great Corneille; but his genius was, in many respects, very strongly contrasted with that of the author of the *Cid*. Of this he has himself enabled us to judge by the feeble and unsuccessful attempts in dramatic poetry, by which he was first known to the world. In these, indeed, as in all his productions, there is an abundance of ingenuity, of elegance, and of courtly refinement; but not the faintest vestige of the *mens divinior*, or of that sympathy with the higher and nobler passions which enabled Corneille to re-

---

[1] Excepting on a few metaphysical points The chief of these were, the question concerning the origin of our ideas, and that relating to the nature of the lower animals On the former of these subjects he has said explicitly " L'Ancienne Philosophie n'a pas toujours eu tort Elle a soutenu que tout ce qui étoit dans l'esprit avoit *passé par les sens*, et nous n'aurions pas mal fait de conserver cela d'elle."—(*Fragment of an intended Treatise on the Human Mind*) On another occasion, he states his own opinion on this point, in language coinciding exactly with that of Gassendi. " A force d'opérer sur les premières idées formées par les sens, d'y ajouter, d'en retrancher, de les rendre de particulières universelles, d'universelles plus universelles encore, l'esprit les rend si différentes de ce qu'elles étoient d'abord qu'on a quelquefois peine à reconnoître leur origine Cependant qui voudra prendre le fil et le suivre exactement, retournera toujours de l'idée la plus sublime et la plus élevée, à quelque idée sensible et grossière"

animate and to reproduce on the stage the heroes of ancient Rome. The circumstance, however, which more peculiarly marks and distinguishes his writings, is the *French mould* in which education and habit seem to have recast all the original features of his mind;—identifying, at the same time, so perfectly the impressions of art with the workmanship of nature, that one would think the PARISIAN, as well as the MAN, had started fresh and finished from her creative hand. Even in his *Conversations on the Plurality of Worlds*, the dry discussions with the Marchioness about the now forgotten vortices of Descartes, are enlivened throughout by a never-failing spirit of light and national gallantry, which will for ever render them an amusing picture of the manners of the times, and of the character of the author. The gallantry, it must be owned, is often strained and affected, but the affectation sits so well on Fontenelle, that he would appear less easy and graceful without it.

The only other production of Fontenelle's youth which deserves to be noticed is his *History of Oracles;* a work of which the aim was to combat the popular belief that the oracles of antiquity were uttered by evil spirits, and that all these spirits became dumb at the moment of the Christian era. To this work Fontenelle contributed little more than the agreeable and lively form in which he gave it to the world; the chief materials being derived from a dull and prolix dissertation on the same subject, by a learned Dutchman. The publication excited a keen opposition among divines, both Catholic and Protestant; and, in particular, gave occasion to a very angry, and, it is said, not contemptible criticism, from a member of the Society of Jesuits.[1] It is mentioned by La Harpe, as an illus-

---

[1] To this criticism, the only reply made by Fontenelle was a single sentence, which he addressed to a *Journalist* who had urged him to take up arms in his own defence. "Je laisserai mon censeur jouir en paix de son triomphe; je consens que le diable ait été prophète, puisque le Jésuite le veut, et qu'il croit cela plus orthodoxe"—(D'Alembert, *Eloge de La Motte*)—We are told by D'Alembert, that the silence of Fontenelle, on this occasion, was owing to the advice of La Motte. "Fontenelle bien tenté de terrasser son adversaire par la facilité qu'il y trouvoit, fut retenu par les avis prudens de La Motte, cet

tration of the rapid change in men's opinions which took place during Fontenelle's life, that a book which, in his youth, was censured for its impiety, was regarded before his death as a proof of his respect for religion.

The most solid basis of Fontenelle's fame is his *History of the Academy of Sciences,* and his *Eloges of the Academicians.* Both of these works, but more especially the latter, possess in an eminent degree all the charms of his former publications, and are written in a much simpler and better taste than any of the others. The materials, besides, are of inestimable value, as succinct and authentic records of one of the most memorable periods in the history of the human mind; and are distinguished by a rare impartiality towards the illustrious dead, of all countries, and of all persuasions. The philosophical reflections, too, which the author has most skilfully interwoven with his literary details, discover a depth and justness of understanding far beyond the promise of his juvenile essays; and afford many proofs of the soundness of his logical views,[1] as well as of his acute and fine discrimination of the varieties and shades of character, both intellectual and moral.

The chief and distinguishing merit of Fontenelle, as the historian of the Academy, is the happy facility with which he adapts the most abstruse and refined speculations to the comprehension of ordinary readers. Nor is this excellence pur-

---

ami lui fit craindre de s'aliéner par sa réponse une société qui s'appeloit *Légion,* quand on avoit affaire au dernier de ses membres." The advice merits the attention of philosophers in all countries, for the spirit of Jesuitism is not confined to the Church of Rome.

[1] An instance of this which happens at present to recur to my memory, may serve to illustrate and to confirm the above remark. It is unnecessary to point out its coincidence with the views which gave birth to the new nomenclature in chemistry.

"If languages had been the work of philosophers, they might certainly be more easily learned. Philosophers would have established everywhere a systematical uniformity, which would have proved a safe and infallible guide; and the manner of forming a derivative word, would, as a necessary consequence, have suggested its signification. The uncivilized nations, who are the first authors of languages, fell naturally into that notion with respect to certain *terminations,* all of which have some common property or virtue, but that advantage, unknown to those who had it in their hands, was not carried to a sufficient extent."

chased by any sacrifice of scientific precision. What he aims at is nothing more than an outline; but this outline is always executed with the firm and exact hand of a master. "When employed in composition, (he has somewhere said,) my first concern is to be certain that I myself understand what I am about to write;" and on the utility of this practice every page of his Historical Memoirs may serve as a comment.[1]

As a writer of *Eloges*, he has not been equalled (if I may be allowed to hazard my own opinion) by any of his countrymen. Some of those, indeed, by D'Alembert and by Condorcet, manifest powers of a far higher order than belonged to Fontenelle; but neither of these writers possessed Fontenelle's incommunicable art of interesting the curiosity and the feelings of his readers in the fortunes of every individual whom he honoured by his notice. In this art it is not improbable that they might have succeeded better had they imitated Fontenelle's self-denial in sacrificing the fleeting praise of brilliant colouring, to the fidelity and lasting effect of their portraits; a self-denial which in *him* was the more meritorious, as his great ambition plainly was to unite the reputation of a *bel-esprit* with that of a philosopher. A justly celebrated academician of the present times, (M. Cuvier,) who has evidently adopted Fontenelle as his model, has accordingly given an interest and truth to his *Eloges*, which the public had long ceased to expect in that species of composition.[2]

---

[1] From this praise, however, must be excepted the mysterious jargon in which (after the example of some of his contemporaries) he has indulged himself in speaking of the geometry and calculus of infinites "Nous le disons avec peine, (says D'Alembert,) et sans vouloir outrager les manes d'un homme célèbre qui n'est plus, il n'y a peut-être point d'ouvrage où l'on trouve des preuves plus fréquentes de l'abus de la métaphysique, que dans l'ouvrage très connu de M. Fontenelle, qui a pour titre *Elémens de la Géométrie de l'Infini;* ouvrage dont la lecture est d'autant plus dangereuse aux jeunes géomètres que l'auteur y présente les sophismes avec une sorte d'élégance et de grace, dont le sujet ne paroissoit pas susceptible "—*Mélanges*, &c, tom. v p 264.

[2] D'Alembert, in his ingenious parallel of Fontenelle and La Motte, has made a remark on Fontenelle's style when he aims at simplicity, of the justness of which *French* critics alone are competent judges "L'un et l'autre ont écrit en prose avec beaucoup de clarté, d'élégance, de simplicité même; mais La Motte avec une simplicité plus naturelle, et Fontenelle avec une simplicité

But the principal charm of Fontenelle's *Eloges* arises from the pleasing pictures which they everywhere present of genius and learning in the scenes of domestic life. In this respect, it has been justly said of them by M. Suard,[1] that "they form the noblest monument ever raised to the glory of the sciences and of letters." Fontenelle himself, in his *Eloge of Varignon*, after remarking, that in *him* the simplicity of his character was only equalled by the superiority of his talents, finely adds, "I have already bestowed so often the same praise on other members of this Academy, that it may be doubted whether it is not less due to the individuals, than to the sciences which they cultivated in common." What a proud reply does this reflection afford to the Machiavellian calumniators of philosophy![2]

The influence of these two works of Fontenelle on the studies of the rising generation all over Europe, can be conceived by those alone who have compared them with similar productions of an earlier date. Sciences which had long been immured in colleges and cloisters, began at length to breathe the ventilated and wholesome air of social life. The union of philosophy and the fine arts, so much boasted of in the schools of ancient Greece, seemed to promise a speedy and invigorated revival. Geometry, Mechanics, Physics, Metaphysics, and Morals, became objects of pursuit in courts and in camps; the accomplishments of a scholar grew more and more into repute among the other characteristics of a gentleman: and (what was of still greater importance to the world) the learned discovered the secret of cultivating the graces of writing, as a necessary passport to truth, in a refined but dissipated age.

---

plus étudiée: car la simplicité peut l'être, et dès lors elle devient manière, et cesse d'être modèle." An idea very similar to this is happily expressed by Congreve, in his portrait of *Amoret*:—

"Coquet and coy at once her air,
  Both studied, though both seem neglected
Careless she is with artful care,
  Affecting to seem unaffected."

[1] *Notice sur la Vie et les Ecrits du Docteur Robertson.* Paris, 1817.

[2] [* Gibbon, whose critical opinions in matters of taste, when he trusts to his own judgment, are not unfrequently erroneous, praises Fontenelle's *History of Oracles*, and even his *Ecloques*, but seems to have been quite insensible to the merits of his *Eloges* See his *Misc. Works*, vol ii p 55]

* Restored —*Ed*

Nor was this change of manners confined to one of the sexes. The other sex, to whom nature has entrusted the first development of our intellectual and moral powers, and who may, therefore, be regarded as the chief *medium* through which the progress of the mind is continued from generation to generation, shared also largely in the general improvement. Fontenelle aspired above all things to be the philosopher of the Parisian circles; and certainly contributed not a little to diffuse a taste for useful knowledge among women of all conditions in France, by bringing it into vogue among the higher classes. A reformation so great and so sudden could not possibly take place, without giving birth to much affectation, extravagance, and folly; but the whole analogy of human affairs encourages us to hope, that the inconveniences and evils connected with it will be partial and temporary, and its beneficial results permanent and progressive.[1]

---

[1] Among the various other respects in which Fontenelle contributed to the intellectual improvement of his countrymen, it ought to be mentioned, that he was one of the first writers in France who diverted the attention of metaphysicians from the old topics of scholastic discussion, to a philosophical investigation of the principles of the fine arts Various original hints upon these subjects are scattered over his works: but the most favourable specimens of his talents for this very delicate species of analysis are to be found in his *Dissertation on Pastorals*, and in his *Theory concerning the Delight we derive from Tragedy* * His speculations, indeed, are not always just and satisfactory; but they are seldom deficient in novelty or refinement Their principal fault, perhaps, arises from the author's disposition to carry his refinements too far; in consequence of which, his theories become chargeable with that sort of sublimated ingenuity which the French epithet *Alambiqué* expresses more precisely and forcibly than any word in our language.

Something of the same philosophical spirit may be traced in Fenelon's *Dialogues on Eloquence*, and in his *Letter on Rhetoric and Poetry* The former of these treatises, besides its merits as a speculative discussion, contains various practical hints, well entitled to the attention of those who aspire to eminence as public speakers; and of which the most apparently trifling claim some regard, as the results of the author's reflections upon an art which few ever practised with greater success

Let me add, that both of these eminent men (who may be regarded as the fathers of philosophical criticism in France) were zealous partisans and admirers of the Cartesian metaphysics It is this *critical* branch of metaphysical

* In the judgment of Mr Hume, " there is not a finer piece of criticism than Fontenelle's *Dissertation on Pastorals*, in which, by a number of reflections and philosophical reasonings, he endeavours to fix the just medium between simplicity and refinement, which is suitable to that species of poetry "

Among the various moral defects imputed to Fontenelle, that of a complete apathy and insensibility to all concerns but his own is by far the most prominent. A letter of the Baron de Grimm, written immediately after Fontenelle's death, but not published till lately, has given a new circulation in this country to some anecdotes injurious to his memory, which had long ago fallen into oblivion or contempt in France. The authority, however, of this adventurer, who earned his subsistence by collecting and retailing, for the amusement of a German Prince, the literary scandal of Paris, is not much to be relied on in estimating a character with which he does not appear to have had any opportunity of becoming personally acquainted; more especially as, during Fontenelle's long decline, the great majority of men of letters in France were disposed to throw his merits into the shade, as an acceptable homage to the rising and more dazzling glories of Voltaire.[1]

science which, in my opinion, has been most successfully cultivated by French writers, although too many of them have been infected (after the example of Fontenelle) with the disease of sickly and of *hyper-metaphysical* subtlety

From this censure, however, must be excepted the Abbé Dubos, whose *Critical Reflections on Poetry and Painting* is one of the most agreeable and instructive works that can be put into the hands of youth. Few books are better calculated for leading their minds gradually from literature to philosophy. The author's theories, if not always profound or just, are in general marked with good sense as well as with ingenuity; and the subjects to which they relate are so peculiarly attractive, as to fix the attention even of those readers who have but little relish for speculative discussions. ' Ce qui fait la bonté de cet ouvrage (says Voltaire) c'est qu'il n'y a que peu d'erreurs, et beaucoup de réflexions vraies, nouvelles, et profondes Il manque cependant d'ordre et sur-tout de précision il auroit pu être écrit avec plus de feu, de grace, et d'élégance, *mais l'écrivain pense et fait penser.*"—*Siècle de Louis XIV*

[1] As to Voltaire himself, it must be mentioned, to his honour, that though there seems never to have been much cordiality between him and Fontenelle, he had yet the magnanimity to give a place to this Nestor of French literature in his catalogue of the eminent persons who adorned the reign of Louis XIV., a tribute of respect the more flattering, as it is the single instance in which he has departed from his general rule of excluding from his list the names of all his living contemporaries Even Fontenelle's most devoted admirers ought to be satisfied with the liberality of Voltaire's eulogy, in which, after pronouncing Fontenelle " the most universal genius which the age of Louis XIV. had produced," he thus sums up his merits as an author "Enfin on l'a regardé comme le premier des hommes dans l'art nouveau de répandre de la lumière et des graces sur les sciences

It is in the Academical Memoirs of D'Alembert and Condorcet (neither of whom can be suspected of any unjust prejudice against Voltaire, but who were both too candid to sacrifice truth to party feelings) that we ought to search for Fontenelle's real portrait:[1] Or rather, (if it be true, as Dr. Hutcheson has somewhere remarked, that "men have commonly the good or bad qualities which they ascribe to mankind,") the most faithful *Eloge* on Fontenelle himself is to be found in those which he has pronounced upon others.

That the character of Fontenelle would have been more amiable and interesting, had his virtues been less the result of cold and prudent calculation, it is impossible to dispute. But his conduct through life was pure and blameless; and the happy serenity of his temper, which prolonged his life till he had almost completed his hundredth year, served as the best comment on the spirit of that mild and benevolent philosophy, of which he had laboured so long to extend the empire.

It is a circumstance almost singular in his history, that since the period of his death, his reputation, both as a man and as an author, has been gradually rising. The fact has been as re-

abstraites, et il a eu du mérite dans tous les autres genres qu'il a traités Tant de talens ont été soutenus par la connoissance des langues et de l'histoire, et *il a été sans contredit au-dessus de tous les sçavans qui n'ont pas eu le don de l'invention*"

[1] Condorcet has said expressly, that his apathy was confined entirely to what regarded himself, and that he was always an active, though frequently a concealed friend, where his good offices could be useful to those who deserved them. "On a cru Fontenelle insensible, parce que sachant maîtriser les mouvemens de son âme il se conduisoit d'après son esprit, toujours juste et toujours sage D'ailleurs, il avoit consenti sans peine à conserver cette réputation d'insensibilité, il avoit souffert les plaisanteries de ses sociétés sur sa froideur, sans chercher à les détromper, parce que, bien sûr que les vraies amis n'en seroit pas la dupe, il voyoit dans cette réputation un moyen commode de se délivrer des indifférens sans blesser leur amour-propre."—*Eloge de Fontenelle, par* Condorcet

Many of Fontenelle's sayings, the import of which must have depended entirely on circumstances of time and place unknown to us, have been absurdly quoted to his disadvantage, in their literal and most obvious acceptation "I hate war, (said he,) for it spoils conversation" Can any just inference be drawn from the levity of this convivial sally, against the humanity of the person who uttered it? Or rather, when connected with the characteristical *finesse* of Fontenelle's wit, does it not lead to a conclusion precisely opposite?

markably the reverse with most of those who have calumniated his memory.

While the circle of mental cultivation was thus rapidly widening in France, a similar progress was taking place, upon a larger scale, and under still more favourable circumstances, in England. To this progress nothing contributed more powerfully than the periodical papers published under various titles by Addison[1] and his associates. The effect of these in reclaiming the public taste from the licentiousness and grossness introduced into England at the period of the Restoration; in recommending the most serious and important truths by the united attractions of wit, humour, imagination, and eloquence; and, above all, in counteracting those superstitious terrors which the weak and ignorant are so apt to mistake for religious and moral impressions,—has been remarked by numberless critics, and is acknowledged even by those who felt no undue partiality in favour of the authors.[2] Some of the papers of Addison, however, are of an order still higher, and bear marks of a mind which, if early and steadily turned to philosophical pursuits, might have accomplished much more than it ventured to undertake. His frequent references to the *Essay on Human Understanding*, and the high encomiums with which they are always accompanied, shew how successfully he had entered into the spirit of that work, and how completely he was aware of the importance of its object. The popular nature of his publications, indeed, which rendered it necessary for him to avoid everything that might savour of scholastic or of metaphysical discussion, has left us no means of estimating his philosophical depth, but what are afforded by the *results* of his thoughts on the particular topics which he has occasion to allude to, and by some of his incidental comments on the scientific merits of preceding authors. But these means are sufficiently ample to justify a very high opinion of his sound and unprejudiced judgment, as well as of the extent and

---

[1] Born in 1672, died in 1719.
[2] See Pope's *Imitations of Horace*, book ii epistle i "Unhappy Dryden," &c. &c.

correctness of his literary information. Of his powers as a logical reasoner he has not enabled us to form an estimate; but none of his contemporaries seem to have been more completely tinctured with all that is most valuable in the metaphysical and ethical systems of his time [1]

But what chiefly entitles the name of Addison to a place in this Discourse, is his *Essays on the Pleasures of Imagination,*— the first attempt in England to investigate the principles of the fine arts; and an attempt which, notwithstanding many defects in the execution, is entitled to the praise of having struck out a new avenue to the study of the human mind, more alluring than any which had been opened before. In this respect, it forms a most important supplement to Locke's *Survey of the Intellectual Powers;* and it has, accordingly, served as a text, on which the greater part of Locke's disciples have been eager to offer their comments and their corrections The progress made by some of these in exploring this interesting region has been great; but let not Addison be defrauded of his claims as a discoverer.

Similar remarks may be extended to the hints suggested by Addison on Wit, on Humour, and on the causes of Laughter. It cannot, indeed, be said of him, that he exhausted any one of these subjects; but he had at least the merit of starting them as problems for the consideration of philosophers; nor would it be easy to name among his successors, a single writer who has

---

[1] I quote the following passage from Addison, *not* as a specimen of his metaphysical acumen, but as a pooof of his good sense in divining and obviating a difficulty which I believe most persons will acknowledge occurred to themselves when they first entered on metaphysical studies —

"Although we divide the soul into several powers and faculties, there is no such division in the soul itself, since it is *the whole soul* that remembers, understands, wills, or imagines Our manner of considering the memory, understanding, will, imagination, and the like faculties, is for the better enabling us to express ourselves in such abstracted subjects of speculation, not that there is any such division in the soul itself" In another part of the same paper, Addison observes, that " what we call the faculties of the soul are only the different ways or modes in which the soul can exert herself."— *Spectator,* No. 600

For some important remarks on the words *Powers* and *Faculties,* as applied to the Mind, see Locke, book ii chap xxi. § 20.

made so important a step towards their solution, as the original proposer.

The philosophy of the papers to which the foregoing observations refer, has been pronounced to be slight and superficial, by a crowd of modern metaphysicians, who were but ill entitled to erect themselves into judges on such a question.[1] The singular simplicity and perspicuity of Addison's style have contributed much to the prevalence of this prejudice. Eager for the instruction, and unambitious of the admiration of the multitude, he everywhere studies to bring himself down to their level; and even when he thinks with the greatest originality, and writes with the most inimitable felicity, so easily do we enter into the train of his ideas, that we can hardly persuade ourselves that we could not have thought and written in the same manner. He has somewhere said of "fine writing," that it "consists of sentiments which are natural, without being obvious:" and his definition has been applauded by Hume, as at once concise and just. Of the thing defined, his own periodical essays exhibit the most perfect examples.

To this simplicity and perspicuity, the wide circulation which his works have so long maintained among all classes of readers, is in a great measure to be ascribed. His periods are not constructed, like those of Johnson, to "elevate and surprise," by filling the ear and dazzling the fancy; but we close his volumes with greater reluctance, and return to the perusal of them with far greater alacrity. Franklin, whose fugitive publications on political topics have had so extraordinary an influence on public opinion, both in the Old and New Worlds, tells us that his style in writing was formed upon the model of Addison: Nor do I know anything in the history of his life which does more honour to his shrewdness and sagacity. The copyist, indeed, did not possess the gifted hand of his master,—*Museo contingens cuncta lepore;* but such is the effect of his plain and seemingly artless manner, that the most profound conclusions of political economy assume, in his hands, the appearance of indisputable truths; and some of them, which had been formerly

[1] See Note RR.

confined to the speculative few, are already current in every country of Europe, as proverbial maxims.[1]

To touch, however slightly, on Addison's other merits, as a critic, as a wit, as a speculative politician, and, above all, as a moralist,[2] would lead me completely astray from my present object. It will not be equally foreign to it to quote the two following short passages, which, though not strictly *metaphysical*, are, both of them, the result of metaphysical habits of thinking, and bear a stronger resemblance than anything I recollect among the wits of Queen Anne's reign, to the best philosophy of the present age. They approach indeed very nearly to the philosophy of Turgot and of Smith.

"Among other excellent arguments for the immortality of the soul, there is one drawn from the perpetual progress of the soul to its perfection, without a possibility of ever arriving at it; which is a hint that I do not remember to have seen opened and improved by others who have written on this subject, though it seems to me to carry a great weight with it. A brute arrives at a point of perfection that he can never pass. In a

---

[1] The expressions "*Laissez nous faire,*" and "*pas trop gouverner,*" which comprise, in a few words, two of the most important lessons of Political Wisdom, are indebted chiefly for their extensive circulation to the short and luminous comments of Franklin.—See his *Political Fragments*, § 4.

[2] [Mr Stewart in his proof had here the words—"and, above all, as the inventor and painter of Sir Roger de Coverley." To this the following note was appended, and both text and comment were deleted merely in pencil, as if doubtful of their propriety.—*Editor.*

In calling Addison the *inventor* of Sir Roger de Coverley, I am perfectly aware, that the second *number* of the Spectator, in which the different members of his Club are first introduced to the reader's acquaintance, is marked with the signature of Steele. But allowing to Steele the whole merit of the original sketches, there yet remains to Addison the undisputed praise of inventing as well as of painting, by far the finest features of the several portraits. This supposition, however, appears to me to ascribe to Steele a great deal too much. Is it conceivable, that Addison should have promised his powerful aid in carrying on so great an undertaking, without taking a very anxious charge of those *prefatory discourses*, on the happy execution of which the success of the infant work was essentially to depend. That Steele held the pen on this occasion is ascertained by the signature, but it seems impossible to doubt, that the great outline of the *Dramatis Personæ* would be furnished by the writer, who of all Steele's associates, was alone equal to the task of filling up the parts. In the case of Sir Roger, more particularly, this conclusion seems almost to amount to a certainty.]

few years he has all the endowments he is capable of; and were he to live ten thousand more, would be the same thing he is at present. Were a human soul thus at a stand in her accomplishments, were her faculties to be full-blown, and incapable of further enlargement, I would imagine it might fall away insensibly, and drop at once into a state of annihilation. But can we believe a thinking being, that is in a perpetual progress of improvement, and travelling on from perfection to perfection, after having just looked abroad into the works of its Creator, and made a few discoveries of his infinite goodness, wisdom, and power, must perish at her first setting out, and in the very beginning of her inquiries?"[1]

The philosophy of the other passage is not unworthy of the author of the *Wealth of Nations*. The *thought* may be traced to earlier writers, but certainly it was never before presented with the same fulness and liveliness of illustration; nor do I know, in all Addison's works, a finer instance of his solicitude for the improvement of his fair readers, than the address with which he here insinuates one of the sublimest moral lessons, while apparently aiming only to amuse them with the geographical history of the muff and the tippet

"Nature seems to have taken a particular care to disseminate her blessings among the different regions of the world, with an eye to the mutual intercourse and traffic among mankind; that the natives of the several parts of the globe might have a kind of dependence upon one another, and be united together by their common interest. Almost every *degree* produces something peculiar to it. The food often grows in one country, and the sauce in another. The fruits of Portugal are corrected by the products of Barbadoes; the infusion of a China plant sweetened with the pith of an Indian cane. The Philippine Islands give a flavour to our European bowls. The single dress of a woman of quality is often the product of a hundred climates.

---

[1] This argument has been prosecuted with great ingenuity and force of reasoning, (blended, however, with some of the peculiarities of his Berkeleian metaphysics,) by the late Dr James Hutton.—See his *Investigation of the Princip'es of Knowledge*, vol iii p. 195, *et seq.* Edin 1794

The muff and the fan come together from the opposite ends of the earth. The scarf is sent from the torrid zone, and the tippet from beneath the pole. The brocade petticoat rises out of the mines of Peru, and the diamond necklace out of the bowels of Indostan"

But I must not dwell longer on the fascinating pages of Addison. Allow me only, before I close them, to contrast the last extract with a remark of Voltaire, which, shallow and contemptible as it is, occurs more than once, both in verse and in prose, in his voluminous writings.

> "Il murit, à Moka, dans le sable Arabique,
> Ce Caffé nécessaire aux pays des frimats,
> Il met la Fièvre en nos climats,
> Et le remède en Amérique."—*Epître au Roi de Prusse*, 1750

And yet Voltaire is admired as a philosopher by many who will smile to hear this title bestowed upon Addison!

It is observed by Akenside, in one of the notes to the *Pleasures of Imagination*, that " Philosophy and the Fine Arts can hardly be conceived at a greater distance from each other than at the Revolution, when Locke stood at the head of one party, and Dryden of the other." · He observes, also, that "a very great progress towards their reunion had been made within these few years." To this progress the chief impulse was undoubtedly given by Addison and Shaftesbury.

Notwithstanding, however, my strong partiality for the former of these writers, I should be truly sorry to think, with Mr. Hume, that "Addison will be read with pleasure when Locke shall be *entirely forgotten*"—*Essay on the Different Species of Philosophy.*

A few years before the commencement of these periodical works, a memorable accession was made to metaphysical science, by the publication of Berkeley's* *New Theory of Vision*, and of his *Principles of Human Knowledge*. Possessed of a mind which, however inferior to that of Locke in depth of reflection

---

* [Born 1684; died 1753 —*Ed*]

and in soundness of judgment, was fully its equal in logical acuteness and invention, and in learning, fancy, and taste, far its superior,—Berkeley was singularly fitted to promote that reunion of Philosophy and of the Fine Arts which is so essential to the prosperity of both. Locke, we are told, despised poetry; and we know from one of his own letters that, among our English poets, his favourite author was Sir Richard Blackmore. Berkeley, on the other hand, courted the society of all from whose conversation and manners he could hope to add to the embellishments of his genius; and although himself a decided and High Church Tory,[1] lived in habits of friendship with Steele and Addison, as well as with Pope and Swift. Pope's admiration of him seems to have risen to a sort of enthusiasm. He yielded to Berkeley's decision on a very delicate question relating to the exordium of the *Essay on Man;* and on his moral qualities he has bestowed the highest and most unqualified eulogy to be found in his writings.

> "Even in a Bishop I can spy desert;
> Secker is decent Rundle has a heart,
> Manners with candour are to Benson given,
> To Berkeley every virtue under Heaven"

With these intellectual and moral endowments, admired and blazoned as they were by the most distinguished wits of his age, it is not surprising that Berkeley should have given a popularity and fashion to metaphysical pursuits which they had never before acquired in England. Nor was this popularity diminished by the boldness of some of his paradoxes; on the contrary, it was in no small degree the *effect* of them, the great bulk of mankind being always prone to mistake a singularity or eccentricity of thinking for the originality of a creative genius.

---

[1] See a volume of Sermons, preached in the chapel of Trinity College, Dublin. See also a Discourse addressed to Magistrates, &c, printed in 1736. In both of these publications, the author carries his Tory principles so far, as to represent the doctrine of passive obedience and non-resistance as an essential article of the Christian faith. "The Christian religion makes every legal constitution sacred, by commanding our submission thereto. *Let every soul be subject to the higher powers*, saith St Paul, *for the powers that be are ordained of God.*"

The solid additions, however, made by Berkeley to the stock of human knowledge were important and brilliant. Among these, the first place is unquestionably due to his *New Theory of Vision;* a work abounding with ideas so different from those commonly received, and, at the same time, so profound and refined, that it was regarded by all but a few accustomed to deep metaphysical reflection, rather in the light of a philosophical romance than of a sober inquiry after truth.[1] Such, however, has been since the progress and diffusion of this sort of knowledge, that the leading and most abstracted doctrines contained in it, form now an essential part of every elementary treatise of optics, and are adopted by the most superficial smatterers in science as fundamental articles of their faith.

Of a theory, the outlines of which cannot fail to be familiar to a great majority of my readers, it would be wholly superfluous to attempt any explanation here, even if it were consistent with the limits within which I am circumscribed. Suffice it to observe, that its chief aim is to distinguish the immediate and natural objects of sight from the *seemingly instantaneous* conclusions which experience and habit teach us to draw from them in our earliest infancy; or, in the more concise metaphysical language of a later period, to draw the line between the *original* and the *acquired perceptions* of the eye. They who wish to study it in detail, will find ample satisfaction, and, if they have any relish for such studies, an inexhaustible fund of entertainment in Berkeley's own short but masterly exposition of his principles, and in the excellent comments upon it by Smith of Cambridge; by Porterfield; by Reid; and, still more lately, by the author of the *Wealth of Nations.*[2]

That this doctrine, with respect to the *acquired perceptions* of sight, was quite unknown to the best metaphysicians of antiquity, we have direct evidence in a passage of Aristotle's *Nicomachian*

---

[1] [* See Bayle, Art *Charron.*]

[2] By this excellent judge, Berkeley's *New Theory of Vision* is pronounced to be "one of the finest examples of Philosophical Analysis that is to be found in our own or any other language."— *Essays on Philosophical Subjects* Lond 1795, p 215

* Restored —*Ed*

Ethics, where he states the distinction between those endowments which are the immediate gift of nature, and those which are the fruit of custom and habit. In the former class, he ranks the perceptions of sense, mentioning particularly the senses of seeing and of hearing. The passage (which I have transcribed in a *Note*) is curious, and seems to me decisive on the subject.[1]

The misapprehensions of the ancients on this very obscure question will not appear surprising, when it is considered, that *forty* years after the publication of Berkeley's *Theory of Vision*, and *sixty* years after the date of Locke's *Essay*, the subject was so imperfectly understood in France, that Condillac (who is, to this day, very generally regarded by his countrymen as the father of genuine logic and metaphysics) combated at great length the conclusions of the English philosophers concerning the *acquired* perceptions of sight; affirming that "the eye judges *naturally* of figures, of magnitudes, of situations, and of distances." His argument in support of this opinion is to be found in the sixth section of his *Essay on the Origin of Human Knowledge*.

It is difficult to suppose, that a person of mature years, who had read and studied Locke and Berkeley with as much care and attention as Condillac appears to have bestowed on them, should have reverted to this ancient and vulgar prejudice, without suspecting that his metaphysical depth has been somewhat overrated by the world.[2] It is but justice,

---

[1] Οὐ γὰρ ἐκ τοῦ πολλάκις ἰδεῖν, ἢ πολλάκις ἀκοῦσαι τὰς αἰσθήσεις ἐλάβομεν, ἀλλ' ἀνάπαλιν, ἔχοντες ἐχρησάμεθα, ὀ χρησάμενοι ἔχομεν — *Ethic Nicomach* lib ii cap 1.

"For it is not from seeing often, or from hearing often, that we get these senses; but, on the contrary, instead of getting them by using them, we use them because we have got them."

Had Aristotle been at all aware of the distinction so finely illustrated by Berkeley, instead of appealing to the perceptions of these two senses as instances of endowments coeval with our birth, he would have quoted them as the most striking of all examples of the effects of custom in apparently identifying our acquired powers with our original faculties

[2] Voltaire, at an earlier period, had seized completely the scope of Berkeley's theory, and had explained it with equal brevity and precision, in the following passage of his *Elements of the Newtonian Philosophy* —

however, to Condillac to add, that, in a subsequent work, he had the candour to acknowledge and to retract his error;—a rare example of that disinterested love of truth, which is so becoming in a philosopher. I quote the passage, (in a literal, though somewhat abridged version,) not only to show, that, in the above statement, I have not misrepresented his opinion, but because I consider this remarkable circumstance in his literary history as a peculiarly amiable and honourable *trait* in his character

" We cannot recall to our memory the ignorance in which we were born. It is a state which leaves no trace behind it. We only recollect our ignorance of those things, the knowledge of which we recollect to have acquired; and to remark what

" Il faut absolument conclure, que les distances, les grandeurs, les situations ne sont pas, à proprement parler, des choses visibles, c'est à dire, ne sont pas les objets propres et immédiats de la vue. L'objet propre et immédiat de la vue n'est autre chose que la lumière colorée tout le reste, nous ne le sentons qu'à la longue et par expérience Nous apprenons à voir, précisément comme nous apprenons à parler et à lire. La différence est, que l'art de voir est plus facile, et que la nature est également à tous notre maître.

" Les jugemens soudains, presque uniformes, que toutes nos âmes à un certain age portent des distances, des grandeurs, des situations, nous font penser, qu'il n'y à qu'à ouvrir les yeux pour voir la manière dont nous voyons. On se trompe, il y faut le secours des autres sens. Si les hommes n'avoient que le sens de la vue, ils n'auroient aucun moyen pour connoître l'étendue en longueur, largeur et profondeur, et un pur esprit ne la connoîtroit peut-être, à moins que Dieu ne la lui révélât [* Il est très difficile de séparer dans notre entendement l'extension d'un objet d'avec les couleurs de cet objet. Nous ne voyons jamais rien que d'étendu, et de-là nous sommes tous portés à croire que nous voyons en effet l'étendue."— *Phys Newton*, Par ii. ch. 5

An attempt was made some years ago in a memoir published in the *Philosophical Transactions*, to discredit the Theory of Berkeley, in consequence of some hasty observations on the case of a boy blind from his birth, upon whom the operation of depressing the cataract had been successfully performed From these observations it was concluded, that the patient was not only able immediately to judge of distances, magnitudes, and figures, but even to apply the names of *colours*, and of the different objects around him, with the most exact propriety, a conclusion, which, by being pushed a 'little too far, defeats completely the author's purpose, and which is indeed not less incredible, (as was remarked to me by an ingenious friend when this memoir first appeared,) than if it had been alleged that a child had come into the world repeating the Athanasian creed."]

* Restored —*Ed*

we acquire, some previous knowledge is necessary. That memory which now renders us so sensible of the step from one acquisition to another, cannot remount to the first steps of the progress; on the contrary, it supposes them already made; and hence the origin of our disposition to believe them connate with ourselves. To say that we have learnt to see, to hear, to taste, to smell, to touch, appears a most extraordinary paradox. It seems to us that nature gave us the complete use of our senses the moment she formed them, and that we have always made use of them without study, because we are no longer obliged to study in order to use them. I retained these prejudices at the time I published my Essay on the *Origin of Human Knowledge;* the reasonings of Locke on a man born blind, to whom the sense of sight was afterwards given, did not undeceive me. and *I maintained against this philosopher that the eye judges naturally of figures, of sizes, of situations, and of distances.*"—Nothing short of his own explicit avowal could have convinced me, that a writer of so high pretensions and of such unquestionable ingenuity as Condillac, had really commenced his metaphysical career under so gross and unaccountable a delusion.

In bestowing the praise of originality on Berkeley's *Theory of Vision,* I do not mean to say, that the *whole* merit of this Theory is exclusively his own. In this, as in most other cases, it may be presumed, that the progress of the human mind has been gradual: And, in point of fact, it will, on examination, be found, that Berkeley only took up the inquiry where Locke dropped it; following out his principles to their remoter consequences, and placing them in so great a variety of strong and happy lights, as to bring a doctrine till *then* understood but by a few, within the reach of every intelligent and attentive reader. For my own part, on comparing these two philosophers together, I am at a loss whether most to admire the powerful and penetrating sagacity of the one, or the fertility of invention displayed in the illustrations of the other. What can be more clear and forcible than the statement of Locke quoted in the Note below; and what an idea does it convey of his superiority to Condillac, when it is considered, that he anticipated à *priori* the same doctrine which was afterwards confirmed by the fine analysis of Berkeley, and demonstrated by the judicious experiments of Cheselden; while the French metaphysician, with all this accumulation of evidence before him, relapsed into a prejudice transmitted to modern times, from the very infancy of optical science![1]

[1] "We are farther to consider," says Locke, "concerning perception, that the ideas we receive by sensation are often in grown people altered by the judgment, without our taking notice of it. When we set before our eyes a round globe, of any uniform colour, *e. g* gold, alabaster, or jet, it is certain that the idea thereby imprinted in our mind is of a flat circle, variously shadowed, with several degrees of light and brightness coming to our eyes. But we having by use been accustomed to perceive what kind of appearance convex bodies are wont to make in us, what alterations are made in the reflections of light by the difference of the sensible figure of bodies; the judgment presently, by an habitual custom, alters the appearances into their causes, so that, from what truly is variety of shadow or colour, collecting the figure it makes it pass for a mark of figure, and frames to itself the perception of a convex figure, and a uniform colour, when the idea we receive from thence is only a plane variously coloured, as is evident in painting.

"But this is not, I think, usual in any of our ideas but those received by sight,* because sight, the most comprehensive of all our senses, conveying to our minds the ideas of lights and colours, which are peculiar only to that sense, and also the far different ideas of space, figure, or motion, the several varieties whereof change the appearances of its proper objects, viz., light and colours, we bring ourselves by use to judge of the one by the other. This, in many cases, by a settled habit in things whereof we have frequent experience, is performed so constantly and so quick, that we take *that* for the perception of our sensation, which is an idea formed by our judgment, so that one, viz., that of sensation, serves only to excite the other, and is scarce taken notice of itself, as a man who reads or hears with attention or understanding, takes little notice of the characters or sounds, but of the ideas that are excited in him by them.

"Nor need we wonder that it is done with so little notice, if we consider how very *quick* the actions of the mind are performed; for as itself is thought to take up no space, to have no extension, so its actions seem to require no time, but many of them seem to be crowded into an instant. I speak this in comparison to the actions of the body. Any one may easily observe this in his own thoughts, who will take the pains to re-

* Mr Locke might, however, have remarked something very *similar* to it in the perceptions of the ear, a very large proportion of its appropriate objects being rather *judged of* than actually *perceived*. In the rapidity (for example) of common conversation, how many syllables, and even words, escape the notice of the most attentive hearer, which syllables and words are so quickly supplied from the relation which they bear to the rest of the sentence, that it is quite impossible to distinguish between the audible and the inaudible sounds! A very palpable instance of this occurs in the difficulty experienced by the most acute ear in catching *proper names* or arithmetical sums, or words borrowed from unknown tongues, the first time they are pronounced.

I believe it would be difficult to produce from any writer prior to Locke, an equal number of important facts relating to the intellectual phenomena, as well observed, and as unexceptionably described, as those which I have here brought under my reader's eye It must appear evident, besides, to all who have studied the subject, that Locke has, in this passage, enunciated, in terms the most precise and decided, the same general conclusion concerning the effect of constant and early *habits*, which it was the great object of Berkeley's *Theory of Vision* to establish, and which, indeed, gives to that work its chief value, when considered in connexion with the Philosophy of the Human Mind.

Berkeley himself, it is to be observed, by no means lays claim to that complete novelty in his *Theory of Vision*, which has been ascribed to it by many who, in all probability, derived their whole information concerning it from the traditional and inexact transcripts of book-making historians. In the introductory sentences of his Essay, he states very clearly and candidly the conclusions of his immediate predecessors on this class of our perceptions; and explains, with the greatest precision, in what particulars his own opinion differs from theirs. "It is, I think, *agreed by all*, that distance, of itself, cannot be seen. For distance being a line directed end-wise to the eye, it projects only one point in the fund of the eye, which point remains invariably the same, whether the distance be longer or shorter.

flect on them. How, as it were in an instant, do our minds with one glance see all the parts of a demonstration, which may very well be called a long one, if we consider the time it will require to put it into words, and step by step shew it to another? Secondly, we shall not be so much surprised that this is done in us with so little notice, if we consider how the facility which we get of doing things by a custom of doing makes them often pass in us without our notice Habits, especially such as are begun very early, come at last to produce actions in us, which often escape our observations How frequently do we in a day cover our eyes with our eye-lids, without perceiving that we are at all in the dark? Men that have by custom got the use of a by-word, do almost in every sentence pronounce sounds, which, though taken notice of by others, they themselves neither hear nor observe, and, therefore, it is not so strange, that our mind should often change the idea of its *sensation* into that of its *judgment*, and make one serve only to excite the other, without our taking notice of it"—Locke's *Works*, vol 1 p 123, et seq

"I find it also acknowledged, that the estimate we make of the distance of objects *considerably remote*, is rather an act of judgment grounded on *experience* than of sense. For example, when I perceive a great number of intermediate objects, such as houses, fields, rivers, and the like, which I have experienced to take up a considerable space, I thence form a judgment or conclusion, that the object I see beyond them is at a great distance. Again, when an object appears faint and small, which, at a near distance, I have experienced to make a vigorous and large appearance, I instantly conclude it to be far off. And this, 'tis evident, is the result of *experience;* without which, from the faintness and littleness, I should not have inferred anything concerning the distance of objects.

"But when an object is placed at *so near a distance*, as that the interval between the eyes bears any sensible proportion to it, it is the received opinion that the two optic axes, concurring at the object, do there make an angle, by means of which, according as it is greater or less, the object is perceived to be nearer or farther off.

"There is another way mentioned by the optic writers, whereby they will have us judge of those distances, in respect of which the breadth of the pupil hath any sensible bigness; and that is, the greater or less divergency of the rays, which, issuing from the visible point, do fall on the pupil; that point being judged nearest, which is seen by most diverging rays, and that remoter, which is seen by less diverging rays."

These (according to Berkeley) are the "common and current accounts" given by *mathematicians* of our perceiving *near distances* by sight. He then proceeds to shew, that they are unsatisfactory; and that it is necessary, for the solution of this problem, to avail ourselves of principles borrowed from a higher philosophy: After which, he explains, in detail, his own theory concerning the *ideas* (*sensations*) which, by experience, become *signs* of distance;[1] or (to use his own phraseology) "by which

---

[1] For assisting persons unaccustomed to metaphysical studies to enter into the spirit and scope of Berkeley's *Theory*, the best illustration I know of is furnished by the phenomena of the *Phantasmagoria*. It is sufficient to hint at

distance is *suggested*[1] to the mind." The result of the whole is, that "a man born blind, being made to see, would not at first have any idea of distance by sight. *The sun and stars, the remotest objects as well as the nearest, would all seem to be in his Eye, or rather in his Mind* "[2]

From this quotation it appears, that, before Berkeley's time, philosophers had advanced greatly beyond the point at which Aristotle stopped, and towards which Condillac, in his first publication, made a retrograde movement. Of this progress some of the chief steps may be traced as early as the twelfth cen-

---

this application of these phenomena, to those who knew anything of the subject

[1] The word *suggest* is much used by Berkeley, in this appropriate and technical sense, not only in his *Theory of Vision*, but in his *Principles of Human Knowledge*, and in his *Minute Philosopher* It expresses, indeed, the cardinal principle on which his *Theory of Vision* hinges; and it is now so incorporated with some of our best metaphysical speculations, that one cannot easily conceive how the use of it was so long dispensed with. Locke (in the passage quoted in the Note, p 344) uses the word *excite* for the same purpose; but it seems to imply an hypothesis concerning the *mechanism* of the mind, and by no means expresses the fact in question with the same force and precision.

It is remarkable, that Dr Reid should have thought it incumbent on him to apologize for introducing into philosophy a word so familiar to every person conversant with Berkeley's works "I beg leave to make use of the word *suggestion*, because I know not one more proper to express a power of the mind, which seems entirely to have escaped the notice of philosophers, and to which we owe many of our simple notions which are neither impressions nor ideas, as well as many original principles of belief I shall endeavour to explain, by an example, what I understand by this word We all know that a certain kind of sound *suggests* immediately to the mind a coach passing in the street, and not only produces the imagination, but the belief, that a coach is passing Yet there is no comparing of ideas, no perception of agreements or disagreements to produce this belief, nor is there the least similitude between the sound we hear, and the coach we imagine and believe to be passing "

So far Dr. Reid's use of the word coincides exactly with that of Berkeley; but the former will be found to annex to it a meaning more extensive than the latter, by employing it to comprehend not only those *intimations* which are the result of experience and habit, but another class of *intimations*, (quite overlooked by Berkeley,) those which result from the original frame of the human mind. See Reid's *Inquiry*, chap ii sect. 7.

[2] I request the attention of my readers to this last sentence, as I have little doubt that the fact here stated gave rise to the theory which Berkeley afterwards adopted, concerning the non-existence of the material world It is not, indeed, surprising that a conclusion, so very curious with respect to the objects of sight, should have been, in the first ardour of discovery, too hastily extended to those qualities also which are the appropriate objects of touch

tury in the Optics of Alhazen;[1] and they may be perceived still more clearly and distinctly in various optical writers since the revival of letters; particularly in the *Optica Promota* of James Gregory.[2] Father Malebranche went still farther, and even anticipated some of the *metaphysical* reasonings of Berkeley concerning the means by which experience enables us to judge of the distances of *near* objects. In proof of this, it is sufficient to mention the explanation he gives of the manner in which a comparison of the perceptions of sight and of touch teaches us gradually to estimate by the eye the distances of all those objects which are within reach of our hands, or of which we are accustomed to measure the distance, by walking over the intermediate ground.

In rendering this justice to earlier writers, I have no wish to detract from the originality of Berkeley. With the single exception, indeed, of the passage in Malebranche which I have just referred to, and which it is more than probable was unknown to Berkeley when his theory first occurred to him,[3] I have ascribed to his predecessors nothing more than what he has himself explicitly acknowledged to belong to them. All that I wished to do was, to supply some links in the historical chain which he has omitted.

The influence which this justly celebrated work has had, not only in perfecting the theory of optics, but in illustrating the astonishing effects of early habit on the mental phenomena in general, will sufficiently account to my intelligent readers for the length to which the foregoing observations upon it have extended.

Next in point of importance to Berkeley's New Theory of

---

[1] Alhazen, lib. ii. NN. 10, 12, 39.

[2] See the end of Prop. 28

[3] Berkeley's *Theory* was published when he was only twenty-five; an age when it can scarcely be supposed that his metaphysical reading had been very extensive.*

* [It was first published in 1709, and in regard to what had previously been done on the theory of the vision of distances, see Charleton's *Physiologia*, book iii chap 3, p 164 . Gassendi *Opera*, tom iii p 455, *seq* In 1733 Berkeley published *The Theory of Vision, &c , Vindicated and Explained*, pp 64, 8vo. An important tract, wholly unknown to his collectors, editors, and biographers, nay, as far as I am aware, to all historians of philosophy, physics, and psychology This, as we have seen, is not a singular case of oblivion in English philosophy —*Ed*]

Vision, which I regard as by far the most solid basis of his philosophical fame, may be ranked his speculations concerning the Objects of General Terms, and his celebrated argument against the existence of the Material World. On both of these questions I have elsewhere explained my own ideas so fully, that it would be quite superfluous for me to resume the consideration of them here.[1] In neither instance are his reasonings so entirely original as has been commonly supposed. In the former they coincide in substance, although with immense improvements in the form, with those of the scholastic nominalists, as revived and modified by Hobbes and Leibnitz. In the latter instance, they amount to little more than an ingenious and elegant development of some principles of Malebranche, pushed to certain paradoxical but obvious consequences, of which Malebranche, though unwilling to avow them, appears to have been fully aware. These consequences, too, had been previously pointed out by Mr. Norris, a very learned divine of the Church of England, whose name has unaccountably failed in obtaining that distinction to which his acuteness as a logician, and his boldness as a theorist, justly entitled him![2]

The great object of Berkeley, in maintaining his system of

---

[1] See *Philosophical Essays*

[2] Another very acute metaphysician of the same church (Arthur Collier, author of a *Demonstration of the Non-existence and Impossibility of an External World*) has met with still greater injustice. His name is not to be found in any of our Biographical Dictionaries In point of date, his publication is some years posterior to that of Norris, and therefore it does not possess the same claims to originality; but it is far superior to it in logical closeness and precision, and is not obscured to the same degree with the mystical theology which Norris (after the example of Malebranche) connected with the scheme of Idealism Indeed, when compared with the writings of Berkeley himself, it yields to them less in force of argument, than in composition and variety of illustration The title of Collier's book is "*Clavis Universalis*, or a New Inquiry after Truth, being a Demonstration, &c &c By Arthur Collier, Rector of Langford Magna, near Sarum (Lond printed for Robert Gosling, at the Mitre and Crown, against St. Dunstan's Church, Fleet Street, 1713 ") The motto prefixed by Collier to his work is from Malebranche, and is strongly characteristical both of the English and French *Inquirer after Truth*. "Vulgi assensus et approbatio circa materiam difficilem est certum argumentum falsitatis istius opinionis cui assentitur"—*Maleb De Inquir Verit.* lib iii p 194   See Note SS.

idealism, it may be proper to remark in passing, was to cut up by the roots the scheme of materialism. "Matter (he tells us himself) being once *expelled out of nature*, drags with it so many sceptical and impious notions . . Without it your Epicureans, Hobbists, and the like, have not even the shadow of a pretence, but become the most cheap and easy triumph in the world."

Not satisfied with addressing these abstract speculations to the learned, Berkeley conceived them to be of such moment to human happiness, that he resolved to bring them, if possible, within the reach of a wider circle of readers, by throwing them into the more popular and amusing form of dialogues [1] The skill with which he has executed this very difficult and unpromising task cannot be too much admired. The characters of his speakers are strongly marked and happily contrasted; the illustrations exhibit a singular combination of logical subtlety and of poetical invention, and the style, while it everywhere abounds with the rich, yet sober colourings of the author's fancy, is perhaps superior, in point of purity and of grammatical correctness, to any English composition of an earlier date.[2]

The impression produced in England by Berkeley's Idealism was not so great as might have been expected; but the novelty of his paradoxes attracted very powerfully the attention of a set of young men who were then prosecuting their studies at Edinburgh, and who formed themselves into a society for the express purpose of soliciting from the author an explanation of

---

[1] I allude here chiefly to *Alciphron*, or the *Minute Philosopher;* for as to the dialogues between *Hylas* and *Philonous*, they aspire to no higher merit than that of the common dialogues between A and B, being merely a compendious way of stating and of obviating the principal objections which the author anticipated to his opinions

[2] Dr Warton, after bestowing high praise on the *Minute Philosopher*, excepts from his encomium "those passages in the fourth dialogue, where the author has introduced his fanciful and whimsical opinions about vision."— (*Essay on the Writings and Genius of Pope*, vol. ii. p 264) If I were called on to point out the most ingenious and original part of the whole work, it would be the argument contained in the passages here so contemptuously alluded to by this learned and (on all questions of taste) most respectable critic.

some parts of his theory which seemed to them obscurely or equivocally expressed. To this correspondence the amiable and excellent prelate appears to have given every encouragement; and I have been told by the best authority, that he was accustomed to say, that his reasonings had been nowhere better understood than by this club of young Scotsmen.[1] The ingenious Dr Wallace, author of the *Discourse on the Numbers of Mankind*, was one of the leading members; and with him were associated several other individuals whose names are now well known and honourably distinguished in the learned world. Mr. Hume's *Treatise of Human Nature*, which was published in 1739, affords sufficient evidence of the deep impression which Berkeley's writings had left upon his mind; and to this juvenile essay of Mr. Hume's may be traced the origin of the most important metaphysical works which Scotland has since produced.

It is not, however, my intention to prosecute farther, at present, the history of Scottish philosophy. The subject may be more conveniently, and I hope advantageously resumed, after a slight review of the speculations of some English and French writers, who, while they professed a general acquiescence in the doctrines of Locke, have attempted to modify his fundamental principles in a manner totally inconsistent with the views of their master. The remarks which I mean to offer on the modern French School will afford me, at the same time, a convenient opportunity of introducing some strictures on the metaphysical systems which have of late prevailed in other parts of the Continent

---

[1] The authority I here allude to is that of my old friend and preceptor, Dr John Stevenson, who was himself a member of the *Rankenian* Club, and who was accustomed for many years to mention this fact in his *Academical Prelections*

SECT. V.—HARTLEIAN SCHOOL.

THE English writers to whom I have alluded in the last paragraph, I shall distinguish by the title of Dr Hartley's School; for although I by no means consider this person as the first author of any of the theories commonly ascribed to him, (the seeds of all of them having been previously sown in the university where he was educated,) it was nevertheless reserved for him to combine them together, and to exhibit them to the world in the imposing form of a system.

Among the immediate predecessors of Hartley, Dr. Law, afterwards Bishop of Carlisle, seems to have been chiefly instrumental in preparing the way for a schism among Locke's disciples. The name of Law was first known to the public by an excellent translation, accompanied by many learned, and some very judicious notes, of Archbishop King's work on the Origin of Evil; a work of which the great object was to combat the Optimism of Leibnitz, and the Manicheism imputed to Bayle. In making this work more generally known, the translator certainly rendered a most acceptable and important service to the world, and, indeed, it is upon this ground that his best claim to literary distinction is still founded.[1] In his own original speculations, he is weak, paradoxical, and oracular;[2]

---

[1] King's argument in proof of the prevalence in this world, both of Natural and Moral Good, over the corresponding Evils, has been much and deservedly admired, nor are Law's Notes upon this head entitled to less praise. Indeed, it is in this part of the work that both the author and his commentator appear, in my opinion, to the greatest advantage.

[2] As instances of this I need only refer to the *first* and *third* of his Notes on King, the former of which relates to the word *substance*, and the latter to the dispute between Clarke and Leibnitz concerning *space* His reasonings on both subjects are obscured by an affected use of hard and unmeaning words, ill becoming so devoted an admirer of Locke. The same remark may be extended to an *Inquiry into the Ideas of Space and Time*, published by Dr Law in 1734

The result of Law's speculations on Space and Time is thus stated by himself: "That our ideas of them do not imply any external *ideatum* or *objective* reality, that these ideas (as well as those of *infinity* and *number*) are *universal* or *abstract* ideas, existing under that *formality* nowhere but in the mind, nor affording a proof of anything, but of the power which the mind has to form

affecting on all occasions the most profound veneration for the opinions of Locke, but much more apt to attach himself to the errors and oversights of that great man, than to enter into the general spirit of his metaphysical philosophy.

To this translation, Dr. Law prefixed a Dissertation concerning the Fundamental Principle of Virtue, by the Reverend Mr. Gay; a performance of considerable ingenuity, but which would now be entitled to little notice, were it not for the influence it appears to have had in suggesting to Dr. Hartley the possibility of accounting for all our intellectual pleasures and pains, by the single principle of the Association of Ideas. We are informed by Dr. Hartley himself, that it was in consequence of hearing some account of the contents of this dissertation, he was first led to engage in those inquiries which produced his celebrated *Theory of Human Nature.*

The other principle on which this theory proceeds, (that of the vibrations and vibratiuncles in the medullary substance of the brain,) is also of Cambridge origin. It occurs in the form of a query in Sir Isaac Newton's *Optics;* and a distinct allusion to it, as a principle likely to throw new light on the phenomena of mind, is to be found in the concluding sentence of Smith's *Harmonies.*

Very nearly about the time when Hartley's *Theory* appeared, Charles Bonnet of Geneva published some speculations of his own, proceeding almost exactly on the same assumptions Both writers speak of vibrations (*ébranlemens*) in the nerves;

them"—(Law's *Trans. of King,* p 7, 4th edit) This language, as we shall afterwards see, approaches very nearly to that lately introduced by Kant. Dr Law's favourite author might have cautioned him against such jargon.— See *Essay on the Human Understanding,* book II chap XIII sect 17, 18

The absurd application of the scholastic word *substance* to empty space, an absurdity in which the powerful mind of Gravesande acquiesced many years after the publication of the *Essay on Human Understanding,* has probably contributed not a little to force some authors into the opposite extreme of maintaining, with Leibnitz and Dr. Law, that our idea of space does not imply any external *ideatum* or objective reality Gravesande's words are these · " Substantiæ sunt aut cogitantes, aut non cogitantes; cogitantes duas novimus, Deum et Mentem nostram · præter has et alias dari in dubium non revocamus. Duæ etiam substantiæ, quæ non cogitant, nobis notæ sunt Spatium et Corpus."— Gravesande, *Introd ad Philosophiam,* sect. 19.

and both of them have recourse to a subtle and elastic ether, co-operating with the nerves in carrying on the communication between soul and body.[1] This fluid Bonnet conceived to be contained in the nerves, in a manner analogous to that in which the electric fluid is contained in the solid bodies which conduct it; differing in this respect from the Cartesians as well as from the ancient physiologists, who considered the nerves as hollow tubes or pipes, within which the animal spirits were included. It is to this elastic ether that Bonnet ascribes the vibrations of which he supposes the nerves to be susceptible; for the nerves themselves, (he justly observes,) have no resemblance to the stretched cords of a musical instrument.[2] Hartley's *Theory* differs in one respect from this, as

---

[1] *Essai Analytique de l'Ame*, chap v. See also the additional notes on the first chapter of the seventh part of the *Contemplation de la Nature*.

[2] "Mais les nerfs sont mous, ils ne sont point tendus comme les cordes d'un instrument, les objets y exciteroient-ils donc les vibrations analogues à celle d'une corde pincée? Ces vibrations se communiqueroient-elles à l'instant au siège de l'âme? La chose paroit difficile à concevoir Mais si l'on admet dans les nerfs un fluide dont la subtilité et l'élasticité approche de celle de la lumière ou de l'éther, on expliquera facilement par le secours de ce fluide, et la célérité avec laquelle les impressions se communiquent à l'âme, et celle avec laquelle l'âme éxécute tant d'opérations différentes "—*Essai Anal* chap v

"Au reste, les physiologistes qui avoient cru que les filets nerveux étoient solides, avoient cédé à des apparences trompeuses Ils vouloient d'ailleurs faire osciller les nerfs pour rendre raison des sensations, et les nerfs ne peuvent osciller. Ils sont mous, et nullement élastiques Un nerf coupé ne se retire point. C'est le fluide invisible que les nerfs renferment, qui est doué de cette élasticité qu'on leur attribuoit, et d'une plus grande élasticité encore."—*Contemp de la Nature*, vii partie, chap i Note at the end of the chapter.

M Quesnai, the celebrated author of the *Economical System*, has expressed himself to the same purpose concerning the supposed vibrations of the nerves: " Plusieurs physiciens ont pensé que le seul ébranlement des nerfs, causé par les objets qui touchent les organes des corps, suffit pour occasioner le mouvement et le sentiment dans les parties où les nerfs sont ébranlés. Ils se représentent les nerfs comme des cordes fort tendus, qu'un léger contact met en vibration dans toute leur étendue Des philosophes, peu instruits en anatomie, ont pu se former une telle idée. ..Mais cette tension qu'on suppose dans les nerfs, et qui les rend si susceptibles d'ébranlement et de vibration, est si grossièrement imaginée qu'il seroit ridicule de s'occuper sérieusement à la réfuter "—*Econ. Animale*, sect 3, c 13.

As this passage from Quesnai is quoted by Condillac, and sanctioned by his authority, (*Traité des Animaux*, chap iii.,) it would appear that the hypothesis which supposes the nerves to perform their functions by means of vibrations was going fast into discredit, both

he speaks of vibrations and vibratiuncles in the medullary substance of the brain and nerves. He agrees, however, with Bonnet in thinking, that to these vibrations in the nerves the co-operation of the ether is essentially necessary; and, therefore, at bottom the two hypotheses may be regarded as in substance the same. As to the trifling shade of difference between them, the advantage seems to me to be in favour of Bonnet.

Nor was it only in their Physiological Theories concerning the nature of the union between soul and body, that these two philosophers agreed. On all the great articles of metaphysical theology, the coincidence between their conclusions is truly astonishing. Both held the doctrine of Necessity in its fullest extent; and both combined with it a vein of mystical devotion, setting at defiance the creeds of all established churches. The intentions of both are allowed, by those who best knew them, to have been eminently pure and worthy; but it cannot be said of either, that his metaphysical writings have contributed much to the instruction or to the improvement of the public. On the contrary, they have been instrumental in spreading a set of speculative tenets very nearly allied to that sentimental and fanatical modification of Spinozism which, for many years past, has prevailed so much, and produced such mischievous effects in some parts of Germany.[1]

among the metaphysicians and the physiologists of France, at the very time when it was beginning to attract notice in England, in consequence of the visionary speculations of Hartley.

[1] In a letter which I received from Dr Parr, he mentions a treatise of Dr. Hartley's which appeared about a year before the publication of his great work, to which it was meant by the author to serve as a precursor Of this rare treatise I had never before heard "You will be astonished to hear," says Dr. Parr, "that in this book, instead of the doctrine of necessity, Hartley openly declares for the indifference of the will, as maintained by Archbishop King." We are told by Hartley himself that his notions upon necessity grew upon him while he was writing his observations upon man, but it is curious, (as Dr. Parr remarks,) that in the course of a year his opinions on so very essential a point should have undergone a complete change.

[* Of this first work of Hartley's, as previously stated, I had never heard before, and from the manner in which Dr. Parr writes of it, I presume it is very little known even in England.

* Restored.—I may also mention, that the collection here referred to, and which was printed previously to Dr Parr's death, has since been published by Mr Lumley —Ed

But it is chiefly by his application of the associating principle to account for all the mental phenomena, that Hartley is known to the world; and upon this I have nothing to add to what I have already stated in another work.—(*Phil. Essays*, Essay IV.) His theory seems to be already fast passing into oblivion; the temporary popularity which it enjoyed in this country having, in a great measure, ceased with the life of its zealous and indefatigable apostle, Dr Priestley [1]

It would be unfair, however, to the translator of Archbishop King, to identify his opinions with those of Hartley and Priestley. The zeal with which he contends for man's free agency is sufficient, of itself, to draw a strong line of distinction between his Ethical System and theirs. (See his Notes on King, *passim*) But I must be allowed to say of him, that the general scope of his writings tends, in common with that of the two other metaphysicians, to depreciate the evidences of Natural Religion, and more especially to depreciate the evidences which the light of nature affords of a life to come ;—" a doctrine equally necessary to comfort the weakness, and to support our lofty ideas of the grandeur of human nature ;"[2] and of which it seems hard to confine exclusively the knowledge to that portion of mankind who have been favoured with the light of Revelation. The influence of the same fundamental error, arising, too, from the

---

(June 1820) I am glad to add that a republication of it, and of some other rare tracts on metaphysical subjects, may soon be expected from this illustrious scholar and philosopher Among these tracts it gives me particular pleasure to mention the *Clavis Universalis* of Arthur Collier, of which I had previously occasion to take notice in speaking of the Idealism of Bishop Berkeley. See p 349 of this Dissertation.]

[1] Dr Priestley's opinion of the merits of Hartley's work is thus stated by himself.—" Something was done in this field of knowledge by Descartes, very much by Mr Locke, but most of all by Dr. Hartley, who has thrown more useful light upon the theory of the mind, than Newton did upon the theory of the natural world."—*Remarks on Reid, Beattie, and Oswald*, p. 2. London, 1774

[2] Smith's *Theory of Moral Sentiments*, 6th ed. vol. i pp. 325, 326.

Dr Law's doctrine of the sleep of the soul, to which his high station in the church could not fail to add much weight in the judgment of many, is, I believe, now universally adopted by the followers of Hartley and Priestley, the theory of vibrations being evidently inconsistent with the supposition of the soul's being able to exercise her powers in a separate state from the body.

same mistaken idea, of thus strengthening the cause of Christianity, may be traced in various passages of the posthumous work of the late Bishop of Llandaff. It is wonderful that the reasonings of Clarke and of Butler did not teach these eminent men a sounder and more consistent logic; or, at least, open their eyes to the inevitable consequences of the rash concessions which they made to their adversaries.[1]

Among the disciples of Law, one illustrious exception to these remarks occurs in Dr. Paley, whose treatise on Natural Theology is unquestionably the most instructive as well as interesting publication on that subject which has appeared in our times. As the book was intended for popular use, the author has wisely avoided, as much as possible, all metaphysical discussions; but I do not know that there exists any other work where the argument from *final causes* is placed in so great a variety of pleasing and striking points of view.

---

[1] Without entering at all into the argument with Dr Law or his followers, it is sufficient here to mention, as a historical fact, their wide departure from the older lights of the English Church, from Hooker downwards "All religion," says Archbishop Tillotson, whom I select as an unexceptionable organ of their common sentiments, "is founded on right notions of God and his perfections, insomuch that Divine Revelation itself does suppose these for its foundations, and can signify nothing to us unless they be first known and believed, so that the principles of natural religion are the foundation of that which is revealed"—(Sermon 41) "There is an intrinsical good and evil in things, and the reasons and respects of moral good and evil are fixed and immutable, eternal and indispensable. Nor do they speak safely who make the Divine will the rule of moral good and evil, as if there were nothing good or evil in its own nature antecedently to the will of God, but, that all things are therefore good and evil because God wills them to be so"—(Sermon 88) "Natural religion is obedience to the natural law, and the performance of such duties as natural light, without any express or supernatural revelation, doth dictate to men These lie at the bottom of all religion, and are the great fundamental duties which God requires of all mankind Those are the surest and most sacred of all other laws; those which God hath rivetted in our souls and written upon our hearts, and these are what we call moral duties, and most valued by God, which are of eternal and perpetual obligation, because they do naturally oblige, without any particular and express revelation from God, and these are the foundation of revealed and instituted religion, and all revealed religion does suppose them and build upon them."—Sermons 48, 49.

SECT. VI.—CONDILLAC, AND OTHER FRENCH METAPHYSICIANS OF
A LATER DATE.

WHILE Hartley and Bonnet were indulging their imagination in theorizing concerning the nature of the union between soul and body, Condillac was attempting to draw the attention of his countrymen to the method of studying the phenomena of Mind recommended and exemplified by Locke.[1] Of the vanity of expecting to illustrate, by physiological conjectures, the manner in which the intercourse between the thinking principle and

---

[1] It may appear to some unaccountable that no notice should have been taken, in this Dissertation, of any French metaphysician during the long interval between Malebranche and Condillac. As an apology for this apparent omission, I beg leave to quote the words of an author intimately acquainted with the history of French literature and philosophy, and eminently qualified to appreciate the merits of those who have contributed to their progress. "If we except," says Mr. Adam Smith, in a *Memoir* published in 1755, "the Meditations of Descartes, I know of nothing in the works of French writers which aspires at originality in morals or metaphysics, for the philosophy of Regis and that of Malebranche are nothing more than the meditations of Descartes unfolded with more art and refinement. But Hobbes, Locke, Dr Mandeville, Lord Shaftesbury, Dr Butler, Dr. Clarke, and Mr. Hutcheson, each in his own system, all different and all incompatible, have tried to be original, at least in some points. They have attempted to add something to the fund of observations collected by their predecessors, and already the common property of mankind This branch of science, which the English themselves neglect at present, appears to have been recently transported into France. I discover some traces of it not only in the *Encyclopédie*, but in the *Theory of Agreeable Sensations*, by M de Pouilly, and much more in the late discourse of M. Rousseau, *On the Origin and Foundation of the Inequality of Ranks among Men.*"

Although I perfectly agree with Mr Smith in his general remark on the sterility of invention among the French metaphysicians posterior to Descartes, when compared to those of England, I cannot pass over the foregoing quotation without expressing my surprise, 1st, To find the name of Malebranche (one of the highest in modern philosophy) degraded to a level with that of Regis; and, 2dly, To observe Mr. Smith's silence with respect to Buffier and Condillac, while he mentions the author of the *Theory of Agreeable Sensations* as a metaphysician of original genius Of the merits of Condillac, whose most important works were published several years before this paper of Mr Smith's, I am about to speak in the text, and those of Buffier I shall have occasion to mention in a subsequent part of this Discourse. In the meantime, I shall only say of him, that I regard him as one of the most original as well as sound philosophers of whom the eighteenth century has to boast.

the external world is carried on, no philosopher seems ever to have been more completely aware; and accordingly, he confines himself strictly, in all his researches concerning this intercourse, to an examination of the general laws by which it is regulated. There is, at the same time, a remarkable coincidence between some of his views and those of the other two writers. All of the three, while they profess the highest veneration for Locke, have abandoned his account of the origin of our ideas for that of Gassendi, and by doing so have, with the best intentions, furnished arms against those principles which it was their common aim to establish in the world.[1] It is much to be regretted, that by far the greater part of those French writers who have since speculated about the human mind, have acquired the whole of their knowledge of Locke's philosophy through this mistaken comment upon its fundamental principle. On this subject I have already exhausted all that I have to offer on the effect of Condillac's writings; and I flatter myself have sufficiently shewn how widely his commentary differs from the text of his author. It is this commentary, however, which is now almost universally received on the Continent as the doctrine of Locke, and which may justly be regarded as the sheet-anchor of those systems which are commonly stigmatized in England with the appellation of French philosophy. Had Condillac been sufficiently aware of the consequences which have been deduced (and I must add *logically* deduced) from his account of the

---

[1] Condillac's earliest work [which was published in 1746] appeared three years before the publication of Hartley's *Theory*. It is entitled, "*Essai sur l'Origine des Connoissances Humaines. Ouvrage où l'on réduit à un seul principe tout ce qui concerne l'entendement humain*." This *seul principe* is the association of ideas. The account which both authors give of the transformation of sensations into ideas is substantially the same. [* A still more curious coincidence may be remarked between the speculations of Condillac and of Bonnet, in their fanciful hypothesis of an animated statue, to illustrate the progress of the mind in acquiring its ideas through the medium of the different senses. The hypothesis is plausible, and does honour to the ingenuity of its authors; but, in my opinion, it throws additional darkness on the difficulties it was intended to elucidate. At any rate, it is of too little moment to deserve particular notice here.]

* Restored.—*Ed.*

origin of our knowledge, I am persuaded, from his known candour and love of truth, that he would have been eager to acknowledge and to retract his error.

In this apparent simplification and generalization of Locke's doctrine, there is, it must be acknowledged, something, at first sight, extremely seducing. It relieves the mind from the painful exercise of abstracted reflection, and amuses it with analogy and metaphor when it looked only for the severity of logical discussion. The clearness and simplicity of Condillac's style add to the force of this illusion, and flatter the reader with an agreeable idea of the powers of his own understanding, when he finds himself so easily conducted through the darkest labyrinths of metaphysical science. It is to this cause I would chiefly ascribe the great popularity of his works They may be read with as little exertion of thought as a history or a novel; and it is only when we shut the book, and attempt to express in our own words the substance of what we have gained, that we have the mortification to see our supposed acquisitions vanish into air.

The philosophy of Condillac was, in a more peculiar manner, suited to the taste of his own country, where (according to Mad. de Staël) "few read a book but with a view to talk of it"[1] Among such a people, speculations which are addressed to the power of reflection can never expect to acquire the same popularity with theories expressed in a metaphorical language, and constantly recalling to the fancy the impressions of the external senses. The state of society in France, accordingly, is singularly unfavourable to the inductive philosophy of the human mind; and of this truth no proof more decisive can be produced, than the admiration with which the metaphysical writings of Condillac have been so long regarded.

On the other hand, it cannot be denied that Condillac has, in many instances, been eminently successful, both in observing and describing the mental phenomena; but, in such cases, he

---

[1] "En France, on ne lit guère un ouvrage que pour en parler."—(*Allemagne*, tom. 1 p 292) The same remark, I am much afraid, is becoming daily more and more applicable to our own island.

commonly follows Locke as his guide; and, wherever he trusts to his own judgment, he seldom fails to wander from his way. The best part of his works relates to the action and reaction of thought and language on each other, a subject which had been previously very profoundly treated by Locke, but which Condillac has had the merit of placing in many new and happy points of view. In various cases, his conclusions are pushed too far, and in others are expressed without due precision; but, on the whole, they form a most valuable accession to this important branch of logic; and (what not a little enhances their value) they have been instrumental in recommending the subject to the attention of other inquirers, still better qualified than their author to do it justice.

In the speculation, too, concerning the origin and the theoretical history of language, Condillac was one of the first who made any considerable advances; nor does it reflect any discredit on his ingenuity, that he has left some of the principal difficulties connected with the inquiry very imperfectly explained. The same subject was soon after taken up by Mr Smith,[1] who, I think, it must be owned, has rather slurred over these difficulties, than attempted to remove them; an omission on his part the more remarkable, as a very specious and puzzling objection had been recently stated by Rousseau, not only to the theory of Condillac, but to all speculations which have for their object the solution of the same problem. "If language," says Rousseau, "be the result of human convention, and if words be essential to the exercise of thought, language would appear to be necessary for the invention of language."[2] "But," continues the same author, "when, by means *which*

---

[1] [* *Dissertation on the Origin of Language;* annexed to the *Theory of Moral Sentiments*]

[2] That men never could have invented an artificial language, if they had not possessed a natural language, is an observation of Dr Reid's, and it is this indisputable and self-evident truth which gives to Rousseau's remark that imposing plausibility, which, at first sight, dazzles and perplexes the judgment. I by no means say, that the former proposition affords a key to *all* the difficulties suggested by the latter; but it advances us at least one important step towards their solution.

* Restored — *Ed*

I cannot conceive, our new grammarians began to extend their ideas, and to generalize their words, their ignorance must have confined them within very narrow bounds. . . . . How, for example, could they imagine or comprehend such words as matter, mind, substance, mode, figure, motion, since our philosophers, who have so long made use of them, scarcely understand them, and since the ideas attached to them, being purely metaphysical, can have no model in nature?"

" I stop at these first steps," continues Rousseau, " and intreat my judges to pause, and consider the distance between the easiest part of language, the invention of physical substantives, and the power of expressing all the thoughts of man, so as to speak in public, and influence society. I entreat them to reflect upon the time and knowledge it must have required to discover numbers, abstract words, aorists, and all the tenses of verbs, particles, syntax, the art of connecting propositions and arguments, and how to form the whole logic of discourse. As for myself, alarmed at these multiplying difficulties, and convinced of the almost demonstrable impossibility of language having been formed and established by means merely human, I leave to others the discussion of the problem, ' Whether a society already formed was more necessary for the institution of language, or a language already invented for the establishment of society?'"[1]

Of the various difficulties here enumerated, *that* mentioned by Rousseau, in the last sentence, was plainly considered by him as the greatest of all, or rather as comprehending under it all the rest. But this difficulty arises merely from his own peculiar and paradoxical theory about the artificial origin of society; a theory which needs no refutation, but the short and luminous aphorism of Montesquieu, that " man is born in society, and there he remains." The other difficulties touched upon by Rousseau, in the former part of this quotation, are much more serious, and have never yet been removed in a manner completely satisfactory: And hence some very ingenious writers have been led to conclude, that language could

[1] *Discours sur l'Origine et les Fondemens de l'Inégalité parmi les Hommes.*

not possibly have been the work of human invention. This argument has been lately urged with much acuteness and plausibility by Dr. Magee of Dublin, and by M. de Bonald of Paris.[1] It may, however, be reasonably questioned, if these philosophers would not have reasoned more logically, had they contented themselves with merely affirming, that the problem has not yet been solved, without going so far as to pronounce it to be absolutely insolvable. For my own part, when I consider its extreme difficulty, and the short space of time during which it has engaged the attention of the learned, I am more disposed to wonder at the steps which have been already gained in the research, than at the number of *desiderata* which remain to employ the ingenuity of our successors. It is justly remarked by Dr. Ferguson, that " when language has attained to that perfection to which it arrives in the progress of society, the speculative mind, in comparing the first and the last stages of the progress, feels the same sort of amazement with a traveller, who, after rising insensibly on the slope of a hill, comes to look down from a precipice, to the summit of which he scarcely believes he could have ascended without supernatural aid."[2]

---

[1] The same theory has been extended to the art of writing, but if *this* art was first taught to man by an express revelation from Heaven, what account can be given of its present state in the great empire of China? Is the mode of writing practised there of divine or of human origin?

[* As to oral language I am at a loss to conceive how the doctrine maintained by Dr Magee and M. de Bonald can be reconciled with the Scripture account of the tower of Babel, or even with what we are told of the arbitrary names assigned by Adam to the beasts of the field and the fowls of the air.]

[2] *Principles of Moral and Political Science,* vol i p 43 Edin 1792 To this observation may be added, by way of comment, the following reflections of one of the most learned prelates of the English Church —" Man, we are told, had a language from the beginning; for he conversed with God, and gave to every animal its particular name But how came man by language? He must either have had it from *inspiration*, ready formed from his Creator, or have *derived* it by the exertion of those faculties of the mind, which were implanted in him as a rational creature, from natural and external objects with which he was surrounded Scripture is silent on the means by which it was acquired We are not, therefore, warranted to affirm, that it was received by *inspiration*, and there is no internal evidence in language to lead us to such a suppo-

* Restored —Ed

With respect to some of the difficulties pointed out by Rousseau and his commentators, it may be here remarked in passing, (and the observation is equally applicable to various passages in Mr. Smith's dissertation on the same subject,) that the difficulty of explaining the theory of any of our intellectual operations affords no proof of any difficulty in applying that operation to its proper practical purpose; nor is the difficulty of explaining the metaphysical nature of any part of speech a proof, that, in its first origin, it implied any extraordinary effort of intellectual capacity. How many metaphysical difficulties might be raised about the mathematical notion of a *line?* And yet this notion is perfectly comprehended by every peasant, when he speaks of the distance between two places; or of the length, breadth, or height of his cottage. In like manner, although it may be difficult to give a satisfactory account of the origin and import of such words as *of* or *by,* we ought not to conclude, that the invention of them implied any metaphysical knowledge in the individual who first employed them.[1] Their import, we

sition On this side, then, of the question, we have nothing but uncertainty, but on a subject, the causes of which are so remote, nothing is more convenient than to refer them to *inspiration,* and to recur to that easy and comprehensive argument,

Διὸς δ' ἐτελείετο βουλή

that is, man enjoyed the great privilege of speech, which distinguished him at first, and still continues to distinguish him as a *rational* creature, so eminently from the brute creation, without exerting those *reasoning* faculties, by which he was in *other* respects enabled to raise himself so much above their level Inspiration, then, seems to have been an argument adopted and made necessary by the difficulty of accounting for it otherwise; and the name of inspiration carries with it an awfulness, which forbids the unhallowed approach of inquisitive discussion "—*Essay on the Study of Antiquities,* by Dr Burgess, 2d edit Oxford, 1782 Pp 85, 86.

It is farther remarked very sagaciously, and I think very decisively, by the same author, that " the supposition of man having received a language ready formed from his Creator, is *actually* inconsistent with the evidence of the origin of our ideas, which exists in language For, as the origin of our ideas is to be traced in the words through which the ideas are conveyed, so the origin of language is referable to the source from whence our (*first*) ideas are derived, namely, *natural* and *external* objects."—*Ibid.* pp. 83, 84.

[1] In this remark I had an eye to the following passage in Mr. Smith's dissertation —" It is worth while to observe, that those prepositions, which, in modern languages, hold the place of the ancient cases, are, of all others, the most general, and abstract, and metaphysical, *and, of consequence, would probably be the last*

see, is fully understood by children of three or four years of age.

In this view of the History of Language I have been anticipated by Dr. Ferguson. "Parts of speech," says this profound and original writer, "which, in speculation, cost the grammarian so much study, are, in practice, familiar to the vulgar. The rudest tribes, even the idiot and the insane, are possessed of them. They are soonest learned in childhood, insomuch that we must suppose human nature, in its lowest state, competent to the use of them; and, without the intervention of uncommon genius, mankind, in a succession of ages, qualified to accomplish in detail this amazing fabric of language, which, when raised to its height, appears so much above what could be ascribed to any simultaneous effort of the most sublime and comprehensive abilities."[1]

---

invented. Ask any man of common acuteness, what relation is expressed by the preposition *above?* He will readily answer, that of *superiority* By the preposition *below?* He will as quickly reply, that of *inferiority*. But ask him what relation is expressed by the preposition *of?* and, if he has not beforehand employed his thoughts a good deal upon these subjects, you may safely allow him a week to consider of his answer."

[1] The following judicious reflections, with which M Raynouard concludes the introduction to his *Elémens de la Langue Romane*, may serve to illustrate some of the above observations The modification of an existing language is, I acknowledge, a thing much less wonderful than the formation of a language entirely new, but the processes of thought, it is reasonable to think, are, in both cases, of the same kind, and the consideration of the one is at least a step gained towards the elucidation of the other.

"La langue Romane est peut-être la seule à la formation de laquelle il soit permis de remonter ainsi, pour découvrir et expliquer le secret de son industrieux mécanisme . . J'ose dire que l'esprit philosophique, consulté sur le choix des moyens qui devraient épargner à l'ignorance beaucoup d'études pénibles et fastidieux, n eut pas été aussi heureux que l'ignorance elle-même, il est vrai qu'elle avoit deux grands maîtres; la NECESSITE et le TEMS

"En considérant à quelle époque d'ignorance et de barbarie s'est formé et perfectionné ce nouvel idiôme, d'après des principes indiqués seulement par l'analogie et l'euphonie, on se dira peut-être comme je me le suis dit, l'homme porte en soi-même les principes d'une logique naturelle, d'un instinct régulateur, que nous admirons quelquefois dans les enfans Oui, la Providence nous a dôté de la faculté indestructible et des moyens ingénieux d'exprimer, de communiquer, d'éterniser par la parole, et par les signes permanens où elle se reproduit, cette pensée qui est l un de nos plus beaux attributs, et qui nous distingue si éminemment et si avantageusement dans l'ordre de la création"—

It is, however, less in tracing the first rudiments of speech, than in some collateral inquiries concerning the genius of different languages, that Condillac's ingenuity appears to advantage. Some of his observations, in particular, on the connexion of natural signs with the growth of a systematical prosody, and on the imitative arts of the Greeks and Romans, as distinguished from those of the moderns, are new and curious; and are enlivened with a mixture of historical illustration, and of critical discussion, seldom to be met with among metaphysical writers.

But through all his researches, the radical error may, more or less, be traced, which lies at the bottom of his system;[1] and

Elémens de la Grammaire de la Langue Romane avant l'an 1000 Pp. 104, 105 A Paris, 1816

In the theoretical history of language, it is more than probable, that some steps will remain to exercise the ingenuity of our latest posterity. Nor will this appear surprising, when we consider how impossible it is for us to judge, from our own experience, of the intellectual processes which pass in the minds of savages. Some instincts, we know, possessed both by them and by infants, (that of imitation, for example, and the use of natural signs,) disappear in by far the greater number of individuals, almost entirely in the maturity of their reason. It does not seem at all improbable, that other instincts connected with the invention of speech, may be confined to that state of the intellectual powers which requires their guidance; nor is it quite impossible, that some latent capacities of the understanding may be evolved by the pressure of necessity. The facility with which infants surmount so many grammatical and metaphysical difficulties, seems to me to add much weight to these conjectures.

In tracing the first steps of the invention of language, it ought never to be forgotten, that we undertake a task more similar than might at first be supposed, to that of tracing the first operations of the infant mind. In both cases, we are apt to attempt an explanation from reason alone, of what requires the co-operation of very different principles. To trace the theoretical history of geometry, in which we know for certain, that all the transitions have depended on *reasoning* alone, is a problem which has not yet been completely solved. Nor has even any satisfactory account been hitherto given of the experimental steps by which men were gradually led to the use of iron. And yet how simple are these problems, when compared with that relating to the origin and progress of language!

[1] A remarkable instance of this occurs in that part of Condillac's *Cours d'Etude*, where he treats of the art of writing: "Vous savez, Monseigneur, comment les mêmes noms ont été transportés des objets qui tombent sous les sens à ceux qui les échappent. Vous avez remarqué, qu'il y en a qui sont encore en usage dans l'un et l'autre acceptation, et qu'il y en a qui sont devenus les noms propres des choses, dont ils avoient d'abord été les signes figurés.

"Les premiers, tel que le *mouvement* de l'âme, son *penchant*, sa *réflexion*,

hence it is that, with all his skill as a writer, he never elevates the imagination, or touches the heart. That he wrote with the best intentions, we have satisfactory evidence; and yet hardly a philosopher can be named, whose theories have had more influence in misleading the opinions of his contemporaries.[1] In

donnent un corps à des choses qui n'en ont pas. Les seconds, tels que la *pensée*, la *volonté*, le *désir*, ne peignent plus rien, et laissent aux idées abstraites cette spiritualité qui les dérobe aux sens Mais si le langage doit être l'image de nos pensées, on a perdu beaucoup, lorsqu' oubliant la première signification des mots, on a effacé jusqu'aux traits qu'ils donnoient aux idées. Toutes les langues sont en cela plus ou moins défectueuses, toutes aussi ont des tableaux plus ou moins conservés "—*Cours d'Etude*, tom. II. p 212, à Parme, 1775

Condillac enlarges on this point at considerable length, endeavouring to shew, that whenever we lose sight of the analogical origin of a figurative word, we become insensible to one of the chief beauties of language " In the word *examen*, for example, a Frenchman perceives only the proper name of one of our mental operations. A Roman attached to it the same idea, and received over and above the image of weighing and balancing. The case is the same with the words *âme* and *anima; pensée* and *cogitatio*.

In this view of the subject, Condillac plainly proceeded on his favourite principle, that all our notions of our mental operations are compounded of sensible images. Whereas the fact is, that the only just notions we can form of the powers of the mind are obtained by abstracting from the qualities and laws of the material world In proportion, therefore, as the analogical origin of a figurative word disappears, it becomes a fitter instrument of metaphysical thought and reasoning —See *Philosophical Essays*, Part I Essay v. chap iii.

[1] A late writer, (M de Bonald,) whose philosophical opinions, in general, agree nearly with those of La Harpe, has, however, appreciated very differently, and, in my judgment, much more sagaciously, the merits of Condillac · " Condillac a eu sur l'esprit philosophique du dernier siècle, l'influence que Voltaire à prise sur l'esprit religieux, et J. J. Rousseau sur les opinions politiques. Condillac a mis de la sécheresse et de la minutie dans les esprits, Voltaire du penchant à la raillerie et à la frivolité, Rousseau les a rendus chagrins et mécontents. . . . Condillac a encore plus faussé l'esprit de la nation, parce que sa doctrine étoit enseignée dans les premières études à des jeunes gens qui n'avoient encore lu ni Rousseau ni Voltaire, et que la manière de raisonner et la direction philosophique de l'esprit s'étendent à tout "—*Recherches Phil.* tom i pp. 187, 188

The following criticism on the supposed perspicuity of Condillac's style is so just and philosophical, that I cannot refrain from giving it a place here: "Condillac est, ou paroit être, clair et méthodique, mais il faut prendre garde que la clarté des pensées, comme la transparence des objets physiques, peut tenir d'un défaut de profondeur, et que la méthode dans les écrits, qui suppose la patience de l'esprit, n'en prouve pas toujours la justesse; et moins encore la fécondité. Il y a aussi une clarté de style en quelque sorte toute matérielle, qui n'est pas incompatible avec l'obscurité dans les idées Rien de plus facile à entendre que les mots de *sensations transformées* dont Condillac s'est servi, parce que ces mots ne parlent qu'à l'imagination, qui se figure à volonté

France, he very early attained to a rank and authority not inferior to those which have been so long and so deservedly assigned to Locke in England; and even in this country, his works have been more generally read and admired, than those of any foreign metaphysician of an equally recent date.

The very general sketches to which I am here obliged to confine myself, do not allow me to take notice of various contributions to metaphysical science, which are to be collected from writers professedly intent upon other subjects. I must not, however, pass over in silence the name of Buffon, who, in the midst of those magnificent views of external nature, which the peculiar character of his eloquence fitted him so admirably to delineate, has frequently indulged himself in ingenious discussions concerning the faculties both of men and of brutes. His subject, indeed, led his attention chiefly to man considered as an animal, but the peculiarities which the human race exhibit in their physical condition, and the manifest reference which these bear to their superior rank in the creation, unavoidably engaged him in speculations of a higher aim, and of a deeper interest. In prosecuting these, he has been accused (and perhaps with some justice) of ascribing too much to the effects of bodily organization on the intellectual powers; but he leads his reader in so pleasing a manner from matter to mind, that I have no doubt he has attracted the curiosity of many to metaphysical inquiries, who would never otherwise have thought of them. In his theories concerning the nature of the brutes, he has been commonly considered as leaning to the opinion of Descartes; but I cannot help thinking without any good reason. Some of his ideas on the complicated operations of insects appear to me just and satisfactory; and while they account for the phenomena, without ascribing to the

des transformations et des changemens Mais cette transformation, appliquée aux opérations de l'esprit, n'est qu'un mot vide de sens, et Condillac lui-même auroit été bien embarrassé d'en donner une explication satisfaisante Ce philosophe me paroit plus heureux dans ses apperçus que dans ses démonstrations. La route de la vérité semble quelquefois s'ouvrir devant lui, mais retenu par la circonspection naturelle à un esprit sans chaleur, et intimidé par la faiblesse de son propre système, il n'ose s'y engager" —*Ibid* tom. 1. pp 33, 34

animal any deep or comprehensive knowledge, are far from degrading him to an insentient and unconscious machine.

In his account of the process by which the use of our external senses (particularly that of sight) is acquired, Buffon has in general followed the principles of Berkeley; and, notwithstanding some important mistakes which have escaped him in his applications of these principles, I do not know that there is anywhere to be found so pleasing or so popular an exposition of the theory of vision. Nothing certainly was ever more finely imagined, than the recital which he puts into the mouth of our first parent, of the gradual steps by which he learned the use of his perceptive organs; and although there are various parts of it which will not bear the test of a rigorous examination, it is impossible to read it without sharing in that admiration, with which we are told the author himself always regarded this favourite effusion of his eloquence.

Nor are these the only instances in which Buffon has discovered the powers of a metaphysician. His thoughts on probabilities (a subject widely removed from his favourite studies) afford a proof how strongly some metaphysical questions had laid hold of his curiosity, and what new lights he was qualified to throw on them, if he had allowed them to occupy more of his attention.[1] In his observations, too, on the peculiar nature of mathematical evidence, he has struck into a train of the soundest thinking, in which he has been very generally followed by our later logicians.[2] Some particular expressions in the passage I refer to are exceptionable; but his remarks on what he calls *Vérités de Définition* are just and important; nor do I remember any modern writer of an earlier date who has touched on the same argument. Plato, indeed, and after him Proclus, had called the definitions of geometry *Hypotheses;* an expression which may be considered as involving the doctrine which Buffon and his successors have more fully unfolded.

---

[1] See his *Essai d'Arithmétique Morale*

[2] See the First Discourse prefixed to his Natural History, towards the end.

What the opinions of Buffon were on those essential questions, which were then in dispute among the French philosophers, his writings do not furnish the means of judging with certainty. In his theory of *Organic Molecules,* and of *Internal Moulds,* he has been accused of entertaining views not very different from those of the ancient atomists; nor would it perhaps be easy to repel the charge, if we were not able to oppose to this wild and unintelligible hypothesis the noble and elevating strain, which in general so peculiarly characterizes his descriptions of nature. The eloquence of some of the finest passages in his works has manifestly been inspired by the same sentiment which dictated to one of his favourite authors the following just and pathetic reflection:—" Le spectacle de la nature, si vivant, si animé pour ceux qui reconnoissent un Dieu, est mort aux yeux de l'athée, et dans cette grande harmonie des êtres où tout parle de Dieu d'une voix si douce, il n'aperçoit qu'un silence éternel."[1]

I have already mentioned the strong bias towards materialism which the authors of the *Encylopédie* derived from Condillac's comments upon Locke. These comments they seem to have received entirely upon credit, without ever being at pains to compare them with the original. Had D'Alembert exercised freely his own judgment, no person was more likely to have perceived their complete futility; and, in fact, he has thrown out various observations which strike at their very root. Notwithstanding, however, these occasional glimpses of light, he

---

[1] Rousseau.—In a work by Hérault de Sechelles, (entitled *Voyages à Montbar, contenant des détails très intéressans sur le caractère, la personne, et les écrits de Buffon,* Paris, 1801,) a very different idea of his religious creed is given from that which I have ascribed to him; but, in direct opposition to this statement, we have a letter, dictated by Buffon, on his death-bed, to Madame Necker, in return for a present of her husband's book, *On the Importance of Religious Opinions.* The letter (we are told) is in the handwriting of Buffon's son, who describes his father as then too weak to hold the pen.—*Mélanges extraits des Manuscrits de Madame Necker* 3 vols, Paris, 1788.

The sublime address to the Supreme Being, with which Buffon closes his reflections on the calamities of war, seems to breathe the very soul of Fénélon. " Grand Dieu! dont la seule présence soutient la nature et maintient l'harmonie des loix de l'univers," &c. &c. &c.

invariably reverts to the same error, and has once and again repeated it in terms as strong as Condillac or Gassendi.

The author who pushed this account of the origin of our knowledge to the most extraordinary and offensive consequences, was Helvetius. His book, *De l'Esprit,* is said to have been composed of materials collected from the conversations of the society in which he habitually lived; and it has accordingly been quoted as an authentic record of the ideas then in fashion among the wits of Paris. The unconnected and desultory composition of the work certainly furnishes some intrinsic evidence of the truth of this anecdote.

According to Helvetius, as all our ideas are derived from the external senses,[1] the causes of the inferiority of the souls

[1] In combating the philosophy of Helvetius, La Harpe (whose philosophical opinions seem, on many occasions, to have been not a little influenced by his private partialities and dislikes) exclaims loudly against the same principles to which he had tacitly given his unqualified approbation in speaking of Condillac. On this occasion he is at pains to distinguish between the doctrines of the two writers; asserting that Condillac considered our senses as only the *occasional* causes of our ideas, while Helvetius represented the former as the *productive* causes of the latter.—(*Cours de Littérature,* tome xv. pp. 348, 349.) But that this is by no means reconcilable with the general spirit of Condillac's works, (although perhaps some detached expressions may be selected from them admitting of such an interpretation,) appears sufficiently from the passages formerly quoted. In addition to these, I beg leave to transcribe the following:—"Dans le système que toutes nos connoissances viennent des sens, rien n'est plus aisé que de se faire une notion exacte des idées. Car elles ne sont que des sensations ou des portions extraites de quelque sensation pour être considérées à part, ce qui produit deux sortes d'idées, les sensibles et les abstraites."—(*Traité des Systèmes,* chap vi) "Puisque nous avons vu que le souvenir n'est qu'une manière de sentir, c'est une conséquence, que les idées intellectuelles ne diffèrent pas essentiellement des sensations mêmes."—(*Traité des Sensations,* chap. viii. § 33) Is not this precisely the doctrine and even the language of Helvetius?

In the same passage of the *Lycée,* from which the above quotation is taken from La Harpe, there is a sweeping judgment pronounced on the merits of Locke, which may serve as a specimen of the author's competency to decide on metaphysical questions: "Locke a prouvé autant qu'il est possible à l'homme, que l'âme est une substance simple et indivisible, et par conséquent immatérielle. Cependant, il ajoute, qu'il n'oseroit affirmer que Dieu ne puisse douer la matière de pensée. Condillac est de son avis sur le premier article, et le combat sur le second. Je suis entièrement de l'avis de Condillac, et *tous les bons métaphysiciens conviennent que c'est la seule inexactitude qu'on puisse relever dans l'ouvrage de Locke.'*—*Cours de Littérature,* tome xv p 149

of brutes to those of men, are to be sought for in the difference between them with respect to bodily organization. In illustration of this remark he reasons as follows:—

" 1 The feet of all quadrupeds terminate either in horn, as those of the ox and the deer, or in nails, as those of the dog and the wolf; or in claws, as those of the lion and the cat. This peculiar organization of the feet of these animals deprives them not only of the sense of touch, considered as a channel of information with respect to external objects, but also of the dexterity requisite for the practice of the mechanical arts.

" 2. The life of animals, in general, being of a shorter duration than that of man, does not permit them to make so many observations, or to acquire so many ideas.

" 3. Animals being better armed and better clothed by nature than the human species, have fewer wants, and consequently fewer motives to stimulate or to exercise their invention. If the voracious animals are more cunning than others, it is because hunger, ever inventive, inspires them with the art of stratagems to surprise their prey.

" 4. The lower animals compose a society that flies from man, who, by the assistance of weapons made by himself, is become formidable to the strongest amongst them.

" 5. Man is the most prolific and versatile animal upon earth. He is born and lives in every climate; while many of the other animals, as the lion, the elephant, and the rhinoceros, are found only in a certain latitude And the more any species of animals capable of making observations is multiplied, the more ideas and the greater ingenuity is it likely to possess.

" But some may ask, (continues Helvetius,) why monkeys, whose paws are nearly as dexterous as our hands, do not make a progress equal to that of man? A variety of causes (he observes) conspire to fix them in that state of inferiority in which we find them:—1. Men are more multiplied upon the earth. 2. Among the different species of monkeys, there are few whose strength can be compared with that of man; and, accordingly, they form only a fugitive society before the human race. 3. Monkeys being frugivorous, have fewer wants, and, therefore, less invention than man. Their life is shorter. And, finally, the organical structure of their bodies keeping them, like children, in perpetual motion, even after their desires are satisfied, they are not susceptible of lassitude, (*ennui*,) which ought to be considered (as I shall prove afterwards) as one of the principles to which the human mind owes its improvement.

"By combining (he adds) all these differences between the nature of man and of beast, we may understand why sensibility and memory, though faculties common to man and to the lower animals, are in the latter only sterile qualities."[1]

The foregoing passage is translated literally from a note on one of the first paragraphs of the book *De l'Esprit ;* and in the sentence of the text to which the note refers, the author triumphantly asks, "Who can doubt, that if the wrist of a man had been terminated by the hoof of a horse, the species would still have been wandering in the forest?"

Without attempting any examination of this shallow and miserable theory, I shall content myself with observing, that it is not peculiar to the philosophers of modern France. From the *Memorabilia* of Xenophon it appears, that it was current among the sophists of Greece; and the answer given it by Socrates is as philosophical and satisfactory as anything that could possibly be advanced in the present state of the sciences.

"And canst thou doubt, Aristodemus, if the gods take care of man? Hath not the privilege of an erect form been bestowed on him alone? Other animals they have provided with feet, by which they may be removed from one place to another; but to man they have also given the use of the hand. A tongue hath been bestowed on every other animal, but what animal,

---

[1] It is not a little surprising that, in the above enumeration, Helvetius takes no notice of the want of *language* in the lower animals; a faculty without which, the multiplication of individuals could contribute nothing to the improvement of the species. Nor is this want of language in the brutes owing to any defect in the organs of speech, as sufficiently appears from those tribes which are possessed of the power of articulation in no inconsiderable degree. It plainly indicates, therefore, some defect in those higher principles which are connected with the use of artificial signs.

except man, hath the power of making his thoughts intelligible to others?

"Nor is it with respect to the body alone that the gods have shown themselves bountiful to man. Who seeth not that he is as it were a god in the midst of this visible creation? So far doth he surpass all animals whatever in the endowments of his body and his mind. For if the body of the ox had been joined to the mind of man, the invention of the latter would have been of little avail, while unable to execute his purposes with facility. Nor would the human form have been of more use to the brute, so long as he remained destitute of understanding. But in thee, Aristodemus, hath been joined to a wonderful soul, a body no less wonderful; and sayst thou, after this, the gods take no care of me? What wouldst thou then more to convince thee of their care?"[1]

A very remarkable passage to the same purpose occurs in Galen's Treatise, *De Usu Partium*. "But as of all animals man is the wisest, so *hands* are well fitted for the purposes of a wise animal. For it is not because he had hands that he is therefore wiser than the rest, as Anaxagoras alleged; but because he was wiser than the rest that he had therefore hands, as Aristotle has most wisely judged. Neither was it his hands, but his reason, which instructed man in the arts The hands are only the organs by which the arts are practised."[2]

The contrast, in point of elevation, between the tone of French philosophy, and that of the best heathen moralists, was long ago remarked by Addison; and of this contrast it would be difficult to find a better illustration than the passages which have just been quoted.

The disposition of ingenious men to pass suddenly from one extreme to another in matters of controversy, has, in no instance, been more strikingly exemplified than in the opposite theories concerning the nature of the brutes, which successively became fashionable in France during the last century. While the prevailing creed of French materialists leads to the rejec-

[1] Mrs Sarah Fielding's Translation. [2] Galen, *De Usu Part*, l 1 c 3

tion of every theory which professes to discriminate the rational mind from the animal principle of action, it is well known that, but a few years before, the disciples of Descartes allowed no one faculty to belong to man and brutes in common, and even went so far as to consider the latter in the light of mere machines. To this paradox the author was probably led, partly by his anxiety to elude the objection which the faculties of the lower animals have been supposed to present to the doctrine of the immortality of the soul, and partly by the difficulty of reconciling their sufferings with the Divine Goodness.

Absurd as this idea may now appear, none of the tenets of Descartes were once adopted with more implicit faith by some of the profoundest thinkers in Europe. The great Pascal admired it as the finest and most valuable article of the Cartesian system; and of the deep impression it made on the mind of Malebranche, a most decisive proof was exhibited by himself in the presence of Fontenelle. "M. de Fontenelle contoit," says one of his intimate friends,[1] " qu'un jour étant allé voir Malebranche aux PP. de l'Oratoire de la Rue St. Honoré, une grosse chienne de la maison, et qui étoit pleine, entra dans la salle où ils se promenoient, vint caresser le P. Malebranche, et se rouler à ses pieds. Aprés quelques mouvemens inutiles pour la chasser, le philosophe lui donna un grand coup de pied, qui fit jetter à la chienne un cri de douleur, et à M de Fontenelle un cri de compassion. Eh quoi (lui dit froidement le P. Malebranche) ne sçavez vous pas bien que cela ne se sent point?"

On this point Fontenelle, though a zealous Cartesian, had the good sense to dissent openly from his master, and even to express his approbation of the sarcastic remark of La Motte, *que cette opinion sur les animaux étoit une débauche de raisonnement.* Is not the same expression equally applicable to the opposite theory quoted from Helvetius?[2]

[1] The Abbé Trublet in the *Mercure de Juillet,* 1757 —See *Œuvres de Fontenelle,* tom. ii. p. 137. Amsterdam, 1764.

[2] In La Fontaine's *Discours à Madame de la Sablière,* (liv. x Fable 1) the good sense with which he points out the extravagance of both these extremes is truly admirable. His argument (in spite of the fetters of rhyme)

From those representations of human nature which tend to assimilate to each other the faculties of man and of the brutes, the transition to atheism is not very wide. In the present instance, both conclusions seem to be the necessary corollaries of the same fundamental maxim. For if all the sources of our knowledge are to be found in the external senses, how is it possible for the human mind to rise to a conception of the Supreme Being, or to that of any other truth either of natural or of revealed religion?

To this question Gassendi and Condillac, it cannot be doubted, were both able to return an answer, which seemed to themselves abundantly satisfactory. But how few of the multitude are competent to enter into these refined explanations? And how much is it to be dreaded, that the majority will embrace, with the general principle, all the more obvious consequences which to their own gross conceptions it seems necessarily to involve? Something of the same sort may be remarked in the controversy about the freedom of the human will. Among the multitudes whom Leibnitz and Edwards have made converts to the scheme of necessity, how comparatively inconsiderable is the number who have acquiesced in their subtle and ingenious attempts to reconcile this scheme with man's accountableness and moral agency?

Of the prevalence of atheism at Paris, among the higher classes, at the period of which we are now speaking, the *Memoirs* and *Correspondence* of the Baron de Grimm afford the most unquestionable proofs.[1] His friend Diderot seems to

---

is stated, not only with his usual grace, but with singular clearness and precision, and considering the period when he wrote, reflects much honour on his philosophical sagacity.

[1] The *Système de la Nature* (the boldest, if not the ablest, publication of the Parisian atheists) appeared in 1770. It bore on the title-page the name of Mirabaud, a respectable but not very eminent writer, who, after long filling the office of perpetual secretary to the French Academy, died at a very advanced age in 1760. (He was chiefly known as the author of very indifferent translations of *Tasso* and *Ariosto*.) It is now, however, universally admitted that Mirabaud had no share whatever in the composition of the *Système de la Nature*. It has been ascribed to various authors, nor am I quite certain, that, among those who are most competent to form a judgment upon this point, there is yet a perfect unanimity. In one of the latest works which has reached this country from France, (the

have been one of its most zealous abettors; who, it appears from various accounts, contributed to render it fashionable, still more by the extraordinary powers of his conversation, than by the odd combination of eloquence and of obscurity displayed in all his metaphysical productions.[1]

In order, however, to prevent misapprehension of my meaning, it is proper for me to caution my readers against supposing that *all* the eminent French philosophers of this period were of the same school with Grimm and Diderot. On this subject many of our English writers have been misled by taking for granted, that to speak lightly of final causes is, of itself, sufficient proof of atheism. That this is a very rash as well as uncharitable conclusion, no other proof is necessary than the manner in which final causes are spoken of by Descartes himself, the great object of whose metaphysical writings

Correspondance inédite de Galiani, 1818,) it seems to be assumed by the editors, as an acknowledged fact, that it proceeded from the pen of the Baron d'Holbach. The Abbé Galiani having remarked, in one of his letters to Madame Epinay, that it appeared to him to come from the same hand with the *Christianisme Dévoilé* and the *Militaire Philosophe,* the editors remark in a note, " On peut rendre homage à la sagacité de l'Abbé Galiani. *Le Christianisme Dévoilé* est en effet le premier ouvrage philosophique du Baron d'Holbach. C'est en vain que la *Biographie Universelle* nous assure, d'après le témoignage de Voltaire, que cet ouvrage est de Damilaville."

Having mentioned the name of Damilaville, I am tempted to add, that the article relating to him in the *Biographie Universelle,* notwithstanding the incorrectness with which it is charged in the foregoing passage, is not unworthy of the reader's attention, as it contains some very remarkable marginal notes on the *Christianisme Dévoilé,* copied from Voltaire's own handwriting

Since writing the above note, I have seen the Memoirs of M. Suard, by M. Garat, (Paris, 1820,) in which the biographer, whose authority on this point is perfectly decisive, ascribes with confidence to Baron d'Holbach the *Système de la Nature,* and also a work entitled *La Morale et La Législation Universelle,* vol i. pp. 210, 211.

According to the same author, the Baron d'Holbach was one of Diderot's proselytes. (*Ibid* p. 208) His former creed, it would appear, had been very different.

[Baron Grimm, anxious for the honour of his friend Diderot, seems disposed to recognise *his* hand in all the finest passages—" Quel est l'homme de lettres qui ne reconnait facilement, et dans le livre de l'Esprit et dans le système de la Nature, toutes les belles pages qui sont, qui ne peuvent être que de Diderot "—*Correspondance* du Baron Grimm]

[1] And yet Diderot, in some of his lucid intervals, seems to have thought and felt very differently. See Note T T.

plainly was, to establish by demonstration the existence of God. The following vindication of this part of the Cartesian philosophy has been lately offered by a French divine, and it may be extended with equal justice to Buffon and many others of Descartes's successors: " Quelques auteurs, et particulièrement Leibnitz, ont critiqué cette partie de la doctrine de Descartes; mais nous la croyons irréprochable, si on veut bien l'entendre, et remarquer que Descartes ne parle que des *Fins totales* de Dieu. Sans doute, le soleil par exemple, et les étoiles, ont été faits pour l'homme, dans ce sens, que Dieu, en les créant, a eu en vue l'utilité de l'homme, et cette utilité a été sa fin. Mais cette utilité a-t-elle été l'unique fin de Dieu? Croit-on qu'en lui attribuant d'autres fins, on affoibliroit la reconnoissance de l'homme, et l'obligation où il est de louer et de bénir Dieu dans toutes ses œuvres? Les auteurs de la vie spirituelle, les plus mystiques même, et les plus accrédités, ne l'ont pas cru."—M. l'Abbé Emery, *Editor of the Thoughts of Descartes upon Religion and Morals*, Paris, 1811, p. 79.

As to the unqualified charge of atheism, which has been brought by some French ecclesiastics against all of their countrymen that have presumed to differ from the tenets of the Catholic Church, it will be admitted, with large allowances, by every candid Presbyterian, when it is recollected that something of the same illiberality formerly existed under the comparatively enlightened establishment of England. In the present times, the following anecdote would appear incredible, if it did not rest on the unquestionable testimony of Dr. Jortin: " I heard Dr. B. say in a sermon, if any one denies the uninterrupted succession of bishops, I shall not scruple to call him a downright atheist. This, when I was young (Jortin adds) was sound, orthodox, and fashionable doctrine."—*Tracts*, vol. i. p 436.[1]

[1] See Note U U.
Of the levity and extravagance with which such charges have sometimes been brought forward, we have a remarkable instance in a tract entitled *Athei Detecti*, by a very learned Jesuit, Father Hardouin. (see his *Opera Varia Posthuma*, Amsterdam, 1733, in fol) where, among a number of other names, re to be found those of Jan-

How far the effects of that false philosophy of which Grimm's correspondence exhibits so dark and so authentic a picture, were connected with the awful revolution which soon after followed, it is not easy to say. That they contributed greatly to blacken its atrocities, as well as to revolt against it the feelings of the whole Christian world, cannot be disputed. The experiment was indeed tremendous, to set loose the passions of all classes of men from the restraints imposed by religious principles; and the result exceeded, if possible, what could have been anticipated in theory. The lesson it has afforded has been dearly purchased; but let us indulge the hope that it will not be thrown away on the generations which are to come.

A prediction, which Bishop Butler hazarded many years before, does honour to his political sagacity, as well as to his knowledge of human nature; that the spirit of irreligion would produce, some time or other, political disorders, similar to those which arose from religious fanaticism in the seventeenth century.[1]

senius, Descartes, Malebranche, Arnauld, Nicole, and Pascal. Large additions, on grounds equally frivolous, have been made in later times, to this list, by authors who, having themselves made profession of Atheism, were anxious, out of vanity, to swell the number of their sect. Of this kind was a book published at Paris, under some of the revolutionary governments, by *Pierre Sylvain Maréchal*, entitled *Dictionnaire des Athées* Here we meet with the names of St. Chrysostom, St. Augustin, Pascal, Bossuet, Fénélon, Bellarmin, Labruyère, Leibnitz, and many others not less unexpected This book he is said to have published at the suggestion of the celebrated astronomer Lalande, who afterwards published a supplement to the Dictionary, supplying the omissions of the author. See the *Biographie Universelle*, Articles *Maréchal, Lalande*.

[* In the article *Lalande*, (subscribed by the respectable name of *Delambre*,) the following characteristical *trait* is mentioned: "Dans ses dernières années, et dès 1789, Lalande affectait de manger avec délices des araignées et des chenilles Il s'en vantait comme d'un trait philosophique."]

[1] "Is there no danger that all this may raise somewhat like that levelling spirit, upon atheistical principles, which, in the last age, prevailed upon enthusiastic ones? Not to speak of the possibility, that different sorts of people may unite in it upon these contrary principles." — *Sermon preached before the House of Lords*, January 30, 1741

As the fatal effects of both these extremes have, in the course of the two

* Restored.—*Ed.*

Nearly about the time that the *Encyclopédie* was undertaken, another set of philosophers, since known by the name of *Economists*, formed themselves into an association for the purpose of enlightening the public on questions of political economy. The object of their studies seemed widely removed from all abstract discussion; but they had, nevertheless, a metaphysical system of their own, which, if it had been brought forward with less enthusiasm and exaggeration, might have been useful in counteracting the gloomy ideas then so generally prevalent about the order of the universe. The whole of their theory proceeds on the supposition that the arrangements of nature are wise and benevolent, and that it is the business of the legislator to study and co-operate with her plans in all his own regulations. With this principle, another was combined, that of the indefinite improvement of which the human mind and character are susceptible; an improvement which was represented as a natural and necessary consequence of wise laws, and which was pointed out to legislators as the most important advantage to be gained from their institutions.

These speculations, whatever opinion may be formed of their solidity, are certainly as remote as possible from any tendency to atheism, and still less do they partake of the spirit of that philosophy which would level man with the brute creation. With their practical tendency in a *political* view we are not at present concerned; but it would be an unpardonable omission, after what has been just said of the metaphysical theories of the same period, not to mention the abstract principles involved in the Economical System, as a remarkable exception to the general observation. It may be questioned, too, if the authors of this system, by incorporating their ethical views with their poli-

---

last centuries, been exemplified on so gigantic a scale in the two most civilized countries of Europe, it is to be hoped that mankind may in future derive some salutary admonitions from the experience of their predecessors. In the meantime, from that disposition common both to the higher and lower orders to pass suddenly from one extreme to another, it is at least possible that the strong reaction produced by the spirit of impiety during the French Revolution may, in the first instance, impel the multitude to something approaching to the puritanical fanaticism and frenzy of the Cromwellian Commonwealth

tical disquisitions, did not take a more effectual step towards discountenancing the opinions to which they were opposed, than if they had attacked them in the way of direct argument.[1]

On the metaphysical theories which issued from the French press during the latter half of the last century, I do not think it necessary for me to enlarge, after what I have so fully stated in some of my former publications. To enter into details with respect to particular works would be superfluous, as the remarks made upon any one of them are nearly applicable to them all.

The excellent writings of M. Prévost and of M. Degerando, will, it is to be hoped, gradually introduce into France a sounder taste in this branch of philosophy.[2] At present, so far as I am acquainted with the state of what is called *Idéologie* in that country, it does not appear to me to furnish much matter either for the instruction or amusement of my readers.

---

[1] For some other observations on the Ethical principles assumed in the Economical System, see *Elements of the Philosophy of the Human Mind*, vol. ii. chap iv sect 6, § 1, towards the end

[2] Some symptoms of such a reformation are admitted already to exist, by an author decidedly hostile to all philosophical systems "Bacon, Locke, Condillac, cherchoient dans nos sens l'origine de nos idées ; Helvetius y a trouvé nos idées elles-mêmes. *Juger*, selon, ce philosophe, *n'est autre chose que sentir* * Aujourd'hui les bons esprits, éclairés par les évènemens sur la secrète tendance de toutes ces opinions, les ont soumises à un examen plus sévère. La *transformation* des sensations en idées ne paroit plus qu'un mot vide de sens On trouve que *l'homme statue* ressemble un peu trop à *l'homme machine,* et Condillac est modifié ou même combattu sur quelques points, par tous ceux qui s'en servent encore dans l'enseignement philosophique "—*Recherches Philosophiques*, &c , par M. de Bonald, tom i pp. 34, 35

[† To the same author we are indebted for the following anecdote —" Vous prétendez que *penser* est *sentir*," disoit M. le Comte de Ségur, Président de l'Institut, répondant à M Destutt Tracy (l'ami de M Cabanis et l'analyste de son ouvrage) c'est là votre principe, et la base de votre système. Mais un sentiment qui résiste à tous les raisonnemens ne consentira pas facilement à vous l'accorder "—(*Ibid* p. 337) The objection to the definition is decisive, and is indeed the only one which Locke or Reid could have stated]

* I was somewhat surprised, in looking over very lately the *Principia* of Descartes, to find (what had formerly escaped me) that the mode of speaking objected to in the above paragraph may plead in its favour the authority of that philosopher " Cogitationis nomine, intelligo illa omnia, quæ nobis consciis in nobis fiunt, quatenus eorum in nobis conscientia est Atque ita non modo intelligere velle, imaginari, sed etiam sentire, idem est hic quod cogitare "—(*Princip Phil.* p 2) Dr Reid, too, has said that "the sensation of colour is a sort of thought," (*Inquiry*, chap vi. § 4 ,) but no names, how great soever, can sanction so gross an abuse of language

After all, there is some difference between saying, that sensation is a sort of thought, and that thought is a sort of sensation

† Restored.—*Ed*

The works of Rousseau have, in general, too slight a connexion with metaphysical science, to come under review in this part of my discourse. But to his *Emile*, which has been regarded as a supplement to Locke's *Treatise on Education*, some attention is justly due, on account of various original and sound suggestions on the management of the infant mind, which, among many extravagances, savouring strongly both of intellectual and moral insanity, may be gathered by a sober and discriminating inquirer. The estimate of the merits of this work, formed by Mr. Gray, appears to me so just and impartial, that I shall adopt it here without a comment.

"I doubt," says he, in a letter to a friend, "you have not yet read Rousseau's *Emile*. Everybody that has children should read it more than once; for though it abounds with his usual glorious absurdity, though his general scheme of education be an impracticable chimera, yet there are a thousand lights struck out, a thousand important truths better expressed than ever they were before, that may be of service to the wisest men. Particularly, I think he has observed children with more attention, knows their meaning, and the working of their little passions, better than any other writer. As to his religious discussions, which have alarmed the world, and engaged their thoughts more than any other parts of his book, I set them all at nought, and wish they had been omitted."—Gray's *Works by Mason*, Letter 49.

The most valuable additions made by French writers to the Philosophy of the Human Mind are to be found, not in their systematical treatises on metaphysics, but in those more popular compositions, which, professing to paint the prevailing manners of the times, touch occasionally on the varieties of intellectual character. In this most interesting and important study, which has been hitherto almost entirely neglected in Great Britain,[1]

---

[1] Many precious hints connected with it may, however, be collected from the writings of Lord Bacon, and a few from those of Mr Locke. It does not seem to have engaged the curiosity of Mr. Hume in so great a degree as might have been expected from his habits of observation and extensive intercourse with the world. The objects of Dr Reid's inquiries led him into a totally different track

Among German writers, Leibnitz has

France must be allowed not only to have led the way, but to remain still unrivalled. It would be endless to enumerate names; but I must not pass over those of Vauvenargues[1] and Duclos.[2] Nor can I forbear to remark, in justice to an author occasionally glanced with a penetrating eye at the varieties of genius; and it were to be wished that he had done so more frequently. How far his example has been followed by his countrymen in later times, I am unable to judge, from my ignorance of their language.

A work expressly on this subject was published by a Spanish physician (Huarte) in the seventeenth century. A French translation of it, printed at Amsterdam in 1672, is now lying before me. It is entitled, *Examen des Esprits pour les Sciences, où se montrent les différences des Esprits, qui se trouvent parmi les hommes, et à quel genre de Science chacun est propre en particulier.* The execution of this work certainly falls far short of the expectations raised by the title; but, allowances being made for the period when it was written, it is by no means destitute of merit, nor unworthy of the attention of those who may speculate on the subject of Education. For some particulars about its contents, and also about the author, see Bayle's *Dictionary,* Art. *Huarte,* and *The Spectator,* No 30.

[1] The Marquis de Vauvenargues, author of a small volume, entitled *Introduction à la Connoissance de l'Esprit Humain.* He entered into the army at the age of eighteen, and continued to serve for nine years; when, having lost his health irrecoverably, in consequence of the fatigues he underwent in the memorable retreat from Prague, in December 1742, he resolved to quit his profession, in the hope of obtaining some diplomatic employment better suited to his broken constitution. Soon after, he was attacked by the small-pox, which unfortunately turned out of so malignant a kind, as to disfigure his countenance, and deprive him almost totally of sight. He died in 1747, at the age of thirty-two. The small volume above mentioned was published the year before his death. It bears everywhere the marks of a powerful, original, and elevated mind; and the imperfect education which the author appears to have received gives it an additional charm, as the genuine result of his own unsophisticated reflections.

Marmontel has given a most interesting picture of his social character: " En le lisant, je crois encore l'entendre, et je ne sais si sa conversation n'avait pas même quelque chose de plus animé, de plus délicat que ses divins écrits." And, on a different occasion, he speaks of him thus: " Doux, sensible, compatissant, il tenait nos âmes dans ses mains. Une sérénité inaltérable dérobait ses douleurs aux yeux de l'amitié. Pour soutenir l'adversité, on n'avoit besoin que de son exemple; et témoin de l'égalité de son âme, on n'osait être malheureux avec lui." See also an eloquent and pathetic tribute to the genius and worth of Vauvenargues, in Voltaire's *Eloge Funèbre des Officiers qui sont morts dans la Guerre de* 1741.

If the space allotted to him in this note should be thought to exceed what is due to his literary eminence, the singular circumstances of his short and unfortunate life, and the deep impression which his virtues, as well as his talents, appear to have left on the minds of all who knew him, will, I trust, be a sufficient apology for my wish to add something to the celebrity of a name, hitherto, I believe, very little known in this country.

[2] The work of Duclos, here referred

whom I have already very freely censured, that a variety of acute and refined observations on the different modifications of genius may be collected from the writings of Helvetius. The soundness of some of his distinctions may perhaps be questioned; but even his attempts at classification may serve as useful guides to future observers, and may supply them with a convenient nomenclature, to which it is not always easy to find corresponding terms in other languages. As examples of this, it is sufficient to mention the following phrases *Esprit juste, Esprit borné, Esprit étendu, Esprit fin, Esprit délié, Esprit de lumière.* The peculiar richness of the French tongue in such appropriate expressions, (a circumstance, by the way, which not unfrequently leads foreigners to overrate the depth of a talkative Frenchman,) is itself a proof of the degree of attention which the ideas they are meant to convey have attracted in that country among the higher and more cultivated classes [1]

The influence, however, of the philosophical spirit on the general habits of thinking among men of letters in France, was in no instance displayed to greater advantage, than in the numerous examples of *theoretical* or *conjectural* history, which appeared about the middle of last century. I have already mentioned the attempts of Condillac and others, to trace upon this plan the first steps of the human mind in the invention of language. The same sort of speculation has been applied with greater success to the mechanical and other necessary arts of civilized life;[2] and still more ingeniously and happily

---

to, has for its title, *Considérations sur les Mœurs de ce Siècle* Gibbon's opinion of this work is, I think, not beyond its merits "L'ouvrage en général est bon. Quelques chapitres (le rapport de l'esprit et du caractère) me paroissent excellens."—*Extrait du Journal.*

I have said nothing of La Rochefoucauld and La Bruyère, as their attention was chiefly confined to manners, and to moral qualities. Yet many of their remarks show, that they had not wholly overlooked the diversities among men in point of intellect. An observer of sagacity equal to theirs might, I should think, find a rich field of study in this part of human nature, as well as in the other.

[1] [*French Encyclopédie. On this subject consult La Harpe, tom. xv. p 90, *et seq*]

[2] Particularly by the President de Goguet, in his learned work, entitled "*De l Origine des Lois, des Arts, et des Sciences, et de leurs Progrès chez les Anciens Peuples*" Paris, 1758.

* Restored —Ed

to the different branches of pure and mixed mathematics. To a philosophical mind, no study certainly can be more delightful than this species of history; but as an organ of instruction, I am not disposed to estimate its practical utility so highly as D'Alembert. It does not seem to me at all adapted to interest the curiosity of novices: nor is it so well calculated to engage the attention of those who wish to enlarge their scientific knowledge, as of persons accustomed to reflect on the phenomena and laws of the intellectual world

Of the application of theoretical history, to account for the diversities of laws and modes of government among men, I shall have occasion afterwards to speak. At present I shall only remark the common relation in which all such researches stand to the Philosophy of the Human Mind, and their common tendency to expand and to liberalize the views of those who are occupied in the more confined pursuits of the subordinate sciences.

After what has been already said of the general tone of French philosophy, it will not appear surprising, that a system so mystical and spiritual as that of Leibnitz never struck its roots deeply in that country. A masterly outline of its principles was published by Madame du Chatelet, at a period of her life when she was an enthusiastic admirer of the author; and a work on such a subject, composed by a lady of her rank and genius, could not fail to produce at first a very strong sensation at Paris; but not long after, she herself abandoned the German philosophy, and became a zealous partisan of the Newtonian School. She even translated into French, and enriched with a commentary, the *Principia* of Newton; and by thus renouncing her first faith, contributed more to discredit it, than she had previously done to bring it into fashion. Since that time, Leibnitz has had few, if any, disciples in France, although some of his peculiar tenets have occasionally found advocates there, among those who have rejected the great and leading doctrines, by which his system is more peculiarly characterized. His opinions and reasonings in particular, on the necessary concatenation of all events, both physical and moral, (which accorded but too well with the philosophy professed by Grimm and Diderot,) have been long incorporated with the doctrines of the French materialists, and they have been lately adopted and sanctioned, in all their extent, by an author, the unrivalled splendour of whose mathematical genius may be justly suspected, in the case of some of his admirers, to throw a false lustre on the dark shades of his philosophical creed.[1]

---

[1] "Les évènemens actuels ont avec les précédens une liaison fondée sur le principe évident, qu'une chose ne peut pas commencer d'être, sans une cause qui la produise. Cet axiome, connu sous le nom de *principe de la raison suffisante*, s'étend aux actions même que l'on juge indifférentes. La volonté la plus libre ne peut, sans un motif déterminant, leur donner naissance; car si, toutes les circonstances de deux positions étant exactement semblables, elle agissoit dans l'une et s'abstenoit d'agir dans l'autre, son choix seroit un effet sans cause,[*] elle seroit alors, dit Leibnitz, le *hazard aveugle* des Epicuriens. L'opinion contraire est une illusion de l'esprit qui perdant de vue les raisons fugitives du choix de la volonté dans les choses indifférentes, se persuade qu'elle s'est déterminée d'elle même et sans motifs.

"Nous devons donc envisager l'état présent de l'univers comme l'effet de son état antérieure, et comme la cause de celui qui va suivre. Une intelligence qui pour un instant donné connoitroit toutes les forces dont la nature est animée, et la situation respective des êtres qui la composent, si d'ailleurs elle étoit assez vaste pour soumettre ces données à l'analyse, embrasseroit dans la même formule, les mouvemens des plus grands corps de l'univers et ceux du plus léger atôme. Rien ne seroit incertain pour elle, et l'avenir comme le passé, seroit présent à ses yeux."—*Essai Philosophique sur les Probabilités*, par Laplace.

Is not this the very spirit of the *Theodicœa* of Leibnitz, and, when combined with the other reasonings in the *Essay on Probabilities*, the very essence of Spinozism?

This, indeed, is studiously kept by the author out of the reader's view; and hence the facility with which some of his propositions have been admitted by many of his *mathematical* disciples, who, it is highly probable, were not aware of the consequences which they necessarily involve.

I cannot conclude this note without recurring to an observation ascribed in the above quotation from Laplace to Leibnitz, "that the *blind chance* of the Epicureans involves the supposition of an effect taking place without a cause." This, I apprehend, is a very incorrect statement of the philosophy taught by Lucretius, which nowhere gives the slightest countenance to such a supposition. The distinguishing tenet of this sect was, that the order of the universe does not imply the existence of *intelligent* causes, but may be accounted for by the active powers belonging to the

---

[*] The impropriety of this language was long ago pointed out by Mr Hume. "They are still more frivolous who say, that every effect must have a cause, because it is implied in the very idea of effect. Every effect necessarily presupposes a cause, effect being a relative term, of which cause is the co-relative. The true state of the question is, whether every object, which begins to exist, must owe its existence to a cause?"—*Treatise of Human Nature*, vol. i. p. 147.

Notwithstanding, however, this important and unfortunate coincidence, no two systems can well be imagined more strongly contrasted on the whole, than the lofty metaphysics of Leibnitz, and that degrading theory concerning the origin of our ideas, which has been fashionable in France since the time of Condillac. In proof of this, I have only to refer to the account of both, which has been already given. The same contrast, it would appear, still continues to exist between the favourite doctrines of the German and of the French schools. " In the French empiricism, (says a most impartial, as well as competent judge, M. Ancillon,) the faculty of feeling, and the faculty of knowing, are one and the same. In the new philosophy of Germany, there is no faculty of knowing, but reason. In the former, taking our departure from individuals, we rise by degrees to ideas, to general notions, to principles. In the latter, beginning with what is most general, or rather with what is universal, we descend to individual existences, and to particular cases. In the one, what we see, what we touch, what we feel, are the only realities In the other, nothing is real but what is invisible and purely intellectual."

" Both these systems (continues M. Ancillon) result from the

atoms of matter; which active powers, being exerted through an indefinitely long period of time, *might* produce, nay, *must* have produced, exactly such a combination of things, as that with which we are surrounded This, it is evident, does not call in question the necessity of a cause to produce every effect, but, on the contrary, virtually assumes the truth of that axiom. It only excludes from those causes the attribute of intelligence. It is in the same way when I apply the words' blind chance (*hazard aveugle*) to the throw of a die, I do not mean to deny that I am ultimately the cause of the particular event that is to take place, but only to intimate that I do not here act as a *designing* cause, in consequence of my ignorance of the various accidents to which the die is subjected, while shaken in the box If I am not mistaken, this *Epicurean Theory* approaches very nearly to the scheme, which it is the main object of the *Essay on Probabilities* to inculcate , and, therefore, it was not quite fair in Laplace to object to the supposition of man's free agency, as favouring those principles which he himself was labouring indirectly to insinuate.

From a passage in Plato's *Sophist*, it is very justly inferred by Mr. Gray, that, according to the *common* opinion then entertained, " the creation of things was the work of blind unintelligent matter, whereas the contrary was the result of philosophical reflection and disquisition believed by a few people only." —(*Gray's Works* by Matthias, vol. ii p 414) On the same subject, see Smith's *Posthumous Essays*, p 106

exaggeration of a sound principle   They are both true and both false in part; true in what they admit, false in what they reject. All our knowledge begins, or appears to begin, in sensation; but it does not follow from this that it is all derived from sensation, or that sensation constitutes its whole amount. The proper and innate activity of the mind has a large share in the origin of our *representations,* our sentiments, our ideas. Reason involves principles which she does not borrow from without, which she owes only to herself, which the impressions of the senses call forth from their obscurity, but which, far from owing their origin to sensations, serve to appreciate them, to judge of them, to employ them as instruments. It would be rash, however, to conclude from hence, that there is no certainty but in reason, that reason alone can seize the mystery of existences and the intimate nature of beings, and that experience is nothing but a vain appearance, destitute of every species of reality."[1]

With this short and comprehensive estimate of the new German philosophy, pronounced by one of the most distinguished members of the Berlin Academy, I might perhaps be pardoned for dismissing a subject with which I have, in some of my former publications, acknowledged myself (from my total ignorance of the German language) to be very imperfectly ac-

[1] *Mélanges de Littérature et de Philosophie,* par F. Ancillon, Préface (à Paris, 1809) The intimacy of M Ancillon's literary connexions both with France and with Germany, entitles his opinions on the respective merits of their philosophical systems to peculiar weight. If he anywhere discovers a partiality for either, the modest account which he gives of himself would lead us to expect his leaning to be in favour of his countrymen. " Placé entre la France et l'Allemagne, appartenant à la première par la langue dans laquelle je hasarde d'écrire, à la seconde par ma naissance, mes études, mes principes, mes affections, et j'ose le dire, par la couleur de ma pensée, je désirerois pouvoir servir de médiateur littéraire, ou d'interprète philosophique entre les deux nations."

In translating from M Ancillon the passage quoted in the text, I have adhered as closely as possible to the words of the original, although I cannot help imagining that I could have rendered it still more intelligible to the English reader by laying aside some of the peculiarities of his German phraseology. My chief reason for retaining these, was to add weight to the strictures which a critic, so deeply tinctured with the German habits of thinking and of writing, has offered on the most prominent faults of the systems in which he had been educated.

quainted; but the impression which it produced for a few years in England, (more particularly while our intercourse with the Continent was interrupted,) makes it proper for me to bestow on it a little more notice in this Dissertation than I should otherwise have judged necessary or useful.

SECT. VII.—KANT AND OTHER METAPHYSICIANS OF THE NEW GERMAN SCHOOL.[1]

The long reign of the Leibnitzian Philosophy in Germany was owing, in no inconsiderable degree, to the zeal and ability with which it was taught in that part of Europe, for nearly half a century, by his disciple Wolfius,[2] a man of little genius, originality, or taste, but whose extensive and various learning, seconded by a methodical head,[3] and by an incredible industry

[1] My ignorance of German would have prevented me from saying anything of the philosophy of Kant, if the extraordinary pretensions with which it was at first brought forward in this island, contrasted with the total oblivion into which it soon after very suddenly fell, had not seemed to demand some attention to so wonderful a phenomenon in the literary history of the eighteenth century. My readers will perceive that I have taken some pains to atone for my inability to read Kant's works in the original, not only by availing myself of the Latin version of Born, but by consulting various comments on them which have appeared in the English, French, and Latin languages. As commentators, however, and even translators, are not always to be trusted to as unexceptionable interpreters of their authors' opinions, my chief reliance has been placed on one of Kant's own compositions in Latin, his Dissertation *De Mundi Sensibilis atque Intelligibilis Forma et Principiis*, which he printed as the subject of a public disputation, when he was candidate for a Professorship in the University of Königsberg. It is far from being improbable, after all, that I may, in some instances, have misapprehended his meaning, but I hope I shall not be accused of wilfully misrepresenting it. Where my remarks are borrowed from other writers, I have been careful in referring to my authorities, that my reader may judge for himself of the fidelity of my statements. If no other purpose, therefore, should be answered by this part of my work, it may at least be of use by calling forth some person properly qualified to correct any mistakes into which I may involuntarily have fallen; and, in the meantime, may serve to direct those who are strangers to German literature, to some of the comments on this philosophy which have appeared in languages more generally understood in this country.

[2] Born 1679, died 1754.

[3] The display of method, however, so conspicuous in all the works of Wolfius, will often be found to amount to little more than an awkward affectation of the

and perseverance, seems to have been peculiarly fitted to command the admiration of his countrymen.[1] Wolfius, indeed, did not profess to follow implicitly the opinions of his master, and on some points laid claim to peculiar ideas of his own; but the spirit of his philosophy is essentially the same with that of Leibnitz,[2] and the particulars in which he dissented from him

phraseology and forms of mathematics, in sciences where they contribute nothing to the clearness of our ideas, or the correctness of our reasonings This affectation, which seems to have been well adapted to the taste of Germany at the time when he wrote, is now one of the chief causes of the neglect into which his writings have fallen. Some of them may still be usefully consulted as dictionaries, but to read them is impossible.

In his own country the reputation of Wolfius is not yet at an end. In the preface to Kant's *Critique of Pure Reason*, he is called "Summus omnium dogmaticorum Philosophus"—(Kantii *Opera ad Philosophiam Criticam*, vol i Præf Auctoris Posterior, p. xxxvi Latine vertit. Fred. Born Lipsiæ, 1796) And by one of Kant's best commentators his name is advantageously contrasted with that of David Hume: "Est autem scientifica methodus aut dogmatica, aut sceptica. Primi generis autorem celeberrimum Wolfium, alterius Davidem Humium nominasse sat est"—*Expositio Philos. Criticæ* Autore Conrado Friderico a Schmidt-Phiseldek Hafniæ, 1796

To the other merits of Wolfius it may be added, that he was one of the first who contributed to diffuse among his countrymen a taste for philosophical inquiries, by writing on scientific subjects in the German language. "Were all Baron Wolf's other merits disputed, there is one (says Michaelis) which must incontestably be allowed him, his having added a new degree of perfection to the German tongue, by applying it to philosophy."— *Dissertation on the Influence of Opinions on Language*, &c English Translation, p. 27

[1] [* "La philosophie (says Degerando) n'a point eu d'écrivain plus fécond que Wolf Ses écrits Latins forment à eux seuls, 23 vols 4to Ceux en langue Allemande sont presque aussi nombreux On peut même assurer que Wolf a beaucoup trop écrit, pour son propre avantage et pour celui des autres." —*Hist. Comp.* tom. ii pp 115, 116]

[2] On the great question of Free Will, Wolfius adopted implicitly the principles of the *Theodicæa*; considering man merely in the light of a *machine*, but (with the author of that work) dignifying this machine by the epithet *spiritual*. This language, which is still very prevalent among German philosophers, may be regarded as a relic of the doctrines of Leibnitz and of Wolfius; and affords an additional proof of the difficulty of eradicating errors sanctioned by illustrious and popular names

When the system of Pre-established Harmony was first introduced by Wolfius into the University of Halle, it excited an alarm which had very nearly been attended with fatal consequences to the professor. The following anecdote on the subject is told by Euler:— "Lorsque du temps du feu Roi de Prusse, M. Wolf enseignoit à Halle le système de l'Harmonie Pré-établie, le Roi s'informa de cette doctrine, qui faisoit grand bruit alors; et un courtisan répondit à sa Majesté, que tous les sol-

* Restored —*Ed*

are too trifling to deserve any notice in the history of literature.[1]

The high reputation so long maintained by Wolfius in Germany suggested at different times, to the bookmakers at Paris, the idea of introducing into France the philosophy which he taught. Hence a number of French abridgments of his logical and metaphysical writings. But an attempt which had failed in the hands of Madame de Chatelet, was not likely to succeed with the admirers and abridgers of Wolfius.[2]

---

dats, selon cette doctrine, n'étoient que des machines, que quand il en désertoit, c'étoit une suite nécessaire de leur structure, et qu'on avoit tort par conséquent de les punir, comme on l'auroit si on punissoit une machine pour avoir produit tel ou tel mouvement. Le Roi se facha si fort sur ce rapport, qu'il donna ordre de chasser M. Wolf de Halle, sous peine d'être pendu s'il s'y trouvoit au bout de 24 heures. Le philosophe se réfugia alors à Marbourg, où je lui ai parlé peu de temps après."— (*Lettres à une Princesse d'Allemagne*, Lettre 84me) We are informed by Condorcet, that some reparation was afterwards made for this injustice by Frederic the Great. "Le Roi de Prusse, qui ne croit pas pourtant à l'Harmonie Pré-établie, s'est empressé de rendre justice à Wolf dès le premier jour de son règne."

[1] Among other novelties affected by Wolfius, was a new modification of the Theory of the Monads. A slight outline of it, but quite sufficient, I should suppose, to gratify the curiosity of most readers, may be found in Euler's *Letters to a German Princess*.

[2] To what was before remarked, of the opposition in matters of philosophy between the taste of the French and that of the Germans, I shall here add a short passage from an author intimately acquainted with the literature of both nations.

" L'école Allemande reconnoit Leibnitz pour chef. Son fameux disciple Wolf régna dans les universités pendant près d'un demi siècle avec une autorité non contestée. On connoit en France cette philosophie par un grand nombre d'abrégés dont quelques-uns sont faits par des auteurs qui seuls auroient suffi pour lui donner de la célébrité.

"Malgré l'appui de tous ces noms, *jamais en France cette philosophie ne s'est soutenue même quelques instans*. La profondeur apparente des idées, l'air d'ensemble et de système, n'ont jamais pu y suppléer à ce qui a paru lui manquer pour en faire une doctrine solide et digne d'être accueillie Outre quelque défaut de clarté, qui probablement en a écarté des esprits pour qui cette qualité de style et de la pensée est devenue un heureux besoin, la forme sous laquelle elle se présente a rebuté bien des lecteurs. Quoiqu'aient pu faire les interprètes, il a toujours percé quelque chose de l'appareil incommode qui l'entoure à son origine. Condillac tourne plus d'une fois en ridicule ces formes et ce jargon scientifique, et il s'applique à montrer qu'ils ne sont pas plus propres à satisfaire la raison que le goût. *Il est au moins certain, que le lecteur Français les repousse par instinct, et qu'il y trouve un obstacle très difficile à surmonter*"— *Reflexions sur les Œuvres Posthumes d'Adam Smith*, par M Prévost de Genève ; à Paris, 1794

From the time of Wolfius till the philosophy of Kant began to attract general notice, I know of no German metaphysician whose speculations seem to have acquired much celebrity in the learned world.[1] Lambert[2] is perhaps the most illustrious name which occurs during this interval. As a mathematician and natural philosopher, his great merits are universally known and acknowleged, but the language in which his metaphysical and logical works were written, has confined their reputation within a comparatively narrow circle. I am sorry that I cannot speak of these from my own knowledge; but I have heard them mentioned in terms of the highest praise, by some very competent judges, to whose testimony I am disposed to give the greater credit, from the singular vein of originality which runs through all his mathematical and physical publications.[3]

---

[1] Madame de Staël mentions Lessing, Hemsterhuis, and Jacobi, as precursors of Kant in his philosophical career. She adds, however, that they had no School, since none of them attempted to found any system; but they began the war against the doctrines of the Materialists.—(*Allemagne*, tome iii p. 98.) I am not acquainted with the metaphysical works of any of the three. Those of Hemsterhuis, who wrote wholly in French, were, I understand, first published in a collected form at Paris, in 1792. He was son of the celebrated Greek scholar and critic, Tiberius Hemsterhusius, Professor of Latin Literature at Leyden

[2] Born at Mulhausen in Alsace in 1728, died at Berlin in 1777.

[3] The following particulars, with respect to Lambert's literary history, are extracted from a *Memoir* annexed by M Prévost to his translation of Mr Smith's *Posthumous Works* —" Cet ingénieux et puissant Lambert, dont les mathématiques, qui lui doivent beaucoup, ne purent épuiser les forces, et qui ne toucha aucun sujet de physique ou de philosophie rationelle, sans le couvrir de lumière Ses *lettres cosmologiques*, qu'il écrivit par forme de délassement, sont pleines d'idées sublimes, entées sur la philosophie la plus saine et la plus savante tout-à-la-fois Il avoit aussi dressé sous le titre *d'Architectonique* un tableau des principes sur lesquels se fondent les connoissances humaines. Cet ouvrage au jugement des hommes les plus versés dans l'étude de leur langue, n'est pas exempt d'obscurité Elle peut tenir en partie à la nature du sujet. Il est à regretter que sa logique, intitulé *Organon*, ne soit traduite ni en Latin, ni en Français, ni je pense en aucune langue Un extrait bien fait de cet ouvrage, duquel on écarteroit ce qui répugne au goût national, exciteroit l'attention des philosophes, et la porteroit sur une multitude d'objets qu'ils se sont accoutumés à regarder avec indifférence."—(Prévost, tome ii pp 267, 268.) [* M Prévost farther informs us, that an abridgment of the *Archetectonik* of Lambert was published by M J Trembley I presume that this is the work referred to by Bonnet in the

* Restored —*Ed*

The *Critique of Pure Reason* (the most celebrated of Kant's metaphysical works) appeared in 1781.[1] The idea annexed to the title by the author, is thus explained by himself: "Criticam rationis puræ non dico censuram librorum et Systematum, sed facultatis rationalis in universum, respectu cognitionum omnium, ad quas, ab omni experientia libera, possit anniti, proinde dijudicationem possibilitatis aut impossibilitatis metaphysices in genere, constitutionemque tum fontium, tum ambitus atque compagis, tum vero terminorum illius, sed cuncta hæc ex principiis."—(Kantii *Opera ad Philosophiam Criticam*, vol. i.

following passage of his *Essai Analytique*. "Ceux de mes lecteurs qui ne possèdent pas la langue Allemande, trouveront un précis très bien raisonné de la Théorie des Forces de M Lambert dans un petit ouvrage publié en Français à La Haye en 1780, sous le titre d'*Exposition de quelques points de la Doctrine des Principes de M. Lambert.*"—*Ess Anal* chap. xiv]

In the article *Lambert*, inserted in the twenty-third volume of the *Biographie Universelle*, (Paris, 1819,) the following account is given of Lambert's logic :—" Wolf, d'après quelques indications de Leibnitz, avoit retiré de l'oubli la syllogistique d'Aristote, science que les scholastiques avoient tellement avilie que ni Bacon ni Locke n'avoient osé lui accorder un regard d'intérêt. Il étoit reservé à Lambert de la montrer sous le plus beau jour et dans la plus riche parure C'est ce qu'il a fait dans son *Novum Organon*, ouvrage qui est un des principaux titres de gloire de son auteur" From the writer of this article, (M. Servois,) we farther learn. that the *Novum Organon* of Lambert was translated into Latin from the German original by a person of the name of Pfleiderer, and that this translation was in the hands of an English nobleman (the late Earl of Stanhope) as lately as 1782 I quote the words of M. Servois,

in the hope that they may attract some attention to the manuscript, if it be still in existence The publication of it would certainly be a most acceptable present to the learned world. " D'après le conseil de Le Sage de Genève, l'ouvrage fut traduit en Latin par Pfleiderer, aux frais d'un savant Italien · cette traduction passa, on ne sait comment, entre les mains de Milford Mahon, qui la possédoit encore en 1782 ; on ignore quel est son sort ultérieur."

[1] [* In a periodical work published in London, (Monthly Magazine for May 1805,) there is a short but interesting Memoir with respect to Kant's life and writings, from which it would appear that his family was originally from Scotland. " He was born " (we are told) " in 1724, at Konigsberg in Prussia His father, John George Kant, though born at Memel, descended from a Scotch family, who spelt their name with a *C*, which our philosopher (and his brother) in early life converted into a *K*, as more conformable to German orthography." The Scottish origin of Kant's family is also mentioned by M. Staffer, author of the article Kant in the *Biographie Universelle* " Sa famille était originaire d'Ecosse, circonstance assez curieuse si nous considérons que c'est aux écrits de David Hume que nous devons le système de Kant "] Kant died in 1804.

* Restored —*Ed*

Præfatio Auctoris Prior, pp. 11, 12.) To render this somewhat more intelligible, I shall subjoin the comment of one of his intimate friends,[1] whose work, we are informed by Dr Willich, had received the sanction of Kant himself. "The aim of Kant's *Critique* is no less than to lead Reason to the true knowledge of itself; to examine the titles upon which it founds the supposed possession of its metaphysical knowledge; and by means of this examination, to mark the true limits, beyond which it cannot venture to speculate, without wandering into the empty region of pure fancy." The same author adds, "The whole *Critique of Pure Reason* is established upon this principle, *that there is a free reason, independent of all experience and sensation.*"

When the *Critique of Pure Reason* first came out, it does not seem to have attracted much notice,[2] but such has been its

---

[1] Mr. John Schulze, an eminent divine at Königsberg, author of the *Synopsis of the Critical Philosophy*, translated by Dr. Willich, and inserted in his *Elementary View of Kant's Works*.—See pp. 42, 43

[2] " Il se passa quelque tems après la première publication de la *Critique de la Pure Raison*, sans qu'on fit beaucoup d'attention à ce livre, et sans que la plupart de philosophes, passionés pour l'éclectisme, soupçonnassent seulement la grande révolution que cet ouvrage et les productions suivantes de son auteur devoient opérer dans la science."—Buhle, *Hist de la Phil. Mod* tom. vi p 573. Paris, 1816

As early, however, as the year 1783, the Philosophy of Kant appears to have been adopted in *some* of the German schools The ingenious M. Trembley, in a memoir then read before the Academy of Berlin, thus speaks of it.— " La philosophie de Kant, qui, *à la honte de l'esprit humain*, paroit avoir acquis tant de faveur dans certaines écoles."—*Essai sur les Préjugés* Reprinted at Neufchatel in 1790

We are further told by Buhle, that the attention of the public to Kant's *Critique of Pure Reason* was first attracted by an excellent analysis of the work, which appeared in the *General Gazette of Literature*, and by the *Letters on Kant's Philosophy*, which Reinhold inserted in the *German Mercury.*—(Buhle, tom vi p 573) Of this last philosopher, who appears, in the first instance, to have entered with enthusiasm into Kant's views, and who afterwards contributed much to open the eyes of his countrymen to the radical defects of his system, I shall have occasion to speak hereafter. Degerando, as well as Buhle, bestows high praise not only on his clearness, but on his eloquence, as a writer in his own language " Il a traduit les oracles Kantiens dans une langue élégante, harmonieuse, et pure. . . . Il a su exprimer avec un langage éloquent, des idées jusqu'alors inintelligibles," &c —(*Histoire Comparée*, &c , tom ii p. 271.) That this praise is not undeserved I am very ready to believe, having lately had an opportunity (through the kindness of my

subsequent success, that it may regarded, according to Madame de Staël,[1] " as having given the impulse to all that has been since done in Germany, both in literature and in philosophy." —*Allemagne*, vol. iii. pp 68, 69.

" At the epoch when this work was published, (continues the same writer,) there existed among thinking men only two systems concerning the human understanding · The one, that

learned and revered friend Dr. Parr) of reading, in the Latin version of Fredericus Gottlob Born, Reinhold's principal work, entitled *Periculum Novæ Theoriæ Facultatis Repræsentativæ Humanæ* In point of perspicuity, he appears to me to be greatly superior to Kant; and of this I conceive myself to be not altogether incompetent to judge, as the Latin versions of both authors are by the same hand.

[1] The following quotation, from the advertisement prefixed to Madame de Staël's posthumous work, (*Considérations sur la Révolution Française*,) will at once account to my readers for the confidence with which I appeal to her historical statements on the subject of German philosophy. Her own knowledge of the language was probably not so critically exact, as to enable her to enter into the more refined details of the different systems which she has described, but her extraordinary penetration, joined to the opportunities she enjoyed of conversing with all that was then most illustrious in Germany, qualified her in an eminent degree to seize and to delineate their great outlines. And if, in executing this task, any considerable mistakes could have been supposed to escape her, we may be fully assured, that the very accomplished person, to whose revision we learn that her literary labours at this period of her life were submitted, would prevent them from ever meeting the public eye. I except, of course, those mistakes into

which she was betrayed by her admiration of the German School Of some of the most important of these, I shall take notice as I proceed, a task which I feel incumbent on me, as it is through the medium of her book that the great majority of English readers have acquired all their knowledge of the new German philosophy, and as her name and talents have given it a temporary consequence in this country which it could not otherwise have acquired.

" Le travail des éditeurs s'est borné uniquement à la révision des épreuves, et à la correction de ces légères inexactitudes de style, qui échappent à la vue dans le manuscrit le plus soigné. Ce travail c'est fait sous les yeux de *M A. W. de Schlegel, dont la rare supériorité d'esprit et de savoir justifie la confiance avec laquelle Madame de Staël le consultoit dans tous ses travaux littéraires*, autant que son honorable caractère mérite l'estime et l'amitié qu'elle n'a pas cessé d'avoir pour lui *pendant une liaison de treize années.*"

If any further apology be necessary for quoting a French lady as an authority on German metaphysics, an obvious one is suggested by the extraordinary and well-merited popularity of her *Allemagne* in this country. I do not know, if, in any part of her works, her matchless powers have been displayed to greater advantage. Of this no stronger proof can be given than the lively interest she inspires, even when discussing such systems as those of Kant and of Fichte

of Locke, ascribed all our ideas to our sensations;[1] the other, that of Descartes and of Leibnitz, had for its chief objects to demonstrate the spirituality and activity of the soul, the freedom of the will,[2] and, in short, the whole doctrines of the

---

[1] That this is a very incorrect account of Locke's philosophy, has been already shown at great length; but in this mistake Madame de Stael has only followed Leibnitz, and a very large proportion of the German philosophers of the present day "The philosophy of sensation," says Frederick Schlegel, "which was unconsciously bequeathed to the world by Bacon, and reduced to a methodical shape by Locke, first displayed in France the true immorality and destructiveness of which it is the parent, and assumed the appearance of a perfect system of Atheism."—(*Lectures on the History of Literature*, from the German of Fred Schlegel Edin 1818, vol ii p 22.) It is evident, that the system of Locke is here confounded with that of Condillac. May not the former be called the philosophy of *reflection*, with as great propriety as the philosophy of *sensation?*

[2] In considering Leibnitz as a partisan of the freedom of the will, Madame de Stael has also followed the views of many German writers, who make no distinction between Materialists and Necessitarians, imagining that to assert the spirituality of the soul, is to assert its free agency On the inaccuracy of these conceptions it would be superfluous to enlarge, after what was formerly said in treating of the metaphysical opinions of Leibnitz. (*Comp* p 265.)

In consequence of this misapprehension, Madame de Stael, and many other late writers on the Continent, have been led to employ, with a very exceptionable latitude, the word *Idealist*, to comprehend not only the advocates for the immateriality of the mind, but those also who maintain the Freedom of the Human Will Between these two opinions, there is certainly no necessary connexion; Leibnitz, and many other German metaphysicians, denying the latter with no less confidence than that with which they assert the former

In England, the word *Idealist* is most commonly restricted to such as (with Berkeley) reject the existence of a material world Of late, its meaning has been sometimes extended (particularly since the publications of Reid) to all those who retain the theory of Descartes and Locke, concerning the immediate objects of our perceptions and thoughts, whether they admit or reject the consequences deduced from this theory by the Berkeleians In the present state of the science, it would contribute much to the distinctness of our reasonings were it to be used in this last sense exclusively

There is another word to which Madame de Staël and other writers on the German philosophy annex an idea peculiar to themselves; I mean the word *experimental* or *empirical*. This epithet is often used by them to distinguish what they call the philosophy of Sensations, from that of Plato and of Leibnitz. It is accordingly generally, if not always, employed by them in an unfavourable sense In this country, on the contrary, the experimental or inductive philosophy of the human mind denotes those speculations concerning mind, which, rejecting all hypothetical theories, rest solely on phenomena for which we have the evidence of consciousness It is applied to the philosophy of Reid, and to all that is truly valuable in the metaphysical works of Descartes, Locke, Berkeley, and Hume.

idealists. . . . Between these extremes reason continued to wander, till Kant undertook to trace the limits of the two empires; of the senses and of the soul; of the external and of the internal worlds The force of meditation and of sagacity, with which he marked these limits, had not perhaps any example among his predecessors."—*Allemagne*, vol. iii. pp. 70, 72.

The praise bestowed on this part of Kant's philosophy, by one of his own pupils, is not less warm than that of Madame de Staël. I quote the passage, as it enters into some historical details which she has omitted, and describes more explicitly than she has done one of the most important steps, which Kant is supposed by his disciples to have made beyond his predecessors. In reading it, some allowances must be made for the peculiar phraseology of the German School.

"Kant *discovered* that the intuitive faculty of man is a compound of very dissimilar ingredients; or, in other words, that it consists of parts very different in their nature, each of which performs functions peculiar to itself; namely, the *sensitive faculty*, and the *understanding*.[1] . . . Leibnitz, indeed,

---

Nor are the words, *experimental* and *empirical*, by any means synonymous in our language The latter word is now almost exclusively appropriated to the practice of Medicine, and when so understood always implies a rash and unphilosophical use of Experience "The appellation Empiric," says the late Dr. John Gregory, " is generally applied to one who, from observing the effects of a remedy in one case of a disease, applies it to all the various cases of that distemper" The same remark may be extended to the word *Empirique* in the French language, which is very nearly synonymous with *Charlatan* In consequence of this abuse of terms, the epithet *experimental*, as well as *empirical*, is seldom applied by foreign writers to the philosophy of Locke, without being intended to convey a censure.

[1] [* In answer to the question, what is meant by the term *understanding*? we are told by Mr Nitsch, that, according to Kant, "it is the faculty which enables a man to perceive the agreement or disagreement of two ideas *immediately*, in distinction from reason, which makes him perceive the same agreement or disagreement of ideas only *mediately*, that is to say, by means of comparing them with a third."—*Nitsch*, p 40

To the English reader it is unnecessary to observe, that this account of the understanding is an exact transcript of Locke's account of Intuition which, however, it may not be superfluous to add, has long been rejected by Locke's most intelligent followers, as one of the weakest parts of his work This has been shown in a most satisfactory man-

* Restored —*Ed*

had likewise remarked the distinction subsisting between the sensitive faculty and the understanding; but he entirely overlooked the essential difference between their functions, and was of opinion that the faculties differed from one another only in degree. . . . In the works of the English and French philosophers, we find this essential distinction between the sensitive and the intellectual faculties, and their combination towards producing one synthetical intuition, scarcely mentioned. Locke only alludes to the accidental limitations of both faculties; but to inquire into the essential difference between them does not at all occur to him. . . . This distinction, then, between the sensitive and the intellectual faculties, forms an essential feature in the philosophy of Kant, and is, indeed, the basis upon which most of his subsequent inquiries are established"—*Elements of the Crit. Phil.* by A. F. M. Willich, M.D., pp. 68-70.

It is a circumstance not easily explicable, that, in the foregoing historical sketch, no mention is made of the name of Cudworth, author of the treatise on *Eternal and Immutable Morality;* a book which could scarcely fail to be known, before the period in question, to every German scholar, by the admirable Latin version of it published by Dr. Mosheim.[1] In

ner by Reid, in his Essays on the Intellectual powers. Nor was Reid the first (as he seems to have imagined) by whom its unsoundness was exposed On looking over Locke's correspondence, I find a letter addressed to Mr. Molyneux by an Irish bishop, in which the most important of Reid's objections are completely anticipated; a coincidence which I remark chiefly, as it affords a very strong presumption, that these objections are well founded]

[1] The first edition of this translation was printed as early as 1732 From Buhle's *History of Modern Philosophy*, (a work which did not fall into my hands till long after this section was written,) I find that Cudworth's *Treatise of Immutable Morality* is now not only well known to the scholars of Germany, but that some of them have remarked the identity of the doctrines contained in it with those of Kant. "Meiners, dans son histoire générale de l'Ethique, nie que le système moral de Cudworth soit identique avec celui de Platon, et prétend au contraire, ' que les principes considérés comme appartenans de la manière la plus spéciale à la morale de Kant, étaient enseignés il y a déjà plusieurs générations par l'école du philosophe Anglais."—(*Hist. de la Phil Moderne*, tom. iii. p 577.) In opposition to this, Buhle states his own decided conviction, " qu' aucune des idées de Cudworth ne se rapproche de celles de Kant."—(*Ibid*) How far this conviction is well founded, the passage from

this treatise, Cudworth is at much pains to illustrate the Platonic doctrine concerning the difference between sensation and intellection; asserting that "some ideas of the mind proceed not from outward sensible objects, but arise from the inward activity of the mind itself;" that "even simple corporeal things, passively perceived by sense, are known and understood only by the active power of the mind;" and that, besides Αἰσθήματα and Φαντάσματα, there must be Νοήματα or intelligible ideas, the source of which can be traced to the understanding alone.[1]

Cudworth, quoted in the text, will enable my readers to judge for themselves.

That Cudworth has blended with his principles a vein of Platonic mysticism, which is not to be found in Kant, is undeniable; but it does not follow from this, that none of Kant's leading ideas are borrowed from the writings of Cudworth.

The assertion of Buhle, just mentioned, is the more surprising, as he himself acknowledges that "La philosophie morale de Price présente en effet une analogie frappante avec celle de Kant," and in another part of his work, he expresses himself thus on the same subject· "Le plus remarquable de tous les moralistes modernes de l'Angleterre est, sans contredit, Richard Price . . . On remarque l'analogie la plus frappante entre ses idées sur les bases de la moralité, et celles que la philosophie critique a fait naître en Allemagne, quoiqu'il ne soit cependant pas possible d'élever le plus petit doute sur l'entière originalité de ces dernières."— (Tom v. p 303) Is there any thing of importance in the system of Price, which is not borrowed from the *Treatise of Immutable Morality*? The distinguishing merit of this learned and most respectable writer is the good sense with which he has applied the doctrines of Cudworth to the sceptical theories of his own times.

In the sequel of Buhle's reflections on Cudworth's philosophy, we are told, that, according to him, "the will of God is only a simple blind power, acting mechanically or accidentally." ("Chez Cudworth la volonté même en Dieu, n'est qu'un simple pouvoir aveugle, agissant mécaniquement ou accidentellement") If this were true, Cudworth ought to be ranked among the disciples, not of Plato, but of Spinoza.

[1] In this instance, a striking resemblance is observable between the language of Cudworth and that of Kant; both of them having followed the distinctions of the Socratic School, as explained in the *Theætetus* of Plato. They who are at all acquainted with Kant's *Critique*, will immediately recognise his phraseology in the passage quoted above

[* In the Philosophy of Kant the name *Æsthetic* is given to the science which treats of the Laws of Sensation, in contradistinction to Logic, or the doctrine of the Understanding. *Nooumenon* denotes an object or thing in itself, in opposition to the term *phænomenon*, which expresses the representation of an object, as it appears to our senses.—*Willich*, pp 139, 170]

* Restored —Ed

In the course of his speculations on these subjects, Cudworth has blended, with some very deep and valuable discussions, several opinions to which I cannot assent, and not a few propositions which I am unable to comprehend; but he seems to have advanced at least as far as Kant, in drawing the line between the provinces of the senses and of the understanding; and although not one of the most luminous of our English writers, he must be allowed to be far superior to the German metaphysician, both in point of perspicuity and of precision A later writer, too, of our own country, (Dr. Price,) a zealous follower both of Plato and of Cudworth, afterwards resumed the same argument, in a work which appeared long before the *Critique of Pure Reason;*[1] and urged it with much force against those modern metaphysicians, who consider the senses as the sources of all our knowledge. At a period somewhat earlier, many very interesting quotations of a similar import had been produced by the learned Mr. Harris, from the later commentators of the Alexandrian School on the philosophy of Aristotle; and had been advantageously contrasted by him with the account given of the origin of our ideas, not only by Hobbes and Gassendi, but by many of the professed followers of Locke. If this part of the Kantian system, therefore, was new in Germany, it certainly could have no claim to the praise of originality, in the estimation of those at all acquainted with English literature.[2]

---

[1] See a review of the *Principal Questions and Difficulties relating to Morals*, by Richard Price, D.D. London, 1758.

[2] I have mentioned here only those works of a modern date, which may be reasonably presumed to be still in general circulation among the learned But many very valuable illustrations of the Platonic distinction between the senses and the understanding, may be collected from the English writers of the seventeenth century Among these it is sufficient to mention at present the names of John Smith and Henry More of Cambridge, and of Joseph Glanvill, the author of *Scepsis Scientifica*

Cudworth's *Treatise of Eternal and Immutable Morality*, although it appears, from intrinsic evidence, to have been composed during the lifetime of Hobbes, was not published till 1731, when the author's manuscript came into the hands of his grandson, Francis Cudworth Masham, one of the Masters in Chancery. This work, therefore, could not have been known to Leibnitz, who died seventeen years before; a circumstance which may help to account for its having attracted so much less

In order, however, to strike at the root of what the Germans call the *philosophy of sensation*, it was necessary to trace, with some degree of systematical detail, the origin of our most important *simple notions;* and for this purpose it seemed reasonable to begin with an analytical view of those faculties and powers, to the exercise of which the development of these notions is necessarily subsequent. It is thus that the simple notions of *time* and *motion* presuppose the exercise of the faculty of memory; and that the simple notions of *truth*, of *belief*, of *doubt*, and many others of the same kind, necessarily presuppose the exercise of the power of reasoning. I do not know that, in this anatomy of the mind, much progress has hitherto been made by the German metaphysicians. A great deal certainly has been accomplished by the late Dr. Reid; and something, perhaps, has been added to his labours by those of his successors.

According to Kant himself, his metaphysical doctrines first occurred to him while employed in the examination of Mr. Hume's *Theory of Causation.* The train of thought by which he was led to them will be best stated in his own words; for it is in this way alone that I can hope to escape the charge of misrepresentation from his followers. Some of his details would perhaps have been more intelligible to my readers, had

attention in Germany than his *Intellectual System*, which is repeatedly mentioned by Leibnitz in terms of the highest praise

From an article in the *Edinburgh Review*, (vol. xxvii p. 191,) we learn that large unpublished manuscripts of Dr Cudworth are deposited in the British Museum. It is much to be regretted, (as the author of the article observes,) that they should have been so long withheld from the public "The press of the two Universities, (he adds,) would be properly employed in works which a commercial publisher could not prudently undertake." May we not indulge a hope that this suggestion will, sooner or later, have its due effect?

In the preface of Mosheim to his Latin version of the *Intellectual System*, there is a catalogue of Cudworth's unpublished remains, communicated to Mosheim by Dr Chandler, then Bishop of Durham. Among these are two distinct works on the Controversy concerning Liberty and Necessity, of each of which works Mosheim has given us the general contents. One of the chapters is entitled, "Answer to the Objection against Liberty, μηδὶν ἐναίτιον" It is not probable that it contains any thing very new or important, but it would certainly be worth while to know the reply made by Cudworth to an objection which both Leibnitz and La Place have fixed upon as decisive of the point in dispute [See Note DDD.—*Ed*]

my plan allowed me to prefix to them a slight outline of Hume's philosophy. But this the general arrangement of my discourse rendered impossible; nor can any material inconvenience result, in this instance, from the order which I have adopted, inasmuch as Hume's *Theory of Causation*, how new soever it may have appeared to Kant, is fundamentally the same with that of Malebranche, and of a variety of other old writers, both French and English.

"Since the *Essays* (says Kant)[1] of Locke and of Leibnitz, or rather since the origin of metaphysics, as far as their history extends, no circumstance has occurred, which might have been more decisive of the fate of this science than the attack made upon it by David Hume.[2] He proceeded upon a single but important idea in metaphysics, the connexion of cause and effect, and the concomitant notions of power and action. He challenged *reason* to answer him what title she had to imagine that anything may be so constituted as that, if it be given, something else is also thereby inferred; for the idea of cause denotes this. He proved beyond contradiction, that it is impossible for reason to think of such a connexion *a priori*, for it contains *necessity;* but it is not possible to perceive how, because something is, something else must necessarily be; nor how the idea of such a connexion can be introduced *a priori*.

"Hence, he concluded, that reason entirely deceives herself with this idea, and that she erroneously considers it as her own child, when it is only the spurious offspring of imagination, impregnated by experience; a *subjective* necessity, arising from habit and the association of ideas, being thus substituted

---

[1] See the Preface of Kant to one of his Treatises, entitled *Prolegomena ad Metaphysicam quamque futuram quæ qua Scientia poterit prodire* I have availed myself in the text of the English version of Dr. Willich, from the German original, which I have carefully compared with the Latin version of Born A few sentences, omitted by Willich, I have thought it worth while to quote, at the foot of the page, from the Latin translation.—*Elem of Critical Philosophy,* by A. F M Willich, M D, p 10, *et seq* London, 1798

[2] "*Humius.*—Qui quidem nullam huic cognitionis parti lucem adfudit, sed tamen excitavit scintillam, de qua sane lumen potuisset accendi, si ea incidisset in fomitem, facile accipientem, cujusque scintillatio diligenter alta fuerit et aucta."

for an *objective* one derived from perception . . However hasty and unwarrantable Hume's conclusion might appear, yet it was founded upon investigation; and this investigation well deserved that some of the philosophers of his time should have united to solve, more happily if possible, the problem in the sense in which he delivered it: A complete reform of the science might have resulted from this solution. But it is a mortifying reflection, that his opponents, Reid, Beattie, Oswald, and lastly, Priestley himself, totally misunderstood the *tendency* of his problem.[1] The question was not, whether the idea of cause be in itself proper and indispensable to the illustration of all natural knowledge, for this Hume had never doubted; but whether this idea be an object of thought through reasoning *a priori;* and whether, in this manner, it possesses internal evidence, independently of all experience; consequently, whether its utility be not limited to objects of sense alone. It was upon this point that Hume expected an explanation.[2]

"I freely own it was these suggestions of Hume's which first, many years ago, roused me from my dogmatical slumber, and gave to my inquiries quite a different direction in the field of speculative philosophy. I was far from being carried away by his conclusions, the fallacy of which chiefly arose from his not forming to himself an idea of the *whole of his problem*, but merely investigating a part of it, the solution of which was impossible without a comprehensive view of the whole. When we proceed on a well founded, though not thoroughly digested thought, we may expect, by patient and continued reflection, to prosecute it farther than the acute genius had done to whom

---

[1] "Non potest sine certo quodam molestiæ sensu percipi, quantopere ejus adversarii, *Reidius, Oswaldus, Beattius,* et tandem *Priestleius,* a scopo quæstionis aberrarent, et propterea quod ea semper acciperent pro concessis, quæ ipse in dubium vocaret, contra vero cum vehementia, et maximam partem cum ingenti immodestia ea probare gestirent, quæ illi nunquam in mentem venisset dubitare, *nutum* ejus ad emendationem ita negligerent, ut omnia in statu pristino maneret, quasi nihil quidquam factum videretur."

[2] Although nothing can be more unjust than these remarks, in the unqualified form in which they are stated by Kant, it must, I think, be acknowledged, that some grounds for them have been furnished by occasional passages which dropped from the pens of most of Mr Hume's Scottish opponents

we are indebted for the first spark of this light. I first inquired, therefore, whether Hume's objection might not be a general one, and soon found, that the idea of cause and effect is far from being the only one by which the understanding *a priori* thinks of the connexion of things; but rather that the science of metaphysics is altogether founded upon these connexions. I endeavoured to ascertain their number; and, having succeeded in this attempt, I proceeded to the examination of those general ideas, which, I was now convinced, are not, as Hume apprehended, derived from experience, but arise out of the pure understanding. This deduction which seemed impossible to my acute predecessor, and which nobody besides him had ever conceived, although every one makes use of these ideas, without asking himself upon what their objective validity is founded; this deduction, I say, was the most difficult which could have been undertaken for the behoof of metaphysics; and what was still more embarrassing, metaphysics could not here offer me the smallest assistance, because that deduction ought first to establish the possibility of a system of metaphysics. As I had now succeeded in the explanation of Hume's problem, not merely in a particular instance, but with a view of the whole power of pure reason, I could advance with sure though tedious steps, to determine completely, and upon general principles, the compass of Pure Reason, both what is the sphere of its exertion, and what are its limits; which was all that was required for erecting a system of metaphysics upon a proper and solid foundation."[1]

---

[1] [* The foregoing remarks and extracts may enable my readers to enter more easily into the idea which led Kant to entitle his book the *Critique of Pure Reason* The fundamental principle on which he proceeds is, that there are various notions and truths, the knowledge of which is altogether independent of experience, and is consequently obtained by the exercise of our rational faculties, unaided by any information derived from without. A systematical exposition of these notions and truths forms (according to him) what is properly called the Science of Metaphysics † To that power of the

* Restored —*Ed*.

† [The object of metaphysics (according to D'Alembert) is precisely the reverse of this "La métaphysique a pour but d'examiner la génération de nos idées, et de prouver qu'elles viennent *toutes* de nos sensations"—(*Elém de Philos* p 143, Mélanges, vol iv) So diametrically opposite to each other are the logical views of German and of French philosophers]

It is difficult to discover anything in the foregoing passage on which Kant could found a claim to the slightest originality. A variety of English writers had, long before this work appeared, replied to Mr. Hume, by observing that the understanding is itself a source of new ideas, and that it is from this source that our notions of cause and effect are derived. "Our certainty (says Dr. Price) that every new event requires some cause, depends no more on experience than our certainty of any other the most obvious subject of intuition. In the idea of every *change*, is included that of its being an *effect*."[1] In the works of Dr. Reid, many remarks of the same nature are to be found; but, instead of quoting any of these, I shall produce a passage from a much older author, whose mode of thinking and writing may perhaps be more agreeable to the taste of Kant's countrymen than the simplicity and precision aimed at by the disciples of Locke.

"That there are some ideas of the mind, (says Dr. Cudworth,) which were not stamped or imprinted upon it from the sensible objects without, and therefore must needs arise from the innate vigour and activity of the mind itself, is evident in that there are, *First*, Ideas of such things as are neither affections of bodies, nor could be imprinted or conveyed by any local motions, nor can be pictured at all by the fancy in any sensible colours; such as are the ideas of wisdom, folly, prudence, imprudence, knowledge, ignorance, verity, falsity, virtue, vice, honesty, dishonesty, justice, injustice, volition, cogitation, nay, of sense itself, which is a species of cogitation, and which is not perceptible by any sense; and many other

understanding, which enables us to form notions and to pronounce judgments *a priori*, without any adventitious lights furnished by experience, Kant gives the name of *Pure Reason*, and the aim of his *Critique* is to assist us in examining the titles which particular supposed truths have to a place in this metaphysical system, or, in other words, to exhibit the extent and to define the limits of that province which *Pure Reason* claims as exclusively her own. See Wilhich, p 38, *et seq*. See also the Preface prefixed to a work entitled, *Prolegomena ad Metaphysicam quamque futuram quæ qua Scientia poterit prodire* Kantii Opera, ex versione Bornii. Lips 1787 Vol ii p 5, *et seq*]

[1] *Review of the Principal Questions and Difficulties in Morals*, chap 1 sect 2 The first edition of this book was printed in 1758

such like notions as include something of cogitation in them, or refer to cogitative beings only; which ideas must needs spring from the active power and innate fecundity of the mind itself,[1] because the corporeal objects of sense can imprint no such things upon it. *Secondly,* In that there are many relative notions and ideas, attributed as well to corporeal as incorporeal things, that proceed wholly from the activity of the mind comparing one thing with another. Such as are CAUSE, EFFECT, means, end, order, proportion, similitude, dissimilitude, equality, inequality, aptitude, inaptitude, symmetry, asymmetry, whole and part, genus and species, and the like."— *Immutable Morality,* pp. 148, 149.

It is not my business at present to inquire into the solidity of the doctrine here maintained I would only wish to be informed what additions have been made by Kant to the reply given to Mr. Hume by our English philosophers, and to direct the attention of my readers to the close resemblance between this part of Kant's system, and the argument which Cudworth opposed to Hobbes and Gassendi considerably more than a century ago.[2]

The following passage, from the writer last quoted, approaches so nearly to what Kant and other Germans have so often repeated of the distinction between *subjective* and *objective* truth, that I am tempted to connect it with the foregoing extract, as an additional proof that there are, at least, some metaphysical points on which we need not search for instruction beyond our own island

" If there were no other perceptive power or faculty distinct from external sense, all our perceptions would be merely relative, seeming, and fantastical, and not reach to the absolute and

---

[1] This is precisely the language of the German School · " Les vérités nécessaires," says Leibnitz, " sont le produit immédiat de l'activité intérieure " —Tom. i p 686, tom ii pp 42, 325 See Degerando, *Hist Comp* tom ii pp 96

[2] In the attempt, indeed, which Kant has made to enumerate all the general ideas which are not derived from experience, but arise out of the pure understanding, he may well lay claim to the praise of originality On this subject I shall only refer my readers to Note X X at the end of this Dissertation

certain truth of anything; and every one would but, as Protagoras expounds, 'think his own private and relative thoughts truths,' and all our cogitations being nothing but appearances, would be indifferently alike true phantasms, and one as another.

"But we have since also demonstrated, that there is another perceptive power in the soul superior to outward sense, and of a distinct nature from it, which is the power of knowing or understanding, that is, an active exertion from the mind itself; and, therefore, has this grand eminence above sense, that it is no idiopathy, not a mere private, relative, seeming, and fantastical thing, but the comprehension of that which absolutely is and is not."[1]

After enlarging on the distinction between the sensitive faculty and the understanding, Kant proceeds to investigate certain essential conditions, without which neither the sensitive faculty nor its objects are conceivable. These conditions are

---

[1] *Immutable Morality,* p 264, *et seq.*
[* A great part of the controversy between the Dogmatists and the Sceptics of Germany with respect to *subjective* and *objective* truths, resolves into the old Cartesian dispute about the veracity of our faculties; a dispute which, as it necessarily appeals to the decision of those very faculties whose authority is called in question, cannot be subjected to logical discussion without the most manifest inconsistency and absurdity, and which, after being so long agitated in the Cartesian schools, one would scarcely have expected to see revived, as a new metaphysical problem, in the end of the eighteenth century. In order to prove that our faculties do not deceive us, Descartes, as my readers will recollect, appealed to the perfect veracity of our Maker, but in this argument it was early and justly objected to him that he reasoned in a *circle* On the other hand, he gave much more countenance than he was aware of to the Sceptics, by representing even necessary truths as entirely dependent upon the Divine Will, affirming that God, if he pleased, could alter the whole theorems of Geometry, and could even make two contradictory propositions to be both true In a letter to Gassendi, he endeavoured to obviate the sceptical consequences which this doctrine seems to threaten, but the evasion he had recourse to was so pitiful, that Cudworth, forgetting for a moment his usual liberality, expresses his doubts "whether he was more in earnest in proposing it, than where he elsewhere attempted to defend Transubstantiation by the principles of his new philosophy."—"As the poets feign (said Descartes) that the Fates were indeed fixed by Jupiter, but that, when they were fixed, he had obliged himself to the preserving of them; so I do not think that the essences of things, and those mathematical truths which can be known of them, are independent on God, but I think, nevertheless, that because God so willed and so ordered, therefore they are immutable and eternal."]

* Restored — *Ed*

time and *space*, which, in the language of Kant, are the *forms* of all phenomena. What his peculiar ideas are concerning their nature and attributes, my readers will find stated in his own words at the end of this Discourse, in an extract from one of his Latin publications.[1] From that extract I cannot promise them much instruction; but it will at least enable them to judge for themselves of the peculiar character of Kant's metaphysical phraseology. In the meantime, it will be sufficient to mention here, for the sake of connexion, that he denies the *objective* reality both of time and of space. The former he considers merely as a *subjective* condition, inseparably connected with the frame of the human mind, in consequence of which, it arranges sensible phenomena according to a certain law, in the order of succession. As to the latter, he asserts that it is nothing *objective* or *real*, inasmuch as it is neither a substance, nor an accident, nor a relation; that its existence, therefore, is only *subjective* and *ideal*, depending on a fixed law, inseparable from the frame of the human mind. In consequence of this law, we are led to conceive all external things as placed in space, or, as Kant expresses it, we are led to consider *space as the fundamental form of every external sensation.*

In selecting Kant's speculations concerning *time* and *space* as a specimen of his mode of writing, I was partly influenced by the consideration that it furnishes, at the same time, a remarkable example of the concatenation which exists between the most remote and seemingly the most unconnected parts of his system. Who could suppose that his opinions on these subjects, the most abstract and the most controverted of any in the whole compass of metaphysics, bore on the great practical question of the freedom of the Human Will? The combination appears, at first sight, so very extraordinary, that I have no doubt I shall gratify the curiosity of some of my readers by mentioning a few of the intermediate steps which, in this argument, lead from the premises to the conclusion.

That Kant conceived the free agency of man to be necessarily implied in his moral nature, (or, at least, that he was anxious

[1] See Note Y Y.

to offer no violence to the common language of the world on this point,) appears from his own explicit declarations in various parts of his works. "Voluntas libera (says he in one instance) eadem est cum voluntate legibus moralibus obnoxia."[1]

In all the accounts of Kant's philosophy which have yet appeared from the pens of his admirers in this country, particular stress is laid on the ingenuity with which he has unloosed this knot, which had baffled the wisdom of all his predecessors. The following are the words of one of his own pupils, to whom we are indebted for the first, and, I think, not the least intelligible, view of his principles, which has been published in our language.[2]

"Professor Kant is decidedly of opinion, that although many strong and ingenious arguments have been brought forward in favour of the freedom of the will, they are yet very far from being decisive. Nor have they refuted the arguments urged by the Necessitarians, but by an appeal to mere feeling, which, on such a question, is of no avail. For this purpose, it is indispensably necessary to call to our assistance the principles of Kant."[3]

"In treating this subject, (continues the same author,) Kant begins with shewing that the notion of a Free Will is not contradictory. In proof of this he observes, that although every human action, as an event in time, must have a cause, and so on *ad infinitum ;* yet it is certain, that the laws of cause and

---

[1] See Born's Latin Translation of Kant's Works, relating to the *Critical Philosophy,* vol. ii. p 325, *et seq.* See also the Preface to vol. iii

[2] *A General and Introductory View of Professor Kant's Principles concerning Man, the World, and the Deity, submitted to the consideration of the Learned,* by F. A. Nitsch, late Lecturer on the Latin Language and Mathematics in the Royal Frederician College at Konigsberg, and pupil of Professor Kant. London, 1796

This small performance is spoken of in terms highly favourable by the other writers who have attempted to introduce Kant's philosophy into England. It is called by Dr. Willich *an excellent publication, (Elements of the Critical Philosophy,* p 62) and is pronounced by the author of the elaborate articles on that subject in the *Encyclopædia Londinensis* to be a *sterling work.* "Though at present very little known, I may venture," says this writer, "to predict that, as time rolls on and prejudices moulder away, this work, like the *E'ements of Euclid,* will stand forth as a lasting monument of PURE TRUTH "—See Note Z Z.

[3] Nitsch, &c. pp. 172, 173

effect can have a place there only where *time* is, for the effect must be consequent on the cause. But neither *time* nor *space* are properties of things; they are only the general *forms* under which man is allowed to view himself and the world. It follows, therefore, that man is not in time nor in space, although the forms of his intuitive ideas are time and space. But if man exist not in time and space, he is not influenced by the laws of time and space, among which those of cause and effect hold a distinguished rank; it is, therefore, no contradiction to conceive that, in such an order of things, man may be free."[1]

In this manner Kant establishes the *possibility* of man's freedom; and farther than this he does not conceive himself warranted to proceed on the principles of the critical philosophy. The first impression, certainly, which his argument produces on the mind is, that his own opinion was favourable to the scheme of necessity. For if the reasonings of the Necessitarians be admitted to be satisfactory, and if nothing can be opposed to them but the incomprehensible proposition, that man neither exists in space nor in time, the natural inference is, that this proposition was brought forward rather to save appearances, than as a serious objection to the universality of the conclusion

Here, however, Kant calls to his aid the principles of what he calls *practical* reason. Deeply impressed with a conviction that morality is the chief concern of man, and that morality and the freedom of the human will must stand or fall together, he exerts his ingenuity to show, that the metaphysical proof already brought of the possibility of free agency, joined to our own consciousness of a liberty of choice, affords evidence of the fact fully sufficient for the practical regulation of our conduct, although not amounting to what is represented as demonstration in the *Critique of Pure Reason*.[2]

---

[1] Nitsch, &c pp. 174, 175

[2] The account of this part of Kant's doctrine given by M Buhle agrees in substance with that of Mr Nitsch "Toute moralité des actions repose uniquement sur la disposition pratique, en tant qu'elle est déterminée par la loi morale seule Si l'on considère cette disposition comme *phénomène* dans la conscience, c'est un évènement naturel, elle obéit à la loi de la causalité, elle repose sur ce que l'homme a éprouvé au-

It is impossible to combine together these two parts of the Kantian system, without being struck with the resemblance they bear to the deceitful sense of liberty to which Lord Kames had recourse, (in the *first* edition of his *Essays on Morality and Natural Religion*,) in order to reconcile our consciousness of free agency with the conclusions of the Necessitarians. In both cases, the reader is left in a state of most uncomfortable scepticism, not confined to this particular question, but extending to every other subject which can give employment to the human faculties.[1]

paravant dans le tems, et elle fait partie du caractère empirique de l'homme. Mais on peut aussi la considérer comme un acte de la liberté raisonnable : Alors elle n'est plus soumise à la loi de la causalité, elle est indépendante de la condition du temps, elle se rapporte à une cause intelligible, la liberté, et elle fait partie du caractère intelligible de l'homme. On ne peut, à la vérité, point acquérir la moindre connoissance des objets intelligibles, mais la liberté n'est pas moins un fait de la conscience. Donc les actions extérieures sont indifférentes pour la moralité de l'homme. La bonté morale de l'homme consiste uniquement dans sa volonté moralement bonne, et celle-ci consiste en ce que la volonté soit déterminée par la loi morale seule "—*Hist de la Philosophie Moderne*, par J. G Buhle, tom vi pp 504, 505.

Very nearly to the same purpose is the following statement by the ingenious author of the article *Leibnitz* in the *Biographie Universelle* :—" Comment accorder le *fatum* et la liberté, l'imputation morale et la dépendance des êtres finies? Kant croit échapper à cet écueil en ne soumettant à la loi de causalité (au *déterminisme* de Leibnitz) que le monde phénoménique, et en affranchissant de ce principe l'âme comme *nou-*

mène ou chose en soi, envisageant ainsi chaque action comme appartenant à un double série à la fois, à l'ordre physique où elle est enchainée à ce qui précède et à ce qui suit par les liens communs de la nature, et à l'ordre morale, où une détermination produit un effet, sans que pour expliquer cette volition et son résultat, on soit renvoyé à un état antécédent."

The author of the above passage is M. Staffer,* to whom we are indebted for the article *Kant* in the same work. For Kant's own view of the subject consult his *Critique of Pure Reason*, *passim*, particularly p. 99, *et seq*. of Born's *Translation*, vol. iii.

[1] The idea of Kant (according to his own explicit avowal) was, that every being, which *conceives* itself to be free, whether it be in reality so or not, is rendered by its own belief a moral and accountable agent "Jam equidem dico: quæque natura, quæ non potest nisi *sub idea libertatis* agere, propter id ipsum, respectu practico, reipsa libera est; hoc est, ad eam valent cunctæ leges, cum libertate arctissime conjunctæ perinde, ac voluntas ejus etiam per se ipsam, et in philosophia theoretica probata, libera declaretur "—*Kanti Opera*, vol. ii p 326

This is also the creed professed by

* [M Maine de Biran? At least among his remains we have, "Exposition de la Doctrine Philosophique de Leibnitz —*Composé pour la Biographie Universelle*,"—and *that article* is attributed to him by M Cousin —*Ed*]

In some respects, the functions ascribed by Kant to his *practical* reason, are analogous to those ascribed to common sense in the writings of Beattie and Oswald. But his view of the subject is, on the whole, infinitely more exceptionable than theirs, inasmuch as it sanctions the supposition, that the conclusions of *pure reason* are, in certain instances, at variance with *that* modification of reason which was meant by our Maker to be our guide in life; whereas the constant language of the other writers is, that all the different parts of our intellectual frame are in the most perfect harmony with each other. The motto which Beattie has prefixed to his book,

"Nunquam aliud natura, aliud sapientia dicit,"

expresses, in a few significant words, the whole substance of his philosophy.

It is to the same *practical* modification of reason that Kant appeals in favour of the existence of the Deity, and of a future state of retribution, both of which articles of belief he thinks derive the whole of their evidence from the moral nature of man. His system, therefore, as far as I am able to comprehend it, tends rather to represent these as useful *credenda*, than as certain or even as probable truths. Indeed, the whole of his moral superstructure will be found to rest ultimately on no better basis than the metaphysical *conundrum*, that the human mind (considered as a *nooumenon* and not as a *phænomenon*) neither exists in space nor in time.

That it was Kant's original aim to establish a system of scepticism, I am far from being disposed to think.[1] The pro-

---

the Abbé Galiani, a much more dangerous moralist than Kant, because he is always intelligible, and often extremely lively and amusing. "L'homme est donc libre, puisqu'il est intimement persuadé de l'être, et que cela vaut tout autant que la liberté Voilà donc le mécanisme de l'univers expliqué clair comme de l'eau de roche" The same author farther remarks, "La persuasion de la liberté constitue l'essence de l'homme On pourroit même définir l'homme un animal qui se croit libre, et ce seroit une définition complète."—*Correspondance de l'Abbé Galiani*, tom 1 pp 339, 340. A Paris, 1818

[1] On the contrary, he declares explicitly, (and I give him full credit for the sincerity of his words,) that he considered his *Critique of Pure Reason* as the only effectual antidote against the opposite extremes of scepticism and of superstition, as well as against various heretical doctrines which at present in-

bability is, that he began with a serious wish to refute the doctrines of Hume; and that, in the progress of his inquiries, he met with obstacles of which he was not aware. It was to remove these obstacles that he had recourse to practical reason; an idea which has every appearance of being an *after-thought*, very remote from his views when he first undertook his work. This, too, would seem, from the following passage, (which I translate from Degerando,) to have been the opinion of one of Kant's ablest German commentators, M. Reinhold: "*Practical Reason* (as Reinhold ingeniously observes) is a wing which Kant has prudently added to his edifice, from a sense of the inadequacy of the original design to answer the intended purpose. It bears a manifest resemblance to what some philosophers call an appeal to *sentiment,* founding belief on the necessity of acting. Whatever contempt Kant may affect for popular systems of philosophy, this manner of considering the subject is not unlike the disposition of those who, feeling their inability to obtain, by the exercise of their reason, a direct conviction of their religious creed, cling to it nevertheless with a blind eagerness, as a support essential to their morals and their happiness." —*Hist. Comparée*, vol. ii. pp. 243, 244.

The extraordinary impression produced for a considerable time in Germany, by the *Critique of Pure Reason*, is very shrewdly, and I suspect justly, accounted for by the writer last quoted: " The system of Kant was well adapted to flatter the weaknesses of the human mind. Curiosity was excited, by seeing paths opened which had never been trodden before. The love of mystery found a secret charm in the obscurity which enveloped the doctrine. The long and troublesome period of initiation was calculated to rouse the ambition of bold and adventurous spirits. Their love of singularity was gratified by the new nomenclature; while their vanity exulted in the idea of being admitted into a privileged sect, exercising, and entitled

fect the schools of philosophy "Hac igitur sola (*Philosophia Critica*) et materialismi, et fatalismi, et Atheismi, et diffidentiæ profanæ, et fanatismi, et superstitionis, quorum virus ad universos potest penetrare, tandemque etiam et idealismi et scepticismi, qui magis scholis sunt pestiferi, radices ipsæ possunt præcidi"—Kant, *Præf. Posterior*, p 35.

to exercise, the supreme censorship in philosophy. Even men of the most ordinary parts, on finding themselves called to so high functions, lost sight of their real mediocrity, and conceived themselves transformed into geniuses destined to form a new era in the history of reason.

"Another inevitable effect resulted from the universal change operated by Kant in his terms, in his classifications, in his methods, and in the enunciation of his problems. The intellectual powers of the greater part of the initiated were too much exhausted in the course of their long novitiate, to be qualified to judge soundly of the doctrine itself. They felt themselves, after so many windings, lost in a labyrinth, and were unable to dispense with the assistance of the guide who had conducted them so far. Others, after so great a sacrifice, wanted the courage to confess to the world, or to themselves, the disappointment they had met with. They attached themselves to the doctrine in proportion to the sacrifice they had made, and estimated its value by the labour it had cost them. As for more superficial thinkers, they drew an inference from the novelty of the form in favour of the novelty of the matter, and from the novelty of the matter in favour of its importance.

"It is a great advantage for a sect to possess a distinguishing garb and livery. It was thus that the Peripatetics extended their empire so widely, and united their subjects in one common obedience. Kant had, over and above all this, the art of insisting, that his disciples should belong exclusively to himself. He explicitly announced, that he was not going to found a school of Eclectics, but a school of his own; a school not only independent, but in some measure hostile to every other, that he could admit of no compromise with any sect whatever; that he was come to overturn every thing which existed in philosophy, and to erect a new edifice on these immense ruins. The more decided and arrogant the terms were in which he announced his design, the more likely was it to succeed; for the human mind submits more easily to an unlimited than to a partial faith, and yields itself up without reserve, rather than consent-to cavil about restrictions and conditions even in favour of its own independence."

With these causes of Kant's success another seems to have powerfully conspired; the indissoluble coherence and concatenation of all the different parts of his philosophy. "It is on this concatenation (says M. Prévost) that the admiration of Kant's followers is chiefly founded." *Grant only* (they boast) *the first principles of the Critical Philosophy, and you must grant the whole system.* The passage quoted on this occasion by M. Prévost is so forcibly expressed, that I cannot do it justice in an English version: "Ab hinc enim capitibus fluere necesse est omnem philosophiæ criticæ rationis puræ vim atque virtutem; namque in ea contextus rerum prorsus mirabilis est, ita ut extrema primis, media utrisque, omnia omnibus respondeant; si prima dederis danda sunt omnia."[1] No worse account could well have been given of a philosophical work on such a subject; nor could any of its characteristical features have been pointed out more symptomatic of its ephemeral reputation. Supposing the praise to be just, it represented the system, however fair and imposing in its first aspect, as vitally and mortally vulnerable (if at all vulnerable) in every point; and, accordingly, it was fast approaching to its dissolution before the death of its author. In Germany, at present, we are told, that a pure Kantian is scarcely to be found[2] But there are many Semi-Kantians and Anti-Kantians, as well as partisans of other schemes built out of the ruins of the Kantian philosophy[3] "In fine, (says a late author,) the *Critique of Pure Reason*, announced with pomp, received with fanaticism, disputed about with fury, after having accomplished the overthrow of the doctrines taught by Leibnitz and Wolff, could no longer support itself upon its own foundations, and has produced no permanent result, but divisions and enmities, and a

---

[1] See some very valuable strictures on Kant, in the learned and elegant sketch of the present state of philosophy, subjoined to M. Prévost's French translation of Mr Smith's posthumous works The Latin panegyric on the critical philosophy is quoted from a work with which I am unacquainted, *Fred Gotilob Bornii De Scientia et Conjectura.*

[2] On this subject, see Degerando, tom ii. p 333

[3] See Degerando and De Bonald

general disgust at all systematical creeds"[1] If this last effect has really resulted from it, (of which some doubts may perhaps be entertained,) it may be regarded as a favourable symptom of a sounder taste in matters of abstract science, than has ever yet prevailed in that country.[2]

To these details, I have only to add a remark of Degerando's, which I have found amply confirmed within the circle of my own experience. It might furnish matter for some useful reflections, but I shall leave my readers to draw their own conclusions from it. "Another remarkable circumstance is, that the defence of the Kantians turned, in general, not upon the *truth* of the disputed proposition, but upon the right interpretation of their master's meaning, and that their reply to all objections has constantly begun and ended with these words, *You have not understood us.*" [* I have myself had the pleasure to be

---

[1] The words in the original are, "Un dégôut générale de toute doctrine." But as the same word *doctrine* is, in a former part of the same sentence, applied to the systems of Leibnitz and of Wolff, I have little doubt, that, in substituting for *doctrine* the phrase *systematical creeds*, I have faithfully rendered the meaning of my author.—See *Recherches Philosophiques*, par M De Bonald, tom. i. pp 43, 44.

[2] The passion of the Germans for *systems* is a striking feature in their literary taste, and is sufficient of itself to show, that they have not yet passed their novitiate in philosophy "To all such (says Mr. Maclaurin) as have just notions of the Great Author of the Universe, and of his admirable workmanship, all complete and finished systems must appear very suspicious" At the time when he wrote, such systems had not wholly lost their partisans in England, and the name of *System* continued to be a favourite title for a book even among writers of the highest reputation. Hence the *System of Moral Philosophy* by Hutcheson, and the *Complete System of Optics* by Smith, titles which, when compared with the subsequent progress of those two sciences, reflect some degree of ridicule upon their authors.

When this affectation of systematical method began, in consequence of the more enlarged views of philosophers, to give way to that aphoristical style so strongly recommended and so happily exemplified by Lord Bacon, we find some writers of the old school complaining of the innovation, in terms not unlike those in which the philosophy of the English has been censured by some German critics. "The best way (says Dr. Watts) to learn any science, is to begin with a regular system. Now, (he continues,) we deal much in essays, and unreasonably despise systematical learning, whereas our fathers had a just value for regularity and systems." Had Dr Watts lived a few years later, I doubt not that his good sense would have led him to retract these hasty and inconsiderate decisions.

* Restored.—*Ed.*

acquainted with some very ingenious as well as zealous Kantians; but I have never yet had the good fortune to meet with two who agreed in giving the same account of their system; nor with any one who would allow any of the attempts to explain it which have hitherto appeared, either in Latin, French, or our own language, to be a genuine exposition of Kant's real principles.[1]

After all, the metaphysics of Kant is well entitled to attention as an article of Philosophical History. If it has thrown no new light on the laws of the intellectual world, the unbounded popularity which it enjoyed for some years in Germany has placed in a new and striking point of view one of the most extraordinary varieties of national character which Europe has exhibited in the eighteenth century; and, while it is kept in remembrance, will preserve to posterity a more perfect idea of the *heads* of its admirers than all the craniological researches of Gall and Spurzheim [2]]

---

[1] [A German philosopher, of the highest rank in his own country, (Reinhold,) whose intimate acquaintance with the doctrines of Kant will not be disputed, has expressed himself on the subject of Kant's obscurity in terms not less strong than those employed by Degerando· "Querelarum omnium, huc usque de critica rationis prolatarum, maxime trita vulgarisque reprehendit in ea obscuritatem Quæ quidem quæstio ex iis quoque auditur, qui systema Kantianum se putant confutasse, et qui ob eam ipsam causam credere deberent, sese illud intellexisse. Nihilominus in copiosis adversariis illius nullus huc usque prodit, qui adsereret, se sensum illius ubivis percepisse, nullusque, quin certe sibi ipse fateri debeat, se multis in locis obscuritatem invincibilem invenisse Plerisque ista obscuritas consequens necessarium videtur apertarum pugnarum, quas in locis sibi perspicuis sese deprehendisse arbitrantur, cum e contrario novi systematis sectatores fontem istarum pugnarum in obscuritate illa sese aperuisse existimant, quæ sibi saltem haud invincibilis fuisse dicitur, ut difficillime vinci eam potuisse fateantur Responsiones illorum ad omnes, quæ huc usque prolatæ sunt objectiones, perinde atque declarationes, quæ Kantius ipse de nonnullis earum protulit, nihil quidquam aliud volunt, quam ut adversarios de sensu criticæ rationis prave intellecto meliora edoceant, quo quidem profecto reprehensionem magis confitentur, quam deprecantur, librum, a tot viris subtilissimis aliasque judicibus justis male intellectum, *summa laborare obscuritate oportere.*"—See Reinhold's Dissertation *de Fatis quæ huc usque experta est Philosophia Kantiana*, prefixed to his *Periculum novæ Theoriæ Facultatis Repræsentativæ Humanæ* Lipsiæ, 1797]

[2] [Those who wish for further information on this subject may consult the several articles relative to it in the *Journal des Sciences*, or *Magazin En-*

Among the various schools which have emanated from that of Kant, those of Fichte and Schelling seem to have attracted among their countrymen the greatest number of proselytes. Of neither am I able to speak from my own knowledge; nor can I annex any distinct idea to the accounts which are given of their opinions by others. Of Fichte's speculations about the philosophical import of the pronoun *I*, (*Qu'est-ce que le moi?* as Degerando translates the question,) I cannot make anything. In some of his remarks, he approaches to the language of those Cartesians who, in the progress of their doubts, ended in absolute *egoism:* but the *ego*[1] of Fichte has a creative power. It creates *existence*, and it creates *science;* two things (by the way) which, according to him, are one and the same. Even *my own* existence, he tells me, commences only with the *reflex act*, by which I think of the pure and primitive *ego*. On this identity of the intelligent *ego* and the existing *ego*, (which Fichte expresses by the formula ego=ego,) all science ultimately rests.—But on this part of his metaphysics it would be idle to enlarge, as the author acknowledges, that it is not to be understood without the aid of a certain *transcendental sense*, the want of which is wholly irreparable; a singular admission enough (as Degerando observes) on the part of those critical philosophers who have treated with so much contempt the appeal to *Common Sense* in the writings of some of their predecessors.[2]

"In the history of beings there are (according to Fichte) three grand epochs; the first belongs to the empire of *chance;* the second is the reign of *nature;* the third will be the epoch of the existence of *God.* For God does not exist yet; he only manifests himself as preparing to exist. Nature tends to an apotheosis, and may be regarded as a sort of divinity in the germ."[3]

cyclopédique, Rédigé par A L. Millin, tom i p 281, tom iii. p. 159; tom. iv p 145, tom v. p 409]

[1] In order to avoid the intolerable awkwardness of such a phrase as *the I*, I have substituted on this occasion the Latin pronoun for the English one.

[2] *Hist. Comparée*, &c tom. ii pp 300, 301. See also the article *Fichte* in the *Encyclopædia Britannica*.

[3] *Hist Comparée*, &c tom ii p 314. The doctrine here ascribed to Fichte by Degerando, although its unparalleled absurdity might well excite some doubts

The account given by Madame de Stael of this part of Fichte's system is considerably different:—"He was heard to say, upon one occasion, that in his next lecture he 'was going to create God,'—an expression which, not without reason, gave general offence. His meaning was, that he intended to show how the idea of God arose and unfolded itself in the mind of man."[1] How far this apology is well founded, I am not competent to judge.

The system of Schelling is, in the opinion of Degerando, but an extension of that of Fichte; connecting with it a sort of Spinozism grafted on Idealism. In considering the primitive *ego* as the source of all reality as well as of all science, and in thus transporting the mind into an intellectual region, inaccessible to men possessed only of the ordinary number of senses, both agree; and to this vein of transcendental mysticism may probably be ascribed the extraordinary enthusiasm with which their doctrines appear to have been received by the German youth. Since the time when Degerando wrote, a new and very unexpected revolution is said to have taken place among

---

about the correctness of the historian, is not altogether a novelty in the history of philosophy. 'It is, in point of fact, nothing more than a return to those gross conceptions of the mind in the infancy of human reason, which Mr Smith has so well described in the following passage:—"In the first ages of the world, the seeming incoherence of the appearances of nature so confounded mankind, that they despaired of discovering in her operations any regular system . . Their gods, though they were apprehended to interpose upon some particular occasions, were so far from being regarded as the creators of the world, that their origin was apprehended to be posterior to that of the world The earth (according to Hesiod) was the first production of the chaos. The heavens arose out of the earth, and from both together all the gods who afterwards inhabited them. Nor was this notion confined to the vulgar, and to those poets who seem to have recorded the vulgar theology. . . The same notion of the spontaneous origin of the world was embraced (as Aristotle tells us) by the early Pythagoreans. . . Mind, and understanding, and consequently Deity, being the most perfect, were necessarily, according to them, the last productions of nature For, in all other things, what was most perfect, they observed, always came last: As in plants and animals, it is not the seed that is most perfect, but the complete animal, with all its members in the one, and the complete plant, with all its branches, leaves, flowers, and fruits, in the other "—Smith's *Post. Essays on Philosophical Subjects*, pp. 106, 107.

[1] *De l'Allemagne*, tom. iii. p 107. Londres, 1813

Schelling's disciples, many of them, originally educated in the Protestant faith, having thrown themselves into the bosom of the Catholic Church.[1] . . . " The union of the faithful of this school forms an invisible church, which has adopted for its symbol and watchword, the Virgin Mary : and hence rosaries are sometimes to be seen in the hands of those who reckon Spinoza among the greatest prophets." It is added, however, with respect to this invisible church, that " its members have embraced the Catholic religion, not as the *true* religion, but as the most *poetical;*" a thing not improbable among a people who have so strong a disposition to mingle together poetry and metaphysics in the same compositions [2] But it is painful to contemplate these sad aberrations of human reason ; nor would I have dwelt on them so long as I have done, had I not been anxious to convey to my readers a general, but I trust not unfaithful, idea of the style and spirit of a philosophy, which, within the short period of our recollection, rose, flourished, and fell ; and which, in every stage of its history, furnished employment to the talents of some of the most learned and able of our contemporaries.[3]

---

[1] See a paper by M. G Schweighauser in the London *Monthly Magazine* for 1804, p 207

[2] " Aussi les Allemands mêlent ils trop souvent la Métaphysique à la Poésie "—(*Allemagne,* vol. iii p 133.) " Nothing (says Mr. Hume) is more dangerous to reason than the flights of imagination, and nothing has been the occasion of more mistakes among philosophers. Men of bright fancies may, in this respect, be compared to those angels whom the scripture represents as covering their eyes with their wings."— *Treatise of Human Nature,* vol i p. 464

[3] According to a French writer, who appears to have resided many years in Germany, and who has enlivened a short Essay on the *Elements of Philosophy* with many curious historical details concerning Kant and his successors, both Fichte and Schelling owed much of their reputation to the uncommon eloquence displayed in their academical lectures —" Cette doctrine sortait de la bouche de Fichte, revêtu de ces ornemens qui donnent la jeunesse, la beauté, et la force au discours On ne se lassait point en l'écoutant "

Of Schelling he expresses himself thus —" Schelling, appelé à l'université de Wirzbourg, y attira par sa réputation un concours nombreux d'auditeurs, qu'il enchainait à ses leçons par la richesse de sa diction et par l'étendue de ses connoissances. De là, il est venu à Munich, où je le revis en 1813. On dit qu'il a embrassé la religion Catholique."—*Essai sur les Elémens de la Philosophie,* par G. Gley, Principal au Collège d'Alençon Paris, 1817, pp. 138, 152.

The space which I have allotted to Kant has so far exceeded what I intended he should occupy, that I must pass over the names of many of his countrymen much more worthy of public attention. In the account given by Degerando of the opponents of the Kantian system, some remarks are quoted from different writers, which convey a very favourable idea of the works from which they are borrowed. Among these I would more particularly distinguish those ascribed to Jacobi and to Reinhold. In the Memoirs, too, of the Berlin Academy, where, as Degerando justly observes, the philosophy of Locke found an asylum, while banished from the rest of Germany, there is a considerable number of metaphysical articles of the highest merit.[1] Nor must I omit to mention the contributions to this science by the University of Göttingen; more especially [those of Michaëlis] on questions connected with the philosophy of language, [which are in an uncommon degree original and instructive.] I have great pleasure, also, in acknowledging the entertainment I have received, and the lights I have borrowed from the learned labours of Meiners and of Herder; but none of these are so closely connected with the history of metaphysics as to justify me in entering into particular details with respect to them. I am ashamed to say that, in Great Britain, the only one of these names which has been much talked of is that of Kant; a circumstance which, I trust, will apologize for the length to which the foregoing observations have extended.[2]

---

[1] In a volume of this collection (for the year 1797) which happens to be now lying before me, [I cannot help pointing out two ingenious and interesting articles by M. Ancillon (le père.) The first of these is a *Dialogue between Hume and Berkeley.* The other is entitled, *Essai Ontologique sur l'Ame*] The same volume contains three profound and important *Memoirs* on *Probabilities*, by M. Prévost and M. l'Huillier. None of these authors, I am aware, is of German origin, but as the Academy of Berlin has had the merit to bring their papers before the public, I could not omit this opportunity of recommending them to the attention of my readers. To a very important observation made by MM. Prévost and l'Huillier, which has been the subject of some dispute, I am happy to avail myself of the same opportunity to express my unqualified assent.—See pp. 15 and 31 of the Memoirs belonging to the *Classe de Philosophie Spéculative.*

[2] See Note A A A

The only other country of Europe from which any contributions to metaphysical philosophy could be reasonably looked for, during the eighteenth century, is Italy; and to this particular branch of science I do not know that any Italian of much celebrity has, in these later times, turned his attention. The metaphysical works of Cardinal Gerdil (a native of Savoy) are extolled by some French writers; but none of them have ever happened to fall in my way.[1] At a more recent period, Genovesi, a Neapolitan philosopher,[2] (best known as a political economist,) has attracted a good deal of notice by some metaphysical publications. Their chief object is said to be to reconcile, as far as possible, the opinions of Leibnitz with those of Locke. "Pendant que Condillac donnait inutilement des leçons à un Prince d'Italie, Genovesi en donnait avec plus de succès à ses élèves Napolitains: il combinait le mieux qu'il lui étoit possible les théories de Leibnitz, pour lequel il eut toujours une prévention favorable, avec celle de Locke, qu'il accrédita le premier en Italie."[3] Various other works of greater

[1] His two first publications, which were directed against the philosophy of Locke, (if we may judge from their titles,) are not likely, in the present times, to excite any curiosity. 1. *The Immateriality of the Soul Demonstrated against Mr Locke, on the same Principles on which this Philosopher has Demonstrated the Existence and the Immateriality of God* Turin, 1747. 2 *Defence of the Opinion of Malebranche, on the Nature and Origin of our Ideas, against the examination of Mr. Locke* Turin, 1748 The only other works of Gerdil which I have seen referred to are, *A Dissertation on the Incompatibility of the Principles of Descartes with those of Spinoza;* and *A Refutation of some Principles maintained in the Emile of Rousseau*

Of this last performance, Rousseau is reported to have said, "*Voilà l'unique écrit publié contre moi que j'ai trouvé digne d'être lu en entier*   (*Nouveau Dict. Hist* article *Gerdil*) In the same article, a reference is made to a public discourse of the celebrated M. Mairan, of the Academy of Sciences, in which he pronounces the following judgment on Gerdil s metaphysical powers · "*Gerdil porte avec lui dans tous ces discours un esprit géométrique, qui manque trop souvent aux géomètres mêmes*"

[2] Born 1712, died 1769.

[3] *Revue Encyclopédique, ou Analyse Raisonnée des Productions les plus Remarquables dans la Littérature, les Sciences, et les Arts* 1 vol 3me livraison, p 515   Paris, Mars 1819. (The writer of the article quoted in the text is M Sarpi, an Italian by birth, who, after having distinguished himself by various publications in his own country, has now (if I am not mistaken) fixed his residence at Paris In his own philosophical opinions he seems to be a follower of Condillac's School,

or less celebrity, from Italian authors, seem to announce a growing taste in that part of Europe for these abstract researches. The names of Francisco Soave, of Biagioli, and of Mariano Gigli, are advantageously mentioned by their countrymen; but none of their works, as far as I can learn, have yet reached Scotland. Indeed, with the single exception of Boscovich, I recollect no writer on the other side of the Alps, whose metaphysical speculations have been heard of in this island. This is the more to be regretted, as the specimens he has given, both of originality and soundness in some of his abstract discussions, convey a very favourable idea of the schools in which he received his education. The authority to which he seems most inclined to lean is that of Leibnitz, but, on all important questions he exercises his own judgment, and often combats Leibnitz with equal freedom and success. Remarkable instances of this occur in his strictures on the principle of the *sufficient reason*, and in the limitations with which he has admitted the *law of continuity*.

The vigour, and, at the same time, the versatility of talents, displayed in the voluminous works of this extraordinary man,

otherwise he would scarcely have spoken so highly as he has done of the French Ideologists. " L'Idéologie qui, d'après sa dénomination récente pourrait être considérée comme spécialement due aux Français, mais qui est aussi ancienne que la philosophie, puisqu'elle a pour objet la génération des idées et l'analyse des facultés qui concourent à leur formation, n'est pas étrangère aux Italiens, comme on pourrait le croire.")

Genovesi is considered by an historian of high reputation, as the reformer of Italian philosophy. If the execution of his *Treatise on Logic* corresponds at all to the enlightened views with which the design seems to have been conceived, it cannot fail to be a work of much practical utility. " Ma chi può veramente dirsi il riformatore dell' Italiana filosofia, chi la fece tosto conoscere, e respettare da' più dotti filosofi delle altre nazioni, chi seppe arricchire di nuovi pregi la logica, la metafisica, e la morale, fu il celebre Genovesi. Tuttochè molti fossero stati i filosofi che cercarono con sottili riflessioni, e giusti precetti d'ajutare la mente a pensare ed a ragionare con esattezza e verità, e Bacone, Malebranche, Loke, Wolfio, e molt' altri sembrassero avere esaurito quanto v'era da scrivere su tale arte, seppe nondimeno il Genovesi trovare nuove osservazioni, e nuovi avvertimenti da preporre, e dare una logica più piena e compiuta, e più utile non solo allo studio della filosofia, e generalmente ad ogni studio scientifico, ma eziandio alla condotta morale, ed alla civile società."—*Dell' Origine, de Progressi, e dello Stato attuale d'Ogni Letteratura* dell' Abate D Giovanni Andies Tomo xv pp 260, 261. Venezia, 1800.

reflect the highest honour on the country which gave him birth, and would almost tempt one to give credit to the theory which ascribes to the genial climates of the south a beneficial influence on the intellectual frame. Italy is certainly the only part of Europe where mathematicians and metaphysicians of the highest rank have produced such poetry as has proceeded from the pens of Boscovich and Stay. It is in this rare balance of imagination, and of the reasoning powers, that the perfection of the human intellect will be allowed to consist; and of this balance a far greater number of instances may be quoted from Italy, (reckoning from Galileo[1] downwards,) than in any other corner of the learned world.

The sciences of ethics and of political economy, seem to be more suited to the taste of the modern Italians, than logic or metaphysics, properly so called. And in the two former branches of knowledge, they have certainly contributed much to the instruction and improvement of the eighteenth century. But on these subjects we are not yet prepared to enter.

In the New World, the state of society and of manners has not hitherto been so favourable to abstract science as to pursuits which come home directly to the business of human life. There is, however, *one* metaphysician of whom America has to boast, who, in logical acuteness and subtility, does not yield to any disputant bred in the universities of Europe. I need not say, that I allude to Jonathan Edwards. But, at the time when he wrote, the state of America was more favourable than it now is, or can for a long period be expected to be, to such inquiries as those which engaged his attention; inquiries, by the way, to which his thoughts were evidently turned, less by the impulse of speculative curiosity, than by his anxiety to defend the theological system in which he had been educated, and to which he was most conscientiously and zealously attached. The effect of this anxiety in sharpening his faculties, and in keeping his

---

[1] See a most interesting account of Galileo's taste for poetry and polite literature in Ginguené, *Histoire Littéraire d'Italie*, tom v pp. 331, *et seq* à Paris 1812

polemical vigilance constantly *on the alert*, may be traced in every step of his argument.[1]

In the meantime, a new and unexpected mine of intellectual wealth has been opened to the learned of Europe, in those regions of the East, which, although in all probability the cradle of civilisation and science, were, till very lately, better known in the annals of commerce than of philosophy. The metaphysical and ethical remains of the Indian sages are, in a peculiar degree, interesting and instructive, inasmuch as they seem to have furnished the germs of the chief systems taught in the Grecian schools. The favourite theories, however, of the Hindoos will, all of them, be found, more or less, tinctured with

---

[1] While this *Dissertation* was in the press, I received a new American publication, entitled, "*Transactions of the Historical and Literary Committee of the American Philosophical Society, held at Philadelphia, for Promoting Useful Knowledge*," vol i Philadelphia, 1819 From an advertisement prefixed to this volume, it appears that, at a meeting of this learned body in 1815, it was resolved, "That a new committee be added to those already established, to be denominated the Committee of History, Moral Science, and General Literature " It was with great pleasure I observed, that one of the first objects to which the committee has directed its attention is to investigate and ascertain, as much as possible, the structure and grammatical forms of the languages of the aboriginal nations of America The *Report* of the corresponding secretary, (M Duponceau,) dated January 1819, with respect to the progress then made in this investigation, is highly curious and interesting, and displays not only enlarged and philosophical views, but an intimate acquaintance with the philological researches of Adelung, Vater, Humboldt, and other German scholars All this evinces an enlightened curiosity, and an extent of literary information, which could scarcely have been expected in these rising states for many years to come

The rapid progress which the Americans have lately made in the art of writing, has been remarked by various critics, and it is certainly a very important fact in the history of their literature Their state papers were, indeed, always distinguished by a strain of animated and vigorous eloquence, but as most of them were composed on the spur of the occasion, their authors had little time to bestow on the niceties, or even upon the purity of diction An attention to these is the slow offspring of learned leisure, and of the diligent study of the best models This I presume was Gray's meaning, when he said, that "good writing not only required great parts, but the very best of those parts,"[*]—a maxim which, if true, would point out the state of the public taste with respect to style, as the surest test among any people of the general improvement which their intellectual powers have received, and which, when applied to our Transatlantic brethren, would justify sanguine expectations of the attainments of the rising generation

[*] Note of Mason on a Letter of Gray s to Dr Wharton, on the death of Dr Middleton.

those ascetic habits of abstract and mystical meditation which seem to have been, in all ages, congenial to their constitutional temperament. Of such habits, an Idealism, approaching to that of Berkeley and Malebranche, is as natural an offspring, as Materialism is of the gay and dissipated manners, which, in great and luxurious capitals, are constantly inviting the thoughts abroad.

To these remains of ancient science in the East, the attention of Europe was first called by Bernier, a most intelligent and authentic traveller, of whom I formerly took notice as a favourite pupil of Gassendi. But it is chiefly by our own countrymen that the field which he opened has been subsequently explored; and of their meritorious labours in the prosecution of this task, during the reign of our late Sovereign, it is scarcely possible to form too high an estimate.

Much more, however, may be yet expected, if such a prodigy as Sir William Jones should again appear, uniting, in as miraculous a degree, the gift of tongues with the spirit of philosophy. The structure of the Sanscrit, in itself, independently of the treasures locked up in it, affords one of the most puzzling subjects of inquiry that was ever presented to human ingenuity. The affinities and filiations of different tongues, as evinced in their corresponding roots and other coincidences, are abundantly curious, but incomparably more easy in the explanation, than the systematical analogy which is said to exist between the Sanscrit and the Greek, (and also between the Sanscrit and the Latin, which is considered as the most ancient dialect of the Greek,) in the conjugations and flexions of their verbs, and in many other particulars of their mechanism; an analogy which is represented as so complete, that, in the versions which have been made from the one language into the other, "Sanscrit," we are told, "answers to Greek, as face to face in a glass."[1] That the Sanscrit did not grow up to the perfection which it now exhibits, from popular and casual modes of speech, the un-

---

[1] Letter from the Reverend David Brown, Provost of the College of Fort William, about the *Sanscrit Edition of the Gospels*, (dated Calcutta, September 1806, and published in some of the *Literary Journals* of the day.)

exampled regularity of its forms seems almost to demonstrate; and yet, should this supposition be rejected, to what other hypothesis shall we have recourse, which does not involve equal if not greater improbabilities? The problem is well worthy of the attention of philosophical grammarians; and the solution of it, whatever it may be, can scarcely fail to throw some new lights on the history of the human race, as well as on that of the human mind.

[* " I have long harboured a suspicion that *some*, perhaps much, of the Indian science was derived from the Greeks of Bactriana."—(Gibbon's *Rom. Hist.* vol. vii. 294.) This is also the opinion of the very learned and judicious Meiners.—(*Hist. Doctrinæ de vero Deo*, pp. 122, seq.) Meiners refers to some arguments in support of it in Bayer's *Historia Regni Græcorum Bactriani*, p. 165.[1] As this author is often quoted by Gibbon, it is not unlikely that he derived the hint from him.—See Robertson's *India*, pp. 33, 34.]

SECT. VIII.—METAPHYSICAL PHILOSOPHY OF SCOTLAND.

It now only remains for me to take a slight survey of the rise and progress of the Metaphysical Philosophy of Scotland; and if, in treating of this, I should be somewhat more minute than in the former parts of this Historical Sketch, I flatter myself that allowances will be made for my anxiety to supply some chasms in the literary history of my country, which could

* Restored.—On Mr. Stewart's speculations touching the Sanscrit, see of this collection, vol iv.—*Editor.*

[1] [The following account of Bayer's Book is given by Klotzins in an epistle prefixed to *Bayeri Opuscula ad Historiam Antiquam, &c Spectantia*, Halæ, 1770.—" Imprimis vero lectoribus persuadere conatur, Indos a Græcis numerorum nomina et mathematicas disciplinas accepisse, et vias, quibus Græcæ artes cum Oriente communicatæ fuerint, indagat Qua in re multum tribui conjecturis, ipse vir olim doctissimus non negavit. Odiosum hoc est saepe suspicari inquit, attamen, ut mea opinio fert, in tempore et loco necessarium atque utile, ut enim in obscurissimis quæstionibus primum est, suspicari, ita, si nihil proficiamus amplius, exstare et cognosci suspiciones nostras convenit, quibus fortasse aliis occasio præbeatur, aut hoc ipsum, aut novum, et diversum iter sibi muniendi, quo proxime ad veritatem perveniatur"]

not be so easily, nor perhaps so authentically, filled up by a younger hand.

The Metaphysical Philosophy of Scotland, and, indeed, the literary taste in general, which so remarkably distinguished this country during the last century, may be dated from the lectures of Dr. Francis Hutcheson, in the University of Glasgow. Strong indications of the same speculative spirit may be traced in earlier writers;[1] but it was from this period that Scotland, after a long slumber, began again to attract general notice in the republic of letters.[2]

The writings of Dr Hutcheson, however, are more closely connected with the history of Ethical than of Metaphysical

---

[1] See Note B B B

[2] An Italian writer of some note, in a work published in 1763, assigns the same date to the revival of letters in Scotland. "Fra i tanti, e si chiari Scrittori che fiorirono nella Gran Bretagna a' tempi della Regina Anna, non se ne conta pur uno, che sia uscito de Scozia . . Francesco Hutcheson venuto in Iscozia, a professarvi la Filosofia, e gli studii di umanità, nella Universita di Glasgow, v'insinuò per tutto il paese colle istruzione a viva voce, e con egregie opere date alle stampe, un vivo genio per gli studii filosofici, e literarii, e sparse qui fecondissimi semi, d'onde vediamo nascere sì felice frutti, e sì copiose "—*Discorso sopra le Vicende della Letteratura, del* Sig Carlo Denina, p 224, Glasgow edition, 1763.

I was somewhat surprised to meet with the foregoing observations in the work of a foreigner, but wherever he acquired his information, it evinces, in those from whom it was derived, a more intimate acquaintance with the traditionary history of letters in this country than has fallen to the share of most of our own authors who have treated of that subject I have heard it conjectured, that the materials of his section on Scottish literature had been communicated to him by Mr Hume

Another foreign writer, much better qualified than Denina to appreciate the merits of Hutcheson, has expressed himself upon this subject with his usual precision "L'école Ecossaise a en quelque sorte pour fondateur Hutcheson, maître et prédécesseur de Smith. C'est ce philosophe qui lui a imprimé son caractère, et qui a commencé à lui donner de l'éclat" In a note upon this passage, the author observes,—"C'est en ce seul sens qu'on peut donner un chef à une école de philosophie qui, comme on le verra, professe d'ailleurs la plus parfaite indépendance de l'autorité"—See the excellent reflections upon the posthumous works of Adam Smith, annexed by M Prévost to his translation of that work

Dr. Hutcheson's first course of lectures at Glasgow was given in 1730. He was a native of Ireland, and is accordingly called by Denina "un dotto Irlandese;" but he was of Scotch extraction, (his father or grandfather having been a younger son of a respectable family in Ayrshire,) and he was sent over when very young to receive his education in Scotland

Science; and I shall, accordingly, delay any remarks which I have to offer upon them till I enter upon that part of my subject. There are, indeed, some very original and important metaphysical hints scattered over his works; but it is chiefly as an ethical writer that he is known to the world, and that he is entitled to a place among the philosophers of the eighteenth century.[1]

Among the contemporaries of Dr. Hutcheson, there was one Scottish metaphysician (Andrew Baxter, author of the *Inquiry into the Nature of the Human Soul*) whose name it would be improper to pass over without some notice, after the splendid eulogy bestowed on his work by Warburton. "He who would see the justest and precisest notions of God and the soul may read this book, one of the most finished of the kind, in my humble opinion, that the present times, greatly advanced in true philosophy, have produced."[2]

To this unqualified praise, I must confess, I do not think Baxter's *Inquiry* altogether entitled, although I readily acknowledge that it displays considerable ingenuity as well as learning. Some of the remarks on Berkeley's argument against the existence of matter are acute and just, and, at the time when they were published, had the merit of novelty.

---

[1] One of the chief objects of Hutcheson's writings was to oppose the licentious system of Mandeville, a system which was the natural offspring of some of Locke's reasonings against the existence of innate practical principles.

As a moralist, Hutcheson was a warm admirer of the ancients, and seems to have been particularly smitten with that favourite doctrine of the Socratic school which identifies the *good* with the *beautiful*. Hence he was led to follow much too closely the example of Shaftesbury, in considering moral distinctions as founded more on sentiment than on reason, and to speak vaguely of virtue as a sort of *noble enthusiasm*. but he was led, at the same time, to connect with his ethical speculations some collateral inquiries concerning Beauty and Harmony, in which he pursued, with considerable success, the path recently struck out by Addison in his *Essays on the Pleasures of the Imagination*. These inquiries of Hutcheson, together with his *Thoughts on Laughter*, although they may not be very highly prized for their depth, bear everywhere the marks of an enlarged and cultivated mind, and, whatever may have been their effects elsewhere, certainly contributed powerfully, in our Northern seats of learning, to introduce a taste for more liberal and elegant pursuits than could have been expected so soon to succeed to the intolerance, bigotry, and barbarism of the preceding century.

[2] See Warburton's *Divine Legation of Moses demonstrated*, p 395 of the first edition.

One of his distinguishing doctrines is, that the Deity [*himself*] is the *immediate* agent in producing the phenomena of the *Material World;* but that, in the *Moral World*, the case is different,—a doctrine which, whatever may be thought of it in other respects, is undoubtedly a great improvement on that of Malebranche, which, by representing God as the only agent in the universe, was not less inconsistent than the scheme of Spinoza with the moral nature of Man. "The Deity (says Baxter) is not only at the head of Nature, but in every part of it. A chain of material causes betwixt the Deity and the effect produced, and much more a series of them, is such a supposition as would conceal the Deity from the knowledge of mortals for ever. We might search for matter above matter, till we were lost in a labyrinth out of which no philosopher ever yet found his way.—This way of bringing in second causes is borrowed from the government of the moral world, where free agents act a part; but it is very improperly applied to the material universe, where matter and motion only (or mechanism, as it is called) comes in competition with the Deity."[1]

Notwithstanding, however, these and other merits, Baxter has contributed so little to the advancement of that philosophy which has since been cultivated in Scotland, that I am afraid the very slight notice I have now taken of him may be considered as an unseasonable digression. The great object of his studies plainly was, to strengthen the old argument for the soul's immateriality, by [* the doctrine of the *inertia* of matter, which had recently attracted general attention, as one of the fundamental principles of the Newtonian Philosophy.] To the intellectual and moral phenomena of Man, and to the laws by which they are regulated, he seems to have paid but little attention.[2]

---

[1] Appendix to the first part of the *Inquiry into the Nature of the Human Soul*, pp 109, 110

* Mr. Stewart had substituted the following for "the new lights furnished by Newton's discoveries"—*Ed.*

[2] Baxter was born at Old Aberdeen, in 1686 or 1687, and died at Whittingham, in East Lothian, in 1750. I have not been able to discover the date of the first edition of his *Inquiry into the Nature of the Human Soul*, but the

While Dr. Hutcheson's reputation as an author, and still more as an eloquent teacher, was at its zenith in Scotland, Mr. Hume began his literary career, by the publication of his *Treatise of Human Nature*. It appeared in 1739, but seems at that time to have attracted little or no attention from the public. According to the author himself, "never literary attempt was more unfortunate. It fell dead-born from the press, without reaching such distinction as even to excite a murmur among the zealots." It forms, however, a very important link in this Historical Sketch, as it has contributed, either directly or indirectly, more than any other single work, to the subsequent progress of the Philosophy of the Human Mind. In order to adapt his principles better to the public taste, the author afterwards threw them into the more popular form of Essays; but it is in the original work that philosophical readers will always study his system, and it is there alone that the relations and bearings of its different parts, as well as its connexion with the speculations of his immediate predecessors, can be distinctly traced. It is there, too, that his metaphysical talents appear, in my opinion, to the greatest advantage; nor am I certain that he has anywhere else displayed more skill or a sounder taste in point of composition.[1]

---

second edition appeared in 1737, two years before the publication of Mr. Hume's *Treatise of Human Nature*.

[1] A gentleman,* who lived in habits of great intimacy with Dr. Reid towards the close of his life, and on whose accuracy I can fully depend, remembers to have heard him say repeatedly, that "Mr Hume, in his *Essays*, appeared to have *forgotten his Metaphysics*." Nor will this supposition be thought improbable, if, in addition to the subtle and fugitive nature of the subjects canvassed in the *Treatise of Human Nature*, it be considered that long before the publication of his *Essays*, Mr. Hume had abandoned all his metaphysical researches In proof of this, I shall quote a passage from a letter of his to Sir Gilbert Elliot, which, though without a date, seems from its contents to have been written about 1750 or 1751. The passage is interesting on another account, as it serves to shew how much Mr Hume undervalued the utility of mathematical learning, and consequently how little he was aware of its importance as an organ of physical discovery, and as the foun-

* This gentleman was Mr Stewart himself. In the proof there is nothing whatever printed corresponding to this But on the opposite blank leaf there appears the following written in pencil — "I remember that in conversation Dr Reid used to say that in his Essays Mr Hume appeared to have *forgotten his Metaphysics* I do not remember whether, in his writings, Dr Reid has expressed this opinion so sharply "—*Ed.*

The great objects of Mr. Hume's *Treatise of Human Nature* will be best explained in his own words

" 'Tis evident that all the sciences have a relation, greater or less, to human nature, and that, however wide any of them

dation of some of the most necessary arts of civilized life " I am sorry that our correspondence should lead us into these abstract speculations. I have thought, and read, and composed very little on such questions of late. Morals, politics, and literature, have employed all my time, but still the other topics I must think more curious, important, entertaining, and useful, than any geometry that is deeper than Euclid "

I have said that it is in Mr. Hume's earliest work that his metaphysical talents appear, in my opinion, to the greatest advantage. From the following advertisement, however, prefixed, in the latest edition of his works, to the second volume of his *Essays* and *Treatises*, Mr Hume himself would appear to have thought differently. "Most of the principles and reasonings contained in this volume were published in a work in three volumes, called *A Treatise of Human Nature;* a work which the author had projected before he left College, and which he wrote and published not long after But not finding it successful, he was sensible of his error in going to the press too early, and he cast the whole anew in the following pieces, where some negligences in his former reasoning, and some in the expression, are, he hopes, corrected. Yet several writers, who have honoured the author's philosophy with answers, have taken care to direct all their batteries against that juvenile work, which the author never acknowledged, and have affected to triumph in any advantage which they imagined they had obtained over it, a practice very contrary to all rules of candour and fair dealing, and a strong instance of those polemical artifices which a bigoted zeal thinks itself authorized to employ. Henceforth, the author desires that the following pieces may alone be regarded as containing his philosophical sentiments and principles."

After this declaration, it certainly would be highly uncandid to impute to Mr. Hume any philosophical sentiments or principles not to be found in his *Philosophical Essays*, as well as in his *Treatise* But where is the unfairness of replying to any plausible arguments in the latter work, even although Mr Hume may have omitted them in his subsequent publications, more especially where these arguments supply any useful lights for illustrating his more popular compositions? The *Treatise of Human Nature* will certainly be remembered as long as any of Mr Hume's philosophical writings, nor is any person qualified either to approve or to reject his doctrines, who has not studied them in the systematical form in which they were originally cast. That Mr Hume's remonstrance may be just with respect to some of his adversaries, I believe to be true; but it is surely expressed in a tone more querulous and peevish than is justified by the occasion.

I shall take this opportunity of preserving another judgment of Mr Hume's (still more fully stated) on the merits of this juvenile work I copy it from a private letter written by himself to Sir Gilbert Elliot, soon after the publication of his *Philosophical Essays*

"I believe the *Philosophical Essays* contain everything of consequence relating to the Understanding, which you would meet with in the *Treatise;* and I give you my advice against reading

may seem to run from it, they still return back by one passage or another. Even Mathematics, Natural Philosophy, and Natural Religion, are in some measure dependent on the science of Man, since they lie under the cognizance of men, and are judged of by their powers and faculties. . .¨. If, therefore, the sciences of Mathematics, Natural Philosophy, and Natural Religion, have such a dependence on the knowledge of man, what may be expected in the other sciences, whose connexion with human nature is more close and intimate ? The sole end of logic is to explain the principles and operations of our reasoning faculty, and the nature of our ideas: morals and criticism regard our tastes and sentiments, and politics consider men as united in society, and dependent on each other. . . . Here, then, is the only expedient from which we can hope for success in our philosophical researches, to leave the tedious lingering method which we have hitherto followed, and, instead of taking now and then a castle or village on the frontier, to march up directly to the capital or centre of these sciences, to human nature itself: which, being once masters of, we may everywhere else hope for an easy victory. From this station, we may extend our conquests over all those sciences which more intimately concern human life, and may afterwards proceed at leisure to discover more fully those which are the objects of pure curiosity. There is no question of importance whose decision is not comprised in the Science of Man, and there is none which can be decided with any certainty before we become acquainted with that science. In pretending, therefore, to explain the principles of Human Nature, we, in effect, propose a complete system of the sciences, built on a foundation almost entirely new, and the only one upon which they can stand with any security.

" And, as the science of man is the only solid foundation for

the latter By shortening and simplifying the questions, I really render them more complete. *Addo dum minuo* The philosophical principles are the same in both; but I was carried away by the heat of youth and invention to publish too precipitately. So vast an undertaking, planned before I was one and twenty, and composed before twenty-five, must necessarily be very defective. I have repented my haste a hundred and a hundred times "

the other sciences, so the only solid foundation we can give to this science itself must be laid on experience and observation. 'Tis no astonishing reflection to consider, that the application of experimental philosophy to moral subjects should come after that to natural, at the distance of above a whole century; since we find, in fact, that there was about the same interval betwixt the origin of these sciences; and that, reckoning from Thales to Socrates, the space of time is nearly equal to that betwixt my Lord Bacon and some late philosophers in England,[1] who have begun to put the science of man on a new ' footing, and have engaged the attention, and excited the curiosity of the public."

I am far from thinking, that the execution of Mr. Hume's work corresponded with the magnificent design sketched out in these observations; nor does it appear to me that he had formed to himself a very correct idea of the manner in which the experimental mode of reasoning ought to be applied to moral subjects. He had, however, very great merit in separating entirely his speculations concerning the philosophy of the mind from all physiological hypotheses about the nature of the union between soul and body; and although, from some of his casual expressions, it may be suspected that he conceived our intellectual operations to result from bodily organization,[2] he had yet much too large a share of good sense and sagacity to suppose, that, by studying the latter, it is possible for human ingenuity to throw any light upon the former. His works, accordingly, are perfectly free from those gratuitous and wild conjectures, which a few years afterwards were given to the world with so much confidence by Hartley and Bonnet[3] And

---

[1] "Mr. Locke, Lord Shaftesbury, Dr Mandeville, Mr Hutcheson, Dr. Butler," &c.

[2] The only expression in his works I can recollect at present, that can give any reasonable countenance to such a suspicion, occurs in his *Posthumous Dialogues*, where he speaks of "that little agitation of the brain which we call thought."—(2d edition, pp. 60, 61) But no fair inference can be drawn from this, as the expression is put into the mouth of Philo the Sceptic, whereas the author intimates that Cleanthes speaks his own sentiments

[3] [* The only exception to this remark that I can recollect in Mr. Hume's Treatise, occurs in vol 1 p 3, *et seq*]

* Restored.—*Ed.*

in this respect his example has been of infinite use to his successors in this northern part of the island. Many absurd theories have, indeed, at different times been produced by our countrymen; but I know of no part of Europe where such systems as those of Hartley and Bonnet have been so uniformly treated with the contempt they deserve as in Scotland.[1]

. Nor was it in this respect alone, that Mr. Hume's juvenile speculations contributed to forward the progress of our national literature. Among the many very exceptionable doctrines involved in them, there are various discussions, equally refined and solid, in which he has happily exemplified the application of metaphysical analysis to questions connected with taste, with the philosophy of jurisprudence, and with the theory of government. Of these discussions some afterwards appeared in a more popular form in his philosophical and literary Essays, and still retain a place in the latest editions of his works; but others, not less curious, have been suppressed by the author, probably from an idea that they were too abstruse to interest the curiosity of ordinary readers. In some of these practical applications of metaphysical principles, we may perceive the germs of several inquiries which have since been successfully prosecuted by Mr. Hume's countrymen; and among others, of those which gave birth to Lord Kames's *Historical Law Tracts*, and to his *Elements of Criticism*.

The publication of Mr. Hume's *Treatise* was attended with another important effect in Scotland. He had cultivated the

---

[1] In no part of Mr. Hume's metaphysical writings is there the slightest reference to either of these systems, although he survived the date of their publication little less than thirty years.

[* Of the general state of Metaphysics and Ethics in Scotland, at the time when the Treatise on Human Nature appeared, some idea may be formed, from the plan adopted by Sir John Pringle, (who was then Professor of Moral Philosophy at Edinburgh,) for his academical course of lectures. It may be presumed that the university of the capital was at least on a footing with any other in the kingdom, that of Glasgow alone excepted, where Dr Hutcheson had shot far a-head of all his contemporaries. Of this plan a record (evidently communicated by Sir John Pringle himself) is preserved in the *Scots Magazine* for 17—, and it appears to me to be an object of sufficient curiosity to justify me in giving a reference to it here.]

* Restored.—*Ed*

art of writing with much greater success than any of his predecessors, and had formed his taste on the best models of English composition. The influence of his example appears to have been great and general; and was in no instance more remarkable than in the style of his principal antagonists, all of whom, in studying his system, have caught in no inconsiderable degree, the purity, polish, and precision of his diction. Nobody, I believe, will deny, that Locke himself, considered as an English writer, is far surpassed, not only by Hume, but by Reid, Campbell, Gerard, and Beattie; and of this fact it will not be easy to find a more satisfactory explanation, than in the critical eye with which they were led to canvass a work, equally distinguished by the depth of its reasonings, and by the attractive form in which they are exhibited.

The fundamental principles from which Mr. Hume sets out, differ more in words than in substance from those of his immediate predecessors. According to him, all the objects of our knowledge are divided into two classes, *impressions* and *ideas*: the former, comprehending our *sensations* properly so called, and also our *perceptions* of sensible qualities, (two things betwixt which Mr. Hume's system does not lead him to make any distinction;) the latter, the objects of our thoughts when we *remember* or *imagine*, or in general exercise any of our intellectual powers on things which are past, absent, or future. These ideas he considers as *copies* of our *impressions*, and the words which denote them as the only *signs* entitled to the attention of a philosopher; every word professing to denote an idea, of which the corresponding impressions cannot be pointed out, being *ipso facto* unmeaning and illusory. The obvious result of these principles is, that what Mr Hume calls *impressions*, furnish, either immediately or mediately, the whole materials about which our thoughts can be employed; a conclusion coinciding exactly with the account of the origin of our ideas borrowed by Gassendi from the ancient Epicureans.

With this fundamental principle of the Gassendists, Mr Hume combined the logical method recommended by their great antagonists the Cartesians, and (what seemed still more remote from his Epicurean starting ground) a strong leaning to the idealism of Malebranche and of Berkeley. Like Descartes, he began with doubting of every thing, but he was too quick-sighted to be satisfied, like Descartes, with the solutions given by that philosopher of his doubts. On the contrary, he exposes the futility not only of the solutions proposed by Descartes himself, but of those suggested by Locke and others among his successors; ending at last where Descartes began, in considering no one proposition as more certain, or even as more probable than another. That the proofs alleged by Descartes of the existence of the material world are quite inconclusive, had been already remarked by many. Nay, it had been shewn by Berkeley and others, that if the principles be admitted on which Descartes, in common with all philosophers, from Aristotle downwards, proceeded, the existence of the material world is impossible. A few bold thinkers, distinguished by the name of Egoists, had gone still further than this, and had pushed their scepticism to such a length, as to doubt of everything but their own existence. According to *these*, the proposition, *cogito, ergo sum*, is the only truth which can be regarded as absolutely certain. It was reserved for Mr. Hume to call in question even this proposition, and to admit only the existence of *impressions* and *ideas*. To dispute against the existence of these he conceived to be impossible, inasmuch as they are the immediate subjects of consciousness. But to admit the existence of the thinking and percipient *I*, was to admit the existence of that imaginary substance called *Mind*, which (according to him) is no more an object of human knowledge than the imaginary and exploded substance called *Matter*.

From what has been already said, it may be seen, that we are not to look in Mr. Hume's *Treatise* for any regular or connected system. It is neither a scheme of Materialism, nor a scheme of Spiritualism, for his reasonings strike equally at the root of both these theories. His aim is to establish a universal scepticism, and to produce in the reader a complete distrust in his own faculties. For this purpose he avails himself of the data assumed by the most opposite sects, shifting his ground skilfully from one position to another, as best suits the scope of his present argument. With the single exception of Bayle, he has carried this sceptical mode of reasoning farther than any other modern philosopher. Cicero, who himself belonged nominally to the same school, seems to have thought, that the controversial habits imposed on the Academical sect by their profession of universal doubt, required a greater versatility of talent and fertility of invention, than were necessary for defending any particular system of tenets;[1] and it is not improbable, that Mr. Hume, in the pride of youthful genius, was misled by this specious but very fallacious idea. On the other hand, Bayle has the candour to acknowledge, that nothing is so easy as to dispute after the manner of the sceptics;[2] and to this proposition every man of reflection will find himself more and more disposed to assent, as he advances in life. It is experience alone that can convince us, how much more difficult it is to make any real progress in the search after truth, than to acquire a talent for plausible disputation.[3]

[1] " Nam si singulas disciplinas percipere magnum est, quanto majus omnes? quod facere iis necesse est, quibus propositum est, veri reperiendi causa, et contra omnes philosophos et pro omnibus dicere —Cujus rei tantæ tamque difficilis facultatem consecutum esse me non profiteor Secutum esse præ me fero."—Cicero, *De Nat. Deor.* l. i *

[* Independently of the love of truth, other considerations, it is probable, contributed to confirm Cicero in his attachment to a sect, which, by accustoming him to employ his ingenuity and eloquence in defence of both sides of a disputed question, prepared him for the exercise of the forensic talents, to which he is chiefly indebted for his immortal fame " Fateor, me, oratorem, si modo sim, aut etiam quicunque sim, non ex rhetorum officinis, sed ex Academiæ spatiis extitisse "—*Orat. ad Brut* in]

[2] See the passage quoted from Bayle, in page 317 of this *Dissertation*.

[3] In the very interesting account, given by Dr. Holland, of Velara, a modern Greek physician, whom he met with at Larissa in Thessaly, a few slight particulars are mentioned, which let us completely into the character of that ingenious person. " It appeared," says Dr Holland, " that Velara had thought much on the various topics of Metaphysics and Morals, and his conversation on these topics bore the same tone of satirical scepticism which was apparent as the general feature of his opinions. We spoke of the questions of Materialism and Necessity, on both of which he declared an affirmative opinion " — (Holland's *Travels in the Ionian Isles*, &c. p 275.) " I passed this evening with Velara at his own house, and sat with him till a late hour.

* Restored —*Ed.*

That this spirit of sceptical argument has been carried to a most pernicious excess in modern Europe, as well as among the ancient Academics, will, I presume, be now very generally allowed; but in the form in which it appears in Mr. Hume's *Treatise,* its mischievous tendency has been more than compensated by the importance of those results for which it has prepared the way. The principles which he assumes were sanctioned in common by Gassendi, by Descartes, and by Locke; and from these, in most instances, he reasons with great logical accuracy and force. The conclusions to which he is thus led are often so extravagant and dangerous, that he ought to have regarded them as a proof of the unsoundness of his data; but if he had not the merit of drawing this inference himself, he at least forced it so irresistibly on the observation of his successors, as to be entitled to share with them in the honour of their discoveries. Perhaps, indeed, it may be questioned if the errors which he adopted from his predecessors would not have kept their ground till this day, had not his sagacity displayed so clearly the consequences which they necessarily involve. It is in this sense that we must understand a compliment paid to him by the ablest of his adversaries, when he says, that "Mr. Hume's premises often do more than atone for his conclusions."[1]

During part of the time our conversation turned upon metaphysical topics, and chiefly on the old Pyrrhonic doctrine of the non-existence of Matter Velara, as usual, took the sceptical side of the argument, in which he showed much ingenuity and great knowledge of the more eminent controversialists on this and other collateral subjects."—(*Ibid.* p 370.) We see here a lively picture of a character daily to be met with in more polished and learned societies, disputing not for truth but for victory, in the first conversation, professing himself a Materialist, and in the second denying the existence of Matter; on both occasions taking up that ground where he was most likely to provoke opposition. If any inference is to be drawn from the conversation of such an individual, with respect to his real creed, it is in favour of those opinions which he controverts These opinions, at least, we may confidently conclude to be agreeable to the general belief of the country where he lives

[1] Mr. Hume himself (to whom Dr. Reid's *Inquiry* was communicated previous to its publication, by their common friend Dr. Blair) seems not to have been dissatisfied with this apology for some of his speculations. "I shall only say, (he observes in a letter addressed to the author,) that if you have been able to clear up these abstruse and important subjects, instead of being

The bias of Mr. Hume's mind to scepticism seems to have been much encouraged, and the success of his sceptical theories in the same proportion promoted, by the recent attempts of Descartes and his followers to demonstrate Self-evident Truths;—attempts which Mr. Hume clearly perceived to involve, in every instance, that sort of paralogism which logicians call *reasoning in a circle*. The weakness of these pretended demonstrations is triumphantly exposed in the *Treatise of Human Nature;* and it is not very wonderful that the author, in the first enthusiasm of his victory over his immediate predecessors, should have fancied that the inconclusiveness of the proofs argued some unsoundness in the propositions which they were employed to support It would, indeed, have done still greater honour to his sagacity if he had ascribed this to its true cause—the impossibility of confirming, by a process of reasoning, the *fundamental laws of human belief;* but (as Bacon remarks) it does not often happen to those who labour in the field of science, that the same person who sows the seed should reap the harvest.

From that strong sceptical bias which led this most acute reasoner, on many important questions, to shift his controversial ground according to the humour of the moment, *one* favourable consequence has resulted—that we are indebted to him for the most powerful antidotes we possess against some of the most poisonous errors of modern philosophy. I have already made a similar remark in speaking of the elaborate refutation of Spinozism by Bayle; but the argument stated by Hume, in his *Essay on the Idea of Necessary Connection,* (though brought forward by the author with a very different view,) forms a still more valuable accession to metaphysical science, as it lays the axe to the very root from which Spinozism springs. The cardinal principle on which the whole of that

mortified, I shall be so vain as to pretend to a share of the praise, and shall think that my errors, by having at least some coherence, had led you to make a more strict review of my principles, which were the common ones, and to perceive their futility."—For the whole of Mr Hume's letter, see *Biographical Memoirs* of Smith, Robertson, and Reid, by the author of this Dissertation, p 417

system turns is, that all events, physical and moral, are *necessarily* linked together as causes and effects; from which principle all the most alarming conclusions adopted by Spinoza follow as unavoidable and manifest corollaries. But, if it be true, as Mr. Hume contends, and as most philosophers now admit, that physical causes and effects are known to us merely as *antecedents* and *consequents ;* still more, if it be true that the word *necessity*, as employed in this discussion, is altogether unmeaning and insignificant, the whole system of Spinoza is nothing better than a rope of sand, and the very proposition which it professes to demonstrate is incomprehensible by our faculties. Mr. Hume's doctrine, in the unqualified form in which he states it, may lead to other consequences not less dangerous : but, if he had not the good fortune to conduct metaphysicians to the truth, he may at least be allowed the merit of having shut up for ever one of the most frequented and fatal paths which led them astray.

In what I have now said, I have supposed my readers to possess that general acquaintance with Mr. Hume's *Theory of Causation* which all well-educated persons may be presumed to have acquired. But the close connexion of this part of his work with some of the historical details which are immediately to follow, makes it necessary for me, before I proceed farther, to recapitulate a little more particularly some of his most important conclusions.

It was, as far as I know, first shown in a satisfactory manner by Mr. Hume, that "every demonstration which has been produced for the necessity of a cause to every new existence, is fallacious and sophistical."[1] In illustration of this assertion,

---

[1] *Treatise of Human Nature*, vol 1 p 144 —Although Mr. Hume, however, succeeded better than any of his predecessors, in calling the attention of philosophers to this discussion, his opinion on the subject does not possess the merit, in point of originality, which was supposed to belong to it either by himself or by his antagonists See the passages which I have quoted in proof of this, in the first volume of the *Philosophy of the Human Mind*, p. 542, *et seq*, fourth edition, and also in the second volume of the same work, p 556, *et seq* , second edition. Among these, I request the attention of my readers more particularly to a passage from a book entitled, *The Procedure, Extent, and Limits of*

he examines three different arguments which have been alleged as proofs of the proposition in question; the first by Mr. Hobbes; the second by Dr. Clarke; and the third by Mr. Locke. And I think it will now be readily acknowledged by every competent judge, that his objections to all these pretended demonstrations are conclusive and unanswerable.

When Mr. Hume, however, attempts to show that the proposition in question is not *intuitively* certain, his argument appears to me to amount to nothing more than a logical quibble. Of this one would almost imagine that he was not insensible himself, from the short and slight manner in which he hurries over the discussion. "All certainty (he observes) arises from the comparison of ideas, and from the discovery of such relations as are unalterable, so long as the ideas continue the same. These relations are *resemblance, proportions in quantity and number, degrees of any quality, and contrariety;* none of which are implied in this proposition, *whatever has a beginning has also a cause of existence.* That proposition, therefore, is not intuitively certain. At least, any one who would assert it to be intuitively certain, must deny these to be the only infallible relations, and must find some other relation of that kind to be implied in it, which it will be then time enough to examine."

Upon this passage, it is sufficient for me to observe, that the whole force of the reasoning hinges on two assumptions, which are not only gratuitous, but false. 1*st*, That all certainty arises from the comparison of ideas. 2*dly*, That *all* the unalterable relations among our ideas are comprehended in his own arbitrary enumeration; *Resemblance, proportions in quantity and number, degrees of any quality, and contrariety.* When the correctness of these two premises shall be fully established, it will be time enough (to borrow Mr. Hume's own words) to examine the justness of his conclusion.

the Human Understanding, published two years before the *Treatise of Human Nature*, and commonly ascribed to Dr Browne, Bishop of Cork. The coincidence is truly wonderful, as it can scarcely, by any possibility, be supposed that this book was ever heard of by Mr Hume.

From this last reasoning, however, of Mr. Hume, it may be suspected, that he was aware of the vulnerable point against which his adversaries were most likely to direct their attacks. From the weakness, too, of the entrenchments which he has here thrown up for his own security, he seems to have been sensible, that it was not capable of a long or vigorous resistance. In the mean time, he betrays no want of confidence in his original position; but repeating his assertion, that " we derive the opinion of the necessity of a cause to every new production, neither from demonstration nor from intuition," he boldly concludes, that " this opinion must necessarily arise from observation and experience."—(Vol. i. p. 147.) Or, as he elsewhere expresses himself, " All our reasonings concerning causes and effects are derived from nothing but custom; and, consequently, belief is more properly an act of the *sensitive* than of the *cogitative* part of our natures."—*Ibid.* p 321.

The distinction here alluded to between the *sensitive* and the *cogitative* parts of our nature, (it may be proper to remind my readers,) makes a great figure in the works of Cudworth and of Kant. By the former it was avowedly borrowed from the philosophy of Plato. To the latter, it is not improbable, that it may have been suggested by this passage in Hume. Without disputing its justness or its importance, I may be permitted to express my doubts of the propriety of stating, so strongly as has frequently been done, the one of these parts of our nature in contrast with the other. Would it not be more philosophical, as well as more pleasing, to contemplate the beautiful harmony between them, and the gradual steps by which the mind is trained by the intimations of the former, for the deliberate conclusions of the latter? If, for example, our conviction of the permanence of the laws of nature be not founded on any process of reasoning, (a proposition which Mr. Hume seems to have established with demonstrative evidence,) but be either the result of an instinctive principle of belief, or of the association of ideas, operating at a period when the light of reason has not yet dawned, what can be more delightful than to find this suggestion of our *sensitive frame*,[1] verified by every step which our reason afterwards makes in the study of physical science; and confirmed with mathematical accuracy by the never-failing accordance of the phenomena of the heavens with the previous calculations of astronomers! Does not this afford a satisfaction to the mind, similar to what it experiences, when we consider the adaptation of the instinct of suction, and of the organs of respiration, to the physical properties of the atmosphere? So far from encouraging scepticism, such a view of human nature seems peculiarly calculated to silence every doubt about the veracity of our faculties.[2]

---

[1] Upon either of these suppositions, Mr. Hume would, with equal propriety, have referred our anticipation of the future event to the *sensitive part of our nature;* and, in point of fact, the one supposition would have answered his purpose as well as the other.

[2] It is but justice to Mr. Hume to remark, that, in his later publications, he has himself suggested this very idea as the best solution he could give of his own doubts. The following passage, which appears to me to be eminently philosophical and beautiful, I beg leave to recommend to the particular attention of Kant's disciples :—

"Here, then, is a kind of pre-established harmony between the course of nature and the succession of our ideas, and though the powers and forces by which the former is governed be wholly unknown to us, yet our thoughts and conceptions have still, we find, gone on in the same train with the other works of nature. Custom is that principle by which this correspondence has been effected ; so necessary to the subsistence of our species, and the regulation of our conduct in every circumstance and occurrence of human life. Had not the presence of an object instantly excited the idea of those objects commonly conjoined with it, all our knowledge must have been limited to the narrow sphere of our memory and senses, and we should never have been able to adjust means to ends, or employ our natural powers, either to the producing of good, or avoiding of evil. Those who delight in the discovery and contemplation of *final causes* have here ample subject to employ their wonder and admiration.

"I shall add, for a further confirmation of the foregoing theory, that, as this operation of the mind, by which we infer like effects from like causes, and *vice versa*, is so essential to the subsistence of all human creatures, it is not probable that it could be trusted to the fallacious deductions of our reason, which is slow in its operations, appears not in any degree during the first years of infancy, and at best is, in every age and period of human life, extremely liable to error and mistake. It is more conformable to the ORDINARY WISDOM OF NATURE to secure so necessary an act of the mind by some instinct or mechanical tendency which may be infallible in its operations, may discover itself at the first appearance of life and thought, and may be independent of all the laboured deductions of the understanding. As nature has taught us the use of our limbs, without giving us the knowledge of the muscles and nerves by which they are actuated,

It is not my business at present to inquire into the soundness of Mr. Hume's doctrines on this subject. The rashness of some of them has, in my opinion, been sufficiently shown by more than one of his antagonists. I wish only to remark the important step which he made, in exposing the futility of the reasonings by which Hobbes, Clarke, and Locke, had attempted to demonstrate the metaphysical axiom, that "everything which begins to exist must have a cause;" and the essential service which he rendered to true philosophy, by thus pointing out indirectly to his successors the only solid ground on which that principle is to be defended. It is to this argument of Hume's, according to Kant's own acknowledgment, that we owe the *Critique of Pure Reason;* and to this we are also indebted for the far more luminous refutations of scepticism by Mr. Hume's own countrymen.

In the course of Mr. Hume's very refined discussions on this subject, he is led to apply them to one of the most important principles of the mind,—our belief of the continuance of the laws of nature; or, in other words, our belief that the future course of nature will resemble the past. And here, too, (as I already hinted,) it is very generally admitted that he has succeeded completely in overturning all the theories which profess to account for this belief, by resolving it into a process of reasoning.[1] The only difference which seems to remain among

so has she implanted in us an instinct which carries forward the thoughts in a correspondent course to that which she has established among external objects, though we are ignorant of those powers and forces on which this regular course and succession of objects totally depends."—See, in the last editions of Mr Hume's *Philosophical Essays,* published during his own lifetime, the two sections entitled *Sceptical Doubts concerning the Operations of the Understanding;* and *Sceptical Solution of these Doubts.* The title of the latter of these sections has, not altogether without reason, incurred the ridicule of Dr. Beattie, who translates it, *Doubtful Solution of Doubtful Doubts.* But the essay contains much sound and important matter, and throws a strong light on some of the chief difficulties which Mr. Hume himself had started. Sufficient justice has not been done to it by his antagonists.

[1] The incidental reference made, by way of illustration, in the following passage, to our *instinctive conviction* of the permanency of the laws of Nature, encourages me to hope that, among candid and intelligent inquirers, it is now received as an acknowledged fact in the Theory of the Human Mind.

"The anxiety men have in all ages

philosophers is, whether it can be explained, as Mr. Hume imagined, by means of the association of ideas; or whether it must be considered as an original and fundamental law of the human understanding;—a question, undoubtedly, abundantly curious, as a problem connected with the *Theory of the Mind;* but to which more practical importance has sometimes been attached than I conceive to be necessary.[1]

That Mr. Hume himself conceived his refutation of the theories which profess to assign *a reason* for our faith in the

---

shewn to obtain a fixed standard of value, and that remarkable agreement of nations, dissimilar in all other customs, in the use of one medium, on account of its superior fitness for that purpose, is itself a convincing proof how essential it is to our social interests The notion of its permanency, although it be conventional and arbitrary, and liable, in reality, to many causes of variation, yet had gained so firm a hold on the minds of men, as to resemble, in its effects on their conduct, that *instinctive conviction of the permanency of the laws of nature which is the foundation of all our reasoning"—A Letter to the Right Hon. R Peel, M P for the University of Oxford*, by one of his Constituents. Second edition, p. 23.

[1] The difference between the two opinions amounts to nothing more than this, whether our expectation of the continuance of the laws of nature results from a principle coeval with the first exercise of the senses; or whether it arises gradually from the accommodation of the order of our thoughts to the established order of physical events "Nature (as Mr. Hume himself observes) *may* certainly produce whatever can arise from habit; nay, habit is nothing but one of the principles of nature, and derives all its force from that origin "—(*Treatise of Human Nature*, vol. i. p 313) Whatever ideas, therefore, and whatever principles we are unavoidably led to acquire by the circumstances in which we are placed, and by the exercise of those faculties which are essential to our preservation, are to be considered as parts of human nature, no less than those which are implanted in the mind at its first formation. Are not the acquired perceptions of sight and of hearing as much parts of human nature as the original perceptions of external objects which we obtain by the use of the hand?

The passage quoted from Mr Hume, in Note 2, p. 444, if attentively considered, will be found, when combined with these remarks, to throw a strong and pleasing light on his latest views with respect to this part of his philosophy

In denying that our expectation of the continuance of the laws of nature is founded on reasoning, as well as in asserting our ignorance of any necessary connexions among physical events, Mr. Hume had been completely anticipated by some of his predecessors. (See the references mentioned in the Note, p 441.) I do not, however, think that, before his time, philosophers were at all aware of the alarming consequences which, on a superficial view, *seem* to follow from this part of his system Indeed, these consequences would never have been apprehended, had it not been supposed to form an essential link in his argument against the commonly received notion of Causation

permanence of the laws of nature, to be closely connected with his sceptical conclusions concerning *causation*, is quite evident from the general strain of his argument; and it is, therefore, not surprising that this refutation should have been looked on with a suspicious eye by his antagonists. Dr. Reid was, I believe, the first of these who had the sagacity to perceive, not only that it is strictly and incontrovertibly logical, but that it may be safely admitted, without any injury to the doctrines which it was brought forward to subvert.

Another of Mr. Hume's attacks on these doctrines was still bolder and more direct. In conducting it he took his vantage ground from his own account of the origin of our ideas. In this way he was led to expunge from his Philosophical Vocabulary every word of which the meaning cannot be explained by a reference to the *impression* from which the corresponding *idea* was originally copied. Nor was he startled, in the application of this rule, by the consideration, that it would force him to condemn as insignificant many words which are to be found in all languages, and some of which express what are commonly regarded as the most important objects of human knowledge. Of this number are the words *cause* and *effect;* at least, in the sense in which they are commonly understood both by the vulgar and by philosophers. "One event (says he) follows another; but we never observe any tie between them. They seem *conjoined*, but never *connected*. And as we can have no idea of anything which never appeared to our outward sense or inward sentiment, the necessary conclusion seems to be, that we have no idea of connexion or power at all; and that these words are absolutely without any meaning, when employed either in philosophical reasonings or common life."—Hume's *Essays*, vol. ii. p. 79. Ed. of Lond 1784.

When this doctrine was first proposed by Mr. Hume, he appears to have been very strongly impressed with its repugnance to the common apprehensions of mankind. "I am sensible (he observes) that of all the paradoxes which I have had, or shall hereafter have occasion to advance in the course of this treatise, the present one is the most violent."—(*Treatise of Human*

Nature, vol. i. p. 291.) It was probably owing to this impression that he did not fully unfold in that work all the consequences which, in his subsequent publications, he deduced from the same paradox; nor did he even apply it to invalidate the argument which infers the existence of an *intelligent* cause from the order of the universe. There cannot, however, be a doubt that he was aware, at this period of his life, of the conclusions to which it unavoidably leads, and which are, indeed, too obvious to escape the notice of a far less acute inquirer.

In a private letter of Mr. Hume's, to one of his most intimate friends,[1] some light is thrown on the circumstances which first led his mind into this train of sceptical speculation. As his narrative has every appearance of the most perfect truth and candour, and contains several passages which I doubt not will be very generally interesting to my readers, I shall give it a place, together with some extracts from the correspondence to which it gave rise, in the Notes at the end of this *Dissertation.* Everything connected with the origin and composition of a work which has had so powerful an influence on the direction which metaphysical pursuits have since taken, both in Scotland[2] and in Germany, will be allowed to form an important

---

[1] Sir Gilbert Elliot, Bart., grandfather of the present Earl of Minto. The originals of the letters to which I refer are in Lord Minto's possession.

[2] A foreign writer of great name (M Frederick Schlegel) seems to think that the influence of Mr Hume's *Treatise of Human Nature* on the Philosophy of England has been still more extensive than I had conceived it to be. His opinion on this point I transcribe as a sort of literary curiosity

"Since the time of Hume, nothing more has been attempted in England than to erect all sorts of bulwarks against the practical influence of his destructive scepticism, and to maintain, by various substitutes and aids, the pile of moral principle uncorrupted and entire. *Not only with Adam Smith, but with all their late philosophers, national welfare is the ruling and central principle of thought;—a principle excellent and praiseworthy in its due situation, but quite unfitted for being the centre and oracle of all knowledge and science."* From the connexion in which this last sentence stands with the context, would not one imagine that the writer conceived the *Wealth of Nations* to be a new *moral* or *metaphysical* system, devised by Mr. Smith for the purpose of counteracting Mr. Hume's scepticism?

I have read this translation of Mr Schlegel's lectures with much curiosity and interest, and flatter myself that we shall soon have English versions of the works of Kant, and of other German authors, from the pens of their English disciples Little more, I am fully per-

article of philosophical history; and this history I need not offer any apology for choosing to communicate to the public rather in Mr. Hume's words than in my own [1]

From the reply to this letter by Mr Hume's very ingenious and accomplished correspondent, we learn that he had drawn from Mr. Hume's metaphysical discussions the only sound and philosophical inference. that the lameness of the proofs offered by Descartes and his successors, of some fundamental truths universally acknowledged by mankind, proceeded, not from any defect in the evidence of these truths, but, on the contrary, from their being *self-evident*, and consequently unsusceptible of demonstration. We learn farther, that the same conclusion had been adopted, at this early period, by another of Mr Hume's friends, Mr. Henry Home, who, under the name of Lord Kames, was afterwards so well known in the learned world. Those who are acquainted with the subsequent publications of this distinguished and most respectable author, will immediately recognise, in the account here given of the impression left on his mind by Mr. Hume's scepticism, the rudiments of a peculiar logic, which runs more or less through all his later works; and which, it must be acknowledged, he has in various instances carried to an unphilosophical extreme.[2]

suaded, is necessary, in this country, to bring down the philosophy of Germany to its proper level.

In treating of literary and historical subjects, Mr Schlegel seems to be more in his element than when he ventures to pronounce on philosophical questions. But even in cases of the former description, some of his dashing judgments on English writers can be accounted for only by haste, caprice, or prejudice "The English themselves (we are told) are now pretty well convinced that Robertson is a careless, superficial, and blundering historian · although they study his works, and are right in doing so, as models of pure composition, extremely deserving of attention during the present declining state of English style . . . With all the abundance of his Italian elegance, what is the overloaded and affected Roscoe when compared with Gibbon? Coxe, although master of a good and classical style, resembles Robertson in no respect so much as in the superficialness of his researches, and the statesman Fox has nothing in common with Hume but the bigotry of his party zeal." Such criticisms may perhaps be applauded by a German auditory, but in this country they can injure the reputation of none but their author.

[1] See Note C C C.
[2] I allude particularly to the unnecessary multiplication, in his philosophical arguments, of internal senses and of instinctive principles

The light in which Mr. Hume's scepticism appears from these extracts to have struck his friends, Sir Gilbert Elliot and Lord Kames, was very nearly the same with that in which it was afterwards viewed by Reid, Oswald, and Beattie, all of whom have manifestly aimed, with greater or less precision, at the same logical doctrine which I have just alluded to. This, too, was the very ground on which Father Buffier had (even before the publication of the *Treatise of Human Nature*) made his stand against similar theories, built by his predecessors on the Cartesian principles. The coincidence between his train of thinking, and that into which our Scottish metaphysicians soon after fell, is so very remarkable that it has been considered by many as amounting to a proof that the plan of their works was, in some measure, suggested by his; but it is infinitely more probable, that the argument which runs in common through the speculations of all of them, was the natural result of the state of metaphysical science when they engaged in their philosophical inquiries.[1]

The answer which Mr. Hume made to this argument, when it was first proposed to him in the easy intercourse of private correspondence, seems to me an object of so much curiosity, as to justify me for bringing it under the eye of my readers

---

[1] Voltaire, in his catalogue of the illustrious writers who adorned the reign of Louis XIV., is one of the very few French authors who have spoken of Buffier with due respect: "Il y a dans ses traités de métaphysique des morceaux que Locke n'aurait pas désavoués, et c'est le seul jésuite qui ait mis une philosophie raisonnable dans ses ouvrages"—Another French philosopher, too, of a very different school, and certainly not disposed to overrate the talents of Buffier, has, in a work published as lately as 1805, candidly acknowledged the lights which he might have derived from the labours of his predecessor, if he had been acquainted with them at an earlier period of his studies Condillac, he also observes, might have profited greatly by the same lights, if he had availed himself of their guidance, in his inquiries concerning the human understanding "Du moins est il certain que pour ma part, je suis fort fâché de ne connoître que depuis très peu de temps ces opinions du Père Buffier, si je les avais vues plutôt énoncées quelque part, elles m'auraient épargné beaucoup de peines et d'hésitations".—"Je regrette beaucoup que Condillac, dans ses profondes et sagaces méditations sur l'intelligence humaine n'ait pas fait plus d'attention aux idées du Père Buffier," &c &c —*Elémens d'Idéologie*, par M. Destutt-Tracy, tom iii pp 136, 137 —See *Elements of the Philosophy of the Human Mind*, vol ii pp. 88, 89, 2d edit

in immediate connexion with the foregoing details. Opinions thus communicated in the confidence of friendly discussion, possess a value which seldom belongs to propositions hazarded in those public controversies where the love of victory is apt to mingle, more or less, in the most candid minds, with the love of truth

"Your notion of correcting subtlety by *sentiment* is certainly very just with regard to morals, which depend upon sentiment: and in politics and natural philosophy, whatever conclusion is contrary to certain matters of fact, must certainly be wrong, and there must some error lie somewhere in the argument, whether we be able to shew it or not. But, in metaphysics or theology, I cannot see how either of these plain and obvious standards of truth can have place. Nothing there can correct bad reasoning but good reasoning; and sophistry must be opposed by syllogism.[1] About seventy or eighty years ago,[2] I observe a principle like that which you advance prevailed very much in France, amongst some philosophers and beaux esprits. The occasion of it was this: The famous M. Nicole of the Port Royal, in his *Perpétuité de la Foi*, pushed the Protestants very hard upon the impossibility of the people's reaching a conviction of their religion by the way of private judgment, which required so many disquisitions, reasonings, researches, erudition, impartiality, and penetration, as not one of a hundred, even among men of education, is capable of M. Claude and the Protestants answered him, not by solving his difficulties, (which seems impossible,) but by retorting them, (which is very easy.) They showed, that to reach the way of authority which the Catholics insist on, as long a train of acute reasoning, and as great erudition was requisite, as would be sufficient for a Protestant. We must first prove all the truths of natural religion, the foundation of morals, the divine autho-

---

[1] May not sophistry be also opposed by appealing to the *fundamental laws of human belief*, and, in some cases, by appealing to *facts* for which we have the evidence of our own consciousness? The word *sentiment* does not express, with sufficient precision, the test which Mr Hume's correspondent had manifestly in view

[2] This letter is dated 1751

rity of the Scripture, the deference which it commands to the Church, the tradition of the Church, &c. &c. The comparison of these controversial writings begat an idea in some that it was neither by reasoning nor authority we learn our religion, but by sentiment; and this was certainly a very convenient way, and what a philosopher would be very well pleased to comply with, if he could distinguish sentiment from education. But, to all appearance, the sentiment of Stockholm, Geneva, Rome, ancient and modern Athens, and Memphis, have not the same characters; and no thinking man can implicitly assent to any of them, but from the general principle, that, as the truth on these subjects is beyond human capacity, and that, as for one's own ease, he must adopt some tenets, there is more satisfaction and convenience in holding to the catechism we have been first taught. Now, this I have nothing to say against. I would only observe, that such a conduct is founded on the most universal and determined scepticism. For more curiosity and research give a direct opposite turn from the same principles."

On this careless effusion of Mr. Hume's pen, it would be unpardonable to offer any critical strictures. It cannot, however, be considered as improper to hint, that there is a wide and essential difference between those articles of faith which formed the subjects of dispute between Nicole and Claude, and those *laws of belief*, of which it is the great object of the *Treatise of Human Nature* to undermine the authority. The reply of Mr. Hume, therefore, is evasive, and although strongly marked with the writer's ingenuity, does not bear upon the point in question.

As to the distinction alleged by Mr. Hume between the *criteria* of truth in natural philosophy and in metaphysics, I trust it will now be pretty generally granted, that however well founded it may be when confined to the metaphysics of the schoolmen, it will by no means hold when extended to the inductive philosophy of the human mind. In this last science, no less than in natural philosophy, Mr. Hume's logical maxim may be laid down as a fundamental principle, that " whatever conclusion is contrary to matter of fact must be wrong, and there must some error lie somewhere in the argument, whether we be able to show it or not."

It is a remarkable circumstance in the history of Mr. Hume's literary life, and a proof of the sincerity with which he was then engaged in the search of truth, that, previous to the publication of his *Treatise of Human Nature*, he discovered a strong anxiety to submit it to the examination of the celebrated Dr. Butler, author of the *Analogy of Religion, Natural and Revealed, to the Constitution and Course of Nature*. For this purpose he applied to Mr. Henry Home, between whom and Dr. Butler some friendly letters appear to have passed before this period. "Your thoughts and mine (says Mr. Hume to his correspondent) agree with respect to Dr. Butler, and I would be glad to be introduced to him. I am at present castrating my work, that is, cutting off its nobler parts; that is, endeavouring it shall give as little offence as possible, before which I could not pretend to put it into the doctor's hands"[1] In another letter, he acknowledges Mr. Home's kindness in recommending him to Dr. Butler's notice. "I shall not trouble you with any formal compliments or thanks, which would be but an ill return for the kindness you have done me in writing in my behalf, to one you are so little acquainted with as Dr. Butler; and, I am afraid, stretching the truth in favour of a friend. I have called on the doctor, with a design of delivering your letter, but find he is at present in the country. I am a little anxious to have the doctor's opinion My own I dare not trust to; both because it concerns myself, and because it is so variable, that I know not how to fix it. Sometimes it elevates me above the clouds; at other times it depresses me with doubts and fears; so that, whatever be my success, I cannot be entirely disappointed."

Whether Mr. Hume ever enjoyed the satisfaction of a personal interview with Dr. Butler, I have not heard From a

---

[1] For the rest of the letter, see *Memoirs of the Life and Writings of Lord Kames*, by Lord Woodhouselee, vol. i. p. 84, *et seq*

letter of his to Mr. Home, dated London 1739, we learn that if any intercourse took place between them, it must have been after the publication of the *Treatise of Human Nature.* " I have sent the Bishop of Bristol a copy; but could not wait upon him with your letter after he had arrived at that dignity. At least, I thought it would be to no purpose after I began the printing."[1] In a subsequent letter to the same correspondent, written in 1742, he expresses his satisfaction at the favourable opinion which he understood Dr. Butler had formed of his volume of *Essays,* then recently published, and augurs well from this circumstance of the success of his book. " I am told that Dr Butler has everywhere recommended them, so that I hope they will have some success."[2]

These particulars, trifling as they may appear to some, seemed to me, for more reasons than one, not unworthy of notice in this sketch. Independently of the pleasing record they afford of the mutual respect entertained by the eminent men to whom they relate, for each other's philosophical talents, they have a closer connexion with the history of metaphysical and moral inquiry in this island, than might be suspected by those who have not a very intimate acquaintance with the writings of both. Dr. Butler was, I think, the first of Mr. Locke's successors who clearly perceived the dangerous consequences likely to be deduced from his account of the origin of our ideas literally interpreted; and although he has touched on this subject but once, and that with his usual brevity, he has yet said enough to show, that his opinion with respect to it was the same with that formerly contended for by Cudworth, in opposition to Gassendi and Hobbes, and which has since been revived in different forms by the ablest of Mr. Hume's antagonists.[3] With these views, it may be reasonably supposed,

---

[1] *Memoirs of the Life and Writings of Lord Kames,* vol 1. p 92.

[2] *Ibid* p. 404. The *Essays* here referred to were the first part of the Essays Moral, Political, and Literary, published in 1742. The elegant author of these Memoirs has inadvertently confounded this volume with the second part of that work, containing the *Political Discourses,* (properly so called,) which did not appear till ten years afterwards

[3] See the short *Essay on Personal Identity,* at the end of Butler's *Ana-*

that he was not displeased to see the consequences of Locke's doctrine so very logically and forcibly pushed to their utmost limits, as the most effectual means of rousing the attention of the learned to a re-examination of this fundamental principle. That he was perfectly aware, before the publication of Mr Hume's work, of the encouragement given to scepticism by the logical maxims then in vogue, is evident from the concluding paragraph of his short *Essay on Personal Identity*. Had it been published a few years later, nobody would have doubted, that it had been directly pointed at the general strain and spirit of Mr. Hume's philosophy.

"But though we are thus certain, that we are the same agents or living beings *now*, which we were as far back as our remembrance reaches: yet it is asked, Whether we may not possibly be deceived in it ? And this question may be asked at the end of any demonstration whatever, because it is a question concerning the truth of perception by memory. And he who can doubt, whether perception by memory can in this case be depended on, may doubt also whether perception by deduction and reasoning, which also includes memory, or indeed whether intuitive perception can. Here then we can go no farther. For it is ridiculous to attempt to prove the truth of those perceptions whose truth we can no otherwise prove than by other perceptions of exactly the same kind with them, and which there is just the same ground to suspect; or to attempt to prove the truth of our faculties, which can no otherwise be proved, than by the use or means of those very suspected faculties themselves." [1]

logy; and compare the second paragraph with the remarks on this part of Locke's *Essay* by Dr Price.—*Review of the Principal Questions and Difficulties relating to Morals*, pp. 49, 50, 3d edit Lond 1787.

[1] I must not, however, be understood as giving unqualified praise to this Essay It is by no means free from the old scholastic jargon, and contains some reasoning which, I may confidently assert, the author would not have employed, had it been written fifty years later. Whoever takes the trouble to read the paragraph beginning with these words, "*Thirdly*, Every person is conscious," &c., will immediately perceive the truth of this remark. I mention it as a proof of the change to the better, which has taken place since Butler's time, in the mode of thinking and writing on Metaphysical questions

It is, however, less as a speculative metaphysician, than as a philosophical inquirer into the principles of morals, that I have been induced to associate the name of Butler with that of Hume. And, on this account, it may be thought that it would have been better to delay what I have now said of him till I come to trace the progress of Ethical Science during the eighteenth century. To myself it seemed more natural and interesting to connect this historical or rather biographical digression, with the earliest notice I was to take of Mr. Hume as an author. The numerous and important hints on metaphysical questions which are scattered over Butler's works, are sufficient of themselves to account for the space I have allotted to him among Locke's successors; if, indeed, any apology for this be necessary, after what I have already mentioned, of Mr. Hume's ambition to submit to his judgment the first fruits of his metaphysical studies.

The remarks hitherto made on the *Treatise of Human Nature* are confined entirely to the first volume. The speculations contained in the two others, on Morals, on the Nature and Foundation of Government, and on some other topics connected with political philosophy, will fall under our review afterwards.

Dr. Reid's *Inquiry into the Human Mind,* (published in 1764,) was the first direct attack which appeared in Scotland upon the sceptical conclusions of Mr. Hume's philosophy. For my own opinion of this work I must refer to one of my former publications.[1] It is enough to remark here, that its great object is to refute the *Ideal Theory* which was then in complete possession of the schools, and upon which Dr. Reid conceived that the whole of Mr. Hume's philosophy, as well as the whole of Berkeley's reasonings against the existence of matter, was founded. According to this theory we are taught, that "nothing is perceived but what is in the mind which perceives it; that we do not really perceive things that are external, but only certain images and pictures of them imprinted upon the mind, which are called impressions and ideas."—" This doctrine, (says

---

[1] *Biographical Account of Reid*

Dr. Reid on another occasion,) I once believed so firmly, as to embrace the whole of Berkeley's system along with it; till finding other consequences to follow from it, which gave me more uneasiness than the want of a material world, it came into my mind, more than forty years ago, to put the question, What evidence have I for this doctrine, that all the objects of my knowledge are ideas in my own mind? From that time to the present, I have been candidly and impartially, as I think, seeking for the evidence of this principle; but can find none, excepting the authority of philosophers."

On the refutation of the ideal theory, contained in this and his other works, Dr. Reid himself was disposed to rest his chief merit as an author. The merit, (says he in a letter to Dr. James Gregory,) of what you are pleased to call *my Philosophy*, lies, I think, chiefly in having called in question the common theory of ideas or images of things in the mind being the only objects of thought; a theory founded on natural prejudices, and so universally received as to be interwoven with the structure of language. Yet were I to give you a detail of what led me to call in question this theory, after I had long held it as self-evident and unquestionable, you would think, as I do, that there was much of chance in the matter. The discovery was the birth of time, not of genius, and Berkeley and Hume did more to bring it to light than the man that hit upon it. I think there is hardly anything that can be called *mine* in the philosophy of the mind, which does not follow with ease from the detection of this prejudice.

" I must, therefore, beg of you, most earnestly, to make no contrast in my favour to the disparagement of my predecessors in the same pursuits. I can truly say of them, and shall always avow, what you are pleased to say of me, that, but for the assistance I have received from their writings, I never could have wrote or thought what I have done."[1]

[1] An ingenious and profound writer, who, though intimately connected with Mr Hume in habits of friendship, was not blind to the vulnerable parts of his Metaphysical System, has bestowed, in the latest of his publications, the following encomium on Dr. Reid's *Philosophical Works*:—

When I reflect on the stress thus laid by Dr. Reid on this part of his writings, and his frequent recurrence to the same argument whenever his subject affords him an opportunity of forcing it upon the attention of his readers, I cannot help expressing my wonder, that Kant and other German philosophers, who appear to have so carefully studied those passages in Reid, which relate to Hume's Theory of Causation, should have overlooked entirely what he himself considered as the most original and important of all his discussions; more especially as the conclusion to which it leads has been long admitted, by the best judges in this island, as one of the few propositions in metaphysical science completely established beyond the reach of controversy. Even those who affect to speak the most lightly of Dr. Reid's contributions to the philosophy of the human mind, have found nothing to object to his reasonings against the ideal theory, but that the absurdities involved in it are too glaring to require a serious examination.[1] Had these

" The author of an *Inquiry into the Mind*, and of subsequent *Essays on the Intellectual and Active Powers of Man*, has great merit in the effect to which he has pursued this history. But, considering the point at which the science stood when he began his inquiries, he has, perhaps, no less merit in having removed the mist of hypothesis and metaphor, with which the subject was enveloped, and, in having taught us to state the facts of which we are conscious, not in figurative language, but in the terms which are proper to the subject. In this it will be our advantage to follow him; the more that, in former theories, so much attention had been paid to the introduction of *ideas* or *images* as the elements of knowledge, that the belief of any external existence or prototype has been left to be inferred from the mere idea or image; and this inference, indeed, is so little founded, that many who have come to examine its evidence have thought themselves warranted to deny it altogether. And hence the scepticism of ingenious men, who, not seeing a proper access to knowledge through the medium of ideas, without considering whether the road they had been directed to take was the true or a false one, denied the possibility of arriving at the end."—*Principles of Moral and Political Science*, by Dr. Adam Ferguson, vol i. pp. 75, 76

The work from which this passage is taken contains various important observations connected with the Philosophy of the Human Mind, but as the taste of the author led him much more strongly to moral and political speculations, than to researches concerning the intellectual powers of man, I have thought it right to reserve any remarks which I have to offer on his philosophical merits for the last part of this Discourse.

[1] I allude here more particularly to Dr Priestley, who, in a work published in 1774, alleged, that when philosophers called ideas the *images* of external things, they are only to be understood as speaking figuratively; and that Dr

reasonings been considered in the same light in Germany, it is quite impossible that the analogical language of Leibnitz, in which he speaks of the soul as *a living mirror of the universe,* could have been again revived; 'a mode of speaking liable to every objection which Reid has urged against the ideal theory. Such, however, it would appear, is the fact. The word *Representation* (*Vorstellung*) is now the German substitute for *Idea;* nay, one of the most able works which Germany has produced since the commencement of its new philosophical era, is entitled *Nova Theoria Facultatis Representativæ Humanæ.* In the same work, the author has prefixed, as a motto to the second book, in which he treats of " the *Representative Faculty* in general," the following sentence from Locke, which he seems to have thought himself entitled to assume as a first principle: " Since the mind, in all its thoughts and reasonings,

Reid has gravely argued against this metaphorical language, as if it were meant to convey a theory of perception. The same remark has been repeated over and over since Priestley's time, by various writers. I have nothing to add in reply to it to what I long ago stated in my Philosophical Essays, (see Note H at the end of that work,) but the following short quotation from Mr. Hume:—

" It seems evident, that, when men follow this blind and powerful instinct of nature, they always suppose the very images, presented by the senses, to be the external objects, and never entertain any suspicion, that the one are nothing but *representations* of the other. . . . But this universal and primary opinion of all men is soon destroyed by the slightest philosophy, which teaches us, that nothing can ever be present to the mind but an *image* or perception, and that the senses are only the inlets through which these images are conveyed, without being able to produce any immediate intercourse between the mind and the object The table which we see seems to diminish as we remove farther from it; but the real table, which exists independent of us, suffers no alteration. It was, therefore, nothing but its image which was present to the mind These are the obvious dictates of reason."—*Essay on the Academical Philosophy*

Is not this analogical theory of perception the principle on which the whole of Berkeley's reasonings against the existence of the material world, and of Hume's scepticism on the same subject, are founded?

The same analogy still continues to be sanctioned by some English philosophers of no small note. Long after the publication of Dr Reid's *Inquiry,* Mr. Horne Tooke quoted with approbation the following words of J. C. Scaliger " Sicut in speculo ea quæ videntur non sunt, sed eorum *species ,* ita quæ intelligimus, ea sunt re ipsa extra nos, eorumque *species* in nobis. EST ENIM QUASI RERUM SPECULUM INTELLECTUS NOSTER , CUI, NISI PER SENSUM REPRESENTENTUR RES, NIHIL SCIT IPSE "— (J C. Scaliger, *de Causis*, L L cap lxvi) *Diversions of Purley,* vol i p 35, 2d edition.

hath no other *immediate* object but its own *ideas* (*representations*) which it alone does or can contemplate, it is evident that our knowledge is only conversant about them."— (Locke's *Essay,* book iv. chap. i.) In a country where this metaphysical jargon still passes current among writers of eminence, it is vain to expect that any solid progress can be made in the inductive philosophy of the human mind. A similar remark may be extended to another country, where the title of *Idéologie* (a word which takes for granted the truth of the hypothesis which it was Reid's great aim to explode) has been lately given to the very science in which the theory of *Ideas* has been so clearly shown to have been, in all ages, the most fruitful source of error and absurdity.[1]

Of the other works by Scottish metaphysicians, which appeared soon after the *Inquiry into the Human Mind,* I have not left myself room to speak. I know of none of them from which something important may not be learned; while several of them (particularly those of Dr. Campbell) have struck out many new and interesting views. To one encomium all of them are well entitled, that of aiming steadily at the advancement of useful knowledge and of human happiness. But the principles on which they have proceeded have so close an affinity to those of Dr. Reid, that I could not, without repeating what I have already said, enter into any explanation concerning their characteristical doctrines.

On comparing the opposition which Mr. Hume's scepticism encountered from his own countrymen, with the account formerly given of the attempts of some German philosophers to refute his Theory of Causation, it is impossible not to be struck with the coincidence between the leading views of his most

---

[1] In censuring these metaphorical terms, I am far from supposing that the learned writers who have employed them have been all misled by the theoretical opinions involved in their language. Reinhold has been more particularly careful in guarding against such a misapprehension. But it cannot, I think, be doubted that the prevalence of such a phraseology must have a tendency to divert the attention from a just view of the mental phenomena, and to infuse into the mind of the young inquirer very false conceptions of the manner in which these phenomena ought to be studied.

eminent antagonists. This coincidence one would have been disposed to consider as purely accidental, if Kant, by his petulant sneers at Reid, Beattie, and Oswald, had not expressly acknowledged, that he was not unacquainted with their writings. As for the great discovery, which he seems to claim as his own—that the ideas of Cause and Effect, as well as many others, are derived from the *pure understanding* without any aid from experience, it is nothing more than a repetition, in very nearly the same terms, of what was advanced a century before by Cudworth, in reply to Hobbes and Gassendi; and borrowed avowedly by Cudworth from the reasonings of Socrates, as reported by Plato, in answer to the scepticism of Protagoras. This recurrence, under different forms, of the same metaphysical controversies, which so often surprises and mortifies us in the history of literature, is an evil which will probably always continue, more or less, even in the most prosperous state of philosophy. But it affords no objection to the utility of metaphysical pursuits. While the sceptics keep the field, it must not be abandoned by the friends of sounder principles; nor ought they to be discouraged from their ungrateful task, by the reflection, that they have probably been anticipated, in everything they have to say, by more than one of their predecessors. If anything is likely to check this periodical return of a mischief so unpropitious to the progress of useful knowledge, it seems to be the general diffusion of that historical information concerning the literature and science of former times, of which it is the aim of these Preliminary Dissertations to present an outline. Should it fail in preventing the occasional revival of obsolete paradoxes, it will, at least, diminish the wonder and admiration with which they are apt to be regarded by the multitude.

And here I cannot refrain from remarking the injustice with which the advocates for truth are apt to be treated, and by none more remarkably than by that class of writers who profess the greatest zeal for its triumph. The importance of their labours is discredited by those who are the loudest in their declamations and invectives against the licentious philosophy of the present age; insomuch that a careless observer would be inclined to imagine (if I may borrow Mr. Hume's words on another occasion) that the battle was fought "not by the men at arms, who manage the pike and the sword; but by the trumpeters, drummers, and musicians of the army."

These observations may serve, at the same time, to account for the slow and (according to some persons) imperceptible advances of the philosophy of the human mind, since the publication of Locke's *Essay*. With those who still attach themselves to that author, as an infallible guide in metaphysics, it is in vain to argue; but I would willingly appeal to any of Locke's rational and discriminating admirers, whether much has not been done by his successors, and, among others, by members of our northern universities, towards the illustration and correction of such of his principles as have furnished, both to English and French sceptics, the foundation of their theories.[1] If this be granted, the way has, at least, been cleared and prepared for the labours of our posterity; and neither the cavils of the sceptic, nor the refutation of them by the sounder logician, can be pronounced to be useless to mankind. Nothing can be juster or more liberal than the following reflection of Reid: "I conceive the sceptical writers to be a set of men, whose business it is to pick holes in the fabric of knowledge wherever it is weak and faulty; and when those places are properly repaired, the whole building becomes more firm and solid than it was formerly."—*Inquiry into the Human Mind.* Dedication.

---

[1] According to Dr. Priestley, the labours of these commentators on Locke have done more harm than good. "I think Mr Locke has been hasty in concluding that there is some other source of our ideas besides the external senses; but the rest of his system appears to me and others to be the corner-stone of all just and rational knowledge of ourselves"

"This solid foundation, however, has lately been attempted to be overturned by a set of pretended philosophers, of whom the most conspicuous and assuming is Dr. Reid, Professor of Moral Philosophy in the University of Glasgow."—(*Exam. of Reid, Beattie, and Oswald*, p 5.) As to Mr Hume, Dr. Priestley says, "In my opinion, he has been *very ably* answered, again and again, upon more solid principles than those of this new *common sense; and I beg leave to refer to the two first volumes of my Institutes of Natural and Revealed Religion*"—*Examination of Reid*, &c Preface, p xxvii

There is, indeed, one point of view, in which it must be owned that Mr. Hume's *Treatise* has had an unfavourable effect (and more especially in Scotland) on the progress of Metaphysical Science. Had it not been for the zeal of some of his countrymen to oppose the sceptical conclusions, which they conceived it to be his aim to establish, much of that ingenuity which has been wasted in the refutation of his sophistry (or, to speak more correctly, in combating the mistaken principles on which he proceeded) would, in all probability, have been directed to speculations more immediately applicable to the business of life, or more agreeable to the taste of the present age. What might not have been expected from Mr. Hume himself, had his powerful and accomplished mind been more frequently turned to the study of some parts of our nature, (of those, for example, which are connected with the principles of criticism,) in examining which, the sceptical bias of his disposition would have had fewer opportunities of leading him astray! In some fragments of this sort, which enliven and adorn his collection of *Essays*, one is at a loss whether more to admire the subtlety of his genius, or the solidity and good sense of his critical judgments.

Nor have these elegant applications of metaphysical pursuits been altogether overlooked by Mr. Hume's antagonists. The active and adventurous spirit of Lord Kames, here, as in many other instances, led the way to his countrymen; and, due allowances being made for the novelty and magnitude of his undertaking, with a success far greater than could have been reasonably anticipated. The *Elements of Criticism*, considered as the first systematical attempt to investigate the metaphysical principles of the fine arts, possesses, in spite of its numerous defects both in point of taste and of philosophy, infinite merits, and will ever be regarded as a literary wonder by those who know how small a portion of his time it was possible for the author to allot to the composition of it, amidst the imperious and multifarious duties of a most active and useful life. Campbell and Gerard, with a sounder philosophy, and Beattie, with a much more lively relish for the Sublime and the

Beautiful, followed afterwards in the same path; and have all contributed to create and diffuse over this island a taste for a higher and more enlightened species of criticism than was known to our forefathers. Among the many advantageous results with which this study has been already attended, the most important, undoubtedly, is the new and pleasing avenue which it has opened to an analysis of the laws which regulate the intellectual phenomena; and the interest which it has thus lent, in the estimation of men of the world, to inquiries which, not many years before, were seldom heard of, but within the walls of a university.

Dr. Reid's two volumes of *Essays on the Intellectual and on the Active Powers of Man*, (the former of which appeared in 1785, and the latter in 1788,) are the latest philosophical publications from Scotland of which I shall at present take notice. They are less highly finished, both in matter and in form, than his *Inquiry into the Human Mind*. They contain also some repetitions, to which, I am afraid, I must add a few trifling inconsistencies of expression, for which the advanced age of the author, who was then approaching to fourscore, claims every indulgence from a candid reader. Perhaps, too, it may be questioned, whether, in one or two instances, his zeal for an important conclusion has not led him to avail himself of some dubious reasonings, which might have been omitted without any prejudice to his general argument. "The value of these volumes, however, (as I have elsewhere remarked,) is inestimable to future adventurers in the same arduous inquiries, not only in consequence of the aids they furnish as a rough draught of the field to be examined, but by the example they exhibit of a method of investigation on such subjects, hitherto very imperfectly understood, even by those philosophers who call themselves the disciples of Locke. It is by the logical rigour of this method, so systematically pursued in all his researches, still more than by the importance of his particular conclusions, that he stands so conspicuously distinguished among those who have hitherto prosecuted analytically the study of man."[1]

[1] *Biographical Account of Reid.*

His acquaintance with the metaphysical doctrines of his predecessors does not appear to have been very extensive; with those of his own contemporaries it was remarkably deficient. I do not recollect that hé has anywhere mentioned the names either of Condillac or of D'Alembert. It is impossible not to regret this, not only as it has deprived us of his critical judgments on some celebrated theories, but as it has prevented him from enlivening his works with that variety of historical discussion so peculiarly agreeable in these abstract researches.

On the other hand, Dr. Reid's limited range of metaphysical reading, by forcing him to draw the materials of his philosophical speculations almost entirely from his own reflections, has given to his style, both of thinking and of writing, a characteristical unity and simplicity seldom to be met with in so voluminous an author. He sometimes, indeed, repeats, with an air of originality, what had been previously said by his predecessors; but on these, as on all other occasions, he has at least the merit of thinking for himself, and of sanctioning, by the weight of his unbiassed judgment, the conclusions which he adopts. It is this uniformity of thought and design, which, according to Dr. Butler, is the best test of an author's sincerity; and I am apt to regard it also, in these abstruse disquisitions, as one of the surest marks of liberal and unfettered inquiry.[1]

In comparing Dr. Reid's publications at different periods of his life, it is interesting to observe his growing partiality for the aphoristical style. Some of his *Essays on the Intellectual and Active Powers of Man* are little more than a series of detached paragraphs, consisting of leading thoughts, of which the reader is left to trace the connexion by his own sagacity. To this aphoristical style it is not improbable that he was

---

[1] [* Among the thoughts which Dr Reid has been accused of borrowing from other writers, not a few have been forced on him by the disgusting revival in the present age of errors, which ought to have been considered as long ago exploded. It is thus, that when he has the appearance of copying Locke in drawing the line between volition and desire, his apology is to be found in the perverse obstinacy with which Priestley and others still persevere in confounding two words so manifestly and so essentially different in their meaning.]

* Restored.—*Ed*

partly led by the indolence incident to advanced years, as it relieved him from what Boileau justly considered as the most difficult task of an author, the skilful management of *transitions*.[1] In consequence of this want of continuity in his compositions, a good deal of popular effect is unavoidably lost; but, on the other hand, to the few who have a taste for such inquiries, and who value books chiefly as they furnish exercise to their own thoughts, (a class of readers who are alone competent to pronounce a judgment on metaphysical questions,) there is a peculiar charm in a mode of writing, so admirably calculated to give *relief* to the author's ideas, and to awaken, at every sentence, the reflections of his readers.

When I review what I have now written on the history of Metaphysics in Scotland, since the publication of Mr. Hume's *Treatise*, and at the same time recollect the laurels which, during the same period, have been won by Scottish authors, in every other department of literature and of science, I must acknowledge that, instead of being mortified at the slender amount of their contributions to the philosophy of the human mind, I am more disposed to wonder at their successful perseverance in cultivating a field of study, where the approbation of a few enlightened and candid judges is the only reward to which their ambition could aspire. Small as their progress may hitherto have been, it will at least not suffer by a comparison with what has been accomplished by their contemporaries in any other part of Europe

It may not be useless to add in this place, that, if little has as yet been done, the more ample is the field left for the industry of our successors. The compilation of a *Manual of Rational Logic*, adapted to the present state of science and of society in Europe, is a *desideratum* which, it is to be hoped, will at no distant period be supplied. It is a work, certainly, of which the execution has been greatly facilitated by the philosophical

---

[1] Boileau is said, by the younger Racine, to have made this remark in speaking of La Bruyère. "Il disoit que La Bruyère s'etoit épargné *le plus diffi-cile d'un ouvrage* en s'épargnant les transitions"—*Mémoire sur la Vie de Jean Racine*

labours of the last century. The varieties of intellectual character among men present another very interesting object of study, which, considering its practical utility, has not yet excited, so much as might have been expected, the curiosity of our countrymen. Much, too, is still wanting to complete the theory of evidence. Campbell has touched upon it with his usual acuteness, but he has attempted nothing more than an illustration of a very few general principles. Nor has he turned his attention to the various illusions of the imagination, and of the passions, by which the judgment is liable to be warped in the estimates it forms of moral evidence in the common affairs of life. This is a most important inquiry, considering how often the lives and fortunes of men are subjected to the decisions of illiterate persons concerning circumstantial proofs; and how much the success or failure of every individual in the conduct of his private concerns turns on the sagacity or rashness with which he anticipates future contingencies. Since the time when Campbell wrote, an attempt has been made by Condorcet[1] and some other French writers, to apply a mathematical calculus to moral and political truths; but though much metaphysical ingenuity, as well as mathematical skill, have been displayed in carrying it into execution, it has not yet led to any useful practical results. Perhaps it may even be questioned, whether, in investigating truths of this sort, the intellectual powers can derive much aid from the employment of such an organ. To define accurately and distinctly the limits of its legitimate province, still remains a *desideratum* in this abstruse part of logic.

Nearly connected with this subject are the metaphysical principles assumed in the mathematical Calculation of Probabilities;[2] in delivering which principles, some foreign mathematicians, with the illustrious La Place at their head, have blended with many unquestionable and highly interesting conclusions, various moral paralogisms of the most pernicious tendency. A critical examination of these paralogisms, which are apt to

[1] *Essai sur l'Application de l'Analyse à la Probabilité des Décisions rendues à la pluralité des Voix*
[2] [See Note E E E.]

escape the attention of the reader amid the variety of original and luminous discussions with which they are surrounded, would, in my humble apprehension, be one of the most essential services which could at present be rendered to true philosophy. In the mind of La Place, their origin may be fairly traced to an ambition, not altogether unnatural in so transcendent a genius, to extend the empire of his favourite science over the moral as well as the material world.[1] I have mentioned but a few out of the innumerable topics which crowd upon me as fit objects of inquiry for the rising generation.[2] Nor have I been guided in my selection of these by any other consideration than their peculiar adaptation to the actual circumstances of the philosophical world.

Should such men as Hume, Smith, and Reid again arise, their curiosity would, in all probability, be turned to some applications of metaphysical principles of a more popular and practical nature than those which chiefly engaged their curiosity. At the same time, let us not forget what a step they made beyond the scholastic philosophy of the preceding age; and how necessary this step was as a preliminary to other researches bearing more directly and palpably on human affairs

The most popular objection hitherto made to our Scottish metaphysicians is, that, in treating of human nature, they have overlooked altogether the corporeal part of our frame. From the contempt which they have uniformly expressed for all physiological theories concerning the intellectual phenomena, it has been concluded, that they were disposed to consider the human mind as altogether independent of the influence of physical causes. Mr. Belsham has carried this charge so far, as to sneer at Dr. Reid's inconsistency, for having somewhere acknow-

---

[1] The paralogisms to which I allude did not fall within the scope of the admirable criticism on this work in the *Edinburgh Review*

[2] Among these, the most prominent is the Natural or Theoretical History of Language, (including under this title *written* as well as *oral* language,) a subject which will probably continue to furnish new problems to human ingenuity, in the most improved state of human knowledge It is not surprising that an art which lays the foundation of all the others, and which is so intimately connected with the exercise of reason itself, should leave behind it such faint and obscure traces of its origin and infancy.

ledged, " in opposition to his systematical principles, that a certain constitution or state of the brain is necessary to memory." In reply to this charge, it may be confidently asserted, that no set of philosophers, since the time of Lord Bacon, have entertained juster views on this subject than the school to which Dr. Reid belonged. In proof of this, I need only appeal to the *Lectures on the Duties and Qualifications of a Physician*, by the late learned and ingenious Dr. John Gregory. Among the different articles connected with the natural history of the human species, which he has there recommended to the examination of the medical student, he lays particular stress on "the laws of union between the mind and body, and the mutual influence they have upon one another." "This, (he observes,) is one of the most important inquiries that ever engaged the attention of mankind, and almost equally necessary in the sciences of morals and of medicine." It must be remarked, however, that it is only the *laws* which regulate the union between mind and body, (the same class of *facts* which Bacon called the *doctrina de fœdere*,) which are here pointed out as proper objects of philosophical curiosity; for as to any *hypothesis* concerning the *manner* in which the union is carried on, this most sagacious writer was well aware, that they are not more unfavourable to the improvement of logic and of ethics, than to a skilful and judicious exercise of the healing art.

I may perhaps form too high an estimate of the progress of knowledge during the last fifty years; but I think I can perceive, within the period of my own recollection, not only a change to the better in the Philosophy of the Human Mind, but in the speculations of medical inquirers Physiological theories concerning the functions of the nerves in producing the intellectual phenomena have pretty generally fallen into contempt. and, on the other hand, a large accession has been made to our stock of well authenticated facts, both with respect to the influence of body on mind, and of mind upon body. As examples of this, it is sufficient to mention the experimental inquiries instituted, in consequence of the pretended cures effected by means of Animal Magnetism and of Tractors; to which may be added, the philosophical spirit evinced in some late publications on Insanity.

Another objection, not so entirely groundless, which has been made to the same school, is, that their mode of philosophizing has led to an unnecessary multiplication of our *internal senses and instinctive determinations*. For this error, I have elsewhere attempted to account and to apologize.[1] On the present occasion I shall only remark, that it is at least a safer error than the opposite extreme, so fashionable of late among our southern neighbours, of endeavouring to explain away, without any exception, all our *instinctive* principles, both speculative and practical. A literal interpretation of Locke's comparison of the infant mind to a *sheet of white paper*, (a comparison which, if I am rightly informed, has not yet wholly lost its credit in all our universities,) naturally predisposed his followers to embrace this theory, and enabled them to shelter it from a free examination, under the sanction of his supposed authority. Dr. Paley himself, in his earliest philosophical publication, yielded so far to the prejudices in which he had been educated, as to dispute the existence of the *moral faculty* ;[2] although in his

---

[1] *Biographical Memoirs*, p. 472.

[2] After relating, in the words of Valerius Maximus, the noted story of Caius Toranius, who betrayed his affectionate and excellent father to the triumvirate, Dr. Paley thus proceeds:—

"Now, the question is, whether, if this story were related to the wild boy caught some years ago in the woods of Hanover, or to a savage without experience and without instruction, cut off in his infancy from all intercourse with his species, and consequently under no possible influence of example, authority, education, sympathy, or habit, whether, I say, such a one would feel, upon the relation, any degree of that *sentiment of disapprobation of Toranius's conduct* which we feel or not?

"They who maintain the existence of a moral sense, of innate maxims, of a natural conscience; that the love of virtue and hatred of vice are instinctive, or the perception of right or wrong intuitive, (all of which are only different ways of expressing the same opinion,) affirm that he would.

"They who deny the existence of a moral sense, &c., affirm that he would not

"And upon this issue is joined."— *Principles of Moral and Political Philosophy*, book i chap. 5

To those who are at all acquainted with the history of this dispute, it must appear evident that the question is here completely mis-stated; and that, in the whole of Dr Paley's subsequent argument on the subject, he combats a phantom of his own imagination. The opinion which he ascribes to his antagonists has been loudly and repeatedly

more advanced years, he amply atoned for this error of his youth, by the ingenuity and acuteness with which he combated the reasonings employed by some of his contemporaries, to invalidate the proofs afforded by the phenomena of *instinct,* of the existence of a designing and provident cause. In this part of his work, he has plainly in his eye the *Zoonomia* of Dr. Darwin,[1] where the same principles, of which Paley and others

disavowed by all the most eminent moralists who have disputed Locke's reasonings against *innate practical principles;* and is, indeed, so very obviously absurd, that it never could have been for a moment entertained by any person in his senses

Did it ever enter into the mind of the wildest theorist to imagine that the sense of seeing would enable a man brought up, from the moment of his birth, in utter darkness, to form a conception of light and colours? But would it not be equally rash to conclude from the extravagance of such a supposition, that the sense of seeing is not an original part of the human frame?

The above quotation from Paley forces me to remark, farther, that, in combating the supposition of a *moral sense,* he has confounded together, as *only different ways of expressing the same opinion,* a variety of systems, which are regarded by all our best philosophers, not only as essentially distinct, but as in some measure standing in opposition to each other The system of Hutcheson, for example, is identified with that of Cudworth. But although, in this instance, the author's logical discrimination does not appear to much advantage, the sweeping censure thus bestowed on so many of our most celebrated ethical theories, has the merit of throwing a very strong light on that particular view of the subject which it is the aim of his reasonings to establish, in contradiction to them all

[1] See his observations on Instinct. —Section xvi. of the *Zoonomia*

[* Mr. Horne Tooke, in his Diversions of Purley, has very ingeniously shewn, that what were called general ideas, are in reality only general terms, or words which signify any parts of a complex object: whence arises much error in our verbal reasoning, as the same word has different significations *And hence those, who can think without words, reason more accurately than those who only compare the ideas suggested by words; a rare faculty, which distinguishes the writers of philosophy from those of sophistry."—Zoonomia,* vol i p 178   3d edit 1801

"By a due attention to circumstances, many of the actions of young animals, which at first sight seemed only referable to an inexplicable instinct, will appear to have been acquired, like all other animal actions that are attended with consciousness, *by the repeated efforts of our muscles under the conduct of our sensations or desires."— Ibid* p. 189.

Our *sensations* and *desires* (it is to be observed) are admitted by Darwin to constitute a part of our system, as our *muscles and bones* constitute another part; and hence they may alike be termed *natural* or *connate;* but neither of them can properly be termed *instinctive;* as the word instinct in its usual acceptation refers only to the *actions* of animals. "The reader (says Darwin) is entreated carefully to attend to this

* Restored —*Ed*

had availed themselves to disprove the existence of instinct and instinctive propensities in man, are eagerly laid hold of to disprove the existence of *instinct* in the brutes. Without such an extension of the argument, it was clearly perceived by Darwin, that sufficient evidences of the existence of a Designing Cause would be afforded by the phenomena of the lower animals; and, accordingly, he has employed much ingenuity to show, that all these phenomena may be accounted for by experience, or by the influence of pleasurable or painful sensations, operating *at the moment* on the animal frame.

In opposition to this theory, it is maintained by Paley, that it is by *instinct*, that is, according to his own definition, " by a propensity prior to experience, and independent of instruction,"—" that the sexes of animals seek each other; that animals cherish their offspring; that the young quadruped is directed to the teat of its dam; that birds build their nest, and brood with so much patience upon their eggs; that insects, which do not sit upon their eggs, deposit them in those particular situations in which the young when hatched find their appropriate food; that it is instinct which carries the salmon, and some other fish, out of the sea into rivers, for the purpose of shedding their spawn in fresh water."[1]

In Dr. Paley's very able and convincing reasonings on these various points, he has undoubtedly approached nearer to the spirit of what has been ironically called *Scottish* philosophy,[2]

---

definition of *instinctive actions*, lest by using the word *instinct* without adjoining any accurate idea to it, he may include the natural desires of love and hunger, and the natural sensations of pain or pleasure under this general term "

According to this explanation, the difference of opinion between Dr Darwin and his opponents is chiefly verbal; for whether we consider the actions of animals commonly referred to *instinct*, as the immediate result of implanted determinations, or as the result of *sensations and desires* which are *natural* or connate, they afford equally manifestations of design and wisdom in the Author of their being; inasmuch as, on both suppositions, they depend on causes either mediately or immediately subservient to the preservation of the creatures to which they belong. On both suppositions, there is an infallible provision and preparation made by the hand of nature, for the effect which she has in view]

[1] Paley's *Natural Theology*, p. 324

[2] May I take the liberty of requesting the reader to compare a few pages of Dr Paley's Section on Instinct, begin-

than any of Mr. Locke's English disciples, since the time of Dr. Butler; a circumstance which, when compared with the metaphysical creed of his earlier years, reflects the greatest honour on the candour and fairness of his mind, and encourages the hope, that this philosophy, where it is equally sound, will gradually and silently work its way among sincere inquirers after truth, in spite of the strong prejudices which many of our southern neighbours still appear to entertain against it The extravagances of Darwin, it is probable, first opened Dr. Paley's eyes to the dangerous tendency of Locke's argument against innate principles, when inculcated without due limitations.[1]

ning " *I am not ignorant of the theory which resolves instinct into sensation,*" &c, with some remarks made by the author of this Dissertation, in an Account of the Life and Writings of Dr. Reid? See the passage in section second, beginning thus, " *In a very original work on which I have already hazarded some criticisms,*" &c. As both publications appeared about the same time, (in the year 1802,) the coincidence, in point of thought, must have been wholly accidental, and as such affords no slight presumption in favour of its soundness

[* Through the whole of Darwin's reasonings on this subject, there seems to me to run a strange inconsistency. On some occasions, he is at pains to represent the brutes as little more than sentient machines; on others, he seems anxious to elevate them to the rank of rational beings. Of the former bias, we have an instance in his theory to account for the operations of birds in the incubation of their eggs; of the latter, in the explanation he proposes of the phenomena exhibited by some of their tribes, in the course of their periodical migrations "It is probable," says he, " that these emigrations were at first undertaken, as accident directed, by the more adventurous of their species, and learned from one another like the discoveries of mankind in navigation."— (Vol i. p. 231) It is curious that the philosopher who started this hypothesis did not also refer the incubation of eggs to the lights afforded by observation and example, aided by those supplied by tradition and by parental instruction This can be accounted for only by his puerile aversion to the word *instinct,* which prompts him always to search for a *cause,* implying either *less* or *more* sagacity, than that word is commonly understood to express]

.[1] When Dr. Paley published his *Principles of Moral and Political Philosophy,* he seems to have attached himself much too slavishly to the opinions of Bishop Law, to whom that work is inscribed. Hence, probably, his anxiety to disprove the existence of the moral faculty Of the length to which Law was disposed to carry Locke's argument against innate principles, he has enabled us to judge by his own explicit declaration: " I take implanted *senses, instincts, appetites, passions, and affections,* &c , to be a remnant of the old philosophy, which used to call every-

With this very faint outline of the speculations of Locke's chief successors in Scotland, prior to the close of Dr. Reid's literary labours, I shall for the present finish my review of the metaphysical pursuits of the eighteenth century. The long period which has since elapsed has been too much crowded with great political events to favour the growth of abstract science in any of its branches; and of the little which appears to have been done, during this interval, in other parts of Europe, towards the advancement of true philosophy, the interrupted communication between this island and the Continent left us for many years in a state of almost total ignorance. This chasm in our information concerning foreign literature, it may not be a difficult task for younger men to supply. At my time of life it would be folly to attempt it; nor, perhaps, is any author who has himself been so frequently before the public, the fittest person to form an impartial estimate of the merits of his living contemporaries. Now, however, when peace is at length restored to the world, it may reasonably be hoped that the human mind will again resume her former career with renovated energy; and that the nineteenth century will not yield to the eighteenth in furnishing materials to those who may hereafter delight to trace the progressive improvement of their species. In the meantime, instead of indulging myself in looking forward to the future, I shall conclude this section with a few general reflections suggested by the foregoing retrospect.

---

thing *innate* that it could not account for, and therefore heartily wish, that they were in one sense all eradicated, which was undoubtedly the aim of that great author last mentioned, (Mr. Locke,) as it was a natural consequence of his first book."—Law's Translation of Archbishop King, *On the Origin of Evil*, p 79, note

In justice, however, to Dr Law, it must be observed, that he appears to have been fully aware that the dispute about innate principles was in a great measure verbal "It will really," says he, "come to the same thing with regard to the moral attributes of God and the nature of virtue and vice, whether the Deity has *implanted* these instincts and affections in us, or has framed and disposed us in such a manner, has given us such powers, and placed us in such circumstances, that we must *necessarily acquire them*"—(*Ibid.*) But if Dr Law was aware of this, why should he and his followers have attached such infinite importance to the controversy?

Among these reflections, what chiefly strikes my own mind is the extraordinary change which has gradually and insensibly taken place, since the publication of Locke's *Essay*, in the meaning of the word *Metaphysics ;* a word formerly appropriated to the ontology and pneumatology of the schools, but now understood as equally applicable to all those inquiries which have for their object to trace the various branches of human knowledge to their first principles in the constitution of our nature.[1] This change can be accounted for only by a change in the philosophical pursuits of Locke's successors; a change from the idle abstractions and subtleties of the dark ages, to studies subservient to the culture of the understanding; to the successful exercise of its faculties and powers; and to a knowledge of the great ends and purposes of our being. It may be regarded, therefore, as a palpable and incontrovertible proof of a corresponding progress of reason in this part of the world.

On comparing together the multifarious studies now classed together under the title of Metaphysics, it will be found difficult

---

[1] The following is the account of Metaphysics given by Hobbes :—"There is a certain *Philosophia prima,* on which all other Philosophy ought to depend, and consisteth principally in right limiting of the significations of such appellations, or names, as are of all others the most universal which limitations serve to avoid ambiguity and equivocation in reasoning, and are commonly called Definitions, such as are the Definitions of Body, Time, Place, Matter, Form, Essence, Subject, Substance, Accident, Power, Act, Finite, Infinite, Quantity, Quality, Motion, Action, Passion, and divers others, necessary to the explaining of a man's conceptions concerning the nature and generation of bodies The explication (that is, the settling of the meaning) of which, and the like terms, is commonly in the schools called *Metaphysics* "— (*Moral and Political Works.* Folio edit Lond 1750, p 399)

[* How very different, and how much more extensive, is the province now assigned to metaphysical science, a title under which is comprehended, not only the inductive philosophy of the human mind, but all the subordinate branches of that study, our logical inquiries (for example) concerning the conduct of the understanding ; our ethical inquiries concerning the theory of morals ; our philological inquiries concerning universal grammar ; our critical inquiries concerning the principles of rhetoric and of the fine arts To these may be added those abstract speculations which relate to the objects of Mathematics and of Physics, and an infinite variety of other general disquisitions to which these sciences have directed the curiosity of the learned As for the researches mentioned by Hobbes, they are no longer to be heard of, even within the walls of our universities]

* Restored —*Ed*

to trace any common circumstance but this, that they all require the same sort of mental exertion for their prosecution; the exercise, I mean, of that power (called by Locke *Reflection*) by which the mind turns its attention inwards upon its own operations, and the subjects of its own consciousness. In researches concerning our intellectual and active powers, the mind directs its attention to the faculties which it exercises, or to the propensities which put these faculties in motion. In all the other inquiries which fall under the province of the metaphysician, the materials of his reasoning are drawn chiefly from his own internal resources. Nor is this observation less applicable to speculations which relate to things external, than to such as are confined to the thinking and sentient principle within him. In carrying on his researches (for example) concerning hardness, softness, figure, and motion, he finds it not less necessary to retire within himself, than in studying the laws of imagination or memory. Indeed, in such cases the whole aim of his studies is to obtain a more precise definition of his *ideas*, and to ascertain the occasions on which they are formed.

From this account of the nature and object of metaphysical science, it may be reasonably expected that those with whom it is a favourite and habitual pursuit, should acquire a more than ordinary capacity of retiring, at pleasure, from the external to the internal world. They may be expected also to acquire a disposition to examine the origin of whatsoever combinations they may find established in the fancy, and a superiority to the casual associations which warp common understandings. Hence an accuracy and a subtlety in their distinctions on all subjects, and those peculiarities in their views which are characteristical of unbiassed and original thinking. But perhaps the most valuable fruit of their researches, is that scrupulous precision in the use of language, upon which, more than upon any one circumstance whatever, the logical accuracy of our reasonings, and the justness of our conclusions, essentially depend. Accordingly it will be found, on a review of the history of the moral sciences, that the most important steps which have been made in some of those apparently the most remote from metaphysical pursuits, (in the science, for example, of political economy,) have been made by men trained to the exercise of their intellectual powers by early habits of abstract meditation. To this fact Burke probably alluded when he remarked, that " by turning the soul inward on itself, its forces are concentered, and are fitted for stronger and bolder flights of science, and that in such pursuits, whether we take, or whether we lose the game, the chase is certainly of service." The names of Locke, of Berkeley, of Hume, of Quesnai, of Turgot, of Morellet, and above all, of Adam Smith, will at once illustrate the truth of these observations, and shew that, in combining together, in this Dissertation, the sciences of Metaphysics, of Ethics, and of Politics, I have not adopted an arrangement altogether capricious.[1]

In farther justification of this arrangement, I might appeal to the popular prejudices so industriously fostered by many, against these three branches of knowledge, as ramifications from one common and most pernicious root. How often have Mr. Smith's reasonings in favour of the freedom of trade been ridiculed as *metaphysical* and visionary! Nay, but a few years have elapsed since this epithet (accompanied with the still more opprobrious terms of Atheistical and Democratical) was applied to the argument then urged against the morality and policy of

---

[1] It furnishes no objection to these remarks, that some of our best treatises on questions of political economy have proceeded from men who were strangers to metaphysical studies. It is enough for my purpose if it be granted, that it was by habits of metaphysical thinking that the minds of those authors were formed, by whom political economy was first exalted to the dignity of a science. To a great proportion even of the learned, the rules of a sound logic are best taught by examples, and when a precise and well-defined phraseology is once introduced, the speculations of the most ordinary writers assume an appearance (sometimes, it must be owned, a very fallacious one) of depth and consistency.

Fontenelle remarks, that a single great man is sufficient to accomplish a change in the taste of his age, and that the perspicuity and method for which Descartes was indebted to his mathematical researches, were successfully copied by many of his contemporaries who were ignorant of mathematics. A similar observation will be found to apply, with still greater force, to the models of metaphysical analysis and of logical discussion exhibited in the political works of Hume and of Smith.

the slave-trade; and, in general, to every speculation in which any appeal was made to the beneficent arrangements of nature, or to the progressive improvement of the human race. Absurd as this language was, it could not for a moment have obtained any currency with the multitude, had there not been an obvious connexion between these liberal doctrines and the well-known habits of logical thinking which so eminently distinguished their authors and advocates. Whatever praise, therefore, may be due to the fathers of the modern science of political economy, belongs, at least in part, (according to the acknowledgment of their most decided adversaries,) to those abstract studies by which they were prepared for an analytical investigation of its first and fundamental principles

Other connexions and affinities between Political Economy and the Philosophy of the Human Mind will present themselves afterwards. At present I purposely confine myself to that which is most obvious and indisputable.

The influence of metaphysical studies may be also perceived in the philosophical spirit so largely infused into the best historical compositions of the last century. This spirit has, indeed, been often perverted to pernicious purposes; but who can doubt that, on the whole, both history and philosophy have gained infinitely by the alliance?

How far a similar alliance has been advantageous to our poetry, may be more reasonably questioned. But on the most unfavourable supposition it must be admitted, that the number of poetical readers has thereby been greatly increased, and the pleasures of imagination proportionally communicated to a wider circle. The same remark may be extended to the study of philosophical criticism If it has not contributed to the encouragement of original genius in the fine arts, it has been followed by a much more beneficial result in diffusing a relish for the beautiful and the elegant, not to mention its influence in correcting and fixing the public taste, by the precision and steadiness of the principles to which it appeals.[1]

---

[1] See some admirable remarks on this subject by Gray, in his comments on the *Io* of Plato —Edition of *Gray*, by Mathias

Another instance, still more important, of the practical influence of metaphysical science, is the improvement which, since the time of Locke, has become general in the conduct of education, both private and public. In the former case, the fact is universally acknowledged. But even in our universities, (notwithstanding the proverbial aversion of most of them to everything which savours of innovation,) what a change has been gradually accomplished since the beginning of the eighteenth century! The studies of Ontology, of Pneumatology, and of Dialectics, have been supplanted by that of the Human Mind, conducted, with more or less success, on the plan of Locke's *Essay*; and, in a few seats of learning, by the studies of Bacon's Method of Inquiry, of the Principles of Philosophical Criticism, and of the Elements of Political Economy. In all this an approach has been made, or attempted, to what Locke so earnestly recommended to parents, "that their children's time should be spent in acquiring what may be useful to them when they come to be men." Many other circumstances, no doubt, have contributed their share in producing this revolution; but what individual can be compared to Locke in giving the first impulse to that spirit of reform by which it has been established?[1]

In consequence of the operation of these causes, a sensible change has taken place in the style of English composition[2]

---

[1] Under this head of education may also be mentioned the practical improvements which, during the course of the last century, have taken place in what Lord Bacon calls *the traditive part of logic* I allude here not only to the new arrangements in the Lancasterian Schools, by which the diffusion of the art of reading among the poorer classes of the community is so wonderfully facilitated and extended, but to those admirable elementary works which have opened a ready and speedy access to the more recondite truths of the severer sciences. How much these have contributed to promote the progress of mathematical knowledge in France may be judged of from an assertion of Condorcet, that two years spent under an able teacher now carry the student beyond the conclusions which limited the researches of Leibnitz and of Newton. The Essays lately published on this subject by M. Lacroix (*Essais sur l'Enseignement en Général, et sur celui des Mathématiques en Particulier*, Paris, 1805) contain many valuable suggestions, and, beside their utility to those who are concerned in the task of instruction, may justly be considered as an accession to the Philosophy of the Human Mind.

[2] See some judicious remarks on this subject, in Mr Godwin's *Inquirer*, p

The number of idiomatical phrases has been abridged; and the language has assumed a form more systematic, precise, and luminous. The transitions, too, in our best authors, have become more logical, and less dependent on fanciful or verbal

274 In the opinion of this author, "the English language is now written with more grammatical propriety than by the best of our ancestors, and with a much higher degree of energy and vigour The spirit of philosophy has infused itself into the structure of our sentences" He remarks farther, in favour of the present style of English composition, "that it at once satisfies the understanding and the ear." The union of these two excellencies certainly constitutes the perfection of writing Johnson boasts, and with truth, in the concluding paper of the *Rambler*, that he had "added something to our language in the elegance of its construction, and something in the harmony of its cadence," but what a sacrifice did he make to these objects, of conciseness, of simplicity, and of (what he has himself called) *Genuine Anglicism*. To accomplish the same ends, without any sacrifice of these higher merits, has been one of the chief aims of the most eminent among his successors

As an instrument of thought and a medium of scientific communication, the English language appears to me, in its present state, to be far superior to the French. Diderot, indeed, (a very high authority,) has, with much confidence, asserted the contrary, and it is but fair to let him speak for himself· "J'ajouterois volontiers que la marche didactique et réglée à laquelle notre langue est assujettie la rend plus propre aux sciences, et que par les tours et les inversions que le Grec, le Latin, l'Italien, l'Anglois, se permettent, ces langues sont plus avantageuses pour les lettres: Que nous pouvons mieux qu' aucun autre peuple faire parler l'esprit, et que le bon sens choisiroit la langue Françoise; mais que l'Imagination et les passions donneroient la préférence aux langues anciennes et à celles de nos voisins· Qu'il faut parler François dans la société et dans les écoles de Philosophie, et Grec, Latin, Anglois, dans les chaires et sur le Théâtre. Que notre langue seroit celle de la vérité, si jamais elle revient sur la terre, et que la Grecque, la Latine, et les autres seroient les langues de la fable et du mensonge Le François est fait pour instruire, éclairer, et convaincre; le Grec, le Latin, l'Italien, l'Anglois, pour persuader, émouvoir, et tromper; parlez Grec, Latin, Italien au peuple, mais parlez François au sage"—*Œuvres de Diderot*, tom. ii pp. 70, 71, Amsterdam, 1772

These peculiar excellencies of the French language are ascribed, in part, by Diderot, to the study of the Aristotelian Philosophy.—(*Ibid.* p. 7) I do not well see what advantage France should, in this respect, have enjoyed over England; and since that philosophy fell into disrepute, it will scarcely be alleged that the habits of thinking cultivated by Locke's disciples have been less favourable to a logical rigour of expression than those of any contemporary sect of French metaphysicians.

A later French writer has, with far greater justice, acknowledged the important services rendered to the French language, by the gentlemen of the Port-Royal Society "L'Ecole de Port-Royal, féconde en penseurs, illustrée par les écrivains les plus purs, par les érudits les plus laborieux du siècle de Louis XIV. eût déjà rendu parmi nous un assez grand service à la philosophie

associations. If by these means our native tongue has been rendered more unfit for some of the lighter species of writing, it has certainly gained immensely as an instrument of thought, and as a vehicle of knowledge. May I not also add, that the study of it has been greatly facilitated to foreigners; and that in proportion to its rejection of colloquial anomalies, more durable materials are supplied to the present generation for transmitting their intellectual acquisitions to posterity?

But granting the truth of these reflections, it may still be asked, what is the amount of the discoveries brought to light by the metaphysical speculations of the eighteenth century? Or rather, where are the principles to be found, of which it can be justly said, that they unite the suffrages, not of the *whole*, but even of the *majority* of our present philosophers? The question has been lately put and urged, with no common ability, by a foreign academician.

" The diversity of doctrines (says M. de Bonald) has increased, from age to age, with the number of masters, and with the progress of knowledge; and Europe, which at present possesses libraries filled with philosophical works, and which reckons up almost as many philosophers as writers; poor in the midst of so much riches, and uncertain, with the aid of all its guides, which road it should follow; Europe, the centre and the focus of all the lights of the world, has yet its *philosophy* only in expectation."[1]

In proof of this assertion, the author appeals to the *Comparative History of Philosophical Systems relative to the Principles of Human Knowledge*, by M Degerando; and after a variety of acute strictures on the contradictory systems there described, sums up his argument in the following words:—

par cela seul qu'elle a puissament concouru à fixer notre langue, à lui donner ce caractère de précision, de clarté, d'exactitude, qui la rend si favorable aux opérations de l'esprit."—*Hist. Comparée*, &c, tom. ii. p 45.

Mr. Gibbon also has remarked, how much " the learned Society of Port- Royal contributed to establish in France a taste for just reasoning, simplicity of style, and philosophical method " The improvement, in all these respects, of our English writers, during the same period, is, in my opinion, much more remarkable.

[1] *Recherches Philosophiques*, &c , p. 2. Paris, 1818

"Thus, the *Comparative History of Philosophical Systems* is nothing else than a *History of the Variations* of philosophical schools, leaving no other impression upon the reader than an insurmountable disgust at all philosophical researches, and a demonstrated conviction of the impossibility of raising an edifice on *a soil so void of consistency, and so completely surrounded by the most frightful precipices.* About what then are philosophers agreed? What single point have they placed beyond the reach of dispute? Plato and Aristotle inquired, What is science? What is knowledge? And we, so many ages after these fathers of philosophy; we, so proud of the progress of human reason, still continue to repeat the same questions, vainly pursuing the same phantoms which the Greeks pursued two thousand years ago."[1]

In reply to this bold attack on the evidence of the moral

---

[1] *Recherches Philosophiques*, &c., pp 58, 59 Paris, 1818.

On the other hand, may it not be asked, if the number of philosophical systems be greater than that of the sects which at present divide the Christian Church? The allusion here made to Bossuet's celebrated *History of the Variations*, shows plainly that the similarity of the two cases had not been overlooked by the ingenious writer, and that the only effectual remedy which, in his opinion, can be applied to either, is to subject once more the reason, both of philosophers and of divines, to the paramount authority of an infallible guide. The conclusion is such as might have been expected from a good Catholic, but I trust that, in this country, it is not likely to mislead many of my readers Some recent conversions to Popery, however, which, in consequence of views similar to those of M de Bonald, have taken place among the philosophers of Germany, afford a proof that, in the present political state of Europe, the danger of a temporary relapse into the superstitions of the Church of Rome, how slight soever, ought not to be regarded as altogether visionary.—See *Lectures on the History of Literature*, by Frederick Schlegel, vol. ii. pp. 65, 88 89, 175, and 187. English Translation, Edinburgh.

[* It is observed by Dr. Mosheim, that "notwithstanding the boasted unity of faith in the Church of Rome, and its ostentatious pretensions to harmony and concord, it was at the time of the Reformation, and is, at this day, divided and distracted with discussions and contests of various kinds The Franciscans and the Dominicans contend with vehemence about several points of doctrine and discipline The Scotists and Thomists are at eternal war . . Nor are the theological colleges and seminaries of learning more exempt from the flame of controversy than the clerical or monastic orders : on the contrary, debates concerning almost all the doctrines of Christianity are multiplied in them without number, and conducted with little moderation"—Maclaine's *Translation*, vol iii pp 462, 463, 2d edition]

* Restored —Ed

sciences, it may suffice to recall to our recollection the state of physical science not more than two centuries ago. The argument of M. de Bonald against the former is, in fact, precisely the same with that ascribed by Xenophon to Socrates against those studies which have immortalized the names of Boyle and Newton, and which, in our own times, have revealed to us all the wonders of the modern chemistry. Whatever contradictions, therefore, may yet exist in our metaphysical doctrines, (and of these contradictions many more than is commonly suspected will be found to be merely verbal,) why should we despair of the success of future ages in tracing the laws of the intellectual world, which, though less obvious than those of the material world, are not less the natural and legitimate objects of human curiosity?

Nor is it at all wonderful that the beneficial effects of metaphysical habits of thinking should have been first perceived in political economy, and some other sciences to which, on a superficial view, they may seem to have a very remote relation; and that the rise of the sap in the tree of knowledge should be indicated by the germs at the extremities of the branches, before any visible change is discernible in the trunk. The sciences, whose improvement during the last century has been generally acknowledged, are those which are most open to common observation; while the changes which have taken place in the state of metaphysics, have attracted the notice of the few alone who take a deep interest in these abstract pursuits. The swelling of the buds, however, affords a sufficient proof that the roots are sound, and encourages the hope that the growth of the trunk, though more slow, will, in process of time, be equally conspicuous with that of the leaves and blossoms.[1]

---

[1] [* The analogy of which I have availed myself in the above paragraph, was suggested to me by the following passage in Descartes "Ainsi, toute la philosophie est comme un arbre, dont les racines sont la Métaphysique, le tronc est la Physique, et les branches qui sortent du tronc sont toutes les autres sciences, qui se réduisent à trois principales, la Médecine, la Mécanique et la Morale j'entends la plus haute et la plus parfaite Morale, qui, présupposant

* Restored —*Ed*

I shall close this part of my Dissertation with remarking, that the practical influence of such speculations as those of Locke and of Bacon is to be traced only by comparing, on a large scale, the state of the human mind at distant periods. Both these philosophers appear to have been fully aware, (and I know of no philosopher before them of whom the same thing can be said,) that the progressive improvement of the species is to be expected less from the culture of the *reasoning powers*, strictly so called, than from the prevention, in early life, of those artificial impressions and associations, by means of which, when once rivetted by habit, the strongest reason may be held in perpetual bondage. These impressions and associations may be likened to the slender threads which fastened Gulliver to the earth; and they are to be overcome, not by a sudden exertion of intellectual force, but by the gradual effect of good education, in breaking them asunder one by one. Since the revival of letters, seconded by the invention of printing, and by the Protestant Reformation, this process has been incessantly going on, all over the Christian world; but it is chiefly in the course of the last century that the result has become visible to common observers. How many are the threads which, even in Catholic countries, have been broken by the writings of Locke! How many still remain to be broken, before the mind of man can recover that moral liberty which, at some future period, it seems destined to enjoy!

une entière connaissance des autres sciences, est le dernier dégré de la sagesse Or, comme ce n'est pas des racines ni du tronc des arbres qu'on cueille les fruits, mais seulement des extrémités de leurs branches, ainsi la principale utilité de la philosophie dépend de celles de ses parties qu'on ne peut apprendre que les dernières."— Préface des *Principes* de la Philosophie.]

DISSERTATION.

PART THIRD.

DISSERTATION.

PART III.

PROGRESS OF ETHICAL AND POLITICAL PHILOSOPHY DURING THE EIGHTEENTH CENTURY.*

CONCLUDING CHAPTER.—A FRAGMENT.

THE slight Historical Sketch which I have now attempted to trace, seems fully to authorize this general inference; that from the Revival of Letters to the present times, the progress of mankind in knowledge, in mental illumination, and in enlarged sentiments of humanity towards each other, has proceeded not only with a steady course, but at a rate continually accelerating When considered, indeed, *partially*, with a reference to local or to temporary circumstances, human reason has repeatedly exhibited the appearance of a pause, if not of a retrogradation; but when its advances are measured upon a scale ranging over longer periods of time, and marking the extent as well as the rapidity of its conquests over the surface of our globe, it may be confidently asserted, that the circle of Science and of Civilisation has been constantly widening since that era.[1] It must

---

* [This was designed (as stated above, p. 202) but never executed, except in the final chapter, now first published, which comprises *Tendencies and Results* The manuscript from which this is printed was thus labelled by Mr Stewart —" The following pages were intended to form the concluding chapter of my *Dissertation* prefixed to the Encyclopædia.—Kinniel, Nov 1816 "—*Editor*]

[1] " Du sein de la féodalité, qui étoit en

be remembered, too, that the obstacles thrown in its way by the crooked policy of Machiavellian statesmen, have generally contributed in the last result, to accomplish those ends which they were intended to defeat,—the *impetus* of the mind, in some cases, forcing for itself a path still shorter and smoother than that in which it was expected to move ; and in others recoiling for a season, to gather an accession of strength for a subsequent spring. Nor must it be overlooked, that in those unfortunate countries where reason and liberality have, for a time, been checked or repressed in their career, the effect has been produced by the influence of despotic power in depriving the people of the means of instruction—in restraining the free communication of mutual lights—and in suppressing or perverting the truths most essential, to human happiness; and consequently, that these apparent exceptions, instead of weakening, tend to confirm the general principles which it has been the chief aim of the foregoing discourse to illustrate.

These reflections naturally carry the thoughts forward, and interest our curiosity in the future fortunes of the human race. A few general observations on this question will not, therefore, I trust, be considered as an improper sequel to the foregoing retrospect.

Before, however, I enter upon this argument, some notice is due to an objection, not unfrequently urged by the disciples of Machiavel and of Hobbes, against the utility of such prospec-

elle même, un système bien moins propre que celui des républiques anciennes au développement de la liberté et à celui de l'esprit humain, sont cependant sorties peu à peu l'abolition presque générale de l'Esclavage, et un tendance vers l'égalité civile qui n'a cessé, qui ne cesse d'agir, et que nous voyons marcher à grands pas à son entier accomplissement La raison publique, gagnant toujours du terrein, a fait des progrès continuels, souvent lents, quelquefois interrompus, mais à la longue surmontant tous les obstacles qui lui étoient opposés, sans se détourner de sa marche, elle a toujours été propageant une répartition plus universelle de l'instruction, ajoutant au trésors des sciences, et malgré quelques vicissitudes momentanées, améliorant nos idées sur la politique, sur la morale, et même, quoiqu'on en dise, sur la religion, qu'elle tend chaque jour, en dépit d'une résistance bien mal calculée à purger de ces impuretés dont la main de l'homme n'a que trop déparé sa divine origine "—*Réflexions sur les Moyens propres à Consolider l'Ordre Constitutionel en France* Par M Xavier de Sade. Paris, 1822.

tive speculations concerning the history of the world. Of what consequence (it has been asked) to the happiness of the existing generation to be told, that a thousand, or even a hundred years hence, human affairs will exhibit a more pleasing and encouraging aspect than at present? How poor a consolation under the actual pressure of irremediable evils! To persons of either of these descriptions I despair of being able to return a satisfactory answer to this question; for we have no common principles from which to argue. But to those who are not systematically steeled against all moral feelings, or who have not completely divested themselves of all concern for an unborn posterity, some of the following may not be unacceptable.[1]

And here I would observe, in the first place,—That if it be grateful to contemplate the order and beauty of the Material Universe, it is so, in an infinitely greater degree, to perceive, amidst the apparent irregularities of the moral world, order beginning to emerge from seeming confusion. In tracing the History of Astronomy, how delightful to see the Cycles and Epicycles of Ptolemy, which drew from Alphonsus his impious censure on the wisdom of the Creator, give way to the perfect and sublime simplicity of the Copernican system! A similar remark may be applied to the discoveries since made by Newton and his followers; discoveries which fully justify what a late eminent writer has said of the argument from final causes for the existence of God, "That it gathers strength with the progress of Human Reason, and is more convincing to-day than it was a thousand years ago."

Is nothing analogous to this to be discovered in the History of Man? Has *no* change taken place in the aspect of human affairs since the revival of letters; since the invention of printing; since the discovery of the New World; and since the Reformation of Luther? Has not the happiness of our species

---

[1] Few, it is to be hoped, would be disposed to close life with avowing the selfish and misanthropical sentiments which Shakespeare has with admirable propriety put into the mouth of Macbeth —

"I'm weary of the sun,
And wish the state of the world were now undone"

Or, as Claudian has expressed the same diabolical feeling —

"Everso juvat orbe mori, solatia letho
Exitium commune dabit"

kept pace, in every country where despotism has not dried up or poisoned the springs of human improvement, with the diffusion of knowledge, and with the triumphs of reason and morality over the superstition and profligacy of the dark ages? What else is wanting, at this moment, to the repose and prosperity of Europe, but the extension to the oppressed and benighted nations around us, of the same intellectual and moral liberty which are enjoyed in this island? Is it possible, in the nature of things, that this extension should not, sooner or later, be effected? Nay, is it possible, (*now* when all the regions of the globe are united together by commercial relations,) that it should not gradually reach to the most remote and obscure hordes of barbarians? The prospect may be distant, but nothing *can* prevent it from being one day realized, but some physical convulsion which shall renovate or destroy the surface of our planet.

It is little more than a hundred years since the following lines were written; at which time they were, in all probability, admired merely as the brilliant vision of a warm and youthful imagination. Already they begin to assume the semblance of a sober philosophical theory; nor is it altogether impossible, that before the end of another century, the most important parts of it shall have become matters of history.

> "The time shall come, when, free as seas or wind,
> Unbounded Thames shall flow for all mankind,
> Whole nations enter with each swelling tide,
> And seas but join the regions they divide,
> Earth's distant ends our glory shall behold,
> And the New World launch forth to seek the Old
> Oh, stretch thy wings, fair Peace, from shore to shore,
> Till conquest cease, and slavery be no more,
> Till the freed Indians in their native groves,
> Reap their own fruits, and woo their sable loves.
> Peru once more a race of kings behold,
> And other Mexicos be roof'd with gold"

In proportion as these and other predictions of the same kind shall be verified; or, in other words, in proportion as the future history of man shall illustrate the inseparable connexion between the diffusion of knowledge and that of human happiness, will not the argument from final causes, for *benevolent* as well as *systematical* design in the moral world, gain an accession of strength, analogous to what it has already gained from the physical discoveries of modern science; and will not an experimental reply be obtained to the most formidable of those cavils which, of old, gave birth to the Manichean hypothesis; and which have, in all ages, been justly regarded as the chief stronghold of the Epicurean theology?[1]

The foregoing observations relate solely to the influence of the doctrine in question, on *individual* happiness. When considered, however, as a *practical principle*, animating and guiding our conduct as members of society, this doctrine opens some views of still higher importance.

I have already hinted, that the Epicurean idea which ascribes entirely to chance the management of human affairs, is altogether irreconcilable with the belief of a progressive system of order and happiness The aim of the policy, accordingly, which is dictated by the lessons of this school, is to leave as little as possible to the operation of natural causes; and to guard with the utmost solicitude against whatever may disturb the artificial mechanism of society, or weaken the authority of those prejudices by which the multitude may more easily be held in subjection. The obvious tendency of these principles is to damp every generous and patriotic exertion, and to unite the timid and the illiberal in an interested league against the progressive emancipation of the human mind. A firm conviction, on the contrary, that the general laws of the moral, as well as of the material world, are wisely and beneficently ordered for the welfare of our species, inspires the pleasing and animating persuasion, that by studying these laws, and accommodating to them our political institutions, we may not only be led to conclusions which no reach of human sagacity could have attained, unassisted by the steady guidance of this polar light, but may reasonably enjoy the satisfaction of considering ourselves, (according to the sublime expression of the philoso-

[1] See Note F F F.

phical emperor,) as *fellow-workers with God* in forwarding the gracious purposes of his government. It represents to us the order of society as much more the result of Divine than of human wisdom; the imperfections of this order as the effects of our own ignorance and blindness; and the dissemination of truth and knowledge among all ranks of men as the only solid foundation for the certain though slow amelioration of the race. Such views, when under the control of a sound and comprehensive judgment, cherish all the native benevolence of the mind, and call forth into exercise every quality both of the head and the heart, by which the welfare of society may be promoted.

I have been led into this train of thinking, by a controversy which has been frequently agitated, during the last fifty years, with respect to the probable issue of the present state of human affairs. The greater part of writers, resting their conclusions chiefly on the *past* history of the world, have taken for granted, that nations, as well as individuals, contain within themselves the seeds of their decay and dissolution;—that there are limits prescribed by nature to the attainments of mankind, which it is impossible for them to pass; and that the splendid exertions of the two preceding centuries in arts, in commerce, and in arms, portend an approaching night of barbarism and misery. The events which we ourselves have witnessed since the period of the American Revolution, have been frequently urged as proofs, that the reign of Science and of Civilisation is already drawing to a close.

In opposition to this very prevalent belief, a few, and but a few, philosophers have ventured to suggest, that the experience of the past does not authorize any such gloomy forebodings;—that the condition of mankind at present differs, in many essential respects, from what it even was in any former age; and that, abstracting entirely from the extravagant doctrine of some of our contemporaries about the indefinite *perfectibility* of the race, the thick cloud which at present hangs over the civilized world, affords no solid argument for despairing of its future destiny.

In the course of those splenetic epistles which were published, a few years ago, from the late King of Prussia to M. d'Alembert, the former of these systems is strenuously inculcated; and it leaves on the mind of the reader an impression of so unsatisfactory and discouraging a nature, as affords of itself no inconsiderable presumption against its truth.[1] The same system is insinuated more or less directly in the writings of most of our modern sceptics; and, as it is unfortunately but too much favoured, on the one hand, by Atheistical or Epicurean prejudices; and, on the other, by that prostitution of religious professions to the purposes of political faction, which has disgraced the present age, it has found numerous, and warm, and powerful advocates among very different descriptions of individuals. It is much to be regretted, that the greater part of those who have opposed it, have suffered themselves to be carried by their enthusiasm, or by their love of paradox, so far towards the other extreme, that they have added weight and authority to the opinion which they wished to explode. Even the grave and philosophical Price has indulged himself in some conjectures concerning the future state of society, which it is difficult to peruse without a smile; nor is it possible to acquit his illustrious correspondent Turgot, of some tendency to the exaggerations of a heated fancy in his benevolent speculations on the same subject. The following outline of his philosophical and political creed, sketched, and perhaps heightened in its colouring, by the masterly hand of one of his most intimate friends, will sufficiently confirm this remark. Making due allowances, however, for these amiable blemishes, how congenial is its general spirit and character to all the best feelings of our nature!

"But is it possible that men will ever conform themselves, in general, to views suggested by sound reason? M. Turgot

---

[1] "L'imperfection tant en morale qu'en physique est le caractere de ce globe que nous habitons; c'est peine perdue d'entreprendre de l'éclairer, et souvent la commission est dangereuse pour ceux qui s'en chargent. Il faut se contenter d'être sage pour soi, si on peut l'être, et abandonner le vulgaire à l'erreur, en tâchant de le détourner des crimes qui dérangent l'ordre de la société."—See the whole passage, Œuv. Post tom. ii. p 66. See also the same vol, p 71; also pp 83, 84.

not only believed that it *is* possible, but he regarded a *constant susceptibility of improvement*[1] as one of the characteristical qualities of the human race. The effects of this susceptibility, always increasing, appeared to him to be infallible. The invention of printing has undoubtedly co-operated with it powerfully, and has rendered a retrograde movement impossible; but this invention was itself a consequence of the taste for reading which had been previously diffused over Europe. The press is by no means the only method now known of multiplying copies; and if it had escaped the ingenuity of the first inventors of the art, they could not have failed to discover some other expedient for accomplishing their purpose. This constant susceptibility of improvement he conceived to belong both to the race and to the individual. He believed, for example, that the progress of physical science and of the art of education, together with improvements in the methods of scientific investigation, or with the discovery of methods yet unknown, would render men capable of an increased accumulation of knowledge, and of combining its materials more extensively and variously

---

[1] I have substituted this circumlocution instead of the word *perfectibilité* which is employed in the original, because the latter word conveys very different ideas to a French and to an English ear. In the French language, it ought to be remarked, there is no verb corresponding to the English verb *improve*, but *perfectionner;* nor any substantive but *perfectionnement*, by which the word *improvement* can possibly be translated. When the French writers, accordingly, represent a constant *perfectibility* as one of the characteristical qualities of our race, they mean nothing more than this, that no limit can be set to the possible improvement of society, a proposition which no philosopher, whether English or French, has yet ventured to dispute. The writers, on the other hand, who have transplanted this doctrine into England, have frequently expressed themselves, as if they conceived that man, both in his individual and political capacity, was destined at last to attain to the *actual perfection of his being,*—an error into which some of them appear to have been partly led by the later extravagances of Condorcet. The ridicule which has been lavished on this last supposition, has been justly merited by those who have given it any countenance; but it ought not to be extended to such a writer as Turgot, and still less to the older philosophers of France, by whom it has been used. I do not know at what period it was first introduced, but it is at least as old as the publications of Buffon, of Rousseau, and of Charles Bonnet, according to whom this *perfectibility* is the characteristic which essentially distinguishes man from the brutes.—See *Bonnet*, tom viii p. 333.

together: He believed also, that their moral sense was susceptible of a similar progress towards perfection.

"According to these principles every useful truth would necessarily at one period or another be generally known and adopted by mankind. All the errors sanctioned by time would gradually disappear, and be replaced by just and enlightened conclusions. And this progress, going on from age to age, if it has any limit, has certainly none, which, in the present state of our knowledge, it is possible to assign.

"He was convinced that the perfection of the social order would necessarily produce one no less remarkable in morals, and that men will continually grow better, in proportion as they shall become more enlightened. He was anxious, therefore, that instead of attempting to graft the virtues of mankind on their prejudices, and to support them by enthusiasm or by exaggerated principles, philosophers would endeavour to convince men, by addressing themselves both to their reason and to their feelings, that a regard to self-interest ought to incline them to the practice of the gentle and the peaceful virtues; and that their own happiness is inseparably connected with that of their fellow-creatures. Neither the fanaticism of liberty, nor of patriotism, appeared to him to be virtuous motives of action; but if these sentiments were sincere, he considered them as respectable qualities of great and elevated minds, which it was proper to enlighten rather than to inflame. He dreaded always, that, if subjected to a severe and philosophical examination, they might be found to originate in pride or the desire of superiority; that the love of liberty might sometimes be, at bottom, a wish for an ascendant over our fellow-citizens, and the love of our country a desire of the personal advantages connected with its greatness; and he fortified himself in this belief, by observing, of how little importance it was to the multitude to possess an influence in public affairs, or to belong to a great and formidable nation.

"He did not doubt that every age, in consequence of the progress of agriculture, of the arts and of the sciences, would increase the enjoyments of all the different classes of society;

would diminish their physical evils; and would furnish the means of preventing or mitigating the misfortunes which may appear to threaten them. The ties which unite nations are every day strengthened and multiplied. In a short period, all the productions of nature, and all the fruits of human industry in different parts of the globe, will become the common inheritance of the human race; and one day or other, all mankind will acknowledge the same principles, possess the same means of information, and combine their exertions for the progress of reason and the happiness of the species.

"M. Turgot saw that the fundamental principles of legislation and of government had already been perceived and recognised by various enlightened writers. He saw that the nature and object of political institutions, the duties of governors and the rights of the governed, were now very generally understood. But he was far from thinking that a system of legislation, regulated by these principles,—a system where the object of government and the rights of individuals were steadily kept in view, had yet been formed or conceived in all its perfection. Time alone and the progress of knowledge could conduct us, not to reach this ultimate limit, but to approximate to it continually. He hoped that the day would come, when men, convinced of the folly of opposing nation to nation, force to force, passion to passion, and crime to crime, would learn to listen with attention to what reason may dictate for the welfare of humanity. Why should not the science of Politics, founded as it is, in common with all the other sciences, on observation and reasoning, advance gradually to perfection in proportion as observations are made with greater delicacy and correctness, and as reasonings are conducted with greater depth and sagacity? Shall we dare to fix a limit to the attainments of genius, cherished by a better education; exercised from infancy in forming more extensive and varied combinations; and accustomed to employ, with address, modes of investigation at once more easy and more general? Let us consider what may be expected from the invigorated powers of that understanding, which we may presume, from the experience of the past, is destined yet to perform wonders; and let us console ourselves for not being witnesses of these fortunate times, by the pleasure of anticipating them in idea; and, if possible, by the still more sublime satisfaction of having contributed to accelerate (were it but by a few moments) the arrival of this too distant era.

"It was thus that, far from believing knowledge to be fatal to mankind, M. Turgot considered the faculty of acquiring it as the only effectual remedy against the evils of life; and as the true justification of that order (imperfect, indeed, to our eyes, but tending always to correct its imperfections) which he observed in human affairs, and in that part of the universe with which we are connected."[1]

I have quoted this passage at length, because it illustrates strongly, when considered in connexion with the events that have since taken place in France, the extreme danger of exhibiting such Utopian pictures of human affairs, as may be supposed, by the most remote tendency, to inflame the passions of the multitude;—a caution more peculiarly necessary in addressing those who have a leaning to that Theory of Morals which resolves the whole of virtue into *Utility*. Engrossed with the magnitude of the beneficent ends which they believe themselves forwarding, men lose gradually all moral discrimination in the selection of means, and are hurried by passions, originally grafted on the love of their country and of mankind, into enormities which would appal those ordinary profligates who act from the avowed motives of interest and ambition. Some of those, it is certain, who professed the enthusiastic sentiments which have just been stated, are accused of having connected themselves, after the overthrow of the French monarchy, with the most violent revolutionary proceedings; and in our own country, during the distractions of the seventeenth century, we know what torrents of blood were shed without remorse by a set of fanatics, who, while they were dreaming that the reign of the saints on earth and the kingdom of the Messias were at hand, found themselves under the iron sceptre of a usurper.[2]

[1] [*Turgot's Life*, by Condorcet.—*Ed*]
[2] With respect to the French Revolution, the fact is more peculiarly remarkable, as the few individuals then

These considerations, however, while they forcibly recommend the calm and dispassionate exercise of our reason in the formation of our practical principles, and illustrate the danger of trusting ourselves to the guidance of imagination, even when warmed by our sublimest moral emotions, afford no reason for rejecting the truth on account of the errors with which it is liable to be blended, or for sacrificing at once all the hopes which both morality and religion encourage us to cherish, to a cold and comfortless system, equally fatal both to public and to private virtue. It is prudent, at least, as well as philosophical, before we embrace opinions so melancholy in their consequences, to consider what the arguments are which are generally urged in their defence.

On this head it will not be necessary for me to insist long, as these arguments rest chiefly on the puerile supposition of an analogy between the natural and political body; or on an empirical retrospect of the past history of mankind, unaccompanied with any consideration of the important peculiarities which so advantageously distinguish the present times. The late celebrated Father Boscovich is the only person, as far as I know, who has attempted a direct proof that the human mind was already at the limit (if, indeed, that limit be not already passed) of its progressive improvement; and even he, by the very mode of reasoning he employs, seems to acknowledge that appearances are in favour of the opposite supposition This reasoning of Boscovich deserves to be mentioned, as one of the most remarkable instances that can be produced, as a misapplication of mathematical theory to the business of human life It occurs in his succinct but masterly commentary on the Latin poem of Benedictus Stay, *De Systemate Mundi;* and is

---

surviving of the school of Turgot and of Quesnai were, in the first instance, so zealously and systematically attached to the old monarchical constitution, that they exposed themselves, during the year 1788, to a very general *odium*, by remonstrating loudly against the Convocation of the States-General, and by the warnings they addressed to those in power, of the confusions in which they were likely to involve their country by subjecting questions of such incalculable moment to the discussions of men so little acquainted with the Theory of Government and the principles of Political Economy.

introduced on occasion of some verses in which the poet seems to express himself favourably to the opposite opinion. "But, for my part," says Boscovich, "my mind, more prone to augur ill than well of the future, is overcast with gloomy presages; presages in which I am farther confirmed by some *Geometrical* considerations afterwards to be explained."[1] Accordingly, he has annexed to the poem an appendix, containing what he calls a *Geometrical Prophecy;* in which he assumes a straight line A B to express the times, and certain ordinates to express the corresponding *states* of knowledge; the curve to which these ordinates belong, receding from the axis A B, or approaching to it, according as the lines denoting the *states* increase or diminish. It is hardly necessary to add, that from the general decrease of the *increments*, during the thirty years preceding the date of his prophecy, he anticipates a succession of *decrements* as about to follow, till the curve expressing the states and vicissitudes of knowledge, shall intersect the axis, and recede from it on the opposite side, with an acceleration growing in proportion to the increase of the distances.[2]

[1] "At mihi contra ad infausta, quæ multo frequentius accidunt, prona mens, animo formidinem incutit. . Quod autem pertinet ad progressum in ætate mox subsecutura, est mihi indicium quoddam a Geometria petitum, quod itidem deteriora divinare jubeat, de quo in Supplemento.'—[Tom i p 93, *seq.* —*Ed.*]

[2] " Si superius decimum septimum sæculum, et primos hujusce decimi octavi annos consideremus quam multis, quam præclaris inventis fœcundum extitit id omne tempus? Quod quidem si cum hoc præsenti tempore comparentur, patebit sane, eo nos jam devenisse, ut fere permanens quidem habeatur status, nisi etiam regressus jam cœperit Qui enim progressus in iis, quæ Cartesius in algebræ potissimum applicatione ad geometriam, Galilæus ac Hugenius, in primis in optica, astronomia, mechanica, invenerunt? Quid ea, quæ Newtonus protulit pertinentia ad analysin, ad geometriam, ad mechanicam, ad opticam, ad astronomiam potissimum, quæ ipse, quæ Leibnitius, quæ universa Bernoulliorum familia in calculo infinitesimali vel inveniendo, vel promovendo prodiderunt. Quam multa ea sunt, cujus ponderis, quantæ utilitatis ? At ea omnia centum annorum circiter intervallo prodierunt, initio quidem plurima confertim, tum sensim pauciora ab annis, jam triginta vix quidquam adjectum est. Aberratio luminis, et nutatio axis accessit astronomiæ, dimensio, graduum ad Telluris formam geographiæ, mira electricorum phenomenorum series, causis tamen adhuc fere latentibus, Physicæ, et si qua alia sunt ejusmodi, quæ sane cum prioribus illis tantis harum disciplinarum incrementis comparari nullo modo possunt. An non igitur eo devenimus, ut incrementis decrescentibus, brevi debeant decrementa

To this reasoning of Boscovich it will not be expected that I should attempt a serious answer; and as to the analogical argument drawn from growth, decline, and mortality of the human body, it is so manifestly grounded on a verbal quibble, that a logical refutation of it is impossible. The only point on which it seems of importance to enlarge, is the essential difference between the present state of society, and any which has occurred in the preceding ages of the world; and on this view of the subject, which forms the very hinge of the controversy, very little stress has hitherto been laid by the advocates for either side of the question. Mr. Gibbon, indeed, in his reflections on the fall of the Roman Empire in the West, has alluded slightly to the changes introduced into the art of war, by the invention of gunpowder, and the consequent improvement in the science of fortification; but as he has passed over entirely various other circumstances of far greater moment—in particular, he has passed over the effects produced by the *invention of printing*, without the co-operation of which, all the other causes he mentions would be insufficient to justify his general conclusions,—I shall, therefore, take this opportunity of illustrating these effects at some length; for, although I have touched on the subject already in a former publication, I have not attempted in that work to examine it with the accuracy which its importance deserves [1]

succedere, ut curva illa linea, quæ exprimit hujus literaturæ statum ac vices, iterum ad axem deflexa delabatur, et præceps ruat?"—[Tom. i. p. 353.—*Ed*]

[1] In an eloquent and philosophical discourse pronounced before the Magistrates of Geneva, on the 20th of June 1814, the author (M. Simonde de Sismondi) has attempted, with great ingenuity and plausibility, to shew, that from the earliest authentic records of the human race, the progress of the world in reason, in virtue, in knowledge, and in civilisation, has been constant and uninterrupted, exhibiting, he acknowledges, on many occasions, the most unequivocal and melancholy symptoms of retrogradation *in particular regions*, but continually embracing a wider and wider circle of the inhabitants of the globe. He even goes so far as to represent the establishment of this cardinal truth as the proper aim of the *Philosophy of History* The object which I have in view at present is comparatively confined, extending no further than to the history of our species during the last three centuries I am far, however, from being disposed to call in question the justness of his very pleasing conclusions. On the contrary, the reasonings which follow are perfectly in unison with his speculations, and so far as they go, tend to confirm, instead

Nor let the following remarks be accused as savouring of what is now sarcastically called *the New Philosophy*. They coincide entirely with the prophetic language of Scripture,[1] as well as with the views of a writer, whose sanguine predictions of invalidating his general argument.—*De la Philosophie de l'Histoire, Discours prononcé devant les Magistrats et le Peuple de la République de Genève, après la Distribution Annuelle des Prix du Collège.* Par J. C. L Simonde de Sismondi Londres, 1814

It is consolatory to compare the spirit of this discourse with a very beautiful but melancholy passage from a prior publication of the same author "Cette immense richesse littéraire des Arabes que nous n'avons fait qu'entrevoir, n'existe plus dans aucun des pays où les Arabes et les Mussulmans dominent Ce n'est plus là qu'il faut chercher ni la renommée de leurs grands hommes, ni leurs écrits Ce qui s'en est sauvé est tout entier entre les mains de leurs ennemis, dans les couvents de moines, ou les bibliothèques des rois de l'Europe. Et cependant ces vastes contrées n'ont point été conquises; ce n'est point l'étranger qui les a dépouillées de leurs richesses, qui a anéanties leur population, qui a détruit leurs lois, leurs mœurs, et leur esprit national. La poison étoit au-dedans d'elles, il s'est développé par lui-même, et il a tout anéanti.

"Qui sait si, dans quelques siècles, cette même Europe, où le règne des Lettres et des Sciences est aujourd'hui transporté, qui brille d'un si grand éclat, qui juge si bien les temps passés, qui compare si bien le règne successif des littérateurs et des mœurs antiques, ne sera pas déserte et sauvage comme les collines de la Mauritanie, les sables de l'Egypte, ou les vallées de l'Anatolie ? Qui sait si, dans un pays entièrement neuf, peut-être dans les hautes contrées d'où découle l'Orenoque ou la fleuve des Amazons, peut-être dans cette enceinte jusqu'à ce jour impénétrable des montagnes de la Nouvelle Hollande, il ne se formera pas des peuples avec d'autres mœurs, d'autres langues, d'autres pensées, d'autres religions, des peuples qui renouvelleront encore une fois la race humaine, qui étudiront comme nous les temps passés, et qui, voyant avec étonnement que nous avons existé, que nous avons su ce qu'ils sauront, que nous avons cru comme eux à la durée et à la gloire, plaindront nos impuissans efforts, et rappelleront les noms des Newton, des Racine, des Tasse, comme exemples de cette vaine lutte de l'homme pour atteindre une immortalité de renommée que la destinée lui refuse "—*De Litter du Midi de l'Europe,* tom. i pp 76, 77 , à Paris, 1813

[1] It may not be improper to observe here that this improvement in the condition of mankind is represented in the sacred writings, not as the consequence of such a miraculous interposition of Providence as was dreamed of by the Cromwellian Millenarians; but as the natural effect of the progress and diffusion of knowledge, resulting from a more enlarged and liberal intercourse among the different nations "Many (it is said) shall go to and fro, and knowledge shall be increased." [Dan xii. 4.] An expression so very congenial in its spirit to that of Bacon's writings, that Montucla has mistaken the Latin version of it for one of Bacon's Aphorisms, and has quoted it as such in the title page of his History of Mathematics *Multi pertransibunt et augebitur Scientia.* The same mistake is committed by Baillet in his Life of Descartes. See book ii chap. 11, end of the chapter (Part i p 149)

concerning the progress of experimental knowledge have been already verified with an almost prophetic precision. "And surely (says Bacon) when I set before me the condition of these times, from the height of men's wits; the excellent monuments of ancient writers which as so many great lights shine before us: THE ART OF PRINTING: THE TRAVERSED BOSOM OF THE OCEAN AND OF THE WORLD: the leisure wherewith the civilized world abounds, and the inseparable quality that attends time itself, which is ever more and more to disclose truth, I cannot but be raised to the persuasion that the learning of this third period of time, blessed beyond former times by sacred and divinely inspired Religion, will far surpass the learning of Greece and of Rome. if men will but well and wisely know their own strength and weakness, and instead of tearing and rending one another with contradictions, and, in a civil rage, bearing arms and waging war against themselves, will conclude a peace, and with joint forces, direct their strength against nature herself, and take her high towers, and dismantle her fortified holds,[1] and thus enlarge the borders of man's dominion, so far as Almighty God of his goodness shall permit."

If this be indeed the spirit of *the New Philosophy*, little are *their* feelings to be envied who still adhere to the Old. It is observed by Aristotle of Anaxagoras, (the first philosopher of the Ionian School, who taught, in opposition to the prevailing atheism of his countrymen, that all things were made and governed by one supreme mind,) *that he talked like a sober man among drunkards.* The same thing may be said of the author of the above passage, when contrasted with the crowd of *vulgar*, or rather of *courtly* politicians.

---

[1] To prevent any misapprehension with respect to the import of these figurative expressions, it is necessary for me to remind my readers, that, according to Bacon himself, "the only way of subduing Nature is by studying and obeying her laws." *Natura enim non imperatur, nisi parendo;*— a maxim which will be found to hold equally true, when applied to the Moral and to the Material World; and which might form the text of a volume on the subject of Political Economy.

The effects of printing in promoting the improvement of society may be referred to two general heads:—

First, Its effect in securing and accelerating the progress of knowledge.

Secondly, Its effect in facilitating the diffusion and dissemination of knowledge among the lower orders.

I. § 1. That the press, by multiplying the copies of every literary production, diminishes to a great degree, or rather reduces to nothing, the chances of a repetition of those accidents which have deprived us of so many of the ancient discoveries, is sufficiently obvious. The waste of intellectual labour which has been thus occasioned in the past history of the world, it is difficult to imagine. Not only have many of the most valuable compositions of Greece and Rome perished in the wreck of ages; but hardly can a vestige be traced of those scientific attainments which, in earlier times, drew to Egypt, from every part of the civilized earth, all those who were anxious to be initiated in the mysteries of Philosophy. The infinite multiplication of books by means of the press; the universal diffusion of the accomplishments of reading and writing; and the stability which the different known languages give to each other by Dictionaries and Translations, (all of them consequences of the same happy invention,) seem to remove completely, in future, the possibility of a similar misfortune. In this respect, the effect of printing may be compared to that of a *catch* in a machine, by which we are enabled to suspend occasionally our exertions, without losing any part of the advantage we have gained.[1]

---

[1] The permanency which the press bestows on the productions of genius, and the security which is thereby added to the reign of civilisation, have not escaped the notice of the ingenious and philosophical poet, to whose pleasing anticipations of the future history of the world I had formerly occasion to allude. The reflections of *Stay* on this head afford him an opportunity, which he appears to me to have managed with peculiar skill, of resuming the subject of his work, after a long digression

Ex aliquo at quoniam jam tempore novimus artem
Eductricem operum servatricemque laborum
Ingenii, possint diffundi ut multiplicati
Præla per et formas, lateque per ora virorum
Spargier, et tanto renovarier incremento
Interdum, ex uno ut nascantur millia multa;
Longius idcirco nobis promittimus ævum,
Immensosque licet quoque spes extendere in annos,
Temporis et sævos labentis temnere morsus

In consequence of this circumstance the progress of knowledge, however slow, can scarcely fail to be at all times advancing; and the longer the progress continues, the more rapid (ceteris paribus) will be the rate at which it proceeds: For, " new knowledge (as Mr. Maclaurin well remarks) does not consist so much in our having access to a new object, as in comparing it with others already known; observing its relations to them, or discerning what it has in common with them, and wherein their disparity consists. Thus, our knowledge is vastly greater than the sum of what all its objects separately could afford; and, when a new object comes within its reach, the addition to our knowledge is the greater the more we already know; so that it increases, not as the new objects increase, but in a much higher proportion."

§ 2. The progress of knowledge must be wonderfully aided by the effect of the press in multiplying the number of scientific inquirers, and in facilitating *a free commerce of ideas* all over the civilized world; effects, not proportioned merely to the increased number of cultivated minds, thus engaged in the search of truth, but to the powers of this increased number, combined with all those arising from the division and distribution of intellectual labour.

Mr. Smith, in his *Inquiry into the Nature and Causes of the Wealth of Nations,* has explained with great ingenuity, and with a peculiar felicity of illustration, in what manner the division of labour, in the mechanical arts, increases the productive powers of human industry. The advantage, however, which from the operation of analogous circumstances is gained in the pursuits of knowledge, is incomparably greater. Different individuals are led, partly by original temperament, partly by early education, to betake themselves to different studies; and hence arise those infinitely diversified capacities of mind, which

---

Magnis præsertim pro rebus, nam levo queis est
Pondus, ferre queant ætatem haud denique multam
Sed quæ fata manent nostros ventura labores ?
Quantum ævi mihi fas optare ? Quid augurer ausis

His immortali de tempore ? Concitat istis
Me quoque promissis, et mentem numine Phœbus
Implet, et incessit, jam, quo feror, impetus
ire est —[Lib. II. v. 92, *seq* —*Ed.*]

we commonly call diversities of *genius*. These diversities of genius, in consequence of the connexions and affinities among the various branches of human knowledge, are all subservient one to another; and when the productions to which they give birth are, by means of the press, contributed to a common stock, all the varieties of intellect, natural and acquired, among men are combined together into one vast engine, operating with a force daily accumulating, on the moral and political destiny of mankind.

But the circumstance which constitutes the chief distinction between the division of labour in the mechanical arts, and in those pursuits which are more purely intellectual, is the small and limited number of individuals who in the former can be made to co-operate in the execution of the same design; whereas in the latter, a combination is formed, by means of the press, among all the powers which genius and industry have displayed, in the most remote nations and ages. How many trains of sublime or of beautiful imagery have been kindled in the minds of our modern poets by sparks struck out by Homer or by Hesiod! And, (not to speak of the mighty effects produced on the Christian world by the truths which Revelation has brought to light,) what an accession to the happiness of many individuals now existing on the globe, might be traced to the Meditations of Marcus Aurelius, to the Maxims of Confucius, or to the familiar sayings which fell from the lips of Socrates on the streets of Athens!

In those scientific researches, however, which rest on observation and experiment solely, and where the reasoning powers are alone concerned, a mutual communication of lights is of still greater importance, than in works of imagination and of sentiment. In studies of the former kind, the force of a single mind, how matchless soever its superiority, can accomplish but little, when compared with the united exertions of an ordinary multitude; and some of the most liberal contributions to our present stock of knowledge have proceeded from men, who, while they were following the impulse of a merely speculative curiosity, were unconsciously sowing the seeds of a rich harvest for a distant posterity. In this point of view, the value of one new fact, or of any new hint, however insulated it may appear at present, may eventually be incalculably great; insomuch, that he who has the merit of ascertaining the one, or of suggesting the other, puts in motion the wheel of a machine, to whose possible effects no human sagacity can fix a limit.

Nor is it only in the sublimer exertions of imagination or of invention, that we may trace the effect of this division of labour on human improvements. What Mr. Smith has so well remarked concerning the astonishing multiplicity of arts which contribute their share in furnishing the peasant with his coarse woollen coat, will be found to apply, in a far greater degree, to the homely furniture of his comparatively unfurnished understanding. In the former instance, something like an enumeration may be attempted; but who can form the most *distant* conception of the number of minds which must have united their lights in discovering and in familiarizing to the apprehensions of the multitude, those elementary truths in morality, in physics, in mechanics, and in natural history, which the lowest of the people, in the actual state of European society, derive insensibly from parental instruction, and from the observation and imitation of the arts which are practised around them!

§ 3. The improvements of the mind, however, must not be estimated merely by the accumulation of facts, or of theoretical conclusions. To correct an error, or to explode a prejudice, is often of more essential importance to human happiness, than to enlarge the boundaries of science.—That there has been a most remarkable progress in this last respect, in all the Protestant states of Europe, since the era of Luther's Reformation, cannot be disputed; nor do I see how it can be explained, but by the effect of a general diffusion of knowledge in gradually clearing truth from that admixture of error, which it had contracted from casual associations, fostered by an ambitious priesthood, during the long period of Gothic darkness. Of this progress, a very striking instance has occurred, in our own northern part of the island, in the rapidity with which the popular belief of witchcraft has vanished in the course of a very few years.[1]

It was not till the year 1735, that a bill, which was passed into a law, was brought into the House of Commons, "repealing the former statutes against witchcraft, Scots as well as English, and prohibiting all future prosecutions for that crime." The law, however, it is well known, gave great offence to a large proportion of very respectable individuals in this country, on account of its daring impiety; and yet, such has since been the progress of information and of good sense, that scarcely does a relic now exist of a superstition, which, sixty or eighty years ago, triumphed very generally over the reason of men of the most unquestionable talents and learning.[2]

---

[1] In the year 1697, we meet with a warrant, issued by the Privy Council of Scotland, to certain Commissioners to try twenty-four persons, male and female, suspected and accused of witchcraft The result was, that seven of the number were consigned to the flames. A trial for the same supposed crime took place at the Dumfries Circuit, as late as 1709, and in the year 1722, a person was brought to the stake, (under the same charge,) in consequence of the sentence of a Sheriff-depute in a remote county.

[2] In the other parts of the United Kingdom, traces of the same superstition continued till an equally recent date. "I know not," says Dr. Parr, "that Judge Powel was a weak or a hard-hearted man, but I do know, that in the Augustan age of English literature and science, when our country was adorned by a Newton, a Halley, a Swift, a Clarke, and an Addison, this Judge, in 1712, condemned Jane Wenman at Hertford, who, in consequence perhaps of a controversy that arose upon her case, rather than from any interposition of Powel, was not executed, and that four years afterwards, he, at Huntingdon, condemned for the same crime, Mary Hicks and her daughter Elizabeth, an infant of eleven years old, who were executed on Saturday the 17th of July 1716. At the beginning of the same century, of which English philosophers and English scholars talk with triumph, two unhappy wretches were hung at Northampton, the 17th of March 1705; and, upon July the 22d, 1712, five other witches suffered the same fate at the same place."—*Characters of Charles James Fox*, p 370

Sir William Blackstone, in mentioning the 9th of George II., which enacts, that no prosecution shall, for the future, be carried on against any person for conjuration, witchcraft, sorcery, or enchantment, does not venture to pronounce decidedly that such crimes exist only in the imaginations of the ignorant and credulous; but, with his usual caution, contents himself with applying to them the epithet of *dubious*. "All prosecutions," he observes, "for these *dubious crimes*, are now at an end."

At a considerably earlier period, a similar regulation had taken place in France, during the reign of Louis XIV, owing probably to the extraordinary

The comparatively harmless prejudices with respect to dreams, apparitions, the second sight, and the influence of the stars on human affairs, have, in like manner, all vanished from Scotland, within the space of a hundred years; and it is of importance to remark, that the extinction of these prejudices, as well as of the popular belief in witchcraft, has been accomplished, not by any new reasonings or discoveries unknown to our forefathers; but by the silent and slow influence of moral causes, more easy to be conceived than enumerated. I shall mention only the effects of Locke's writings, in recommending to parents a more judicious and vigilant attention to the casual associations, and to the natural credulity of the infant mind. The circulation among the lower ranks of society, of a certain portion of historical information and of experimental science, and (in consequence of these and other circumstances) the universal prevalence of a spirit of free inquiry and discussion, unexampled in former times.

With this effect of printing in gradually undermining esta-

extent to which prosecutions for sorcery had been carried in that country On this subject there is a curious insinuation of President Hénault, which the high and deserved reputation of the writer induces me to transcribe. "Urbain Grandier, atteint et convaincu, du crime de magie par une commission particulière, est brulé vif 1634 On demandoit à La Peyrère, auteur des Préadamites, mais qui d'ailleurs a composé une histoire de Grœenland fort estimée, pourquoi il y avoit tant de sorciers dans le nord; c'est, disoit-il, que les biens de ces prétendus sorciers, que l'on fait mourir, sont en partie confisqués au profit de leurs juges."—*Abrégé Chronologique*

It is observed by Lord Hailes, that in the ancient history of Scotland, there is little mention of *magic*, and scarcely any vestiges of *witchcraft*. The first capital punishment for *witchcraft* (according to Pinkerton) was in 1479.

The triumph of this absurd and cruel superstition was reserved for the gloomy fanaticism of the Covenanters "The fanaticism," says Hume, "which prevailed (1650) being so full of sour and angry principles, and so overcharged with various antipathies, had acquired a new object of abhorrence: these were the *sorcerers*. So prevalent was the opinion of witchcraft, that great numbers, accused of that crime, were burnt, by sentence of the Magistrates, throughout all parts of Scotland. In a village near Berwick, which contained over fourteen houses, fourteen persons were punished by fire; and it became a science, everywhere much studied and cultivated, to distinguish a true witch by proper trials and symptoms."—Vol. vii p. 186

According to Beccaria, there have been a hundred thousand witches condemned to die, by tribunals calling themselves Christian.

blished prejudices, the general diffusion of wealth among the lower orders, in consequence of the progress of commerce, has very powerfully co-operated. Without this auxiliary circumstance, the art of printing must have been a barren invention; for before men read, they must have felt the desire of knowledge,—and this desire is never strong, till a certain degree of independence and of affluence is obtained.

But it is chiefly by the active intercourse which commerce gives rise to between different and remote regions, that it contributes to the intellectual and moral improvement of mankind; —diminishing, all over the world, the virulence of national antipathies and of religious bigotry, and uniting men together by their common interest. In this respect its influence extends to classes of the people who have neither leisure nor inclination to cultivate their minds. To be able to profit by reading, a man must previously possess a certain measure of information, as well as of speculative curiosity; but to profit by travelling, (so far at least as is sufficient to open and to humanize the mind,) requires only the use of the external senses; and the lights which it affords are much stronger and more permanent in their effect, than those which are derived from books. What, indeed, is that large portion of book-learning which relates to the institutions and manners of foreign countries, but an imperfect substitute for actual experience and observation?

The ocean, which at first view appears intended to separate the inhabitants of this globe into unconnected and mutually unknown communities, is found, in the progress of the commercial arts, to be a part of the same mighty plan of which I have now been attempting to trace the outlines; and the winds, with all their irregularities, conspire to the accomplishment of its beneficent purposes. "They blow from all quarters, (as Seneca has well observed,) that the peculiar advantages of every different climate might contribute to the enjoyments of mankind in common; that an interchange of good offices should extend over the whole earth; and that nations the most remote should be connected together by their mutual wants and their mutual interests." "A wonderful provision (he beautifully adds) for augmenting the sum of human happiness; if the bad passions of men did not convert the blessings of heaven into instruments of hostility and destruction."[1]

II. The remarks which I have offered on this last head lead me to consider more particularly, the effects of the press in diffusing knowledge among the great body of a people.

Prior to the invention of printing, the advantages of education must have everywhere been exclusively confined to a small and privileged circle; the discoveries which from time to time genius and industry added to the stock of human information, must have spread by very slow degrees among the multitude; and the labours of inquisitive men must have been carried on, without any of the aids now afforded by the extensive and rapid communication of literary intelligence. Of this some idea may be formed from the gratitude with which Pliny mentions the name of Asinius Pollio, a celebrated orator and patron of letters in the Augustan age, who first opened a library at Rome for the general use of the city; and thereby (to use the words of Pliny) "made the genius of individuals the property of the public."[2] With how much greater force does this expression apply to the inventor of an art, which multiplies copies in proportion to the number of readers, and enables us, at all times, and in all places, to appropriate to ourselves the accumulated experience and wisdom of the remotest nations and ages!

In order, however, to give to this invention that full and universal efficacy which alone can render it a blessing to the world, it is necessary that the lower orders should have easy access to the elementary parts of education; in particular, that they should be taught to read at so early a period of life that they may afterwards have recourse to books as an enjoyment rather than as a task. It was for this reason, that I formerly mentioned the general diffusion of wealth produced by commerce, as a circumstance which had co-operated powerfully

---

[1] [*Nat. Qu* v 18?—*Ed*]

[2] "Asinii Pollionis hoc Romæ inventum, qui primus Bibliothecam dicando ingenia hominum rem publicam fecit." —*Hist Nat.* l xxxv c. 1

with the press in enlightening modern Europe. But this alone is not sufficient; for beside the general ease and security of the people, some arrangements are necessary, on the part of government, to provide the proper means of public instruction.[1] In England, there cannot be a doubt, that the mass of the community enjoy the comforts of animal life much more amply than in Scotland; and yet, in the latter country, in consequence of the footing on which our parochial schools are established, there is scarcely a person of either sex to be met with who is not able to read, and very few who do not possess, to a certain degree, the accomplishments of writing and of cyphering; whereas, in the southern part of the island, there are many parishes where the number of those who can read, bears a very inconsiderable proportion to the whole body of inhabitants. In most other parts of Europe, (not excepting France itself,[2]) the proportion is probably much less

[1] The following passage, written seventy years ago, by an eminent English prelate, exhibits a pleasing contrast to the spirit displayed at a much more recent period, by some political divines, in both parts of the island "Till within a century or two, all ranks were nearly on a level as to the learning in question. THE ART OF PRINTING APPEARS TO HAVE BEEN PROVIDENTIALLY RESERVED TILL THESE LATTER AGES, AND THEN PROVIDENTIALLY BROUGHT INTO USE, AS WHAT WAS TO BE INSTRUMENTAL FOR THE FUTURE IN CARRYING ON THE APPOINTED COURSE OF THINGS. The alterations which this art has already made in the face of the world, are not inconsiderable. By means of it, whether immediately or remotely, the methods of carrying on business are, in several respects, improved, *knowledge has been increased;* and some sort of literature is become general. And if this be a blessing, we ought to let the poor, in their degree, share it with us If we do not, it is certain that they will be upon a greater disadvantage, on many accounts, especially in populous places, than they were in the dark ages, for they will be more ignorant, comparatively with the people about them, than they were then. And therefore to bring up the poor in their former ignorance, would be, not to keep them in the same, but to put them into a lower condition of life than what they were in formerly. Nor let people of rank flatter themselves, that ignorance will keep their inferiors more dutiful and in greater subjection to them, for surely there must be danger that it will have a contrary effect, under a free government such as ours, and in a dissolute age."—*Sermon preached at Christchurch*, London, 1745, by Bishop Butler

[2] In a book of M. Daubenton's, entitled *Instruction pour les Bergers*, (published in 1782,) there is a passage from which we may form some estimate on this subject In the first *Lesson*, the question is proposed, (for the book is written in the form of a catechism,) "Whether it be necessary that a shepherd should be able to read?" To this

The universal diffusion of the rudiments of knowledge among the Scottish peasantry, when contrasted with the prevailing ignorance of the same class on the other side of the Tweed, affords a decisive proof that, in such a state of society as ours, some interference on the part of government is indispensably necessary to render the art of printing, even when aided by the congenial tendencies of commerce, completely effectual in extending the benefits of elementary education to the mass of a large community. How much more might be accomplished by a government aiming systematically, and on enlightened principles, at the instruction and improvement of the multitude, it is not easy to imagine.

But although a great deal yet remains in prospect to animate our exertions, much, it must be remembered, has already been done. The number of readers is, I believe, in almost every part of the island, rapidly on the increase; and to *these* useful knowledge is every day presented, in a form more and more accessible, and more and more alluring. One circumstance (which has, indeed, been operating more or less during two centuries, but of which, in our times, the influence has been more peculiarly remarkable) is not undeserving of notice; I mean the wide circulation of occasional pamphlets,[1] and of

question the following answer is given:—" A shepherd who can read possesses a superior facility in acquiring information, but this cannot be considered as indispensably necessary, since he may employ others to read to him what has been published for his instruction He will be able, perhaps, to find some person in the same house with him, or at least in the neighbourhood, who can read, and who will be willing to instruct him The schoolmasters in the village will do it for a trifling gratification, and sometimes a spirit of charity or of patriotism, will induce the curates or surgeons to undertake this good office "

In one of the Revolutionary Assemblies of France, a proposition was made, which, if I recollect right, passed into a law, that no soldier should be promoted to the rank of an officer who was not able to read and to write. Is it surprising that a people, among whom such a law was thought necessary, should so easily have become the dupes and instruments of the most shallow and unprincipled demagogues? And yet a very distinguished English statesman, in one of his Parliamentary speeches, drew an argument against the expediency of popular instruction, from the atrocities committed by the Parisian mobs, whom he described as "mobs composed of *savans* and *philosophers.*"

[1] The first appearance of pamphlets in England is said to have been at the time of the Protestant Reformation, and there can be little doubt that they contributed more to the establishment of

periodical journals,—those cheap and enticing vehicles of instruction, which, adapting themselves to the rapid and often capricious changes of general curiosity, communicate, even to the indolent and the dissipated, some imperfect knowledge of the course of political events, and of the progress of scientific improvement. The peculiar attractions which periodical journals derive from their miscellaneous nature, and the quick regularity of their succession, may be judged of from the extent to which this branch of bookselling speculation has been carried both here and on the Continent. A late very eminent mathematician, Mr. Simpson of Woolwich, speaking of a monthly publication, begun in the year 1704, under the title of the *Ladies' Diary;* and which, among a humble collection of *Rebuses, Conundrums,* and *Acrostics,* includes some very ingenious mathematical problems, has asserted, that "for upwards of half a century, this small performance, sent abroad in the poor dress of an Almanack, has contributed more to the study of the mathematicks than half the books written professedly on the subject." What, then, may we suppose to be the influence of periodical miscellanies conducted by men of superior genius and learning, and which address the public on subjects more immediately connected with the business of human life? "The people (as an eloquent writer observes) cannot be profound; but the truths which regulate the moral and political relations of man are at no great distance from the surface. The great works in which discoveries are contained cannot be read by the people, but their substance passes, through a variety of minute and circuitous channels, to the shop and the hamlet. The con-

---

the new opinions than all the profound and systematical works which issued from the press about the same period, in opposition to the corruptions of the Romish Church. During the reign of Charles I, (which is called by Dr. Johnson the age of pamphlets,) the same weapons were zealously employed by the contending parties, and although their influence was not such as to prevent a final appeal to violence and arms, yet they certainly accustomed men to the exercise of reason on those questions which had formerly been decided by a reference to authority, and gave a beginning to that freedom of political discussion, to which England is indebted for that system of regulated liberty which was established at the Revolution

version of the works of unproductive splendour into latent use and unobserved activity, resembles the process of nature in the external world. The expanse of a noble lake, the course of a majestic river, imposes on the imagination by every impression of dignity and sublimity. But it is the moisture that insensibly arises from them, which, gradually mingling with the soil, nourishes all the luxuriance of vegetation, fructifies and adorns the surface of the earth."

Some other causes, too, which naturally result from the general progress of society, have conspired with the circumstances now under our consideration, in extending and quickening the circulation of knowledge. The multiplication of high roads, and the establishment of regular posts and couriers, have virtually contracted the dimensions of the countries where they have been introduced; communicating to them the advantages arising from the animated discussions and the contagious public spirit of a small community, combined with the order and stability connected with a population spread over an extended territory. The happy invention of the telegraph, and the application of the steam-engine to the purposes of navigation, afford a proof that the resources of human ingenuity for accomplishing these important purposes, have not been completely exhausted by our forefathers.

I am aware of an objection which presents itself to these speculations; that the *inventions* which I have dignified with the name of *improvements,* are equally instrumental in the circulation of error and of truth. But, not to insist on the advantage which the latter may confidently be expected to gain over the former, wherever there is a perfectly fair field opened for controversy, it will be found (as I already hinted) that the collision and contention of different and opposing prejudices, are the means which, in the ordinary course of events, bring mankind at last to a general acquiescence in reasonable and just opinions. The *first* effect may, indeed, be a tendency to universal doubt; but so distempered and unnatural a state of mind cannot long exist in the great body of a people; and it is far less adverse to the progress of reason and humanity, than a spirit of unenlightened and intolerant bigotry. The active friends of truth and of mankind, however few in number, will continue, slowly but surely, to extend their conquests, and will gradually draw to their standard, the unprejudiced and uncorrupted judgments of the rising generation. In the meantime, it is comfortable to reflect, that inconsiderable as the body of such men may appear to be in the eye of the world, they are more firmly and zealously united together than any other description of individuals can possibly be;—united not merely by the same benevolent intentions, but by the systematic consistency and harmony of those doctrines which it is their common aim to illustrate. Mr. Hume himself has stated it as an undoubted principle, "that Truth is *one* thing, but errors numberless;" and we may add, as an obvious and important consequence of his maxim, that, while the advocates for false systems are necessarily at variance with each other, and have a tendency to correct each other's deviations, a combination is no less necessarily formed among all those minds which are sincerely engaged in the pursuit of solid and of useful knowledge.

I need scarcely add, that all I have now said proceeds on the supposition, that an unlimited freedom of the press is enjoyed. In consequence of the restraints imposed on it in some parts of Europe, the invention of printing has hitherto continued not merely sterile and useless, but it may be questioned, whether it has not furnished those who have monopolized the use of it, with additional resources for prolonging the reign of superstition and darkness. The objections which are commonly urged to such an unlimited freedom might, in a great measure, be obviated by a regulation (perfectly compatible with the principles of genuine liberty) which, while it left the press open to every man who was willing to avow his opinions, rendered it impossible for any individual to publish a sentence without the sanction of his name.

Such then are the effects of the press in accelerating the progress and in promoting the diffusion of knowledge. But what is the tendency of these two circumstances with respect to the *wellbeing* of society ? It is to this test, that, in all our political arguments, the ultimate appeal must be made.

It has been often alleged, that in proportion as knowledge advances and spreads, originality of genius decays ; and that no proof more certain of its decline can be produced, than the multiplication of commentators, compilers, and imitators. Hence it has been inferred, that the diffusion of knowledge is not even so favourable to the advancement of science as might at first be imagined ; the advantages resulting from the growing crowd of authors being more than compensated by the decreasing value of their productions. Voltaire has, I think, placed this fact in its proper light by remarking, that " original genius occurs but seldom in a nation where the literary taste is formed. The number of cultivated minds which there abound, like the trees in a thick and flourishing forest, prevent any single individual from rearing his head far above the rest. Where trade is in few hands, we meet with a small number of overgrown fortunes in the midst of a general poverty. In proportion as it extends, opulence becomes general, and great fortunes rare. It is precisely," he adds, " because there is at present much light and much cultivation in France, that we are led to complain of the want of original genius."

In this remark of Voltaire it seems to be implied, that the apparent mediocrity of talent in times of general cultivation is partly owing to the great number of individuals who, by rising above the ordinary standard, diminish the effect of those who attain to a still greater eminence. But granting the fact to be as it is commonly stated, and that the diffusion of knowledge is accompanied with a *real* decline in point of genius, no inference can be deduced from this in favour of less enlightened ages ; for the happiness of mankind at any particular period is to be estimated, not by the materials which it affords for literary history, but by the degree in which a capacity for intellectual enjoyment is imparted to the great body of the people. In this point of view, what a spectacle does our own country afford during the last forty years ! Literary societies, composed of manufacturers and of agriculturists, arising in various provincial towns of the kingdom, and publishing, from time to time, their united contributions; and a multitude of female authors, in every department of learning and of taste, disputing the palm of excellence with the most celebrated of their countrymen Amidst such a profusion of productions, there will, of course, be much to call forth and to justify the severity of criticism; but the Philosopher will trace with pleasure, in the humblest attempts to instruct or to amuse the world, the progress of science and of philanthropy in widening the circle of their operation; and even where he finds little to admire or to approve, will reflect with satisfaction, that the delights of study, and the activity of public spirit, are not confined to the walks of academical retirement, or to the great theatre of Political Ambition. To those who consider the subject in this light, the long list of obscure and ephemeral publications which swell the monthly catalogue in our literary journals, is not without its interest; and to collect the rays of fancy or the sparks of tenderness in the rude verses of a milkmaid or of a negro girl, affords an occupation not less gratifying to the understanding and the heart, than to catch the inspirations of more cultivated and exalted minds.

Nor let it be supposed that any danger is to be apprehended from this quarter, in withdrawing men from active professions and imperious duties to the pursuits of literature and science. It is wisely ordered by Providence, in every age and in every state of society, that while a small number of minds are captivated with the luxury of intellectual enjoyments, the great mass of the people are urged, by motives much more irresistible, to take a share in the busy concerns of human life. The same wisdom which regulates the physical condition of man, watches also (we may presume) over all the other circumstances of his destiny; and as it preserves invariably that balance of the sexes which is essential to the social order, so it mingles, in their due proportion, the elements of those moral and intellectual qualities on which the wellbeing and stability of the political system depends. To vary these proportions by legislative arrangements is surely not, in any instance, the business of an enlightened statesman; and, least of all, in those cases where his interference may have the effect to bury in obscurity those seeds of genius which are so sparingly sown among the human race, and which, with careful culture, might have ripened into a harvest to improve and to bless generations yet unborn.

These views of the effects resulting from the diffusion of knowledge, in opening to the multitude new sources of refined and ennobling pleasures, become still more satisfactory when we attend to the mighty influence of the same circumstance on public morals, and on the good order of society.

In almost every species of manual labour, a considerable part of the day must be devoted to relaxation and repose; and, unless some exercise or amusement be provided for the mind, these intervals of bodily rest will naturally be filled up with intemperance and profligacy The task of speculative thinking is far beyond the capacities of those who have not received the advantages of education ; and, where the curiosity has not been excited, and the faculties exercised in early life, is of all mental efforts the most painful. Such, at the same time, is the activity of our nature, that a state of perfect listlessness is the completion of suffering, and seldom fails to suggest some expedient, however desperate, for a remedy. Hence the indolence and languor of the savage, when his animal powers are unemployed, and hence that melancholy vacuity of thought, which prompts him to shorten his hours of inaction with the agitations of gaming and the *delirium* of intoxication. All this applies more or less to uncultivated minds in every state of society; and it can be prevented only by those early habits, which render some degree of intellectual exertion a sort of want or necessary of life. Nor is this mere theory. Wherever the lower orders enjoy the benefits of education, they will be found comparatively sober and industrious; and in many instances, the establishment of a small library in the neighbourhood of a manufactory has produced a sensible and rapid reformation in the morals of the workmen The cultivation of mind, too, which books communicate, naturally inspires that desire and hope of advancement which, in all the classes of society, is the most steady and powerful motive for economy and industry. The book-societies in different parts of Scotland, England, and America, abundantly illustrate and confirm the truth of these observations.

But it is not merely as a resource against "the pains and penalties of idleness" that habits of reading and of thinking are favourable to the morals of the lower orders. The great source of the miseries and vices which afflict mankind is in their prejudices and speculative errors; and every addition which is made to the stock of their knowledge has a tendency to augment their virtue and their happiness.

The exceptions which seem to contradict the universality of this remark will, I am persuaded, be found, upon examination, to be rather apparent than real.

It cannot be disputed, that there are various prejudices, both of a political and of a moral nature, which a philosopher who wishes well to the world, would touch with a very cautious and timorous hand. But, in cases of this sort, it will always be found, that the prejudice derives its *utility* from some mixture which it involves of important truth. The truth, probably, in the first instance, from its congeniality with the principles of human nature, served to consecrate the prejudice; but frequently this order of things comes to be reversed, and the prejudice to perform the office of an auxiliary to the truth. Where such a combination exists, the indulgence shewn to the error is but an additional mark of homage to the truths with which it is associated in the imaginations of the multitude.

With a view to the solution of the same difficulty, it may be further observed, that the progress of scepticism ought not to be confounded with the progress of knowledge; nor a want of fixed principles with a superiority to vulgar prejudices. There is, indeed, a certain species of *scepticism* which is a necessary step towards the discovery of truth. It is that anxious and unsettled state of mind which immediately succeeds to an implicit faith in established opinions; and which seems to have been intended as a *stimulus* to our inquiries, till doubt gives way to the permanent convictions of reason. But it is not in *this* sense that the word scepticism is now commonly understood, or in which I would be understood to employ it at present. On the contrary, the scepticism to which I object, is a mental disease much more nearly allied to the infectious credulity of fashion, than to a spirit of free and bold inquiry; and which, so far from indicating that manliness and vigour of intellect which result from a consciousness of the connexion between *knowledge and power,* is a relapse towards the ignorance, the inefficiency, and the imbecility of childhood.

With these apparent exceptions, I do not hesitate to repeat it as an incontrovertible proposition, that the discovery of *philosophical truth,* (under which term I comprehend the *general* laws of nature both in the physical and moral worlds,) always adds to the sum of human happiness. That there are many *particular facts,* a knowledge of which tends only to disturb our tranquillity, without bringing any accession of good to compensate the uneasiness which it occasions, our daily experience is sufficient to demonstrate. But the *general* laws of nature, as far as they have yet been traced, appear all so wisely and beneficently ordered, as to entitle us to reject, on this very principle, every theory which represents either the physical or the moral order of the universe, in a light calculated to damp the hopes, or to slacken the exertions of the friends of humanity. This is a conclusion, not resting on hypothesis, but on an incomparably broader induction from particular instances, than what serves as the foundation of any one of the *data* on which we reason in natural philosophy.

It is from this tendency of philosophical studies to cultivate habits of *generalization,* that their chief utility arises, accustoming those who pursue them to regard events, less in relation to their own immediate and partial concerns, than to the general interests of the human race; and thus rendering them at once happier in themselves, and more likely to be extensively useful in the discharge of their social duties

Among the manifold obstacles which stand in the way of these encouraging prospects, none is nearly so formidable as the selfish and turbulent *impatience* of that unprincipled crowd, who, during every short gleam of sunshine in the political world, never fail to press into the foremost ranks among the friends of reason and humanity. To such men it is of little consequence to contemplate any advantage to mankind, of which themselves are not to reap some immediate share in the benefit; and, accordingly, they are ever eager to hasten to their object, in spite of all the impediments which ancient establishments and deep-rooted opinions may oppose to their progress. The calamitous events which in the first instance resulted from the French Revolution, afford an awful and never to be forgotten comment on the truth of this remark.

These observations naturally lead me to take notice of the mischievous consequences which have, in many instances, been produced by the indiscriminate zeal of some modern philosophers against what they choose to consider as the prejudices of education; a zeal warranted (as has been imagined) by the indefeasible right of every individual to the use of his own *unbiassed* judgment on all questions whatever. It appears to me that this doctrine has been carried to a length, equally inexpedient in the practical result, and inconsistent with the principles of sound philosophy; indeed, hardly less so, than if it were proposed that each individual should be abandoned to the exercise of his own ingenuity in re-inventing all the necessary and useful arts of life. For what is the provision made by nature to secure the progressive improvement of the species, but that every successive generation should build on the experience and wisdom of the former? And although, in this way, a mixture of error *must* be transmitted from one generation to another, yet should parents and instructors refuse to inculcate what appears to their private judgment to be conducive to the happiness of their offspring, from a distrust in the attainments of their own times, when compared with the possible discoveries of future ages, how would it be possible for mankind to advance either in knowledge or in morals? In such an age, more especially as the present, we need not be apprehensive that the errors we communicate will be of long duration. The evil to be dreaded is not implicit credulity, but a general disregard of those moral principles which have been hitherto cherished by the wise and good in all ages of the world.

To the prevalence of the spirit which I am now attempting to oppose, may be traced a looseness and want of system in the modern plans of education, and an inattention to that important part of our constitution, called by philosophers the *Association of Ideas;* a law of the human mind by which Nature plainly meant to put into the hands of every successive generation, the culture of the moral principles, and the formation of the moral habits of those to whom they have given existence. The melancholy consequences to which it sometimes led in times of darkness, only place in a more striking point of view, the happy effects it might produce in times comparatively enlightened; and in the natural progress of the species towards further improvement, its unavoidable inconveniences would become every day less and less perceptible, while the sphere of its utility would keep pace in its enlargement with the diffusion of right principles and of mental cultivation among all the various orders of society. "Opinionum enim commenta delet dies, naturæ judicia confirmat."[1]

That these ideas are not altogether visionary is demonstrated by the proverbial inefficacy of speculative conclusions of the understanding, when opposed to early habit, or even to the fashions of the times An argument is often drawn from this circumstance against the most important truths, as if their evidence or certainty were to be judged of from their influence on the character and manners of those who profess to believe them. The just inference is, that reason considered as a principle of action is of inferior force to habit; and that truth itself can become a steady and uniform motive to human conduct, only by being inculcated so early as to be identified with the essential principles of our constitution Hence the obvious necessity of fortifying the lessons of parental wisdom by early associations and impressions, if we would wish that a progress

---

[1] [At this place Miss Stewart had inserted—" Here my father's own handwriting ceases, the rest is in mine— Maria D Stewart "—*Ed*]

in good morals should accompany the progress of mankind in useful knowledge. In consequence of that law of the human mind which I have just mentioned, combined with the ever active principle of curiosity, a beautiful provision is made on the one hand, for the final triumph of truth over error; and, on the other hand, against the mischief of a sudden revolution in the established habits of mankind And it is the business of a calm and enlightened philosophy in this, as in every other instance, to consult as an oracle the laws and intentions of Nature, contenting itself with aiding and facilitating the means which she has appointed for conducting us, by slow but certain steps, through the future stages of our progress. To loosen with a violent hand the foundations of opinions which "come home to the business and bosoms of men," even when they involve a mixture of prejudices, must be always a hazardous experiment, lest we should weaken the influence of what is true and salutary, in a greater proportion than we are able to correct what is hurtful or erroneous; or, (as it is beautifully expressed in the Sacred Writings,) lest "in pulling up the tares we should pull up the wheat also." For these reasons I have always thought, not only that a religious veneration is due to such fundamental maxims as the united experience of past ages has proved to be essential to the existence of the social order, but that even prejudices which involve a mixture of sound and useful principles, should seldom or ever be attacked directly; and that the philosopher should content himself with exhibiting the truth pure and unadulterated, leaving it to the operation of time and of reflection to secure its future triumph. In this manner the errors which prevail in the world, whether on political or moral subjects, will gradually decay, without ever unsettling the opinions of the multitude, or weakening the influence of those truths that are essential to human happiness; and the scaffolding will appear to vulgar eyes to add to the stability of the fabric, till, the frail materials mouldering into dust, the arch exhibit its simple and majestic form.

APPENDIX.

As a supplement to the foregoing argument, it may not be improper to remark the illustration which it affords of Bacon's maxim that *Knowledge is Power*. It is indeed the only species of power which the people can exercise without the possibility of danger to themselves Under all governments, even the most despotic, the superiority in point of physical force must belong to the multitude; but, like the physical force of the brutes, it is easily held in subjection by the reason and art of higher and more cultivated minds. *Vis consilii expers mole ruit suâ.* In proportion as public opinion becomes enlightened, the voice of the people becomes the voice of reason; or, to use the old proverbial phrase, it becomes the voice of God; and in the same proportion it becomes like the voice of God, unchangeable, irresistible, and omnipotent. It is by truth alone that the multitude, who are otherwise united by a rope of sand, can be led to direct their common efforts to any useful object; and hence the origin and foundation of that infallible secret of state policy, *Divide et impera*. Of the practical efficacy of this secret, examples are not wanting even in our own times, but yet I cannot help thinking that there are symptoms of a growing disposition in men to rally around some general and fundamental principles. The progress indeed would be infinitely more rapid, were it not for the miserable vanity which misleads so many, both in philosophy and in politics, from the standards of those who are willing and able to lead them.

Among the various remarkable effects which have already resulted from the general diffusion of light and liberality in the principal nations of Europe, none is more deserving of attention than the change which has taken place in the language employed by the rulers of mankind in addressing their subjects. "Nothing in the history of the world," said the late Emperor of the French, at the moment of his usurpation, "resembles the close of the eighteenth century;" and the reflection which was everywhere applauded as at once just and profound, seemed to men of sanguine hopes to promise a government in harmony with the prevailing spirit and principles of the times. Had these expectations been realized, he would have saved himself the mortification (whatever might have been the issue of his personal fortunes) of having been the undisputed author of his own ruin. It will be happy for posterity if the sad comment which his history has left on the shortsightedness of his Machiavellian policy, shall leave a lasting impression on the minds of his conquerors.

The most memorable illustration, however, which has yet appeared of the influence of public opinion over the councils of princes, is the manifesto published by the Allied Sovereigns at the gates of Paris [1]

[1] The public and solemn testimony which, on various occasions, has been borne, by those statesmen who are generally supposed not to have been most favourable to popular rights, to the truth and soundness of the most liberal principles of commercial policy, is another important fact which leads to favourable presages with respect to the future This testimony, indeed, has not been always accompanied with a disposition to adopt, at the present moment, the line of conduct suitable to its professions; but it is at least something gained to the good cause, when such public and official homage is rendered to it from all quarters, and encourages the hope that at no distant period the cause itself will be everywhere triumphant The following brief report of a Parliamentary conversation is, in this point of view, not unworthy of a place in this Appendix.*

"The House then resolved itself into a Committee.

"Lord Castlereagh said, that after the full discussion which the late Treaty with Spain, respecting the abolition of the Slave Trade, underwent on a former evening, and the almost unanimous approbation it received, he had little doubt of the assent of the Committee to the proposition growing out of that Treaty, for granting the sum of £400,000. He should, therefore, merely move the resolution to that effect, being ready to answer any subsequent questions which Gentlemen might wish to put to him.

"Mr. Lyttelton said, that it was with reluctance he rose to offer any observations at all calculated to disturb the unanimity which the object of the Treaty so justly obtained. There was no more sincere friend to the progress of that great cause of humanity than he was But he took the opportunity, from instructions that he had received, to ask the noble Lord some questions, materially connected with our commercial intercourse with Spain. He saw by the provisions of that Treaty, that a sum of £400,000 was to be paid by this country, as a *bonus* to the Spanish nation. When we were evincing such a disposi-

* This last paragraph, it may be observed, was written in Mr Stewart's own hand, after March 1821, and before August 1822 The rest of the note was cut from the newspaper —*Ed*

" Inhabitants of Paris! The allied armies are under your walls. The object of their march to the capital of France, is founded on the hope of a sincere and durable pacification with her. For twenty years Europe has been deluged with blood tion to that Government, it could not be inopportune to advert to the state of our commercial relations with that Power. And he must say, from what he was taught to believe, this country was, as to those relations, in a state rather remote from a very cordial amity with Spain. The British merchants were not alone treated with severity, but with a caprice the most destructive to the continuance of a commercial intercourse In the export of cotton goods, one of our principal articles, we were met with a total prohibition. Although he lamented that circumstance, he was still ready to admit that such prohibition could not form the ground of any hostile remonstrance. Woollens and linens were most highly taxed, but in respect to our iron trade, the duties on which were augmented in a proportion of 110 per cent on the value, changes the most sudden were so frequently introduced, that the British merchant had no previous notice, until his vessel entered the ports of that country, although, according to the ancient usage, six months' notice of these changes were given. There were, indeed, instances where cargoes just arrived found a rate of duty so different from what they had a right to expect, that time was not allowed to prevent shipments made on their faith It was of the first consideration—of the very essence of commercial intercourse, that regulations affecting it should never be clandestine. He wished therefore to know, whether up to the present period, any representations had been made to the Spanish Government relative to these severities and restrictions, and whether any modification might be expected in the commercial tariff between the two countries?

" Lord Castlereagh felt a difficulty on the distinct proposition before the House, to hazard a premature explanation on the complicated question of our commercial intercourse with Spain. He sincerely lamented the continuance in that country of those erroneous principles of commerce which were happily exploded in our own. Some indulgence ought, however, to be extended to that error, when it was recollected that for a succession of years those principles were cherished in this country in their fullest vigour, and how long we ourselves had been reaping the bitter fruits of such a policy. Every endeavour had been made to awaken Spain to the adoption of a more enlightened and prosperous system, but he was sorry to add that, from their attachment to a code of restrictions and high duties, no great progress had yet been made in that desirable pursuit With regard to the cotton trade, the admission it had for some time received was a relaxation from the former usage, and therefore the prohibition must be considered as a return to the standard laid down in former treaties, such as it was in the year 1792 The truth was, that we ourselves were embarrassed in our mercantile relations with foreign countries, by our own prohibitive code Still representations as strong as he felt assured the honourable member would wish were made by his Majesty's Government, and nothing would be left untried to convince foreign nations that the freest and most unrestricted intercourse was the certain means to reciprocal advantage. We should, however,

and tears. Every attempt to put an end to these calamities has proved vain, for this reason, that in the very government which oppresses you, there has been found an insurmountable obstacle to peace. Who among you is not convinced of this truth? The Allied Sovereigns desire to find in France a beneficent government, which shall strengthen her alliance with all nations; and, therefore, in the present circumstances, it is the duty of Paris to hasten the general pacification. We await the expression of your opinion, with a degree of impatience proportioned to the mighty consequences which must result from your deliberation. The preservation of your city and of your tranquillity, shall be the object of the prudent measures which the Allies will not fail to take, in concert with such of your authorities as enjoy the general confidence. Troops shall not be quartered on you. Such are the sentiments with which Europe, arrayed before your walls, now addresses you Hasten to justify her confidence in your patriotism and prudence."

To these professions, indeed, it must be owned, that subsequent events exhibit but a melancholy contrast, but this affords no ground for despair in future An instructive lesson has been given to the governed as well as to their governors, and in the course of another century, the latter may find it expedient to carry into practical effect those principles to which they have already been forced to give the solemn sanction of their theoretical authority.

recollect, that at no very remote period, that restrictive system was as strictly exercised between two parts of our own empire, Great Britain and Ireland, as between this kingdom and any foreign nation

"Mr Lyttelton expressed his high satisfaction at the sound and enlightened views of the Noble Lord, and he hailed their annunciation as propitious to the commercial interests of the country. He trusted they would be acted upon in the Councils of the nation, as soon as was compatible with the public expediency What he had principally complained of, in regard to Spain, was the capricious manner in which the change of duties without notification was made."—*Morning Chronicle*, 12th February 1818

NOTES AND ILLUSTRATIONS.

The chief purpose of these Notes and Illustrations, is to verify some of the more important views contained in the foregoing Historical Sketch. The errors into which I have frequently been led by trusting to the information of writers, who, in describing philosophical systems, profess to give merely the general results of their researches, unauthenticated by particular references to the original sources, have long convinced me of the propriety, on such occasions, of bringing under the eye of the reader, the specific authorities on which my statements proceed. Without such a check, the most faithful historian is perpetually liable to the suspicion of accommodating facts to his favourite theories; or of unconsciously blending with the opinions he ascribes to others, the glosses of his own imagination. The quotations in the following pages, selected principally from books not now in general circulation, may, I hope, at the same time, be useful in facilitating the labours of those who shall hereafter resume the same subject, on a scale more susceptible of the minuteness of literary detail.

For a few short biographical digressions, with which I have endeavoured to give somewhat of interest and relief to the abstract and unattractive topics which occupy so great a part of my Discourse, I flatter myself that no apology is necessary, more especially, as these digressions will in general be found to throw some additional light on the philosophical or the political principles of the individuals to whom they relate.

TO DISSERTATION, PART FIRST.—NOTES FROM A TO R

Note A, p 28.

Sir Thomas More, though towards the close of his life, he became "a persecutor even unto blood, defiling with cruelties those hands which were never polluted with bribes,"[1] was, in his earlier and better days, eminently distinguished by the humanity of his temper, and the liberality of his opinions Abundant proofs of this may be collected from his Letters to Erasmus and from the sentiments, both religious and political, indirectly inculcated in his *Utopia*. In contempt for the

[1] Burnet

ignorance and profligacy of the monks, he was not surpassed by his correspondent, and against various superstitions of the Romish church, such as the celibacy of priests, and the use of images in worship, he has expressed himself more decidedly than could well have been expected from a man placed in his circumstances. But *these* were not the whole of his merits. His ideas on Criminal Law are still quoted with respect by the advocates for a milder code than has yet been introduced into this country, and on the subject of toleration, no modern politician has gone farther than his Utopian Legislators.

The disorders occasioned by the rapid progress of the Reformation, having completely shaken his faith in the sanguine speculations of his youth, seem at length, by alarming his fears as to the fate of existing establishments, to have unhinged his understanding, and perverted his moral feelings. The case was somewhat the same with his friend Erasmus, who, as Jortin remarks, "began in his old days to act the zealot and the missionary with an ill grace, and to maintain, that there were *certain* heretics who might be put to death as blasphemers and rioters," (pp 428, 481.) In the mind of Erasmus, other motives, it is not improbable, concurred, his biographer and apologist being forced to acknowledge, that "he was afraid lest Francis, and Charles, and Ferdinand, and George, and Henry VIII., and other persecuting princes, should suspect that he condemned their cruel conduct."—*Ibid* p 481

Something, it must at the same time be observed, may be alleged in behalf of these two illustrious persons *not*, indeed, in extenuation of their unpardonable defection from the cause of religious liberty, but of their estrangement from some of their old friends, who scrupled not to consider as apostates and traitors all those who, while they acknowledged the expediency of ecclesiastical reform, did not approve of the violent measures employed for the accomplishment of that object. A very able and candid argument on this point may be found in Bayle, Article *Castellan*, Note Q.

Note B, p 30

The following short extract will serve to convey a general idea of Calvin's argument upon the subject of usury

"Pecunia non parit pecuniam. Quid mare? quid domus, ex cujus locatione pensionem percipio? an ex tectis et parietibus argentum proprie nascitur? Sed et terra producit, et mari advehitur quod pecuniam deinde producat, et habitationis commoditas cum certa pecunia parari commutarive solet. Quod si igitur plus ex negotiatione lucri percipi possit, quam ex fundi cujusvis proventu, an feretur qui fundum sterilem fortasse colono locaverit ex quo mercedem vel proventum recipiat sibi, qui ex pecunia fructum aliquem perceperit, non feretur? et qui pecunia fundum acquirit, annon pecunia illa generat alteram annuam pecuniam? Unde vero mercatoris lucrum? Ex ipsius, inquies, diligentia atque industria. Quis dubitat pecuniam vacuam inutilem omnino esse? neque qui a me mutuam rogat, vacuam apud se habere a me acceptam cogitat. Non ergo ex pecunia illa lucrum accedit, sed ex proventu. Illæ igitur rationes subtiles quidem sunt, et speciem quandam habent, sed ubi propius expenduntur, reipsa concidunt. Nunc igitur concludo, judicandum de usuris esse, non ex particulari aliquo Scripturæ loco, sed tantum ex æquitatis regula."—Calvini *Epistolæ*

NOTE C, p 43.

The prevailing idea among Machiavel's contemporaries and immediate successors certainly was, that the design of the *Prince* was hostile to the rights of mankind; and that the author was either entirely unprincipled, or adapted his professed opinions to the varying circumstances of his own eventful life. The following are the words of Bodinus, born in 1530, the very year when Machiavel died, an author whose judgment will have no small weight with those who are acquainted with his political writings "Machiavel s'est bien fort mésconté, de dire que l'éstat populaire est le meilleur.[1] et néantmoins ayant oublié sa première opinion, il a tenu en un autre lieu,[2] que pour restituer l'Italie, en sa liberté, il faut qu'il n'y ait qu'un Prince, et de fait, il s'est efforcé de former un éstat le plus tyrannique du monde, et en autre lien[3] il confesse, que l'éstat de Venise est le plus beau de tous, lequel est une pure Aristocratie, s'il en fût onques tellement qu'il ne sçait à quoi se tenir"—(*De la République,* liv vi chap iv Paris, 1576.) In the Latin version of the above passage, the author applies to Machiavel the phrase, *Homo levissimus ac nequissimus*

One of the earliest apologists for Machiavel was Albericus Gentilis, an Italian author, of whom some account will be given afterwards. His words are these "Machiavel, a warm panegyrist and keen assertor of democracy, born, educated, promoted under a republican government, was in the highest possible degree hostile to tyranny. The scope of his work, accordingly, is not to instruct tyrants; but, on the contrary, by disclosing their secrets to their oppressed subjects, to expose them to public view, stripped of all their trappings." He afterwards adds, that "Machiavel's real design was, under the mask of giving lessons to sovereigns, to open the eyes of the people, and that he assumed this mask in the hope of thereby securing a freer circulation to his doctrines."—(*De Legationibus,* lib iii. c ix Lond. 1585.) The same idea was afterwards adopted and zealously contended for by Wicquefort, the author of a noted book entitled the *Ambassador;* and by many other writers of a later date.[4] Bayle, in his *Dictionary,* has stated ably and impartially the arguments on both sides of the question, evidently leaning, however, very decidedly, in his own opinion, to that of Machiavel's apologists.

The following passage from the excellent work of M Simonde de Sismondi on the Literature of the South, appears to me to approach very near to the truth in the estimate it contains both of the spirit of the *Prince,* and of the character of the author "The real object of Machiavel cannot have been to confirm upon the throne a tyrant whom he detested, and against whom he had already conspired; nor is it more probable that he had a design to expose to the people the maxims of tyranny, in order to render them odious. Universal experience made them at that time sufficiently known to all Italy; and that infernal policy which Machiavel reduced to principles, was, in the sixteenth century, practised by every government. There is rather, in his manner of treating it, a universal bitterness against mankind, a contempt of the whole human race, which makes him address them in the language to which they had debased themselves. He speaks to the interests of

---

[1] *Discourses upon Livy*
[2] *Prince,* book i. c ix
[3] *Discourses upon Livy*
[4] See in particular Rousseau, *Du Contrat Social,* liv iii. c. vi.

men, and to their selfish calculations, as if he thought it useless to appeal to their enthusiasm or to their moral feelings."

I agree perfectly with M. de Sismondi in considering the two opposite hypotheses referred to in the above extract, as alike untenable; and have only to add to his remarks, that, in writing the *Prince*, the author seems to have been more under the influence of spleen, of ill-humour, and of blasted hopes, than of any deliberate or systematical purpose, either favourable or adverse to human happiness. The prevailing sentiment in his mind probably was, *Si populus vult decipi, decipiatur* [1]

According to this view of the subject, Machiavel's *Prince*, instead of being considered as a new system of political morality, invented by himself, ought to be regarded merely as a digest of the maxims of state policy then universally acted upon in the Italian courts. If I be not mistaken, it was in this light that the book was regarded by Lord Bacon, whose opinion concerning it being, in *one* instance, somewhat ambiguously expressed, has been supposed by several writers of note (particularly Bayle and Mr Roscoe) to have coincided with that quoted above from Albericus Gentilis. To me it appears, that the very turn of the sentence appealed to on this occasion is rather disrespectful than otherwise to Machiavel's character. "Est itaque quod gratias agamus Machiavelho et *hujusmodi scriptoribus*, qui aperte et indissimulanter proferunt, quid homines facere soleant, non quid debeant." —(*De Aug. Scient.* lib. vii cap ii.) The best comment, however, on these words, is to be found in another passage of Bacon, where he has expressed his opinion of Machiavel's moral demerits in terms as strong and unequivocal as language can furnish. "Quod enim ad *malas artes* attinet, si quis Machiavelho se dederit in disciplinam, qui præcipit," &c. &c. See the rest of the paragraph, (*De Aug Scient.* lib. viii. cap ii.) See also a passage in book vii chap. viii, beginning thus "An non et hoc verum est, juvenes multo minus *Politicæ* quam *Ethicæ* auditores idoneos esse, antequam religione et doctrina de moribus et officiis plane imbuantur, ne forte judicio depravati et corrupti, in eam opinionem veniant, non esse rerum differentias morales veras et solidas, sed omnia ex utilitate —Sic enim Machiavellio dicere placet, *Quod si contigisset Cæsarem bello superatum fuisse, Catilina ipso fuisset otiosior,*" &c &c. After these explicit and repeated declarations of his sentiments on this point, it is hard that Bacon should have been numbered among the apologists of Machiavel, by such high authorities as Bayle and the excellent biographer of Lorenzo de Medicis.

It has been objected to me, that in the foregoing observations on the design of the *Prince*, I have taken no notice of the author's vindication of himself and his writings, in his letter to Zenobius Buondelmontius, annexed to the old English translation of Machiavel, printed at London in 1675 and 1680. In the preface to this translation, we are told, that the letter in question "had never before been published in any language, but lurked for above eighty years in the private cabinets of his own kindred, or the descendants of his admirers in Florence, till, in the Pontificate of Urban VIII, it was procured by the Jesuits and other busy bodies,

---

[1] Many traces of this misanthropic disposition occur in the historical and even in the dramatic works of Machiavel. It is very justly observed by M de Sismondi, that "the pleasantry of his comedies is almost always mingled with gall His laughter at the human race is but the laughter of contempt."

and brought to Rome with an intention to divert that wise Pope from his design of making one of Nicholas Machiavel's name and family cardinal, as (notwithstanding all their opposition) he did, not long after. When it was gotten into that city, it wanted not those who had the judgment and curiosity to copy it, and so at length came to enjoy that privilege which all rare pieces (even the sharpest libels and pasquins) challenge at that court, which is to be sold to strangers, one of which, being a gentleman of this country, brought it over with him at his return from thence in 1645, and having translated it into English, did communicate it to divers of his friends, and by means of some of them, it hath been my good fortune to be capable of making thee a present of it, and let it serve as an apology for our author and his writings, if thou thinkest he need any."

As the translation of Machiavel, from which this advertisement is copied, is still in the hands of many readers in this country, it may not be improper to mention here, that the letter in question is altogether of English fabrication, and (as far as I can learn) is quite unknown on the Continent. It is reprinted at the end of the second volume of Farneworth's Translation of Machiavel's works, 1762, with the following statement prefixed to it [1]

"The following letter having been printed in all the editions of the old translation, it is here given to the reader, though it certainly was not written by Machiavel. It bears date in 1537, and his death is placed by all the best historians in 1530. There are, besides, in it many internal marks, which to the judicious will clearly prove it to be the work of some other writer, vainly endeavouring at the style and manner of our excellent author. The letter is indeed a spirited and judicious defence of Machiavel and his writings, but it is written in a style too inflated, and is utterly void of that elegance and precision which so much distinguish the works of the Florentine secretary."

To the author of this last translation we are farther indebted for a very curious letter of Dr Warburton's, which renders it probable that the forgery was contrived and carried into execution by the Marquis of Wharton. I shall transcribe the letter in Warburton's words.

'There is at the end of the English translation of Machiavel's works, printed in folio, 1680, a translation of a pretended letter of Machiavel to Zenobius Buondelmontius, in vindication of himself and his writings. I believe it has been generally understood to be a feigned thing, and has by some been given to Nevil, he who wrote, if I do not mistake, the *Plato Redivivus*. But many years ago, a number of the famous Marquis of Wharton's papers (the father of the Duke) were put into my hands. Amongst these was the press copy (as appeared by the printer's marks, where any page of the printed letter began and ended) of this remarkable letter in the Marquis's handwriting, as I took it to be, compared with other papers of his. The person who intrusted me with these papers, and who I understood had given them to me, called them back out of my hands. This anecdote I communicated to the late Speaker, and, at his desire, wrote down the substance of what I have told you, in his book of the above edition.—W. Gloucester.' [2]

---

[1] In a book published 1816, this letter is referred to without any expression of doubt as to its authenticity.—See Miller's *Lectures on the Philosophy of Modern History*. Dublin, 1816, p. 17.

[2] In a letter from Warburton to the Reverend

From a memoir read before the French Institute in July 1814, by M. Daunou,[1] it appears that some new light has been lately thrown on the writings and life of Machiavel by the discovery of some of his unpublished papers. The following particulars cannot fail to be gratifying to many of my readers.

"M. Ginguené continue son Histoire de la Littérature Italienne, et vient de communiquer à la classe l'un des articles qui vont composer le septième tome de cette histoire. C'est un tableau de la vie et des écrits de Nicolas Machiavel. La vie de cet écrivain célèbre est le véritable commentaire de ses livres; et jusqu'ici ce commentaire étoit resté fort incomplet. Par exemple, on se bornait à dire, que la république de Florence, dont il étoit le secrétaire, l'avoit chargé de diverses missions politiques à la cour de France, à la cour de Rome, auprès du Duc de Valentinois, auprès de l'Empereur, au camp de Pise, &c &c. M. Ginguené le suit année par année dans toutes ses légations, il en fait connoître l'objet et les principales circonstances. Cette vie devient ainsi une partie essentielle de l'histoire de Florence, et tient même à celle des puissances qui étoient alors en relation avec cette république. On lit peu dans la collection des Œuvres de Machiavel, ses correspondances politiques, qui néanmoins offrent tous ces détails et jettent un grand jour sur son caractère et sur ses intentions. Malheureusement, ce jour lui est peu favorable, et ne nous éclaire que trop sur le véritable sens dans lequel doit être pris son Traité du Prince si diversement jugé. L'une des pièces les plus curieuses et les plus décisives est une lettre qu'il écrivit de la campagne où il s'étoit retiré après la rentrée des Médicis à Florence. Il venoit d'être destitué de ses emplois, impliqué dans une conspiration contre ces princes, il avoit été incarcéré, mis à la torture, et jugé innocent, soit qu'il le fut en effet, soit que les tourmens n'eussent pu lui arracher l'aveu de sa faute. Il trace dans ce lettre le tableau de ses occupations et de ses projets, des travaux et des distractions qui remplissent ses journées. Pour sortir d'une position voisine de la misère, il sent la nécessité de rentrer en grâce avec les Médicis, et n'en trouve pas de meilleur moyen que de dédier le Traité du Prince qu'il vient d'achever à Julien le Jeune, frère du Léon X, et à qui ce Pape avoit confié le gouvernement de Florence. Machiavel croit que son Traité ne peut manquer d'être agréable et utile à un prince, et surtout à un nouveau prince. Quelque tems après, il fit en effet hommage de ce livre, non à Julien, mais à Laurent II. Cette lettre, qui n'est connue en Italie, que depuis peu d'années, étoit encore ignorée en France. M Ginguené l'a traduite; il pense qu'elle ne laisse aucune incertitude sur le but et les intentions de l'auteur du Traité du Prince."—Some farther details on this subject are to be found in a subsequent memoir by the same author, read before the French Institute in July 1815.

Soon after reading the above passage in M. Daunou's *Report*, I received nearly

---

Mr Birch, there is the following passage:—"I told you, I think, I had several of old Lord Wharton's papers. Amongst the rest is a manuscript in his own handwriting, a pretended translation of a manuscript apologetical epistle of Machiavel's, to his friend Zenobio. It is a wonderful fine thing. There are the printer's marks on the manuscript, which makes me think it is printed. There is a postscript of Lord Wharton's to it, by which it appears this pretended translation was designed to prefix to an English edition of his works. As I know nothing of the English edition of Machiavel, I wish you would make this out, and let me know."—*Illustrations of the Literary History of the Eighteenth Century*, intended as a sequel to the *Literary Anecdotes* by John Nichols, vol ii p 88

[1] *Rapport sur les Travaux de la Classe d'Histoire*, &c 1 Juillet, 1814

the same information from the North of Italy. It cannot be so well expressed as in the words of the writer:—

"Pray tell Mr Stewart that there is a very remarkable letter of Machiavel's lately published, written to a private friend at the very time he was engaged in the composition of the *Prince*, and not only fixing the date of that work, but explaining in a manner disgraceful to the author, the use he made of it, in putting it into the hands of the Medicis family. The letter is besides full of character, and describes, in a very lively manner, the life he was leading when driven away from Florence This particular letter may be read at the end of the last volume of Pignotti's *Storia della Toscana*; a book published here, but which was in all the London shops before I came away It is to be found also with several others, which are entertaining and curious, in a new collection published at Florence in 1814, of Machiavel's public dispatches and familiar letters By the way, I must likewise tell Mr. Stewart, that my late reading has suggested a slight criticism upon one expression of his with regard to Machiavel's *Prince*, where he calls it one of the 'latest of his publications.' The fact is, that the three great works were none of them published in his lifetime, nor for four years after his death. They appear to have been all written at the same period of his life, during the eight or ten years of leisure that were forced upon him, and I believe it may be made out from the works themselves, that the *Prince* was composed and finished first of the three, then the *Discourses*, and last of all the *History*. This and the first having been written for the Medicis family, the MSS were in their hands, and they published them, the *Discourses* were printed by the care of some of his personal friends If Mr Stewart wishes to have the proof of all this in detail, I can draw it out without any trouble "

The foregoing passage will be read by many with no common interest, when it is known that it formed part of a letter from the late Francis Horner, written a very few weeks before his death Independently of the satisfaction I feel in preserving a memorial of his kind attention to his friends, at a period when he was himself an object of such anxious solicitude to his country, I was eager to record the opinion of so perfect and accomplished a judge on a question which, for more than two centuries, has divided the learned world; and which his profound admiration of Machiavel's genius, combined with the most unqualified detestation of Machiavel's principles, had led him to study with peculiar care. The letter is dated Pisa, December 17, 1816

The united tribute of respect already paid by Mr. Horner's political friends and his political opponents, to his short but brilliant and spotless career in public life, renders all additional eulogies on his merits as a statesman, equally feeble and superfluous. Of the extent and variety of his learning, the depth and accuracy of his scientific attainments, the classical (perhaps somewhat severe) purity of his taste, and the truly philosophical cast of his whole mind, none had better opportunities than myself to form a judgment, in the course of a friendship which commenced before he left the University, and which grew till the moment of his death But on these rare endowments of his understanding, or the still rarer combination of virtues which shed over all his mental gifts a characteristical grace and a moral harmony, this is not the proper place to enlarge. Never certainly was more completely realized the ideal portrait so nobly imagined by the Roman poet. " A calm devotion to reason and justice, the sanctuary of the heart undefiled, and a breast glowing with inborn honour."

> Compositum jus fasque animi, sanctosque recessus
> Mentis, et incoctum generoso pectus honesto.

Note D, p. 53.

The charge of plagiarism from Bodin has been urged somewhat indelicately against Montesquieu, by a very respectable writer, the Chevalier de Filangieri. "On a cru, et l'on croit peut-être encore, que Montesquieu a parlé le premier de l'influence du climat. Cette opinion est une erreur. Avant lui, le délicat et ingénieux Fontenelle s'étoit exercé sur cet objet. Machiavel, en plusieurs endroits de ses ouvrages, parle aussi de cette influence du climat sur le physique et sur le moral des peuples. Chardin, un de ces voyageurs qui savent observer, a fait beaucoup de réflexions sur l'influence physique et moral des climats. L'Abbé Dubos a soutenu et développé les pensées de Chardin, et Bodin, qui peut-être avoit lu dans Polybe que le climat détermine les formes, la couleur, et les mœurs des peuples, en avoit déjà fait, cent cinquante ans auparavant, la base de son système, dans son livre de la République, et dans sa Méthode de l'Histoire. Avant tous ces écrivains, l'immortel Hippocrate avoit traité fort au long cette matière dans son fameux ouvrage *de l'air, des eaux, et des lieux*. L'auteur de l'Esprit des Lois, sans citer un seul de ces philosophes, établit à son tour un système; mais il ne fit qu'altérer les principes d'Hippocrate, et donner une plus grande extension aux idées de Dubos, de Chardin, et de Bodin. Il voulut faire croire au public qu'il avoit eu le premier quelques idées sur ce sujet, et le public l'en crut sur sa parole." —*La Science de la Législation, ouvrage traduit de l'Italien*. Paris, 1786, tom. i. pp. 225, 226.

The enumeration here given of writers whose works are in everybody's hands, might have satisfied Filangieri, that, in giving his sanction to this old theory, Montesquieu had no wish to claim to himself the praise of originality. It is surprising, that, in the foregoing list, the name of Plato should have been omitted, who concludes his fifth book, *De Legibus*, with remarking, that "all countries are not equally susceptible of the same sort of discipline; and that a wise legislator will pay a due regard to the diversity of national character, arising from the influence of climate and of soil." It is not less surprising, that the name of Charron should have been overlooked, whose observations on the moral influence of physical causes discover as much originality of thought as those of any of his successors.— See *De la Sagesse*, livre i. chap. xxxvii.

Note E, p. 57.

Innumerable instances of Luther's credulity and superstition are to be found in a book entitled *Martini Lutheri Colloquia Mensalia*, &c., first published, according to Bayle, in 1571. The only copy of it which I have seen, is a translation from the German into the English tongue by Captain Henric Bell.—(London, 1652.) This work, in which are "gathered up the fragments of the divine discourses which Luther held at his table with Philip Melanchthon, and divers other learned men," bears to have been originally collected "out of his holy mouth" by Dr. Anthony Lauterbach, and to have been afterwards "digested into commonplaces" by Dr Aurifaber. Although not sanctioned with Luther's name, I do not know that the slightest doubts of its details have been suggested, even by such of his followers as have regretted the indiscreet communication to the public, of his unreserved *table-talk* with his confidential companions. The very accurate Seckendorff has not called in question its authenticity, but, on the contrary, gives it his indirect sanction, by remarking, that it was collected with little prudence, and not less imprudently printed. "Libro *Colloquiorum Mensalium* minus quidem cautè composito et vulgato" (Bayle, article Luther, Note L.) It is very often quoted as an authority by the candid and judicious Dr Jortin.

In confirmation of what I have said of Luther's credulity, I shall transcribe, in the words of the English translator, the substance of one of Luther's *Divine Discourses*, "concerning the devil and his works." "The devil," said Luther, "can transform himself into the shape of a man or a woman, and so deceiveth people; insomuch that one thinketh he lieth by a right woman, and yet is no such matter, for, as St Paul saith, the devil is strong by the child of unbelief. But inasmuch as children or devils are conceived in such sort, the same are very horrible and fearful examples. Like unto this it is also with what they call the *Nix* in the water, who draweth people unto him as maids and virgins, of whom he begetteth devils' children. The devil can also steal children away, as sometimes children within the space of six weeks after their birth are lost, and other children, called *supposititii*, or changelings, laid in their places. Of the Saxons they were called *Killcrops*.

"Eight years since," said Luther, "at *Dessau*, I did see and touch such a changed child, which was twelve years of age, he had his eyes, and all members, like another child, he did nothing but feed, and would eat as much as two clowns were able to eat. I told the Prince of Anhalt, if I were prince of that country, I would venture *homicidium* thereon, and would throw it into the river Moldau. I admonished the people dwelling in that place devoutly to pray to God to take away the devil. The same was done accordingly, and the second year after the changeling died.

"In Saxony, near unto Halberstadt, was a man that also had a *killcrop*, who sucked the mother and five other women dry, and besides devoured very much. This man was advised that he should, in his pilgrimage at Halberstadt, make a promise of the *killcrop* to the Virgin Marie, and should cause him there to be rocked. This advice the man followed, and carried the changeling thither in a basket. But going over a river, being upon the bridge, another devil that was below in the river, called and said, *Killcrop! Killcrop!* Then the child in the basket (which never before spoke one word) answered, Ho, ho. The devil in the water asked further, Whither art thou going? The child in the basket said, I am going towards Hocklestadt to our loving mother, to be rocked. The man being much affrighted thereat, threw the child, with the basket, over the bridge into the water. Whereupon the two devils flew away together, and cried Ho, ho, ha, tumbling themselves over one another, and so vanished."—Pp 386, 387.

With respect to Luther's Theological Disputes with the Devil, see the passages quoted by Bayle, Art *Luther*, Note U.

Facts of this sort, so recent in their date, and connected with the history of so great a character, are consolatory to those who, amid the follies and extravagancies of their contemporaries, are sometimes tempted to despair of the cause of truth, and of the gradual progress of human reason.

Note F, p. 76

Ben Jonson is one of the few contemporary writers by whom the transcendent genius of Bacon appears to have been justly appreciated, and the only one I know of who has transmitted any idea of his forensic eloquence,—a subject on which, from his own professional pursuits, combined with the reflecting and philosophical cast of his mind, Jonson was peculiarly qualified to form a competent judgment. "There happened," says he, "in my time, one noble speaker, who was full of gravity in his speaking. No man ever spoke more neatly, more pressly, more weightily, or suffered less emptiness, less idleness in what he uttered. No member of his speech but consisted of its own graces. His hearers could not cough or look aside from him without loss. He commanded where he spoke, and had his judges angry and pleased at his devotion. The fear of every man that heard him was, that he should make an end." No finer description of the perfection of this art is to be found in any author, ancient or modern.

The admiration of Jonson for Bacon (whom he appears to have known intimately[1]) seems almost to have blinded him to those indelible shades in his fame, to which, even at this distance of time, it is impossible to turn the eye without feelings of sorrow and humiliation. Yet it is but candid to conclude, from the posthumous praise lavished on him by Jonson and by Sir Kenelm Digby,[2] that the servility of the courtier, and the laxity of the judge, were, in the relations of private life, redeemed by many estimable and amiable qualities. That man must surely have been marked by some rare features of moral as well as of intellectual greatness, of whom, long after his death, Jonson could write in the following words:—

"My conceit of his person was never increased toward him by his place or honours, but I have and do reverence him, for the greatness that was only proper to himself, in that he seemed to me ever, by his works, one of the greatest men, and most worthy of admiration, that had been in many ages. In his adversity, I ever prayed that God would give him strength, for greatness he could not want. Neither could I condole in a word or syllable for him, as knowing no accident could do harm to virtue, but rather help to make it manifest."

In Aubrey's anecdotes of Bacon,[3] there are several particulars not unworthy of the attention of his future biographers. One expression of this writer is more peculiarly striking. "In short, all that were *great and good* loved and honoured him." When it is considered, that Aubrey's knowledge of Bacon was derived chiefly through the medium of Hobbes, who had lived in habits of the most intimate friendship with both, and whose writings shew that he was far from being an idolatrous admirer of Bacon's philosophy, it seems impossible for a candid mind, after reading the foregoing short but comprehensive eulogy, not to feel a strong

---

[1] Jonson is said to have translated into Latin great part of the books *De Augmentis Scientiarum*. Dr Warton states this (I do not know on what authority) as an undoubted fact.—*Essay on the Genius and Writings of Pope*.

[2] See his letters to M. de Fermat, printed at the end of Fermat's *Opera Mathematica*, Tolosæ, 1679.

[3] Lately published in the extracts from the Bodleian Library.

inclination to dwell rather on the fair than on the dark side of the Chancellor's character, and, before pronouncing an unqualified condemnation, carefully to separate the faults of the age from those of the individual.

An affecting allusion of his own, in one of his greatest works, to the errors and misfortunes of his public life, if it does not atone for his faults, may, at least, have some effect in softening the asperity of our censures. " Ad literas potius quam ad aliud quicquam natus, et ad res gerendas nescio quo fato contra genium suum abreptus."—*De Aug Scient* lib. viii cap iii.

Even in Bacon's professional line, it is now admitted by the best judges that he was greatly underrated by his contemporaries. " The Queen did acknowledge," says the Earl of Essex, in a letter to Bacon himself, " you had a great wit, and an excellent gift of speech, and much other good learning But *in law*, she rather thought you could make show to the utmost of your knowledge, than that you were deep "

" If it be asked," says Dr. Hurd, "how the Queen came to form this conclusion, the answer is plain. It was from Mr. Bacon's having a great wit, an excellent gift of speech, and much other good learning "—Hurd's *Dialogues*

The following testimony to Bacon's legal knowledge, (pointed out to me by a learned friend,) is of somewhat more weight than Queen Elizabeth's judgment against it · "What might we not have expected,' says Mr Hargrave, after a high encomium on the powers displayed by Bacon in his " Reading on *the Statute of Uses;*"—" what might we not have expected from the hands of such a master, if his vast mind had not so embraced within its compass the whole field of science as very much to detach him from professional studies!"

It was probably owing in part to his court disgrace that so little notice was taken of Bacon, for some time after his death, by those English writers who availed themselves without any scruple of the lights struck out in his works. A very remarkable example of this occurs in a curious, though now almost forgotten book, (published in 1627,) entitled, *An Apology or Declaration of the Power and Providence of God in the Government of the World,* by George Hakewill, D D., Archdeacon of Surrey It is plainly the production of an uncommonly liberal and enlightened mind, well stored with various and choice learning, collected both from ancient and modern authors Its general aim may be guessed at from the text of Scripture prefixed to it as a motto—" Say not thou, what is the cause that the former days are better than these, for thou dost not inquire wisely concerning this," and from the words of Ovid, so happily applied by Hakewill to the " common error touching the golden age,"

" Prisca juvent alios, ego me nunc denique natum
Gratulor "——

That the general design of the book, as well as many incidental observations contained in it, was borrowed from Bacon, there cannot, I apprehend, be a doubt, and yet I do not recollect more than one or two references (and these very slight ones) to his writings through the whole volume. One would naturally have expected that, in the following passage of the epistle dedicatory, the name of the late unfortunate Chancellor of England, who had died in the course of the preceding year, might have found a place along with the other *great clerks* there enumerated " I do not believe that all regions of the world, or all ages in the same region, afford wits always alike, but *this* I think, (neither is it my opinion alone, but of Scaliger, Vives, Budæus, Bodin, and other *great clerks,*) that the wits of these latter ages, being manured by industry, directed by precepts, and regulated by method, may be as capable of deep speculations, and produce as masculine and lasting births, as any of the ancienter times have done. But if we conceive them to be giants, and ourselves dwarfs, if we imagine all sciences already to have received their utmost perfection, so as we need not but translate and comment on what they have done, surely there is little hope that we should ever come near them, much less match them. The first step to enable a man to the achieving of great designs, is to be persuaded that he is able to achieve them; the next not to be persuaded, that whatsoever hath not yet been done, cannot therefore *be* done. Not any one man, or nation, or age, but rather *mankind* is it, which, in latitude of capacity, answers to the universality of things to be known." In another passage Hakewill observes that, "if we will speak properly and punctually, antiquity rather consists in old age, than in the infancy or youth of the world." I need scarcely add, that some of the foregoing sentences are almost literal transcripts of Bacon's words.

The philosophical fame of Bacon in his own country may be dated from the establishment of the Royal Society of London, by the founders of which, as appears from their colleague, Dr Sprat, he was held in so high estimation, that it was once proposed to prefix to the history of their labours some of Bacon's writings, as the best comment on the views with which they were undertaken. Sprat himself, and his illustrious friend Cowley, were among the number of Bacon's earliest eulogists; the latter in an Ode to the Royal Society, too well known to require any notice here; the former in a very splendid passage of his History, from which I shall borrow a few sentences, as a conclusion and ornament to this note.

"For it is not wonderful, that he who had run through all the degrees of that profession, which usually takes up men's whole time; who had studied, and practised, and governed the common law, who had always lived in the crowd, and borne the greatest burden of civil business, should yet find leisure enough for these retired studies, to excel all those men, who separate themselves for this very purpose? He was a man of strong, clear, and powerful imaginations; his genius was searching and inimitable; and of this I need give no other proof than his style itself, which as, for the most part, it describes men's minds, as well as pictures do their bodies, so it did his above all men living. The course of it vigorous and majestical, the wit bold and familiar, the comparisons fetched out of the way, and yet the more easy.[1] In all expressing a soul equally skilled in men and nature."

Note G, p. 80.

The paradoxical bias of Hobbes's understanding is never so conspicuous as when he engages in physical or in mathematical discussions. On such occasions, he expresses himself with even more than his usual confidence and arrogance. Of the Royal Society (*the Virtuosi,* as he calls them, *that meet at Gresham College*) he writes thus: "Conveniant, studia conferant, experimenta faciant quantum

---

[1] By the word *easy,* I presume Sprat here means the native and spontaneous growth of Bacon's own fancy, in opposition to the traditionary similes borrowed by commonplace writers from their predecessors.

volunt, nisi et principiis utantur meis, nihil proficient." And elsewhere. "Ad causas autem propter quas proficere ne paullum quidem potuistis nec poteritis, accedunt etiam alia, ut odium Hobbii, quia nimium libere scripserat de academis veritatem. Nam ex eo tempore irati physici et mathematici veritatem ab eo venientem non recepturos se palam professi sunt." In his English publications, he indulges in a vein of coarse scurrility, of which his own words alone can convey any idea. "So go your ways," says he, addressing himself to Dr Wallis and Dr. Seth Ward, two of the most eminent mathematicians then in England, "you uncivil ecclesiastics, inhuman divines, de-doctors of morality, unasinous colleagues, egregious pair of *Issachars*, most wretched *indices* and *vindices academiarum*; and remember Vespasian's law, *that it is unlawful to give ill language first, but civil and lawful to return it.*"

Note H, p 83.

With respect to the *Leviathan*, a very curious anecdote is mentioned by Lord Clarendon. "When I returned," says he, "from Spain by Paris, Mr Hobbes frequently came to me, and told me that his book, which he would call *Leviathan*, was then printing in England, and that he received every week a sheet to correct, and thought it would be finished within a little more than a month. He added, that he knew when I read the book I would not like it, and thereupon mentioned some conclusions; upon which I asked him why he would publish such doctrines; to which, after a discourse between jest and earnest, he said, '*The truth is, I have a mind to go home.*'" In another passage, the same writer expresses himself thus:—"The review and conclusion of the *Leviathan* is, in truth, a sly address to Cromwell, that, being out of the kingdom, and so being neither conquered nor his subject, he might, by his return, submit to his government, and be bound to obey it. This review and conclusion he made short enough to hope that Cromwell might read it, where he should not only receive the pawn of his new subject's allegiance, by declaring his own obligations and obedience, but by publishing such doctrines as, being diligently infused by such a master in the art of government, might secure the people of the kingdom (over whom he had no right to command) to acquiesce and submit to his brutal power."

That there is no exaggeration or misrepresentation of facts in these passages, with the view of injuring the character of Hobbes, may be confidently presumed from the very honourable testimony which Clarendon bears, in another part of the same work, to his moral as well as intellectual merits. "Mr. Hobbes," he observes, "is a man of excellent parts, of great wit, of some reading, and of somewhat more thinking, one who has spent many years in foreign parts and observations, understands the learned as well as modern languages, hath long had the reputation of a great philosopher and mathematician, and in his age hath had conversation with many worthy and extraordinary men. In a word, he is one of the most ancient acquaintance I have in the world, and of whom I have always had a great esteem, as a man, who, besides his eminent learning and knowledge, hath been always looked upon as a man of probity, and of a life free from scandal."

Note I, p 117

It is not easy to conceive how Descartes reconciled, to his own satisfaction, his frequent use of the word *substance*, as applied to the mind, with his favourite doctrine, that the *essence* of the mind consists in *thought.* Nothing can be well imagined more unphilosophical than this last doctrine, in whatever terms it is expressed; but to designate by the name of *substance,* what is also called *thought,* in the course of the same argument, renders the absurdity still more glaring than it would otherwise have been.

I have alluded, in the text, to the difference between the popular and the scholastic notion of *substance.* According to the latter, the word *substance* corresponds to the Greek word οὐσία, as employed by Aristotle to denote the first of the predicaments, in which technical sense it is said, in the language of the schools, to signify *that* which supports attributes, or which is *subject to accidents.* At a period when every person liberally educated was accustomed to this barbarous jargon, it might not appear altogether absurd to apply the term *substance* to the human soul, or even to the Deity. But, in the present times, a writer who so employs it may be assured, that, to a great majority of his readers, it will be no less puzzling than it was to Crambe, in Martinus Scriblerus, when he first heard it thus defined by his master Cornelius.[1] How extraordinary does the following sentence now sound even to a philosophical ear? and yet it is copied from a work published little more than seventy years ago, by the learned and judicious Gravesande. "Substantiæ sunt aut cogitantes, aut non cogitantes, cogitantes duas novimus, Deum et mentem nostram. Duæ etiam substantiæ, quæ non cogitant, nobis notæ sunt, spatium et corpus."—*Introd. ad Phil.* § 19.

The Greek word οὐσία (derived from the participle of εἰμί) is not liable to these objections. It obtrudes no sensible image on the fancy, and, in this respect, has a great advantage over the Latin word *substantia.* The former, in its logical acceptation, is an extension to Matter, of an idea originally derived from Mind. The latter is an extension to Mind, of an idea originally derived from Matter.

Instead of defining *mind* to be a thinking *substance,* it seems much more logically correct to define it a thinking *being.* Perhaps it would be better still, to avoid, by the use of the pronoun *that,* any substantive whatever, "Mind is *that* which thinks, wills," &c.

The foregoing remarks afford me an opportunity of exemplifying what I have elsewhere observed concerning the effects which the scholastic philosophy has left on the present habits of thinking, even of those who never cultivated that branch of learning. In consequence of the stress laid on the *predicaments,* men became accustomed in their youth to imagine, that in order to know the nature of anything, it was sufficient to know under what *predicament* or *category* it ought to be arranged; and that, till this was done, it remained to our faculties a subject merely of ignorant wonder.[2] Hence the impotent attempt to comprehend under some com-

---

[1] "When he was told a *substance* was that which was *subject to accidents,* then soldiers, quoth Crambe, are the most substantial people in the world." Let me add, that, in the list of philosophical reformers, the authors of Martinus Scriblerus ought not to be overlooked. Their happy ridicule of the scholastic Logic and Metaphysics is universally known, but few are aware of the acuteness and sagacity displayed in their allusions to some of the most vulnerable passages in Locke's Essay. In this part of the work it is commonly understood that Arbuthnot had the principal share.

[2] [So far was this idea carried, at a very recent period, that as late as 1560, we read of a public dispute held at Weimar between two Lutheran divines, Flacius and Strigelius, on the following question :—"Whether original sin is to be placed in the class of *substances* or of *ac-*

mon name (such as that of *substance*) the heterogeneous existences of *matter*, of *mind*, and even of *empty space;* and hence the endless disputes to which the last of these words has given rise in the Schools.

In our own times, Kant and his followers seem to have thought that they had thrown a new and strong light on the nature of *space*, and also of *time*, when they introduced the word *form (forms of the intellect)* as a common term applicable to both Is not this to revert to the scholastic folly of verbal generalization? And, is it not evident, that of things which are *unique* (such as *matter, mind, space, time*) no classification is practicable? Indeed, to speak of classifying what has nothing in common with anything else, is a contradiction in terms It was thus that St Augustine felt when he said, " Quid sit tempus, si nemo quærat a me, scio, si quis interroget, nescio " His idea evidently was, that although he annexed as clear and precise a notion to the word *time* as he could do to any object of human thought, he was unable to find any term more general under which it could be comprehended, and, consequently, unable to give any definition by which it might be explained

NOTE K, p 117.

"Les Méditations de Descartes parûrent en 1641 C'étoit, de tous ses ouvrages, celui qu'il estimoit le plus Ce qui caractérise surtout cet ouvrage, c'est qu'il contient sa fameuse démonstration de Dieu par l'idée, démonstration si répétée depuis, adoptée par les unes, et rejettée par les autres, et *qu'il est le premier où la distinction de l'esprit et de la matière sont parfaitement développée*, car avant Descartes on n'avoit encore bien approfondi les preuves philosophiques de la spiritualité de l'âme."—*Eloge de Descartes*, par M Thomas Note 20.

If the remarks in the text be correct, the characteristical merits of Descartes' *Meditations* do not consist in the novelty of the proofs contained in them of the *spirituality* of the soul, (on which point Descartes has added little or nothing to what had been advanced by his predecessors,) but in the clear and decisive arguments by which they expose the absurdity of attempting to explain the mental phenomena by analogies borrowed from those of matter Of this distinction, neither Thomas, nor Turgot, nor D'Alembert, nor Condorcet, seem to have been at all aware.

I quote from the last of these writers an additional proof of the confusion of ideas upon this point, still prevalent among the most acute logicians. "Ainsi *la spiritualité de l'âme*, n'est pas une opinion qui ait besoin de preuves, mais le résultat simple et naturel d'un analyse exacte de nos idées, et de nos facultés."—(*Vie de M Turgot.*) Substitute for *spirituality* the word *immateriality*, and the observation becomes equally just and important

NOTE L, p. 118

The following extract from Descartes might be easily mistaken for a passage in the *Novum Organon*

" Quoniam infantes nati sumus, et varia de rebus sensibilibus judicia prius tulimus, quam integrum nostræ rationis usum haberemus, multis præjudiciis a veri

cidents ?" Which dispute, ludicrous as it may now seem, appears from Mosheim to have spread so wide a flame as to have retarded, while it lasted, the progress of the Lutheran Reformation —*Mosheim*, translated by Maclaine, vol 1 pp 43, 44]

cognitione avertimini, quibus non aliter videmur posse liberari, quam si semel in vita, de iis omnibus studeamus dubitare, in quibus vel minimam incertitudinis suspicionem reperiemus

"Quin et illa etiam, de quibus dubitabimus, utile erit habere pro falsis, ut tanto clarius, quidnam certissimum et cognitu facillimum sit, inveniamus

"Itaque ad serio philosophandum, veritatemque omnium rerum cognoscibilium indagandam, primo omnia præjudicia sunt deponenda, sive accurate est cavendum, ne ullis ex opinionibus olim a nobis receptis fidem habeamus, nisi prius, iis ad novum examen revocatis, veras esse comperiamus"—*Princ Phil Pars Prima,* §§ lii. lxxv

Notwithstanding these and various other similar coincidences, it has been asserted, with some confidence, that Descartes had never read the works of Bacon "Quelques auteurs assurent que Descartes n'avoit point lu les ouvrages de Bacon, et il nous dit lui-même dans une de ses lettres, qu'il ne lut que fort tard les principaux ouvrages de Galilée"—(*Éloge de Descartes,* par Thomas) Of the veracity of Descartes I have not the slightest doubt; and therefore I consider this last fact (however extraordinary) as completely established by his own testimony. But it would require more evidence than the assertions of those nameless writers alluded to by Thomas, to convince me that he had never looked into an author so highly extolled as Bacon is, in the letters addressed to himself by his illustrious antagonist, Gassendi At any rate, if this was actually the case, I cannot subscribe to the reflection subjoined to the foregoing quotation by his eloquent eulogist "Si cela est, il faut convenir, que la gloire de Descartes en est bien plus grande."

[When the first edition of this Dissertation was sent to the press, I had not an opportunity of consulting either the letters of Descartes, or his life by Baillet, otherwise I should have expressed myself more decidedly with respect to the sentence quoted above from Thomas The following passage is from Baillet — "Quoique Descartes se fut fait une route toute nouvelle, avant que d'avoir jamais oui parler de ce grand homme, (Bacon,) ni de ses desseins, il paroit néanmoins que ses écrits ne lui furent pas entièrement inutiles. L'on voit en divers endroits de ses lettres qu'il ne désapprouvoit point sa méthode," &c [p. 149] In confirmation of this remark, the following references (which I have not yet had it in my power to verify) are quoted in the margin —Tom. ii de *Lettres,* pp 330, 494, and p 324]

Note M, p 131

From the indissoluble union between the notions of colour and extension, Dr Berkeley has drawn a curious, and, in my opinion, most illogical argument in favour of his scheme of idealism,—which, as it may throw some additional light on the phenomena in question, I shall transcribe in his own words.

"Perhaps, upon a strict inquiry, we shall not find, that even those who, from their birth, have grown up in a continued habit of seeing, are still irrevocably prejudiced on the other side, to wit, in thinking what they see to be at a distance from them For, at this time, it seems agreed on all hands, that *colours,* which are the proper and immediate objects of sight, are not without the mind. But then, it will be said, by sight we have also the ideas of extension, and figure, and motion, all which may well be thought *without,* and at some distance from the mind, though colour should not In answer to this, I appeal to any man's experi-

NOTE N.   545

ence, whether the visible extension of any object doth not appear *as near* to him as the colour of that object, nay, whether they do not both seem to be in the same place. Is not the extension we see coloured, and is it possible for us, so much as in thought, to separate and abstract colour from extension? Now, where the extension is, there surely is the figure, and there the motion too. I speak of those which are perceived by sight."[1]

Among the multitude of arguments advanced by Berkeley, in support of his favourite theory, I do not recollect any that strikes me more with the appearance of a wilful sophism than the foregoing. It is difficult to conceive how so very acute a reasoner should not have perceived that his premises, in this instance, lead to a conclusion directly opposite to what he has drawn from them. Supposing all mankind to have an irresistible conviction of the *outness* and distance of extension and figure, it is very easy to explain, from the association of ideas, and from our early habits of inattention to the phenomena of consciousness, how the sensations of colour should appear to the imagination to be transported *out* of the mind. But if, according to Berkeley's doctrines, the constitution of human nature leads men to believe that extension and figure, and every other quality of the material universe, exists only within themselves, whence the ideas of *external* and of *internal;* of *remote* or of *near?* When Berkeley says, "I appeal to any man's experience, whether the visible extension of any object doth not appear *as near* to him as the colour of that object;" how much more reasonable would it have been to have stated the indisputable fact, that the colour of the object appears as *remote* as its extension and figure? Nothing, in my opinion, can afford a more conclusive proof, that the natural judgment of the mind is against the inference just quoted from Berkeley, than the problem of D'Alembert, which has given occasion to this discussion.

NOTE N, p. 138.

It is observed by Dr Reid, that "the system which is now generally received with regard to the mind and its operations, derives not only its spirit from Descartes, but its fundamental principles; and that, after all the improvements made by Malebranche, Locke, Berkeley, and Hume, it may still be called *the Cartesian system.*"—*Conclusion of the Inquiry into the Human Mind.*

The part of the Cartesian system here alluded to is the hypothesis, that the communication between the mind and external objects is carried on by means of *ideas* or *images;—not,* indeed, transmitted *from without,* (as the Aristotelians supposed,) through the channel of the senses, but nevertheless bearing a relation to the qualities perceived, analogous to that of an impression on wax to the seal by which it was stamped. In this last assumption, Aristotle and Descartes agreed perfectly; and the chief difference between them was, that Descartes palliated, or rather kept out of view, the more obvious absurdities of the old theory, by rejecting the unintelligible supposition of *intentional species,* and by substituting, instead of the word *image,* the more indefinite and ambiguous word *idea.*

But there was another and very important step made by Descartes, in restricting the ideal Theory to the *primary* qualities of matter, its *secondary* qualities (of colour, sound, smell, taste, heat, and cold) having, according to him, no more *resemblance* to the sensations by means of which they are perceived, than arbitrary

[1] *Essay toward a New Theory of Vision,* p. 255.

VOL. I.   2 M

sounds have to the things they denote, or the edge of a sword to the pain it may occasion. (*Princ* Pars iv §§ 197, 198) To this doctrine he frequently recurs in other parts of his works.

In these modifications of the Aristotelian Theory of Perception, Locke acquiesced entirely, explicitly asserting, that "the *ideas* of *primary* qualities are resemblances of them, but that the *ideas* of secondary qualities have no resemblance to them at all "—*Essay*, B ii c viii § 15.

When pressed by Gassendi to explain how images of extension and figure can exist in an unextended mind, Descartes expresses himself thus : " Quæris quomodo existimem in me subjecto inextenso recipi posse speciem ideamve corporis quod extensum est Respondeo nullam speciem corpoream in mente recipi, sed puram intellectionem tam rei corporeæ quam incorporeæ fieri absque ulla specie corporea , ad imaginationem vero, quæ non nisi de rebus corporeis esse potest, opus quidem esse specie quæ sit verum corpus, et *ad quam mens se applicet*, sed non quæ in mente recipiatur "—*Responsio de iis quæ in sextam Meditationem objecta sunt*, § 4.

In this reply it is manifestly assumed as an indisputable principle, that the immediate objects of our thoughts, when we *imagine* or *conceive* the primary qualities of extension and figure, are *ideas* or *species* of these qualities; and, of consequence, are themselves extended and figured. Had it only occurred to him to apply (*mutatis mutandis*) to the perception of *primary* qualities, his own account of the perception of *secondary* qualities, (that it is obtained, to wit, by the *media* of sensations more analogous to arbitrary signs, than to stamps or pictures,) he might have eluded the difficulty started by Gassendi, without being reduced to the disagreeable necessity of supposing his *ideas* or *images* to exist in the brain, and not in the mind The language of Mr Locke, it is observable, sometimes implies the one of these hypotheses, and sometimes the other

It was plainly with the view of escaping from the dilemma proposed by Gassendi to Descartes, that Newton and Clarke were led to adopt a mode of speaking concerning perception, approaching very nearly to the language of Descartes. " Is not," says Newton, " the sensorium of animals the place where the sentient substance *is present;* and to which the sensible *species* of things are brought, through the nerves and brain, that there they may be perceived by the mind *present in that place?*" And still more confidently Dr- Clarke : " Without being *present to the images* of the things perceived, the soul could not possibly perceive them. A living substance can only there perceive where it is present. Nothing can any more act or be acted upon *where* it is not present, than it can *when* it is not " The distinction between primary and secondary qualities was afterwards rejected by Berkeley, in the course of his argument against the existence of matter, but he continued to retain the language of Descartes concerning *ideas*, and to consider them as the *immediate*, or rather as the *only* objects of our thoughts, wherever the external senses are concerned. Mr Hume's notions and expressions on the subject are very nearly the same

I thought it necessary to enter into these details, in order to show with what limitations the remark quoted from Dr Reid in the beginning of this note ought to be received. It is certainly true, that the Cartesian system may be said to form the groundwork of Locke's Theory of Perception, as well as of the sceptical conclusions deduced from it by Berkeley and Hume, but it is not the less true, that it forms also the groundwork of all that has since been done towards the substitution, in place of this scepticism, of a more solid fabric of metaphysical science.

NOTE O, p 139

After the pains taken by Descartes to ascertain the *seat* of the soul, it is surprising to find one of the most learned English divines of the seventeenth century (Dr. Henry More) accusing him as an abettor of the dangerous heresy of *Nullibism.* Of this heresy Dr. More represents Descartes as the chief author; and, at the same time, speaks of it as so completely extravagant, that he is at a loss whether to treat it as a serious opinion of the philosopher, or as the jest of a buffoon "The chief author and leader of the Nullibists," he tells us, "seems to have been *that pleasant wit, Renatus Descartes,* who, by his *jocular* metaphysical meditations, has luxated and distorted the rational faculties of some otherwise sober and quick-witted persons."—[It is not easy (considering the acknowledged simplicity and integrity of More's character) to reconcile these sarcastic and contemptuous expressions, with the unqualified praise lavished on Descartes in the course of their epistolary correspondence —(See *Cartesii Epist.* Pars i. Ep 66, *et seq*) In a letter, too, addressed to M. Clerseher, five years after the death of Descartes, More expresses himself thus —" In neminem aptius quadrat, quam in divinum illum virum, Horatianum illud,—' *Qui nil molitur inepte* ' " At the end of this letter, he subscribes himself, " *Tibi Cartesianisque omnibus addictissimus, H M* " With respect to these inconsistencies in the language of More, see Baillet, *Vie de Descartes,* livre vii. chap. 15] To those who are at all acquainted with the philosophy of Descartes, it is unnecessary to observe, that, so far from being a Nullibist, he valued himself not a little on having fixed the precise *ubi* of the soul with a degree of accuracy unthought of by any of his predecessors. As he held, however, that the soul was *unextended*, and as More happened to conceive that nothing which was unextended could have any reference to place, he seems to have thought himself entitled to impute to Descartes, in direct opposition to his own words, the latter of these opinions as well as the former. "The true notion of a spirit," according to More, " is that of an extended penetrable substance, logically and intellectually divisible, but not physically discernible into parts."

Whoever has the curiosity to look into the works of this once admired, and, in truth, very able logician, will easily discover that his alarm at the philosophy of Descartes was really occasioned, not by the scheme of *nullibism,* but by the Cartesian doctrine of the *non-extension* of mind, which More thought inconsistent with a fundamental article in his own creed—the existence of witches and apparitions. To hint at any doubt about either, or even to hold any opinion that seemed to weaken their credibility, appeared to this excellent person quite a sufficient proof of complete atheism.

The observations of More on "the true notion of a spirit" (extracted from his *Enchiridion Ethicum*) were afterwards republished in Glanvill's book upon witchcraft,—a work (as I before mentioned) proceeding from the same pen with the *Scepsis Scientifica*, one of the most acute and original productions of which English philosophy had then to boast.

If some of the foregoing particulars should, at first sight, appear unworthy of attention in a historical sketch of the progress of science, I must beg leave to remind my readers, that they belong to a history of still higher importance and dignity—that of the progress of Reason, and of the Human Mind

Note P, p. 141

For an interesting sketch of the chief events in the life of Descartes, see the Notes annexed to his Eloge by Thomas, where also is to be found a very pleasing and lively portrait of his moral qualities. As for the distinguishing merits of the Cartesian philosophy, and more particularly of the Cartesian metaphysics, it was a subject peculiarly ill adapted to the pen of this amiable and eloquent, but verbose and declamatory academician.

I am doubtful, too, if Thomas has not gone too far, in the following passage, on a subject of which he was much more competent to judge than of some others which he has ventured to discuss. "L'imagination brillante de Descartes se décèle partout dans ses ouvrages, et s'il n'avoit voulu être ni géomètre ni philosophe, il n'auroit tenu qu'à lui d'être le plus bel esprit de son temps." Whatever opinion may be formed on this last assertion, it will not be disputed by those who have studied Descartes, that his *philosophical* style is remarkably dry, concise, and severe. Its great merit lies in its singular precision and perspicuity; a perspicuity, however, which does not dispense with a moment's relaxation in the reader's attention, the author seldom repeating his remarks, and hardly ever attempting to illustrate or to enforce them either by reasoning or by examples. In all these respects, his style forms a complete contrast to that of Bacon's.

In Descartes' *epistolary* compositions, indeed, ample evidences are to be found of his vivacity and fancy, as well as of his classical taste. One of the most remarkable is a letter addressed to Balzac, in which he gives his reasons for preferring Holland to all other countries, not only as a tranquil, but as an agreeable residence for a philosopher: and enters into some very engaging details concerning his own petty habits. The praise bestowed on this letter by Thomas is by no means extravagant, when he compares it to the best of Balzac's. "Je ne sçais s'il y a rien dans tout Balzac où il y ait autant d'esprit et d'agrément."

Note Q, p. 147

It is an error common to by far the greater number of modern metaphysicians, to suppose that there is no medium between the innate ideas of Descartes, and the opposite theory of Gassendi. In a very ingenious and learned essay on Philosophical Prejudices, by M. Trembley,[1] I find the following sentence:—"Mais l'expérience dément ce système des idées innées, puisque la privation d'un sens emporte avec elle la privation des idées attachées à ce sens, comme l'a remarqué l'illustre auteur de *l'Essai Analytique sur les Facultés de l'Ame*."

What are we to understand by the remark here ascribed to Mr. Bonnet? Does it mean nothing more than this, that to a person born blind no instruction can convey an idea of colours, nor to a person born deaf, of sounds? A remark of this sort surely did not need to be sanctioned by the united names of Bonnet and of Trembley. Nor, indeed, does it bear in the slightest degree on the point in dispute. The question is not about our ideas of the *material* world, but about those

[1] *Essai sur les Préjugés*, &c. Neufchatel, 1790.

ideas on *metaphysical* and *moral* subjects, which may be equally imparted to the blind and to the deaf; enabling them to arrive at the knowledge of the same truths, and exciting in their minds the same moral emotions The *signs* employed in the reasonings of these two classes of persons will of course excite by association, in their respective fancies, very different *material images*, but whence the origin of the physical and moral *notions* of which these signs are the vehicle, and for suggesting which, *all* sets of signs seem to be equally fitted? The astonishing, scientific attainments of many persons, blind from their birth, and the progress lately made in the instruction of the deaf, furnish palpable and incontestable proofs of the flimsiness of this article of the Epicurean philosophy, so completely verified is now the original and profound conclusion long ago formed by Dalgarno—"That the soul can exert her powers by the ministry of any of the senses: And, therefore, when she is deprived of her principal secretaries, the eye and the ear, then she must be contented with the service of her lackeys and scullions, the other senses, which are no less true and faithful to their mistress than the eye and the ear, but not so quick for dispatch."—*Didascalocophus*, &c, Oxford, 1680.

I was once in hopes of being able to throw a still stronger light on the subject of this note, by attempting to ascertain experimentally the possibility of awakening and cultivating the dormant powers of a boy destitute of the organs both of sight and of hearing, but unexpected occurrences have disappointed my expectations.

I have just learned that a case somewhat similar, though not quite so favourable in all its circumstances, has recently occurred in the state of Connecticut in New England; and I have the satisfaction to add, there is some probability that so rare an opportunity for philosophical observations and experiments will not be overlooked in that quarter of the world

Note R, p 149

Of Gassendi's orthodoxy as a Roman Catholic divine, he has left a very curious memorial, in an inaugural discourse pronounced in 1645, before Cardinal Richelieu,* when he entered on the duties of his office as Regius Professor of Mathematics at Paris. The great object of the oration is to apologize to his auditors for his having abandoned his ecclesiastical functions, to teach and cultivate the profane science of geometry. With this view, he proposes to explain and illustrate the saying of Plato, who, being questioned about the employment of the Supreme Being, answered Γιωμιτρεῖν τὸν Θεόν. In the prosecution of this argument, he expresses himself thus on the doctrine of the Trinity —

"Anne proinde hoc adorandum Trinitatis mysterium habebimus rursus ut sphæram, cujus quasi centrum sit Pater Æternus, qui totius divinitatis fons, origo, principium accommodate dicitur, circumferentia Filius, in quo legitur habitare plenitudo Divinitatis; et radii centro circumferentiæque intercedentes Spiritus Sanctus, qui est Patris et Filii nexus, vinculumque mutuum? Anne potius dicendum est eminere in hoc mysterio quicquid sublime magnificumque humana geometria etiamnum requirit? Percelebre est latere eam adhuc, quam quadraturam circuli vocant; atque idcirco in eo esse, ut describat triangulum, cujus si basin ostenderit circuli ambitui æqualem, tum demum esse circulo triangulum æquale demonstrat At in hoc mysterio augustissimo gloriosissima Personarum

* [The words "before Cardinal Richelieu," are deleted in his copy by Mr Stewart —*Ed*]

Trias ita infinitæ essentiæ, ipsiusque fœcunditati, tanquam circulo exæquatur, seu, ut sic loquar, et verius quidem, penitus identificatur; ut cum sit omnium, et cujusque una, atque eadem essentia, una proinde ac eadem sit immensitas, æternitas, et perfectionum plenitudo.

"Sic, cum nondum norit humana geometria trisecare angulum, divideréve, et citra accommodationem mechanicam, ostendere divisum esse in tria æqualia, habemus in hocce mysterio unam essentiam non tam trisectam, quam integram communicatam in tria æqualia supposita, quæ cum simul, sigillatimque totam individuamque possideant, sint inter se tamen realiter distincta."

The rest of the oration is composed in exactly the same taste.

The following interesting particulars of Gassendi's death are recorded by Sorbière:—

"Extremam tamen horam imminentem sentiens, quod reliquum erat vinum impendendum existimavit præparando ad mortem animo. Itaque significavit, ut quamprimum vocaretur Sacerdos, in cujus aurem, dum fari poterat, peccata sua effunderet. . Dein, ut nihil perfectæ Christiani militis armaturæ deesset, sacro inungi oleo efflagitavit. Ad quam cæremoniam animo attendens, cum sacerdos aures inungens pronuntiaret verba solennia, et lapsu quodam memoriæ dixisset, *Indulgeat tibi Dominus quidquid per odoratum peccasti,* reposuit statim æger, *imo per auditum;* adeo intentus erat rei gravissimæ, et eluendarum sordium vel minimarum cupidum se et sitibundum gerebat."—Sorberi *Præfatio.*

Having mentioned in the text the avowed partiality of Gassendi for the Epicurean ethics, it is but justice to his memory to add, that his own habits were, in every respect, the reverse of those commonly imputed to this school. "Ad privatam Gassendi vitam sæpius attendens," says Sorbière, "anachoretam aliquem cernere mihi videor, qui media in urbe vitam instituit plane ad monachi severioris normam; adeo paupertatem, castitatem et obedientiam coluit, quanquam sine ullo voto tria ista vota solvisse videatur.—Abstemius erat sponte sua, ptisanam tepidam bibens pulmoni refrigerando humectandoque. Carne raro, herbis sæpius, ac macerata offa mane et vespere utebatur."—*Ibid.*

TO DISSERTATION, PART SECOND.—NOTES FROM S TO EEE.

NOTE S, p 216.

It deserves to be remarked, as a circumstance which throws considerable light on the literary history of Scotland during the latter half of the eighteenth century, that, from time immemorial, a continued intercourse had been kept up between Scotland and the Continent. To all who were destined for the profession of law, an education either at a Dutch or French university was considered as almost essential. The case was nearly the same in the profession of physic; and, even among the Scottish clergy, I have conversed, in my youth, with some old men who had studied theology in Holland or in Germany. Of our smaller country gentlemen, resident on their own estates, (an order of men which, from various causes, has now, alas! totally vanished,) there was scarcely one who had not enjoyed the benefit of a university education; and very few of those who could afford the expense of foreign travel, who had not visited France and Italy. Lord Monboddo somewhere mentions, to the honour of his father, that he sold part of his estate to enable himself (his eldest son) to pursue his studies at the University of Groningen. The constant influx of information and of liberality from abroad, which was thus kept up in Scotland in consequence of the ancient habits and manners of the people, may help to account for the sudden burst of genius, which to a foreigner must seem to have sprung up in this country by a sort of enchantment, soon after the Rebellion of 1745 The great step *then* made was in the art of English composition. In the mathematical sciences, where the graces of writing have no place, Scotland in proportion to the number of its inhabitants, was never, from the time of Neper, left behind by any country in Europe, nor ought it to be forgotten, that the philosophy of Newton was publicly taught by David Gregory at Edinburgh, and by his brother James Gregory at St Andrew's, before it was able to supplant the vortices of Descartes in that very university of which Newton was a member [1] The case was similar in every other liberal pursuit, where an ignorance of the delicacies of the English tongue was not an insuperable bar to distinction. Even in the study of eloquence, as far as it was attainable in their own vernacular idiom, some of the Scottish pleaders, about the era when the two kingdoms were united, seem ambitiously, and not altogether unsuccessfully, to have formed themselves upon models, which, in modern times, it has been commonly supposed to be more safe to admire than to imitate [2] Of the progress made in this part of the island in Metaphysical and Ethical Studies, at a period long prior to that which is commonly considered as the commencement of our literary history, I shall afterwards have occasion to speak. At present, I shall only observe, that it was in the Scottish universities that the philosophy of Locke, as well as that of Newton, was first adopted as a branch of academical education.

NOTE T, p. 220.

Extract of a letter from M Allamand to Mr Gibbon.—See Gibbon's *Miscellaneous Works*

"Vous avez sans doute raison de dire que les propositions évidentes dont il s'agit, ne sont pas de simples idées, mais des jugemens. Mais ayez aussi la complaisance de reconnoître que M Locke les alléguant en exemple d'idées qui passent pour innées, et qui ne le sont pas selon lui, s'il y a ici de la méprise, c'est lui qu'il

[1] For this we have the authority of Whiston, the immediate successor of Sir Isaac Newton in the Lucasian Professorship at Cambridge; and of Dr Reid, who was a nephew of the two Gregorys "Mr. Gregory had already caused several of his scholars to keep Acts, as we call them, upon several branches of the Newtonian Philosophy, while we at Cambridge, poor wretches, were ignominiously studying the fictitious hypotheses of the Cartesians."—Whiston's *Memoirs of his own Life*

"I have by me," says Dr. Reid, "a *Thesis* printed at Edinburgh, 1690, by James Gregory, who was at that time Professor of Philosophy at St. Andrew's, containing twenty-five positions, the first three relating to logic, and the abuse of it in the Aristotelian and Cartesian philosophy The remaining twenty-two positions are a compend of Newton's *Principia* This *Thesis*, as was the custom at that time in the Scottish Universities, was to be defended in a public disputation, by the candidates, previous to their taking their degree"—Hutton's *Mathematical Dictionary—Supplement* by Dr Reid to the article *Gregory*

[2] See a splendid eulogium in the Latin language, by Sir George Mackenzie, on the most distinguished pleaders of his time at the Scottish bar Every allowance being made for the flattering touches of a friendly hand, his portraits can scarcely be supposed not to have borne a strong and characteristical resemblance to the originals from which they were copied

faut relever la-dessus, et non pas moi, qui n'avois autre chose à faire qu'à réfuter sa manière de raisonner contre l'innéité de ces idées ou jugemens là D'ailleurs, Monsieur, vous remarquerez, s'il vous plait, que dans cette dispute il s'agit en effet, de savoir si certaines vérités évidentes et communes, et non pas seulement certaines idées simples, sont innées ou non   Ceux qui affirment, ne donnent guère pour exemple d'idées simples qui le soyent, que celles de Dieu, de l'unité, et de l'existence; les autres exemples sont pris de propositions complètes, que vous appellez jugemens

"Mais, dites vous, y aura-t-il donc des jugemens innés ? Le jugement est il autre chose qu'un acte de nos facultés intellectuelles dans la comparaison des idées ? Le jugement sur les vérités évidentes, n'est il pas une simple vue de ces vérités là, un simple coup-d'œil que l'esprit jette sur elles ? J'accorde tout cela. *Et de grace, qu'est ce qu' idée ? N'est ce pas vue, ou coup d'œil, si vous voulez ?* Ceux qui définissent l'idée autrement, ne s'éloignent-ils pas visiblement du sens et de l'intention du mot ? Dire que les idées sont les *espèces* des choses imprimées dans l'esprit, comme l'image de l'objet sensible est tracée dans l'œil, n est ce pas jargonner plutôt que définir ? Or c'est la faute, qu'ont fait tous les métaphysiciens, et quoique M. Locke l'ait bien sentie, il a mieux aimé se fâcher contre eux, et tirer contre les girouettes de la place, que s'appliquer à démêler ce galimatias   Que n'a-t-il dit, non seulement il n'y a point d'idées innées dans le sens de ces Messieurs, mais *il n'y a point d'idées du tout dans ce sens là, toute idée est un acte, une vue, un coup-d'œil de l'esprit*. Dès lors demander s'il y a des idées innées, c'est demander s il y a certaines vérités si évidentes et si communes que tout esprit non stupide puisse naturellement, sans culture et sans maître, sans discussion, sans raisonnement, les reconnoître d'un coup-d'œil, et souvent même sans s'apercevoir qu'on jette ce coup d'œil L'affirmative me paroit incontestable, et selon moi, la question est vuidée par là

"Maintenant prenez garde, Monsieur, que cette manière d'entendre l'affaire, va au but des partisans des idées innées, tout comme la leur; et par la même contredit M. Locke dans le sien. Car pourquoi voudroit-on qu'il y a eu des idées innées? C'est pour en opposer la certitude et l'évidence au doute universel des sceptiques, qui est ruiné d'un seul coup, s'il y a des vérités dont la vue soit nécessaire et naturelle à l'homme   Or vous sentez, Monsieur, que je puis leur dire cela dans ma façon d'expliquer la chose, tout aussi bien que les partisans ordinaires des idées innées dans la leur. Et voilà ce que semble incommoder un peu M. Locke, qui, sans se déclarer Pyrrhonien, laisse apercevoir un peu trop de foible pour le Pyrrhonisme, et a beaucoup contribué à le nourrir dans ce siècle   A force de vouloir marquer les bornes de nos connoissances, ce qui étoit fort nécessaire, il a quelquefois tout mis en bornes "

Note U, p 222

"A decisive proof of this is afforded by the allusions to Locke's doctrines in the dramatic pieces then in possession of the French stage," &c

In a comedy of Destouches, (entitled *La Fausse Agnes*,) which must have been written long before the period in question,[1] the heroine, a lively and accomplished

---

[1] This little piece was first published in 1757, three years after the author s death, which took place in 1754, in the seventy-fourth year of his age. But we are told by D Alembert, that from

NOTE X.   553

girl, supposed to be just arrived from Paris at her father's house in Poitou, is introduced as first assuming the appearance of imbecility, in order to get rid of a disagreeable lover, and, afterwards, as pleading her own cause in a mock trial before an absurd old president and two provincial ladies, to convince them that she is in reality not out of her senses. In the course of her argument on this subject, she endeavours to astonish her judges by an ironical display of her philosophical knowledge; warning them of the extreme difficulty and nicety of the question upon which they were about to pronounce "Vous voulez juger de moi! mais, pour juger sainement, il faut une grande étendue de connoissances, encore est il bien douteux qu'il y en ait de certaines. . . . Avant donc que vous entrepreniez de prononcer sur mon sujet, je demande préalablement que vous examiniez avec moi nos connoissances en général, les degrés de ces connoissances, leur étendue, leur réalité, que nous convenions de ce que c'est que la vérité, et si la vérité se trouve effectivement   Après quoi nous traiterons des propositions universelles, des maximes, des propositions frivoles, et de la foiblesse, ou de la solidité de nos lumières. . . . Quelques personnes tiennent pour vérité, que l'homme naît avec certains principes innés, certaines notions primitives, certains caractères qui sont comme gravés dans son esprit, dès le premier instant de son existence. Pour moi, j'ai longtemps examiné ce sentiment, et j'entreprends de la combattre, de le réfuter, de l'anéantir, si vous avez la patience de m'écouter." I have transcribed but a part of this curious pleading, but, I presume, more than enough to show, that every sentence, and almost every word of it, refers to Locke's doctrines. In the second and third sentences, the titles of the principal chapters in the fourth book of his *Essay* are exactly copied. It was impossible that such a scene should have produced the slightest comic effect, unless the book alluded to had been in very general circulation among the higher orders, I might perhaps add, in much *more* general circulation than it ever obtained among that class of readers in England. At no period, certainly, since it was first published, (such is the difference of national manners,) could similar allusions have been made to it, or to any other work on so abstract a subject, with the slightest hope of success on the London stage   And yet D'Alembert pronounces *La Fausse Agnes* to be a piece, *pleine de mouvement et de gaieté.*

NOTE X, p. 227.

"Descartes asserted," says a very zealous Lockist, M. de Voltaire, "that the soul, at its coming into the body, is informed with the whole series of metaphysical notions; knowing God, infinite space, possessing all abstract ideas; in a word, completely endued with the most sublime lights, which it unhappily forgets at its issuing from the womb.

"With regard to myself," continues the same writer, "I am as little inclined as Locke could be to fancy that, some weeks after I was conceived, I was a very learned soul; knowing at that time a thousand things which I forgot at my birth;

---

the age of sixty, he had renounced, from sentiments of piety, all thoughts of writing for the stage.—(*Eloge de Destouches*) This carries the date of *all* his dramatic works, at least as far back as 1740   As for Destouches's own familiarity with the writings of Locke, it is easily accounted for by his residence in England from 1717 to 1723, where he remained, for some time after the departure of Cardinal Dubois, as *Chargé d'Affaires*   Voltaire did not visit England till 1727

and possessing, when in the womb, (though to no manner of purpose,) knowledge which I lost the instant I had occasion for it ; and which I have never since been able to recover perfectly "—*Letters concerning the English Nation.* Letter 13.

Whatever inferences may be deducible from some of Descartes's expressions, or from the comments on these expressions by some who assumed the title of Cartesians, I never can persuade myself that the system of *innate ideas,* as conceived and adopted by *him,* was meant to give any sanction to the absurdities here treated by Voltaire with such just contempt. In no part of Descartes's works, as far as I have been able to discover, is the slightest ground given for this extraordinary account of his opinions. Nor was Descartes the first person who introduced this language. Long before the date of his works it was in common use in England, and is to be found in a *Poem* of Sir John Davis, published four years before Descartes was born. (See sect. xxvi. of *The Immortality of the Soul.*) The title of this section expressly asserts, That *there are innate ideas in the soul.*

In one of Descartes's letters, he enters into some explanations with respect to this part of his philosophy, which he complains had been very grossly misunderstood or misrepresented. To the following passage I have no doubt that Locke himself would have subscribed. It strikes myself as so very remarkable, that, in order to attract to it the attention of my readers, I shall submit it to their consideration in an English translation.

" When I said that the idea of God is innate in us, I never meant more than this, that Nature has endowed us with a faculty by which we may know God, but I have never either said or thought that such ideas had an actual existence, or even that they were *species* distinct from the faculty of thinking. I will even go farther, and assert that nobody has kept at a greater distance than myself from all this trash of scholastic entities, insomuch that I could not help smiling when I read the numerous arguments which Regius has so industriously collected to shew that infants have no actual knowledge of God while they remain in the womb. Although the idea of God is so imprinted on our minds, that every person has within himself the faculty of knowing him, it does not follow that there may not have been various individuals who have passed through life without ever making this idea a distinct object of apprehension; and, in truth, they who think they have an idea of a plurality of Gods, have no idea of God whatsoever "—Cartesii *Epist.* Pars i. Epist. xcix.

- [* In another letter, Descartes says still more explicitly—" Licet idea Dei *sit menti humanæ ita impressa,* ut nemo non habeat in se facultatem illum cognoscendi, tamen fieri potest ut plurimi nunquam sibi hanc ideam distincte repræsentarint; et revera ii qui putant se habere multorum Deorum ideam, nequaquam habent ideam Dei "—(*Ibid.* Epist. cxvii.) And in another work—" Idea est ipsa res cogitata, quatenus est *objectiva* in intellectu." By way of comment on this, Descartes tells us afterwards, in reply to a difficulty started by one of his correspondents, " ubi advertendum, me loqui de Idea quæ nunquam ut extra intellectum, et ratione cujus esse objectivi non aliud significet, quam esse in intellectu eo modo quo objecta in illo esse solent "—*Responsio ad primas objectiones in Meditationes Cartesii.*

In this instance, the distinction between *subjective* and *objective* seems to be

* Restored.—*Ed.*

merely grammatical, analogous to that between the verb and noun, when we make use of such a circumlocution as *thinking and thought*]

After reading this passage from Descartes, may I request of my readers to look back to the extracts, in the beginning of this note, from Voltaire's letters? A remark of Montesquieu, occasioned by some strictures hazarded by this lively but very superficial philosopher on the *Spirit of Laws*, is more peculiarly applicable to him when he ventures to pronounce judgment on metaphysical writers "Quant à Voltaire, il a *trop d'esprit pour m'entendre;* tous les livres qu'il lit, il les fait, après quoi il approuve ou critique ce qu'il a fait "—(*Lettre à M. l'Abbé de Guasco*) The remark is applicable to other critics as well as to Voltaire.

The prevailing misapprehensions with respect to this and some other principles of the Cartesian metaphysics, can only be accounted for by supposing that the opinions of Descartes have been more frequently judged of from the glosses of his followers than from his own works It seems to have never been sufficiently known to his adversaries, either in France or in England, that, after his philosophy had become fashionable in Holland, a number of Dutch divines, whose opinions differed very widely from his, found it convenient to shelter their own errors under his established name, and that some of them went so far as to avail themselves of his authority in propagating tenets directly opposite to his declared sentiments Hence a distinction of *the Cartesians* into the *genuine* and the *pseudo*-Cartesians; and hence an inconsistency in their representations of the metaphysical ideas of their master, which can only be cleared up by a reference (seldom thought of) to his own very concise and perspicuous text (Fabricii, *Bib Gr.* lib. iii. cap vi. p. 183 Heinecc *El Hist Phil* § cx)

Many of the objections commonly urged against the *innate ideas* of Descartes are much more applicable to the *innate ideas* of Leibnitz, whose language concerning them is infinitely more hypothetical and unphilosophical, and sometimes approaches nearly to the enthusiastic theology of Plato and of Cudworth. Nothing in the works of Descartes bears any resemblance, in point of extravagance, to what follows "Pulcherrima multa sunt Platonis dogmata, . . . esse in divina mente mundum intelligibilem, quem ego quoque vocare soleo regionem idearum, objectum sapientiæ esse τὰ ὄντως ὄντα, substantias nempe simplices, quæ a me *monades* appellantur, et semel existentes semper perstant, πρῶτα δικτικὰ τῆς ζωῆς, id est, Deum et Animas, et harum potissimas mentes, producta a Deo simulacra divinitatis . . . Porro quævis mens, ut recte Plotinus, quendam in se mundum intelligibilem continet, imo mea sententia et hunc ipsum sensibilem sibi repræsentat . . Sunt in nobis *semina eorum*, quæ discimus, ideæ nempe, et quæ inde nascuntur, æternæ veritates . Longe ergo præferendæ sunt Platonis *notitiæ innatæ*, quas *reminiscentiæ* nomine velavit, tabulæ rasæ Aristotelis et Lockii, aliorumque recentiorum, qui ἐξωτερικῶς philosophantur.'—Leib. *Opera*, tom. ii. p. 223.

Wild and visionary, however, as the foregoing propositions are, if the names of Gassendi and of Hobbes had been substituted instead of those of Aristotle and of Locke, I should have been disposed to subscribe implicitly to the judgment pronounced in the concluding sentence. The metaphysics of Plato, along with a considerable alloy of poetical fiction, has at least the merit of containing a large admixture of important and of ennobling truth, while that of Gassendi and of Hobbes, besides its inconsistency with facts attested, every moment, by our own consciousness, tends directly to level the rational faculties of man with the instincts of the brutes.

In the *Acta Eruditorum* for the year 1684, Leibnitz observes, that " in the case of things which we have never thought of, the *innate ideas* in our minds may be compared to the figure of Hercules in a block of marble." This seems to me to prove, that the difference between him and Locke was rather in appearance than in reality, and that, although he called those ideas *innate* which Locke was at pains to trace to sensation or to reflection, he would have readily granted, that our first knowledge of their existence was coeval with the first impressions made on our senses by external objects. That this was also the opinion of Descartes is still more evident, notwithstanding the ludicrous point of view in which Voltaire has attempted to exhibit this part of his system.

Note Y, p. 228.

Mr Locke seems to have considered this use of the word *reflection* as peculiar to himself, but it is perfectly analogous to the κινήσεις κυκλικαί of the Greek philosophers, and to various expressions which occur in the works of John Smith of Cambridge, and of Dr. Cudworth. We find it in a *Poem on the Immortality of the Soul*, by Sir John Davis, Attorney-General to Queen Elizabeth; and probably it is to be met with in English publications of a still earlier date.

> All things without which round about we see,
>   We seek to know, and have wherewith to do,
> But that whereby we reason, live, and be,
>   Within ourselves, we strangers are thereto.
>
> Is it because the mind is like the eye,
>   Through which it gathers knowledge by degrees,
> Whose rays *reflect* not, but spread outwardly,
>   Not seeing itself, when other things it sees?
>
> No, doubtless, for the mind can backward cast
>   Upon herself her understanding light,
> But she is so corrupt, and so defac'd,
>   As her own image doth herself affright.
>
> As is the fable of the Lady fair,
>   Which for her lust was turned into a cow,
> When thirsty, to a stream she did repair,
>   And saw herself transform'd, she wist not how.
>
> At first she startles, then she stands amaz'd,
>   At last with terror she from hence doth fly,
> And loathes the wat'ry glass wherein she gaz'd,
>   And shuns it still, although for thirst she die.
>
> For even at first *reflection* she espies
>   Such strange chimeras and such monsters there;
> Such toys, such antics, and such vanities,
>   As she retires and shrinks for shame and fear.

I have quoted these verses, chiefly because I think it not improbable that they may have suggested to Gray the following very happy allusion in his fine Fragment *De Principiis Cogitandi* :—

> Qualis Hamadryadum quondam si forte sororum
> Una, novos peragrans saltus, et devia rura,
> (Atque illam in viridi suadet procumbere ripa
> Fontis pura quies, et opaci frigoris umbra)
> Dum prona in latices speculi de margine pendet,
> Mirata est subitam venienti occurrere Nympham.
> Mox eosdem, quos ipsa, artus, eadem ora gerentem
> Unà inferre gradus, unà succedere sylvæ
> Aspicit alludens; seseque agnoscit in undis
> Sic sensu interno rerum simulacra suarum
> Mens ciet, et proprios observat conscia vultus

NOTE Z, p. 251.

The chief attacks made in England on Locke's *Essay*, during his own lifetime, were by Edward Stillingfleet, Bishop of Worcester; John Norris,[1] Rector of Bemerton; Henry Lee, B.D., and the Reverend Mr Lowde, (author of a *Discourse concerning the Nature of Man*.) Of these four writers, the first is the only one whose objections to Locke are now at all remembered in the learned world, and for this distinction, Stillingfleet is solely indebted (I speak of him here merely as a metaphysician, for in some other departments of study his merits are universally admitted) to the particular notice which Locke has condescended to take of him, in the Notes incorporated with the later editions of his *Essay* The only circumstance which renders these Notes worthy of preservation, is the record they furnish of Locke's forbearance and courtesy, in managing a controversy carried on, upon the other side, with so much captiousness and asperity. An Irish bishop, in a letter on this subject to Mr Molyneux, writes thus. "I read Mr. Locke's letter to the Bishop of Worcester with great satisfaction, and am wholly of your opinion, that he has fairly laid the great bishop on his back, but it is with so much gentleness, as if he were afraid not only of hurting him, but even of spoiling or tumbling his clothes."

[* In the case of one antagonist alone, Dr. William Sherlock, (afterwards Bishop of London,) Locke seems to have been disposed to judge somewhat uncharitably. In a work of Sherlock's with which I am unacquainted, some severe strictures having been introduced on the doctrine which rejects *connate ideas or inbred notions*, Locke takes occasion thus to express himself in a letter to Mr. Molyneux "A man of no small name, as you know Dr. *Sherlock* is, has been pleased to declare against my doctrine of no innate ideas from the pulpit in the Temple, but as I have been told, charged it with little less than Atheism. Though the Doctor be a great man, yet that would not much fright me, because I am told that he is not always obstinate against opinions which he has condemned more publicly than in

---

[1] Of this person, who was a most ingenious and original thinker, I shall have occasion afterwards to speak

* Restored.—*Ed.*

a harangue to a Sunday's auditory. But that it is possible he may be firm here, because it is also said, he never quits his aversion to any tenet he has once declared against, till change of times bringing change of interest, and fashionable opinions open his eyes and his heart; and then he kindly embraces what before deserved his aversion and censure."—Locke's *Works*, vol ix p 396]

The work of Lee is entitled "*Anti-scepticism*, or Notes upon each chapter of Mr. Locke's *Essay concerning Human Understanding*, with an explanation of all the particulars of which he treats, and in the same order. By Henry Lee, B D, formerly Fellow of Emanuel College in Cambridge, now Rector of Tichmarsh in Northamptonshire."—London, 1702, in folio.

The strictures of this author, which are often acute and sometimes just, are marked throughout with a fairness and candour rarely to be met with in controversial writers. It will appear remarkable to modern critics that he lays particular stress upon the charms of Locke's style, among the other excellences which had conspired to recommend his work to public favour. "The celebrated author of the *Essay on Human Understanding* has all the advantages desirable to recommend it to the inquisitive genius of this age, an avowed pretence to new methods of discovering truth and improving learning, an unusual coherence in the several parts of his scheme; a singular clearness in his reasonings; and, *above all*, a natural elegancy of style; an unaffected beauty in his expressions, a just proportion and tuneable cadence in all his periods"—See the *Epistle Dedicatory*.

NOTE A A, p 257.

For the information of some of my readers, it may be proper to observe, that the word *influx* came to be employed to denote *the action* of body and soul on each other, in consequence of a prevailing theory which supposed that this action was carried on by something intermediate, (whether material or immaterial was not positively decided,) *flowing* from the one substance to the other. It is in this sense that the word is understood by Leibnitz, when he states as an insurmountable objection to the theory of *influx*, that "it is impossible to conceive either material particles or immaterial qualities to pass from body to mind, or from mind to body"

Instead of the term *influx*, that of *influence* came gradually to be substituted by our English writers, but the two words were originally synonymous, and were used indiscriminately as late as the time of Sir Matthew Hale —See his *Primitive Origination of Mankind*.

In Johnson's *Dictionary*, the primitive and radical meaning assigned to the word *influence* (which he considers as of French extraction) is "the power of the celestial aspects operating upon terrestrial bodies and affairs," and in the *Encyclopædia* of Chambers, it is defined to be "a quality supposed to *flow* from the bodies of the stars, either with their heat or light, to which astrologers vainly attribute all the events which happen on the earth." To this astrological use of the word, Milton had plainly a reference in that fine expression of his *L'Allegro*,

"Store of ladies whose bright eyes
Rain *influence*."[1]

[1] The explanation of the word *influence*, given in the *Dictionary* of the French Academy, accords perfectly with the tenor of the above remarks "Vertu qui, suivant les Astrologues découle des Astres sur les corps sublunaires."

NOTE BB.   559

It is a circumstance worthy of notice, that a word thus originating in the dreams of astrologers and schoolmen, should now, in our language, be appropriated almost exclusively to politics. "Thus," says Blackstone, "are the electors of one branch of the legislature secured from any undue *influence* from either of the other two, and from all external violence and compulsion, but the greatest danger is that in which themselves co-operate by the infamous practice of bribery and corruption.' And again, "The crown has gradually and imperceptibly gained almost as much in *influence* as it has lost in prerogative."

In all these cases, there will be found at bottom one common idea, the existence of some secret and mysterious connexion between two things, of which connexion it is conceived to be impossible or unwise to trace what Bacon calls the *latens processus*.

NOTE B B, p. 259.

After these quotations from Locke, added to those which I have already produced from the same work, the reader may judge of the injustice done to him by Leibnitz, in the first sentence of his correspondence with Clarke.

" Il semble que la religion naturelle même s'affoiblit extrèmement. Plusieurs font les âmes corporelles, d'autres font Dieu lui-même corporel."

" M. Locke et ses sectateurs, *doutent* au moins, si les âmes ne sont matérielles, et naturellement périssables"

Dr Clarke, in his reply to this charge, admits that "*some* parts of Locke's writings may justly be suspected as intimating his doubts whether the soul be immaterial or no, but herein (he adds) he has been followed only by some Materialists, enemies to the mathematical principles of philosophy, and who approve little or nothing in Mr Locke's writings, but his errors"

To those who have studied with care the *whole* writings of Locke, the *errors* here alluded to will appear in a very venial light when compared with the general spirit of his philosophy. Nor can I forbear to remark farther on this occasion, that supposing Locke's *doubts* concerning the immateriality of the soul to have been as real as Clarke seems to have suspected, this very circumstance would only reflect the greater lustre on the soundness of his *logical* views concerning the proper method of studying the mind;—in the prosecution of which study, he has adhered much more systematically than either Descartes or Leibnitz to the exercise of *reflection*, as the sole medium for ascertaining the internal phenomena; describing, at the same time, these phenomena in the simplest and most rigorous terms which our language affords, and avoiding, in a far greater degree than any of his predecessors, any attempt to explain them by analogies borrowed from the perceptions of the external senses

I before observed, that Leibnitz greatly underrated Locke as a metaphysician. It is with regret I have now to mention, that Locke has by no means done justice to the splendid talents and matchless erudition of Leibnitz. In a letter to his friend Mr. Molyneux, dated in 1697, he expresses himself thus · "I see you and I agree pretty well concerning Mr. Leibnitz, and this sort of fiddling makes me hardly avoid thinking that he is not that very great man as has been talked of him." And in another letter, written in the same year to the same correspondent, after referring to one of Leibnitz's Memoirs in the *Acta Eruditorum*, (De Primæ Philosophiæ Emendatione,) he adds, "From whence I only draw this inference, that even great parts will not master any subject without great thinking, and that even the largest minds have but narrow swallows."

Let me add, that in my quotations from English writers, I adhere scrupulously to their own phraseology, in order to bring under the eye of my readers, specimens of English composition at different periods of our history. I must request their attention to this circumstance, as some expressions in the former part of this Dissertation, which have been censured as Scotticisms, occur in extracts from authors who, in all probability, never visited this side of the Tweed.

NOTE C C, p 270

After studying, with all possible diligence, what Leibnitz has said of his *monads* in different parts of his works, I find myself quite incompetent to annex any precise idea to the word as he has employed it I shall, therefore, aim at nothing more in this note, but to collect, into as small a compass as I can, some of his most intelligible attempts to explain its meaning.

" A substance is a thing capable of action It is simple or compounded A simple substance is that which has no parts. A compound substance is an aggregate of simple substances or of *monads*.

" Compounded substances, or bodies, are multitudes Simple substances, lives, souls, spirits, are units [1] Such simple substances must exist everywhere, for without simple substances there could be no compounded ones. All nature therefore is full of life "—Tom ii p 32

" *Monads*, having no parts, are neither extended, figured, nor divisible. They are the real *atoms* of nature, or, in other words, the elements of things "—Tom ii. p 20.

(It must not, however, be imagined, that the *monads* of Leibnitz have any resemblance to what are commonly called *atoms* by philosophers. On the contrary, he says expressly that " *monads* are *not* atoms of *matter*, but atoms of *substances*;— real units, which are the first principles in the composition of things, and the last elements in the analysis of substances,—of which principles or elements, what we call *bodies* are only the *phenomena* ")—Tom ii pp. 53, 325

In another passage we are told, that " a *monad* is not a *material* but a *formal* atom, it being impossible for a thing to be at once material, and possessed of a real unity and indivisibility. It is necessary, therefore," says Leibnitz, " to revive the obsolete doctrines of *substantial forms*, (the essence of which consists in *force*,) separating it, however, from the various abuses to which it is liable "—*Ibid* p 50

" Every *monad* is a living mirror, representing the universe, according to its particular point of view, and subject to as regular laws as the universe itself "

" Every *monad*, with a particular body, makes a living substance."

" The knowledge of every *soul* (*âme*) extends to infinity, and to all things, but this knowledge is confused As a person walking on the margin of the sea, and listening to its roar, hears the noise of each individual wave of which the whole noise is made up, but without being able to distinguish one sound from another, in like manner, our confused perceptions are the result of the impressions made upon us by the whole universe The case (he adds) is the same with each *monad*."

" As for the reasonable soul or mind, (*l'esprit*,) there is something in it more

[1] " Les substances simples, les vies, les âmes, les esprits, sont des unités."

NOTE D D.

than in the *monads*, or even than in those souls which are simple. It is not only a mirror of the universe of created things, but an image of the Deity Such minds are capable of reflected acts, and of conceiving what is meant by the words *I*, *substance, monad, soul, mind*, in a word, of conceiving *things and truths* unconnected with matter, and it is this which renders us capable of science and of demonstrative reasoning

"What becomes of these *souls*, or *forms*, on the death of the animal? There is no alternative (replies Leibnitz) but to conclude, that not only the soul is preserved, but that the *animal also with its organical machine* continues to exist, although the destruction of its grosser parts has reduced it to a smallness as invisible to our eyes as it was before the moment of conception. Thus neither animals nor souls perish at death, nor is there such a thing as *death*, if that word be understood with rigorous and metaphysical accuracy. The soul never quits completely the body with which it is united, nor does it pass from one body into another with which it had no connexion before, a *metamorphosis* takes place, but there is no *metempsychosis*"—Tom ii pp 51, 52.

On this part of the Leibnitzian system D'Alembert remarks, that it proves nothing more than that the author had perceived better than any of his predecessors, the impossibility of forming a distinct idea of the nature of *matter*, a subject, however, (D'Alembert adds,) on which the theory of the monads does not seem calculated to throw much light. I would rather say, (without altogether denying the justness of D'Alembert's criticism,) that this theory took its rise from the author's vain desire to explain the nature of *forces;* in consequence of which he suffers himself perpetually to be led astray from those *sensible effects* which are exclusively the proper objects of *physics*, into conjectures concerning their *efficient causes*, which are placed altogether beyond the reach of our research

NOTE D D, p 276

The *metaphysical* argument advanced by the Leibnitzians in proof of the *law of continuity*, has never appeared to me to be satisfactory. "If a body at rest (it has been said) begins, *per saltum*, to move with any finite velocity, then this body must be at the same indivisible instant in two different states, that of rest and of motion, which is impossible."[1]

As this reasoning, though it relates to a *physical fact*, is itself wholly of a *metaphysical* nature ; and as the inference deduced from it has been generalized into a

---

[1] "Si toto tempore," says Father Boscovich, speaking of the Law of Continuity in the Collision of Bodies, "ante contactum subsequentis corporis superficies antecedens habuit 12 gradus velocitatis, et sequenti 9, saltu facto momentaneo ipso initio contactus, in ipso momento ea tempora dirimente debuissent habere et 12 et 9 simul, quod est absurdum. Duas enim velocitates simul habere corpus non potest."— *Theoria Phil Nat. &c*

Boscovich, however, it is to be observed, admits the existence of the Law of Continuity in the phenomena of Motion alone, (§ 143,) and rejects it altogether in things co-existent with each other, (§ 142) In other cases, he says, Nature does not observe the Law of Continuity with mathematical accuracy, but only *affects it*, by which expression he seems to mean, that, where she is guilty of a *saltus*, she aims at making it as moderate as possible The expression is certainly deficient in metaphysical precision, but it is not unworthy of attention, inasmuch as it affords a proof, that Boscovich did not (with the Leibnitzians) conceive Nature, or the Author of Nature, as obeying an *irresistible necessity* in observing or not observing the Law of Continuity

LAW, supposed to extend to all the various branches of human knowledge, it is not altogether foreign to our present subject briefly to consider how far it is demonstratively conclusive, in this simplest of all its possible applications.

On the above argument, then, I would remark,—1. That the ideas both of *rest* and of *motion*, as well as the more general idea conveyed by the word *state*, all of them necessarily involve the idea of *time* or *duration*; and, consequently, a body cannot be said to be in a *state* either of rest or of motion, at an *indivisible* instant. Whether the body be supposed (as in the case of motion) to *change* its place from one instant to another; or to *continue* (as in that of rest) for an instant in the same place; the idea of some finite portion of time will, on the slightest reflection, be found to enter as an essential element into our conception of the physical fact

2. Although it certainly would imply a contradiction to suppose a body to be in two different *states* at the same instant, there does not appear to be any inconsistency in asserting that an indivisible instant may form the limit between a state of rest and a state of motion Suppose one half of this page to be painted white, and the other black, it might, I apprehend, be said with the most rigorous propriety, that the transition from the one colour to the other was made *per saltum;* nor do I think it would be regarded as a valid objection to this phraseology, to represent it as one of its implied consequences, that the mathematical line which forms their common limit must at once be both black and white.[1] It seems to me quite impossible to elude the force of this reasoning, without having recourse to the existence of something intermediate between *rest* and *motion*, which does not partake of the nature of either

Is it conceivable that a body can exist in any *state* which does not fall under one or other of the two predicaments, rest or motion? If this question should be answered in the negative, will it not follow that the transition from one of these *states* to the other must, of necessity, be made *per saltum*, and must consequently violate the supposed law of continuity? Indeed, if such a law existed, how could a body at rest *begin* to move, or a body in motion come to a state of rest?

But farther, when it is said that "it is impossible for a body to have its state changed from motion to rest, or from rest to motion, without passing through all the intermediate degrees of velocity," what are we to understand by the *intermediate degrees of velocity between rest and motion?* Is not *every* velocity, how small soever, a *finite* velocity, and does it not differ as essentially from a state of rest, as the velocity of light?

It is observed by Mr Playfair, (*Dissertation on the Progress of Mathematical and Physical Science*, Part i sect. iii), that Galileo was the first who maintained the existence of the *law of continuity*, and who made use of it as a principle in his

---

[1] [* In reply to this remark, it has been urged by a late critic, that " the *boundary* between the two colours is a *mathematical line*, a mere *conception, an abstract idea*, whereas we are talking of a *physical fact* subjected to the cognizance of the senses, and therefore the analogy is not in point "—(*Edinburgh Magazine* for October, 1821) To myself, I acknowledge that the analogy between the two cases appears to me perfect Is not an *indivisible instant* of time a *mere abstraction* of the mind, as well as a *mathematical line*?]

* Restored.—*Ed.*

reasonings on the phenomena of motion. Mr. Playfair, however, with his usual discrimination and correctness, ranks this among the *mechanical* discoveries of Galileo. Indeed, it does not appear that it was at all regarded by Galileo (as it avowedly was by Leibnitz) in the light of a metaphysical and necessary *law*, which could not by any possibility be violated in any of the phenomena of motion.[1] It was probably first suggested to him by the diagram which he employed to *demonstrate*, or rather to *illustrate*, the uniformly accelerated motion of falling bodies,[2] and the numberless and beautiful exemplifications of the same law which occur in *pure geometry*, sufficiently account for the disposition which so many mathematicians have shewn to extend it to all those branches of physics which admit of a mathematical consideration.

My late illustrious friend, who, to his many other great and amiable qualities, added the most perfect fairness and candour in his inquiries after truth, has (in the Second Part of his *Dissertation*) expressed himself with considerably greater scepticism concerning the law of continuity, than in his *Outlines of Natural Philosophy*. In that work he pronounced the metaphysical argument, employed by Leibnitz to prove its *necessity*, "to be conclusive." (Sect. vi. § 99, b.) In the Second Part of his *Dissertation*, (Sect. ii), he writes thus on the same subject —

"Leibnitz considered this principle as known *a priori*, because, if any *saltus* were to take place, that is, if any change were to happen without the intervention of time, the thing changed must be in two different conditions at the same individual instant, which is obviously impossible. Whether this reasoning be quite satisfactory or no, the conformity of the law to the facts generally observed cannot but entitle it to great authority in judging of the explanations and theories of natural phenomena."

The phrase, *Law of Continuity*, occurs repeatedly in the course of the correspondence between Leibnitz and John Bernouilli, and appears to have been *first* used by Leibnitz himself. The following passage contains some interesting particulars concerning the history of this law: "*Lex Continuitatis*, cum usque adeo sit rationi et naturæ consentanea, et usum habeat tam late patentem, mirum tamen est eam a nemine (quantum recorder) antea adhibitam fuisse. Mentionem ejus

---

[1] [* A learned and ingenious writer has lately expressed himself to the same purpose with Leibnitz "A body does not acquire its celerity in an instant Nothing material can exist but what is finite, and the beautiful *law of continuation*, by which changes are produced by imperceptible shades, *can never be violated*" (See a very valuable Essay by Mr Leslie, *On the Construction and Effect of Machines*, in the second volume of Dr Brewster's edition of Ferguson's *Lectures*, p 353) To myself, I own it appears that the first clause of this sentence leads to a conclusion directly opposite to what is here inferred in the second ']

[2] Descartes seems, from his correspondence with Mersenne, to have been much puzzled with Galileo's reasonings concerning the descent of falling bodies, and in alluding to it, has, on different occasions, expressed himself with an indecision and inconsistency of which few instances occur in his works (Vide Cartesii *Epist.* Pars ii. Epist. xxxiv xxxv xxxvii xci) His doubts on this point will appear less surprising, if compared with a passage in the article *Mécanique* in D'Alembert's *Elémens de Philosophie* "Tous les philosophes paroissent convenir, que la vitesse avec laquelle les corps qui tombent commencent a se mouvoir est absolument nulle," &c &c.—See his *Mélanges*, tom iv pp 219, 220

* Restored —*J d*

aliquam teceram olim in Novellis Reipublicæ Literariæ (Juillet, 1687, p 744,) occasione collatiunculæ cum Malebranchio, qui ideo meis considerationibus persuasus, suam de legibus motus in Inquisitione Veritatis expositam doctrinam postea mutavit, quod brevi libello edito testatus est, in quo ingenue occasionem mutationis exponit. Sed tamen paullo promptior, quam par erat, fuit in novis legibus constituendis in eodem libello, antequam mecum communicasset; nec tantum in veritatem, sed etiam in illam ipsam Legem Continuitatis, etsi minus aperte, denuo tamen impegit, quod nolui viro optimo objicere, ne viderer ejus existimationi detrahere velle "—*Epist* Leibnit. ad Joh Bernouilli, 1697

From one of John Bernouilli's letters to Leibnitz, it would appear that he had himself a conviction of the truth of this law, before he had any communication with Leibnitz upon the subject.

" Placet tuum criterium pro examinandis regulis motuum, quod *legem continuitatis* vocas; est enim per se evidens, et velut a natura nobis inditum, quod evanescente inæqualitate hypothesium, evanescere quoque debeant inæqualitates eventuum Hinc multoties non satis mirari potui, qui fieri potuerit, ut tam incongruas, tam absonas, et tam manifeste inter se pugnantes regulas, excepta sola prima, potuerit condere Cartesius, vir alias summi ingenii. Mihi videtur vel ab infante falsitatem illarum palpari posse, eo quod ubique saltus ille, naturæ adeo inimicus, manifeste nimis elucet "—*Epist* Bernouilli ad Leib. 1696 *Vide* Leibnitzii et Jo Bernouilli *Comm Epist* 2 vols. 4to Lausannæ et Genevæ, 1745.

[* The reasoning of John Bernouilli in support of the *Law of Continuity*, strikes me as obviously inconsequential "Tous ceux qui sont convaincus que tous les genres de quantité sont divisibles à l'infini, auront-ils de la peine à diviser la plus insensible durée en un nombre infini de petites parties, et à y placer tous les degrés possibles de vitesse, depuis le repos jusqu'à un mouvement déterminé " They who hold the infinite divisibility of extension would be the last, I should conceive, to admit the force of this argument. If the least conceivable mathematical line be, in idea, as much susceptible of an endless division as the diameter of the earth's orbit, does it not follow that the *gap* which separates an *indivisible part* from the former, is of the same kind, however inferior in degree, to that which separates the *point* from the latter? Is there anything intermediate between a point and a line, to assist the imagination in conceiving what is meant by "*tous les degrés possibles de vitesse, depuis le repos jusqu'à un mouvement déterminé ?*"]

NOTE E E, p 276.

Mais il restoit encore la plus grande question, de ce que ces âmes ou ces formes deviennent par la mort de l'animal, ou par la destruction de l'individu de la substance organisé Et c'est ce qui embarrasse le plus; d'autant qu'il paroit peu raisonnable que les âmes restent inutilement dans un chaos de matière confuse. Cela m'a fait juger enfin qu'il n'y avoit qu'un seul parti raisonnable à prendre, et c'est celui de la conservation non seulement de l'âme, mais encore de l'animal même, et de la machine organique ; quoique la destruction des parties grossières l'ait réduit à une petitesse qui n'échappe pas moins à nos sens que celle où il étoit avant que de naître —Leib *Op* tom ii p 51.

. Des personnes fort exactes aux expériences se sont déjà aperçues de notre

* Restored.—*Ed.*

tems,[1] qu'on peut douter, si jamais un animal tout à fait nouveau est produit, et si les animaux tout en vie ne sont déjà en petit avant la conception dans les semences aussi bien que les plantes. Cette doctrine étant posée, il sera raisonnable de juger, que ce qui ne commence pas de vivre ne cesse pas de vivre non plus, et que la mort, comme la génération, n'est que la transformation du même animal qui est tantôt augmenté, et tantôt diminué.—*Ibid* pp 42, 43.

. Et puisqu' ainsi il n'y a point de première naissance ni de génération entièrement nouvelle de l'animal, il s'ensuit qu'il n'y en aura point d'extinction finale, ni de mort entière prise à la rigueur métaphysique; et que, par conséquent, au lieu de la transmigration des âmes, il n'y a qu'une transformation d'un même animal, selon que les organes sont pliés différemment, et plus ou moins développés.—*Ibid* p 52

Quant à la Métempsycose, je crois que l'ordre ne l'admet point, il veut que tout soit explicable distinctement, et que rien ne se fasse par saut Mais le passage de l'âme d'un corps dans l'autre seroit un saut étrange et inexplicable. Il se fait toujours dans l'animal ce qui se fait présentement C'est que le corps est dans un changement continuel, comme un fleuve, et ce que nous appellons génération ou mort, n'est qu'un changement plus grand et plus prompt qu'à l'ordinaire, tel que seroit le saut ou la cataracte d'une rivière Mais ces sauts ne sont pas absolus et tels que je désaprouve, comme seroit celui d'un corps qui iroit d'un lieu à un autre sans passer par le milieu. *Et de tels sauts ne sont pas seulement défendus dans les mouvemens, mais encore dans tout ordre des choses ou des vérités.*—The sentences which follow afford a proof of what I have elsewhere remarked, how much the mind of Leibnitz was misled, in the whole of this metaphysical theory, by habits of thinking formed in early life, amidst the hypothetical abstractions of pure geometry, a prejudice (or *idol of the* mathematical *den*) to which the most important errors of his philosophy might, without much difficulty, be traced —Or comme dans une ligne de géométrie il y a certains points distingués, qu'on appelle sommets, points d'inflexion, points de rebroussement, ou autrement, et comme il y en a des lignes qui en ont une infinité, c'est ainsi qu'il faut concevoir dans la vie d'un animal ou d'une personne les tems d'un changement extraordinaire, qui ne laissent pas d'être dans la règle générale, de même que les points distingués dans la courbe se peuvent déterminer par sa nature générale ou son équation. On peut toujours dire d'un animal *c'est tout comme ici*, la différence n'est que du plus ou moins — Tom v p 18

Note FF, p. 282.

The praise which I have bestowed on this Memoir renders it necessary for me to take some notice of a very exceptionable proposition which is laid down in the first paragraph as a fundamental maxim,—that "all proper names were at first appellatives;" a proposition so completely at variance with the commonly received opinions among later philosophers, that it seems an object of some curiosity to inquire, how far it is entitled to plead in its favour the authority of Leibnitz Since the writings of Condillac and of Smith, it has, so far as I know, been universally acknowledged, that, if there be any one truth in the *Theoretical History* of Language, which we are entitled to assume as an incontrovertible fact, it is the direct

[1] The experiments here referred to are the observations of Swammerdam, Malpighi, and Lewenhoeck

contrary of the above proposition. Indeed, to assert that all proper names were at first appellatives, would appear to be nearly an absurdity of the same kind as to maintain, that *classes* of objects existed before *individual* objects had been brought into being.

When Leibnitz, however, comes to explain his idea more fully, we find it to be something very different from what his words literally imply, and to amount only to the trite and indisputable observation, that, in simple and primitive languages, all proper names (such as the names of persons, mountains, places of residence, &c.) are descriptive or significant of certain prominent and characteristical features, distinguishing them from other objects of the same class,—a fact, of which a large proportion of the surnames still in use, all over Europe, as well as the names of mountains, villages, and rivers, when traced to their primitive roots, afford numerous and well known exemplifications.

Not that the proposition, even when thus explained, can be assumed as a general maxim. It holds, indeed, in many cases, as the Celtic and the Saxon languages abundantly testify in our own island; but it is true only under certain limitations, and it is perfectly consistent with the doctrine delivered on this subject by the greater part of philologers for the last fifty years.

In the history of language, nothing is more remarkable than the aversion of men to coin words out of unmeaning and arbitrary sounds, and their eagerness to avail themselves of the stores already in their possession, in order to give utterance to their thoughts on the new topics which the gradual extension of their experience is continually bringing within the circle of their knowledge. Hence metaphors, and other figures of speech, and hence the various changes which words undergo, in the way of amplification, diminution, composition, and the other transformations of elementary terms which fall under the notice of the etymologist. Were it not, indeed, for this strong and universal bias of our nature, the vocabulary of every language would, in process of time, become so extensive and unwieldy, as to render the acquisition of one's mother tongue a task of immense difficulty, and the acquisition of a dead or foreign tongue next to impossible. It is needless to observe, how immensely these tasks are facilitated by that etymological system which runs, more or less, through every language; and which everywhere proceeds on certain analogical principles, which it is the business of the practical grammarian to reduce to general rules, for the sake of those who wish to speak or to write it with correctness.

In attempting thus to trace backwards the steps of the mind towards the commencement of its progress, it is evident, that we must at last arrive at a set of elementary and primitive roots, of which no account can be given, but the arbitrary choice of those who first happened to employ them. It is to this *first* stage in the infancy of language that Mr Smith's remarks obviously relate, whereas the proposition of Leibnitz, which gave occasion to this note, as obviously relates to its subsequent stages, when the language is beginning to assume somewhat of a regular form, by compositions and other modifications of the materials previously collected.

From these slight hints it may be inferred, 1*st*, That the proposition of Leibnitz, although it may seem, from the very inaccurate and equivocal terms in which it is expressed, to stand in direct opposition to the doctrine of Smith, was really meant by the author to state a fact totally unconnected with the question under Smith's consideration 2*dly*, That even in the sense in which it was understood by the author, it fails entirely, when extended to that *first* stage in the infancy of language, to which the introductory paragraphs in Mr. Smith's discourse are exclusively confined

Note G G, p. 285.

" Je viens de recevoir une lettre d'un Prince Régnant de l'Empire, où S A. me marque avoir vu deux fois ce printems à la dernière foire de Leipsig, et examiné avec soin un chien qui parle. Ce chien a prononcé distinctement plus de trente mots, répondant même assez à propos à son maître : il a aussi prononcé tout l'alphabet excepté les lettres m, n, x "—Leib *Opera*, tom v. p 72.

Thus far the fact rests upon the authority of the German prince alone. But from a passage in the *History of the Academy of Sciences*, for the year 1706, it appears that Leibnitz had himself seen and heard the dog. What follows is transcribed from a report of the Academy upon a letter from Leibnitz to the Abbé de St. Pierre, giving the details of this extraordinary occurrence

" Sans un garant tel que M Leibnitz, témoin oculaire, nous n'aurions pas la hardiesse de rapporter, qu'auprès de Zeitz dans la Misnie, il y a un chien qui parle. C'est un chien de Paysan, d'une figure des plus communes, et de grandeur médiocre Un jeune enfant lui entendit pousser quelques sons qu'il crut ressembler à des mots Allemands, et sur cela se mit en tête de lui apprendre à parler. Le maître, qui n'avoit rien de mieux à faire, n'y épargna pas le tems ni ses peines, et heureusement le disciple avoit des dispositions qu'il eut été difficile de trouver dans un autre. Enfin, au bout de quelques années, le chien sçut prononcer environ une trentaine de mots · de ce nombre sont *Thé*, *Caffé*, *Chocolat*, *Assemblée*, mots François, qui ont passé dans l'Allemand tels qu'ils sont. Il est à remarquer, que le chien avoit bien trois ans quand il fut mis à l'école. Il ne parle que par écho, c'est a dire, après que son maître a prononcé un mot, et il semble, qu'il ne repète que par force et malgré lui, quoiqu'on ne le maltraite pas. Encore une fois, M. Leibnitz l'a vu et entendu "

(Exposé d'une lettre de M. Leibnitz à l'Abbé de St. Pierre sur un chien qui parle) " Cet exposé de la lettre de M Leibnitz se trouve dans l'Histoire de l'Académie des Sciences, année 1706. Ce sont les Auteurs de l'Histoire de l'Académie qui parlent "—Leib *Opera*, vol. ii p 180, Part ii.

May not all the circumstances of the above story be accounted for, by supposing the master of the dog to have possessed that peculiar species of imitative power which is called *Ventriloquism ?* Matthews, I have no doubt, would find little difficulty in managing such a deception, so as to impose on the senses of any person who had never before witnessed any exhibition of the same kind.

Note H H, p 285

When I speak in favourable terms of the *Philosophical Spirit*, I hope none of my readers will confound it with the spirit of that false philosophy, which, by unhinging every rational principle of belief, seldom fails to unite in the same characters the extremes of scepticism and of credulity. It is a very remarkable fact, that the same period of the eighteenth century, and the same part of Europe which were most distinguished by the triumphs of Atheism and Materialism, were also distinguished by a greater number of visionaries and impostors than had ever appeared before, since the revival of letters. Nor were these follies confined to persons of little education. They extended to men of the highest rank, and to many individuals of distinguished talents. Of this the most satisfactory proofs might be produced, but I have room here only for one short quotation. It is from the pen of the Duc de Levis, and relates to the celebrated Maréschal de Richelieu, on whom Voltaire has lavished so much of his flattery. "Ce dont je suis positivement certain, c'est que cet homme spirituel (le Maréschal de Richelieu) étoit superstitieux, et qu'il croyoit aux prédictions des astrologues et autres sottises de cet espèce. Je l'ai vu refusant à Versailles d'aller faire sa cour au fils aîné de Louis XVI. en disant sérieusement, *qu'il savoit* que cet enfant n'étoit point destiné au trône. Cette crédulité superstitieuse, générale pendant la ligue, étoit encore très commune sous la régence lorsque le Duc de Richelieu entra dans le monde, par la plus bizarre des inconséquences, elle s'allioit très bien avec la plus grande impiété, et la plupart des matérialistes croyoient aux *esprits*, aujourd'hui, ce genre de folie est très rare, mais beaucoup de gens, qui se moquent des astrologues, croient à des prédictions d'une autre espèce."—*Souvenirs et Portraits*, par M. de Levis, à Paris, 1813.

Some extraordinary facts of the same kind are mentioned in the *Memoirs of the Marquis de Bouillé*. According to him, Frederic the Great himself was not free from this sort of superstition.

A similar remark is made by an ancient historian, with respect to the manners of Rome at the period of the Gothic invasion. "There are many who do not presume either to bathe, or to dine, or to appear in public, till they have diligently consulted, according to the rules of astrology, the situation of Mercury, and the aspect of the Moon. It is singular enough that this vain credulity may often be discovered among the profane sceptics, who impiously doubt or deny the existence of a Celestial Power."—Gibbon, from Ammianus Marcellinus, *Decline and Fall of the Roman Empire*, vol. v. p. 278.

Note II, p. 286

The following estimate of Leibnitz, considered in comparison with his most distinguished contemporaries, approaches, on the whole, very nearly to the truth although some doubts may be entertained about the justness of the decision in the last clause of the sentence. "Leibnitz, aussi hardi que Descartes, aussi subtil que Bayle, peut-être moins profond que Newton, et moins sage que Locke, mais seul universel entre tous ces grands hommes, paroit avoir embrassé le domaine de la raison dans toute son étendue, et avoir contribué le plus à répandre cet esprit philosophique que fait aujourd'hui la gloire de notre siècle."—Bailly, *Eloge de Leibnitz*.

I have mentioned in the text only a part of the learned labours of Leibnitz. It remains to be added, that he wrote also on various subjects connected with chemistry, medicine, botany, and natural history; on the philosophy and language of the Chinese, and on numberless other topics of subordinate importance. The philological discussions and etymological collections, which occupy so large a space among his works, would (even if he had produced nothing else) have been no inconsiderable memorials of the activity and industry of his mind.

Manifold and heterogeneous as these pursuits may at first appear, it is not difficult to trace the thread by which his curiosity was led from one of them to another. I have already remarked a connexion of the same sort between his different metaphysical and theological researches, and it may not be altogether uninteresting to extend the observation to some of the subjects enumerated in the foregoing paragraph.

The studies by which he first distinguished himself in the learned world (I pass over that of jurisprudence,[1] which was imposed on him by the profession for which he was destined) were directed to the antiquities of his own country, and more particularly to those connected with the history of the House of Brunswick. With this view he ransacked, with an unexampled industry, the libraries, monasteries, and other archives, both of Germany and of Italy, employing in this ungrateful drudgery several of the best and most precious years of his life. Mortified, however, to find how narrow the limits are, within which the range of written records is confined, he struck out for himself and his successors a new and unexpected light, to guide them through the seemingly hopeless darkness of remote ages. This light was the study of etymology, and of the affinities of different tongues in their primitive roots,—a light at first faint and glimmering, but which, since his time, has continued to increase in brightness, and is likely to do so more and more as the world grows older. It is pleasing to see his curiosity on this subject expand, from the names of the towns, and rivers, and mountains in his neighbourhood, till it reached to China and other regions in the east, leading him, in the last result, to some general conclusions concerning the origin of the different tribes of our species, approximating very nearly to those which have been since drawn from a much more extensive range of *data* by Sir William Jones, and other philologers of the same school.

As an additional light for illustrating the antiquities of Germany, he had recourse to natural history: examining, with a scientific eye, the shells and other marine bodies everywhere to be found in Europe, and the impressions of plants and fishes (some of them unknown in this part of the world) which are distinctly legible, even by the unlettered observer, on many of our fossils. In entering upon this research, as well as on the former, he seems to have had a view to Germany alone ; on the state of which, (he tells us,) prior to all historical documents, it was his purpose to prefix a discourse to his History of the House of Brunswick. But his imagination soon took a bolder flight, and gave birth to his *Protogœa;*—a dissertation which (to use his own words) had for its object " to ascertain the original face of the earth, and to collect the vestiges of its earliest history from the monuments which nature herself has left of her successive operations on its surface. It is a work which, wild and extravagant as it may now be regarded, is spoken of by

---

[1] Bailly, in his *Eloge on Leibnitz*, speaks of him in terms of the most enthusiastic praise, as a philosophical jurist, and as a man fitted to become the legislator of the human race. To me, I must own, it appears, that there is no part of his writings in which he discovers less of his characteristical originality, than where he professes to treat of the law of nature. On these occasions, how inferior does he appear to Grotius, not to speak of Montesquieu and his disciples!

Buffon with much respect, and is considered by Cuvier as the groundwork of Buffon's own system on the same subject

In the connexion which I have now pointed out between the Historical, the Philological, and the Geological speculations of Leibnitz, Helvetius might have fancied that he saw a new exemplification of *the law of continuity*, but the true light in which it ought to be viewed, is as a faithful picture of a philosophical mind emancipating itself from the trammels of local and conventional details, and gradually rising from subject to subject, till it embraces in its survey those nobler inquiries which, sooner or later, will be equally interesting to every portion of the human race [1]—[* With this unparalleled range of knowledge treasured up in a mind peculiarly fond of combining the most remote affinities, it is not wonderful that Leibnitz should have conceived the idea of compiling an *Encyclopedia*. The groundwork of his undertaking was to be the Encyclopedia published in 1620 by *Alstedius;* a work, of which he seems to have thought more highly than most of the learned have done There is, I should think, but little reason to regret that this design proved abortive,—when we consider, first, that he proposed to insert, *entire*, in his Dictionary, the tracts of Hobbes *De Jure* and *De Corpore*, and, secondly, that in one of his letters to a friend, he has suggested the advantages of composing an Encyclopedia in verse How vast the distance of these imperfect glimmerings from the views opened in the preliminary discourse of D'Alembert, and what a proof does this contrast furnish of the astonishing progress of the human mind during the first half of the eighteenth century !]

NOTE K K, p. 296

Of Locke's affectionate regard for Collins, notwithstanding the contrariety of their opinions on some questions of the highest moment, there exist many proofs in his letters, published by M Des Maizeaux. In one of these, the following passage is remarkable It is dated from Oates in Essex, 1703, about a year before Locke's death

"You complain of a great many defects, and that very complaint is the highest recommendation I could desire to make me love and esteem you, and desire your friendship. And if I were now setting out in the world, I should think it my

---

[1] In the above note, I have said nothing of Leibnitz's project of a philosophical language, founded on an alphabet of Human Thoughts, as he has nowhere given us any hint of the principles on which he intended to proceed in its formation, although he has frequently alluded to the practicability of such an invention in terms of extraordinary confidence (For some remarks on these passages in his works, see *Philosophy of the Human Mind*, vol ii p 143, *et seq*) In some of Leibnitz's expressions on this subject, there is a striking resemblance to those of Descartes in one of his letters. See the preliminary discourse prefixed to the Abbé Emery's *Pensées de Descartes*, p 14, *et seq.*

In the ingenious essay of Michaelis, *On the Influence of Opinions on Language, and of Language on Opinions*, (which obtained the prize from the Royal Society of Berlin in 1759,) there are some very acute and judicious reflections on the impossibility of carrying into effect, with any advantage, such a project as these philosophers had in view The author's argument on this point seems to me decisive, in the present state of human knowledge, but who can pretend to fix a limit to the possible attainments of our posterity !

[This Essay, which obtained the prize from the Royal Academy of Berlin, originally appeared in German, but has been very well translated into French by an anonymous writer The translation was printed at Bremen in 1762]

* Restored —*Ed*

great happiness to have such a companion as you, who had a true relish for truth, would in earnest seek it with me, from whom I might receive it undisguised, and to whom I might communicate what I thought true freely Believe it, my good friend, to love truth for truth's sake, is the principal part of human perfection in this world, and the seed-plot of all other virtues, and, if I mistake not, you have as much of it as ever I met with in anybody. What, then, is there wanting to make you equal to the best, a friend for any one to be proud of?" . . . The whole of Locke's letters to Collins are highly interesting and curious, more particularly *that* which he desired to be delivered to him after his own death. From the general tenor of these letters, it may be inferred, that Collins had never let Locke fully into the secret of those pernicious opinions which he was afterwards at so much pains to disseminate.

Note LL, p 299.

In addition to the account of Spinoza given in Bayle, some interesting particulars of his history may be learnt from a small volume, entitled *La Vie de B de Spinoza, tirée des écrits de ce Fameux Philosophe, et du témoignage de plusieurs personnes dignes de foi, qui l'ont connu particulièrement. par* JEAN COLERUS, *Ministre de l Eglise Luthérienne de la Haye:* 1706.[1] The book is evidently written by a man altogether unfit to appreciate the merits or demerits of Spinoza as an author, but it is not without some value to those who delight in the study of human character, as it supplies some chasms in the narrative of Bayle, and has every appearance of the most perfect impartiality and candour

According to this account, Spinoza was a person of the most quiet and inoffensive manners; of singular temperance and moderation in his passions; contented and happy with an income which barely supplied him with the necessaries of life, and of too independent a spirit to accept of any addition to it, either from the favour of princes, or the liberality of his friends. In conformity to the law, and to the customs of his ancestors, (which he adhered to, when he thought them not unreasonable, even when under the sentence of excommunication,) he resolved to learn some mechanical trade; and fortunately selected that of grinding optical glasses, in which he acquired so much dexterity, that it furnished him with what he conceived to be a sufficient maintenance He acquired also enough of the art of designing, to produce good portraits in chalk and china-ink of some distinguished persons

For the last five years of his life he lodged in the house of a respectable and religious family, who were tenderly attached to him, and from whom his biographer collected various interesting anecdotes. All of them are very creditable to his private character, and more particularly show how courteous and amiable he must have been in his intercourse with his inferiors. In a bill presented for payment after his death, he is styled by Abraham Keveling, his barber-surgeon, *Benedict Spinoza of blessed memory;* and the same compliment is paid to him by the tradesman who furnished gloves to the mourners at his funeral.

These particulars are the more deserving of notice, as they rest on the authority of a very zealous member of the Lutheran communion—[* a man certainly not of

---

[1] The Life of Spinoza by Colerus, with some other curious pieces on the same subject, is reprinted in the complete edition of Spinoza's Works, published at Jena, in 1802

* Restored —*Ed*

very superior powers, but who seems to have felt more than most divines either of the Roman Catholic or of the Reformed Churches, the force of the Scripture precept—"not to violate the truth even in the cause of God." The manifest pleasure with which he records the numerous testimonies in favour of Spinoza's moral qualities does honour to his own heart, and adds weight and dignity to the severity with which he reprobates his theological tracts] They coincide exactly with the account given of Spinoza by the learned and candid Mosheim "This man (says he) observed in his conduct, the rules of wisdom and probity much better than many who profess themselves Christians; nor did he ever endeavour to pervert the sentiments or to corrupt the morals of those with whom he lived, or to inspire, in his discourse, a contempt of religion or virtue" . . . *Eccles History*, translated by Dr. Maclaine, vol. iv p. 252.

Among the various circumstances connected with Spinoza's domestic habits, Colerus mentions one very trifling singularity, which appears to me to throw a strong light on his general character, and to furnish some apology for his eccentricities as an author The extreme feebleness of his constitution (for he was consumptive from the age of twenty) having unfitted him for the enjoyment of convivial pleasures, he spent the greater part of the day in his chamber alone, but when fatigued with study, he would sometimes join the family party below, and take a part in their conversation, however insignificant its subject might be One of the amusements with which he was accustomed to unbend his mind, was that of entangling flies in a spider's web, or of setting spiders a-fighting with each other, on which occasions (it is added) he would observe their combats with so much interest, that it was not unusual for him to be seized with immoderate fits of laughter. Does not this slight *trait* indicate very decidedly a tendency to insanity, a supposition by no means incompatible (as will be readily admitted by all who have paid any attention to the phenomena of madness) with that logical *acumen* which is so conspicuous in some of his writings?

His irreligious principles he is supposed to have adopted, in the first instance, from his Latin preceptor, Vander Ende, a physician and classical scholar, of some eminence; but it is much more probable that his chief school of atheism was the synagogue of Amsterdam, where, without any breach of charity, a large proportion of the more opulent class of the assembly may be reasonably presumed to belong to the ancient sect of *Sadducees* (This is, I presume, the idea of Heineccius in the following passage: " Quamvis Spinoza Cartesii principia methodo mathematica demonstrata dederit; Pantheismum tamen ille non ex Cartesio didicit, sed *dom habuit, quos sequeretur*" In proof of this, he refers to a book entitled *Spinozismus in Judaismo*, by Wachterus.) The blasphemous curses pronounced upon him in the sentence of excommunication were not well calculated to recall him to the faith of his ancestors, and when combined with his early and hereditary prejudices against Christianity, may go far to account for the indiscriminate war which he afterwards waged against priests of all denominations

The ruling passion of Spinoza seems to have been the love of fame. "It is owned," says Bayle, "that he had an extreme desire to immortalize his name, and would have sacrificed his life to that glory, though he should have been torn to pieces by the mob"—Art *Spinoza*.

NOTE M M, p. 307.

In proof of the impossibility of Liberty, Collins argues thus :—

"A second reason to prove man a necessary agent is, because all his actions have a beginning: for, whatever has a beginning must have a cause, and every cause is a necessary cause

"If anything can have a beginning, which has no cause, then nothing can produce something And if nothing can produce something, then the world might have had a beginning without a cause; which is an absurdity not only charged on atheists, but is a real absurdity in itself Liberty, therefore, or a power to act or not to act, to do this or another thing under the same causes, is an *impossibility and atheistical*.[1]

"And as Liberty stands, and can only be grounded on the absurd principles of Epicurean atheism, so the Epicurean atheists, who were the most popular and most numerous sect of the atheists of antiquity, were the great assertors of liberty, as, on the other side, the Stoics, who were the most popular and numerous sect among the religionaries of antiquity, were the great assertors of *fate* and *necessity*"
—Collins, p 54

As to the above *reasoning* of Collins, it cannot be expected that I should, in the compass of a Note, "boult this matter to the bran " It is sufficient here to remark, that it derives all its plausibility from the unqualified terms in which the maxim ($\mu\eta\delta\grave{\epsilon}\nu$ $\dot{\alpha}\nu\alpha\acute{\iota}\tau\iota o\nu$) has frequently been stated "In the idea of every *change*, (says Dr. Price, a zealous advocate for the freedom of the will,) is included that of its being an *effect* "—(*Review, &c.*, p. 30, 3d edition) If this maxim be literally admitted without any explanation or restriction, it seems difficult to resist the conclusions of the Necessitarians. The proper statement of Price's maxim evidently is, that "in every *change* we perceive in *inanimate* matter, the idea of its being an *effect* is necessarily involved," and that he himself understood it under this limitation appears clearly from the application he makes of it to the point in dispute As to intelligent and active beings, to affirm that they possess the power of self-determination, seems to me to be little more than an identical proposition. Upon an accurate analysis of the meaning of words, it will be found that the idea of an *efficient* cause implies the idea of *Mind*, and, consequently, that it is absurd to ascribe the volitions of the *mind* to the efficiency of causes foreign to itself To do so must unavoidably involve us in the inconsistencies of Spinozism by forcing us to conclude that everything is passive, and nothing active in the universe, and, consequently, that the idea of a *First* Cause involves an impossibility —But upon these hints I must not enlarge at present, and shall, therefore, confine myself to what falls more immediately within the scope of this Discourse, Collins's Historical Statement with respect to the tenets of the Epicureans and the Stoics

In confirmation of his assertion concerning the former, he refers to the following well-known lines of Lucretius —

" Denique si semper motus connectitur omnis," &c &c
Lucret. Lab 2, v 251

On the obscurity of this passage, and the inconsistencies involved in it, much

---

[1] To the same purpose Edwards attempts to show, that "the scheme of free-will (by affording an exception to that dictate of common sense which refers every event to a cause) would destroy the proof *a posteriori* for the being of God"

might be said, but it is of more importance, on the present occasion, to remark its complete repugnance to the whole strain and spirit of the Epicurean philosophy. This repugnance did not escape the notice of Cicero, who justly considers Epicurus as having contributed more to establish, by this puerile subterfuge, the authority of Fatalism, than if he had left the argument altogether untouched. "Nec vero quisquam magis confirmare mihi videtur non modo fatum, verum etiam necessitatem et vim omnium rerum, sustulisseque motus animi voluntarios, quam hic qui aliter obsistere fato fatetur se non potuisse nisi ad has commenticias declinationes confugisset."—*Liber de Fato*, cap. 20.

On the noted expression of Lucretius (*fatis avolsa voluntas*) some acute remarks are made in a note on the French translation by M. de la Grange. They are not improbably from the pen of the Baron d'Holbach, who is said to have contributed many notes to this translation. Whoever the author was, he was evidently strongly struck with the inconsistency of this particular tenet with the general principles of the Epicurean system.

"On est surpris qu' Epicure fonde la liberté humaine sur la déclinaison des atomes. On demande si cette déclinaison est nécessaire, ou si elle est simplement accidentelle. Nécessaire, comment la liberté peut elle en être le résultat? Accidentelle, par quoi est elle déterminée? Mais on devrait bien plutot être surpris, qu'il lui soit venu en idée de rendre l'homme libre dans un système qui suppose un enchainement nécessaire de causes et d'effets. C'étoit une recherche curieuse, que la raison qui a pu faire d'Epicure l'Apôtre de la Liberté." For the theory which follows on this point, I must refer to the work in question.—See *Traduction Nouvelle de Lucrèce, avec des Notes*, par M. de la Grange, vol. i. pp. 218-220: à Paris, 1768.

But whatever may have been the doctrines of some of the *ancient* Atheists about man's free-agency, it will not be denied, that in the *History of* MODERN *Philosophy*, the schemes of Atheism and of Necessity have been hitherto always connected together. Not that I would by any means be understood to say, that every Necessitarian must *ipso facto* be an Atheist, or even that any presumption is afforded by a man's attachment to the former sect, of his having the slightest bias in favour of the latter; but only that every modern Atheist I have heard of has been a Necessitarian. I cannot help adding, that the most consistent Necessitarians who have yet appeared, have been those who followed out their principles till they ended in *Spinozism*, a doctrine which differs from Atheism more in words than in reality.

In what Collins says of the Stoics in the above quotation, he plainly proceeds on the supposition that all Fatalists are of course Necessitarians,[1] and I agree with him in thinking, that this would be the case if they reasoned logically. It is certain, however, that a great proportion of those who have belonged to the first sect have disclaimed all connexion with the second. The Stoics themselves furnish one very remarkable instance. I do not know any author by whom the liberty of the will is stated in stronger and more explicit terms, than it is by Epictetus in

---

[1] Collins states this more strongly in what he says of the Pharisees. "The Pharisees, who were a religious sect, ascribed all things to fate or to God's appointment, and it was the first article of their creed, that Fate and God do all, and consequently, they could not assert a true liberty when they asserted a liberty together with this fatality and *necessity* of all things."—Collins, p. 54.

the very first sentence of the Enchiridion. Indeed, the Stoics seem, with their usual passion for exaggeration, to have carried their ideas about the freedom of the will to an unphilosophical extreme

If the belief of man's free-agency has thus maintained its ground among professed Fatalists, it need not appear surprising that it should have withstood the strong arguments against it, which the doctrine of the eternal decrees of God, and even that of the Divine prescience, appear at first sight to furnish. A remarkable instance of this occurs in St. Augustine, (distinguished in ecclesiastical history by the title of *the Doctor of Grace*,) who has asserted the liberty of the will in terms as explicit as those in which he has announced the theological dogmas with which it is most difficult to reconcile it. Nay, he has gone so far as to acknowledge the essential importance of this belief, as a motive to virtuous conduct. " Quocirca nullo modo cogimur, aut retenta præscientia Dei, tollere voluntatis arbitrium, aut retento voluntatis arbitrio, Deum, quod nefas est, negare præscium futurorum, sed utrumque amplectimur, utrumque fideliter et veraciter confitemur : illud, ut bene credamus ; *hoc ut bene vivamus.*" [* In the Confession of Faith of the Church of Scotland, (the Articles of which are strictly Calvinistic,) the freedom of the human will is asserted as strongly as the doctrine of the eternal decrees of God " God (it is said, Chap. iii.) from all eternity did, by the most wise and holy counsel of his own will, freely and unchangeably ordain whatsoever comes to pass Yet so as thereby neither is God the author of sin, *nor is violence offered to the will of his creatures*, nor is the liberty or contingency of second causes taken away, but rather established " And still more explicitly in Chap. ix., " God hath endued the will of man with that natural liberty, that it is neither forced, nor by any absolute necessity of nature determined to do good or evil."]

Descartes has expressed himself on this point nearly to the same purpose with St Augustine. In one passage he asserts, in the most unqualified terms, that God is the cause of all the actions which depend on the Free-will of Man ; and yet, that the Will is really free, he considers as a fact perfectly established by the evidence of consciousness. " Sed quemadmodum existentiæ divinæ cognitio non debet liberi nostri arbitrii certitudinem tollere, quia illud in nobismet ipsis experimur et sentimus, ita neque liberi nostri arbitrii cognitio existentiam Dei apud nos dubiam facere debet. Independentia enim illa quam experimur, atque in nobis persentiscimus, et quæ actionibus nostris laude vel vituperio dignis efficiendis sufficit, non pugnat cum dependentia alterius generis, secundum quam omnia Deo subjiciuntur " —(Cartesii *Epistolæ*, Epist. viii. ix Pars 1) These letters form part of his correspondence with the Princess Elizabeth, daughter of Frederick, King of Bohemia, and Elector Palatine.

We are told by Dr. Priestley, in the very interesting *Memoirs of his own Life*, that he was educated in the strict principles of Calvinism ; and yet it would appear, that while he remained a Calvinist, he entertained no doubt of his being a free-agent. "The doctrine of Necessity," he also tells us, "he *first* learned from Collins,[1] and

---

* Restored.—*Ed*

[1] We are elsewhere informed by Priestley, that " It was in consequence of reading and studying the *Inquiry* of Collins, he was first convinced of the truth of the doctrine of Necessity, and was enabled to see the fallacy of most of the arguments in favour of Philosophical Liberty though (he adds) I was much more confirmed in this principle by my acquaintance with Hartley's *Theory of the Human Mind*, a work to which I owe much more than I am able to express "—*Preface*, &c &c p xxvii

was established in the belief of it by Hartley's *Observations on Man*."—(*Ibid* p 19.) He farther mentions in another work, that "he was not a ready convert to the doctrine of Necessity, and that, like Dr. Hartley himself, he gave up his liberty with great reluctance*"—Preface to the Doctrine of Philosophical Necessity Illustrated*, 2d edit. Birmingham, 1782, p. xxvii

These instances afford a proof, I do not say of the compatibility of man's free-agency with those schemes with which it seems most at variance, but of this compatibility in the opinion of some of the profoundest thinkers who have turned their attention to the argument. No conclusion, therefore, can be drawn against a man's belief in his own free-agency, from his embracing other metaphysical or theological tenets, with which it may appear to ourselves impossible to reconcile it.

As for the notion of liberty, for which Collins professes himself an advocate, it is precisely that of his predecessor Hobbes, who defines a free-agent to be, "he that can do if he will, and forbear if he will."—(Hobbes's *Works*, p 484, fol ed.) The same definition has been adopted by Leibnitz, by Gravesande, by Edwards, by Bonnet, and by all our later Necessitarians. It cannot be better expressed than in the words of Gravesande · "*Facultas faciendi quod libuerit, quæcunque fuerit voluntatis determinatio.*"—*Introd ad Philosoph* sect. 115

Dr. Priestley ascribes this peculiar notion of free-will to Hobbes as its author,[1] but it is, in fact, of much older date even among modern metaphysicians; coinciding exactly with the doctrines of those scholastic divines who contended for the *Liberty of Spontaneity*, in opposition to the *Liberty of Indifference* It is, however, to Hobbes that the partisans of this opinion are indebted for the happiest and most popular illustration of it that has yet been given "I conceive," says he, "liberty to be rightly defined,—The absence of all the impediments to action that are not contained in the nature and intrinsical quality of the agent As, for example, the water is said to descend *freely*, or to have liberty to descend by the channel of the river, because there is no impediment that way but *not* across, because the banks are impediments. And, though water cannot ascend, yet men never say, it wants the *liberty* to ascend, but the *faculty* or power, because the impediment is in the nature of the water, and intrinsical So also we say, he that is tied wants the *liberty* to go, because the impediment is not in him, but in his hands ; whereas we say not so of him who is sick or lame, because the impediment is in himself"—*Treatise of Liberty and Necessity*

According to Bonnet, "moral liberty is the power of the mind to obey without constraint the impulse of the motives which act upon it" This definition, which

---

[1] "The doctrine of philosophical necessity," says Priestley, "is in reality a modern thing, not older, I believe, than Mr Hobbes Of the Calvinists, I believe Mr. Jonathan Edwards to be the first."—*Illustrations of Philosophical Necessity*, p 195

Supposing this statement to be correct, does not the very modern date of Hobbes's alleged *discovery* furnish a very strong presumption against it ?

[* The question to which it relates is subjected to the examination of every person capable of reflection , and it is a question (according to the acknowledgment of all parties) so deeply interesting to human happiness, that no person able to comprehend its import can be supposed to have passed through life without forming some opinion concerning it It would be strange indeed, if Hobbes should have been the first to place a *fact* of this nature in its true light.]

* Restored.—*Ed*

is obviously the same in substance with that of Hobbes, is thus very justly, as well as acutely, animadverted on by Cuvier. "N'admettant aucune action sans motif, comme dit-il, il n'y a aucun effet sans cause, Bonnet définit la *liberté morale* le pouvoir de l'âme de suivre sans contrainte les motifs dont elle éprouve l impulsion, et résout ainsi les objections que l'on tire de la prévision de Dieu, mais peut-être aussi détournent-t-il l'idée qu'on se fait d'ordinaire de la liberté. Malgré ces opinions que touchent au Matérialisme et au Fatalisme, Bonnet fut très religieux."— *Biographie Universelle*, à Paris, 1812.—Art *Bonnet*

From this passage it appears, that the very ingenious writer was as completely aware as Clarke or Reid of the unsoundness of the definition of *moral liberty* given by Hobbes and his followers, and that the ultimate tendency of the doctrine which limits the free-agency of man to (what has been called) the *liberty of spontaneity*, was the same, though in a more disguised form, with that of fatalism.

For a complete exposure of the futility of this definition of *liberty*, as the word is employed in the controversy about man's free-agency, I have only to refer to Dr. Clarke's remarks on Collins, and to Dr. Reid's *Essays on the Active Powers of Man* In this last work, the various meanings of this very ambiguous word are explained with great accuracy and clearness.

The only two opinions which, in the actual state of metaphysical science, ought to be stated in contrast, are that of Liberty (or free-will) on the one side, and that of Necessity on the other As to the *Liberty of Spontaneity*, (which expresses a fact altogether foreign to the point in question,) I can conceive no motive for inventing such a phrase, but a desire in some writers to veil the scheme of necessity from their readers, under a language less revolting to the sentiments of mankind, and in others, an anxiety to banish it as far as possible from their own thoughts, by substituting, instead of the terms in which it is commonly expressed, a circumlocution which seems, on a superficial view, to concede something to the advocates for liberty.

If this phrase (the *Liberty of Spontaneity*) should fall into disuse, the other phrase, (the *Liberty of Indifference*,)[1] which is commonly stated in opposition to it, would become completely useless; nor would there be occasion for qualifying with any epithet, the older, simpler, and much more intelligible word, *Free-will*

The distinction between *physical* and *moral* necessity I conceive to be not less frivolous than those to which the foregoing animadversions relate On this point I agree with Diderot, that the word *necessity* (as it ought to be understood in this dispute) admits but of *one* interpretation

Note NN, p 307

To the arguments of Collins, against man's free-agency, some of his successors have added, the inconsistency of this doctrine with the known *effects of education* (under which phrase they comprehend the moral effects of all the external circumstances in which men are involuntarily placed) in forming the characters of individuals.

---

[1] Both phrases are favourite expressions with Lord Kames in his discussions on this subject See in particular the Appendix to his *Essay on Liberty and Necessity*, in the last edition of his *Essays on Morality and Natural Religion*

The plausibility of this argument (on which much stress has been laid by Priestley and others) arises entirely from the mixture of truth which it involves, or, to express myself more correctly, from the evidence and importance of the *fact* on which it proceeds, when that fact is stated with due limitations.

That the influence of *education*, in this comprehensive sense of the word, was greatly underrated by our ancestors, is now universally acknowledged; and it is to Locke's writings, more than to any other single cause, that the change in public opinion on this head is to be ascribed. On various occasions he has expressed himself very strongly with respect to the *extent* of this influence; and has more than once intimated his belief, that the great majority of men continue through life what early education had made them. In making use, however, of this strong language, his object (as is evident from the opinions which he has avowed in other parts of his works) was only to arrest the attention of his readers to the practical lessons he was anxious to inculcate, and not to state a metaphysical fact, which was to be literally and rigorously interpreted in the controversy about liberty and necessity. The only sound and useful *moral* to be drawn from the *spirit* of his observations, is the duty of gratitude to Heaven for all the blessings, in respect of education and of external situation, which have fallen to our own lot: the impossibility of ascertaining the involuntary misfortunes by which the seeming demerits of others may have been in part occasioned, and in the same proportion diminished, and the consequent obligation upon ourselves, to think as charitably as possible of their conduct, under the most unfavourable appearances. The truth of all this I conceive to be implied in these words of Scripture, " To whom much is given, of him much will be required;" and, if possible, still more explicitly and impressively, in the parable of the Talents.

Is not the use which has been made by Necessitarians of Locke's *Treatise on Education*, and other books of a similar tendency, only one instance more of that disposition, so common among metaphysical Sciolists, to appropriate to themselves the conclusions of their wiser and more sober predecessors, under the startling and imposing disguise of universal maxims, admitting neither of exception nor restriction? It is thus that Locke's judicious and refined remarks on the *Association of Ideas* have been exaggerated to such an extreme in the coarse *caricatures* of Hartley and of Priestley, as to bring, among cautious inquirers, some degree of discredit on one of the most important doctrines of modern philosophy. Or, to take another case still more in point; it is thus that Locke's reflections on the effects of education in modifying the intellectual faculties, and (where skilfully conducted) in supplying their original defects, have been distorted into the puerile paradox of Helvetius, that the mental capacities of the whole human race are the same at the moment of birth. It is sufficient for me here to throw out these hints, which will be found to apply equally to a large proportion of other theories started by modern metaphysicians.

Before I finish this note, I cannot refrain from remarking, with respect to the argument for Necessity drawn from the Divine prescience, that, if it be conclusive, it only affords an additional confirmation of what Clarke has said concerning the identity of the creed of the Necessitarians with that of the Spinozists. For, if God certainly foresees all the future volitions of his creatures, he must, for the same reason, foresee all *his own* future volitions; and if this knowledge infers a *necessity* of volition in the one case, how is it possible to avoid the same inference in the other?

NOTE O O, p 309

A similar application of St. Paul's comparison of the *potter* is to be found both in Hobbes and in Collins. Also, in a note annexed by Cowley to his ode entitled *Destiny*; an ode written (as we are informed by the author) " upon an extravagant supposition of two angels playing a game at chess, which, if they did, the spectators would have reason as much to believe that the pieces moved themselves, as we have for thinking the same of mankind, when we see them exercise so many and so different actions. It was of old said by Plautus, *Dii nos quasi pilas homines habent,* ' We are but tennis-balls for the gods to play withal, which they strike away at last, and still call for new ones, and St Paul says, ' *We are but the clay in the hand of the potter* ' "

For the comparison of the *potter,* alluded to by these different writers, see the Epistle to the Romans, chap ix. verses 18, 19, 20, 21 Upon these verses the only comment which I have to offer is a remark of the apostle Peter, that " In the epistles of our beloved brother Paul are some things hard to be understood, which they that are unlearned and unstable wrest unto their own destruction."

[* May I be permitted, at the same time, without being accused of trespassing on the province of the theological critic, to request my readers to compare the above passage from St. Paul with the sixth and following verses of the second chapter of the same epistle; recommending to their attention as a canon of Biblical criticism, which, although the reverse of that commonly adhered to in practice, I presume will not be disputed by the most orthodox divines,—that when two passages of Scripture have *the appearance* of being somewhat at variance with each other, the darker ought to be interpreted by the clearer, and not the clearer by the darker. To which canon, it may, by way of supplement, be added, that when one passage is in unison with the conclusions of our own reason, and with the dictates of our own moral feelings, while another, when literally understood, offers equal violence to both, the former is justly entitled to be preferred to the latter, as a rule of faith and of practice]

The same similitude of the *potter* makes a conspicuous figure in the writings of Hobbes, who has availed himself of this, as of many other insulated passages of Holy Writ, in support of principles which are now universally allowed to strike at the very root of religion and morality. The veneration of Cowley for Hobbes is well known, and is recorded by himself in the ode which immediately precedes that on Destiny It cannot, however, be candidly supposed, that Cowley understood the whole drift of Hobbes' doctrines. The contrary, indeed, in the present instance, is obvious from the ode before us; for while Cowley supposed the angels to move, like chess-men, the inhabitants of this globe, Hobbes (along with Spinoza) plainly conceived that the angels themselves, and even that Being to which he impiously gave the name of *God,* were all of them moved, like knights and pawns, by the invisible hand of fate or necessity.

Were it not for the serious and pensive cast of Cowley's mind, and his solemn appeal to the authority of the apostle, in support of the doctrine of *destiny,* one would be tempted to consider the first stanzas of this ode in the light of a *jeu*

* Restored —*Ed.*

d'esprit, introductory to the very characteristical and interesting picture of himself, with which the poem concludes

Note P P, p 312

"Tout ce qui est doit être, par cela même que cela est. Voilà la seule bonne philosophie Aussi longtemps que nous ne connaîtrons pas cet univers, comme on dit dans l'école, *a priori*, tout est nécessité. La liberté est un mot vide de sens, comme vous allez voir dans la lettre de M. Diderot."—*Lettre de Grimm au Duc de Saxe-Gotha*

"C'est ici, mon cher, que je vais quitter le ton de prédicateur pour prendre, si je peux, celui de philosophe. Regardez-y de près, et vous verrez que le mot liberté est un mot vide de sens, qu'il n'y a point, et qu'il ne peut y avoir d'êtres libres; que nous ne sommes que ce qui convient à l'ordre général, à l'organisation, à l'éducation, et à la chaîne des évènemens Voilà ce qui dispose de nous invinciblement. On ne conçoit non plus qu'un être agisse sans motif, qu'un des bras d'une balance agisse sans action d'un poids, et le motif nous est toujours extérieur, étranger, attaché ou par une nature ou par une cause quelconque, qui n'est pas nous. Ce qui nous trompe, c'est la prodigieuse variété de nos actions, jointe à l'habitude que nous avons prise tout en naissant, de confondre le volontaire avec le libre Nous avons tant loué, tant repris, nous l'avons été tant de fois, que c'est un préjugé bien vieux que celui de croire que nous et les autres voulons, agissons librement. Mais s'il n'y a point de liberté, il n'y a point d'action qui mérite la louange ou le blâme; il n'y a ni vice, ni vertu, rien dont il faille récompenser ou châtier. Qu'est ce qui distingue donc les hommes? La bienfaisance ou la malfaisance. Le malfaisant est un homme qu'il faut détruire et non punir, la bienfaisance est une bonne fortune, et non une vertu. Mais quoique l'homme bien ou malfaisant ne soit pas libre, l'homme n'en est pas moins un être qu'on modifie, c'est par cette raison qu'il faut détruire le malfaisant sur une place publique. De là les bons effets de l'exemple, des discours, de l'éducation, du plaisir, de la douleur, des grandeurs, de la misère, &c., de là une sorte de philosophie pleine de commisération, qui attache fortement aux bons, qui n'irrite non plus contre le méchant, que contre un ouragan qui nous remplit les yeux de poussière Il n'y a qu'une sorte de causes à proprement parler, ce sont les causes physiques Il n'y a qu'une sorte de nécessité, c'est la même pour tous les êtres Voilà ce qui me réconcilie avec le genre humain, c'est pour cette raison que je vous exhortais à la philanthropie. Adoptez ces principes si vous les trouvez bons, ou montrez-moi qu'ils sont mauvais. Si vous les adoptez, ils vous réconcilieront aussi avec les autres et avec vous-même; vous ne vous saurez ni bon ni mauvais gré d'être ce qui vous êtes Ne rien reprocher aux autres, ne se repentir de rien, voilà les premiers pas vers la sagesse. Ce qui est hors de là est préjugé, fausse philosophie."—*Correspondance Littéraire, Philosophique, et Critique, addressée au Duc de Saxe-Gotha*, par le Baron de Grimm et par Diderot. Première Partie, tom i pp. 300, 304, 305, 306. Londres, 1814

Note Q Q, p 323

See in Bayle the three articles *Luther*, *Knox*, and *Buchanan*. The following passage concerning Knox may serve as a specimen of the others It is quoted by

Bayle from the *Cosmographie Universelle* of Thevet, a writer who has long sunk into the contempt he merited, but whose zeal for legitimacy and the Catholic faith raised him to the dignity of almoner to Catherine de Medicis, and of historiographer to the King of France. I borrow the translation from the English *Historical Dictionary*.

"During that time the Scots never left England in peace, it was when Henry VIII. played his pranks with the chalices, relics, and other ornaments of the English churches; which tragedies and plays have been acted in our time in the kingdom of Scotland, by the exhortations of Noptz,[1] the first Scots minister of the bloody Gospel. This firebrand of sedition could not be content with barely following the steps of Luther, or of his master, Calvin, who had not long before delivered him from the galleys of the Prior of Capua, where he had been three years for his crimes, unlawful amours, and abominable fornications, for he used to lead a dissolute life, in shameful and odious places, and had been also found guilty of the particide and murder committed on the body of the Archbishop of St Andrew's, by the contrivances of the Earl of Rophol, of James Lescle, John Lescle, their uncle, and William du Coy. This simonist, who had been a priest of our church, being fattened by the benefices he had enjoyed, sold them for ready money, and finding that he could not make his cause good, he gave himself up to the most terrible blasphemies. He persuaded also several devout wives and religious virgins to abandon themselves to wicked adulterers Nor was this all During two whole years, he never ceased to rouse the people, encouraging them to take up arms against the Queen, and to drive her out of the kingdom, which he said was elective, as it had been formerly in the time of heathenism. . The Lutherans have churches and oratories Their ministers sing psalms, and say mass, and though it be different from ours, yet they add to it the Creed, and other prayers, as we do And when their ministers officiate, they wear the cope, the chasuble, and the surplice, as ours do, being concerned for their salvation, and careful of what relates to the public worship. Whereas the Scots have lived these twelve years past without laws, without religion, without ceremonies, constantly refusing to own a king or a queen, as so many brutes, suffering themselves to be imposed upon by the stories told them by this arch-hypocrite Noptz, a traitor to God and to his country, rather than to follow the pure Gospel, the councils, and the doctrine of so many holy doctors, both Greek and Latin, of the Catholic Church."

If any of my readers be yet unacquainted with the real character and history of this distinguished person, it may amuse them to compare the above passage with the very able, authentic, and animated account of his life, lately published by the reverend and learned Dr. M'Crie.

Note R R, p 335.

Dr Blair, whose estimate of the distinguishing beauties and imperfections of Addison's style, reflects honour on the justness and discernment of his taste, has allowed himself to be carried along much too easily, by the vulgar sneers at Addison's want of philosophical depth. In one of his lectures on rhetoric, he has even

---

[1] Thus Thevet (says Bayle) writes the name of Knox.

gone so far as to accuse Addison of misapprehending, or, at least, of *mis-stating*, Locke's doctrine concerning *secondary qualities* But a comparison of Dr Blair's own statement with that which he censures, will not turn out to the advantage of the learned critic; and I willingly lay hold of this example, as the point at issue turns on one of the most refined questions of metaphysics. The words of Addison are these —

"Things would make but a poor appearance to the eye, if we saw them only in their proper figures and motions And what reason can we assign for their exciting in us many of those ideas which are different from anything that exists in the objects themselves, (for such are light and colours,) were it not to add supernumerary ornaments to the universe, and make it more agreeable to the imagination?"

After quoting this sentence, Dr. Blair proceeds thus —

"Our author is now entering on a theory, which he is about to illustrate, if not with much philosophical accuracy, yet with great beauty of fancy and glow of expression. A strong instance of his want of accuracy appears in the manner in which he opens the subject For what meaning is there in things *exciting in us many of those ideas which are different from anything that exists in the objects?* No one, sure, ever imagined that our ideas exist in the objects Ideas, it is agreed on all hands, can exist nowhere but in the mind What Mr. Locke's philosophy teaches, and what our author should have said, is, *exciting in us many ideas of qualities which are different from anything that exists in the objects*"

- Let us now attend to Locke's theory, as stated by himself —

"From whence I think it is easy to draw this observation, That the *ideas* of primary qualities of bodies are *resemblances* of them, *and their patterns do really exist in the bodies themselves*, but the *ideas* produced in us by these secondary qualities have *no resemblance* of them at all There is nothing *like* our ideas existing in the bodies themselves They are in the bodies we denominate from them, only a power to produce these sensations in us And what is sweet, blue, or warm in *idea*, is but the certain bulk, figure, and motion of the insensible parts in the bodies themselves, which we call so."

The inaccuracy of Locke in conceiving that our *ideas* of primary qualities are *resemblances* of these qualities, and that the *patterns* of such ideas exist in the bodies themselves, has been fully exposed by Dr Reid But the *repetition* of Locke's inaccuracy (supposing Addison to have been really guilty of it) should not be charged upon him as a *deviation* from his master's doctrine To all, however, who understand the subject, it must appear evident, that Addison has, in this instance, *improved* greatly on Locke, by keeping out of view what is most exceptionable in his language, while he has retained all that is solid in his doctrine For my own part, I do not see how Addison's expressions could be altered to the better, except, perhaps, by substituting the words *unlike to*, instead of *different from* But in this last phrase Addison has been implicitly followed by Dr Blair, and certainly would not have been disavowed as an interpreter by Locke himself Let me add, that Dr. Blair's proposed emendation, ("exciting in us many ideas *of qualities*, which are different from anything that exists in the objects,") if not wholly unintelligible, deviates much farther from Locke's meaning than the correspondent clause in its original state The additional words *of qualities* throw an obscurity over the whole proposition, which was before sufficiently precise and perspicuous.¹

My principal reason for offering these remarks in vindication of Addison's account of secondary qualities, was to prepare the way for the sequel of the passage animadverted on by Dr Blair.

"We are everywhere entertained with pleasing shows and apparitions. We discover imaginary glories in the heavens and in the earth, and see some of this visionary beauty poured out upon the whole creation. But what a rough unsightly sketch of nature should we be entertained with, did all her colouring disappear, and the several distinctions of light and shade vanish?² In short, our souls are delightfully lost and bewildered in a pleasing delusion, and we walk about like the enchanted hero of a romance, who sees beautiful castles, woods, and meadows, and, at the same time, hears the warbling of birds and the purling of streams, but, upon the finishing of some secret spell, the fantastic scene breaks up, and the disconsolate knight finds himself on a barren heath, or in a solitary desert"

In this passage one is at a loss whether most to admire the author's depth and refinement of thought, or the singular felicity of fancy displayed in its illustration. The image of the *enchanted hero* is so unexpected, and, at the same time, so exquisitely appropriate, that it seems itself to have been conjured up by an enchanter's wand. Though introduced with the unpretending simplicity of a poetical simile, it has the effect of shedding the light of day on one of the darkest corners of metaphysics Nor is the language in which it is conveyed unworthy of the attention of the critic; abounding throughout with those natural and happy graces, which appear artless and easy to all but to those who have attempted to copy them.³

---

¹ Another passage, afterwards quoted by Dr Blair, might have satisfied him of the clearness and accuracy of Addison's ideas on the subject.

"I have here supposed that my reader is acquainted with that great modern discovery, which is, at present, universally acknowledged by all the inquirers into Natural Philosophy; namely, that light and colours, *as apprehended by the imagination*, are only ideas in the mind, and not qualities that have any existence in matter As this is a truth which has been proved incontestably by many modern philosophers, if the English reader would see the notion explained at large, he may find it in the eighth book of Mr Locke's *Essay on Human Understanding*"

I have already taken notice (*Elements of the Philosophy of the Human Mind*, vol. 1 Note P) of the extraordinary precision of the above statement, arising from the clause printed in Italics. By a strange slip of memory, I ascribed the merit of this very judicious qualification, not to Addison, but to Dr Akenside, who transcribed it from the Spectator

The last quotation affords me also an opportunity of remarking the correctness of Addison's information about the history of this doctrine, which most English writers have conceived to be an original speculation of Locke's. From some of Addison's expressions, it is more than probable that he had derived his first knowledge of it from Malebranche

² On the supposition made in this sentence, the face of Nature, instead of presenting a "rough unsightly sketch," would, it is evident, become wholly invisible. But I need scarcely say, this does not render Mr Addison's allusion less pertinent.

³ [* " Ut sibi quivis
Speret idem , sudet multum, frustraque laboret
Ausus idem "

Dr Blair objects to the clause, (*the fantastic scene breaks up*,) remarking that "the expression is lively, but not altogether justifiable." "An assembly, (he adds,) *breaks up*, a scene *closes* or *disappears*"

To this criticism I cannot assent One of the oldest and most genuine meanings of the verb *break up*, is to dissolve or vanish, nor do I know any word or phrase in our language which could here be substituted in its place, without

* Restored.—*Ed*

The praise which I have bestowed on Addison as a commentator on this part of Locke's Essay, will not appear extravagant to those who may take the trouble to compare the conciseness and elegance of the foregoing extracts with the prolixity and homeliness of the author's text. (See Locke's *Essay*, book ii. chap. viii. sects. 17, 18.) It is sufficient to mention here, that his chief illustration is taken from "the effects of manna on the stomach and guts."

Note S S, p. 349.

For the following note I am indebted to my learned friend, Sir William Hamilton, Professor of Universal History in the University of Edinburgh.

The *Clavis Universalis* of Arthur Collier, though little known in England, has been translated into German. It is published in a work entitled "*Samlung,*" (sic) &c. &c., literally, "A Collection of the most distinguished Authors who deny the existence of their own bodies, and of the whole material world, containing the dialogues of Berkeley, between Hylas and Philonous, and Collier's *Universal Key* translated, with Illustrative Observations, and an Appendix, wherein the Existence of Body is demonstrated, by John Christopher Eschenbach, Professor of Philo-

impairing the effect of the picture. It is a favourite expression of Bacon's in this very sense.

"These and the like conceits, when men have cleared their understanding by the light of experience, will scatter and *break up* like mist."— "The speedy depredation of air upon watery moisture, and version of the same into air appeareth in nothing more visible than the sudden discharge or vanishing of a little cloud of breath or vapour from glass or any polished body, for the mistiness scattereth and *breaketh up* suddenly." And elsewhere, "But ere he came near it, the pillar and cross of light *brake up*, and cast itself abroad, as it were, into a firmament of many stars."

Of the charm attached to such appropriate or specific idioms, no English writers have been more aware than Addison and Burke, but, in general, they are employed with far greater taste and judgment by the former than by the latter. The use of them is indeed hazardous to all who have been educated at a distance from the seat of government, and, accordingly, the best of our Scotch writers have thought it safer to lean to the opposite extreme. Fénélon has remarked something similar to this among the *provinciaux* of his own country. "On a tant de peur d'être bas, qu'on est ordinaire *sec et vague* dans les expressions. Nous avons là-dessus une fausse politésse, semblable à celle de certains provinciaux qui se piquent de bel esprit, et qui croiraient s'abaisser en nommant les choses par leur nom."

In applying, however, this very judicious observation, it ought not to be forgotten, that Fénélon had from his youth moved exclusively in that privileged circle of society which gives law to speech, and, of consequence, that in the selection of his idioms he might trust to his ear with a confidence which few of our southern neighbours (I least of all, except those purists whose taste has been formed within the sound of *Bow-bell*) are entitled to feel. How many of these, while they fancy they are rivalling the easy and graceful Anglicism of Addison, unconsciously betray the secret of those early habits and inveterate associations which they are so anxious to conceal!

The passage of Addison which suggested this note, has been versified and expanded by Akenside, but there is a conciseness, simplicity, and freshness in the original, which it is impossible to preserve in any poetical version.

" So fables tell,
Th' adventurous hero, bound on hard exploits,
Beholds, with glad surprise, by secret spells
Of some kind sage, the patron of his toils,
A visionary paradise disclosed
Amid the dubious wild, wild streams and shades,
And airy songs, th' enchanted landscape smiles,
Cheers his long labours and renews his frame."

The reflection, however, of the philosophical poet, on the accession to the sum of our enjoyments, arising from this arbitrary adaptation of the human frame to the constitution of external objects, is, so far as I know, exclusively his own.

" Not content
With every food of life to nourish man,
By kind illusions of the wondering sense,
Thou mak'st all mature beauty to his eye
And music to his ear."]

sophy in Rostock"—(Rostock, 1756, 8vo) The remarks are numerous, and show much reading The Appendix contains.—1 An exposition of the opinions of the Idealists, with its grounds and arguments. 2 A proof of the external existence of body. The argument on which he chiefly dwells to show the existence of matter is the same with that of Dr Reid, in so far as he says, "a direct proof must not here be expected; in regard to the fundamental principles of human nature this is seldom possible, or rather is absolutely impossible." He argues at length, that the Idealist has no better proof of the existence of his soul than of the existence of his body "When an Idealist says, *I am a thinking being; of this I am certain from internal conviction;*—I would ask from whence he derives this certainty, and why he excludes from this conviction the possibility of deception? He has no other answer than this, *I feel it It is impossible that I can have any representation (Vorstellung, presentation) of self without the consciousness of being a thinking being.* In the same manner, Eschenbach argues (right or wrong) that the *feeling* applies to the existence of body, and that the ground of belief is equally strong and conclusive, in respect to the reality of the *objective*, as of the *subjective* in perception."

NOTE T T, p. 377.

"*And yet Diderot, in some of his lucid intervals, seems to have thought and felt very differently*"

The following passage (extracted from his *Pensées Philosophiques*) is pronounced by La Harpe to be not only one of the most eloquent which Diderot has written, but to be one of the best comments which is anywhere to be found on the Cartesian argument for the existence of God. It has certainly great merit in point of reasoning, but I cannot see with what propriety it can be considered as a comment upon the argument of Descartes, nor am I sure if, in point of eloquence, it be as well suited to the English as to the French taste.

"Convenez qu'il y auroit de la folie à refuser à vos semblables la faculté de penser. Sans doute, mais que s'ensuit-il de là? Il s'ensuit, que si l'univers, que dis-je l'univers, si l'aile d'un papillon m'offre des traces mille fois plus distinctes d'une intelligence que vous n'avez d'indices que votre semblable a la faculté de penser, il est mille fois plus fou de nier qu'il existe un Dieu, que de nier que votre semblable pense Or, que cela soit ainsi, c'est à vos lumières, c'est à votre conscience que j'en appelle. Avez-vous jamais remarqué dans les raisonnemens, les actions, et la conduite de quelque homme que ce soit, plus d intelligence, d'ordre, de sagacité, de conséquence, que dans le mécanisme d'un insecte? La divinité n'est elle pas aussi clairement empreinte dans l'œil d'un ciron, que la faculté de penser dans les écrits du grand Newton? Quoi! le monde formé prouverait moins d'intelligence, que le monde expliqué? Quelle assertion! l'intelligence d'un premier être ne m'est pas mieux démontrée par ses ouvrages, que la faculté de penser dans un philosophe par ses écrits? Songez donc que je ne vous objecte que l'aile d'un papillon, quand je pourrais vous écraser du poids de l'univers "

This, however, was certainly not the creed which Diderot professed in his more advanced years The article, on the contrary, which immediately follows the foregoing quotation, there is every reason to think, expresses his real sentiments on the subject. I transcribe it at length, as it states clearly and explicitly the same

argument which is indirectly hinted at in a late publication by a far more illustrious author

"J'ouvre les cahiers d'un philosophe célèbre, et je lis : 'Athées, je vous accorde que le mouvement est essentiel à la matière ; qu'en concluez-vous ? que le monde résulte du jet fortuit d'atomes ? J'aimerois autant que vous me disiez que l'Iliade d'Homère ou la Henriade de Voltaire est un résultat de jets fortuits de caractères?' Je me garderai bien de faire ce raisonnement à un athée. Cette comparaison lui donneroit beau jeu. Selon les lois de l'analyse des sorts, me diroit-il, je ne dois être surpris qu'une chose arrive, lorsqu'elle est possible, et que la difficulté de l'évènement est compensée par la quantité des jets Il y a tel nombre de coups dans lesquels je gagerois avec avantage d'amener cent mille six à la fois avec cent mille dés. Quelle que fût la somme finie de caractères avec laquelle on me proposeroit d'engendrer fortuitement l'Iliade, il y a telle somme finie de jets qui me rendroit la proposition avantageuse ; mon avantage seroit même infini, si la quantité de jets accordée étoit infinie —[*Vous voulez bien convenir avec moi, continueroit-il, que la matière existe de toute éternité, et que le mouvement lui est essentiel Pour répondre à cette faveur, je vais supposer avec vous que le monde n'a point de bornes, que la multitude des atomes est infinie, et que cet ordre qui nous étonne ne se dément nulle part. Or, de ces aveux réciproques, il ne s'ensuit autre chose, si non que la possibilité d'engendrer fortuitement l'univers est très petite, mais que la quantité de jets est infinie, c'est-à-dire, que la difficulté de l'évènement est plus que suffisamment compensée par la multitude des jets Donc si quelque chose doit répugner à la raison, c'est la supposition que la matière s'étant mue de toute l'éternité, et qu'ayant peut-être dans la somme infinie de combinaisons possibles, un nombre infini d'arrangemens admirables, il ne se soit rencontré aucun de ces arrangemens admirables dans la multitude infinie de ceux qu'elle a pris successivement Donc l'esprit doit être plus étonné de la durée hypothétique du chaos, que de la naissance réelle de l'univers."]—*Pensées Philosophiques*, par Diderot, xxi

My chief reason for considering this as the genuine exposition of Diderot's own creed is, that he omits no opportunity of suggesting the same train of thinking in his other works. It may be distinctly traced in the following passage of his *Traité du Beau*, the substance of which he has also introduced in the article *Beau* of the *Encyclopédie*.

"Le beau n'est pas toujours l'ouvrage d'une cause intelligente, le mouvement établit souvent, soit dans un être considéré solitairement, soit entre plusieurs êtres comparés entr'eux, une multitude prodigieuse de rapports surprenans Les cabinets d'histoire naturelle en offrent un grand nombre d'exemples. Les rapports sont alors des résultats de combinaisons fortuites, du moins par rapport à nous. La nature imite en se jouant, dans cent occasions, les productions d'art, et l'on pourroit demander, je ne dis pas si ce philosophe qui fût jeté par une tempête sur les bords d'une Ile inconnue, avoit raison de se crier, à la vue de quelque figures de géométrie; '*Courage, mes amis, voici des pas d'hommes ;*' mais combien il faudroit remarquer de rapports dans un être, pour avoir une certitude complète qu'il est l'ouvrage d'un artiste[1] (en quelle occasion, un seul défaut de symmétrie

---

* Restored —*Ed*

[1] Is not this precisely the sophistical mode of questioning known among Logicians by the name of *Sorites* or *Acervus?* "Vitiosum sane," says Cicero, " et captiosum genus "—*Acad. Quæst.*, lib. iv. xvi.

NOTE TT.   587

prouveroit plus que toute somme donnée de rapports,) comment sont entr'eux le temps de l'action de la cause fortuite, et les rapports observés dans les effets produits, et si (à l'exception des œuvres du Tout-Puissant)[1] il y a des cas où le nombre des rapports ne puisse jamais être compensé par celui des jets."

With respect to the passages here extracted from Diderot, it is worthy of observation, that if the atheistical argument from chances be conclusive in its application to that order of things which we behold, it is not less conclusive when applied to every other possible combination of atoms which imagination can conceive, and affords a mathematical proof, that the fables of Grecian mythology, the tales of the genii, and the dreams of the Rosicrucians, *may*, or rather *must*, all of them, be somewhere or other realized in the infinite extent of the universe: a proposition which, if true, would destroy every argument for or against any given system of opinions founded on the reasonableness or the unreasonableness of the tenets involved in it; and would, of consequence, lead to the subversion of the whole frame of the human understanding.[2]

Mr. Hume, in his *Natural History of Religion*, (Sect. xi.), has drawn an inference from the internal evidence of the Heathen Mythology, in favour of the supposition that it may not be altogether so fabulous as is commonly supposed.

---

[1] To those who enter fully into the spirit of the foregoing reasoning, it is unnecessary to observe, that this parenthetical clause is nothing better than an ironical *salvo*. If the argument proves anything, it leads to this general conclusion, that the apparent order of the universe affords no evidence whatever of the existence of a designing cause.

[2] The atheistical argument here quoted from Diderot is, at least, as old as the time of Epicurus.

Nam certe neque consilio primordia rerum
Ordine se quæque, atque sagaci mente locarunt
Nec quos quæque darent motus pepigere profecto,
Sed quia multimodis, multis, mutata, per omne
Ex infinito vexantur percita plagis,
Omne genus motus, et cœtus experiundo,
Tandem deveniunt in talens disposituras,
Qualibus hæc rebus consistit summa creata.
Lucret. lib 1 l 1026

And still more explicitly in the following lines:—

Nam cum respicias immensi temporis omne
Præteritum spatium, tum motus materiai
Multimodi quam sint facile hoc adcredere possis,
Semina sæpe in eodem, ut nunc sunt, ordine posta.
Ibid lib iii l 857

[* The whole of this reasoning (if it deserves that name) proceeds evidently on the supposition that the atoms, or *semina*, considered by Epicurus as the *Primordia Rerum*, are *finite* in their number, and that this was also the idea of Diderot in the passage last quoted, appears from the concluding words, in which he speaks of the possibility of the number of *rapports* being compensated by the number of *jets*. If we suppose the number of atoms to be *infinite*, the whole of this Epicurean speculation falls at once to the ground. Dr Bentley seems, indeed, to have thought, that this last supposition involves a contradiction *in terminis*, inasmuch as it implies the possibility of an *innumerable number* or a *sumless sum*; but this cavil is, I think, obviated in a very satisfactory manner by Sir Isaac Newton, who plainly leaned to the opinion, that the matter of the universe is scattered over the immensity of space. See his Third Letter to Dr Bentley.

The idea of a *finite universe* presents, to my mind at least, as great a difficulty as that which staggered Dr Bentley. But to what purpose employ our faculties on subjects so far above their reach as all those manifestly are in which the notions of infinity or of eternity are concerned?

I have said, that if we suppose the number of atoms to be infinite, the whole of this Epicurean speculation falls at once to the ground. This, however, does not seem to have been attended to by Lucretius, who expressly teaches, that the universe is without bounds, and that the number of atoms is infinite.—Lucret. lib i v 957, *et seq*. Diderot also thinks, that he may safely make this concession, without weakening his argument. "Pour répondre à cette faveur je vais supposer avec vous que le monde n'a point de bornes et *que la multitude des atòmes est infinie*."

* Restored.—*Ed.*

"The whole mythological system is so natural, that in the vast variety of planets and worlds contained in this universe, *it seems more than probable*, that somewhere or other it is really carried into execution." The argument of Diderot goes much farther, and leads to an extension of Mr Hume's conclusion to all conceivable systems, whether *natural* or not.

But further, since the human mind, and all the numberless displays of wisdom and of power which it has exhibited, are ultimately to be referred to a fortuitous concourse of atoms, why might not the Supreme Being, such as we are commonly taught to regard him, have been Himself (as well as the Gods of Epicurus)[1] the result of the continued operation of the same blind causes? or rather, *must* not such a Being have necessarily resulted from these causes operating from all eternity, through the immensity of space?—a conclusion, by the way, which, according to Diderot's own principles, would lead us to refer the era of his origin to a period indefinitely more remote than any given point of time which imagination can assign, or, in other words, to a period to which the epithet *eternal* may with perfect propriety be applied. The amount, therefore, of the whole matter is this, that the atheistical reasoning, as stated by Diderot, leaves the subject of natural, and, I may add, of revealed religion, precisely on the same footing as before, without invalidating, in the very smallest degree, the evidence for any one of the doctrines connected with either, nay more, superadding to this evidence, a mathematical demonstration of the *possible* truth of all those articles of belief which it was the object of Diderot to subvert from their foundation.

It might be easily shown, that these principles, if pushed to their legitimate consequences, instead of establishing the just authority of reason in our constitution, would lead to the most unlimited credulity on all subjects whatever; or (what is only another name for the same thing) to that state of mind, which, in the words of Mr Hume, "does not consider any one proposition as more certain, or even as more probable, than another."

The following curious and (in my opinion) instructive anecdote has a sufficient connexion with the subject of this note, to justify me in subjoining it to the foregoing observations. I transcribe it from the Notes annexed to the Abbé de Lille's poem, entitled *La Conversation*. à Paris, 1812.

"Dans la société du Baron d'Holbach, Diderot proposa un jour de nommer un *avocat de Dieu*, et on choisit l'Abbé Galiani. Il s'assit et débuta ainsi :

"Un jour à Naples, un homme de la Basilicate prit devant nous, six dés dans un cornet, et paria d'amener rafle de six. Je dis cette chance étoit possible. Il l'amena sur le champ une seconde fois, je dis la même chose. Il remit les dés dans le cornet trois, quatre, cinq fois, et toujours rafle de six. *Sangue di Bacco,* m'écriai-je, *les dés sont pipés ;* et ils l'étoient.

"Philosophes, quand je considère l'ordre toujours renaissant de la nature, ses lois immuables, ses révolutions toujours constantes dans une variété infinie, cette chance unique et conservatrice d'un univers tel que nous le voyons, qui revient sans cesse, malgré cent autres millions de chances de perturbation et de destruction possibles, je m'écrie. *certes la nature est pipée !*"

The argument here stated strikes me as irresistible; nor ought it at all to weaken its effect, that it was spoken by the mouth of the Abbé Galiani.

[1] Cic. *de Nat Deor* lib i xxiv

NOTE U U.   589

Whatever his own professed principles may have been, this theory of the *loaded die* appears evidently, from the repeated allusions to it in his familiar correspondence, to have produced a very deep impression on his mind —See *Correspondance inédite de* l'Abbé Galiani, &c , vol i pp 18, 42, 141, 142   à Paris, 1818.

As the old argument of the atomical atheists is plainly that on which the school of Diderot are still disposed to rest the strength of their cause, I shall make no apology for the length of this note The *sceptical* suggestions on the same subject which occur in Mr. Hume's *Essay on the Idea of Necessary Connexion*, and which have given occasion to so much discussion in this country, do not seem to me to have ever produced any considerable impression on the French philosophers.

[* M Daunou observes, that Galiani is so celebrated for his Dialogues on the Corn Trade, published at Paris in 1770, that his correspondence cannot but excite the curiosity of men of letters. But though these letters contain some interesting passages, especially remarks on the dramatic art, which he had particularly studied, on fatalism, religion, incredulity, ambition, ennui, education, on Cicero, Louis XIV , and other celebrated persons, yet these two volumes are on the whole very futile ; and if any service has been done by their publication, it is certainly not to the memory of Galiani, who paints himself in colours that do him little honour , an egotist by character and system , actuated, in all the relations of life, by the grossest self-interest , laughing at his own doctrine and those who think it *profound*, whereas, says he, "*it is hollow, and there is nothing in it*," yet foaming with rage against those who contradicted it, loading them with insults and calumnies, denouncing them as seditious, and seriously complaining that they are not sent to the Bastille , exercising himself, beyond all bounds, in freedom of ideas, and sometimes of expression, yet recommending the most rigid intolerance , and who, when charged at Naples with the *censure* of the drama, beginning by prohibiting the performance of Tartuffe , lastly, boasting of admitting no other policy than "*pure Machiavelism, sans mélange, cru, vert, dans toute sa force, dans toute son apreté.*"

The inedited Correspondence of Abbé Ferd Galiani with Madame d'Epinay, Baron d'Holbach, &c. (from the *Journal des Savans*, January, 1819).]

Note U U, p 378.

Among the contemporaries of Diderot, the author of the *Spirit of Laws* is entitled to particular notice, for the respect with which he always speaks of natural religion A remarkable instance of this occurs in a letter to Dr Warburton, occasioned by the publication of his *View of Bolingbroke's Philosophy*. The letter, it must be owned, savours somewhat of the political religionist , but how fortunate would it have been for France, if, during its late revolutionary governments, such sentiments as those here expressed by Montesquieu had been more generally prevalent among his countrymen ! " Celui qui attaque la religion révélée n'attaque que la religion révélée , mais celui qui attaque la religion naturelle attaque toutes les religions du monde . . . Il n'est pas impossible d'attaquer une religion révélée, parce qu'elle existe par des faits particuliers, et que les faits par leur nature

---

* At the end of the volume, Mr Stewart had inserted the following extract, written by a stranger-hand.—*Ed*

peuvent être une matière de dispute, mais il n'en est pas de même de la religion naturelle; elle est tirée de la nature de l'homme, dont on ne peut pas disputer encore. J'ajoute à ceci, quel peut-être le motif d'attaquer la religion révélée en Angleterre ? On l'y a tellement purgé de tout préjugé destructeur qu'elle n'y peut faire de mal et qu'elle y peut faire, au contraire, une infinité de bien Je sais, qu'un homme en Espagne ou en Portugal que l'on va bruler, ou qui craint d'être brulé, parce qu'il ne croit point de certains articles dépendans ou non de la religion révélée, a un juste sujet de l'attaquer, parce qu'il peut avoir quelque espérance de pourvoir à sa défense naturelle : mais il n'en pas de même en Angleterre, où tout homme qui attaque la religion révélée l'attaque sans intérêt, et où cet homme, quand il réussiroit, quand même il auroit raison dans le fond, ne feroit que détruire une infinité de biens pratiques, pour établir une vérité purement spéculative."— For the whole letter, see the 4to edit of Montesquieu's *Works* Paris, 1788 Tome v p 391 Also Warburton's *Works*, by Hurd, vol. vii. p. 553 London, 1758

In the foregoing passage, Montesquieu hints more explicitly than could well have been expected from a French magistrate, at a consideration which ought always to be taken into the account in judging of the works of his countrymen, when they touch on the subject of religion; I mean, the corrupted and intolerant spirit of that system of faith which is immediately before their eyes. The eulogy bestowed on the Church of England is particularly deserving of notice, and should serve as a caution to Protestant writers against making common cause with the defenders of the Church of Rome

With respect to Voltaire, who, amidst all his extravagances and impieties, is well known to have declared open war against the principles maintained in the *Système de la Nature*, it is remarked by Madame de Stael, that two different epochs may be distinguished in his literary life; the one, while his mind was warm from the philosophical lessons he had imbibed in England; the other, after it became infected with those extravagant principles which, soon after his death, brought a temporary reproach on the name of Philosophy. As the observation is extended by the very ingenious writer to the French nation in general, and draws a line between two classes of authors who are frequently confounded together in this country, I shall transcribe it in her own words

"Il me semble qu'on pourroit marquer dans le dix-huitième siècle, en France, deux époques parfaitement distinctes, celle dans laquelle l'influence de l'Angleterre s'est fait sentir, et celle où les esprits se sont précipités dans la destruction Alors les lumières se sont changées en incendie, et la philosophie, magicienne irritée, a consumé le palais où elle avoit étalé ses prodiges.

"En politique, Montesquieu appartient à la première époque, Raynal à la seconde, en religion, les écrits de Voltaire, qui avoit la tolérance pour but, sont inspirés par l'esprit de la première moitié du siècle, mais sa misérable et vaniteuse irréligion a flétri la seconde."—*De l'Allemagne*, tom iii pp 37, 38

Nothing, in truth, can be more striking than the contrast between the spirit of Voltaire's early and of his later productions. From the former may be quoted some of the sublimest sentiments anywhere to be found, both of religion and of morality In some of the latter, he appears irrecoverably sunk in the abyss of fatalism. Examples of both are so numerous, that one is at a loss in the selection In making

choice of the following, I am guided chiefly by the comparative shortness of the passages.

> "Consulte Zoroastre, et Minos, et Solon,
> Et le sage Socrate, et le grand Cicéron ·
> Ils ont adoré tous un maître, un juge, un père,—
> Ce système sublime à l'homme est nécessaire.
> C'est le sacré lien de la société,
> Le premier fondement de la sainte équité,
> Le frein du scélérat, l'espérance du juste.
> Si les cieux, dépouillés de leur empreinte auguste,
> Pouvoient cesser jamais de le manifester,
> Si Dieu n'existoit pas, il faudroit l'inventer."[1]

Nor is it only on this fundamental principle of religion that Voltaire, in his better days, delighted to enlarge. The existence of a natural law engraved on the human heart, and the liberty of the human will, are subjects which he has repeatedly enforced and adorned with all his philosophical and poetical powers. What can be more explicit, or more forcible, than the following exposition of the inconsistencies of fatalism?

> "Vois de la liberté cet ennemi mutin,
> Aveugle partisan d'un aveugle destin;
> Entends comme il consulte, approuve, ou délibère,
> Entends de quel reproche il couvre un adversaire,
> Vois comment d'un rival il cherche à se venger,
> Comme il punit son fils, et le veut corriger.
> Il le croyoit donc libre?—Oui, sans doute, et lui-même
> Dément à chaque pas son funeste système.
> Il mentoit à son cœur, en voulant expliquer
> Ce dogme absurde à croire, absurde à pratiquer.
> Il reconnoit en lui le sentiment qu'il brave,
> Il agit comme libre et parle comme esclave."[2]

This very system, however, which Voltaire has here so severely reprobated, he lived to avow as the creed of his more advanced years. The words, indeed, are put into the mouth of a fictitious personage; but it is plain that the writer meant to be understood as speaking his own sentiments. "Je vois une chaine immense, dont tout est chainon, elle embrasse, elle serre aujourd'hui la nature," &c. &c.

---

[1] A thought approaching very nearly to this occurs in one of Tillotson's Sermons. "The being of God is so comfortable, so convenient, so necessary to the felicity of mankind, that (as Tully admirably says) *Dii immortales ad usum hominum fabricati pene videantur*—If God were not a necessary being of himself, he might almost be said to be made for the use and benefit of Man." For some ingenious remarks on this quotation from Cicero, see Jortin's *Tracts*, vol. i. p. 371.

[2] These verses form part of a *Discourse on the Liberty of Man*, and the rest of the poem is in the same strain. Yet so very imperfectly did Voltaire even then understand the metaphysical argument on this subject, that he prefixed to his Discourse the following advertisement:—"On entend par ce mot *liberté*, le pouvoir de faire ce qu'on veut. Il n'y a, et ne peut y avoir d'autre *liberté*." It appears, therefore, that in maintaining the *liberty of spontaneity*, Voltaire conceived himself to be combating the scheme of Necessity, whereas *this* sort of liberty no Necessitarian or Fatalist was ever hardy enough to dispute.

"Je suis donc ramené malgré moi à cette ancienne idée, que je vois être la base de tous les systèmes, dans laquelle tous les philosophes retombent apres mille détours, et qui m'est démontré par toutes les actions des hommes, par les miennes, par tous les évènemens que j'ai lus, que j'ai vus, et aux-quelles j'ai eu part, c'est le Fatalisme, c'est la Nécessité dont je vous ai déjà parlé."—*Lettres de Memmius à Cicéron* See *Œuvres* de Voltaire, *Mélanges*, tome iv p 358 4to edit. Genève, 1771.

"En effet, (says Voltaire, in another of his pieces,) il seroit bien singulier que toute la nature, tous les astres, obéissent à des lois éternelles, et qu'il y eut un petit animal haut de cinq pieds, qui au mépris de ces lois pût agir toujours comme il lui plairoit au seul gré de son caprice."

To this passage Voltaire adds the following acknowledgment:—"L'ignorant qui pense ainsi n'a pas toujours pensé de même,[1] mais il est enfin contraint de se rendre"—*Le Philosophe Ignorant.*

Notwithstanding, however, this change in Voltaire's philosophical opinions, he continued to the last his zealous opposition to atheism[2] But in what respects it is more pernicious than fatalism, it is not easy to discover.

A reflection of La Harpe's, occasioned by some strictures of Voltaire's upon Montesquieu, applies with equal force to the numberless inconsistencies which occur in his metaphysical speculations "Les objets de méditation étoient trop étrangers à l'excessive vivacité de son esprit Saisir fortement par l'imagination les objets qu'elle ne doit montrer que d'un côté, c'est ce qui est du Poète, les embrasser sous toutes les faces, c'est ce qui est du Philosophe, et Voltaire étoit trop exclusivement l'un pour être l'autre"—*Cours de Littérat.* tom xv. pp 46, 47.

A late author[3] has very justly reprobated that *spiritual deification of nature* which has been long fashionable among the French, and which, according to his own account, is at present not unfashionable in Germany. It is proper, however, to observe, that this mode of speaking has been used by two very different classes of writers; by the one with an intention to keep as much as possible the Deity out of their view, while studying his works; by the other, as a convenient and well understood metaphor, by means of which the frequent and irreverent mention of the name of God is avoided in philosophical arguments It was with this last view, undoubtedly, that it was so often employed by Newton, and other English

---

[1] In proof of this he refers to his *Treatise of Metaphysics*, written forty years before, for the use of Madame du Châtelet.

[2] See the *Dict Philosophique*, Art *Athéisme* See also the Strictures on the *Système de la Nature* in the *Questions sur l'Encyclopédie*, the very work from which the above quotation is taken

[* The same work contains the following observations on Final Causes —

"Je sais bien que plusieurs philosophes, et surtout *Lucrèce* ont nié les causes finales, et je sais que Lucrèce, quoique peu châtié, est un très grand poète dans ses déscriptions, et dans son morale, mais en philosophie il me paraît, je l'avoue, fort au dessous d'un portier de collège et d'un bedeau de paroisse Affermir que ni l'œil n'est fait pour voir, ni l'oreille pour entendre, ni l'estomac pour digérer, n'est ce pas là la plus énorme absurdité, la plus révoltante folie qui soit jamais tombée dans l'esprit humaine? Tout douteux que je suis, cette démence me paraît évidente, et je le dis

"Pour moi je ne vois dans la nature comme dans les arts, que des causes finales, et je crois un pommier fait pour porter des pommes, comme je vois un montre faite pour marquer l'heure"]

[3] Frederick Schlegel *Lectures on the History of Literature*, vol ii. p 169 Edinburgh, 1818

* Restored —*Ed*

philosophers of the same school. In general, when we find a writer speaking of the *wise* or of the *benevolent intentions* of nature, we should be slow in imputing to him any leaning towards atheism. Many of the finest instances of Final Causes, it is certain, which the eighteenth century has brought to light, have been first remarked by inquirers who seem to have been fond of this phraseology, and of these inquirers, it is possible that some would have been less forward in bearing testimony to the truth, had they been forced to avail themselves of the style of theologians. These speculations, therefore, concerning the *intentions* or *designs of Nature*, how reprehensible soever and even absurd in point of strict logic the language may be in which they are expressed, may often be, nay, have often been, a step towards something higher and better; and, at any rate, are of a character totally different from the blind chance of the Epicureans, or the conflicting principles of the Manicheans.

Note XX, p. 406

"*In the attempt, indeed, which Kant has made to enumerate the general ideas which are not derived from experience, but arise out of the pure understanding, Kant may well lay claim to the praise of originality.*" The object of this problem is thus stated by his friend, Mr. Schulz, the author of the Synopsis formerly quoted. The following translation is by Dr Willich, *Elements*, &c p. 45.

"To investigate the whole store of original notions discoverable in our understanding, and which lie at the foundation of all our knowledge, and, at the same time, to authenticate their true descent, by showing that they are not derived from experience, but are pure productions of the understanding.

"1 The perceptions of objects contain, indeed, the matter of knowledge, but are in themselves blind and dead, and not knowledge, and our soul is merely passive in regard to them.

"2 If these perceptions are to furnish knowledge, the understanding must think of them, and this is possible only through notions, (conceptions,) which are the peculiar form of our understanding, in the same manner as space and time are the form of our sensitive faculty

"3. These notions are active representations of our understanding faculty, and as they regard *immediately* the perceptions of objects, they refer to the objects themselves only mediately.

"4 They lie in our understanding as pure notions à *priori*, at the foundation of all our knowledge. They are necessary forms, radical notions, categories, (predicaments,) of which all our knowledge of them must be compounded: And the table of them follows.

"*Quantity;* unity, plurality, totality.

"*Quality;* reality, negation, limitation.

"*Relation;* substance, cause, reciprocation

"*Modality;* possibility, existence, necessity.

"5 Now, to think and to judge is the same thing; consequently, every notion contains a particular form of judgment concerning objects There are *four* principal *genera of judgments*. They are derived from the above four possible functions of the understanding, each of which contains under it *three species;* namely, with respect to—

"*Quantity*, they are universal, particular, singular judgments
"*Quality*, they are affirmative, negative, infinite judgments
"*Relation*, they are categorical, hypothetical, disjunctive judgments
"*Modality*, they are problematical, assertory, apodictical judgments"
These tables speak for themselves without any comment

Note Y Y, p 408

Kant's notions of *Time* are contained in the following seven propositions:
"1. *Idea temporis non oritur sed supponitur a sensibus* 2 *Idea temporis est singularis*, non generalis. Tempus enim quodlibet non cogitatur, nisi tanquam pars unius ejusdem temporis immensi. 3. *Idea itaque temporis est intuitus*, et quoniam ante omnem sensationem concipitur, tanquam conditio respectuum in sensibilibus obviorum, est *intuitus*, non sensualis, sed *purus* 4 *Tempus est quantum continuum* et legum continui in mutationibus universi principium 5 *Tempus non est objectivum aliquid et reale*, nec substantia, nec accidens, nec relatio, sed subjectiva conditio, per naturam mentis humanæ necessaria, quælibet sensibilia, certa lege sibi co-ordinandi, et *intuitus purus* 6 Tempus est conceptus verissimus, et, per omnia possibilia sensuum objecta, in infinitum patens, intuitivæ repræsentationis conditio. 7. Tempus itaque est *principium formale mundi sensibilis* absolute primum"

With respect to *Space*, Kant states a series of similar propositions, ascribing to it very nearly the same metaphysical attributes as to *Time*, and running as far as possible a sort of parallel between them "A *Conceptus spatii non abstrahitur a sensationibus externis* B. *Conceptus spatii est singularis repræsentatio* omnia in se comprehendens, non *sub se* continens notio abstracta et communis. C *Conceptus spatii itaque est intuitus purus*, cum sit conceptus singularis; sensationibus non conflatus, sed omnis sensationis externæ forma fundamentalis. D. *Spatium non est aliquid objectivi* et realis, nec substantia, nec accidens, nec relatio, sed *subjectivum* et ideale, e natura mentis stabili lege proficiscens, veluti schema, omnia omnino externe sensa sibi co-ordinandi. E. Quanquam *conceptus spatii*, ut objectivi alicujus et realis entis vel affectionis, sit imaginarius, nihilo tamen secius *respective ad sensibilia quæcunque*, non solum est *verissimus*, sed et omnis veritatis in sensualitate externa fundamentum."

These propositions are extracted from a Dissertation written by Kant himself in the Latin language [1] Their obscurity therefore, cannot be ascribed to any misapprehension on the part of a translator It was on this account that I thought it better to quote them in his own unaltered words, than to avail myself of the corresponding passage in Born's Latin version of the *Critique of Pure Reason*.

To each of Kant's propositions concerning Time and Space I shall subjoin a short comment, following the same order in which these propositions are arranged above

1. That the idea of *Time* has no resemblance to any of our sensations, and that it is, therefore, not derived from sensation immediately and directly, has been very often observed, and if nobody had ever observed it, the fact is so very obvious,

---

[1] *De Mundi Sensibilis atque Intelligibilis forma et principiis* Dissertatio pro loco professionis Log et Metaph. Ordinariæ rite sibi vindicando, quam, exigentibus statutis Academicis, publice tuebitur Immanuel Kant.—Regiomonti, 1770

that the enunciation of it could not entitle the author to the praise of much ingenuity. Whether "this idea be *supposed* in all our sensations," or (as Kant explains himself more clearly in his third proposition,) "be *conceived* by the mind prior to all sensation," is a question which seems to me at least doubtful, nor do I think the opinion we form concerning it a matter of the smallest importance. One thing is certain, that this idea is an inseparable concomitant of every act of memory with respect to past events, and that, in whatever way it is acquired, we are irresistibly led to ascribe to the thing itself an existence independent of the will of any being whatever.

2 On the second proposition I have nothing to remark. The following is the most intelligible translation of it that I can give "The idea of Time is singular, not general, for any particular length of Time can be conceived only as a part of one and the same immense whole"

3. From these premises (such as they are) Kant concludes, that the idea of Time is *intuitive*, and that this intuition, being prior to the exercise of the senses, is not empirical but pure The conclusion here must necessarily partake of the uncertainty of the premises from which it is drawn, but the meaning of the author does not seem to imply any very erroneous principle. It amounts, indeed, to little more than an explanation of some of his peculiar terms

4 That Time is a *continued quantity* is indisputable. To the latter clause of the sentence I can annex no meaning but this, that Time enters as an essential element into our conception of the law of continuity, in all its various applications to the changes that take place in Nature.

5. In this proposition Kant assumes the truth of that much contested, and, to me, incomprehensible doctrine, which denies the objective reality of Time He seems to consider it merely as a subjective *condition*, inseparably connected with the frame of the Human Mind, in consequence of which it arranges sensible phenomena, according to a certain law, in the order of succession.

6 What is meant by calling Time *a true conception*, I do not profess to understand, nor am I able to interpret the remainder of the sentence in any way but this, that we can find no limits to the range thus opened in our conceptions to the succession of sensible events.

7. The conclusion of the whole matter is, that Time is "absolutely the first formal principle of the sensible world" I can annex no meaning to this, but I have translated the original, word for word, and shall leave my readers to their own conjectures

---

A. It appears from this, that, in the opinion of Kant, the idea of Space is connate with the mind, or at least, that it is prior to any information received from the senses [* Mr Smith, from some passages in his Essay on the External Senses, appears to have had a notion somewhat similar. He repeatedly hints, that some confused conception of *Externality* or *Outness*, is prior to the exercise of any of our perceptive powers] But this doctrine seems to me not a little doubtful In deed, I rather lean to the common theory, which supposes our first ideas of Space or Extension to be formed by abstracting this attribute from the other qualities of matter. The idea of Space, however, in whatever manner formed, is manifestly

* Restored —*Ed*

accompanied with an irresistible conviction, that Space is necessarily existent, and that its annihilation is impossible, nay, it appears to me to be also accompanied with an irresistible conviction, that Space cannot possibly be extended in more than three dimensions. Call either of these propositions in question, and you open a door to universal scepticism.

B. I can extract no meaning from this, but the nugatory proposition, that our conception of Space leads us to consider it as *the place* in which all things are comprehended

C "The conception of Space, therefore, is a *pure intuition*" This follows as a necessary corollary (according to Kant's own definition) from Prop A What is to be understood by the clause which asserts, that Space is the fundamental *form* of every external sensation, it is not easy to conjecture Does it imply merely that the conception of *Space* is necessarily involved in all our notions of things external? In this case, it only repeats over, in different and most inaccurate terms, the last clause of Prop. B What can be more loose and illogical than the phrase *external sensation* ?

D That Space is neither a *substance*, nor an *accident*, nor a *relation*, may be safely granted, but does it follow from this that it is nothing *objective*, or, in other words, that it is a mere creature of the imagination? This, however, would seem to be the idea of Kant, and yet I cannot reconcile it with what he says in Prop. E, that the conception of Space is the foundation of all the truth we ascribe to our perceptions of external objects (The author's own words are—" omnis veritatis in sensualitate externa fundamentum ")[1]

Upon the whole, it appears to me, that, among these various propositions, there are some which are quite unintelligible; that others assume, as first principles, doctrines which have been disputed by many of our most eminent philosophers, that others, again, seem to aim at involving plain and obvious truths in darkness and mystery, and that not one is expressed with simplicity and precision, which are the natural results of clear and accurate thinking In considering time and space as the *forms* of all sensible phenomena, does Kant mean any thing more but this,—that we necessarily refer every sensible phenomenon to some point of space, or to some instant of time? If this was really his meaning, he has only repeated over, in obscurer language, the following propositions of Newton " Ut ordo partium temporis est immutabilis, sic etiam ordo partium spatii. Moveantur hæc de locis suis, et movebuntur (ut ita dicam) de seipsis *Nam tempora et spatia sunt sui ipsorum et rerum omnium quasi loca In tempore, quoad ordinem succes-*

---

[1] Mr Nitsch has remarked this difficulty, and has attempted to remove it "The most essential objection (he observes) to Kant's system is, that it leads to scepticism; because it maintains that the figures in which we see the external objects clothed are not inherent in those objects, and that consequently space is something *within*, and not without the mind," —(pp. 144, 145) " It may be further objected, (he adds,) that, if there be no external space, there is also no external world. But this is concluding by far too much from these premises If there be no external space, it will follow, that we are not authorized to assign *extension* to external things, but there will follow no more,"—(p 149) Mr. Nitsch then proceeds to obviate these objections, but his reply is far from satisfactory, and is indeed not less applicable to the doctrine of Berkeley than to that of Kant. This point, however, I do not mean to argue here The concessions which Nitsch has made are quite sufficient for my present purpose They serve at least to satisfy my own mind, that I have not misrepresented Kant's meaning

sionis, in spatio, quoad ordinem situs locantur universa De illorum essentia est ut sint loca · et loca primaria moveri absurdum est"

I have quoted this passage, not from any desire of displaying the superiority of Newton over Kant, but chiefly to show how very nearly the powers of the former sink to the same level with those of the latter, when directed to inquiries unfathomable by the human faculties. What abuse of words can be greater than to say, That neither the parts of time nor the parts of space can be *moved* from their *places*?[1] In the *Principia* of Newton, however, this incidental discussion is but a spot on the sun [* The same thing may, in particular, be said of various passages in the general scholium at the end, amongst others of the following sentence :—" Cum unaquæque spatii particula sit *semper*, et unumquodque durationis indivisibile momentum *ubique*, certe rerum omnium fabricator ac dominus, non erit *nunquam*, *nusquam*."] In the *Critique of Pure Reason*, it is a fair specimen of the rest of the work, and forms one of the chief pillars of the whole system, both metaphysical and moral.

[* " Plus d'un homme de lettres (says M. Prévost) s'occupe en ce moment à faire connaitre en notre langue les principes de la philosophie *Kantienne*. Mais l'entreprise est fort difficile, son langage est obscur ; et avant tout le lecteur François demande une clarté parfaite. Telle est la différence des goûts et des habitudes intellectuelles des deux nations, que les ouvrages de *Kant*, qui ont eu en Allemagne un succès si prodigieux, écrits en Français du même style, n'auraient, je crois, pas trouvé de lecteurs

"La langue Allemande, forte de sa richesse et de ses tours hardis et variés, s'est accoutumée à supporter des violences qui effrayent une langue plus sévère et plus défiante Celle-ci repousserait des néologismes étranges, qui tantôt se rapprochent du jargon de l'école, tantôt se rapportent à des conceptions particulières, même bizarres Elle fuit un langage fatiguant par son obscurité ; tel même qu'il faut, de l'aveu de ceux qui l'emploient, une assez longue étude pour l'entendre

"Si, malgré ces difficultés, je voulais anticiper sur les travaux entrepris par d'autres, et tracer l'esquisse de cette nouvelle philosophie, j'insisterai surtout sur la distinction à faire entre ce qui lui est propre, et ce qu'elle s'est approprié Certainement il doit y avoir dans le génie de son auteur de quoi justifier l'enthousiasme d'une nation éclairée et judicieuse, et les éloges de quelques savans profonds et ingénieux Mais ces richesses naturelles, n'ont elles pas été grossies imperceptiblement d'autres richesses empruntées ? Et celles-ci ne font-elles point quelquefois le principal mérite de cette doctrine qu'on admire ? Je m'expliquerais mieux par un exemple

"M. *Kant*, après avoir distingué la sensibilité de l'intelligence, observe que les notions de tems et d'espace sont comme les formes naturelles de la faculté sensible de l'âme, que ces notions ne peuvent venir de l'extérieur ; que ce sont des dispositions primitives ; qu'en conséquence de cette structure de l'esprit humain, toute impression faite sur lui vient nécessairement se loger à-la-fois dans l'une et l'autre

---

[1] Was it not to avoid the palpable incongruity of this language that Kant was led to substitute the word *forms* instead of *places*, the former word not seeming to be so obviously inapplicable as the latter to time and space in common or, to speak more correctly, being, from its extreme vagueness, equally unmeaning when applied to both ?

* Restored —*Ed*

de ces formes, et ceci fait une partie importante de ses principes. Mais en nous bornant un instant à l'espace, *Locke* avant M. *Kant*, avoit observé que l'étendue est une qualité primaire, c'est-à-dire, que l'âme la juge nécessairement extérieure et indépendante de la sensation.[1] Ce même philosophe et ses successeurs, en particulier *Condillac*, avaient beaucoup insisté sur ce point, que nous ne connaissons les choses extérieures que relativement à la constitution particulière de notre esprit; que la nature intime et absolue des substances nous est inconnue.[2] Si notre âme reconnaît l'étendue comme extérieure et toujours existante, si cette conception est purement relative à sa constitution, elle est donc une forme constante et qui dépend de sa nature. Jusques-là les deux philosophies semblent ne différer que par l'expression.[3] Il n'y a de propre à celle de Kant que cette remarque par laquelle il représente l'âme comme rapportant nécessairement tous les phénomènes à quelque point de l'espace. Remarque plutôt négligée qu'inaperçue. Il y a des assertions plus nouvelles sans doute dans cette partie de la doctrine Kantienne, qui s'occupe de la division des notions et de jugemens, ou des formes de l'intelligence, mais aussi des assertions plus disputables.[4] En voyant s'élever sur ces principes des théories nouvelles de morale, ou d'autres relatives à des objets importans, mais comme épuisés, on ne peut s'empêcher de concevoir quelque défiance. Les conséquences dépendent-elles bien des principes? La liaison du système est elle aussi réelle et aussi solide que ses défenseurs le supposent?[5] N'y a-t-il point lieu de soupçonner que les découvertes, ou les recherches du moins qu'on rassemble ailleurs sans prétention, viennent ici s'enchâsser dans un cadre où elles prennent un air de nouveauté? Ces doutes, ou ces indications, ont pour but de donner un intérêt particulier aux traductions projetées des ouvrages relatifs à la philosophie *Kantienne*. Si les auteurs de ses traductions parviennent à démêler ce qui est propre à cette philosophie, de ce qui est commun à toutes; si dans ce qui lui est propre, ils facilitent le choix à faire, ils auront contribué sans doute aux progrès de l'esprit humain, et ceux qui, comme moi, sont imparfaitement instruits de cette nouvelle doctrine, chercheront avec avidité des lumières dégagées de fausses ombres, et ré-

---

[1] *Essai sur l'Entendement Humain*, liv. ii chap. viii. Voyez aussi la *Dissertation de Smith sur les sens externes*.

[2] *Ibid* liv. iv chap. vi § 11, et suivans. *Art de Penser*, chap xi. &c.

[3] On disait du chef des Stoïciens: Zenonem non tam rerum inventorem fuisse, quam novorum verborum.—*Cic de Fin*. Sans appliquer ce jugement au philosophe moderne, on doit au moins s'efforcer de distinguer ce qui, dans la doctrine, est entièrement, de ce qui est seulement revêtu d'un nouvel appareil de mots.

[4] Voyez entr'autres le mémoire de M. Selle, sur *la réalité et l'idéalité des objets de nos connaissances*, inséré dans les Mémoires de l'Académie de Berlin pour 1786 et 1787, en particulier à la page 601 et suivantes.

[5] C'est en effet cette liaison, cet enchaînement indissoluble qu'ils semblent le plus admirer, en particulier dans cette fameuse *Critique de la Raison Pure*, qui est le premier et le principal corps de doctrine de cette secte philosophique.

Voilà comme s'en exprime un de ses professeurs le plus zélé: "Ab hisce enim capitibus fluere necesse est omnem philosophiæ criticæ rationis puræ vim atque virtutem: namque in ea contextus rerum prorsus mirabilis est, ita ut extrema primis media utrisque, omnia omnibus respondeant, si prima dederis danda sunt omnia."—(Frid. Gottlob Born *De Scientia et Conjectura*, p. 91.) No worse account could, in my opinion, have been given of a philosophical work on such a subject, nor could any of its characteristic features have been pointed out more prophetic of its ephemeral reputation. Supposing the praise to be just, it represented the system, however fair and imposing in its first aspect, as not only vulnerable, but vitally and mortally vulnerable in every point, and, accordingly, it was fast approaching to its dissolution before the death of its author. Its rapid decline and untimely end are recorded by the same pen from which I borrowed the sketch of its first rise and progress.

pandues avec discernement."—*Historical Appendix to M Prévost's Translation of the Posthumous Works of Adam Smith*, p. 262, *et seq*]

Note ZZ, p 409

The following quotation will account for the references which I have made to Mr Nitsch among the expounders of Kant's Philosophy. It will also serve to shew that the *Critique of Pure Reason* has still *some* admirers in England, not less enthusiastic than those it had formerly in Germany.

"In submitting this fourth Treatise on the Philosophy of Kant to the reader," (says the author of these articles in the *Encyclopædia Londinensis*,) " I cannot deny myself the satisfaction of publicly acknowledging the great assistance which I have derived, in my literary pursuits, from my excellent and highly valued friend, Mr Henry Richter To him I am indebted for the clearness and perspicuity with which the thoughts of the immortal Kant have been conveyed to the public. Indeed, his comprehensive knowledge of the system, as well as his enthusiastic admiration of its general truth, render him a most able and desirable co-operator Should, therefore, any good result to mankind from our joint labours in the display of this vast and profound system, he is justly entitled to his share of the praise. It is with sincere pleasure that I reflect upon that period, now two-and-twenty years ago, when we first studied together under the same master, Frederic Augustus Nitsch, who originally imported the seeds of TRANSCENDENTAL PHILOSOPHY from its native country, to plant them in our soil; and though, as is usually the case, many of those seeds were scattered by the wind, I trust that a sufficient number have taken root to maintain the growth of this vigorous and flourishing plant, till the time shall come when, by its general cultivation, England may be enabled to enrich other nations with the most perfect specimens of its produce. Professor Nitsch, who thus bestowed upon our country her first attainments in the department of *Pure Science*, has paid the debt of nature I confess it is some reflection upon England, that she did not foster and protect this immediate disciple of the father of philosophy; but the necessities of this learned and illustrious man unfortunately compelled him to seek that subsistence elsewhere which was withheld from him here. At Rostock, about the year 1813, this valuable member of society, and perfect master of the philosophy he undertook to teach, entered upon his immortal career as a reward for his earthly services. It is with the most heartfelt satisfaction that I add my mite of praise to his revered memory. But for him, I might ever have remained in the dark regions of sophistry and uncertainty "—[Mr. Wirgman.—*Ed*]

Note AAA, p 421

Among the secondary mischiefs resulting from the temporary popularity of Kant, none is more to be regretted than the influence of his works on the habits, both of thinking and of writing, of some very eminent men, who have since given to the world histories of philosophy That of Tennemann in particular (a work said to possess great merit) would appear to have been vitiated by this unfortunate bias in the views of its author. A very competent judge has said of it, that "it affords as far as it is completed, the most accurate, the most minute, and the most rational view we yet possess of the different systems of philosophy; but that the critical philosophy being chosen as the vantage ground from whence the survey of former systems is taken, the continual reference in Kant's own language to his peculiar doctrines, renders it frequently impossible for those who have not studied the dark works of this modern Heraclitus to understand the strictures of the historian on the systems even of Aristotle or Plato."—(See the Article *Brucker* in the *Encyclopædia Britannica*, 7th edition.) We are told by the same writer, that "among the learned of Germany, Brucker has never enjoyed a very distinguished reputation." This I can very easily credit, but I am more inclined to interpret it to the disadvantage of the German taste, than to that of the historian. Brucker is indeed not distinguished by any extraordinary measure of depth or of acuteness; but his industry, fidelity, and sound judgment, he has few superiors—qualities of infinitely greater value in the undertaker of a historical work, than that passion for systematical refinement, which is so apt to betray the best intentioned writers into false glosses on the opinions they record.

When the above passage was written, I had not seen the work of Buhle. I have since had an opportunity of looking into the French translation of it, published at Paris in 1816; and I must frankly acknowledge that I have seldom met with a greater disappointment. The account there given of the Kantian system, to which I turned with peculiar eagerness, has, if possible, involved to *my* apprehension, in additional obscurity, that mysterious doctrine. From this, however, I did not feel myself entitled to form an estimate of the author's merits as a philosophical historian, till I had read some other articles of which I considered myself better qualified to judge. The following short extract will, without the aid of any comment, enable such of my readers as know anything of the literary history of Scotland to form an opinion upon this point for themselves.

"Reid n'attaqua les systèmes de ses prédécesseurs et notamment celui de Hume, que parce qu'il se croyait convaincu de leur défaut de fondement. Mais un autre antagoniste, non moins célèbre, du scepticisme de Hume, fut, en outre, guidé par la haine qu'il avoit vouée à son illustre compatriote, *lequel lui répondit avec beaucoup d'aigreur et d'animosité*. James Beattie, *professeur de morale à Edimbourg*, puis ensuite, de logique et de morale à l'Université d'Aberdeen, *obtint la préférence sur Hume lorsqu'il fut question de remplir la chaire vacante à Edimbourg.* Cette circonstance devint *sans doute* la principale source de l'inimitié que les deux savans conçurent l'un pour l'autre, et qui influa même sur le ton qu'ils employèrent dans les raisonnemens par lesquels ils se combattirent."—Tom. v. p. 235.

To this quotation may I be pardoned for adding a few sentences relative to myself? "L'ouvrage de Dugald Stewart, intitulé, *Elements of the Philosophy of the Human Mind*, est un syncrétisme des opinions de Hartley et de Reid. Stewart borne absolument la connoissance, tant de l'âme que des choses extérieures, à ce que le sens commun nous en apprend, et croit pouvoir ainsi mettre l'étude de la métaphysique à l'abri du reproche de rouler sur des choses qui dépassent la sphère de notre intelligence, ou qui sont tout-a-fait inutiles dans la pratique de la vie . . . Les chapitres suivans renferment le développement du principe de l'association des idées. Ils sont presqu' entièrement écrits d'après Hartley. Stewart fait dériver de ce principe toutes les facultés intellectuelles et pratiques de l'homme."—Tom v. pp. 330, 331.

Of the discrimination displayed by Buhle in the classification of systems and of authors, the title prefixed to his 19th chapter may serve as a specimen: "*Philosophy of Condillac, of Helvetius, of Baron d'Holbach, of Robinet, of Bonnet, of Montesquieu, of Burlemaqui, of Vattel, and of Reid*"

But the radical defect of Buhle's work is the almost total want of references to original authors. We are presented only with the general results of the author's reading, without any guide to assist us in confirming his conclusions when right, or in correcting them when wrong. This circumstance is of itself sufficient to annihilate the value of any historical composition.

Sismondi, in mentioning the history of Modern literature by Bouterwek, takes occasion to pay a compliment (and, I have no doubt, a very deserved one) to German scholars in general, observing that he has executed his task—"avec une étendue d'érudition, et une *loyauté* dans la manière d'en faire profiter ses lecteurs, qui semblent propres aux savans Allemands"—(*De la Litt. du Midi de l'Europe*, tom. i. p 13 · à Paris, 1813.) I regret that my ignorance of the German language has prevented me from profiting by a work of which Sismondi has expressed so favourable an opinion, and still more, that the only history of philosophy from the pen of a contemporary German scholar, which I have had access to consult, should form so remarkable an exception to Sismondi's observation.

The contents of the preceding note lay me under the necessity, in justice to myself, of taking some notice of the following remark, by an anonymous critic, on the first part of this *Dissertation*, published in 1815.—See *Quarterly Review*, vol. xvii p 42.

"In the plan which Mr. Stewart has adopted, if he has not consulted his *strength*, he has at least consulted his *ease;* for, supposing a person to have the requisite talent and information, the task which our author has performed, is one which, with the historical abstracts of Buhle or Tennemann, cannot be supposed to have required any very laborious meditation."

On the insinuation contained in the foregoing passage, I abstain from offering any comment I have only to say, that it was not till the summer of 1820 that I saw the work of Buhle, and that I have never yet had an opportunity of seeing that of Tennemann. From what I have found in the one, and from what I have heard of the other, I am strongly inclined to suspect, that when the anonymous critic wrote the above sentence, he was not less ignorant than myself of the works of these two historians. Nor can I refrain from adding, (which I do with perfect confidence,) that no person competent to judge on such a subject can read with attention this Historical Sketch, without perceiving that its merits and defects, whatever they may be, are at least all my own

NOTE BBB, p 428.

Of the Scottish authors who turned their attention to metaphysical studies, prior to the union of the two kingdoms, I know of none so eminent as George Dalgarno of Aberdeen, author of two works, both of them strongly marked with sound philosophy, as well as with original genius The one published at London, 1660, is entitled, "*Ars signorum, vulgo character universalis et lingua philosophica, qua poterunt homines diversissimorum idiomatum, spatio duarum septimanarum, omnia animi sui sensa (in rebus familiaribus) non minus intelligibilter, sive scribendo, sive loquendo, mutuo communicare, quam linguis propriis vernaculis. Præterea, hinc etiam poterunt juvenes, philosophiæ principia, et veram logicæ praxin, citius et facilius multo imbibere, quam ex vulgaribus philosophorum scriptis*" The other work of Dalgarno is entitled, "*Didascalocophus, or the Deaf and Dumb Man's Tutor*." Printed at Oxford, 1680. I have given some account of the former in the notes at the end of the first volume of the *Philosophy of the Human Mind;* and of the latter, in a *Memoir* published in vol vii of the *Transactions of the Royal Society of Edinburgh.* As they are now become extremely rare, and would together form a very small octavo volume, I cannot help thinking that a bookseller who should reprint them would be fully indemnified by the sale The fate of Dalgarno will be hard indeed, if, in addition to the unjust neglect he experienced from his contemporaries, the proofs he has left of his philosophical talents shall be suffered to sink into total oblivion.

Lord Stair's *Physiologia Nova Experimentalis* (published at Leyden in 1686) is also worthy of notice in the literary history of Scotland. Although it bears few marks of the eminent talents which distinguished the author, both as a lawyer and as a statesman, it discovers a very extensive acquaintance with the metaphysical as well as with the physical doctrines, which were chiefly in vogue at that period, more particularly with the leading doctrines of Gassendi, Descartes, and Malebranche. Many acute and some important strictures are made on the errors of all the three, and at the same time complete justice is done to their merits; the writer everywhere manifesting an independence of opinion and a spirit of free inquiry, very uncommon among the philosophers of the seventeenth century The work is dedicated to the Royal Society of London, of the utility of which institution, in promoting experimental knowledge, he appears to have been fully aware

The limits of a note will not permit me to enter into farther details concerning the state of philosophy in Scotland, during the interval between the union of the Crowns and that of the Kingdoms. The circumstances of the country were indeed peculiarly unfavourable to it. But memorials still exist of a few individuals, sufficient to show, that the philosophical taste, which has so remarkably distinguished our countrymen during the eighteenth century, was in some measure an inheritance from their immediate predecessors Leibnitz, I think, somewhere mentions the number of learned Scotchmen by whom he was visited in the course of their travels. To one of them (Mr. Burnet of Kemney) he has addressed a most interesting letter, dated in 1697, on the general state of learning and science in Europe, opening his mind on the various topics which he introduces, with a freedom and confidence highly honourable to the attainments and character of his correspondent. Dr. Arbuthnot, who was born about the time of the Restoration, may serve as a fair specimen of the very liberal education which was then to be had in some of the Scottish Universities. The large share which he is allowed to have contributed to the *Memoirs of Martinus Scriblerus*, abundantly attests the variety of his learning, and the just estimate he had formed of the philosophy of the schools; and in one or two passages, where he glances at the errors of his contemporaries, an attentive and intelligent reader will trace, amid all his pleasantry, a metaphysical depth and soundness which seem to belong to a later period.—Is there no Arbuthnot now, to chastise the follies of our craniologists?

NOTE CCC, p. 449

The letter which gives occasion to this note was written twenty years after the publication of the *Treatise of Human Nature*. As it relates, however, to the history of Mr Hume's studies previous to that publication, I consider this as the proper place for introducing it. The Dialogue to which the letter refers was plainly that which appeared after Mr. Hume's death, under the title of *Dialogues on Natural Religion*.

"NINEWELLS, *March* 19, 1751.

"DEAR SIR,—You would perceive by the sample I have given you, that I make Cleanthes the hero of the Dialogue. Whatever you can think of to strengthen that side of the argument will be most acceptable to me. Any propensity you imagine I have to the other side crept in upon me against my will, and it is not long ago that I burned an old manuscript book, wrote before I was twenty, which contained, page after page, the gradual progress of my thoughts on that head. It begun with an anxious search after arguments to confirm the common opinion, doubts stole in, dissipated, returned, were again dissipated, returned again, and it was a perpetual struggle of a restless imagination against inclination, perhaps against reason.

"I have often thought that the best way of composing a dialogue would be for two persons that are of different opinions about any question of importance, to write alternately the different parts of the discourse, and reply to each other. By this means that vulgar error would be avoided of putting nothing but nonsense into the mouth of the adversary; and, at the same time, a variety of character and genius being upheld, would make the whole look more natural and unaffected. Had it been my good fortune to live near you, I should have taken on me the character of Philo in the Dialogue, which you'll own I could have supported naturally enough, and you would not have been averse to that of Cleanthes. I believe, too, we could both of us have kept our tempers very well, only you have not reached an absolute philosophical indifference on these points. What danger can ever come from ingenious reasoning and inquiry? The worst speculative sceptic ever I knew was a much better man than the best superstitious devotee and bigot. I must inform you too, that this was the way of thinking of the ancients on this subject. If a man made profession of philosophy, whatever his sect was, they always expected to find more regularity in his life and manners than in those of the ignorant and illiterate. There is a remarkable passage of Appian to this purpose. That historian observes, that, notwithstanding the established prepossession in favour of learning, yet some philosophers who have been trusted with absolute power have very much abused it, and he instances in Critias, the most violent of the Thirty, and Aristion, who governed Athens in the time of Sylla. But I find, upon inquiry, that Critias was a professed Atheist, and Aristion an Epicurean, which is little or nothing different, and yet Appian wonders at their corruption as much as if they had been Stoics or Platonists. A modern zealot would have thought that corruption unavoidable.

"I could wish that Cleanthes's argument could be so analyzed as to be rendered quite formal and regular. The propensity of the mind towards it, unless that propensity were as strong and universal as that to believe in our senses and experience, will still, I am afraid, be esteemed a suspicious foundation. 'Tis here I wish for your assistance. We must endeavour to prove that this propensity is somewhat different from our inclination to find our own figures in the clouds, our face in the moon, our passions and sentiments even in inanimate matter. Such an inclination may and ought to be controlled, and can never be a legitimate ground of assent.

"The instances I have chosen for Cleanthes are, I hope, tolerably happy, and the confusion in which I represent the sceptic seems natural But, *si quid novisti rectius*, &c.

"You ask me, *if the idea of cause and effect is nothing but vicinity?* (you should have said constant vicinity or regular conjunction)—*I would gladly know whence is that farther idea of causation against which you argue?* The question is pertinent; but I hope I have answered it. We feel, after the constant conjunction, an easy transition from one idea to the other, or a connexion in the imagination, and, as it is usual for us to transfer our own feelings to the objects on which they are dependent, we attach the internal sentiment to the external objects. If no single instances of cause and effect appear to have any connexion, but only repeated similar ones, you will find yourself obliged to have recourse to this theory.

"I am sorry our correspondence should lead us into these abstract speculations I have thought, and read, and composed very little on such questions of late. Morals, politics, and literature, have employed all my time; but still the other topics I must think more curious, important, entertaining, and useful than any geometry that is deeper than Euclid If, in order to answer the doubts started, new principles of philosophy must be laid, are not these doubts themselves very useful? Are they not preferable to blind and ignorant assent? I hope I can answer my own doubts; but, if I could not, is it to be wondered at? To give myself airs and speak magnificently, might I not observe that Columbus did not conquer empires and plant colonies?

"If I have not unravelled the knot so well in these last papers I sent you, as perhaps I did in the former, it has not, I assure you, proceeded from want of good will But some subjects are easier than others; and sometimes one is happier in one's researches and inquiries than at other times Still I have recourse to the *si quid novisti rectius*, not in order to pay you a compliment, but from a real philosophical doubt and curiosity"[1]

An unfinished draught of the letter to which the foregoing seems to have been the reply, has been preserved among Sir Gilbert Elliot's papers This careless fragment is in his own handwriting, and exhibits an interesting specimen of the progress made in Scotland among the higher classes, seventy years ago, not only in sound philosophy, but in purity of English style

[* What follows has not hitherto (so far as I know) been urged in opposition to Mr Hume, and to my mind is more satisfactory than any view of the subject that

---

[1] The original is in the possession of the Earl of Minto.

* I am not sure that this addition should have been inserted here. It appears to have been written before the intention of publishing fully in this Note the preceding letter of Hume, and it was thrown in at the page corresponding to p 377 above,—probably for consideration —*Ed*

has yet been taken by his opponents It is however, after all, little more than a comment on some *concessions* made in the course of the argument by the sceptical Philo , of which I think Cleanthes might have availed himself more than he has done   It must always be remembered that the latter is the hero of the Dialogue, and is to be understood as speaking Mr Hume's real opinions. (See a confidential letter of his to his friend, Sir Gilbert Elliot, which I have published in the second volume of the Philosophy of the Human Mind, Note C, p 532, 3d edition, [and more fully on preceding page —*Ed*]   I think it fair to recall this to the reader's memory, as the reasonings of Philo have often been quoted as parts of Hume's philosophical system, although the words of Shylock or Cahban might, with equal justice, be quoted as speaking the real sentiments of Shakespeare]

" DEAR SIR,—Inclosed I return your papers, which, since my coming to town, I have again read over with the greatest care   The thoughts which this last perusal of them has suggested I shall set down, merely in compliance with your desire, for I pretend not to say anything new upon a question which has already been examined so often and so accurately. I must freely own to you, that to me it appears extremely doubtful if the position which Cleanthes undertakes to maintain can be supported, at least in any satisfactory manner, upon the principles he establishes and the concessions he makes. If it be only from effects exactly similar that experience warrants us to infer a similar cause, then I am afraid it must be granted, that the works of Nature resemble not so nearly the productions of man as to support the conclusion which Cleanthes admits can be built only on that resemblance. The two instances he brings to illustrate his argument are indeed ingenious and elegant—the first, especially, which seemingly carries great weight along with it; the other, I mean that of the Vegetating Library, as it is of more difficult apprehension, so I think it is not easy for the mind either to retain or to apply it   But, if I mistake not, this strong objection strikes equally against them both.   Cleanthes does no more than substitute two artificial instances in the place of natural ones : but if these bear no nearer a resemblance than natural ones to the effects which we have experienced to proceed from men, then nothing *can* justly be inferred from them , and if this resemblance be greater, then nothing farther *ought* to be inferred from them. In one respect, however, Cleanthes seems to limit his reasonings more than is necessary even upon his own principles Admitting, for once, that experience is the only source of our knowledge, I cannot see how it follows, that, to enable us to infer a similar cause, the effects must not only be similar, but exactly and precisely so   Will not experience authorize me to conclude, that a machine or piece of mechanism was produced by human art, unless I have happened previously to see a machine or piece of mechanism exactly of the same sort ?   Point out, for instance, the contrivance and end of a watch to a peasant who had never before seen anything more curious than the coarsest instruments of husbandry, will he not immediately conclude, that this watch is an effect produced by human art and design ? And I would still further ask, does a spade or a plough much more resemble a watch than a watch does an organized animal ? The result of our whole experience, if experience indeed be the only principle, seems rather to amount to this There are but two ways in which we have ever observed the different parcels of matter to be thrown together , either at random, or with design and purpose   By the first we have never seen produced a regular complicated effect, corresponding to a certain end, by the second, we uniformly have. If, then, the works of nature, and the productions of man, resemble each other in this one general characteristic, will not even experience sufficiently warrant us to ascribe to both a similar though proportionable cause? If you answer, that abstracting from the experience we acquire in this world, order and adjustment of parts is no proof of design, my reply is, that no conclusions, drawn from the nature of so chimerical a being as man, considered abstracted from experience, can at all be listened to. The principles of the human mind are clearly so contrived as not to unfold themselves till the proper objects and proper opportunity and occasion be presented. There is no arguing upon the nature of man but by considering him as grown to maturity, placed in society, and become acquainted with surrounding objects. But if you should still farther urge, that, with regard to instances of which we have no experience, for aught we know, matter may contain the principles of order, arrangement, and the adjustment of final causes, I should only answer, that whoever can conceive this proposition to be true, has exactly the same idea of matter that I have of mind. I know not if I have reasoned justly upon Cleanthes's principles, nor is it indeed very material. The purpose of my letter is barely to point out what to me appears the fair and philosophical method of proceeding in this inquiry. That this universe is the effect of an intelligent designing cause, is a principle which has been most universally received in all ages and in all nations; the proof uniformly appealed to is, the admirable order and adjustment of the works of nature. To proceed, then, experimentally and philosophically, the first question in point of order seems to be, what is the effect which the contemplation of the universe, and the several parts of it, produces upon a considering mind? This is a question of fact, a popular question, the discussion of which depends not upon refinements and subtlety, but merely upon impartiality and attention. I ask, then, what is the sentiment which prevails in one's mind, after having considered not only the more familiar objects that surround him, but also all the discoveries of Natural Philosophy and Natural History, after having considered not only the general economy of the universe, but also the most minute parts of it, and the amazing adjustment of means to ends with a precision unknown to human art, and in instances innumerable? Tell me, (to use the words of Cleanthes,) does not the idea of a contriver flow in upon you with a force like that of sensation? Expressions how just! (yet in the mouth of Cleanthes you must allow me to doubt of their propriety.) Nor does this conviction only arise from the consideration of the inanimate parts of the creation, but still more strongly from the contemplation of the faculties of the understanding, the affections of the heart, and the various instincts discoverable both in men and brutes all so properly adapted to the circumstances and situation both of the species and the individual. Yet this last observation, whatever may be in it, derives no force from experience. For who ever saw a mind produced? If we are desirous to push our experiments still farther, and inquire, whether the survey of the universe has regularly and uniformly led to the belief of an intelligent cause? Shall we not find, that, from the author of the book of Job to the preachers at Boyle's Lecture, the same language has been universally held? No writer, who has ever treated this subject, but has either applied himself to describe, in the most emphatical language, the beauty and order of the universe, or else to collect together and place in the most striking light, the many instances of contrivance and design which have been discovered by observation and experiment. And when they have done this, they seem to have imagined that their task was finished, and their demonstration complete, and indeed no wonder,—for it seems to me, that we are scarce more assured of our own existence, than that this well-ordered universe is the effect of an intelligent cause.

" This first question, then, which is indeed a question of fact, being thus settled upon observations which are obvious and unrefined, but not on that account the less satisfactory, it becomes the business of the philosopher to inquire, whether the conviction arising from these observations be founded on the conclusions of reason, the reports of experience, or the dictates of feeling, or possibly upon all these together, but if his principles shall not be laid so wide as to account for the fact already established upon prior evidence, we may, I think, safely conclude, that his principles are erroneous. Should a philosopher pretend to demonstrate to me, by a system of optics, that I can only discern an object when placed directly opposite to my eye, I should certainly answer, your system must be defective, for it is contradicted by matter of fact"

[* In another letter to Mr. Hume, the same very ingenious and accomplished person expresses himself thus.—

" I admit that there is no writing or talking of any subject, which is of importance enough to become the object of reasoning, without having recourse to some degree of subtilty or refinement "]

Note D D D, p. 401

[† It will not, I hope, be considered as altogether foreign to the object of this Discourse, if I hazard a few hints of my own towards a solution of the same difficulty

Inconsistency remarked by Reid and others in Mr Hume's reasoning in favour of the scheme of Necessity, with his objection to the argument for the existence of God, founded on the maxim, that every change in Nature implies the operation of a cause. The same charge retorted on Reid, by a very ingenious writer in the *Edinburgh Review*.—" We may be permitted to remark, that it is somewhat extraordinary to find the dependence of human actions on motives so positively denied by those very Philosophers with whom the doctrine of Causation is of such high authority."—*Edinburgh Review*, vol ii p 284.

Although I am far from admitting the logical justness of this retort, I must candidly acknowledge, that it possesses a sufficient degree of plausibility to be entitled to a careful examination, nay farther, I admit, that too much ground for it has been afforded by the unqualified terms in which the maxim ($\mu\eta\delta\grave{\epsilon}\nu$ $\alpha\nu\alpha\acute{\iota}\tau\iota o\nu$) has frequently been stated [Then after the same observations in regard to Price which appear on p. 573, and as far as the word " impossibility," Mr Stewart goes on —*Ed*]

It would perhaps contribute to render our reasonings on this subject more distinct, if, instead of speaking of the influence of motives on *the Will*, we were to speak (agreeably to the suggestion of Locke)[1] of the influence of motives on *the*

---

* Restored —*Ed*
† Restored—though in part apparently only memoranda —*Ed*
[1] *Essay on Human Understanding*, book ii chap 21, § 16, *et seq* " The question is not proper, whether the Will be free, but whether a Man be free "—*Ibid* § 21 For some remarks on the words *faculties* and *powers*, when applied to the mind, see the same chapter, § 20

Agent We are apt to forget what *the Will* is, and to consider it as something inanimate, which can have its state changed only by the operation of some foreign cause

---

Part of the obscurity in which this question has been involved may be justly ascribed to the inaccurate use that has been made of the words *active* and *activity*. A remarkable instance of this occurs in the following sentence of Lord Kames — " Chemistry discovers various powers in matter of the most *active* kind, and every man who is conversant with the operations of Chemistry, must have a strong impression that matter is extremely *active*."—(*Essay on Motion*, printed in the Essays Physical and Literary, by a Society in Edinburgh, vol i p 9) Into this mode of speaking the author was evidently led by confounding together the ideas of *action* an l of *motion*, which two words (he afterwards tells us) he considers as synonymous.[1] The amount, therefore, of what Kames has observed concerning the phenomena of Chemistry, is merely this, that in the processes of that art, sudden and (to the novice) unexpected *motions* often take place, in consequence of the mixture of substances formerly quiescent. But do these motions take place in that irregular or capricious way which indicates *activity* and *volition?* On the contrary, may they not all be predicted by the experienced chemist, with a confidence equal to that with which the astronomer predicts the precise moment when a solar or lunar eclipse is to happen? Indeed, if matter were not universally regarded in this light, how could the belief of the permanency of the course of nature have been so firmly established in the human mind? Does not this belief obviously proceed on the supposition, that matter never changes its state but in consequence of its being acted upon? Were the fact otherwise, it would be a vain attempt to ascertain those general conclusions which are known by the name of *the Laws of Motion* Have we not, therefore, in the one case as well as in the other, complete evidence that these motions are the *effects* of powers which cannot belong to mere matter, or, in other words, that in the phenomena of chemistry, as well as of physics, matter is entirely inert and passive?

I have said before, that the idea of an *efficient cause* implies the idea of mind, and I have since added, that the regularity of the phenomena exhibited in physics and in chemistry, evinces the operation of powers which cannot belong to unintelligent matter. In opposition to this it may be argued, (in the words of Lord Kames, *Essay on Motion*, p 8,) " that a power of beginning visible motion is no more connected with a power of thinking, than it is with any other property of matter or spirit." The remark is certainly just, if understood merely to assert that the power of the mind to move body is known to us by experience alone, and that it is possible for us to conceive intelligent beings to whom this power does not belong But, in order to render the remark applicable to the present argument, it is necessary to establish the *converse* of the proposition, by shewing that a power of beginning motion does not imply a power of thinking The contrary of this seems to me self-evident, for, without thought, how could the velocity or the direction of the motion be determined?]

NOTE E E E, p 467.

[* Under the general title of the doctrine of *Probabilities*, two very different subjects are confounded together by Laplace, as well as by many other writers of an

---

[1] " Motion, by the very conception of it, is action —*Ibid* p 19   * Restored —*Ed*

earlier date. The one is, the purely mathematical theory of chances, the other, the inductive anticipations of future events, deduced from observations on the past course of nature. The calculations about dice furnish the simplest of all examples of the first sort of theory. The conclusions to which they lead are as rigorously exact as any other arithmetical theorems; amounting to nothing more than a numerical statement of the ways in which a given event *may* happen, compared with those in which it *may not* happen. Thus, in the case of a single die, (supposing it to be made with mathematical accuracy,) the chance that *ace* shall turn up at the first throw, is to the chance against that event as one to five. The more complicated cases of the problem all depend on the application of the same fundamental principle. This principle, as Condorcet has well remarked, (*Essai sur l'Application de l'Analyse*, &c. p. 7,) is only a definition, (une Vérité de définition,) and, therefore, the calculations founded on it are all rigorously true.

To this theory of chances Laplace labours, through the whole of his work, to assimilate all the other cases in which mathematics are applied to the *calculus* of probabilities; and I have no doubt that he would have readily subscribed to the following proposition of Condorcet, although I do not recollect that he has anywhere sanctioned it expressly by his authority. "Le motif de croire que sur dix millions de boules blanches mêlées avec une noire, ce ne sera point la noire que je tirerai du premier coup, est de la même nature que le motif de croire que le soleil ne manquera pas de se lever demain, et les deux opinions ne diffèrent entre elles que par le plus et le moins de probabilité."—*Essai sur l'Application de l'Analyse*, &c., Disc. Prelim p. 11.

According to Degerando, (*Hist Comp* tom ii pp 151, 152,) Mendelsohn was the first who thought of opposing Mr. Hume's scepticism concerning cause and effect, by considerations drawn from the calculus of probabilities. This statement is confirmed by Lacroix, who refers for farther information on the subject to Mendelsohn's Treatise on Evidence, which obtained the prize from the Academy of Berlin in 1763. Degerando himself, in his Treatise *Des Signes et de l'Art de Penser*, (published l'an viii.) has adopted the same view of the subject, without being then aware (as he assures us himself) that he had been anticipated in this speculation by Mendelsohn, (*Hist. Comparée*, tom ii p. 155.) Lacroix, in his *Traité Elémentaire du Calcul des Probabilités*, remarks the coincidence of opinion of these different authors, with some hints suggested by Helvetius in a note on the first chapter of the first discourse, in his work entitled *L'Esprit*.

The only foreign writers, so far as I know, by whom this doctrine has yet been controverted, are MM Prévost and L'Huillier of Geneva, in a very able paper published in the Memoirs of the Royal Academy of Berlin for the year 1796. After quoting from Condorcet the passage I have transcribed above, these learned and ingenious philosophers proceed thus —

"La persuasion Analogique qu'éprouve tout homme de voir se répéter un événement naturel (tel que le lever du soleil) est d'un genre différent de la persuasion représentée par une fraction dans la théorie des probabilités. Celle-ci peut lui être ajoutée, mais l'une peut exister sans l'autre. Elles dépendent de deux ordres de facultés différents. Un enfant, un animal éprouve la première, et ne forme aucun calcul explicite, ni même implicite il n'y a aucune dépendance nécessaire entre ces deux persuasions. Celle que le calcul apprécie est raisonnée, et même, jusqu'à un certain point, artificielle. L'autre est d'instinct et naturelle. Elle dépend de quelques facultés intellectuelles dont l'analyse n'est pas facile, et probablement en très grande partie du principe de la liaison des idées"—*Mémoires de Berlin*, tom. xxiii. Classe de Philosophie Spéculative, p. 15.

"Je veux prouver maintenant, que tout cet appareil de méthode, si beau et si utile, par lequel on arrive à calculer la probabilité des causes par les effets, suppose une estimation antérieure de cette même probabilité, et qu'en particulier dans toutes les applications intéressantes qu'on peut faire de ce calcul, nous sommes toujours nécessairement guidés par un instinct de persuasion, inappréciable en degré, et que tous nos raisonnemens sur cet objet dépendent de notre confiance en un principe de croyance que le calcul des probabilités ne peut estimer."

". . Je dis donc qu'il y a dans l'homme un principe (qu'on peut nommer *instinct de croyance*) que suppose toute application du calcul des probabilités Tant qu'on raisonne dans l'abstrait, on n'est point appelé à se rendre compte des raisons sur lesquelles on fonde l'estimation de la probabilité d'un chance Mais dans tous les cas concrets ou particuliers, on ne peut déterminer cette probabilité que par voie d'expérience. Or les cas passés n'étant pas liés aux cas à venir, nous ne les envisageons comme devant donner les mêmes résultats, que par le sentiment, sourd mais irrésistible, qui nous fait admettre la constance des lois de la nature. Si l'on prend l'exemple d'un dé, on verra que pour arriver à lui donner la construction que le joueur a en vue, l'artiste finalement n'a pu se guider que par quelques expériences antérieures sur de tels instrumens aléatoires, et sur celui-là en particulier. Lors donc qu'il espère les mêmes effets, il se fonde sur une prévoyance dont la raison ne peut être appréciée par le calcul. Et c'est en vain qu'on voudroit sortir de ce cercle en remontant de cause en cause. car finalement, toute probabilité qu'on voudra estimer Stochastiquement, se réduira à cet emblême. On détermine la probabilité de vie par des tables empiriques : il en est de même de la probabilité des phénomènes météorologiques, et autres."

Dr Price, in his *Dissertation on Historical Evidence*, and also in an Essay published in vol. liii. of the *Philosophical Transactions*, has fallen into a train of thinking exactly similar to that quoted above from Condorcet —(See Price's *Dissertations*, p. 389, *et seq*) The passage here referred to is well worthy of perusal, but, on the slightest examination, it must appear to every intelligent reader to be liable to the very same objections which have been so strongly urged against Condorcet's principle, by MM. Prévost and L'Huillier.

"We trust experience, (says Dr. Price,) and expect that the future should resemble the past in the course of nature, *for the very same reason* that, supposing ourselves otherwise in the dark, we should conclude that a die which has turned an ace oftenest in *past* trials, is mostly marked with aces, and, consequently, should expect that it will go on to turn the same number oftenest in *future* trials."—(P. 392) "And so far is it from being true that the understanding is *not* the faculty which teaches us to rely on experience, that it is capable of determining, *in all cases*, what conclusions ought to be drawn from it, and what *precise degree* of confidence should be placed in it."—(P 398)

Nothing can be more evident than this, that it is not upon any *reasoning* of this sort that children proceed, when they anticipate the continuance of those laws of nature, a knowledge of which is indispensably necessary for the preservation of their animal existence. Mr. Hume, although he plainly leaned to the opinion that this anticipation may be accounted for by the association of ideas, has yet, with the most philosophical propriety, given it the name of *an instinct;* inasmuch as it manifests itself in infants long before the dawn of reason, and is as evidently the result of an arrangement of Nature, as if it were implanted immediately in their frame by her own hand. It is, indeed, an *instinct* common to man, and to the brute creation.

That we are able, in many cases, to calculate, with mathematical precision, the probability of future events, is so far from affording an argument against the existence of this instinctive anticipation, that all these calculations take for granted (as M. Prévost has observed) that uniformity in the course of nature which we are thus led to anticipate The *calculations*, it is true, imply at every step the exercise of the understanding, but that no process of the understanding can account for the origin of the fundamental assumption on which they proceed, has been shown by Mr Hume (according to the best of my judgment) with demonstrative evidence.

"Au milieu (says Laplace) des causes variables et inconnues que nous comprenons sous le nom de hazard, et qui rendent incertaine et irrégulière, la marche des évènemens; on voit naître à mesure qu'ils se multiplient, une régularité frappante qui semble tenir à un dessein, et que l'on a considéré comme une preuve de la providence qui gouverne le monde. Mais en y réfléchissant, on recouroit bientôt que cette régularité n'est que le développement des possibilités respectives des évènemens simples qui doivent se présenter plus souvent, lorsqu'ils sont plus probables. Concevons, par exemple, une urne qui renferme des boules blanches et des boules noires, et supposons qu'à chaque fois que l'on en tire une boule, on la remette dans l'urne pour procéder à un nouveau tirage. Le rapport du nombre des boules blanches extraites, au nombre des boules noires extraites, sera le plus souvent très irrégulier dans les premiers tirages, mais les causes variables de cette irrégularité, produisent des effets alternativement favorables et contraires à la marche régulière des évènemens, et qui se détruisent mutuellement dans l'ensemble d'un grand nombre de tirages, laissent de plus en plus apercevoir le rapport des boules blanches aux boules noires contenues dans l'urne, ou les possibilités respectives d'en extraire une boule blanche ou une boule noire à chaque tirage. De là résulte le Théorème suivant.

"La probabilité que le rapport du nombre des boules blanches extraites, au nombre total des boules sorties, ne s'écarte pas au delà d'un intervalle donné, du rapport du nombre des boules blanches, au nombre total des boules contenues dans l'urne, approche indéfiniment de la certitude, par la multiplication indéfinie des évènemens quelque petit que l'on suppose cet intervalle."

* * * * * * *

"On peut tirer du théorème précédent cette conséquence qui doit être regardée comme une loi générale, savoir, que les rapports des effets de la Nature, sont à fort peu près constans, quand ces effets sont considérés en grand nombre. Ainsi, malgré la variété des années, la somme des productions pendant un nombre d'années considérable, est sensiblement la même; en sorte que l'homme par une utile prévoyance, peut se mettre à l'abri de l'irrégularité des saisons, en répandant également sur tous les temps que la nature distribue d'une manière inégale Je n'excepte pas de la loi précédente, les effets dus aux causes morales. Le rapport des naissances annuelles à la population, et celui des mariages aux naissances, n'éprouvent que de très-petites variations. à Paris, le nombre des naissances annuelles a toujours été le même à peu près, et j'ai oui dire qu'à la poste, dans les temps ordinaires, le nombre des lettres mises au rebut par les défauts des addresses, change peu chaque année ; ce qui a été pareillement observé à Londres.

"Il suit encore de ce Théorème, que dans une série d'évènemens, indéfiniment prolongée, l'action des causes régulières et constantes doit l'emporter à la longue, sur celle des causes irrégulières...

"Si l'on applique ce Théorème au rapport des naissances des garçons à celles des filles, observé dans les diverses parties de l'Europe, on trouve que ce rapport, partout à peu près égal à celui de 22 à 21, indique avec une extrême probabilité, une plus grande facilité dans les naissances des garçons. En considérant ensuite qu'il est le même à Naples qu'à Pétersbourg, on verra qu'à cet égard, l'influence du climat est insensible. On pouvait donc soupçonner contre l'opinion commune, que cette supériorité des naissances masculines subsiste dans l'orient même. J'avais en conséquence invité les savans Français envoyés en Egypte, à s'occuper de cette question intéressante ; mais la difficulté d'obtenir des renseignemens précis sur les naissances, ne leur a pas permis de la résoudre. Heureusement, Humboldt n'a point négligé cet objet dans l'immensité des choses nouvelles qu'il a observées et recueillies en Amérique, avec tant de sagacité, de constance, et de courage. Il a retrouvé entre les tropiques, le même rapport des naissances des garçons à celles des filles, que l'on observe à Paris, *ce qui doit faire regarder la supériorité des naissances masculines, comme une loi générale de l'espèce humaine.* Les lois que suivent à cet égard, les diverses espèces d'animaux, me paroissent dignes de l'attention des naturalistes."—*Essai Philos.* p. 73, *et seq.*

From these quotations it appears, that the constancy in the proportion of births to the whole population of a country, in that of births to marriages, and in that of male children to females, are considered by Laplace as facts of the *same kind*, and to be accounted for in the same way, with the very narrow limits within which the number of misdirected letters in the general post-office of Paris varies from year to year. The same thing, he tells us, has been observed in the dead-letter office at London. But as he mentions both these last facts merely on the authority of a *hearsay*, I do not know to what degree of credit they are entitled ; and I shall, therefore, leave them entirely out of our consideration in the present argument. The meaning which Laplace wished to convey by this comparison cannot be mistaken.

Among the different facts in Political Arithmetic here alluded to by Laplace, that of the constancy in the proportion of male to female births (which he himself pronounces to be a general law of our species) is the most exactly analogous to the example of the urn containing a mixture of white and of black balls, from which he deduces his general theorem. I shall, accordingly, select this in preference to the others. The intelligent reader will at once perceive that the same reasoning is equally applicable to all of them.

Let us suppose, then, that the white balls in Laplace's urn represent male infants, and the black balls female infants ; upon which supposition, the longer that the operation (described by Laplace) of drawing and returning the balls is continued, the nearer will the proportion of white to black balls approach to that of 22 to 21. What inference (according to Laplace's own theorem) ought we to deduce from this, but that the *whole* number of white balls in the urn, is to the whole number of black balls, in the same proportion of 22 to 21; or, in other words, that this is the proportion of the whole number of unborn males to the whole number of unborn females in the womb of futurity? And yet this inference is regarded by Laplace as a proof, that the approximation to equality in the numbers of the two sexes affords no evidence of design and contrivance.

"La constance de la supériorité des naissances des garçons sur celles des filles, à Paris et à Londres, depuis qu'on les observe, a paru à quelques savans, être une preuve *de la providence* sans laquelle ils ont pensé que les causes irrégulières qui troublent sans cesse la marche des évènemens, aurait du plusieurs fois, rendre les naissances annuelles des filles, supérieures à celles des garçons.

"Mais cette preuve est un nouvel exemple de l'abus que l'on a fait si souvent des causes finales qui disparaissent toujours par un examen approfondi des questions, lorsqu'on a les données nécessaires pour les résoudre La constance dont il s'agit, est un résultat des CAUSES REGULIERES qui donnent la supériorité aux naissances des garçons, et que l'emportent sur les anomalies dues au hasard, lorsque le nombre des naissances annuelles est considérable."—*Ibid.* pp 84, 85.

With the proposition announced in the last sentence, I perfectly agree That the constancy of the results in the instance now in question, depends on *regular causes*, (which, in this case, is merely a synonymous expression with *general laws*,) the most zealous advocates for a designing cause will readily admit; and if Laplace means nothing more than to say, that the uniformity of the effect, when observed on a large scale, may be explained without supposing the miraculous interference of Providence *in each individual birth*, the question does not seem worthy of a controversy. If the person who put the white and black balls into the urn, had wished to secure the actual result of the drawing, what other means could he have employed for the purpose, than to adjust to each other the relative proportions of these balls *in the whole number of both?* Could any proof more demonstrative be given, that this was the very end he had in view?

Nor do I think that the authors whom Laplace opposes ever meant to dispute the operation of these *regular causes* Dr. Arbuthnot, certainly one of the earliest writers in this country who brought forward the regular proportion between male and female births as an argument in favour of providence, not only agrees in this point with Laplace, but has proposed a physical theory to explain this regularity. The theory is, indeed, too ludicrous to deserve a moment's consideration,[1] but it at least shews, that Laplace has advanced nothing in favour of his conclusions which had not been previously granted by his adversaries]

[The following appears only in the First Edition.—*Ed*]

When this *Dissertation* was nearly ready for the press, the posthumous works of my late very learned, ingenious, and amiable friend, Dr. Thomas Brown, were

---

[1] "There seems (says Dr Arbuthnot) no more probable cause to be assigned in Physics for this equality of the births, than that in our first parents' seed there were at first formed an equal number of both sexes "—*Abridgment of the Philosophical Transactions*, vol. v part ii pp 240-242.

published. The contributions which the philosophy of the human mind owes to his talents and industry, belong exclusively to the literary history of the nineteenth century, and will, I doubt not, receive ample justice from the pens of some of his numerous pupils. On certain points on which we differed in opinion, more particularly on the philosophical merits of Lord Bacon and of Dr Reid, I should have been tempted to offer some additional explanations, if the circumstance of his recent and much lamented death had not imposed silence on me, upon all questions of controversy between us. The state of my health, besides, has been such during the winter, that I have found the task of correcting the press more than sufficient to furnish employment both to my mind and body, and, in fact, I have been forced to deny myself the satisfaction of reading Dr. Brown's *Lectures*, till my own performance shall be in the hands of the public.

TO DISSERTATION, PART THIRD.—NOTE F F F.

NOTE F F F, p. 491.

The well-known lines of Claudian on the Fall and Death of Rufinus, express a train of thought and of feeling which has probably passed more than once through every contemplating mind

" Sæpe mihi dubiam traxit sententia mentem,
Curarent superi terras, an nullus inesset
Rector, et incerto fluerent mortalia casu.
Nam cum dispositi quæsissem fœdera mundi
Præscriptosque mari fines, annisque meatus,
Et lucis noctisque vices, tunc omnia rebar
Consilio firmata Dei, qui lege moveri
Sidera, qui fruges diverso tempore nasci,
Qui variam Phœben alieno jusserit igni
Compleri, Solemque suo. porrexerit undis
Litora. tellurem medio libraverit axe
Sed cum res hominum tanta caligine volvi
Adspicerem, lætosque diu florere nocentes,
Vexarique pios. rursus labefacta cadebat
Relligio.
　　　*　　　*　　　*　　　*　　　*
Abstulit hunc tandem Rufini pœna tumultum,
Absolvitque Deos."

To the conclusiveness of this inference in favour of Providence, drawn from *one* particular instance of retributive justice, some strong, and in my opinion, just objections, are stated by Bayle, in a long, grave, and elaborate argument. I am doubtful, however, whether, on the present occasion, this formidable and unsparing critic has fully entered into the spirit of the passage which he censures. The whole poem in question, it ought to be remembered, is professedly an invective against the memory of Rufinus, and, therefore, the author is to be considered rather in the light of a declaimer and wit, than of a philosopher anxious to explain, with logical precision, the grounds of his own theological creed. In the passage quoted above, the gravity and solemnity of the introductory lines were evidently meant as a preparation for the satirical stab at the close;—the poetical effect of which is not in the least diminished by its inconsistency with sound and enlarged views of the order of the universe. It is sufficient, in such cases, if the poet speak a language which accords with the natural and universal prejudices of the multitude.

Let me add, that the popular error (unjustly as I conceive) imputed by Bayle to Claudian, arises from a mistaken expectation, that good or bad fortune is always to be connected, *in particular instances*, with good or bad actions; an expectation manifestly incompatible with those *general laws* by which both the material and the moral worlds are governed. It is from the tendency of these *general laws* alone that any inferences can fairly be deduced with respect to the ultimate designs of Providence; and for this purpose a much more enlarged and prolonged observation of the course of events is necessary, than can be expected from men whose minds are unenlightened by science, or whose views are circumscribed within the narrow circle of their own personal concerns. This consideration will, I hope, apologize for the space allotted in the text to the present discussion.

SUPPLEMENT.

[The following letter, addressed to Mr Stewart by his illustrious friend, M. Prévost, with the accompanying observations on Part II of the Dissertation, were inserted at the end of his own copy of that work, and merit preservation. This letter is in some parts mutilated.—*Ed.*

"A Geneve, 23 *Novembre*, 1821.

"Monsieur et ancien ami,—Aucun don littéraire ne pouvait m'être plus agréable que celui de votre *Dissertation*. La 2de partie répond bien à l'attente qu'avoit produite la 1ère. Je l'ai lue avec une attention recueillie, et un intérêt soutenu. Il s'en faut bien que les courtes remarques . . le feuillet joint à cette lettre, indiquent tous les sujets . . . que cette lecture m'a fournis, et je me suis interdis d'y . . . l'effet général qu'elle a produit chez moi et les sentiments qu'elle a provoqués. Indépendamment de l'ordre et de la clarté qui y règnent de l'union si rare d'une vaste étendue de connoissances et d'une saine philosophie, il y a dans le ton et dans le style une si juste mesure, et cependant une chaleur et une élévation, qui captivent et entraînent, au milieu de quelques discussions en apparence fort arides. Vous avez aussi mis dans vos jugements une équité et même une impartialité remarquables. Et sous plusieurs de ces rapports, ce tableau est un beau pendant à celui qu'a tracé votre illustre ami Playfair. J'ai été touché du soin que vous avez pris de me donner çà et là dans cet ouvrage (comme vous l'aviez fait dans d'autres) une honorable place.

"Conservez-moi, Monsieur, celle que vous m'avez accordée dans votre amitié, et puisse votre santé se soutenir au milieu de tant de pénibles et utiles travaux.—Votre dévoué,   P Prevost"

"DISSERTATION, ETC., PART II

" P 421 Ces mémoires furent insérés dans ceux pour 1796 et 1797. C'est à ceux pour 1796, que se rapporte la citation des pages 15 et 31 indiquées dans cette note

" Pp 284-286 A l'appui de ces remarques, je ne peux m'empêcher d'ajouter celle-ci comment est-il arrivé que Leibnitz, armé aussitôt que Newton de l'instrument du calcul, n'ait réellement rien fait en physique ?

" P. 356, l. 14 *But I must—a life to come* Bien que, j'aie vécu dans un temps, dans un lieu et dans une société, où l'admiration pour Ch. Bonnet étoit une espèce de religion, je n'ai jamais pu goûter beaucoup sa métaphysique. Je dois dire cependant, en réponse à l'accusation dans laquelle il se trouve compris, que ce philosophe a cru, par sa *Palingénésie*, y avoir pleinement répondu. En ce point encore, il a suivi d'assez près la marche de Leibnitz ; mais il mettoit un grand prix au trait qui distinguoit son opinion de celle de son prédécesseur. Et en effet (système pour système) elle est plus spécieuse.

" P. 369, l 18. *His thoughts—attention* J'ai quelque regret à cet éloge, que je ne crois pas mérité Dès le temps où parut ce volume, sous le titre assez fastueux *d'arithmétique morale*, m'étant empressé de l'étudier, j'y reconnus un tissu de paralogismes Il s'y trouve, il est vrai, des assertions incontestables , et comment auroit il pu ne pas énoncer en conclusion des vérités reconnues ? Mais ses ridicules expériences à un jeu frivole, et les conséquences absurdes ou mal déduites qu'il en dérive, n'ont aucune valeur Je supposai, dans le temps, que cet auteur (qui, sans être mathématicien, n'étoit point étranger aux mathématiques) avoit, vers la fin de sa vie, perdu l'habitude du raisonnement ferme, qu'exige le genre d'application qu'il avoit entrepris.

" P. 373, l 4 J'éprouve ici deux surprises . 1º pourquoi, si les Anglois manquent du mot *ennui*, ne le font-ils pas ? 2º le mot *lassitude* est-il donc en Anglois un synonyme d'*ennui*, chose en François si différente ?

" P. 596, l. 31. *Forms . . . Does Kant mean*, &c. 1º Le mot *forme*, appliqué à la sensibilité, est expliqué, tom 1 p 25, de la trad de Born, *In viso*, &c , et d'une manière plus générale, par les deux caractères de la connoissance *a priori*, p. 3, l. dern. *Hinc itaque*,'&c Ce mot ne semble pas trop mal imaginé, pour représenter ce qui constitue les *lois* de notre nature spirituelle, comme Bacon l'emploie à signifier les lois de la nature A la vérité c'est moins de Bacon que d'Aristote que Kant me semble l'avoir emprunté Quoiqu'il en soit, se faisant Kantien, il convenoit d'avoir un mot qui s'appliquât aux trois facultés de l'esprit, pour exprimer ce qui lui est propre, ce qui n'est point acquis par l'expérience 2ª A la question— *Does Kant*, &c ; je répondroit Kant veut dire que le concept de l'espace est *nécessaire*, c'est-à-dire, que nous ne pouvons pas le dépouiller , et de plus, qu'il est *universel*, c d qu'il s'applique à tous les phénomènes des sens externes Et dès qu'une fois il a conçu ce qu'il a conçu, il n'a pas trop mal fait de substituer le mot *forme* à ce double caractère —C'est par pure justice, que je fais cette remarque, n'étant pas Kantien , et en particulier ayant, dès long temps, analysé tout autrement les idées de *temps* et *d'espace*

" P. 429, note 1 La réflexion finale est bien juste Je l'ai souvent faite sans avoir eu le bonheur de voir l'Ecosse, et j'ai toujours attribué à la philosophie de cette école une partie des honorables traits que distinguent les sentiments, les mœurs et le caractère de ceux qui en sont le plus rapprochés. Je ne peux parler à la vérité que des personnes et des livres à moi connus.

"P 446, l 5 *But to which*, &c J'adopte avec empressement cette opinion Je l'étends même un peu au delà, et je l'applique volontiers à d'autres écarts. C'est un principe de tolérance."

There is also annexed by Mr. Stewart, to his own copy of the Dissertation, a long extract against *chance*, from the work of Kepler, *De Stella Nova in pede Serpentarii*. It was transcribed by the late Dr Nicoll, from a copy in the Bodleian Library, in 1820 The edition of the book is Prague, 1606, 4to; and the extract commences, p. 140, "Age igitur," and terminates by the words "hoc ordine." The quotation probably had reference, in the author's mind, to the opinion of Diderot and Hume, as stated in Note T T, pp 586, 587, but, though curious, it has been thought too long to be here appended.—*Ed*]

INDEX.

DISSERTATION, (PARTS I. II. III.) FROM BEGINNING TO PAGE 528.
NOTES AND ILLUSTRATIONS, FROM PAGE 529 TO END.

ADDISON, beneficial influence exerted by him and his associates, 333-338, on his accuracy and power of philosophical exposition, 581-584
Æsthetic, in the Kantian Philosophy, 399
Alembert, (D',) *see* D'Alembert
Allamand, whether self-evident propositions be simple ideas or judgments, (and his approximation to Reid,) 551, 552.
Allied Sovereigns, their manifesto on entering Paris in 1815, 525.
American (North) thinkers, 424, 425
Ancillon, (le père,) praised, 421.
Ancillon, (le fils,) quoted as contrasting the French and German philosophies, 387, 388
Arbuthnot, (Dr,) favourably noticed, 602, *et alibi;* as one of the earliest speculators on the doctrine of probabilities, 614
Aristotle, quoted 109
Arnauld, (Anthony,) a practical observer of men, 153; in his book *On True and False Ideas* an opponent to Malebranche, 162; coincides with Reid in respect of the Ideal Theory, 162, 163; principal author of the *Port-Royal Logic*, 163; the value of that work, 163, 164, his essential correspondence with Locke in regard to the origin of our ideas, 225, 226.
Association of Ideas, great importance of, in education, 522, *alibi*
Atheism, from what philosophical opinions it more immediately results, 376, directly from the doctrine of Neces-

sity, 376, 574, prevalence of, in Paris about the middle of last century, 376, 377, absurd imputation of, 378, 379, irreligion and fanaticism analogous in their political effects, 379; deification of Nature reprobated, 592, but to be cautiously interpreted, 593.
Augustine, on Cicero, 48; maintained the doctrine of Free-will, 575

BACON, on his arrangement of the sciences, 1, *seq.*; on his Philosophy in general, 63-78, on his Physics, 64, on his Psychology, 64-68, two errors noted, 69, on his Ethical Disquisitions, 69; on his Political Philosophy, 71-75, on his views of Education, 75, on his Philosophy of Law, 189, his maxim that *Knowledge is Power*, 502, 524; testimonies touching, 538-540.
Barrow, his learning and intellectual vigour, 90, 91, his rapidity and inconsistency, 92.
Baxter, (Andrew,) his *Inquiry into the Nature of the Human Soul* considered, 429, 430
Bayle, refutation of Spinoza, 300; led the way in the misapplication of the term Spinozism, 304; on his genius, influence, and opinions in general, 313-324, specimen of his lives, in that of Knox, as drawn from Catholic writers, 580, 581.
Beattie, praised with qualification, 463
Beaumarchais, quoted as speaking in his comedy the doctrine of Necessity, 312

Belsham, quoted in favour of Necessity, 312.
Bentham, quoted on Grotius, Puffendorf, and Burlamaqui, 184, on universal jurisprudence, 187; on the authority of our ancestors, 192.
Berkeley, his doctrine of visual distance, 131, 132, on his doctrine concerning the indissoluble connexion of our notions of Colour and Extension, 544, 545; specially on his *New Theory of Vision*, and how far original therein, 340-348, unknown pamphlet of, entitled "*The Theory of Vision, &c., Vindicated and Explained*," 348; on him, in general, 338-350, his character and accomplishments, 339, gave popularity to metaphysical pursuits which they had never possessed in England, 339; on his doctrine touching the objects of general terms, 349, on his argument against the existence of the material world, 349, on the intention and defect of his Idealism, 350, 351
Berlin Academy, 421.
Bernouilh, (John,) on the Law of Continuity, 275, 563, 564
Blair, (Rev Dr,) his criticism of Addison considered, 581-583
Bodinus, his resemblance to Bacon, 53, 55, his anticipation of Montesquieu, 53, 536; liberality of his political principles, 54, 55, his belief in witchcraft and astrology, only the usual belief of the greatest thinkers before and after him, as Melanchthon, Erasmus, Luther, Kepler, Tycho Brahe, &c., 56, 57
Bonald, (M de,) quoted touching Kant, 415; holds, that philosophy is as yet only in expectation, 481.
Bondwill, *see* Necessity
Bonnet, (Charles,) a follower of Leibnitz, 265; in favour of the Law of Continuity, 277, 278, quoted as an advocate of Necessity, 308, 309, his theory of vibrations in the nerves, 353, 354, compared with Hartley generally, 355; his coincidence with Condillac in the hypothesis of an animated statue, 359, remark on, by Prévost, 616
Boscovich, praised, 423, 424; refutation of his mathematical argument against the progress of mankind, 498, 499; on the Law of Continuity, 561.
Breadthless lines as realized to sense, ix
Brown, (Dr. Thomas,) notice of, 613.

Buchanan, his political doctrine, 61, 62.
Budæus, 58
Buffier, on the Secondary Qualities of matter, 127.
Buffon, on his contributions to metaphysical science, his merits and demerits, 368-370; notice of, by Prévost, 616
Buhle, his blunders, 600, 601.
Burnet, (of Kemney,) noticed, 602
Butler, (Bishop,) notice of, in relation to Hume, 453, 454, was the first to detect the dangerous consequences from Locke's account of the origin of our ideas, if literally interpreted, 454, 455, on the art of printing, 511.

CALVIN, on usury, 30, 503; on some theological tenets of, 40, opinion on the Popes, 44, his participation in the judicial murder of Servetus, 54
Campanella, an original speculator, notice of, 50, *seq*
Campbell, (Principal,) on his Nomenclature of the Sciences, 17, praised as a metaphysician, 460, 463, 467.
Cape of Good Hope, (passage to India by,) 34
Carmichael, (Professor Gershom,) quoted, on Grotius and Puffendorf, 177, 178
Cartes, (Des,) *see* Descartes
Cause and Effect, according to Kant, 402, *seq*, to Price, 403; to Cudworth, 406; notion of an efficient cause implies the notion of mind, 573, 608
Character, (varieties of intellectual,) works delineating, common in France, 382
Charron, friend of Montaigne, 105, how he has attempted to supply an antidote to Montaigne's scepticism, 106; character of his work *On Wisdom*, 106.
Chatelet, (Madame du,) notice of her works and opinions, 385
Cicero, 48.
Clarendon, (Earl of,) his testimonies as to Hobbes, 541
Clarke, (Dr Samuel,) on his opinions in general, 287-298, relation to Newton, 287, 288; on his controversy with Leibnitz, 288, on Space and Time, Immensity and Eternity, 291-294; his polemic as an advocate of Free-will, 295, *seq*, his controversy with Collins on this question, 306,

INDEX.   621

seq ; how his heart was in the controversy of liberty and necessity, 308
Claudian, his verses on the fall of Rufinus criticised, but defended against Bayle, 614, 615
Coccen, (Henry and Samuel,) on Grotius, 185
Coke, (Lord,) his saying, that to trace an error to its origin, is to refute it, 192.
Collier, (Arthur,) on his merits as a speculator, 349, *see* 855, 356, notice of his *Clavis Universalis*, of its German translation, and translator's notes, 584, 585
Collins, (Anthony,) 272 ; as an advocate for Necessity, 297, 573-577, on his controversy with Clarke on this opinion, 306, *seq ;* unknown treatise by, *On Liberty and Necessity*, 1729, being a vindication of his *Inquiry*, 307, Locke's affection for, 570, 571, his notion of Liberty, (as that of Hobbes, Leibnitz, S'Gravesande, Edwards, Bonnet, &c &c,) is only the Liberty of Spontaneity—of doing what we will. 576, 577.
Condillac, supposed in France to be a genuine disciple of Locke, but not so, 238, 239, 359; on his philosophy in general, 358, *seq ;* sterility of invention between Descartes and Condillac, 358, preceded Hartley in applying the Association of Ideas as the one explanatory principle in Psychology, 359, his coincidence with Bonnet in the hypothesis of an animated statue, 359, probably not aware of the logical consequences of his theory of the origin of our knowledge, 359, 360, his lucid style of writing, and the tenor of his philosophy, peculiarly suited to the taste of his countrymen, 360, his analysis of the mental phenomena often very successful, 360 ; especially in explaining the mutual action and reaction of thought and language, 361 ; in his theoretical history of language made considerable advances, 361 ; a radical error in his system noticed, 366-368, compared with Kant in regard to the notion of Space, 598
Condorcet, erroneous opinion as to the foundation of our belief in the constancy of nature, 609
Confession of Faith of the Church of Scotland asserts the Free-will of man, 575
Continuity, (Law of,) 561-564, only the old and common law—that nature does not operate *per saltum* on, 279.
Copernicus and his system, 37.
Cowley, on his *Ode to Destiny*, 579
Crousaz, his merits, 218-220
Cudworth, an antagonist of Hobbes, 85, his ethics, 86-88, his plastic medium, 89, resemblance to Kant, 398-400, an advocate for Free-will, 401
Cumberland, on the law of nature, 93.
Cuvier, aware, that the liberty of Spontaneity was only a disguised form of Fatalism, 577.

D'ALEMBERT, strictures on his arrangement of the sciences, or touching his Encyclopedical Tree, 1-22, on Montesquieu, 189, blindly follows Condillac's interpretation of Locke, 370.
Dalgarno, favourable notice of his works, 601, 602.
Darwin, on Instinct, 471-473, *alibi*.
Death, Leibnitian theory of, 564, 565.
Definition, words expressing notions incapable of analysis undefinable, this held by Descartes, 124
Degerando, praised, 381 ; quoted touching Kant, 413, 416, coincides with Mendelsohn in refuting Hume's doctrine of Causation by the calculus of probabilities, 609, 610.
Descartes, on his Philosophy in general, 112-141, whether he, or Bacon, or Galileo, be the father of free inquiry in modern Europe, 112, 113, father of modern experimental Psychology, 113, prior to Locke in the employment of Reflection, 113, merit in asserting the immateriality of the human mind, 114-117, whether he had read the works of Bacon, 118, 543, 544, his process of doubt and its results, 118-121; according to Stewart, the first who recognised that our knowledge of mind is only relative, 121 ; how great his merit in this respect, 122, 123 ; his Psychological observations made when very young, 123, his great glory is to have pointed out the true method of studying mind, 124, 543 ; the principal articles of the Cartesian Philosophy are,—1°. his limitation of verbal definition, 124 ; 2°. observations on our prejudices, 124, 3°. the paramount authority of consciousness, 125, 4° clear distinction of the Primary and Secondary qualities of matter, 125, *seq ,* esta-

blished the great principle, that imagination can throw no light on the operations of thought, 136, 137; his errors,—1°. in rejecting the speculation about Final Causes, 138, 2°. in considering the brutes as mere machines, 138, compare 375; 3°. his doctrine of Innate Ideas, 138, 4°. his placing the essence of mind in thinking, 138; 5°. his placing the essence of matter in extension, 138, 6°. his new modification of the Ideal Theory of perception, adopted by Malebranche. Locke, Berkeley, and Hume, 138, 545; his theory of the communication of mind and body groundless, 139, this originated the hypothesis of Hartley, which is however also to be traced to some queries of Sir Isaac Newton, 140, how far the sect of the Egoists is a legitimate offshoot of Cartesianism, 160, his meaning of Innate Ideas commonly misunderstood, and misunderstood by Locke, 227, 236, 553-556, defence of his rejection of Final Causes, 377, 378, uses *thought* (cogitatio) for every thing of which we are conscious, 381; holds that philosophy is as a tree of which metaphysics are the root, &c., 483, his use of the term *substance*, 541-543; thought the *Meditations* his best book, 543, merit in rejecting all explanation of the mental phenomena by material analogies, 543, misunderstanding of his doctrine in this respect, 543, on his opinion touching sensible ideas, 545, 546; on the seat of the soul, 547; falsely charged by Dr Henry More with Nullibism, 547; on his genius as a *bel esprit*, 548; common error in supposing there is no medium between the Innate Ideas of Descartes, and the opposite theory of Gassendi, 548; he asserts Free-will, 575.

Determinism, *see* Necessity.

Diderot, quoted as an advocate of Necessity, 311, 580; was he an author of the *Système de la Nature?* 377, inconsistent in his philosophy, 585, his ultimate philosophy rank atheism, 585-589; his reasoning inconclusive, 588.

Duclos, as a delineator of character, 383

Economists, their opinions and merits, 380.

Edwards, (Dr Jonathan,) as an advocate of Necessity, 307, 573, noticed as the only American metaphysician, 424

Efficiency, the conception of, implies the notion of mind, 573, 608

Egoism, how far a legitimate development of Cartesianism, 160

Elliot, (Sir Gilbert,) remarkable letter of, in regard to Hume, 605-607, compare 448

Empirical, on the word, 396, 397.

Encyclopédie, authors of, their tendency to Materialism blindly derived from Condillac's comments upon Locke, 370

England, rapid progress in intellectual cultivation between 1588 and 1640, 77

Epicureans, error of the statement,— that their Chance involves the supposition of an effect without a cause, 386, 387, on their doctrine of Liberty, 573, 574

Erasmus, noticed, 27, his temporizing liberality, 530.

Ethics, degraded state into which they had fallen, 179; ethical and political philosophy during the eighteenth century, sketch of, intended by author, 202.

Experiment, (sciences of,) 33.

Fearn, (Mr John,) his attack upon the author, groundless, ix.

Fenelon, on, in general, 167-169, his doctrine of religious toleration and liberty of conscience, 168, 169

Fichte, on his opinions, 418, 419.

Filangieri, (Chevalier de,) charges Montesquieu with plagiarizing from Bodinus, 536.

Final Causes, their neglect an insufficient proof of atheism, 377

Fontenelle, on his influence and opinions, 324-332

Freedom of action, *see* Free-will.

Free-will, doctrine of, as held by Augustine, 575, by Clarke, 295, *seq.*; by Cudworth, 401; by Cuvier, 577; by Descartes, 575, by the Epicureans, 573, 574, by Kant, 408, *seq.*, by Law, (Bishop,) 356, by Locke, 296, 297, by Price, 573, a deceitful sense of, asserted, 411.

French selfish Philosophy originated before the Regency, 110, 111; French tongue, its peculiar richness in the delineation of character, 384.

INDEX. 623

GALIANI, (Abbé,) anecdote of, in defence of theism, 588, 589, his character, 589.

Galileo, on the Law of Continuity, 562, 563

Gassendi, on his Philosophy in general, 141-149, his character, 141, 142, 549, 550; his physics, 142, 143, an advocate for the investigation of Final Causes, 143, his Metaphysics and Ethics, 144, 145, his attachment to Hobbes, 145, a Sensationalist, 145; how far he anticipated Locke, 146, 147, his doctrine on the origin of our ideas, 224; his orthodoxy and self-denial, 549, 550.

General terms, are they prior in the order of knowledge to proper names, 565, 566

Genovesi, (Antonio,) 422, 423

Gentilis, (Albericus,) 50, 531.

Gerard, favourably noticed, 463

Gerdil, (Cardinal,) 422.

Ginguené, on Machiavel, 534.

Glanvill, 79, on the Secondary Qualities of matter, 127

Gley, (G.,) quoted as to Fichte and Schelling, 420.

God, the so-called Divinity of Hobbes, Spinoza, &c, subject to fate or necessity, 579.

Goettingen Royal Society, 421.

Greek refugees, 27

Gregory, (Dr. John,) his views on the union of soul and body favourably noticed, 469

Grimm, (Baron de,) quoted in favour of Necessity, 310.

Grotius, 76, influence of his writings, 93, his work *De Jure Belli et Pacis*, the merits and defects of this work, 170-187.

HAMILTON, (Sir William,) 584

Harpe, (La,) quoted against Helvetius, 371.

Hartley, his theory of vibrations to be traced through a query of Newton's to Descartes' theory of animal spirits, &c., 140, 289, 353, favourably noticed, but criticised, 237; quoted in favour of Necessity, 312, Hartleian school, 352, *seq.;* adopts from Gay the Association of Ideas as the single explanatory principle, 353; in what respect his theory of vibrations differs from Bonnet's, 353, originally a Libertarian, 355, 576, compared with Bonnet generally, 355

Helvetius, 110; on his extension of the Law of Continuity, 279, 280; on his doctrines in general, 371, *seq ;* maintains that all our ideas are derived from the external senses, and that the inferiority of the brutal to the human soul lies in the differences of organization, 371-373, this opinion refuted, 373, 374; this crotchet in extreme contrast to the paradox of the Cartesians, in regard to the brutes as mere machines, 375, his merit as a delineator of character, 384.

Hobbes, on his philosophy in general, 79-85; his political writings, 80-83; his ethical principles, 83, a Necessitarian, 84, *et pluries;* his deity subject to fate, 579, his Psychology, 84, 85, relation to the Antinomians, 86, to the ancient Sceptics, 89; not deficient in reading, 89, on his doctrine of national jurisprudence, 181, contrasted with Locke, in regard to the origin of our ideas, 235; herein corresponds with Gassendi, 235, on his personal character, 297, his paradoxical bias, 540, 541, not a stickler in his political opinions, 541

Holbach, (Baron d',) as author of the *Système de la Nature*, a scheme of Necessity and Atheism, 377.

Home, (Henry,) *see* Kames.

Hooker, noticed, 78

Hopital, (Chancellor De l',) his principles of toleration, 52

Horner, (Mr. Francis,) on Machiavel's *Prince*, 535; character of Mr Horner himself, by the author, 535

Huarte, notice of, as a delineator of character, 383

Huillier, (M l',) on Probabilities, praised, 421; he and Prévost, against Condorcet's (and Laplace's) theory of our anticipation of nature, 610, 611

Hume, his tendency to Materialism, 137; but more strongly to Idealism, or even Egoism, 437, on his works and opinions, 431-456; scope of his speculation, 432-434, his merit in renouncing all physiological hypotheses in explanation of the phænomena of mind, 434, 435; he originated various inquiries which he himself did not further pursue, 435; his merit in regard to an improved style of composition in Scotland, 435, 436, his fundamental principles nearly the same as those of his predecessors, 436, his scepticism, 437, 438; his influence perhaps more beneficial than pernicious, 439, 440, 462, 463, his doctrine of Causation, 441, *seq ;* anticipations of his doctrine on this point, 441, 442, his account of the necessity we are conscious of to think a cause for whatever begins to be, 443, 444; he fairly disproved the reasonings of Hobbes, Clarke, and Locke, in explanation of this, 445, to him we owe Kant's *Critique of Pure Reason,* 445, bold attempt to expunge every *idea* which was not derived from a preceding *impression,* 447; he was fully aware of the consequences of this doctrine, 447, 448; how he was led into his sceptical speculation, 448, 449, how he regarded the argument from Common Sense, 450-452; his sincerity in regard to the sceptical argument, 453, notice of his correspondence with Butler, 453, 454, remarkable coincidence between the arguments of his Scottish and German opponents, 460, 461, the former have been unjustly treated, 461, 462; in favour of the heathen mythology, 587, 588; Cleanthes, in the Dialogues of Natural Religion, expresses Hume's own opinions, 603, despised mathematics, 604, curious letter to Sir Gilbert Elliot, upon Cause, Effect, &c, 603, 604. reply by Sir Gilbert Elliot, 605-607.

Hutcheson, (Dr. Francis,) influence of, 428, 429

Idealist, on the word, 396

Ideas, (Innate,) in what sense understood by Descartes and the philosophers, 553-556.

Ideas, (Sensible,) theory of, what is the import of, as held by Descartes and other philosophers, 545, 546

Idéologie, the French doctrine designated by that term of little value, 381, founded on the Ideal Theory which Reid refuted, 460.

Indian (Hindoo) Philosophy, 425-427.

Indifference, liberty of, *see* Liberty.

Influence or *Influx,* their supposed derivation in a philosophical application, 558, 559

Intercourse between nations, 36, 502, 509.

Italian Physics, Philosophy, &c, 195; philosophers, merits of, 424

JACOBI, praised, 421.

Johnson, (Ben,) his testimony touching Bacon, 538

KAMES, (Lord,) a Necessitarian, asserts a deceitful sense of Free-will, 411, the spirit of his writings praised, 463, holds matter to be most active, 608.

Kant, a Scotsman by descent, 393, on his philosophy in general, 389-418; his *Critique of Pure Reason,* 393, *seq.;* formed an epoch both in German literature and philosophy 395, a Libertarian and Non-Sensationalist, 396, *seq.;* analogy to Cudworth, 398, *seq.,* 405, 406, *seq ;* to Price, 399, 400, 405, to the Cambridge Platonists in general, 400, roused to speculation from his dogmatic slumber by Hume's theory of Causation, 401, *seq ;* theory of Space and Time, 408, 594-598, asserts Free-will, 408, *seq ;* his Practical Reason, 410, *seq.,* this how far analogous to the Common Sense of Beattie and Oswald, 412, his obscurity, 416, 417, 597, table of his notions *a priori,* or Categories of the Understanding, 593, 594, tendency of his doctrine to scepticism, 596, contrasted with Newton, 596, 597, compared with Locke in regard to the notion of Space, 598, with Condillac in respect of the same notion, 598, on his application of the term *form,* 596, 616

Kepler, against Chance, noticed, 617.

LAMBERT, on his philosophical merits, 392, 393

Lampredi, on Grotius and Puffendorf, 172

Language, (theoretical history of,) Rousseau's puzzling objection, 361-365

Laplace, pernicious philosophy of, in fact, a Spinozism, 386, 467, 463, 586; his merit in the calculation of Probabilities, 467, 468, but there confounds the mathematical theory of chances and the inductive anticipation of future events, deduced from an observation of the past, 609-614, criticism of his argument from Probabilities in the superseding of Providence and Final Causes, 613, 614

Law, (Bishop of Carlisle,) on, 352, his speculations on Space and Time, 352; contends strongly for man's Free-agency, 356, yet how analogous in some respects are his opinions with those of Hartley and Priestley, 356, shewn to depreciate the evidences of Natural Religion, 356, 357

Law of Nature, abstract code of the, unphilosophical, 187, 188.

Lee, as an antagonist of Locke, 557, 558

Leibnitz, his superstitious veneration of the Roman Law, 186, his eminence as a thinker, 196, Leibnitz (with Locke) opens the metaphysical history of the eighteenth century, 204, to correct certain misapprehensions touching the opinions of these two philosophers is proposed by the author, 204, 205, Leibnitz's injustice to Locke, 233, 234, 559, Leibnitz's famous reservation (*nisi ipse intellectus*) little more than a translation from Aristotle, 234, contrasted with Locke, 252, 258, 259; influence in promoting a mutual communication of intellectual lights and moral sympathies, 252, 253, how far his doctrine touching the origin of our knowledge coincides with the Innate Ideas of the Cartesians, 253, 254; his system of *Pre-established Harmony*, 254, *seq.*; this scheme more untenable than the doctrine of *Occasional Causes*, 255, 256, why the old doctrine of the mutual *influence* of soul and body was rejected by the Cartesians and Leibnitians, 256, 257; the Pre-established Harmony involves a mechanism, 257, 258; his Optimism, 260; this abolishes all moral distinctions, 261, his zeal in maintaining the doctrine of Necessity, 263, *seq.*; though holding the mind to be a mere machine, maintains it to be immaterial, 263, 264, the identification of Materialism and Necessitarianism inaccurate, 265, 396, Leibnitz trained in the school of Plato, 265, 266, regarded the Newtonian Physics as a mere romance, 266, evil effects of his *Theodicœa* in propagating Fatalism throughout Europe, 267, on his letter to Pfaff, 267, 268; his principle of the *Sufficient Reason* discussed, 269-272, in the employment of this he has shewn great dexterity, 272, his principle of the *Law of Continuity* redargued, 273-281, see also 561-564; defects of his intellectual habits may be traced to his early and excessive study of Mathematics, 281, 565; his merits in regard to the study of Etymology, 281; of German Antiquities, of Roman Jurisprudence, of Theology, &c, 282, 283, defects of his character, 284; remark on, by Prévost, 616, like Locke, his credulity too great, 285, 567; on Space and Time, 293, 294, as a delineator of character, 383; his philosophy, as a whole, diametrically opposed to the Sensationalist Philosophy of France, 387, his doctrine of Monads, 560, 561, his theory of death, 564, 567; held all proper names to be at first appellatives, 565, 566, general estimate of Leibnitz, 568-570.

Leslie, (Sir John,) on the Law of Continuity, 563

Liberty, see *Free-will;* Liberty of Spontaneity and Liberty of Indifference, or from Necessity, 297, 306, 576, 577.

Locke, his distribution of the sciences, 15, *seq.;* one of the first speculators upon Trade, 97, Locke and Leibnitz open the metaphysical history of the eighteenth century, 204; to correct certain misapprehensions touching the opinions of these two philosophers is proposed by the author, 204, 205, Locke, on his opinions in general, 206-251, his study of medicine, effect of it on his mind, 207, 208, his attention turned to politics by his intimacy with the Earl of Shaftesbury, 208, how the Essay on Human Understanding originated, 209, 210; this Essay composed by snatches, 212; appears to have studied diligently Hobbes and Gassendi, and to have been no stranger to Montaigne, Bacon, and Malebranche, 212; familiar also with the Cartesian system, 212; but in his Essay mentions none of these authors, 213; his style, that of a man of the world, 213, his Essay, how received at the English Universities, 214, 215; how in Scotland, 216, how on the Continent, 216-223, how his philosophical acceptation was affected by his political opinions, 216, 217; his letters on Toleration, 217, how Locke estimated by Leibnitz and others, 218; coincidence between the doctrines of Locke and Gassendi, facilitated the circulation of Locke's opinions in France, 221, 222; inculcates always a free use of reason, 223, his opinion as to two fundamental doctrines, 1°, *the Origin of our Ideas;* 2°, *the Immu-*

VOL. I. 2 R

tability of Moral distinctions, has been grossly misapprehended, 223, 224; contrast of Locke's real doctrine concerning the Origin of our Ideas and the doctrine of the Sensationalists, as Gassendi, Hobbes, Condillac, Diderot, Condorcet, Hartley, Tucker, Horne Tooke, &c, 224-237, the stress laid by him on *Reflection*, as a source of our ideas different from Sense, distinguishes him from the mere Sensationalists, 227-233, 396; Locke misrepresented, among others, by Leibnitz, 233, 234, 559, in regard to the immutability of moral distinctions and power of moral perception, his real opinion vindicated, 238-243, Shaftesbury and Sir Isaac Newton on Locke's Moral doctrine, 242-244; his tracts on Education and on the Conduct of the Understanding, 244, 245, defects in his intellectual character, 247-250, his writings on Money, Trade, and Government, 251, on the *Scale of Beings*, 280, as a maintainer of Free-will, 296, 297, slow progress of Philosophy after the publication of his Essay, 462, proof of the popularity of Locke's philosophy in France in the eighteenth century, 552, 553, Locke's first antagonists noted—Stillingfleet, Norris, Lee, Lowde, also Sherlock, 557, 558, compared with Kant, in regard to the notion of Space, 598, notices that we should not say the *Will* is free, but that the *Man* is free, 608

Logic, want of a competent Manual of Logic, Rational or Applied, 466, 467
Lowde, as an antagonist of Locke, 557.
Lower Orders, (rise of,) 32.
Luther, 29, on certain of his theological opinions, 39; examples of his credulity and superstition, 536, 537.

MACHIAVEL, on his character and doctrines, 41-48, 531-535
Maclaurin, against the Law of Continuity, 275.
Malebranche, on the Cartesian doctrine of the Secondary Qualities of matter, 126, 129; on his Philosophy in general, 149-161, his accomplishments, 149, his *Search after Truth*, 150, displays strong imagination, 150, blends theology with metaphysics, 151, mystical, 151; otherwise bold and free in speculation, 151, remarkable in his generation for a disbelief of sorcery, 152; an acute observer of character, 153, on the Cartesian Theory of Vision, 156, on the nature of habits, 157; his doctrine of Occasional Causes, and making the Deity himself the efficient and immediate cause exclusively of every effect, 157-160, objections to this theory not satisfactory, 158, 160; how far followed by Berkeley, 160, their conversation and its result, 161, remarks on it by Warburton, 162
Mathematics, their early and excessive study pervert the mind, 281, 498-500, 565
Matter, is it active? 608, 609
Melanchthon, 30, 38, his approbation of the execution of Servetus, 54
Mendelsohn, an opponent of Hume's scepticism as to Causation, by reasons drawn from the calculus of Probabilities, 609
Metaphysics, change in the meaning of the word since the publication of Locke's Essay, 475, 476; conjunction of the sciences of Metaphysics, of Ethics, and of Politics, vindicated, 477, 478, influence of metaphysical studies on historical writing, 478, on poetry, 478, on criticism, 478, on education, 479, on the style of composition, 479-481, what is the amount of truth obtained by the metaphysical speculations of the eighteenth century? 481-484, is philosophy only in expectation? 481-483, metaphysics are the root of the tree of philosophy, 483.
Metaphysical and Moral Sciences, 38.
Microscope, (invention of,) 36.
Middle Ages, 25.
Montaigne, on his opinions in general, 98-104, characteristic of his Essays, his self-study, 98, 99, severely criticised in the *Port-Royal Logic*, 99; his scientific knowledge, 100, his education by Buchanan, 100, lively and paradoxical, 100, sceptical on religion, 101, but a bigot towards the close of life, 101, character of his scepticism, 102, his Apology for Raimond de Sebonde, 103, 104
Montesquieu, his historical speculation as to the origin and relations of laws, 188-192; the popularity of his *Spirit of Laws* was fatal to the study of Natural Jurisprudence, 193, was he a plagiarist? 536, speaks always respectfully of Natural Religion, 589

INDEX. 627

More, (Dr Henry,) 79, quoted, 294
More, (Sir Thomas,) his liberality and toleration, 529, 530.
Motives, as identified with causes, in support of the scheme of Necessity, 607, *seq*

NAPOLEON, saying of, that "nothing in history resembles the close of the eighteenth century," 524
Nature, on the ground of our expectation of its constancy, 609-614.
Necessity of human actions, admits but of one interpretation, 577, leads to Atheism, 376, 574, according to Priestley is a merely modern opinion, 576; as supposed to be proved by the influence of education, 577, 578, by the Divine prescience, 578, by the scriptural comparison of the potter, 309, 579; supersedes remorse, 312; as held by Beaumarchais, 312; by Belsham, 312; by Bonnet, 308, 309; by Collins, 297, 573-577; by Diderot, 311, 580, by Edwards, 307, 578, by Grimm, 310; by Hartley, 312; by Hobbes, 84, *et pluries*; by Holbach, 377, by Hume, 607; by Kames, 411; by Leibnitz, 257, 258, *et alibi*; by Priestley, 575, 576, by Spinoza, 298, 579; by Voltaire, (inconsistently,) 591, 592, by Wolf, 391.
Necessity, (quality of, *i.e.*, the impossibility of not thinking so or so,) the criterion of *native* cognitions, 406.
New World, (Discovery of,) 34.
Newton, (Sir Isaac,) made no research into the cause of Gravitation, 148; on his opinions in general, 287-294; affords the germ of Clarke's *a priori* argument for the existence of God, 290, misrepresented as thinking with Spinoza, 303; his philosophy was taught in the Scottish Unversities before it was admitted into the English, 551; contrasted with Kant and criticised, 596, 597
Nizolius, (Marius,) an original speculator in philosophy, 49.
Nooumenon in the Kantian Philosophy, 399.
Norris, on his merits as a philosopher, 349; an antagonist of Locke, 557

OBJECTIVE and Subjective Truths, 407.
Occam, 38

PALEY, an exception among the disciples of Dr. Law, 357, on his opinions concerning instinct, 470-473
Paracelsus, 33
Pascal, on his character and doctrines, 165-167.
Patricius, (Franciscus,) a philosophical reformer, 49.
Philosophical studies, chief use of, to cultivate habits of generalization, 520
Plato, revival of his philosophy, 48, his Optimism 261.
Playfair, on the Law of Continuity, 562, 563.
Politics, Political Economy, among its earliest cultivators, English merchants, 97, Political and Ethical Philosophy, sketch of their progress during the eighteenth century, intended by author, 202.
Pope, (Alex.) a dangerous vindicator of the ways of God, 262, 263; on Clarke's argument, *a priori*, 290
Prévost, praised, 381, 421, quoted touching Kant, 415, 597-599, touching Hutcheson, 428, and L'Huilier, against Condorcet's (and Laplace's) theory of our anticipation of the constancy of nature, 610, 611; Letter to Mr. Stewart, 615; his observation on Leibnitz, 616, on Bonnet, 616; on Buffon, 616; on the words *ennui* and *lassitude*, 616, on the Kantian application of the term *form*, 616, on the Scottish philosophers, 617, on the principle of our belief in the constancy of nature, 617
Price, resemblance to Kant, 399, 400, his admission that the idea of every *change* supposes it to be an *effect*, 573, a stout advocate for Free-will, 573, coincides with Condorcet (and Laplace) in regard to the ground of our confidence in the course of nature, 611
Priestley, a Necessitarian, but originally a Libertarian, 575, 576; he supposes the doctrine of philosophical Necessity to be a merely modern opinion, 576.
Pringle, (Sir John,) referred to as shewing the general state of Metaphysical speculation in Scotland, 435.
Printing, (Invention of,) 30, *seq*
Prior, (Matthew,) quoted, 140
Probabilities, calculation of, 467, 468, 609-614.
Progress of Mankind in illumination, humanity, and happiness, upon the whole steady and accelerating, 487-527, objection considered, 488, *seq*;

circumstances contributing to this improvement—Revival of Letters—Invention of Printing—Geographical Discoveries — Intercourse between Nations—Religious Reformation, 489, *seq*; probability of such a progress, 491, *seq.*; anticipation from the character of the Divine Agency, 491, *seq.*; counter inference refuted, 492, *seq*; true nature of the problem stated, 493, 494; Turgot's opinion relative to, 493-497; fallacious doctrines on the question, 497, 498, misapplication of mathematical theory in opposition to this progress by Boscovich, 498, 499; Sismondi, his opinion in favour of, 500, 501; printing, its effect specially considered, 501, *seq.*, 503, *seq.*; Stay, his verses on this effect, 503, effect of printing in securing and accelerating the progress of knowledge, 503, *seq*; by the multiplication of books, 503, by a free commerce of ideas, 504, by the division of intellectual labour, and a combination of all powers through all ages, 505, in correcting errors and exploding prejudices, 506, *seq*; this assisted by the diffusion of independence and affluence, 509; by active intercourse between remote regions, 509, *seq*; the ocean, how it contributes to this end, 509; effect of printing in diffusing knowledge among the great body of a people, 510, institution of libraries, 510; means of popular instruction, 511, 512, the wide circulation of pamphlets and journals, 512, 513, other concurring causes—multiplication of roads, posts, and couriers, 514; objection from the possible circulation of error, 514, *seq*; freedom of the press supposed, 515, as knowledge advances and spreads, does originality decrease as Voltaire supposed, 516; even granting the objection to be true, the diffusion still beneficial, 517-519; progress of knowledge not to be confounded with the progress of scepticism, 519, advancement of philosophy gives as an incontrovertible result the advancement of human happiness, 520, pernicious zeal of some modern philosophers against what they regard as prejudice, 521; defects of our modern education, 522, importance of the Association of Ideas in training the mind, 522, 523, important admission by the Emperor Napoleon, 524, and by the Allied Sovereigns on entering Paris, 525-527, and in the British Parliament, 525-527

Propositions, self-evident, Allamand's doctrine regarding, 551, 552

Puffendorf, his work on the law of Nature and Nations, characteristics of this work, 172-187.

QUALITIES, Primary and Secondary, distinction of, 125, *seq*

Quarterly Review, article in, on Part I of this Dissertation, noticed, 601

RALEIGH, (Sir Walter,) on, 78

Ramus, of his doctrine, 59, 60.

Reflection, Mr Stewart, who thinks the philosophical employment of the word *Reflection* modern, gives examples of its use, 556

Reformation, (Protestant,) 28

Reid, his historical statement in regard to the distinction between Primary and Secondary Qualities of Matter, 126, his apparent inconsistency in regard to colour, 131-134, his opinion quoted as to Clarke's speculations concerning Space, Time, &c. 291, he was the first to see clearly the purport of Hume's scepticism touching Causation, 447; on his opinions in general, 456-466, his *Inquiry into the Human Mind* and refutation of the Ideal Theory, 456, *seq*; not a mere mistake of the figurative for the real, 458, 459; his *Essays on the Intellectual and on the Active Powers of Man*, 464-466

Reinhold, on his merits, 394, 395, 421; quoted touching Kant, 417.

Remorse, fallacious feeling of, superseded by the doctrine of Necessity, 312

Revival of Letters, 27

Robins, against the Law of Continuity, 275, 276

Rochefoucauld, (Duke of La,) character of his Maxims, 107; holds that self-love is the spring of all our actions and thus unfavourable to morality, 108, but personally a model of propriety, 108, not to be forgotten that he wrote within the vortex of a court, 109

Roman Law, 26.

Rousseau, his merits and defects as a writer on education, 382.

INDEX.   629

Royal Academy of Sciences, Paris, its influence, 94, 95.
Royal Society of London, its influence, 94, 95.

SAGE, (M Le,) against the Law of Continuity, 278, 279
Scepticism, how useful, 439, 440, 462, scepticism and credulity often united, 567, 568.
Schelling, on his doctrine, 419, 420.
Schlegel, (Frederick,) quoted and corrected in regard to Locke, 396.
Schulz, (not Schulze,) author of the Synopsis of the Kantian Philosophy, noticed, 593
Scotland, resort of Scotsmen to the Continent for education, 550.
Scottish Confession, *see* Confession, &c
Scottish Metaphysical Philosophy, 427-473, 601, 602, objection that Scottish Metaphysicians have neglected Physiology as a mean of Psychological explanation, 468, 469; also objected that they have multiplied unnecessarily our internal senses and instinctive determinations, 470-473.
Secondary Qualities of Matter, Cartesian doctrine of, slowly admitted in England, 127, *seq*.
Seneca, that nothing necessary for our improvement or happiness is recondite, 295
Sherlock, an antagonist of Locke, 557, 558.
Signs, merely act as hints, 131-135.
Sismondi, his opinion in favour of the continued progress of mankind, 500, 501, on the character of Machiavel and scope of the *Prince*, 531, on German accuracy and learning, 601.
Smith, (Adam,) on the distribution of the Sciences, 17, quoted, 174, 175, 178; evades Rousseau's puzzling objection touching the history of language, 361, 362, analogy to Kant in his doctrine of Space, 595.
Smith, (John, of Cambridge,) 79, 140, quoted, 122.
Space and Time, (theory of,) by Clarke, 291-294, by Kant, 408, 594-598, the author leans to an empirical genesis of the notion of Space, 595
Spanish criticism and literature, 194, 195
Spinoza, advocates the most tenable system of Necessity, in fact, the doctrine of Necessity must ultimately result in the Atheism of Spinoza, 298,
his Deity subject to fate, 579; history of his opinions, 299; not a declared atheist, but a real, 300, 301; in this respect generally misunderstood, 301-305, his political doctrines, 302; his life and character, 571, 572
Spontaneity, *see* Liberty of.
Stael, (Madame de,) quoted on the German Philosophers, 392, 395, 419.
Stair, (Lord,) notice of his *Physiologia Nova Experimentalis*, 602, *et alibi*.
Stay, (Benedict,) praised, 424, his verses on the effect of printing, 503
Stewart, (Dugald,) how he limits the present Dissertation, 23, 24, Letter to Reid about our perceptions of colour as the means of our perception of visible figure, 138, leans to an empirical genesis of the notion of Space, 595, holds that the notion of efficiency supposes mind, 608, 609.
Stillingfleet, as antagonist of Locke, 557.
Stoics, on their doctrine of Fatalism, 574.
Subjective and Objective Truths, 407.
System, on the love of, 416.

TELESCOPE, (invention of,) 86
Tennemann, on his History, 599, 600.
Theoretical History, value of, 384, 385.
Thuanus, his liberality, 52
Tillotson, (Archbishop,) quoted in contrast to Law and his followers, 357
Toleration, long imperfectly admitted, 54, 217
Trade, as an object of Political Philosophy altogether modern, 97.
Tucker, (Abraham, = Edward Search, Esq.,) noticed, 236.
Turgot, his doctrine as to the progress of mankind, 493-497.

VALLA, (Laurentius,) an independent thinker, 49, quotation from his dialogue on Free-will, 261, 262.
Vauvenargues, as a delineator of character, 383.
Vernacular tongues, (usage of, in writing,) 33
Vives, (Ludovicus,) anticipates Bacon in foreseeing the great progress of the human mind, 58
Voltaire, quoted, 106, 107, 178, *et passim*; what his merits in making known in France the philosophy of Locke, 220, on his raillery of the Optimism

of Leibnitz, 262, quoted as to the Innate Ideas of Descartes, 553; two epochs to be distinguished in his philosophical life, 590, 591, always opposed to the atheism of the *Système de la Nature*, 590-592; asserts Final Causes, 592; at an earlier period an advocate of Free-will, at a later of Necessity, 591, 592; but imperfectly informed as to the Metaphysical arguments, 591.

WARBURTON, characterized and quoted, 161, 162; on Machiavel's *Prince*, 533

Wilkins, on his universal language, 92

Will, confounded with Desire by Priestley and other Necessitarians, 465, we ought not to say that the *Will* is free, but that the *Man* is free, 608.

Wirgman, (Mr) quoted as to Kant, &c., 599.

Witt, (John de,) earliest writer on commerce as a matter of Political interest, 97

Wolf, (Christian,) as a systematizer of the Leibnitian system, and on his merits in general, 389-391; follows Leibnitz as considering the soul in the light of a *machine*, 390, 391

PROSPECTUS.

In handsome 8vo, with Portraits, &c., price 12s per Volume,

COMPLETE EDITION OF THE WORKS

OF

DUGALD STEWART, ESQ.,

COMPRISING, AMONG OTHER LARGE ADDITIONS, A CONCLUDING
CHAPTER OF HIS DISSERTATION, LECTURES ON
POLITICAL ECONOMY, &c &c

WITH A BIOGRAPHICAL MEMOIR OF THE AUTHOR
By SIR WILLIAM HAMILTON, Bart.

AFTER the death of Reid, DUGALD STEWART was the head of what has been denominated "The Scottish School of Philosophy;" long before his death he was, indeed, universally acknowledged as the most distinguished living philosopher of Great Britain, and likewise as one of the best writers in the language. His published works are considerable, both in number and extent, and are also conversant with the most important parts of Philosophy,—historical, speculative, and practical. Of these works, the earlier have been frequently reprinted; but from circumstances, merely private, and which it is unnecessary to specify, new editions of his later writings have been withheld, and a collection of the whole, which ought long ago to have appeared, has only now become possible.

This Collection, which it is proposed forthwith to publish, will appear in handsome 8vo, and may extend to nine, perhaps to ten, volumes. It will not be merely a uniform re-impression of the former Publications. These it will of course comprise,—following the most authentic Edition, with the Author's Manuscript Corrections, and his frequent and important Additions;—but in the extensive literary remains of Mr. STEWART, besides the Writings thus left prepared for the Press, there are others which may afford valuable extracts to be incorporated in the already published Treatises,—or to be otherwise annexed to them.

The work of selecting from the Manuscripts, and, in general, of editing the Collection, has been undertaken by Sir WILLIAM HAMILTON, who will likewise supply a Memoir of the Author.

The contents of the Publication are as follows; and, in so far as at present appears, they will occupy Nine volumes.

1 DISSERTATION, EXHIBITING A GENERAL VIEW OF THE PROGRESS OF METAPHYSICAL, ETHICAL, AND POLITICAL PHILOSOPHY.
> This will comprise numerous and extensive Additions, and a Chapter hitherto unpublished, exhibiting a concluding view of "Tendencies and Results."

2, 3, 4. ELEMENTS OF THE PHILOSOPHY OF THE HUMAN MIND. 3 vols.
> To this will be prefixed Part I. of the OUTLINES OF MORAL PHILOSOPHY, containing the Outline of the Philosophy of Mind The first volume will contain the relative Addenda published in the third, which are still in copyright. In the second volume will appear various Insertions and Corrections. The OUTLINES also have some additions

5. PHILOSOPHICAL ESSAYS.
> This volume may be considered as almost a part of the last work —Large additions

6, 7 PHILOSOPHY OF THE ACTIVE AND MORAL POWERS. 2 vols.
> There will be prefixed Part II. of the OUTLINES OF MORAL PHILOSOPHY, containing the Outline of the Ethical Philosophy. Considerable Additions

8. LECTURES ON POLITICAL ECONOMY.
> That is, on Political Philosophy in its widest signification. Now first published. Part III. of the OUTLINES OF MORAL PHILOSOPHY, containing the Outline of the Political Philosophy, will be prefixed.

9 BIOGRAPHICAL MEMOIRS OF SMITH, ROBERTSON, AND REID.
> Additions; with Memoir of the Author by Sir WILLIAM HAMILTON, which will be paged by itself, and may be prefixed to volume first.

INDICES WILL BE ANNEXED

General Laws in Plato p 260 | Study of Law (Roman) p. 26.
Law of continuity. p 274. | Reference to Bacon on mind. Bk. I. p.
No doubt p 276. | Rest of Locke p 67.
Development p 277-8. | Aristotle. "nihil ipse intellectus" p 87
Prediction of Laplace, ibid.
Hume on physical
   explanations. p. 259.